SENSIBLE ECSTASY

RELIGION AND POSTMODERNISM
A series edited by Mark C. Taylor

RECENT BOOKS IN THE SERIES

Ellen T. Armour, *Deconstruction, Feminist Theology, and the Problem of Difference*, 1999

Thomas A. Carlson, *Indiscretion: Finitude and the Naming of God*, 1999

Mark C. Taylor, *About Religion: Economies of Faith in Virtual Culture*, 1999

Edith Wyschogrod, *An Ethics of Remembering: History, Heterology, and the Nameless Others*, 1998

Mark C. Taylor, *Hiding*, 1997

Jonathan Boyarin, *Thinking in Jewish*, 1996

Jacques Derrida, *Archive Fever: A Freudian Impression*, 1996

William Franke, *Dante's Interpretive Journey*, 1996

SENSIBLE ECSTASY   MYSTICISM, SEXUAL DIFFERENCE,
AND THE DEMANDS OF HISTORY

AMY HOLLYWOOD

The University of Chicago Press
Chicago and London

BV
5083
.H55
2002

A M Y   H O L L Y W O O D is associate professor of religion at Dartmouth
College. She is the author of *The Soul as Virgin Wife: Mechthild of Magdeburg,
Marguerite Porete, and Meister Eckhart* (Notre Dame, 1995), which won the
International Congress on Medieval Studies' Otto Gründler Prize for the
best book in medieval studies.

The University of Chicago Press, Chicago 60637
The University of Chicago Press, Ltd., London
© 2002 by The University of Chicago
All rights reserved. Published 2002
Printed in the United States of America

11 10 09 08 07 06 05 04 03 02   1 2 3 4 5

ISBN: 0–226–34951–9 (cloth)
ISBN: 0–226–34952–7 (paper)

Library of Congress Cataloging-in-Publication Data

Hollywood, Amy M., 1963–
   Sensible ecstasy : mysticism, sexual difference, and the demands of
history / Amy Hollywood.
      p. cm. — (Religion and postmodernism)
   Includes bibliographical references and index.
   ISBN 0-226-34951-9 (cloth : alk. paper) — ISBN 0-226-34952-7
(paper : alk. paper)
      1. Mysticism—Psychology—History.   2. Women mystics—
Psychology—History.   3. Philosophy, French—20th century.
4. Psychoanalysis and religion—France—History—20th century.
I. Title.   II. Series.

BV5083 .H55 2002
248.2'2'09—dc21

                                        2001037603

⊗ The paper used in this publication meets the minimum requirements
of the American National Standard for Information Sciences—
Permanence of Paper for Printed Library Materials, ANSI Z39.48–1992.

FOR REED

....

Conceived in this sense, History is what hurts, it is what refuses

desire and sets inexorable limits to individual as well as collective

praxis, which its "ruses" turn into grisly and ironic reversals of their

overt intentions. But this History can be apprehended only through

its effects, and never directly as some reified force. This is indeed

the ultimate sense in which History as ground and untranscendable

horizon needs no particular theoretical justification: we may be sure

that its alienating necessities will not forget us, however much we

might prefer to ignore them.

FREDRIC JAMESON, *The Political Unconscious*

It is the dream of the body—to know a place bodily and say so. To take words into and

out of itself. To have words assume bodily shape, *salamander* or *milk,* it doesn't matter. To

inhabit a shore, a fabulous body of water, debris, insects drilled in the sand.

Where in the world can the body say, I am in my element?

The body strips to its flesh, and flame, and dives. When air gives out,

and blues and greens simplify into dark, lips open the way lips open for kisses.

But the body, more fully desirous, recalcitrant in the extreme, says,

even there, No, this is not the world I dreamed of. This is not the world.

JANET KAUFFMAN, *The Body in Four Parts*

I don't know if in this way I express human helplessness—or my own.

GEORGES BATAILLE, *On Nietzsche*

CONTENTS

Acknowledgments   xi

List of Abbreviations   xiii

Introduction   1

....

1   GEORGES BATAILLE, *MYSTIQUE*

INTRODUCTION: *"THE PHILOSOPHER* —SARTRE—AND ME"   25

1   The Scandal of the Real   36

2   Mysticism, Trauma, and Catastrophe in Angela of Foligno's Book
          and Bataille's *Atheological Summa*   60

3   From Image to Text: Photography, Writing, and Communication   88

....

2   (EN)GENDERING MYSTICISM

INTRODUCTION: FROM WOUNDEDNESS TO CASTRATION;

          OR, ON THE GENDER OF MYSTICISM   113

4   "Mysticism is tempting": Simone de Beauvoir on Mysticism,
          Metaphysics, and Sexual Difference   120

5   Jacques Lacan, *Encore*: Feminine Jouissance, the Real,
          and the Goal of Psychoanalysis   146

....

3   FEMINISM, MYSTICISM, AND BELIEF

INTRODUCTION: FEMINISM AND PSYCHOANALYSIS IN FRANCE   173

6   From Lack to Fluidity: Luce Irigaray, *La Mystérique*   187

7   Sexual Difference and the Problem of Belief   211

8   Ventriloquizing Hysteria: Fetishism, Trauma,
          and Sexual Difference   236

Conclusion   274

Notes   279

Index   359

ACKNOWLEDGMENTS

Many people and institutions helped make this book possible. Bernard McGinn, Stephanie Paulsell, and Charles Stinson read the entire manuscript and, together with Mark Taylor and two anonymous readers from the University of Chicago Press, offered suggestions and encouragement. The book came together in the year I spent as a Women's Studies Research Associate at Harvard Divinity School. Ann Braude, the director of that program, and my fellow research associates, Ann Mongoven, Susan Starr Sered, Ulrike Strasser, and Gail Sutherland, read chapters and helped me think through how the book as a whole should be organized. These conversations helped me to write an immeasurably better book than I would have done otherwise. Some of the thinking in the book dates from my years as a student at the University of Chicago. For their influence on this and other projects, I thank my teachers: Bernard McGinn, Françoise Meltzer, Paul Ricoeur, and David Tracy. My students at Dartmouth College and at the Harvard Divinity School enriched the project and helped me clarify my thinking. Alan Thomas and Randy Petilos of the University of Chicago Press are a pleasure to work with, and David Toole's exceptional copyediting has made this a much better book. For help with chapters, translation tips, suggestions for reading, and trips to the beach, I am also deeply grateful to Susan Ackerman, Amy Allen, Maria Arbusto, Ellen Armour, Matthew Bagger, Ehud Benor, Katharine Conley, Jonathan Crewe, Mary Desjardins, Michael Drompp, Ken Fox, Nancy Frankenberry, Robert Henricks, Susannah Heschel, Marianne Hirsch, Paul Iappini, Alexander Irwin, Serene Jones, Cleo Kearns, Jeffrey Kripal, Paul Lachance, Sam Levey, Reed Lowrie, Kevin Madigan, Barbee Majors, Cynthia

Marshall, Michelle Meyers, Catherine Mooney, Jerry Sanders, Susan St. Ville, Brenda Silver, Susan Simonaitis, Richard Stamelman, Christine Thomas, Peter Travis, Barbara Will, Mark Williams, Elliot Wolfson, Melissa Zeiger, and my families: the Hollywoods, Pooles, Wilsons, and Lowries.

I have been extraordinarily fortunate to have received research funding and leave time to write. My thanks to the Dartmouth College Religion Department for its generosity and support. Also at Dartmouth College, I have been the beneficiary of numerous funds, including the Dickinson Fund, the Burke Grant, the Carson Fund, the McLane Family Fellowship, the Karen Wetterhahn Prize, and the Junior Faculty Fellowship. In addition to the Harvard Divinity School Women's Studies Program, the American Academy of Religion provided research support for the project. I thank all those donors whose generosity makes my work and that of other scholars possible, and the colleagues and administrators who have entrusted me with these precious resources.

Chapter 1 will appear in a slightly different form as "Georges Bataille and the Scandal of the Real," in *Method as Path: Religious Experience and Hermeneutical Discourse*, edited by Jeffrey Kripal and Elliott Wolfson (New York: Seven Bridges Press, forthcoming). Portions of chapter 2 appeared in "'Beautiful as a Wasp': Angela of Foligno and Georges Bataille," *Harvard Theological Review* 92 (1999): 224–32; and in "Bataille and Mysticism: A 'Dazzling Dissolution,'" *Diacritics* 26, no. 2 (1996): 375–84. © The Johns Hopkins University Press. Some of the work on Irigaray in chapters 6 and 7 appeared in "Beauvoir, Irigaray, and the Mystical," *Hypatia* 9, no. 4 (1994): 163–72, © Indiana University Press; and in "Deconstructing Belief: Irigaray and the Philosophy of Religion," *Journal of Religion* 78 (1998): 236–44. Portions of the material on Beatrice of Nazareth in chapter 8 are taken, in revised form, from "Inside Out: Beatrice of Nazareth and Her Hagiographer," in *Gendered Voices: Medieval Saints and Their Interpreters*, edited by Catherine M. Mooney (Philadelphia: University of Pennsylvania Press, 1999). My thanks to these publishers for permission to reprint this material.

The following texts are cited parenthetically within the text. For stylistic continuity and accuracy, I have used my own translations of the French texts unless otherwise noted. I have been greatly aided by existing English translations, however, and cite them after the original for ease of reference.

AE   Luce Irigaray, *An Ethics of Sexual Difference*, trans. Carolyn Burke
          and Gillian C. Gill (Ithaca, N.Y.: Cornell University Press,
          1993).

CA   Georges Bataille, "Concerning the Accounts Given by the
          Residents of Hiroshima," trans. Alan Keenan, in *Trauma:
          Explorations in Memory*, ed. Cathy Caruth (Baltimore, Md.:
          Johns Hopkins University Press, 1995).

CS   Luce Irigaray, *Ce Sexe qui n'en est pas un* (Paris: Minuit, 1977).

DS I–II   Simone de Beauvoir, *Le Deuxième sexe*, 2 vols. (Paris: Galli-
          mard, 1949).

E   Jacques Lacan, *Le Séminaire de Jacques Lacan, Livre XX, Encore*,
          1972–73, ed. Jacques-Alain Miller (Paris: Seuil, 1975).

EDS   Luce Irigaray, *Ethique de la différence sexuelle* (Paris: Minuit,
          1984).

FA   Simone de Beauvoir, *La force de l'âge* (Paris: Gallimard,
          1960).

G	Georges Bataille, *Guilty*, trans. Bruce Boone (San Francisco: Lapis Press, 1988).
IE	Georges Bataille, *Inner Experience*, trans. Leslie Anne Boldt (Albany: State University of New York Press, 1988).
ILTY	Luce Irigaray, *I Love to You*, trans. Alison Martin (New York: Routledge, 1996).
JAT	Luce Irigaray, *J'aime à toi* (Paris: Grasset, 1992).
JTN	Luce Irigaray, *je, tu, nous: Toward a Culture of Difference*, trans. Alison Martin (New York: Routledge, 1993).
JTNP	Luce Irigaray, *je, tu, nous: Pour une culture de la différence* (Paris: Grasset, 1990).
LBN	*The Life of Beatrice of Nazareth*, translated and annotated by Roger DeGanck (Kalamazoo, Mich.: Cistercian Publications, 1991).
LCA	Thomas of Cantimpré, *The Life of Christina Mirabilis*, trans. Margot H. King (Toronto: Peregrina Publishing, 1986).
LMO	Jacques de Vitry, *The Life of Marie d'Oignies*, trans. Margot H. King (Toronto: Peregrina Publishing, 1989).
LTD	Luce Irigaray, *Le Temps de la différence: Pour une révolution pacifique* (Paris: Librairie Générale Française, 1989).
MDD	Simone de Beauvoir, *Memoirs of a Dutiful Daughter*, trans. James Kirkup (New York: Harper and Row, 1959).
MJF	Simone de Beauvoir, *Mémoires d'une jeune fille rangée* (Paris: Gallimard, 1958).
NM	Jean-Paul Sartre, "Un nouveau mystique," in *Situations*, vol. 1 (Paris: Gallimard, 1947).
OC I–XII	Georges Bataille, *Oeuvres complètes*, 12 vols. (Paris: Gallimard, 1970–88).
ON	Georges Bataille, *On Nietzsche*, trans. Bruce Boone (New York: Paragon House, 1992).
PL	Simone de Beauvoir, *The Prime of Life*, trans. Peter Green (Harmondsworth: Penguin, 1962).

SA	Luce Irigaray, *Speculum de l'autre femme* (Paris: Minuit, 1974).
SG	Luce Irigaray, *Sexes and Genealogies*, trans. Gillian C. Gill (New York: Columbia University Press, 1993).
SE	Georges Bataille, *Story of the Eye*, trans. Joachim Neugroschel (San Francisco: City Lights, 1987).
SML	Beatrice of Nazareth, "There Are Seven Manners of Loving," trans. Eric Colledge, in *Medieval Women's Visionary Literature*, ed. Elizabeth Alvilda Petroff (Oxford: Oxford University Press, 1986).
SMM	Beatrice of Nazareth, *Seven Manieren van Minne*, ed. L. Reypens and J. Van Mierlo (Leuven: S. V. de Vlaamsche Boekenhalle, 1926).
SO	Luce Irigaray, *Speculum of the Other Woman*, trans. Gillian C. Gill (Ithaca, N.Y.: Cornell University Press, 1985).
SP	Luce Irigaray, *Sexes et parentés* (Paris: Minuit, 1987).
SS	Simone de Beauvoir, *The Second Sex*, trans. H. M. Parshley (1952; reprint, New York: Vintage, 1974).
S XX	Jacques Lacan, *On Feminine Sexuality, the Limits of Love and Knowledge, 1972–73, Encore: The Seminar of Jacques Lacan, Book XX*, trans. Bruce Fink (New York: W. W. Norton, 1998).
TD	Luce Irigaray, *Thinking the Difference*, trans. Karin Montin (New York: Routledge, 1994).
TS	Luce Irigaray, *This Sex Which Is Not One*, trans. Catherine Porter (Ithaca, N.Y.: Cornell University Press, 1985).
VCM	Thomas of Cantimpré, *Vita S. Christinae Mirabilis*, in *Acta Sanctorum*, ed. J. Bolland et al. (Brussels: Culture et civilisation, 1965–70), vol. 31 (July 5): 637–60.
VMO	Jacques of Vitry, *Vita Mariae Oignacensis*, in *Acta Sanctorum*, ed. J. Bolland et al. (Brussels: Culture et civilisation, 1965–70), vol. 23 (June 4): 630–66.

THREE MYSTICAL MOMENTS

On a day sometime in the late thirteenth century, a woman came through the portals of the church of St. Francis in Assisi and began to scream. Her companions, a holy man and other "very good men and women," waited and watched over her with great reverence. Only her confessor and counselor, a blood relative who lived at the adjacent Franciscan friary, was embarrassed by her behavior. Unable to approach her because he was so ashamed at her outburst, he waited until she stopped screaming and came to him. Even then, he later wrote, "I could hardly speak to her calmly. I told her that, henceforth, she should never again dare come to Assisi, since this was the place where this evil seized her. I also told her companions never to bring her there again."[1]

This man, known to historians only as Brother A., was convinced that on that day in Assisi his kinswoman, Angela of Foligno, was possessed by evil spirits. Yet for some reason he pursued her to Foligno and asked her to explain to him how she understood what had occurred to her. Eventually, he not only came to believe that her experiences had a divine rather than demonic origin, but undertook to write down her words as a guide for her companions and other religious people. Although Angela complained that Brother A.'s Latin transcriptions of her speech were almost unrecognizable to her, she continued to collaborate with him in the production of her *Memorial.*

On that particular day in Assisi, she told him, God had promised to be present to her until the moment when she entered the church for a second time:

Then, on this second time, as soon as I had genuflected at the entrance of the church and when I saw a stained-glass window depicting St. Francis being closely held by Christ, I heard him [God] telling me: "Thus I will hold you closely to me and much more closely than can be observed with the eyes of the body. And now the time has come, sweet daughter, my temple, my delight, to fulfill my promise to you. I am about to leave you in the form of this consolation, but I will never leave you if you move me."

After seeing God in "such immense majesty" that she did "not know how to describe it," Angela explains, God "very gently" and "very gradually" withdrew. At that point, she began to scream and to cry out "Love still unknown, why do you leave me?"—although with so much intensity and such a choked throat that her words were unintelligible to those around her.[2] According to Angela, her screams were not occasioned by the devil, but by the intensity of her experience of God and her anguish at his withdrawal from her.

In February 1896 a devout forty-two-year-old woman entered Paris's Salpêtrière Hospital, already famous as a center for the study of hysteria. Madeleine, as she chose to be known, had been extremely religious since childhood, dedicating herself to a life of voluntary poverty and care for the sick. She once even served a prison sentence for refusing to give her real name to the authorities. What brought her to the Salpêtrière was a peculiar contraction of the leg muscles that enabled her to walk only on tiptoe. Although she believed that this posture was caused by her imminent assumption into heaven, her doctor, the esteemed psychologist Pierre Janet, had different views. For Janet, Madeleine was "a poor contemporary mystic" whose ecstasies, crucifixion postures, and bleeding wounds (stigmata) were signs of delirium and other pathologies.[3] What earlier mystics described as moments in the soul's relationship to the divine, Janet read as abnormal states (of consolation, ecstasy, temptation, dryness, and torture) in need of a cure—or at least of resolution into some kind of sustained equilibrium.

Yet Janet was much more sensitive to Madeleine's religious beliefs and practices than many of his contemporaries, most notably his teacher and collaborator, the neurologist Jean-Martin Charcot, who used retrospective diagnosis as a way of dismissing the religious claims of mystics (as well as of demoniacs).[4] Janet allowed a religious advisor to administer to Madeleine while she was in the hospital.[5] He also noted her creativity, delicacy of mind, and intelligence.

"It is these same qualities, although more developed, that have allowed certain mystics with the same pathological problems to carry out nevertheless some remarkable works."[6] After her discharge in 1904, Madeleine stayed in close touch with Janet until her death in 1918. Yet battles raged around her case after its initial publication. Many Catholic theologians charged Janet with atheism and irreligion, while others accepted Janet's assessment of Madeleine as a neurotic, arguing that "psychopathology and genuine religious feeling" could exist side by side.[7] What Madeleine thought was not recorded.[8]

In an exchange published in 1975, Hélène Cixous, an affiliate of *Psych et Po* (a psychoanalytically oriented branch of the French women's movement) and the Marxist feminist Catherine Clément debated the political value of hysteria. Their conversation closes a volume in which Clément compares the sixteenth-century witch hunts with the nineteenth- and twentieth-century phenomenon of hysteria and Cixous links female characters from Kleist and Shakespeare with Teresa of Avila and Freud's Dora, the classic psychoanalytic case study of hysteria. "I was Saint Teresa of Avila," Cixous writes, "that madwoman who knew more than all the men. And who knew how to become a bird by dint of loving." Teresa, Cixous suggests, is a hysteric, and "the hysterics," she claims, "are my sisters. . . . But I am what Dora would have been if the history of women had begun."[9] The hysteric declares that she wants "everything" (*tout*). But "the world does not offer her people who are everything/all/whole [*tout*]; they are always very little pieces. What she projects as a demand for totality, for strength, for infallibility, requires others in a manner that is intolerable to them and stops them from functioning as they function, without their restricted little economy. She breaks/destroys calculation."[10]

Clément, whose essay carefully balances recognition of the witch's and hysteric's creativity and power with their ultimate containment by male-dominant society, challenges what she sees as Cixous's valorization of the hysteric. Clément argues that what Dora "broke" through her bodily symptoms "was strictly individual and limited." Cixous insists that she does not "fetishize" Dora but uses her as "the name of a certain unsettling force, which makes the little circus not work anymore."[11] In hysteria, repressed desire erupts: "I think that what cannot be oppressed, even in the class struggle, is the libido—desire; it is in taking off from desire that you will revive the need for things really to change. Desire never dies, but it can be stifled for a long time. For example, in peoples who are denied speech and who are in the last gasp. One ceases to move the moment one no longer communicates."[12]

Yet Clément worries that desire can be destructive in ways inimical to the emancipatory political projects to which she and Cixous are both committed. The obsessive person, she argues, through the force of his or her desire, destroys by adding to "the rigidity of structures" and to "ritual" rather than by loosening their hold. For Cixous, however, the obsessive and the hysteric must be kept distinct: "When Freud says that the obsessive, on the cultural level, yields the religious and that what is hysterical yields art, that seems exactly right to me. The religious on the contrary is something that consolidates, that will re-enclose, that will seal and fasten everything that is rigid in the social realm. There is a difference between what makes things move and what stops them; it is what moves things that changes them."[13]

The mystics,[14] or at least "that madwoman" Teresa of Avila, are aligned not with religion but with hysteria. Cixous's argument leads to the conclusion that mystics, in that they are *religious*, are obsessive-compulsives, whereas in that they are *hysterical*, they are artists and revolutionaries. Cixous effects here a transvaluation of values, a radical reversal of the deployment of medical and psychoanalytic categories against Christian mystics—in particular women mystics—by means of which their texts and experiences are rendered pathological.[15] In other words, where earlier readings of some Christian mystics as hysterical reduced affective and erotic forms of mysticism to disease, thereby potentially, if not explicitly, undermining their religious value, Cixous argues that hysteria—and hence the mystical forms associated with it—marks the return of repressed desire and so unleashes a liberating force that works against the conservative and rigidifying power of religious belief and practice. She does not challenge the perceived gap between certain types of mysticism and religion, but instead reverses the valuations placed on the two. Her brief juxtaposition of mysticism and hysteria, then, works within an opposition between repressive and oppressive dominant social structures (including religion) and desire, the site, for Cixous, of a disrupting and liberatory mystical excess.

SENSIBLE ECSTASY

Cixous's evocation of mysticism is brief, but the juxtaposition of mysticism and femininity recurs within texts produced in and around the French women's movement. Under the influence of both Simone de Beauvoir, who includes a discussion of mysticism as a justification for women's existence in *The Second Sex* (1949), and the psychoanalyst Jacques Lacan, whose seminar *Encore* (delivered in 1972–1973) links femininity, hysteria, and mysticism, Cixous, Clément, the literary theorist and psychoanalyst Julia Kristeva, and the philosopher and psychoanalyst Luce Irigaray all discuss mysticism at various points in their work.[16] Yet Clément's objections to the valorization of mysticism, particularly as it is linked to hysteria, raise crucial questions about what is at stake for feminists in returning to the writings of Christian women mystics like Angela of Foligno and Teresa of Avila; for as Clément suggests, the writings of Christian women mystics always operate within, although often in ways dangerously subversive of, male-dominant society. Angela disrupts the calm liturgical life of the little church at Assisi, but she is able to do so only because she received the approbation of a "holy man" and eventually of Brother A.

The ambivalent relationship between mysticism and feminism is articulated most fully in the work of Luce Irigaray. She argues both that mysticism is the first site in which a feminine imaginary and potential symbolic appear[17] and that, at least in its Christian forms, it is inadequate to the needs of contemporary feminism. Yet despite this assertion, Irigaray returns again and again to the mystical in ways that both generate and suggest potential resolutions of key tensions within her work. These moments of creative tension are themselves, I will argue, moments in which she mimes mystical modes of writing.

What fascinates Irigaray about mysticism, as she understands it, is its insistence both on recognizing the other as another and on overcoming boundaries between the self and that other. This is a peculiar understanding of the mystical, one that sees mysticism as rooted in the particularity of the body even as it moves through the senses toward an intimate apprehension of other beings.[18] The emphasis on corporeality and the emotions links Irigaray's mystical turn with modern scholarly distinctions between affective or erotic forms of mysticism, usually associated with women, and more speculative or intellectual forms of mysticism associated with men. Unlike most secular scholarship, however, which until recently has denigrated affective and bodily forms of mysticism in favor of the speculative (Beauvoir, for example, does so, although with important exceptions), Irigaray follows a countertradition in French secular thought that looks to mysticism as an affective encounter with the other that marks the apex of the ethical and religious life. First seen in the wartime writings of the novelist, essayist, theorist, and provocateur Georges Bataille, the tradition moves through the work of Simone de Beauvoir and Jacques Lacan to that of Irigaray.

Sensible Ecstasy is the history of this twentieth-century fascination with emotional, bodily, and excessive forms of mysticism. Mysticism plays a crucial role in the work of other secular twentieth-century French intellectuals, among them Henri Bergson, Maurice Blanchot, Michel Foucault, and Jacques Derrida.[19] What is particular to Bataille, Beauvoir, Lacan, and Irigaray is their attention to the forms of mysticism associated with women, whether they explicitly theorize this relationship (as do Beauvoir, Lacan, and Irigaray) or not (as in the case of Bataille, although the gendering of mysticism and inner experience lies always just below the surface of his texts). This book asks why a handful of twentieth-century, resolutely secular, even anti-Christian intellectuals have been among the rare exceptions to the widespread denigration of affective and bodily forms of mysticism.[20] Bataille, Lacan, and Irigaray (and at times Beauvoir) read these women not as pathological, emotionally excessive escapists, but as unique in their ability to bring together action and contemplation, emotion and reason, body and soul. Or perhaps better, these twentieth-century intellectuals admire a figure like Angela of Foligno because she subverts the very distinctions between action and contemplation, emotion and reason, and body and soul, effecting through her words a disruption of the boundaries between them.

In this book I trace this attraction to a feminized and embodied mystical figure and ask what work the figure of the medieval and early modern mystic performs, both epistemologically and affectively, for these secular, twentieth-century intellectuals. As my opening stories show, the meaning of the woman mystic's experience—in particular her bodily experience—has always been the site of competing interpretations and claims to authority. Angela, like many other medieval and early modern women, actively struggled to maintain interpretative control over her experience against the continual encroachment of male clerical elites; so although the work of these twentieth-century intellectuals can be elucidated by attention to their fascination with medieval mysticism, at the same time, medieval women's texts proleptically resist some of these readings in their contestation of the cultural roles prescribed for women in the Middle Ages. Any feminist assessments of the contemporary turn to the mystical must take seriously the words of those women whose writings purportedly, if often only elliptically, give rise to this turn, for the very antithesis between affective and speculative forms of mysticism, as well as the resistance to the gendering of that distinction, has its roots in texts written by and addressed to medieval women.

MYSTICISM AND GENDER

Both Beauvoir and Irigaray argue that mysticism is the sole place within the history of the West where women have achieved full and autonomous subjectivity. Although I would challenge the claims to uniqueness, it is true that with few exceptions the first women to write in the West (by which I mean the classical Mediterranean world and Europe) were Christian mystics, that is, women who claimed to have extraordinary experiences of the divine and/or of union with God that both authorized their writing and served as its subject matter.[21] Women were not, of course, the only Christian mystics. But they were central to the medieval and early modern Christian mystical traditions and produced a number of texts in a wide variety of genres (letters, poems, visionary books, mystical treatises, allegorical dramas, etc.) that have survived. (No doubt many other texts were produced that have been lost or are still covered in anonymity.) Women mystics were often leaders and innovators not only within women's religious communities, but also within larger communities that included men. Their spheres of influence were as small as circles of family, close friends, and confessors or as wide as European Christianity itself. In the twelfth century, Hildegard of Bingen went on preaching tours throughout Germany and Swabia. Mechthild of Magdeburg warned both religious and secular leaders of the spiritual dangers to which she saw thirteenth-century Germany succumbing.[22] In the fourteenth century, Catherine of Siena, a lay woman, advised religious leaders— even the pope.

In less extraordinary cases, historians often overlook women's influence. The work of the thirteenth- and early fourteenth-century Dominican preacher and theologian known as Meister ("Master") Eckhart, for example, has traditionally been read in light of its relationship to scholastic theology, patristic and Neoplatonic antecedents to high medieval mysticism, the developing pastoral theology of the Dominican order, and the traditions of German mysticism that followed it. Yet Herbert Grundmann argued as early as 1935 that the mystical and theological innovations central to Eckhart's work first appear in the women's religious movement of the thirteenth century—in particular, in the writing, thought, and practice of the beguines, semireligious women who devoted themselves to lives of prayer and mutual exhortation without taking formal vows.[23] Only recently, however, has more sustained analysis of the surviving beguinal texts by Hadewijch, Mechthild of Magdeburg, and Marguerite Porete allowed scholars to assess the extent of that influence and its importance for understanding Eckhart's thought.[24]

These kinds of influence have gone unnoticed not only because of a general tendency to ignore women's writings, but also because of traditional lines of gendered interpretation in which the kind of mysticism found among women and that found among men (often exemplified by Eckhart) are deemed antithetical. Mysticism tends to be gendered in one of two ways. Either mysticism (again, extraordinary experiences of divine presence or of union with God) is simply associated with femininity or with women and so denigrated, or a distinction is made between good and bad, acceptable and unacceptable, non-pathological and pathological forms of mysticism, with the first category in each case associated with masculinity and men and the second with femininity and women.

This gendering process began in the medieval period. Thus in 1415 the French prelate Jean Gerson, himself an author of mystical treatises and guidebooks, bemoaned women's religious teaching and writing, claiming that there is "hardly any other calamity more apt to harm or that is more incurable. If its only consequence were the immense loss of time, this would already be sufficient for the devil. But you must know that there is something else to it! The insatiable itch to see and to speak, not to mention . . . the itch to touch."[25] Gerson attacked women's visionary, auditory, and sensory experiences of the divine, as well as the teaching, preaching, and writing that these experiences authorized.[26] Although Gerson himself did not wish to silence women entirely but merely to "bridle" their speech with tight clerical control, the basis for later denigrating distinctions between male and female styles of mysticism was clearly already in place in the early fifteenth century.

Modern scholars pick up on distinctions like those made by Gerson and tend to divide mysticism into two general types: the feminine—affective, emotional, visionary, and often erotic; and the masculine—speculative, intellectual, and often explicitly antivisionary.[27] The distinction, we should note, does not quite fit the evidence. The twelfth-century Cistercian Bernard of Clairvaux, the greatest of the many male monastic commentators on the Song of Songs, both initiated and provided the vocabulary and images for the erotic mysticism of the thirteenth and fourteenth centuries. The thirteenth-century beguine, Marguerite Porete, on the other hand, eschewed visionary experience and erotic ecstasies in favor of an absolute union of the annihilated soul with the divine. Eckhart, often taken as the greatest of speculative mystics (especially by philosophical readers unconcerned with questions of orthodoxy),[28] was profoundly influenced by women, both by those of a visionary and ecstatic nature and by Porete.

The distinction between feminine and masculine types of mysticism is rendered even more problematic by the fact that the most visionary and ecstatic mystics usually include within their texts the call for a move through the visionary to another kind of more ineffable experience of union with the divine. So the thirteenth-century beguine visionary Hadewijch describes a vision in which the Eucharist comes to her in human form and then is "naughted" as the soul and Christ become indistinguishable from each other.[29] Similarly, as we will see in chapter 2, Angela of Foligno's *Memorial* is an extended record of her movement from ecstatic, spiritually apprehended experiences of God's presence to their "unsaying" in the darkness of Christ's eyes.[30]

This conception of the relationship between the visionary and other spiritual senses and their "unsaying" emerges out of a distinction most influentially disseminated in Christian mystical theology by the anonymous sixth-century author known throughout the Middle Ages as Dionysius the Areopagite.[31] Dionysius distinguishes two modes of naming God: the cataphatic, in which names are positively attributed of the divine, and the apophatic, in which all attributes are "unsaid" or denied in order to mark the illimitability of God's being. For Dionysius, this distinction works itself out in terms of an interplay between the biblical and philosophical names for God and their negation in the movement of mystical theology. Eckhart, one of the greatest Christian apophatic thinkers, also works with attributes derived from the Bible and from philosophical speculation on the nature of God.

Women, however, were prohibited by the church from engaging in the interpretation of scripture and did not generally have access to philosophical education. Medical, philosophical, and theological opinion throughout the Middle Ages, moreover, proclaimed that women were more porous and imaginative than men and, therefore, open to possession (whether divine or demonic) and to spiritual visions, auditions, and other sensations. Denied access to the sacrament of holy orders, women were acknowledged to be possible recipients of extraordinary experiences of the spirit.[32] In this situation, women's experiences of God's presence become the text that they interpret, both cataphatically and apophatically, in order to apprehend and write about the divine. These experiences, in turn, derive from women's intense sacramental, liturgical, and meditative practices. (Angela, remember, hears God's voice on entering a church and seeing a pictorial representation of Francis of Assisi in God's arms.) I will show in chapters 2 and 8 how medieval women like Angela and Beatrice of Nazareth imaginatively recreate the suffering of Christ on the cross in order to make those horrible experiences real in their own bodies and souls. Just as Dionysius and Eckhart ground their apophatic practice in the reading of scripture, women like Angela and Beatrice use their daily liturgical and meditative practices—both biblically based—to engender authorizing experiences that then become texts to be unsaid in the pursuit of a closer, less limited and mediated experience of the divine.[33]

The denigration of mysticism, and particularly of those affective, visionary, and ecstatic forms of mysticism most often associated with women, is also tied to its putative escapism. The issue is rooted in a long Christian debate about the relationship between action and contemplation in the religious life. Following Jesus' approbation of Mary (who sits at his feet to listen to his teaching) over Martha (who rushes to prepare a meal for her visitor), medieval commentaries argue that the life of contemplation is higher than that of action. Yet they still often worry about how to continue to act in the ways required for one's own salvation and that of others.[34] The potential danger of mysticism is that it turns one too completely away from the cares of this world.

The thirteenth- and fourteenth-century women's movement in northern Europe grappled with just this problem. The beguines, in particular, desired, like Francis's and Dominic's new orders, to live actively in the world, serving others and bringing souls to God. Medieval views, however, insisted that women were bodily porous and weak, susceptible to physical (read sexual) and spiritual danger if not enclosed within the walls of a convent. The kind of active ministry pursued by Francis and his male followers—preaching, hearing confessions, and caring for the sick and poor in the new city centers—was deemed untenable for women. The lives of the early beguines evince a continual struggle between their desire to serve others and to live in absolute poverty, dependent on alms or the labor of their own hands for survival, and the demands of local bishops and monastic authorities that religious women be enclosed (which generally required that they own sufficient property, either individually or as a group, to support themselves).[35] This conflict is consistently interpreted in terms of the contrast between Mary and Martha (or the typologically related one between Rachel and Leah), and so between contemplation and action. Insofar as they aspired to a life of action, the beguines stood with Martha.

Yet many of the beguines also pursued, through meditative practice, asceticism, and prayer, experiences of divine presence and union. Indeed, in response to the peculiar dilemmas posed by the church for religious women, the beguines sought to bring together the active and the contemplative lives in new ways. For these women, the life of contemplation was itself a form of action through which they redeemed souls from purgatory and cared for their spiritual children on earth. Even more radically, Marguerite Porete argues that those activities generally associated with action (care for the poor, the sick, one's religious community) and those associated with contemplation (participation in the sacramental system, asceticism, meditation, prayer) were all forms of action from which the soul seeking annihilation must become detached. This tradition culminates in Eckhart's Sermon 86, a radical rereading of the story of Mary and Martha in which he argues that *Martha* was favored by Christ, for she was so detached from all creaturely things, and hence so fully one with the divine in the ground of her soul, that she was able to work in the world as Christ himself.

The insistence on the ethical demands and consequences of mysticism within thirteenth-century women's texts has consistently been ignored in the modern study of mysticism, skewing accounts of the relationship between ethics and mysticism and upholding the picture of "women's" erotic and visionary mysticism as particularly escapist in its pursuit of spiritually sensory experiences of the divine. Yet the impetus toward this critical reading of visions and ecstasies emerges out of texts like those of Porete and Eckhart, who argue that enjoying the delights of the spiritual senses and experiences of God's special presence ultimately distract the soul from the pursuit of annihilation or detachment (thus Mary is less advanced than Martha, for she still becomes so caught up in spiritual delights as to be unable to do anything else). For Porete and Eckhart, then, the union of action and contemplation depends in part on a denigration of ecstatic and visionary experience in favor of apophasis, annihilation, and detachment. Porete is characteristically vigorous and unyielding in her language. She describes seven stages of the soul, the fourth representing what many, she claims, wrongly take to be the heights of the religious life:

> The fourth state occurs when the Soul is drawn up by the height of love into the delight of thought through meditation and relinquishes all labors of the outside and of obedience to another through the height of contemplation. . . . So the Soul holds that there is no higher life than to have this over which she has lordship. For Love has so greatly satisfied her with delights that she does not believe that God has a greater gift to give to this soul here below than such a love as Love has poured out within her through love.[36]

This state, representative of the visions and ecstasies that follow meditative practice, is the most dangerous for the soul. Many become "lost" there, "merchants" who believe that they can exchange suffering, asceticism, and meditative practices for Love's presence. Freedom comes only with the death of the spirit, which requires an attitude of detachment toward both external and internal works. The soul then becomes, both Porete and Eckhart argue, the place where God works in the world.

Neither Porete nor Eckhart gender the distinction between action and contemplation, or that between ecstasy and apophasis; both speak to women and assume that women are capable of attaining the heights of the mystical life. Nor do they understand visionary and ecstatic experience and apophasis as antithetical to each other. Even Porete, who is a vocal critic of "spiritual delights," recognizes that they represent a necessary stage on the path toward annihilation.[37] Porete, then, did not directly influence the gendering of mysticism that we find in theologians like Gerson in the fifteenth century and that continues in the modern study of mysticism.[38] Porete does, however, make it apparent that the distinction between visionary and ecstatic experience and apophasis, which requires annihilation or detachment, appears already in debates about the nature of religious experience emerging from the thirteenth-century women's religious movement.

Porete was condemned as a relapsed heretic and burned at the stake in Paris's Place de Greve in 1310. Despite the edict commanding that all copies of her book be destroyed, it survived anonymously, to be rediscovered by the Italian scholar Romana Guarnieri just after the Second World War. As I have argued elsewhere, the condemnation of Porete and of certain of Eckhart's teachings, particularly those dealing with an uncreated aspect of the soul that is always one with the ground of the divine, point to the dangers of these views for women. Within the Middle Ages, as I will argue at length in chapter 8, women's religious authority depended on extraordinary visionary, auditory, or somatic experiences of the divine presence. Without that legitimatizing experience and its approbation by clerical authorities increasingly trained to "read" the female body and soul, women had no voice within medieval religious culture. Hence the proliferation of visionary, ecstatic, and "autohagiographical" texts in the centuries following Porete's condemnation, and the resulting association of these forms of visionary, ecstatic, and corporeal spirituality with women (although not, it should be noted, without signs of continued resistance on the part of some women).[39] The association of women with certain styles of mysticism is the result, then, not of some universal feminine traits but of the specific set of social and cultural constraints that women faced in the late medieval and early modern periods.

As the case of Porete makes evident, the putative distinction between affective and intellectual mysticism can be traced to medieval debates about the value and role of visionary and ecstatic experiences of the divine. Such experiences invariably are followed by the desolation of God's absence. For Angela and many other medieval women and men, this desolation itself becomes part of the mystical life, a repetition of Christ's suffering in intensifying spirals of abjection and ecstasy. This is the life from which Porete hopes to free the soul through the abnegation of desire. Yet even for Porete, annihilation occurs through a contest between Love and the soul in which the intensity of the soul's desire leads to her death. God asks the soul what she would do if he should wish that the soul love another better than himself, if he could love another soul better than her, and finally, "if it could be that he would will that another love me better than he." To all these questions, the soul does "not know what to answer"; her mind fails her, and the will is annihilated.[40] The affective here works directly toward its own destruction. Whether through an ecstatic renunciation of the will or through a process of detachment from desire (as in Eckhart) a potential antithesis is created between the will and desire, on one hand, and the life of the annihilated, free, or detached soul on the other. This antithesis leads in the modern era to the denigration of those forms of mysticism that seem hopelessly mired in the emotions, eroticism, and the body.[41]

A PREVIEW

In the modern era, affective forms of mysticism were denigrated; yet for Georges Bataille, interested during the 1930s and 1940s in discovering ways in which the affective might be expressed, the writings of women like Angela of Foligno were deeply compelling. This desire to find a place in which the pleasures and pains of the (speaking) body might be apprehended, even as the impossibility of pure self-presence is acknowledged, marks one line of continuity between Bataille, Beauvoir, Lacan, and Irigaray. The relationship between the four thinkers is not, however, without tensions and contradictions. To get at the complexity of the interactions both between these intellectuals and between their work and medieval and early modern mysticism, I will proceed both chronologically and thematically; thus I have divided the book into three parts, each of which opens with a brief introduction. Part 1 is devoted to Bataille, whose fascination with mysticism is fundamental to his work. Part 2 will describe the self-conscious gendering of mysticism in the work of Beauvoir and Lacan. Part 3 will turn to Irigaray's feminist appropriation and critique of these forms of material mysticism, and to the implications of her work for feminist theory and the study of religion.

Bataille's fascination with mysticism is linked to a radical rethinking of politics, history, and communication. His insistence on the necessity of releasing the excessive desire and anguish of the body in the face of its own mortality gives rise almost immediately to concern about the potential threat to reason and rationally guided political projects. In the face of fascism's violence, Bataille's turn to mysticism looks, at worst, like an abdication to the emotional forces undermining reason and, at best, like an evasion of the responsibilities of history. These issues are raised cogently by one of Bataille's earliest critics, Jean-Paul Sartre, whose 1943 review of Bataille's *Inner Experience* argues that Bataille confuses emotion and reason and the existential and the objective in ways that subvert ethics, politics, and communication.

As we will see, Sartre mistakes Bataille's desire to apprehend that he is not "everything" with the desire to be "everything," which, for Sartre, suggests that Bataille wants to escape history in the immediacy of the experienced moment. Yet at the same time, Sartre recognizes—and is quietly appalled by—Bataille's "fleshly promiscuity," a mysticism not of the other world but of this one in all of its bodily particularity, and a conception of history as that which is irreducible to rational projects. For Sartre, this fleshly promiscuity leads, paradoxically, both to Bataille's uneasily strong powers of communication and to a form of particularism that makes communication impossible.

Chapter 1, then, explores the "scandal" of Bataille's work through an analysis of his understanding of "experience." For Sartre, Bataille is scandalous because he confuses philosophical and scientific language with that of personal experience. For many of Bataille's subsequent readers, his texts are scandalous because of the nature of the experience described within them. This judgment is tied to a tendency to read Bataille autobiographically—to insist on the reality of that about which he writes. Yet for Bataille, as I will show through an analysis of his early novel *Story of the Eye*, the kind of autobiographical realism to which many commentators and critics subject his work is itself an evasion of the "real"—that in experience that resists narrativization. In *Story of the Eye*, as in other texts dealing more directly with religion and mysticism, Bataille continually attempts to elicit the real through the shattering of subjectivity, both literally and psychically. Violence, then, and in *Story of the Eye* particularly sexualized violence, marks a moment of masochistic self-shattering in which the languages of philosophy, science, and experience are deployed in order to be "unsaid."

Chapter 2 shows that this masochistic self-shattering is both ethical and religious and is modeled directly on the meditative practices of late medieval mysticism. In his three-volume *Atheological Summa*, written during the Second World War, Bataille suggests that the Christian mystical tradition is double. On the one hand, the mystic desires to be "everything/all/whole" (*tout*) and thus to find a place within a scheme of salvation that redeems human suffering and renders the body immortal. On the other hand, the very strength of the mystic's desire and her insistence on apprehending death and mortality in the figure of

Christ marks the mystical as the site in which the human being recognizes that she cannot and never will be "everything."

For Bataille, these practices of traumatic repetition, in which meaning-giving narratives are eschewed in the face of "that which is," provide the key ethical and affective insights of Christian mysticism. Bataille both links his work to that of the Christian mystical tradition and insists on his difference from that tradition (in that it returns to salvation), for he seeks an "inner experience" without God and without hope of redemption. "Inner experience" is an encounter, affective and ecstatic, with the other in his or her bodily specificity, as mortal and lacerated, but also as the source of joy and the simultaneous pleasure and annihilation of the senses. Bataille understands mysticism not as a flight from history but as the apprehension of the other in his or her bodily specificity and particularity—a form of communication necessary before more goal-directed political projects can be usefully or meaningfully undertaken.

Yet the kinds of contemplative practice that lead to Bataille's inner experience —particularly his meditation on the photographic image of a Chinese man who is being tortured and executed—raise complex ethical questions about the nature of the communication engendered through those practices. These questions lead back to Sartre's final critique, in which he argues that Bataille's experience is so personal and immediate as to be incommunicable. Sartre refuses to acknowledge that Bataille's practice finds its ethical basis in his desire to apprehend the suffering and laceration of the other and to live fully the "guilty" consequences of survival. Yet even when these "hyper-moral" insights are acknowledged, the question remains unresolved as to what it means to communicate with the image of a man who is now dead. For Bataille, as for his friend Maurice Blanchot and, later, for the philosopher Jacques Derrida, this is the problem posed by writing itself.

Chapter 3 returns to Bataille's mystical models to show how writing replaces —or perhaps better, supplements—practices of meditation in Bataille's wartime work. Through writing, Bataille attempts to affect his own and the reader's psychic laceration. Shattered subjects then recognize themselves and each other in their contingent existences, enabling the ecstatic anguish that is, for Bataille, communication.

Bataille does not explicitly gender his conception of mysticism, although the introduction to part 2 demonstrates that he does so in a number of implicit ways.[42] Beauvoir follows Sartre in misreading Bataille's desire as a desire to be "everything" and reads it in explicitly gendered terms. This reading of Bataille is allied with her reading of mysticism as tied to femininity. For Beauvoir, in fact, mysticism is one of the few places within the West in which women have been able to give free rein to their desire to be everything, a desire thwarted, she argues, by man's conception of woman as other. Yet given her existentialist ethics, which demands that we renounce this desire to be everything, Beauvoir remains deeply ambivalent about mysticism.

Beauvoir recognizes that mystical experience historically granted some extraordinary women limited forms of authority. Yet for Beauvoir, mysticism merely serves as a justification for women's political oppression within male-dominant society. She understands the authority granted to women mystics as a compensation for their secondary status, a compensation grounded in their belief in a delusory divine and therefore one that renders women unable to challenge actual social conditions. Beauvoir accepts, moreover, the denigratory association of mysticism and hysteria, reading most women mystics in pathological terms. Teresa of Avila is the great exception.

Beauvoir argues that the very strength of Teresa's desire enables her to confront profound metaphysical questions, and so to achieve a degree of free subjectivity unprecedented among women. In chapter 4 I show that what Teresa encounters is death, mortality, and loss, thereby marking her confrontation with the real as the site of her autonomy. Although Beauvoir presents Teresa as an existentialist heroine, I argue that it is precisely the power of belief in a God who enables her to be "everything" that enables Teresa to act in the face of death. Without strong cultural support for their subjectivity, perhaps women— even Beauvoir—still need belief in order to attain freedom.

Lacan also ties the mystical explicitly to sexual difference; like his friend and associate Bataille, Lacan sees mysticism as the apprehension of human lack and mortality. Chapter 5 reads Lacan's *Seminar XX* as a theorization, in terms of psychoanalysis's emphasis on sexual difference, of Bataille's account of the deep divide within Christian mysticism. Bataille's work raises the question of how mysticism can be the site of both the desire to be everything, to escape the particularity, limitations, and constraints of the body, and of the recognition that one is not everything, of embodied subjectivity in all of its pleasurable and painful affects. For Lacan, this doubleness is rooted in the nature of human language as both bodily and irreducible to the materiality of the body and in the nature of human subjectivity as embodied and yet always also split from the body. Like Freud, moreover, although in crucially new ways, Lacan will insist that sexual difference is foundational to the constitution of the speaking subject. Yet Lacan's work also opens the possibility of undermining that same set of associations, for he insists that the goal of psychoanalysis—like that of mysticism in its apophatic moments—is to refuse the claims to mastery and wholeness on which male-dominant culture, society, and their unconscious rest.

Part 3 turns to the work of Luce Irigaray. Chapter 6 demonstrates how she both takes up and crucially recasts Lacan's understanding of the relationship between femininity, mysticism, and the body, finding in the Christian mystical tradition precisely what Lacan believes is impossible—an imaginary, and hence a possible symbolic, grounded in the form of the female body. Yet Irigaray also contests the value of this conception of the imaginary, grounded as it is in an understanding of woman as "not all," as lacking, wounded, or lacerated. Irigaray here critiques the psychoanalytic reading of sexual difference in terms of the penis/phallus, arguing that it is only when we think in terms of having or not having the penis/phallus that not having one gets read as lack. In other words, Lacan's embrace of lack and his reading of "woman" as emblematic of the human condition (as always already split and "not all") is itself dependent on the normativity of the phallus (for Lacan, always irreducible to the penis, although iconically tied to it). Insofar as Christian mysticism is dependent on a similar conception of lack, Irigaray subjects it to the same critique she levels at psychoanalysis.

Yet as I have already suggested, Irigaray does not reject mysticism entirely; she returns repeatedly to evocations of the mystical—although not explicitly to the Christian mystical tradition—in her attempt to articulate a theory of embodied (inter)subjectivity. Chapter 7 argues that this tendency in Irigaray's thought is at odds with her insistence on the primacy of sexual difference, which is unable to account for the complexity and multiplicity of lived bodily experience. The problem of sexual difference is tied to that of belief, already posed by Beauvoir and taken up by Irigaray in relationship to Feuerbach. Feuerbach argued that religion emerges from emotion, fear of mortality and limitation, and the desire for immortality and transcendence of the limitations of individual embodied existence. Against the reification and alienation of human beings in a divine other, he called for a recognition that God's predicates are in fact attributes of humanity in its species being, and that faith in God is thus "belief in the absolute reality of subjectivity."[43] Finite limitations are submerged within this new object of belief. For Irigaray, sexual difference (in her early work, woman) takes the place of Feuerbach's "subjectivity"; thus she calls for female divinities that will serve as the support of feminine subjectivity. Although she understands sexual difference as the mark of mortality itself, its structural position within her work leads to the reification of sexual difference and, paradoxically, to the potential evasion of mortality, limitation, and particularity.

Chapter 8 returns to the later Middle Ages and to that era's explicit association of the body and its mortality, fragility, and limitations with women and femininity.[44] The mystic, crying out in anguish as God departs from her soul, becomes a mystically marked, hysterical body. In the hagiographical and auto-hagiographical traditions that emerge out of the women's religious movement in the north and the Franciscan tradition in the south, women bear the weight, in and on their anguished bodies, of human mortality and of the hope for redemption. Because the body and its mortality are associated with women, in other words, men's (and women's) anxieties about disease, pain, and death are projected onto women's bodies. These bodies are the site of repressed desires and traumatic emotions—at times taken on willingly, at other times resisted, although usually without lasting success. Irigaray, by maintaining the primacy of the association of the body with sexual difference, is in danger of facilitating just such a debilitating equation of sexual difference and woman with the body and death. The potential for this conflation of woman with death is the basis for the continued uneasiness Irigaray's work elicits in some feminist circles (despite the fact that such feminist critiques of Irigaray are often based on misreadings and misapprehensions of the philosophical and psychoanalytic subtleties of her work).

If mysticism works through the "unsaying" of cataphatic utterances and experiences of the (divine) other, and if feminine subjectivity has no discourse, no imaginary or symbolic to serve as its support, then feminism is in the unenviable position of needing both to articulate a cataphatic conception of the divine and to engage in its unsaying. In other words, Irigaray might argue, everything in our culture works to support the subjectivity and claims to wholeness of white, educated, European men like Bataille and Lacan. Bataille's and Lacan's primary project then becomes pursuit of the real through the negation of those illusory supports. But women's subjectivities are not similarly upheld by the culture around them. Irigaray's work raises the question of whether feminism can successfully engage in the emotional and affective work of providing imaginary and symbolic supports for women and at the same time be the site of their unsaying through deployment of the excessive desires of the speaking body.[45] Irigaray insists that sexual difference must be the primary site of difference—but does this reification work against the very political and philosophical projects to which Irigaray is committed? Might the speaking body, in all the complexities of its pleasurable and painful subjectification, be a better object of belief for feminism? Irigaray, at her most complex and moving, suggests as much.

Bataille, Beauvoir, Lacan, and Irigaray, although each in a different way, all turn to Christian mysticism as a potent site for philosophical reflection and for its disruption through bodily affect. They all hope somehow to translate aspects of medieval women mystics' experiences, texts, and practices into modern, non-theistic terms (although Beauvoir and Irigaray with much more ambivalence than Bataille and Lacan). In other words, they claim that medieval mystical texts can still be useful and meaningful—even if in highly mediated forms—in the modern world. In their readings of figures like Angela of Foligno and Teresa of Avila, moreover, they suggest that mysticism is itself an event. What they uncover, and try to resurrect, is an idea of mysticism as an encounter with human suffering, illness, death, and mortality that is itself an encounter with the sacred or the divine. For Angela and Hadewijch (privileged figures within Bataille's and Lacan's texts) the mystical event occurs through meditation on the broken and suffering body of Christ; for Bataille, through meditation on the tortured, lacerated bodies and/or psyches of other human beings; for La-can, through recognition of the always missed encounter with the unattainable and unnameable Other (that may in fact be simply our own bodies in their pleasurable and painful mortality).

One catches glimpses of this same vision in Beauvoir and Irigaray. Beauvoir praises Teresa as the one woman who has grappled with human finitude and emerged out of that experience able to act. What Beauvoir admires, however, also remains mysterious to her—the power of a belief that enables Teresa to engage with the world even in the face of death. Although Beauvoir sees that belief as an illusion, she is also nostalgic, in a way that Bataille and Lacan apparently are not, for that belief and for the authority with which it invests Teresa. Their lack of nostalgia is tied to the existence, within Christianity and Western philosophically grounded cultures, of symbolic support for straight, white, elite male subjectivities.

Irigaray also evokes throughout her work the idea of a mystical encounter in which the other is apprehended in his or her finitude and particularity, yielding a kind of ecstatic (or en-static) transcendence toward and of the other. Irigaray, however, wants always to emphasize finitude as possibility, rather than as lack and loss. Yet this move loses site of the emotional work performed by such encounters, which enable human beings to grapple with the bodily felt realities of loss and limitation. Irigaray is poised between two positions—one in which she emphasizes a mystical encounter with the real, experienced as both pleasure and pain, and another governed by a utopic drive that tends to efface the reality of suffering, illness, mortality, and death through a hypostatization of sexual difference.

The human experience of mortality and bodily limitation, as we currently experience it, is always sexed or gendered, but it need not necessarily be so (or at least not in the binary terms that are the only ones now available to us). If, with Irigaray, we continue to associate bodiliness first and foremost with sexual difference, the dangerous association of women and femininity—which ineluctably bear the mark of that difference within male-dominant society— with bodies, limitation, and death remains. Irigaray criticizes Lacan's emphasis on loss and lack and maintains—even strengthens—psychoanalysis's claims to the primacy of sexual difference. Feminism, however, needs to leave room for the tragic or, as Beauvoir would say, the metaphysical, but in ways that dissociate it from, and look toward an end of, the regime of binary sexual difference. We need to articulate responses to suffering, illness, death, and mortality that give attention to the role gender plays within our experience, but that also enable us to recognize these human realities as themselves irreducible to sexual difference.

The twentieth-century fascination with Christian mysticism is, I think, a response to this need and to this desire to come to terms with suffering and death. The mystic who cries out in anguish when Christ leaves her recognizes, in a way many of us today do not, that loss is experienced in the body. As Freud would learn working with hysterical patients at the Salpêtrière, if emotional responses to trauma and loss are repressed, they return in other, more fully somatic forms. In chapter 8 I argue that one of the crucial differences between the medieval mystic and the modern hysteric is that the former insists—often against strong ecclesial opposition—on her ability to interpret her own symptoms, thereby recasting repression as sublimation and the forces of the unconscious as God (even if, as in the case of Angela, this is a God who will be radically "unsaid"). Regardless of our ontological commitments, the modern fascination with the mystical exhibits a nostalgia for a time when there were ritual means to deal with the traumatic effects of loss, limitation, and death. Ritual and the body, contrary to many modern conceptions of mysticism, are crucial to that process, for it is through bodily practices and the affective work that they perform with and on the body that we work through loss. Psychoanalysis argues that we are formed and supported as subjects through such experiences of loss and ritual compensation. Careful analysis of Irigaray's work raises the questions of whether loss must be defined as constitutive of subjectivity and whether the means to deal with loss (i.e., mourning, bodily repetition, melancholic incorporation, and fetishization) and the imaginary and symbolic supports for our subjectivity should be the same.

We need to pay attention to death and its rituals, working to undo the association of sex and gender with death and the pernicious consequences this association has for women. Yet we cannot deny the reality of death itself in a utopic flight from the real, history, and the limitations of the human body. The opposition Cixous assumes between desire and ritual is undermined by the medieval story with which I began. Angela's vision is sparked by a ritual image (the stained glass representation of Christ and St. Francis), and her screams burst out in a ritual center. She both participates in the ritual life of the medieval church and disrupts it through the intensity of the desire it elicits. Bataille understands this relationship between ritual and desire. He outlines (with the proviso that method alone does not ensure success) a theory of practice that, if carried out, might give rise to inner experience. Similarly, Lacan argues that psychoanalysis, as he understands it, is a form of practice that elicits mystical jouissance. Both Bataille and Lacan assume the hegemony of the salvific and supportive narratives they unsay through their practices. Medieval women find such support, as I will show, through the feminized figure of the Son. In rejecting the feminized Godman, Beauvoir and Irigaray are left seeking feminine avatars of the divine that will help women face death. Feminism needs to find a place for the rituals that help human beings sustain loss and support subjectivity. At the same time, feminism requires a place for the apophatic, the ritual unsaying of those imaginary and symbolic supports that work to efface death's reality—and with it, the deep pleasures and pains of the speaking body.

GEORGES BATAILLE, *MYSTIQUE*

1

"THE PHILOSOPHER—SARTRE—AND ME"

In early 1944, Simone de Beauvoir and Jean-Paul Sartre were poised to emerge as France's most well-known and influential postwar intellectuals. In the final months of the European conflict, they sensed the possibility of Allied victory, and so began to enjoy a loosening of the tensions brought about by the war and its material deprivations. In this climate of hope and expectation, Beauvoir and Sartre made new friends among the writers, artists, and intellectuals gathered in Paris to wait out the occupation. At the home of the anthropologist and "dissident" surrealist writer Michel Leiris, Beauvoir first met Georges Bataille, the author of Inner Experience (1943), a book she recalls having found both irritating and deeply moving. Beauvoir, Sartre, Bataille, Leiris, Raymond Queneau, Albert Camus, Pablo Picasso, Dora Maar, and others then began to celebrate a series of what Leiris called "fiestas." According to Beauvoir, the first fete took place in Georges Bataille's apartment, where the Jewish musician René Leibovitz and his wife were in hiding. More followed in the weeks and months to come.

When Beauvoir describes these drunken, carnivalesque nights in her 1960 memoir, The Prime of Life, she refers readers to the theories of the festival first developed before the war by Bataille and his friend and intellectual associate, the anthropologist Roger Caillois.[1] But there is a curious disjunction in her deployment of these theories, particularly concerning the issues of time and history. Beauvoir argues, first, that for her "the festival is before all else an ardent apotheosis of the present, in face of inquietude concerning the future" (FA 655; PL 573). Still aware of the dangers that surround them, she and her friends engage in a festival through which "death, during one resplendent moment, is reduced to nothing" (FA 656; PL 573). Beauvoir insists that there was no self-deception in their pleasure: "We did not deceive ourselves: we only wanted to snatch from this confusion some nuggets of joy and to get drunk from their brightness, in defiance of the disillusions that lay ahead" (FA 656; PL 573).

Yet she goes on to argue that a victorious future was made present in the fiestas themselves. According to Beauvoir, she and her friends

> became a sort of fraternity, performing its secret rites sheltered from the world. And the fact is, it was necessary for us to invent magic spells, for the landings had not yet taken place, Paris was not liberated, and Hitler not killed: how to celebrate events that are not yet accomplished? There exist magical conductors that abolish distances of space and time: the emotions. We worked up a vast collective emotion that fulfilled our longings without delay: victory became tangible in the fever that emotion kindled. (FA 656; PL 574)

Here there is no older, wiser, Beauvoir, aware of the horrors that await at the end of the war; we seem closer to the enthusiasm and sense of future possibilities that run throughout Beauvoir's and Sartre's writings in the mid-1940s.

Beauvoir's initial account of the fetes evinces a struggle between her desire both to maintain the value of these celebrations—fueled as they were by alcohol, sleeplessness, song and dance—and to deny that they represent a rejection of history. These few minutes snatched out of the present were valuable, she recalls, in reawakening a sense of life's pleasures and possibilities. Yet she insists that they never completely deceived her or her companions into believing that harsh wartime realities had been overcome. To be so deceived would be to think that the festivals negated history, taking one out of time into a realm in which death has no reality; Beauvoir is then careful to argue that neither she nor her companions ever fully succumbed to this atemporal, ahistorical emotionality.

Yet in Beauvoir's second account, the fetes made present the future—an Allied victory and the possibilities opened by that victory. Only in light of subsequent experience does Beauvoir recognize the gap between the future's reality and its evocation in the festival. According to this account, the fetes do not take her out of time and history, even for a moment, but into a hoped for future. Only when she comes to recognize that her vision of the future was wrong does Beauvoir reinterpret the festival as the erasure of time itself—

although always only in part and provisionally. In other words, I think that Beauvoir understood the festival initially as itself a historical event (a making present of the future); only later, in order to elide her own optimistic earlier self (a self the older Beauvoir no doubt sees as embarrassingly naïve), does she reread the festival as taking—or perhaps better, giving the illusion of taking—its participants out of time. In this version, her concern for maintaining responsibility to history leads Beauvoir to claim that she and her companions never fully succumbed to the emotional festivities they enjoyed in the final months of the war.

These two conceptions of the festival and its relationship to time and history sit side by side in Beauvoir's text, perhaps, as I have suggested, marking different moments in her understanding of the temporality of the wartime fiestas. There is a similar disjunction between Bataille's understanding of temporality and ecstasy in *Inner Experience* and Sartre's interpretation of that text in his review essay "Un nouveau mystique," first published in 1943 in the resistance journal *Cahiers du Sud*; moreover, Sartre's essay itself manifests a crucial ambivalence in its reading of Bataille.

At the level of explicit critique, Sartre claims that Bataille evokes the temporality and historicity of the human condition only in order to attempt an escape from that condition through the instantaneous. Bataille, Sartre argues, is a "new mystic" or a "pantheist *noir*," who claims to confront human contingency, history, and the death of God only in order to evade them in a flight to the transcendent. By hypostatizing negation and nothingness as the unknown, Sartre claims, even Bataille's experience of the void becomes a space in which the transcendent might emerge. Bataille simultaneously denies God and mysticism and returns to a transcendent reality and a new kind of mystical, atemporal communion with it; for Sartre, these contradictions convincingly demonstrate Bataille's bad faith. Yet beneath Sartre's explicit analysis of *Inner Experience* lies another reading of Bataille's work, one in which the problem is not Bataille's desire to escape history, but the inordinate nature of his historically situated desire. Not surprisingly, Sartre suggests this alternative reading of Bataille in a discussion of the festival.

By 1943, Sartre had published his important philosophical novel, *Nausea* (1938), and his long account of "phenomenological ontology," *Being and Nothingness* (1943), as well as a number of shorter philosophical studies. In the final years of the war, he wrote a series of review essays in which he assesses the major writers among his contemporaries, thereby establishing his own position as a central critical voice in postwar France. In these reviews, Sartre asserts mastery over French philosophy and literature, creates alliances with like-minded thinkers, and carefully differentiates his positions from those of his contemporaries. "A New Mystic" should be read in the context of this critical enterprise, which was closely tied to the postwar purge of writers and intellectuals.

As Philip Watts shows, the spirit of the purge emerged well before the end of the war. As early as 1942, Sartre and others associated with the resistance to German occupation and the Vichy regime demanded retribution from those who collaborated with the Germans. In that year the resistance journal *Les Lettres françaises* proclaimed: "French letters are under attack," and "we will defend them."[2] This defense required identification of those who served the cause of France and those who betrayed her; an essential part of Sartre's self-appointed critical task lay in making and supporting such judgments. Only in this way could the ground be cleared of old, destructive influences and opened for the dissemination of new intellectual, artistic, and political projects.

Bataille, who in the late 1920s and in the 1930s was an active, if often dissident, participant in the world of surrealism, literary and artistic reviews, and left-wing politics, might seem to represent the old Parisian scene rather than the new world to which Sartre looks in the mid-1940s.[3] Sartre suggests as much when he dismisses Bataille's desire to lose himself as "rigorously *dated*; one recalls the thousand experiences of the young people of 1925: drugs, eroticism, and all those lives tossed up to chance out of the hatred of project" (NM 173–74). Sartre here betrays his familiarity with Bataille's prewar writings and suggests the deeper reasons for his rejection of (although with lingering signs of fascination, as I will show) Bataille's work:

> What one glimpses under the icy exhortations of this solitary is nostalgia for one of those primitive festivals where a whole tribe gets drunk, laughs and dances and couples by chance, one of those festivals that are consummation and consumption, and where each one, in the frenzy of running amok, in joy, lacerates himself and mutilates himself, gaily destroys a year's worth of patiently amassed wealth, and finally loses himself, rips himself up like a piece of cloth, gives himself to death while singing—without God, without hope, carried by wine and cries and sex [*le rut*] to the extremes of generosity, killing himself *for nothing*. (NM 174)

Sartre glimpses the excesses of Bataille's prewar work on the festival in Bataille's wartime writing; he here acknowledges that Bataille's desire is exorbitant, without limits, and uncontainable. Yet Sartre immediately asks whether Bataille is *sincere* in this desire and argues, ultimately, that he is not. Despite denying salvation, Sartre avers, Bataille claims to find it.

Thus it is less the prewar excesses of Bataille (and the other surrealists and dissident surrealists with whom Sartre associates him) that Sartre explicitly rejects than it is Bataille's complicity, as Sartre sees it, with a certain "totalitarian thought" (NM 149)—despite the fragmentation of Bataille's text. "Monsieur Bataille," Sartre writes, "wants to exist wholly and immediately: in the instant" (NM 147). Sartre has no grounds for claiming Bataille's complicity with fascism;[4] he recognizes, moreover, that the form of Bataille's text seems antithetical to totalitarian thought and practice. Yet beneath *Inner Experience*'s fragmentation and heterogeneity, Sartre purports to glimpse a thinking grounded in the absolute, the transcendent, and the denial of history and project. Sartre does not repeat the heavily incriminating term "totalitarian";[5] yet his three interlocking criticisms of Bataille's text are linked by this early, seemingly passing, denunciation.

Sartre begins by criticizing Bataille for confusing scientific and existentialist claims. Bataille writes a "martyr-essay" grounded in interior experience and revolt, but at the same time purports to speak scientifically and objectively about nature and the human condition. Moreover, he believes that scientific facts give rise to and explain human experiences of anguish and revolt. "Monsieur Bataille," Sartre writes, "simultaneously takes on two contradictory points of view" (NM 162) and hence cannot escape error and absurdity. Bataille's ideas are "soft" and "unformed" (*informe*, a crucial term in the early Bataille's lexicon),[6] Sartre complains, in sharp contrast to the "hardness" of his emotions (NM 171). By continually reinterpreting Bataille's arguments in terms of German existentialism (to the extent that Sartre implies Bataille's thought must be translated into German to be rendered coherent), Sartre suggests that what Bataille lacks is the existentialist, phenomenological method through which subjective consciousness can be philosophically described. In other words, to make sense of the quasi-existentialist aspect of Bataille's thought, Sartre needs the method and descriptive ontology that he himself provides in *Being and Nothingness*.[7]

Sartre goes on to argue that Bataille's description of the human condition does not lie at the heart of his text, an argument that leads Sartre to his second critique of Bataille. Although Bataille pretends to locate human beings fully in history, speaking of the human condition rather than of human nature and underscoring the contingency and historicity of human existence, he simultaneously claims to step outside of history in the instantaneous moment. The turn to history, Sartre suggests, is merely a vestige of Bataille's Catholic past. As in the Catholic tradition, history will ultimately be overcome through a salvific apotheosis (NM 150). Bataille asserts the death of God and the end of salvation, Sartre argues, but reinstates the transcendent as nothingness or the unknown and then claims a mystical union with that unknown:

> By naming nothing the unknown, I turn it into an existence whose essence is to escape my knowing; and if I add that I know nothing, that signifies that I communicate with this existence in some way other than by knowing. . . . It appears that abandonment to this night is ravishing: I am hardly astonished. This is a way, in effect, to dissolve oneself into *nothing*. But this nothing is easily managed in such a way as to be *all*. (NM 184)

From Sartre's perspective, Bataille's desire to be all is itself a form of totalitarian thinking.

According to Sartre, then, Bataille's methodological confusions are intimately related to his "bad faith" concerning God, salvation, and mysticism, for his desire to stand outside the human condition and history is reflected in his claim to scientific objectivity. "M. Bataille vainly attempts to integrate himself into the machinery that he has set up [*montée*]: he remains outside, with Durkheim, with Hegel, with God the Father" (NM 166). By claiming scientific objectivity, Sartre argues, Bataille allies himself with the absolute and thereby attempts to escape the very human condition he describes; he wants to escape history, engagement with history, and hence politics.

Sartre's and Bataille's opposing attitudes toward human projects are crucial here. Sartre insists that to be human is to engage in projects; Bataille argues that inner experience is the opposite of project; thus he generates endlessly recursive negations of his own attempt to provide a method for attaining inner experience. As Jean-François Louette argues, for Sartre

> a project unifies the course of time and gives it the form of an intention that wants to inscribe itself in the course of things. Sartre, in maintaining against Bataille the notion of project, defends at the same time his ontology of time and the condition for the possibility of politics. This is defined at the same time as putting the self into play without hope of winning everything . . . ; and as a non-ecstatic, because not instantaneous, temporality, one which forms

"the framework of new enterprises" for "a new humanity who will surpass itself toward new ends."[8]

Louette here cites Sartre's closing injunction to Bataille. For Sartre, if inner experience does not give rise to new enterprises it is worth nothing more than "the pleasure of drinking a glass of alcohol or of warming oneself in the sun at the beach" (NM 187). Such experiences are, for Sartre, "useless."

Finally, Sartre accuses Bataille of claiming to wish to communicate while writing with a contempt for his audience that blocks communication. Sartre outlines Bataille's constant queries about how silence and interior experience can be communicated and suggests that Bataille, who was for a brief period a devout Christian, remains a crypto-Christian despite his overt atheism.[9] Bataille writes only for the "apprentice mystic"; but even such "preaching to the converted" causes him distress (NM 151–52). Ultimately, like the evangelist possessed of a truth that he is required to share, "the communication that he wants to establish is without reciprocity. He is in the heights, we are down below. He delivers us a message: he receives it who can. But that which adds to our trouble, is that the summit from which he speaks to us is at the same time the profound 'abyss' of abjection" (NM 152). Once again, we see the interrelation of Sartre's three critiques, for to stand on the heights bestowing a message on those below is to stand outside the human condition with a truth one must convey to those still trapped within it. The injunction to speak or to write generates endless paradoxes, according to Sartre, for Bataille must move from a singular experience of eternity back into time in order to speak to those still immersed within history. The paradoxes generated by the demand for speech give rise, Sartre suggests, to Bataille's "hatred of discourse" and to the fragmentation and disdain of his writing.

And yet, Sartre claims, there is much "to praise in this mode of expression: [Bataille] offers the essayist an example and a tradition; he brings us back to the sources, to Pascal, to Montaigne, and, at the same time, he proposes a language, a syntax more adapted to the problems of our epoch" (NM 152). On one reading, these words of praise structure Sartre's review, for he opens with the claim that the contemporary essay "is in crisis" (NM 143). Essayists (unlike novelists), Sartre argues, have not found a language adequate to the contemporary world; even that language in which Sartre himself writes is, he claims, an outdated one, "preserved up until our time by the university tradition" (NM 143). Bataille, following the tradition of Pascal, Nietzsche, and the surrealists, offers an alternative, a language that operates through emotion rather than through (or perhaps better, in addition to) reason. Such a nonliterary literature seeks, Sartre writes, "direct access." Sartre makes his most revealing comments about Bataille's style in a brief discussion of André Breton.[10] Breton's constant oscillation between cold, theoretical discourse and an exhibitionism that "destroys all literature" evinces a desire to uncover "the true monster" behind those imitated by art. This monster, uncovered through the "direct access" of a language without restraint, establishes "between the author and the reader a sort of fleshly promiscuity [*promiscuité charnelle*]" (NM 145).

These comments on the "martyr-essay" and the vitality of its language once again evoke Bataille's account of the festival as a frenzy of affect through which "conviction" is generated. In praising the power of Bataille's language, more-over, Sartre seems to embrace affect as the site of contemporaneity. Sartre's comments clarify the crucial difference between Beauvoir and Bataille on the festival, for whereas Beauvoir, in her initial account of the wartime fetes, argues that the festival makes the future present, Sartre rightly suggests that for Bataille one speaks through emotion directly to the present moment. The problem with Bataille, Sartre argues, is that he tries to bring this emotion-laden language together with rational, scientific forms of discourse; in other words, Bataille attempts to universalize the particular and to make the subjective objective. In choosing history against metaphysics (NM 149), Sartre suggests, Bataille must eschew any claim to universality and objectivity. The subjective language of af-fect and emotion, Sartre argues, necessarily remains on the level of the "flesh" (*promiscuité charnelle*) and of the present; if not carefully directed toward a mean-ingful project, it is in danger of offering merely idiosyncratic pleasure and emo-tion. In other words, Bataille's style has contemporary relevance—it speaks to the present in a way Sartre's own scholarly and reflective language cannot—but what Bataille communicates through that style is either fundamentally confused (and potentially fascistic) or evanescent and useless (like the festival, for Sartre; thus we see his slightly different attitude toward emotional conflagrations from that found in Beauvoir's memoir).[11] Bataille suffers, one might say, from being *too* contemporary.

By describing so vividly the communicative power of Bataille's style, how-ever, Sartre raises questions about his own subsequent assertion that Bataille does not communicate. I think the real issue for Sartre is *what* is communicated —idiosyncratic affect or something useful that can give rise to projects produc-tive of a new world (in the wake of the war's destruction of the old). Sartre claims that Breton (and, by implication, Bataille) establishes a "fleshly promis-cuity" with his readers—the problem for Sartre is precisely the carnality and excess of this communication and its refusal to be contained by any political or literary project. Bataille calls for an immersion in the present that seems in danger, Sartre suggests, of eliding the future. Just as Beauvoir exhibits ambivalence toward the emotional excess of the wartime fetes (expressed through her slide between present and future and her attempt to delimit the extent to which the emotions take over and/or take her out of history), so Sartre admires the "martyr-essay" and its grounding in affect but at the same time profoundly distrusts the excesses it reflects and to which it gives rise.[12] Only if these excesses are contained by project can they be meaningful and useful.

Arguably, Sartre's reading of Bataille as desiring to be all is a moment of just such containment—better a totalitarian thinker than one who radically challenges any conception of totality and limitation. Sartre claims that Bataille never undermines the totalitarian desire for immediacy and pure presence, for Sartre reads Bataille's excesses as an embrace of emotion, corporeality, and plenitude. Unable "to exist wholly and immediately" through the homogenizing power of reason, Sartre implies, Bataille renounces reason for the emotions, those "magical conductors," according to Beauvoir, "that abolish distances of space and time." In other words, Sartre reads Bataille's excesses as contained by his desire for wholeness. Seen in this light, Sartre fears Bataille's embrace of a fascistic subordination of reason to the immediacy of the emotions.

Sartre's reservations are not without warrant, and I will return to them in the following chapters. Yet Sartre refuses to acknowledge that Bataille worries about another form of subordination, one that, he would argue, is equally amenable to fascistic or totalitarian manipulation—the subordination of the present to a projected future. From this perspective, what bothers Sartre about Bataille may be less the latter's putative desire to escape history than the relentlessness of his immersion in history and in the flesh, an immersion that seems to deny—or at least to suspend—the rationality of human existence. For Sartre, human existence in its givenness is absurd, but human beings can and must project themselves into futures grounded in human will, desire, and reason.[13] To live authentically is to live in conscious pursuit of one's own projects. It is precisely this future-oriented and consciously crafted life that Bataille's encounter with history and pursuit of excessive desire most radically challenge.

Bataille's response to Sartre suggests that he understands the true source of Sartre's unease. He replies to Sartre in On Nietzsche (1945), the third and final volume of his Atheological Summa. The response takes two forms. Part 3 of On Nietzsche is entitled "Diary February–August 1944." In the midst of a fragmented discussion of asceticism ("I loathe monks"), Bataille offers his own brief account of the festivals in which he engaged with Sartre, Camus, and others:

> Happy to remember the night when I drank and danced—danced alone, like a peasant, like a faun, in the midst of couples.
>
> Alone? To tell the truth, we were dancing face to face, in a potlatch of absurdity, the philosopher—Sartre—and me. (OC VI 90; ON 75)

Here Bataille seems to implicate Sartre (who as a philosopher Bataille may see as committed to monkish asceticism, despite Sartre's own unruly practices) in the fleshly promiscuity of the festival, to remind Sartre that he too participated in the fiesta. Bataille's drunken and dancing Sartre is, perhaps, even in danger of a nonheterosexual, nonproductive fleshly encounter.[14]

Later in On Nietzsche, amid a series of appendixes, Bataille replies to Sartre more directly. Most of the reply is made up of long quotations from Sartre's essay. After citing at length the passage in which Sartre accuses Bataille of contradiction and bad faith, Bataille writes: "Sartre aptly describes my movements of spirit, basing himself on my book, underlining their foolishness from the outside better than I could from the inside (I was moved): insights, dissected by an indifferent lucidity—I must say that the painful character of my thought is comically (as it should be) marked" (OC VI 196; ON 181). By underlining Sartre's objectivity, his externality to the experience described, Bataille immediately raises questions about the adequacy of Sartre's categories. For Bataille, as I will show, the contradictions between inner and outer, existential and scientific, and subjective and objective themselves enact or engender the movements of inner experience. Sartre, in attempting to maintain a rigid distinction between the two forms of discourse or knowledge, may adequately describe Bataille's confusion, but he will never understand his experience: "My vertiginous fall and the difference it introduces into the spirit can not be grasped by one who has not experienced it in themselves" (OC VI 199; ON 183). The movement through the contradictions of Bataille's texts engender this experience in the reader.

Bataille's response to Sartre's methodological critique leads directly to his reply to the second charge Sartre makes against him: "From that [lack of experience] one can, as Sartre does, successively reproach me for ending up with God, ending up with the void! These contradictory reproaches support my affirmation: I never end up anywhere!" (OC VI 199; ON 184). Whereas Sartre contrasts

Bataille's mystical rejection of language with Camus's terrorist revolt, Bataille insists that rather than desiring to be all, he rejects totality and totalization:

> In other words, the moment of revolt inherent in the will to knowledge beyond practical ends cannot be indefinitely prolonged: to be the whole of the universe, humanity has to let go of its principle: to accept nothing of that which is, except the tendency to go beyond that which is. This being [être] that I am is a revolt against being, it is indefinite *desire*: God was, for it, only a stage—and now here he is, grown large from an immeasurable experience, comically perched on a stake. (OC VI 202; ON 187)

Desire is not emotion as pure presence but a continual interplay of presence and absence. The desire to be all subverts itself in immeasurable, unending, and indefinite desire. Here Bataille both contests Sartre's explicit reading and suggests the real fear of excess that underlies Sartre's rejection of inner experience.

We can read Bataille, then, as demonstrating both what he *has* communicated to Sartre and where his efforts at communication fail; insofar as Sartre has glimpsed the excess, the fleshly promiscuity and unbounded emotion of Bataille's inner experience, communication takes place. Sartre's rejection of that experience in the name of philosophical coherence, universalizability, and project, however, marks the failure of Bataille's text. He has not elicited inner experience in his reader and so, ultimately, his text (or his reader?) fails.[15]

In calling Bataille a mystic, Sartre wants to underline Bataille's purported desire to be all, to escape time and history, and to become one with the unknown. This "totalitarian" reading of Bataille's writing and experience is, then, closely linked to the claim that in turning to mysticism, Bataille walks away from history and politics. In the following chapters, I will argue that what is most mystical in Bataille is, on the contrary, the excessive desire and fleshly promiscuity periodically glimpsed within Sartre's critique. The gap between Sartre's understanding of Bataille's mysticism and my own suggests a doubleness within the mystical, which Bataille—and following him Beauvoir and Lacan—indicates is marked both by the desire to be all and the recognition that one cannot be everything. Bataille does not desire to escape history and temporality but to engage with them differently, and he makes use of the ambiguities of his mystical sources to help him think, write, and live a new relationship to history and to the other. This new relationship involves a continual contestation of the distinctions between content and form, mysticism and history, and atheism and theism on which Sartre's critique rests.

THE SCANDAL OF

THE REAL

· ·

Language is, by nature, fictional.

ROLAND BARTHES, *Camera Lucida*

The I has no importance. For a reader, I am any being: name, identity, the historical don't change anything. He (reader) is anyone and I (author) am anyone.

GEORGES BATAILLE, *Inner Experience*

Bataille, la peur—Bataille, fear

Bataille, after all, affects me little enough: what have I to do with laughter, devotion, poetry, violence? What have I to say about "the sacred," about "the impossible"?

Yet no sooner do I make all this (alien) language coincide with that disturbance in myself which I call *fear* than Bataille conquers me all over again: then everything he *inscribes describes* me: it sticks.

ROLAND BARTHES, *Roland Barthes*

THE PROBLEM OF EXPERIENCE

For Sartre, one of the many scandalous aspects of Bataille's work is its confusion of two kinds of language, a quasi-existential language grounded in emotion and personal experience, and the language of scientific objectivity. The experiences of what Sartre presumes to be the autobiographical subject of *Inner Experience* further scandalize Sartre (as they have many subsequent readers) in their exces-

36

sive corporeality and essential uselessness. Bataille's response to the claim that he moves illegitimately from the personal to the scientific appears at first sight evasive:

> I don't know if in this way I express human powerlessness—or my own. . . . I don't know, but I have little hope of coming to a conclusion, even if it were one that comes from outside. But isn't there an advantage in doing philosophy the way I do it: a flash in the night, the language of a short instant? . . . Maybe on this subject, the latest moment contains a simple truth. (OC VI 201–2; ON 186)

Bataille here claims ignorance about the objective value of his writing, an ignorance that is constitutive of his mode of thinking itself. Yet if Bataille does not wish to claim scientific universality and objectivity for his account of the human condition, why does he couch portions of his argument in that language? And if, as I will argue below, he ultimately refuses to legitimize his texts through appeals to personal experience, why does he also continuously gesture toward the autobiographical? The two problems, as I will show, are intimately related and tied directly to Bataille's conception of the interplay between communication and experience.

In response to Sartre's claim that Bataille's hypostatization of nothingness represents a "black pantheism," Bataille insists on the conditional nature of that accusation:

> At this point, I should reprimand Sartre: *would be*, it is necessary to say, *a pantheism noir* . . . it would be, if, let us say, my infinite turbulence did not deprive from me in advance any possibility of stopping. . . . Without a doubt, I myself perceived (under some form) these inextricable difficulties—*my thought, its movement taking off from them*—but it was like the countryside seen from a rapid train [*d'un rapide*] and what I always saw was the dissolution of these difficulties in movement, their rebirth under other forms accelerating with a disastrous rapidity. (OC VI 198; ON 182–83)

Bataille emphasizes the movement of his thinking, writing, and experience. His thinking emerges out of contradictions yet cannot keep these generative contradictions in sight because of its rapidity and unstoppable trajectory. There is a movement here, Bataille implies, that cannot be stopped from the outside. Sartre condemns inner experience as useless because it does not lead to new enterprises. This is right, according to Bataille; but he then goes on to insist that

> it is precisely because they [inner experiences] are such—leaving
> one empty—that they prolong themselves in me as anguish. What
> I try to describe in *Inner Experience* is this movement, which, losing
> all possibility of being stopped, falls easily victim to a critique that
> believes it can stop the movement from the outside, because the
> critique is not *taken* into the movement. (OC VI 199; ON 183)

Sartre has not experienced what Bataille describes; he stands outside inner experience and believes he can halt it with a view to the future. In other words, Sartre has not gotten on the train, allowing the contradictions of Bataille's text to start a movement of thought and writing that engenders new kinds of experience. For Bataille, the success of his writing depends on its eliciting inner experience in his readers. The key to his use of objective, scientific language lies here—it is not that he wishes to make his subjective experience objective, but that he wants to move the reader from the language of science to that of experience. Precisely the contradictions in his use of scientific language (and the contradiction between scientific and existential language) work to engender inner experience (and hence, paradoxically, to render Bataille's writing general).

The paradoxical interplay of exterior and interior, objective and subjective, general and particular runs throughout Bataille's work, particularly when he writes about mysticism, religion, and eroticism. In his 1957 study of eroticism, Bataille claims that "without private experience we could discuss neither eroticism nor religion."[1] To have a genuine understanding of the forms and practices of eroticism, Bataille argues, one must be effected bodily by them; objectivity, which would require the absence of subjective response, marks an inability to understand the erotic. Similarly, knowledge of religious beliefs, rites, and practices, if it is to be genuine, must be joined by inner experience, a subjective response to these phenomena.[2] Hence the "scientific" study of eroticism and of religion is always thwarted by the intrusion of subjectivity into its objective analysis. This methodological insight points, for Bataille, to the deeper relationship between the erotic and the religious. Bataille distinguishes three forms of eroticism—physical, emotional, and religious—and thus argues that the religious is a subset of the erotic. Physical, emotional, and religious experiences are fundamentally tied together in that all three bring about the dissolution of the self and hence of the boundaries between inner and outer that Bataille's own appeal to experience seems, paradoxically, to erect.

One might argue, then, that Bataille's erotic fictions are the key to under-standing his theories of physical and emotional eroticism and that his journals and other apparently first-person accounts of religious experience (particularly those collected in his three-volume *Atheological Summa*) are the key to understanding his theory of religion and of religious eroticism. We might, for example, read the "Diary" sections of Bataille's wartime publication *On Nietzsche* (the third volume of the *Atheological Summa*) as exemplifying the kinds of experience that gave rise to his posthumously published *Theory of Religion*. This reading would be only slightly complicated by the recognition of Bataille's claim that eroticism and religion are closely related and that his erotic fiction is crucial to under-standing his other writings. Bataille insists, for example, that *Madame Edwarda*, in which the protagonist sees God in a prostitute's genitals, is so "closely linked" to *Inner Experience* (the first volume of the *Atheological Summa*) that "one cannot understand one without the other" (OC V 421; IE 168). It appears, then, that any understanding of Bataille's "experience" as constitutive of his "theories" would have to look at his accounts of both inner experience and eroticism.

Yet the move from "experience" to "theory" assumes that Bataille's erotic and religious texts offer accounts of his own experience and that there is a close tie between Bataille's apparently experiential writing and the genre of autobiography, understood within a realist mode.[3] This assumption is displayed in commentaries on Bataille's work, which tend to read them—novels, articles, poems, aphoristic and expository writings—as records of his own experience. Although only occasionally described as autobiographical (the second part of Bataille's first published book, *Story of the Eye* [1928], is one crucial exception), Bataille's works are continually read autobiographically, that is, as texts that both record Bataille's experiences and reflect and effect those of the reader.[4] Such interpretations assume that the theoretical is grounded in the experiential. To craft such interpretations, commentators rely on and simultaneously undermine the distinctions between private and public, subjective and objective, and inner and outer that are central to Bataille's methodological claims in *Erotism*. Yet if experience grounds Bataille's theory, then objectivity is undermined and theory itself becomes merely another aspect of Bataille's subjective experience. In this case, Sartre's initial critique stands, and we are forced to ask on what grounds Bataille moves from his own idiosyncratic experience to a general theory of religion and eroticism.

The contradictions these autobiographical interpretations produce suggest that Bataille is working toward an understanding of experience at odds with that deployed by most philosophers and theorists. To read Bataille's texts as autobiographical presumes that there is an experience recoverable behind his texts. Experience is taken as self-evident and "construed as unified, holistic, coherent, and present to itself."[5] As Martin Jay explains, within nineteenth- and twentieth-century philosophy and cultural studies, experience is generally understood to embody these qualities in one of two ways: "as a marker for the immediacy of lived, prereflexive encounters between self and world privileged by the tradition of *Lebensphilosophie* from Dilthey on under the rubric of *Erlebnis*, or as a marker for the cumulative wisdom over time produced by the interaction of self and world that is generally called *Erfahrung*."[6] According to poststructuralist critics, Jay continues, the appeal to experience is an ill-conceived attempt to recover a presence, immediacy, and self-identity that never existed in the first place.[7]

Bataille, however, seeks to deconstruct common notions of experience, even as he appeals to them. He insists, for example, that experience shatters the self and its history, destroying any pretense to self-presence and immediacy. Thus any reading of the relationship between Bataille's "experiential" and theoretical texts must take into account the particularity of Bataille's deployment of experience, which systematically subverts prevailing phenomenological accounts of experience as immediacy and self-presence (despite and against Sartre's assertion that Bataille's notion of experience is best exemplified by the German term *Erlebnis*). Moreover, we must bear in mind that Bataille's work effects this subversion through writing itself, and so we must pay careful attention to the relationship between his writing strategies and the idea of experience. As I will show, in a number of texts Bataille explicitly invokes the autobiographical subject only in order to subvert it.

Jacques Derrida has perhaps gone furthest in demonstrating the self-subverting quality of Bataille's appeal to experience. According to Derrida, Bataille is best read in light of his critique of Hegel. The crucial feature of Bataille's anti-Hegelianism is not his explicit critiques of the phenomenology of mind, reason, and experience central to Hegel's enterprise, but his doubling of that discourse, a doubling that unleashes an excessive other disruptive of the closed Hegelian system. Bataille's writing practice opens Hegel's system to nonmeaning and radical negativity, destabilizing and unsettling reason itself. As Derrida shows, Bataille's writing is always double; it works with the terms of Hegelian philosophy—hence whole portions of Bataille's texts appear to offer a classical philosophy of the subject and of voluntarism—yet "the *same* concepts, apparently unchanged in themselves, will be subject to a mutation of meaning, or rather will be struck by (even though they are apparently indifferent), the loss of sense toward which they slide, thereby ruining themselves immeasurably."[8] The scientific language to which Sartre objects is subject to the same subversive doubling movement.

Perhaps most important, Bataille subjects experience itself, as Derrida notes, to this sliding movement:

> That which *indicates itself* as interior experience is not an experience, because it is related to no presence, to no plenitude, but only to the 'impossible' it 'undergoes' in torture. This experience above all is not interior: and if it seems to be such because it is related to nothing else, to no exterior (except in the modes of non-relation, secrecy and rupture), it is also completely *exposed*—to torture— naked, open to the exterior, with no interior reserve or feelings, profoundly superficial.[9]

Not only does Bataille subvert the language of philosophical and scientific objectivity by placing it in uneasy proximity to emotion and subjectivity, he also calls into question philosophical accounts of subjectivity and experience. His quasi-existential language of experience is itself unsettled and unsettling (as Sartre's reference to its "fleshly promiscuity" attests), refusing any final halt to the movement of that experience. To effect the subversion of the concept of experience as immediacy and interiority, however, the *appeal* to interior experience must be made. This movement is exemplified by Bataille's appeals to an autobiographical subject that is subverted by the very same movement of writing by which it is constructed.

Autobiographical readings of Bataille's work, then, are not simply mistaken; his texts consistently point the reader to such interpretations, often at their most scandalous moments. (Again, Sartre initiates such autobiographical readings when, at the close of "Un nouveau mystique," he suggests that what Bataille really needs is a good—presumably existentialist—psychoanalyst [NM 187– 88].) Not only does Bataille explicitly use the journal form in his aphoristic writings (particularly in the *Atheological Summa*), but in *Story of the Eye* and other fictions he offers what seem to be keys suggesting the autobiographical roots of central images and events in the primary narrative. Moreover, in *Erotism* he insists that any theory of eroticism and religion has to be grounded in experience.

Yet as Derrida indicates, there are reasons to distrust the transparency of these autobiographical gestures and to read them as strategic. An inveterate wearer of masks, concerned with the dissolution of the self through erotic (and) religious experience, Bataille incessantly problematizes the relationship between himself and the texts that bear his name. Even those texts most widely accepted as unproblematically autobiographical, most prominently "Coincidences," the second part of Story of the Eye, are fraught with referential difficulties. For instance, any easy identification of Bataille's erotic writing with his own experience is immediately problematized by the fact that these texts are fictions; moreover, they always appeared pseudonymously during Bataille's lifetime. One might argue that this pseudonymity was simply a pragmatic precaution; given French obscenity laws, pornographic texts often used such safeguards to protect against prosecution. In addition, as a functionary of the state (Bataille was a librarian at the Bibliothèque Nationale in Paris and later in the municipal library at Orléans), Bataille might well have wished to avoid scandal. Yet careful analysis of Bataille's writing strategies suggests the centrality of pseudonymity to his work. Moreover, even those texts that are apparently nonfiction (some of which appear within the pseudonymous works) and those that bear his name are infected by the complexity of his notion of experience and its relationship to fictionality.

In short, there can be no easy movement from writing to experience and from the "experiential" to the "theoretical" in Bataille's corpus, for these distinctions are continually subverted by his writing practice. The scandal of Bataille's texts may lie less in their putatively autobiographical subject matter than in the operations through which that subjectivity is simultaneously effaced and communicated. In order to analyze these operations, let me turn to Story of the Eye and to the relationship between its two parts: the violently erotic "Tale" with which the book begins, and "Coincidences," the self-reflexive, seemingly autobiographical commentary that follows.[10]

REALITY EFFECTS

As Linda Williams recounts in Hard Core: Power, Pleasure, and the "Frenzy of the Visible," rumors about snuff films began to circulate in New York City during 1975. Word was out that police had confiscated underground films from South America said to include footage of women being murdered. These rumors seemed to be confirmed by the 1976 release of a movie called Snuff. The main body of the movie shares features with the slasher genre. Filmed in South America, it depicts the murderous activities of a Charles Manson-esque cult leader and his followers. The movie culminates in a bloodbath and the stabbing of a pregnant actress; it is the epilogue, however, that earns the film its title. Williams describes the scene after the actress's murder:

The camera pulls back to reveal a movie set with camera, crew, and director. A "script girl" admires the director's work and tells him she was turned on by the scene. He invites her to have sex; she complies until she realizes that this scene, too, is being filmed. When she tries to pull away, the director grabs the knife from the previous scene, looks directly at the camera and says, presumably to the operator, "You want to get a good scene?" and proceeds to slice off first her fingers, then her hand, and then the rest of her. The sequence culminates in the director cutting open the women's abdomen, pulling out her inner organs, and holding them over his head in triumph while the sound track mixes heavy panting with the beat of a throbbing heart. The organs seem to convulse. The image goes black as a voice says, "Shit, we ran out of film." Another says, "Did you get it all?" "Yeah, we got it. Let's get out of here." No credits roll.[11]

The movie generated outraged responses from feminist antipornography activists, who believed these closing shots were of the script girl's actual murder.[12] For many, the apparently real violence of Snuff signaled the logical outcome of pornography.

Yet as investigators for the *New York Times* and the New York City district attorney's office soon discovered, *Snuff* was a hoax (or just a movie?). The actress who played the script girl was alive and well and interviewed by officials. The epilogue was the work of an opportunistic producer (Alan Shakleton) who, inspired by the recent rumors about snuff films from South America, had added it to a shelved 1971 exploitation film by Roberta and Michael Findlay. People fell for the snuff claims in part because of the scene's self-reflexive gestures (pulling back to show the movie set and shifting suddenly from sex to violence) and documentary signs (the director's speech to the camera, the claim that the film had run out). These are cinematic narrative conventions intended to fool the viewer; in some way—and presumably for some viewers—the thrills and pleasures of horror are enhanced by the claim that what is happening on the screen is real.[13]

Hard-core porn, according to Williams, rests on the unique relationship between the thing (the erect and ejaculating penis and its penetration of the vagina) and its representation. Given the specificities of the filmic apparatus, the "realness" of the sex it depicts becomes crucial to distinguishing hard-core porn as a genre.[14] Apparently, "the money shot" (an ejaculating penis) cannot be faked. Or at least this is the convention on which hard-core as a genre rests.[15] Williams is interested in *Snuff* because of the genre confusions surrounding it within the antipornography debates; although the movie galvanized many feminists in their fight against pornography, it does not, strictly speaking, belong to the hard-core genre. It contains only soft-core (hence simulated) sex and none of the conventional hard-core shots or heavily choreographed routines. Yet perhaps when exploitation, horror, and violence purport to be shown "for real," they become hard-core, suggesting that what makes a film hard-core is not necessarily the sex but the claims for the realness of what is seen. (Although clearly the shocking nature of that which is displayed—sex and violence—also plays a crucial role in defining the genre.) The fact that the violence as well as the sex in *Snuff* were faked reestablishes boundaries that the movie's reality effects seek to undermine.

Bataille's *Story of the Eye* includes a similar self-reflexive movement and concomitant reality effect, as well as a mingling of sex and violence (moreover, the slicing of the "script girl" in *Snuff* is reminiscent of Bataille's descriptions, in *Guilty* and *Inner Experience*, of pictures of a torture victim on which he meditates in pursuit of inner experience). The often scandalized responses to this and other texts by Bataille are similar to those with which *Snuff* was greeted in 1976 and seem to depend in large part on a conflation of Bataille with the narrator(s) of his book(s). Furthermore, the reality effects in *Story of the Eye* and other texts are almost always taken literally—by both detractors and advocates. I have yet to hear anyone accuse Bataille of murder—the double narrative of *Story of the Eye* protects him from this charge, as we will see—but there is a general assumption that anyone who produces such "sick" narratives must himself be sick.[16]

Despite the tendency to confuse Bataille with the first-person narrator of *Story of the Eye*, the text actually has multiple narrators, and it is not clear that any of them can be identified with Bataille. Both the 1928 and 1944 editions are divided into two parts: "The Tale" ("Récit") and "Coincidences" (changed in 1944 to "Réminiscences"). In the 1928 edition, on which I focus here, there is no indication that the two parts should be read differently—no change in typography or page layout or indication of the subordination of one part to another. Yet "Coincidences" is self-reflexive in the style of *Snuff*'s final scene. The first-person narrator steps back from the story just told, distancing himself from it and at the same time suggesting the autobiographical roots of the sexual obsessions that mark "The Tale." The "I" of "Coincidences" (I will call him N2, and the narrator of "The Tale" N1) claims that when he began writing his story, he "believed . . . that the character who spoke in the first person had no relationship with me" (OC I 73; SE 89). By chance, however, certain images remind N2 that one of the central scenes of "The Tale" has origins in his own experience; thus he unravels a set of autobiographical references for N1's obsessions with eyes, eggs, and the testicles of a bull. N1, then, if not identical to N2, is linked to him through the psychoanalytic association of images.

Readers persistently identify N2 with N1 and both with Bataille. Even Bataille's biographer, Michel Surya, bases his account of Bataille's early life almost entirely on statements made in "Coincidences," although there is no external evidence to support these claims (of a paralyzed, blind, mad, syphilitic father and a periodically mad mother), nor any compelling internal reasons for reading "Coincidences" as any less fictive than "The Tale."[17] Furthermore, the self-reflexive account of childhood events offered in "Coincidences" was challenged by Bataille's brother Martial after a 1961 interview in which Madeleine Chapsal repeated these stories and declared them to be authentic accounts of Bataille's childhood.[18] In the face of this tendency to conflate the narrators of *Story of the Eye* with Bataille, it is worth noting that during Bataille's lifetime, the author of the "The Tale" and "Coincidences" was Lord Auch or, when the novel was included in *Le Petit*, Louis Trente. These pseudonyms suggest the continued disjunction between the confessing narrator of "Coincidences" and Bataille.

Susan Suleiman has pointed out the dangers of taking N2's autobiographical confessions as statements about Bataille and has argued that "Coincidences," no less than "The Tale," should be read as fiction.[19] Although I agree with Suleiman, I want to take this analysis further and ask why Bataille generates narrative voices that insist on and simultaneously subvert their own veracity. He often repeats the move, even as he undermines it. In a preface to the version of *Story of the Eye* printed with *Le Petit*, the narrator describes masturbating next to his mother's corpse (a scene often repeated in Bataille's work and reminiscent of the narrator's deflowering of Simone next to the dead body of Marcelle in *Story of the Eye*) and then parenthetically asserts the literality of this preface and of "Coincidences": "A few people, reading "Coincidences," wondered whether it did not have the fictional character of the tale itself. But, like this "Preface," "Coincidences" has a literal exactness: many people in the village of R. could confirm the material; moreover, some of my friends did read *W.C.*" (OC III 60; SE 99). This claim is followed by a continuation and intensification of the familial account begun in "Coincidences," suggesting the continuities between their narrators. Although, as I will show, N2 crucially undermines his own authority, problematizing these claims to "literal exactness," we still need to ask why Bataille has his narrators make them.[20] What is at stake, for Bataille, in these claims to reality?

In a letter written after Martial Bataille's response to Chapsal's interview, Bataille points to the more complicated way in which all of his writing is a writing of his own experience:

> But I want to tell you this today, that what happened nearly fifty years ago still makes me tremble and it doesn't surprise me that I didn't find any other way to get myself out of that than by expressing it anonymously. I was under the care of a doctor (my state being serious) who told me that the way I was using, despite everything, was the best that I could find. You could see him: I am sure that he would tell you. (OC I 644)

This "way out" was through erotic fictions, only published, during Bataille's lifetime, pseudonymously. Endemic to Bataille's experience is the need to efface the self through the use of pseudonyms and through the practice of modes of writing that shatter the self. This self-annihilation, moreover, is central to his understanding of eroticism, mysticism, and religion. The constantly repeated crisis is, for Bataille, the encounter with death; he argues that it is necessary for the subject to

> live at the moment when it truly dies, or it is necessary for him to live with the impression of truly dying. This difficulty foreshadows the necessity of the *spectacle*, or generally of *representation*, without the repetition of which we could remain foreign to and ignorant of death, as animals apparently remain. In effect, nothing is less animal than the fiction, more or less removed from reality, of death.[21]

As Derrida argues: "In order to run this risk in language [that of the death of the subject and the encounter with absolute negativity and nonmeaning], in order to save that which does not want to be saved—the possibility of play and absolute risk—we must redouble language and have recourse to ruses, to stratagems, to simulacra. To masks."[22] So even as Bataille and his narrators claim to expose themselves fully ("You could see him: I am sure that he would tell you") they (he) retreat behind masks. Through representation, fiction, and spectacle, Bataille repeatedly reenacts that death he can never experience directly.

The doctor to whom Bataille refers is the psychoanalyst Adrien Borel, which suggests that Bataille's writing is a kind of therapy, one in which selves are dissolved as they are constructed.[23] Bataille's relationship to psychoanalysis—a peculiarly twentieth-century therapy of the self confronting death—is crucial, then, to understanding the ways in which he wrote the dissolution of his self and "got himself out of" the serious state in which he found himself in the late 1920s. Unlike those readers who take Bataille's "Coincidences" as an attempt to locate certain crucial images in events within Bataille's life, I will argue that Bataille tells stories about (fictional) selves in order to mask and dissolve the self (the letter might itself be a further incidence of this). "Coincidences," then, is as much a therapy of the dissolving subject as is "The Tale" and demands equal analytic attention. Rather than providing a key to the narrative, it doubles and decenters it in crucial ways.

PHALLUS OR FETISH?

At this point, it might be helpful to offer a summary of "The Tale." Although its episodic nature defies easy synopsis, and the recurrence of key metaphors is perhaps more important than the plot itself, some account of the sexuality and violence of the narrative is necessary for assessing the import of the re-visionary interpretation contained in "Coincidences." "The Tale" is told by an anonymous first-person narrator who recalls his adolescent sexual escapades with Simone, a teenage girl whose family is distantly related to his own. The narrator and Simone are fascinated with the emotionally unstable Marcelle. They stage a drunken orgy with other local youth, during which they sexually manipulate Marcelle, who goes mad and is placed in a sanitarium, from which they eventually "rescue" her. When Marcelle realizes that her rescuers are also her sexual tormentors, she kills herself. The narrator and Simone then run away to Spain, where they encounter an English nobleman, Lord Edmund, go to a bullfight that ends tragically, and brutalize and murder a priest. The three make their escape through Spain, and from Gibraltar "they set sail toward new adventures with a crew of blacks" (OC I 69; SE 85).[24]

Unlike the epilogue of Snuff, "Coincidences" at first seems to de-sensationalize the proceeding narrative. Rather than reiterating and intensifying its constantly escalating sexuality and violence (the sexual license of the narrator and Simone; the death of an unnamed woman hit by their car; Marcelle's sexual humiliation, madness, and suicide; the enucleation and death of the bullfighter, Granero; the rape, torture, and murder of the Spanish priest, Don Aminado), "Coincidences" locates the source of these fictional incidents and the images that run through them in the seemingly more commonplace experience of its narrator.[25] For example, a scene in which N1 and Simone see a sheet, wet with urine, hanging from Marcelle's window at the mental hospital has its roots, according to N2, in a prank in which his older brother pretended to be a ghost. As N2 comments: "I was very surprised to have substituted, without any consciousness of it, a perfectly obscene image for a vision that seemed deprived of all sexual implication" (OC I 74; SE 91). N2 uses psychoanalytic techniques as a way of anchoring subjectivity, but he works against psychoanalytic premises in that he moves away from the radical dissolution or destabilization of the subject through sex and violence that recurs in "The Tale."

N2 goes on to describe the role of an event found in the tale and generally believed to have been witnessed by Bataille: the enucleation and death of the bullfighter, Granero. Yet N2's description immediately alerts the reader to his unreliability:

> I had already thought out all the details of the scene in the sacristy in Seville, in particular the incision made across the ocular orbit of the priest whose eye was ripped out, when, *aware already of the relationship between this narrative and my own life*, I amused myself by introducing the description of a tragic bullfight that I had really attended. *Curiously, I made no connection between the two episodes before having described with precision the wound the bull made on Manuel Granero (a real person)*, but at the very moment when I arrived at this death scene, I remained entirely dumbfounded [*je demeurai tout à faite stupide*]. (OC I 74; SE 91; my emphasis)

N2 claims that the scene of the priest's enucleation reminds him of that of the bullfighter and thus leads him to include the bullfight in the novel; yet in the very next line he claims to understand the "historical" source of the Seville sacristy scene only as he describes Granero's enucleation. This flat contradiction surrounding the one moment described in "Coincidences" for which external evidence survives (Granero was enucleated and killed by a bull while Bataille was in Spain, although we do not know for sure if he attended that fight) undermines N2's historical veracity when it should be most fully secured. The reader is "dumbfounded" by this contradiction, one that N2's stupefaction itself, perhaps, keeps him from seeing.

Having located the eyes, eggs, and testicles imagery in two traumatic (adolescent and adult) experiences, N2, in good psychoanalytic fashion, digs deeper into the past, seeking out the family romance from which these obscene images emerge. In a passage that has become crucial for accounts of Bataille's childhood, he first elucidates the relationship between eyes, eggs, and urine that runs throughout the tale:

I was born of a father who was suffering from general paralysis and was already blind when he conceived me, and who, shortly after my birth, was confined to his chair by a sinister illness. Unlike most male babies, however, who are in love with their mother, I was in love with my father. Now to his paralysis and to his blindness was tied the following fact. He couldn't go urinate in the WC like everyone else, but was obliged to do it in his chair into a little receptacle, and as he had to go often, he wasn't troubled by doing it in front of me under a blanket, which, being blind, he generally positioned badly. But the strangest thing was surely his manner of looking while he was pissing. As he saw nothing, his pupils very often looked up into space, under his eyelids, and that happened particularly in the moment when he pissed. He had very big eyes always very open in a faced marked with an eagle's beak and these great eyes were almost entirely white when he pissed, with an entirely stunning expression of abandon and wandering in a world that he alone could see and which gave him a vague and sardonic laugh. (OC I 75–76; SE 93)

Not only the association between eyes, eggs (the whites of the eyes), and urine is given here, as N2 explains, but also the association of these images with an ecstatic and abandoned sexuality. The eyes thrown back into the head mark, throughout Bataille's fiction, the figure of jouissance, an ecstatic and tortured sexuality.

At about fourteen, according to N2, he began to hate his father, delighting in his pain, his stench (he now shat himself), and his powerlessness; this "hate," then, is marked by its own pleasures. At this time, the father loses his mind. A doctor is sent for, and after examining the patient he goes into another room with the mother. The father cries out, "Tell me, doctor, when you have finished fucking my wife!" N2 comments on the effect of these words:

For me, this sentence, which destroyed in the blink of an eye the demoralizing effects of a severe education, left after it a sort of constant obligation, involuntary and unconsciously submitted to up until now: the necessity to find continually its equivalent in all the situations in which I find myself; this in large part explains *Story of the Eye*. (OC I 77; SE 94–95)

Behind (yet subsequently, within the narrative and the account of N2's life) the ecstatic dissolution of the pissing father lies the sexuality of the mother and the need to see that sexuality enacted in every situation in which N2 finds himself. This reading of the tale is underlined by N2's subsequent association of Marcelle with the mother, particularly in madness and death (the mother attempts suicide by hanging, paralleling Marcelle's successful suicide). The mother is also associated with Simone through descriptions of their wet dresses, which expose their genitalia. What remains unspoken here is the association of the Spanish priest—arguably also a double for the narrator himself—with Marcelle and hence also with the mother.

Although the interpretative movement through association of images is grounded in psychoanalytic practice, the family romance N2 describes diverges from the classic Oedipal narrative (if not from the mobility of the Freudian text).[26] Rather than loving his mother and hating his father—a scenario resolved through the castration complex and internalization of the threatening father—N2 claims to love his father before turning away from him in adolescence. The trauma he cites as decisive is the uncovering of the mother's sexuality, a sexuality exposed by the ravings of a lunatic and now despised father. For N2, it appears, the father is castrated by the sexualized, phallic mother.[27] Hence what we have described as the father's jouissance now becomes the ravings of a lunatic. According to N2, the secret of Story of the Eye is its obsessive repetition of the sexualization of the mother and the threat this poses to the father and, by extension, to the son. (Yet, as I will show, the threat is also always a promise. This ambivalence can be seen most clearly in the simultaneous fear and excitation N1 feels toward Simone.) According to N2, the sexualization of his memories follows the same trajectory as this "primal scene":

> I never linger over memories of this sort, because for a long time now they have lost for me any emotional characteristic. It was impossible for me to restore life to them except after having transformed them to the point where they were unrecognizable at first sight to my eyes and solely because they had taken in the course of this transformation the most obscene meaning. (OC I 78; SE 96)

Every memory must be retroactively transformed by knowledge of the mother's sexuality, a sexuality that renders the mother phallic. Only this transformation can give them life and emotional cogency.

Viewed from another angle, however, Story of the Eye appears to be a fetishistic narrative in which part objects—various body parts or inanimate objects that substitute for the lost object of desire—proliferate in an endless attempt to cover

over the gap in the real, the absence of the mother's phallus.[28] This fetishiza-tion, it should be said, like N2's oedipalization of his narrative, is exceedingly mobile and avoids the reification often associated with the fetish. Yet if "The Tale" is read as fetishistic, *Story of the Eye* becomes deeply ironic, for the real-ity effects of "Coincidences" occur after a narrative concerned primarily with the evasion of reality (i.e., the castration of the mother). Perhaps as a result of this tension, "Coincidences" points the reader to the other, nonfetishistic reading of "The Tale" outlined above. At the most overt level (I'll argue shortly for the viability of other readings of "Coincidences"), N2 reads the prolifera-tion of obscene images and scenes in "The Tale" as an attempt to control the sexuality of the mother through its continual staging, whereas the fetishistic reading of the narrative highlights the parceling out of the female body in an attempt to cover its lack.[29] The first reading would interpret the scenes of vi-olent outrage in "The Tale" as a punishment of the phallic mother, whereas in the second these scenes would be read as a fetishistic attempt to deny the mother's lack.

SADOMASOCHISTIC SPECTACLES

The two readings of the narrative (my provisional, "phallic" interpretation of N2's reading and the widespread fetishistic accounts) partially parallel Laura Mulvey's account of the male gaze constructed within classic cinema. For Mul-vey, the problem from which this cinema protects the subject is the castration of the mother, experienced as displeasure by the male viewer for whom it rep-resents a threat to his own phallus. In response to this threat, two possibilities emerge: the sadistic-voyeuristic look in which women are punished for their lack of a penis and the fetishistic-scopophilic look in which the female body is fetishized and itself substitutes for the lack that constitutes it.[30] In one reading of *Story of the Eye*, N2 imputes a phallic sexuality to the mother and demands her castration so that he, the son, can retain/attain masculinity. This reading marks a revision of the sadistic-voyeuristic look as described by Mulvey, for N2 does not fear but desires the mother's castration. N2 then might be seen as offering a sadistic-voyeuristic look in which Marcelle and the feminized priest have to be punished in order to establish their lack.[31]

In an analysis of horror films, Carol Clover argues that Mulvey's thesis re-quires elaboration and correction in order to explain the effects and appeal of the genre. Although horror might appear to be exhausted by the sadistic-voyeuristic look, Clover argues that there is also significant identification with the victim. Following David Rodowick, Clover suggests that the blind spot of much important film theory, including Mulvey's, is the relationship between fetishization and masochism. According to Rodowick, Mulvey "defines fetishistic scopophilia as an overvaluation of the object, a point which Freud would support. But he would also add that this phenomenon is one of the fundamental sources of *authority* defined as passive submission to the object: in sum, *masochism*."[32] According to Clover, horror is crucially concerned with the failure of the male, controlling gaze and its submission to a masochistic frenzy of victim-identification. Fetishization, rather than simply covering over the reality of the mother's castration, can be the mark of masochistic identification with that lack and the decentering of the subject effected by it. The horror film's victim, moreover, is usually female, suggesting, as Clover argues, that within the essentially conservative horror genre, sex follows gender.[33] Clover stresses the necessity of recognizing cross-identifications if one is to understand horror and its pleasures, which depend on male viewers' projection of their masochism onto female victims.

For Clover, masochism is feminine in that it is associated with femininity and figured by women within the horror genre. The adolescent boys who make up the primary audience for slasher films are able to identify with the victim while at the same time her female body creates a needed distance between that masochism and the viewer. Moreover, the victim-hero of the slasher film is a masculinized female body, one that does not fully succumb to masochistic dissolution but fights back and survives. Crucially, she is not sexualized. The point about cross-identifications is important in reading Bataille's fiction—readers tend unproblematically to identify Bataille's "experience" and viewpoint with that of the first-person narrator(s), who is (are) male, ignoring the obvious textual investment in characters such as Simone, Marcelle, and Don Aminado.[34] Many readers who assume the identification of Bataille with his first-person narrators invest him with control over the text's meanings. Yet to say that Bataille *is* the narrator(s) ignores the crucial cross-identifications (both of the first-person narrator and of the reader) that structure *Story of the Eye*. Moreover, to argue that N2 is N1 is to allow N2 to control the interpretation of N1's narrative, precisely the bid made by the self-reflexive moves that govern "Coincidences." Yet to do so is, potentially, to reassert a voyeuristic-sadistic gaze into the narrative of the tale and thereby to refuse the radical shattering of subjectivity depicted in and evoked by the bullfight and sacristy scenes.[35]

These scenes mark the slide from a fetishistic attempt to cover over the mother's lack to a masochistic submission to castration. This submission, moreover, is experienced as ecstatic. N1, then, depicts and enacts a form of ecstatic sexuality most closely akin to the image of the pissing father, with his "entirely stunning expression of abandon and wandering in a world he alone could see." Despite N2's claims, his initial account of the father describes him as blind and symbolically castrated before the birth of the narrator, suggesting that the mother has always been phallic and the father's jouissance always somehow "beyond the phallus." In witnessing the violent deaths of Granero and Don Aminado, similarly, N1 loses normal forms of consciousness or subjectivity. This loss is evoked stylistically. In the bullfight episode, before providing a rapid account of the avalanche of bizarre events that accompany Granero's enucleation, the narrator claims: "The events that followed occurred without transition and as if without connection, not because they really were disconnected, but because my attention, as absent, remained absolutely dissociated" (OC I 55–56; SE 64). After the murder and enucleation of Don Aminado, the narrator sees his eye, as if it were the eye of Marcelle, in Simone's vulva and is rendered speechless (textually rendered as two lines of ellipses).

The analogy between "The Tale" and Clover's analysis of horror films breaks down at crucial points; not only is there a seemingly more complete immersion in sadomasochistic fantasies within Bataille's work, but every aspect of Bataille's narrative is sexualized. I think something more complicated and potentially more subversive is happening in Story of the Eye than simply a movement between sadistic-voyeurism and fetishistic-scopophilia, something that subverts the very distinction between phallic and fetishized representations of women and that simultaneously undermines the emphasis on the look or the gaze so crucial to film theorists like Mulvey and Clover.[36] The father is blind; Granero and Don Aminado enucleated. Male masochism is marked, most crucially, by blindness. This shattering of vision marks the shattering of the self.[37] The association of fetishism with masochism enables us to see that N1 participates in the masochism of his and Simone's victims and that this masochism shatters the subject and his claims to either sadistic or fetishistic mastery.[38]

Yet in attempting to control the reading of "The Tale," N2 seems to hope to deflect his own complicity with the sadism, the masochism, and/or the fetishism of that narrative. Readers of Story of the Eye have followed N2 in their identifications of his voice with that of Bataille. According to these biographical constructions, Bataille is not complicitous with murder (as is N1) but constructs this murderous sexualized narrative as a result of the crimes of his father (exposure, madness, and elsewhere, it is suggested, rape). N2 successfully deflects attention away from his own masochistic and sadistic pleasure toward the other world in which his father lives and in which the father sexualizes the mother (and, by implication, the child).[39] The drive toward reality is, then, a drive toward covering up the real. The verisimilitude of realist narratives, of auto-biography and the diary, is always in danger not of exposing inner experience and the shattering of the self, but of covering them back up again.

As I suggested earlier, if the drive toward reality in "Coincidences" subverts the real, then it again stands in tension with "The Tale." This point is clari-fied by a further analysis of the relationship between sadism and masochism within the latter narrative. In a brilliant series of rereadings of Freud, in which the dissolution of the theoretical is traced within his texts, Leo Bersani ar-gues for the primacy of masochism in Freud's understanding of sexuality.[40] Following a suggestion made by Jean Laplanche, Bersani hypothesizes that sexuality

> would be that which is intolerable to the structured self. From
> this perspective, the distinguishing feature of infancy would be
> its *susceptibility to the sexual*. The polymorphously perverse nature of
> infantile sexuality would be a function of the child's vulnerability
> to being shattered into sexuality. . . . In sexuality, satisfaction is
> inherent in the painful need to find satisfaction.[41]

On this reading, sexuality is itself traumatic. Masochism is not a secondary phe-nomenon, a disordered experience of sexuality, but is primary to its constitu-tion; subjects are always in tension with themselves, desiring autonomy and yet at the same time finding their pleasure in the shattering of subjectivity. This is the account of sexuality we will see challenged by Irigaray. It is one that leads Bersani to offer a radically revised account of sublimation. On the one hand, Freud clearly argues that sublimation is the repression of libidinal energy through its diversion to other pursuits, giving rise to symptomatic readings of works of art as records of libidinal repression. Bersani suggests another under-standing of sublimation, hinted at by Freud, in which art itself is libidinally invested with a masochistic impulse toward the shattering of the self in sex-uality. *Story of the Eye* is the record of this tension, for while the tale recounts the shattering of the self in violent sexuality, "Coincidences" is—at least on the surface—an attempt to place responsibility for that masochism/sexuality onto the father/mother.

Yet before accepting this reading of N2's narrative, we must remember that the father with whom N2 identifies and onto whom he deflects his own fascina-tion with pain and pleasure is himself always already castrated, that is, his ecstasy goes beyond the phallus in some crucial way.[42] The father's castration suggests that the bid for mastery is always undermined and ironized within Bataille's work—or that there are elements within the text that subvert the bid for mastery also found there. Meditation on the figure of the blind, pissing father shatters the subject just as does the blasphemous murder of Don Aminado. N2's apparently sadistic hatred for the father masks his masochistic identification with the father. N2's unreliability only furthers these suspicions. Unlike the Freudian analyst, who looks for the hidden and repressed sexuality lying behind seemingly nonsexual events, "The Tale" is a sexual narrative in need of interpretation. In claiming his educated innocence before the father's lewd words, N2 claims to be sexualized by the parent. Yet the very phrasing of this complaint suggests that sexuality is not generated by the father's words but merely reactivated by them.[43] The narrative of "The Tale" suggests that this Oedipal configuration is itself secondary. Bersani quotes Freud, at the moment in which he comes closest to repudiating his own Oedipal theory: "The ambivalence displayed in the relations to the parents should be attributed entirely to bisexuality and that is not, as I have represented above, developed out of identification in consequence of rivalry."[44] This ambivalence then gives rise to a secondary construction of masochism and guilt quite different from the jouissance of masochistic shattering that marks infantile sexuality. Bataille's tale emerges from this masochistic, infantile sexuality, even as N2 conspires to cover it over. (And arguably, this primary masochistic self-shattering also undermines developmental models of the psyche.)[45]

This masochistic sexuality represents the encounter with the other, that which cannot be negotiated or protected against, the emergence of the real (in the Lacanian sense) against which reality effects attempt to protect the subject. For the reader who takes refuge in these reality effects, the ironic shattering of Bataille's text is effaced. Maybe this is an out Bataille himself needed in 1928. Or, taking off from the blindness of the father and the unreliability of the narrator, one might read "Coincidences" as ironic; a parody of the claims to mastery of the male subject who is in fact always already castrated. The father's blindness, like that of Granero and Don Aminado, shatters the self in a masochistic frenzy and decenters the voyeuristic-sadistic gaze, which, precisely as sadistic, identifies with these masochistic moments.[46] The two readings of "Coincidences"—as voyeuristic-sadistic mastery and fetishistic-masochistic (rather than scopophilic), self-subverting ironization—stand side by side; one cannot, finally, decide between them. Similarly, although it is difficult to write—even at the level of the sentence—keeping both possibilities in view, we can never decide conclusively whether the text subverts itself despite

Bataille's attempt at mastery (through N2) or whether this self-ironizing is intentional. Intentional claims are shown here to be both inescapable and forever undecidable. In forcing us to this recognition, Bataille's text simultaneously posits and shatters the autobiographical subject.[47] At the same time, it both posits and shatters the reader who identifies with that subject, suggesting that, for Bataille, "experience" is as much that of the reader as the writer.

ECSTASY, MASOCHISM, AND THE THEORY OF RELIGION

This same shattering of the subject—both as writer and reader—is enacted in the *Atheological Summa* and underlies Bataille's theory of religion. Before the war, Bataille understood sacrifice as a site of self-dissolution. In the "world without myth" revealed by war, Bataille turns to a form of meditative practice, based on medieval models, that clarifies the identificatory processes with which the fictions engage:

> The method of meditation is close to the technique of sacrifice. The point of ecstasy is laid bare if I smash interiorly the particularity that encloses me within myself: in the same fashion, the *sacred* is substituted for the animal at the moment the priest kills it, destroys it.

> An image of torture falls under my eyes; I can, in my fright, turn away. But I am, if I look at it, *outside of myself*. . . . The sight, horrible, of a torture victim opens the sphere in which is enclosed (is limited) my personal particularity, it opens it violently, lacerates it. (OC V 272; G 35)

This representation of suffering, like Christ's crucifixion within Christianity, becomes the projected image through which the subject experiences his or her own dissolution.

> I didn't choose God as object, but humanly, the young condemned Chinese man that some photographs show me streaming with blood, while the executioner tortures him (the blade in the bone of his knee). To that afflicted one, I was tied by ties of horror and of friendship. But if I looked at the image *up to the point of harmony*, it suppressed in me the necessity of being myself alone: at the same time this object that I had chosen came undone in an immensity, lost itself in a storm of pain. (OC V 283; G 46)

I will discuss this meditative practice at greater length in the next chapter. For now we can read this passage in Bersani's terms; Bataille denies taking any sadistic pleasure in the torture victim's suffering because he recognizes that the sadistic is itself masochistic. He denies taking pleasure in this meditative practice, insofar as pleasure is understood in its secondary genital sense, yet his ruin is a source of what Lacan would call jouissance, an ecstasy that goes beyond, dissolving the subject and those secondary formations of subjectivity—masochism and sadism—that attempt to protect it.

The religious and the erotic come together here.[48] Both mark the limits of experience yet seem to require some lingering subjectivity (the body that reacts?) if that dissolution is to be lived and communicated. Inner experience requires dramatization and meditation—"images of explosion and of being lacerated—ripped to pieces" (OC V 269; G 32)—yet the subject can never itself be literally ripped to pieces, or jouissance could not be communicated. The demand for dramatization raises the ethical problem of whether the dismemberment of the other is the necessary screen on or through which the subject experiences jouissance.[49] Before the war, Bataille suggested that sacrifice is a voluntary submission of the victim through whose death the community experiences a vicarious self-dissolution.[50] He hoped, moreover, to reintroduce sacrifice into the modern world. Bataille's fascination with violence reached its height just before the Second World War. The texts he wrote for the short-lived journal Acéphale celebrate war and the sacrificial laceration of the subject as a way of returning sacrality to Europe and generating a community without a head that can counter the rising tide of fascism. Both the secret society, Acéphale, and the public College of Sociology were engaged in this project. Moreover, in Bataille's writings from this time and in the wartime text On Nietzsche, he reads Christ as voluntarily submitting to torture and death, hence making communication possible. Bataille does not desire a return to Christianity, however, but a generalization of its logic and a rejection of the dualism by which it attempts to negate (through naming as evil) the violence necessary to its instantiation.[51]

Before and after the war, Bataille writes about sacrifice as engendering the sacred. Yet in the face of the extraordinary and clearly involuntary suffering brought about by the Second World War, his attitude toward violence changes in ways that suggest a divergence between his pre- and postwar discussions of the sacred. I argue in the next chapter that during the war years, Bataille meditates on images of extreme physical suffering as a traumatic response to the ethical call of the other, those suffering violently throughout Europe and the world.[52] In much of Inner Experience and Guilty, he seems more interested in the particularity of the suffering other than in the sacrality that emerges from contemplation of that figure (although as the parallels with Christianity's meditation on Christ's suffering suggest, the two cannot be fully disentangled).[53] Both in these texts and in Bataille's postwar writings, he recognizes that communication cannot be grounded in literal sacrifice, for death makes communication impossible. Thus in the *Atheological Summa* and in his postwar fictional and theoretical work, Bataille follows the lead set by *Story of the Eye* and turns to writing as the site of self-laceration and dissolution, and so of communication with the other. Through writing, one does not encounter literal suffering but its textual effects; Bataille effaces the writerliness and fictionality of his own texts so that their portrayal of the dissolution of the narrator's subjectivity may become meditative objects for his readers.[54] The narrators' claims to "reality" are necessary to their effect on the reader, just as these effects ultimately undermine their claims to "reality" in the emergence of the "real."

These textual paradoxes parallel the problem of religion that Bataille describes in his *Theory of Religion*: "The constant problem posed by the impossibility of being human without being a thing and of escaping the limits of things without returning to animal slumber receives the limited solution of the festival."[55] For human beings, transcendence is discontinuity, that which separates us from the world and other creatures. Subjectivity depends on this discontinuity, yet we desire communication between creatures and a return to immanence and radical continuity. The question becomes how we can encounter continuity (and hence communion between beings) without the death that would end life and communication. Bataille argues that in premodern religious communities, through the sacrifice of another (whether human or animal), the subject vicariously dissolves and encounters immanence and continuity without dying. In the modern world, however, sacrifice, the festival, and the sacred have been lost. In the 1940s and 1950s, Bataille looked on his earlier desire to reinvoke the sacred as misguided and naive.[56] The literality of that desire involves a violence Bataille can no longer sanction after the Second World War, for it endangers the very communication he wishes to enact. Yet his recognition that violence fascinates and that it is, paradoxically, tied to freedom and to communication remains. To recognize the other's suffering and to release the violence of the passions, he turns (or perhaps better, given my reading of *Story of the Eye*, returns) to writing.[57]

On the level of the textuality to which Bataille had recourse throughout his writing career, but most explicitly during and after the Second World War, sacrifice (and witness) can be enacted without death; through the fictionality of language and the wearing of masks, fictional or "autobiographical," the subject is sacrificed while writing and communication remain. I will return to these issues in chapter 3. At this point, it is crucial to recognize that experience, for Bataille, is not absolute immanence, immediacy, or self-presence, but the self-shattering that occurs through identification with the lacerated (textual) other. Through the interplay of "autobiographical" and "fictional" selves, Bataille's texts enact their own shattering dissolution, starting in motion the catastrophic training of the reader's self-shattering experience. Similarly, Bataille mixes claims to scientific objectivity with "autobiographical" evocations of excess, carnality, and emotion in order to shatter reason.

We started with Jean-Paul Sartre's objection to Bataille's use of scientific language. Jürgen Habermas and Martin Jay repeat Sartre's question with regard to Bataille's textual practice: "Is it . . . a contradiction to privilege subject-annihilating ecstatic experience and at the same time try to talk about that experience "objectively" and impersonally?"[58] What the philosophers miss is the strategic value, for Bataille, in claiming to write objectively—it is only by inhabiting the language of science, philosophy, and experience that it can be shattered. It is only by dancing with the philosophers that the philosophers can be made to dance. For Bataille, the contradiction between objective and subjective, like that between the fictional and the autobiographical, allows his theoretical texts themselves to become "operations" of ecstasy; they continually erect and overturn distinctions between "experience" and "theory," "subjective" and "objective," "inner" and "outer," making the writing of theory itself an erotic, mystical, religious exercise.

MYSTICISM, TRAUMA, AND CATASTROPHE IN ANGELA OF FOLIGNO'S *BOOK* AND BATAILLE'S *ATHEOLOGICAL SUMMA*

. . . .

[St. John of the Cross] is an *enragé*. That's what he has in common with the surrealists, and in my view is the essence of surrealism: a sort of rage . . . against the existing state of things. A rage against life as it is.
GEORGES BATAILLE, "Interview with Madeleine Chapsal"

If the unrelieved instant before me, or rather within me, with each throw carries eternity in its fall, like a roll of the dice—if there is no salvation and if the rationalized future of the world cannot alter the world's being open to all that is possible—then nothing counts *beyond* this cry, which fills the air like the wind or the light and, however lacking in virility, leaves no room for fear, that is to say, for worrying about the future.
GEORGES BATAILLE, "Concerning the Accounts Given by the Residents of Hiroshima"

MYSTICISM AND HISTORY

The opening lines of *Guilty*, the second volume of Georges Bataille's three part *Atheological Summa*, mark the crucial, if often oblique, conjunction of historical events and mysticism in his wartime writings (the textual history is complex, but these are the first lines to be written explicitly for this project):

> The date on which I am beginning to write (September 5, 1939) is not a coincidence. I am beginning because of these

events, but not in order to talk about them. I write these notes incapable of anything else. From now on it's necessary for me to let myself go to the movements of liberty, of caprice. Suddenly, the moment has come for me to speak without circumlocution.

It is impossible for me to read—at least most books. I don't have the desire. Too much work tires me. My nerves are shattered. I get drunk a lot. I feel faithful to life if I eat and drink what I want. Life is an enchantment, a feast, a festival: an oppressing, unintelligible dream, adorned nevertheless with a charm that I enjoy. The sentiment of chance demands that I look a difficult fate in the face. It would not be about chance if there were not an incontestable madness.

I began to read, standing on a crowded train, Angela of Foligno's *Book of Visions*.

I'm copying it out, not knowing how to say how fiercely I burn—the veil is torn in two, I emerge from the fog in which my impotence flails. (OC V 245; G 11)

Bataille opens his exploration of ecstatic anguish at the moment when World War II begins and claims that the war itself necessitates his text. Despite "living like a pig in the eyes of Christians," moreover, Bataille finds his own tormented desire—the very anguish that compels him to write—reflected in Angela's pages. Angela, the most important of the Christian mystics for Bataille, surpasses him in the pursuit of abjection and ecstasy.[1] He wants to be like her in her desire for and proximity to death: "I suffer from not myself burning to the point of coming close to death, so close that I inhale it like the breath of a loved being" (OC V 246; G 12).

War and mysticism, then, converge in Bataille's texts. Yet as these lines suggest, Bataille refers only elliptically to the war in *Inner Experience* and *Guilty*. He had, in fact, little direct experience of armed conflict. From 1939 to 1943, Bataille lived in relative isolation; often ill, he moved between Paris and the French countryside.[2] Michel Surya and Susan Suleiman point out that Bataille would have been aware of numerous acts of Nazi violence against resistance fighters and Jews, yet occupation censors would have made it impossible for him to discuss such atrocities directly within his published work.[3] Nonetheless, Sarah Wilson claims that *Madame Edwarda* and "The Torture," a central section of *Inner Experience*, were both sparked by the intensified Nazi hostage-taking and reprisal shootings of September and October 1941. Similarly, I argue in what follows that the images of a Chinese torture victim central to the meditative practice Bataille describes in the *Atheological Summa* stand in for these victims of Nazi violence.[4] Only in *On Nietzsche*, the third volume of the *Atheological Summa* published after the end of the war, was Bataille able to deal directly with the war and its effects on civilian bystanders.

What I hope to show is that during a historical moment in which concrete political action seemed hopeless and the threat of death pervasive, Bataille turned to mysticism as an alternative form of community-building. Bataille's own chance survival of the war and his inability to participate in the movements of history generated intense guilt.[5] In response, Bataille recreated a mystical path of contemplation made up of "compassion, pain, and ecstasy" (OC V 273; G 36). Rather than marking a willed rejection of history, mysticism offers a form of community and action in the face of chance events that lie outside the control of individual subjects.[6]

Bataille suggests a connection between the historical moment and his feelings of political impotence in the introduction to *Guilty*, written in 1961. There he claims that the impetus for his wartime writing was "to ask oneself before another: how does he appease in himself the desire to be everything [tout]? . . . No longer to desire to be everything [tout] is to put everything [tout] into question" (OC V 10; G xxxii). These words respond directly to and challenge Sartre's reading of *Inner Experience* as grounded in a desire to be "everything." For Sartre, as for other early critics of Bataille, mysticism is a form of intellectual and spiritual solipsism; Bataille's turn to mysticism, then, represents an attempt to evade history, politics, and responsibility. Sartre was not the first to make these accusations against Bataille. Bataille tells us in his final lecture for the College of Sociology that Roger Caillois, with whom Bataille had founded the college, was critical of Bataille's turn to mysticism. The letter in which Caillois voices his concerns has been lost, but he too seems to have equated Bataille's mysticism with a rejection of politics. Similarly, Sartre rejects Bataille's claim that nothingness and the unknowable radically destabilize the theological and soteriological assertions of traditional Christian mysticism; to the contrary, Sartre claims, Bataille reifies nothingness and makes it God. This nihilism, according to Sartre, is the result of Bataille's attempt to escape temporality, historicity, and responsibility through inner experience.[7] Both Caillois and Sartre, then, note the importance of Christian mysticism to Bataille's work from the late 1930s on, contest or ignore Bataille's warnings against an easy assimilation of his writings with those of the mystics, and reject his work precisely *as* mystical.

Caillois and Sartre set the tone for later commentators, who continually reiterate this opposition between mysticism and politics. Francis Marmande, for example, argues in *Georges Bataille politique* that Bataille's multiple and fragmented body of writing can be tied together by its political aims. Marmande remains uneasy, however, with the *Atheological Summa*. The turn to mysticism, Marmande writes, clearly marks a break with the flurry of overt prewar political activities in which Bataille engaged during the 1930s (participation in Boris Souvarine's Trotskyite Democratic Communist circle and its journal, *La Critique sociale*; the shorted-lived rapprochement with André Breton and the surrealists in Contre Attaque; the secret society Acéphale and the College of Sociology, both founded by Bataille in order to pursue the study of the sacred and its revitalization in the modern world, specifically as a response to fascism). Moreover, Marmande does not limit Bataille's politics to such overt political activity; he insists that the resistance of Bataille's writing, his focus on the use of words rather than simply their meaning, is itself a form of antiauthoritarian and contestatory political engagement (no doubt an attenuated understanding of politics for Sartre and others). Thus, according to Marmande, *Inner Experience* maintains the refractory power of Bataille's writing. Marmande argues, however, that the political character of this text emerged in response to "personal dramas and illness."[8] By confining *Inner Experience* to the realm of the "personal," Marmande follows the lead of Bataille's early critics and crucially ignores the centrality of historical events to Bataille's mystical "turn."

The perceived opposition in Bataille's writing between the personal and the historical, mysticism and politics, has a basis both in Western intellectual traditions and in Bataille's own texts. There is a long tradition in the West dealing with the apparent conflict between contemplation and action, and Bataille himself wrestles with the relationship between his meditative, ecstatic practice and historical action. Moreover, the mode of his relationship with the real—that in history unassimilable to its salvific narratives[9]—suggests that history, like mysticism and action, is itself at least double.[10] Bataille acknowledges his proximity to mysticism and his rejection of action, but at the same time he insists that inner experience is something other, something more than, mysticism and that it is a mode of action with ethical ramifications.[11] He thus uses crucial terms—mysticism, action, history—in at least two ways, and much of the apparent confusion in his writings is generated by these double meanings.

So, for example, Bataille remains ambivalent toward the term mysticism and its Christian usage, wishing to differentiate the kind of community it engenders from that which he seeks. In *Guilty*, this ambivalence takes the form of an almost compulsive repetition of his proximity to and distance from Angela's experience. After citing Angela's book, for example, Bataille states that "Angela of Foligno, speaking of God, speaks in servitude" (OC V 251; G 16). In this way, he marks his distance from Angela's text, insisting on the sovereignty of inner experience, which rejects any authority external to itself. Yet he then cites Angela at length and claims that "if laughter is violent enough, there is no limit" (OC V 251; G 17). In other words, the extremity of Angela's experience breaks through the bonds of servitude marked by God's presence, thereby bringing her experience into greater proximity with his own understanding of a community without authority.[12]

Inner Experience, the first published volume of the *Atheological Summa*, in which Bataille offers more discursive accounts of his own mystical path, similarly circles around Bataille's ambivalent attitude toward mysticism. The book opens with a section entitled "Critique of Dogmatic Servitude (and of Mysticism)." Here Bataille makes clear his oft repeated objections to the term "mysticism":

> By *inner experience* I understand that which one usually calls *mystical experience*: states of ecstasy, of rapture, at least of meditated emotion. But I am thinking less of *confessional* experience, to which one has had to adhere up to now, than of an experience laid bare, free of attachments, even of origin, of any confession whatsoever. This is why I don't like the word *mystical*. (OC V 15; IE 3)

Insofar as mystical traditions are concerned with salvation, with project, and with ends external to experience itself, Bataille insists on their divergence from inner experience. God is rejected because claims to the existence of God are tied to the promise of salvation (OC V 126; IE 107–8). Yet Bataille does not reject the term "mystical" so much as appropriate it; he claims that inner experience better captures the mystics' experiences than do their own dogmatic utterances. Part 4 of *Inner Experience* is entitled "Post-Scriptum to the Torment/Torture [*supplice*] (or the New Mystical Theology)." Bataille thus operates with two conceptions of the mystical and suggests that both are operative within at least some texts of the Christian mystical tradition.

Before I offer an account of Bataille's new mystical theology, it might be helpful to look briefly at one voice that dissents from the insistence that mysticism marks a flight from history.[13] In his 1972–1973 seminar *Encore* (which I discuss at length in part 2), Jacques Lacan turns to the questions of love, woman, history, and mysticism. Before associating his own work with mystical texts, he wants to make clear that mysticism is not to be associated with the early twentieth-century French religious and political right.[14] Nor does he associate mysticism with obscurantism and antinomianism, as do many commentators throughout the early twentieth century (including, at times, Bataille):

> Me, I don't use the world mystic as Péguy used it. Mysticism is not all [*pas tout*] that which is not politics. It is something serious, about which certain people teach us, and most often women, or gifted people like Saint John of the Cross—because one is not forced when one is male, to place oneself on the side of the [phallic function]. One can also place oneself on the side of the not all [*pas-tout*]. There are men who are as good as women. It happens. And who at the same time feel good about it. Despite, I don't say their phallus, despite that which encumbers them under that title, they catch a glimpse, they sense the idea that there must be a jouissance that goes beyond. That's who one calls "mystics." (S XX 70; E 76)

Like those men who take the side of the "not all/whole"—who reject their place in a symbolic (cultural, political, and social realm) governed by the phallus (and hence, symbolically and literally, by men)—mysticism is itself "not all/whole." Rather than marking a nostalgia for lost plenitude and wholeness (supported by the conflation of imaginary and symbolic realms), mysticism (like psychoanalysis, according to Lacan) is the site in which such desires are renounced.[15] As such, it is not that which is not political but is arguably the place where ethics (and a particular sort of politics?) receives its most stringent expression.

Lacan does not mention Georges Bataille in *Seminar XX*; yet I suspect that in naming those "men who are as good as women" in their renunciation of plenitude and wholeness, Lacan alludes to his longtime friend (who died in 1962). Even without such an association, however, I think that Bataille's wartime writings can be read usefully in light of Lacan's understanding of mysticism as the "not all/whole," that is, as a rejection of fantasies of wholeness and plenitude through which what Lacan calls "the real" is apprehended.[16] As Lacan shows in *Encore*, male subjectivity is supported in its illusory wholeness by the primacy of the phallus as signifier of mastery, meaning, and power; the gap between the penis and the phallus is real, and yet—as we all know—they look an awful lot alike. This resemblance gives verisimilitude to men's claims to overcome the gap in being that is intrinsic, Lacan argues, to every speaking subject. Only through a rejection of this fantasmatic association, however, can "the real"—what I will associate, following Lacan, with that in history that is unassimilable to its meaning-giving and salvific narratives—be apprehended.

This brief synopsis of Lacan allows me to situate *Inner Experience* and *Guilty* as texts that are markedly indebted to the mystical work most important to Bataille, the *Book* of the thirteenth-century Umbrian Franciscan tertiary Angela of Foligno.[17] Following Angela, Bataille offers an account of the modes of contemplation that lead to ecstasy. Bataille's texts can be read as his attempt to repeat Angela's experience, to bring himself "close to death," creating a new sacred community through embracing the "not all" and contemplating "the real."[18] In reading and rewriting (repeating) Angela's texts, moreover, Bataille creates a community with her in which the reader might also come to share. He argues that through contemplation, the laceration of subjectivity required by communication occurs. This communication grounds new communities, which themselves are the fruit—the work or action—of Bataille's texts. So for Bataille, as for a central strand of the medieval Christian mystical tradition, contemplation is itself a form of action, one that generates a community brought together through their shared contemplation of the real (what Bataille in *Guilty* refers to as the catastrophe, which can be linked to contemporary discussions of trauma). Uncovering the relationship between *Inner Experience*, *Guilty*, and Angela's *Book*—and between Angela's *Book* and broader Christian practices of meditation—offers important insight into the political, ethical, and religious import of Bataille's "project that is not a project" and raises a new set of questions about the viability of his political, ethical, and religious claims.

TOWARD A NEW MYSTICAL THEOLOGY

Bataille begins his new mystical theology with a reminder to the reader of its divergences from the old. He writes that, like Maurice Blanchot in *Thomas the Obscure*, he seeks a new theology "which has only the unknown for its object" (OC V 120; IE 102). Such a theology must

—have its principles and its end in the absence of salvation, in the renunciation of all hope,
—affirm of inner experience that it is authority (but all authority expiates itself),
—be contestation of itself and non-knowledge. (OC V 120; IE 102)

Bataille wants to develop a mystical theology without God, an atheology in which God (as this concept is understood, according to Bataille, within the modern Christian West) is subverted through a radical experience of the limit and the unknowable, what, in *Guilty*, Bataille will call the catastrophe. He follows this demand for a new mystical theology with a series of chapters on

God and the philosophical conceptions of God, knowledge, and totality found in Descartes and Hegel. As Sartre points out in his 1943 review essay, these philosophical reflections are framed by accounts of inner experience and the anguished ecstasy of the writing subject in the face of the unknowable. For Sartre, this approach marks a confusion of the subjectivity of experience with claims to objectivity (whether philosophical or scientific). For Bataille, once again, subjective experience decenters and subverts the very claims to objectivity on which systematic philosophy is based.

The God of the mystics, Bataille suggests, is a God without aim, project, salvation, or knowledge—hence not God at all, at least as that concept is deployed within the mainstream of Christian theology and philosophy. Christian mystics experience the limit that undermines conceptions of the divine central to Western philosophical traditions. Yet their continued reliance on traditional conceptions of God, despite the textual shattering of these concepts in accounts of mystical experience, gives rise to ambiguities within their writings. These same ambiguities are reflected in Bataille's work; at times he describes the mystics' God from the standpoint of shattering experience, whereas at other times he emphasizes the mystics' return to salvific conceptions of God. The section in "Post-Scriptum to the Torment/Torture (or the New Mystical Theology)" entitled "God" plays on this ambiguity. On the basis of the mystics' experience of divine darkness and unknowing, Bataille subverts the concept of God as the omniscient, omnipotent, and fully self-present source of unchanging transcendence and salvation.

Bataille begins with the startling claim that God hates himself. Only when human beings are exhausted by existence and full of self-loathing do they turn to God as a source of salvation. Human self-hatred is reflected in the self-hatred of God. Bataille argues that "within human thought," God always conforms to humanity, which suggests that human conceptions of the divine are projections of human desire. Bataille subverts such conceptions of the divine and also shows how mystical experience itself deconstructs these cultural constructs. God, as the projection of human desire, can never find rest and satisfaction because human desire is contradictory, as is apparent in mystical conceptions of the divine. Human beings desire fulfillment, and yet the fulfillment of that desire would mark the end of desire itself. Following many of the mystics, Bataille posits human desire as ceaseless, endless, and only capable of momentary appeasement. For God (as desire) to know himself as God (as the fulfillment of all desire) would imply a satisfaction that God (as desire) cannot allow; thus God himself is, according to Bataille, an atheist. The mystics' experience of divine insatiability, darkness, and unknowability becomes the basis for Bataille's atheological assertions. Although God may be a cultural construct, a projection of human desire, the interrogation of the conception of God reveals a crucial aspect of human experience.

This section, in which Bataille undermines traditional conceptions of the divine, begins and ends with appeals to the mystics—first Meister Eckhart and, at much greater length, Angela of Foligno. Bataille cites central passages that occur at the end of the *Memorial*; here Angela describes the twenty-sixth transformation in which she is immersed in God "in and with darkness." Bataille chooses texts that stress the "nothingness" of that which Angela encounters in this final transformation:

> Saint Angela of Foligno says: "One time my soul was elevated and I saw God in a clarity and a fullness that I had never known to that point in such a full way. And I did not see any love there. I lost then that love that I bore in myself; I was made into nonlove. And then after that I saw him in a darkness, for he is a good so great that he cannot be thought or understood. And nothing of that which can be thought or understood attains or approaches him" (*Livre de l'expérience* I, 105). A little further on, " . . . The soul sees a nothingness and sees all things (*nihil videt et omnia videt*); my body is asleep; language is cut off. All the numerous and unspeakable signs of friendship God has given me, and all the words that he has spoken to me . . . are, I perceive, so below this good encountered in a darkness so great that I do not put my hope in them, that my hope may not rest in them" (id., 106). (OC V 122; IE 104)[19]

Although in *Guilty* Bataille contrasts mystical and erotic experience, arguing that the former can be perfected, whereas eroticism is marked by insatiability and ceaseless desire, here Bataille points to a moment in which Angela's erotic mystical experience subverts the limits of more traditional mysticisms. Angela's soul passes beyond experiences of loving union with God and into a darkness in which there is no pretense of satisfaction or completion.

Yet once again Bataille is ambivalent about Angela, who he reads as herself ambivalent—servile in her hope for salvation, yet lacerating and sovereign in her description and enactment of the sacred annihilation of self and God. As in *Guilty*, Bataille argues that "it is difficult to tell to what extent belief is an obstacle to the experience, to what extent the intensity of the experience overturns the obstacle" (OC V 122; IE 104). Bataille presumes a gap between inner experience and the dogmatic utterances found in Angela's *Book*, but is not clear whether her beliefs obstruct her ability to achieve inner experience or simply distort her accounts of it. Inner experience, Bataille suggests, necessarily lacerates dogma, just as it does the subject. From this perspective, Angela's desire for abject suffering and death becomes emblematic of the corrosive quality of the mystical (OC V 122; IE 104). A similar ambivalence emerges, as Bataille shows, in Angela's reported last words—"Oh unknown nothingness ! (*o nihil incognitum!*)" (OC V 122; IE 104).[20] "Nothingness" here is ambiguous; whereas the text of the *Instructions* interprets Angela's words as referring to the nothingness of her created being, Bataille suggests that they may refer to the nothingness of the divine. His own account of inner experience, moreover, demonstrates the inextricability of the two; Angela's nothingness and that of the divine are one in ecstasy.

TOWARD A NEW MEDITATIVE PRACTICE

After sections on Descartes, Hegel, and a fragmentary and interrupted account of a "partly-failed" inner experience (one described, Bataille tells us, in order better to evoke a successful experience),[21] Bataille introduces two digressions that are particularly indebted to Angela's *Book*—"First Digression on Ecstasy before an Object: The Point" and "Second Digression on Ecstasy in the Void."[22] In characteristic fashion, these "digressions" are the heart of Bataille's book. Without here naming Angela, Bataille relies on a distinction central to her account of the twenty-sixth transformation of the soul. After having emphasized the role of suffering in her experience and its relationship to Christ's incarnation and passion, Angela describes the movement from that object-centered and desirous loving relationship to the encounter with darkness in which she is made into nonlove and lies in the abyss:

> When I am in that darkness I do not remember anything about anything human, or the God-man, or anything which has a form. Nevertheless, I see all and I see nothing. As what I have spoken of withdraws and stays with me, I see the God-man. He draws my soul with great gentleness and he sometimes says to me; "You are I and I am you." I see, then, those eyes and that face so gracious and attractive as he leans to embrace me. In short, what proceeds from those eyes and that face is what I said that I saw in that previous darkness that comes from within, and that delights me so that I can say nothing of it. When I am in the God-man my soul is alive. And

I am in the God-man much more than in the other vision of seeing God with darkness. The soul is alive in that vision concerning the God-man. The vision with darkness, however, draws me so much more that there is no comparison.[23]

Angela here articulates the relationship between her experience of unity with Christ in his suffering and that with the divine abyss of darkness, nothingness, and unknowing. She asserts a relationship between these two forms of experience, but she does not completely elucidate the nature of the link between them. She explains, however, that she sees the darkness in the eyes and face of Christ, suggesting a causal connection between her meditation and identification with the passion of Christ and her experience of the dissolution of self and other into ecstatic darkness. Similarly, Bataille seeks to articulate the relationship between an ecstasy generated before an object and out of love for an other and that experienced in the void.

Bataille's conception of the self-subverting nature of the divine suggests that there will be no place for a positive object of meditation in his practice.[24] But instead of rejecting such an object, Bataille reinterprets it, arguing that the object contemplated by the mystic is not a divine object of emulation but a projection of the self, a dramatization of the self's dissolution.[25] In making this claim, Bataille also draws out explicitly what Angela had adumbrated regarding the relationship between ecstasy before an object and that before the void or darkness:

> I will say this, although it is obscure: the object in the experience is first the projection of a dramatic loss of self. It is the image of the subject. The subject attempts at first to go to one like itself. But having entered into inner experience, the subject is in quest of an object like itself, reduced to its interiority. In addition, the subject whose experience is in itself and from the beginning dramatic (it is loss of self) needs to objectify this dramatic character. . . .
>
> But it is only a question there of a fellow human being. The point, before me, reduced to the most paltry simplicity, is a person. At each instant of experience, this point can radiate arms, cry out, set itself ablaze. (OC V 137; IE 118)

The extremity of the other's suffering leads not only to his or her own dissolution, but also to that of the contemplator or viewer. It is through this laceration and loss of self that communication between the self and the other occurs. The practice of dramatization or meditation is a necessary (although not sufficient) condition if one is to stand out of the self and open oneself to the other—if one is, in other words, to attain ecstasy and communication.

Bataille explicitly ties ecstasy before the object to the practice of meditation described by Ignatius of Loyola and other Christian mystics. Denise Despres displays the character of such meditation in her study of late medieval meditative practices and their relationship to visionary literature. Despres shows, in particular, that Franciscan devotional literature advocates a form of sensible meditative practice designed to be penitential and participatory. Responding to the vexed question of the relationship between the active and contemplative lives, Franciscan authors emphasize that contemplation is itself a form of action and that living in accordance with the life of Christ is itself a form of contemplation.[26] Thus contemplation and action do not stand in tension; rather, meditation on the life of Christ brings about sensible identification with Christ's suffering and, hence, true contrition (the emotional component) and the moral actions required by it.[27] Meditation, then, as Mary Carruthers shows brilliantly with regard to the early medieval monastic culture out of which Franciscan practice emerges, is an art of memory and memorialization.

Memory is the key to both contemplative and active lives, for both moral and religious dispositions depend on a well-stocked and ordered memory. Meditative practice, according to Carruthers, is a type of memory work that generates emotion, which in turn facilitates the act of memorialization. The beginning of the meditative life for monastics, Franciscans, and the lay audiences for whom Franciscans often wrote (among them Angela of Foligno) lies in the inculcation of guilt (and with it contrition), which leads to further acts of meditation (including, for the Franciscans, actions imitative of Christ) through which that guilt is expiated.

This form of memory work and of exegetical meditative practice is crucial to understanding Angela of Foligno. Comparing Angela's Book to the late thirteenth-century meditative primer Meditations on the Life of Christ, Robyn O'Sullivan demonstrates both Angela's debt to the Franciscan tradition and her divergences from it. Although thirteenth-century Franciscan authors typically call for the believer to identify with various witnesses to the events of Christ's life through the imaginative recreation of key moments in the Gospel narratives (perhaps reflecting a shift from monastic practice to texts designed for the laity), Angela moves from identification with St. John and Mary, the mother of God, to identification with Christ himself.[28] Like the thirteenth-century beguine mystics of northern Europe, Hadewijch and Mechthild of Magdeburg, Angela desires an unmediated relationship with Christ. Angela's desire for mystical union with Christ and the Godhead is reflected in her meditative practice, which gradually elides the gap between onlooker and object.[29]

Angela's accounts of Christ's suffering, like those of many others in the later Middle Ages, attempt to explore fully the details of Christ's torture in order to make his suffering come alive for herself and for the reader. Meditation on the details of Christ's abjection is essential to the mystic's and the reader's identification with him:

> Once when I was meditating on the great suffering Christ endured on the cross, I was considering the nails, which, I had heard it said, had driven a little bit of the flesh of his hands and feet into the wood. And I desired to see at least that small amount of Christ's flesh which the nails had driven into the wood. And then such was my sorrow over the pain that Christ had endured that I could no longer stand on my feet. I bent over and sat down; I stretched out my arms on the ground and inclined my head on them. Then Christ showed me his throat and arms.[30]

Angela does not just meditate on the figure of a crucified Christ but on the bits and pieces of his lacerated body. Moreover, the gap between herself as onlooker and the object of her contemplation dissipates in the fragmentation of Christ's body. Attention to these fragments molds her body into the very cruciform pattern of Christ's torment, suggesting her complete identification with his anguish. Her suffering at the sight of the cross is immediate and inescapable (she tells us early in her book that she screams and cries out whenever she sees the cross), and ultimately the cross itself is permanently inscribed in her heart. Through the imaginative recreation of Christ's passion, Angela moves from sensible identification with his suffering body to the incorporation of that body within her own. This fragmentation, incorporation, and repetition of Christ's suffering, moreover, leads to her joyful ecstasy.

Angela's Book suggests that in rendering herself Christ-like she potentially shares in Christ's redemptive activity. Her meditation is thus salvific, for herself and others (a move made much more explicitly by Hadewijch and Mechthild of Magdeburg). Bataille argues, to the contrary, that the other is simply a projection of the self. Hence Angela's meditation on the images of Christ's suffering displays her own desire to dissolve the self, to approach death, and to open herself to the lacerating wounds required for communication. In his own meditative practice, Bataille uses other images:

In any case, we can only project the object-point by drama. I had
recourse to upsetting images. In particular, I would gaze at the
photographic image—or sometimes the memory I have of it—of a
Chinese man who must have been tortured in my lifetime. Of this
torture, I had had in the past a series of successive representations.
In the end, the patient writhed, his chest flayed, arms and legs
cut off at the elbows and at the knees. His hair standing on end,
hideous, haggard, striped with blood, beautiful as a wasp. (OC V
139; IE 119)[31]

The fragility of the human body displayed in moments of supreme suffering
becomes the basis of Bataille's ecstatic drama. Some of the most shocking aspects
of Bataille's text mimic in the modern world (or as Bataille would put it, after the
death of God) Angela's contemplation of Christ's suffering. The image of Christ
on the cross is analogous to the photos of the cut-apart body of a torture victim
(the contemporary figure of ignominy and abjection so central to Inner Experience
and Guilty) on which Bataille meditates (just as Bataille's aestheticization of that
figure mirrors, in profoundly troubling ways, the aestheticization of Christ's
passion within the Christian tradition).

Bataille's meditations mimic but do not simply repeat those of the Christian
mystic. In order to reenact the meditative and writing practices of medieval
mysticism, Bataille must defamiliarize the crucifixion, whose cultural ubiquity
has come to obscure the horrors of the bodily torture that it represents. More
importantly, if the theocentrism and Christocentrism of Angela's experience is
to be decentered, other images of woundedness and laceration must take the
place of the Christ figure. The "object-point," as Bataille tells us, is simply a
"person," "a fellow human being":

The young and seductive Chinese man of whom I have spoken, left
to the work of the executioner—I loved him with a love in which
the sadistic instinct played no part: he communicated his pain to
me or perhaps the excessive nature of his pain, and it was precisely
that which I was seeking, not so as to take pleasure in it, but in
order to ruin in me that which is opposed to ruin. (OC V 140;
IE 120)[32]

What is central about the cross, Bataille suggests, is neither who is on it, nor
the salvific nature of his suffering, but the suffering itself, which serves as
the projected image through which the subject experiences his or her own

dissolution. What we cannot ruin directly in ourselves, Bataille argues, we can (must?) ruin through identification with the other's bodily laceration.

The torture of the other's body serves as a dramatization that leads to greater ecstasy in the void.[33] Here we see the move from ecstasy before the object, parallel to Angela's meditations on the figure of Christ, to ecstasy before the void, which is analogous to Angela's account of the darkness of the divine:

> The movement prior to the ecstasy of non-knowledge is the ec-
> stasy before an object (whether the latter be the pure point—as
> the renouncing of dogmatic beliefs would have it—or some up-
> setting image). If this ecstasy before the object is at first given (as
> a "possible") and if I suppress afterwards the object—as "contes-
> tation" inevitably does—if for this reason I enter into anguish—
> into horror, into the night of non-knowledge—ecstasy is near
> and, when it sets in, sends me further into ruin than anything
> imaginable. If I had not known of the ecstasy before the object,
> I would not have reached ecstasy in night. But *initiated* as I was in
> the object—and my initiation had represented the furthest pene-
> tration of what is possible—I could, in night, only find a deeper
> ecstasy. From that moment night, non-knowledge, will each time
> be the path of ecstasy into which I will lose myself. (OC V 144;
> IE 123–24)

Bataille's text itself attempts, like Angela's, to engender in writing and in the reader the dissolution of subject and object that is inner experience. Through this dissolution, communication occurs and a new community emerges—between Angela and Bataille, and between Bataille and his projected readers (and, more problematically, between Bataille and the torture victim). Moreover, Angela and her book become objects on to which Bataille can project his own dissolution, leading to the greater dissolution of self before the void. As I will show in the next chapter, Bataille and his books in turn become such objects for his readers.

MEDITATION AND TRAUMATIC MEMORY

These meditative practices—those found both in medieval texts like the *Medi-*
tations on the Life of Christ and Angela of Foligno's *Book* and in Bataille's twentieth-
century revisionings—bear a curious similarity to contemporary discussions of memory and traumatic suffering. Angela and Bataille both use meditative techniques to reenact and to experience sensibly, emotionally, and viscerally

the extraordinary physical suffering of another;[34] meditation on the fragmented bodies of torture victims gives rise to the dissolution of the subject and to his or her lacerating openness to the other. In the twentieth century, the literature on extraordinary suffering and its aftereffects focuses primarily on the victims of trauma and on attempts to alleviate the hyperarousal, intrusive memories, and constrictions of world that result from overwhelming events (as well as on the question of why certain experiences give rise to such symptoms and other, seemingly similar, experiences do not). Clearly there is a gulf between bodily memories of the sort Angela and Bataille experienced through medi- tation and the memories of trauma victims, whose bodies and psyches were actually subject to physical and mental abuse. Nonetheless, the relationship be- tween the memories of trauma victims and those induced by meditative prac- tices raises interesting questions, not unlike those Freud encountered in his attempt to explain the compulsion among shell shock victims to repeat trau- matic memories.

For Freud, who understood dreams and compulsions in terms of the desire for pleasure and its repression, compulsively repeated memories and dreams about physical horrors and the threat of death were inexplicable. To explain traumatic memories, therefore, Freud, in conjunction with his late theory of primary masochism, posits a death drive in addition to and "beyond" the plea- sure principle. Freud suggests that there is a drive to escape subjectivity or to shatter the self that stands in tension with the pleasure principle (although, arguably, pleasure, untouched by the reality principle, itself dissolves subjec- tivity). For many contemporary theorists, the danger of Freud's view is that it ignores or covers over the harsh realities of victimization; if we read self- dissolution as desired, we are in danger of replacing trauma, the inescapable suffering inflicted on human beings, with masochism, the embrace of shattering affliction.[35] A similar danger haunts any reading of Angela's and Bataille's texts. To get at the issues involved here, we need to begin by clarifying the relationship between medieval and modern meditative practices and contemporary theories of bodily or traumatic memory.

Pierre Janet introduced the distinction between narrative and traumatic memory as a way to highlight the abnormality of vivid, intrusive memories, laden with sensory and iconic motifs, that are common among survivors of traumatic events:

> [Normal memory] like all psychological phenomena, is an ac-
> tion; essentially it is the action of telling a story. . . . A situation

has not been satisfactorily liquidated . . . until we have achieved, not merely an outward reaction through our movements, but also an inward reaction through the words we address to ourselves, through the organization of the recital of the event to others and to ourselves, and through the putting of this recital in its place as one of the chapters in our personal history. . . . Strictly speaking, then, one who retains a fixed idea of a happening cannot be said to have a "memory." . . . It is only for convenience that we speak of it as a "traumatic memory."[36]

The highly sensory nature of these memories and the absence of verbal narrative make them similar to the memories of young children.[37] Yet unlike normal memories from early childhood, traumatic memories (and the associated phenomenon of traumatic dreams) are experienced as involuntary, having a "driven, tenacious quality" and a repetitive dimension.[38] Current research suggests that in situations of hyperarousal, particularly those for which the subject is unable to prepare, memory is encoded in a different, more viscerally experiential manner than normal. These bodily memories are not assimilated to consciousness and thus impinge on it in uncontrollable and intrusive ways. The best available treatment for such memories seems to be narrativization, through which bodily memories are relived and reordered in meaningful narrative forms.

Thus researchers, psychiatrists, and psychotherapists working with trauma survivors have developed complex therapies of reenactment and narrativization in which subjects remember in controlled environments, enabling them to order and make sense out of their experience:

> Out of the fragmented components of frozen imagery and sensation, patient and therapist slowly reassemble an organized, detailed, verbal account, oriented in time and historical context. The narrative includes not only the event itself but also the survivor's response to it and the responses of important people in her life. . . . The completed narrative must include a full and vivid description of the traumatic imagery. . . . The ultimate goal, however, is to put the story, including its imagery, into words.[39]

Psychiatrist and psychotherapist Judith Herman, who offers this account of the therapeutic process involved in recovery from post-traumatic stress disorder (PTSD), also insists that the (re)creation of a narrative of the traumatic event "includes a systematic review of the meaning of the event." The survivor must "reconstruct a system of belief that makes sense of her undeserved suffering"; such a system of belief, to be effective, must also result in action, often involving social activism against suffering and injustice.[40]

Medieval meditative practices reverse this pattern, moving through narrative memory in order, through imaginative recreation, to induce sensory and emotive suffering and horror in the face of catastrophic loss—in this case the death of the Godman on the cross. Medieval memory work involves making this historically distant yet cosmologically and soteriologically central event one's own by inducing something like traumatic memories of events that have not occurred to the subject but to Christ. We see this work, for example, in Angela's focus on the gruesome details of Christ's crucifixion, through which she makes present, emotionally and sensorially, the experience of Christ's suffering. Moreover, Angela stresses the extent to which these emotive and visceral responses become involuntary and inescapable. This sensory and emotionally laden contemplation generates the guilt of survival, and with it contrition and the penitential acts that will—in theory—allay that guilt. Angela thus moves from intense sorrow at Christ's suffering to the desire not simply to witness but to share in the suffering, even to intensify it:

> Then I would beg him to grant me this grace, namely, that since Christ had been crucified on the wood of the cross, that I be crucified in a gully, or in some very vile place, and by a very vile instrument. Moreover, since I did not desire to die as the saints had died, that he make me die a slower and even more vile death than theirs. I could not imagine a death vile enough to match my desire.[41]

This desire is answered on the spiritual level, making Angela's suffering soul itself an object of contemplation for the reader:

> Concerning the torments of the soul which demons inflicted upon her, she found herself incapable of finding any other comparison than that of a man hanged by the neck who, with his hands tied behind him and his eyes blindfolded, remains dangling on the gallows and yet lives, with no help, no support, no remedy, swinging in the empty air.[42]

Angela's repeated accounts of her own abject suffering and her desire for pain and death suggest the viability of Bataille's claim that the image of the suffering

Christ serves as a projection through which the subject comes to experience her own dissolution.[43] Angela seems less intent on the "recovery" made possible through narrativization (in this case the soteriological narrative of Christianity) than on a dissolution of self desired "beyond the pleasure principle" (although, arguably, the Christian narrative allows for both recovery and dissolution simultaneously, as Angela is lost in Christ and, through sharing in his suffering, redeems her own—and the world's—guilt).

We see, then, that a central feature of traumatic memory, its lack of a meaning-giving narrative framework, is generally absent from the work of medieval meditation, for in monastic meditative texts and in Franciscan meditative guides the narrative of salvation history is the constant backdrop against which Jesus' life and death is reenacted. In this context, the making visceral of Christ's suffering in the soul (and, at least occasionally, on the body with phenomenon like the stigmata) of the believer is a means of inducing emotion only in order to redeploy that suffering toward certain narrative and salvific ends. Medieval meditative techniques, on this reading, induce something like traumatic memory—or perhaps better, make visceral the catastrophe of God's death on the cross—only in order to relocate and redeploy that bodily response within the terms of salvation history. The central question raised by Angela's text is whether in her case the reenactment of the divine catastrophe of the cross does not overwhelm the redemptive story that frames her meditative practice, bringing her closer, once again, to Bataille than her place within the Christian tradition might initially suggest.

Though I do not mean to deny the power and efficacy of narrativization, it is important to see that both Angela's and Bataille's texts raise the question of that which is left out of Herman's therapeutic account of trauma and my use of it to read medieval meditative practices—the refusal, on the part of many survivors of traumatic or catastrophic events, to accept any palliating or explanatory narrative for their suffering. Victims often express the fear that the imposition of salvific or other explanatory narratives onto their experience undercuts the onlooker's ability to understand and identify with the severity of victims' suffering.[44] In addition, a sense of obligation to co-sufferers who have not survived sometimes causes victims to reject meaning-giving narratives on explicitly ethical grounds.[45] And even if victims of trauma do not consciously reject the narrativization of their suffering, the guilt often associated with survival can block such attempts at healing. It is precisely in the face of this rejection and failure of redemptive narratives that Bataille's texts, even more than Angela's *Book*, share something crucial with the experiences of at least some trauma survivors. With his explicit rejection of salvific narratives and his insistence on the dissolution of subjectivity in the face of bodily trauma, Bataille uses meditative practices of traumatic recreation not to inculcate and then allay guilt, but to intensify and embrace guilt-ridden anguish (a move still only suggested by aspects of Angela's *Book*). However, given his distance from the catastrophes of war and experiences of bodily torture like those on which he meditates, we must ask whether Bataille's pursuit of bodily memory and the concomitant dissolution of the subject marks, as Sartre and others suggest, mere self-indulgence and escapism from the demands of history.

AN ETHICS OF CATASTROPHE

Following Lacan, Cathy Caruth argues that the refusal to accept redemptive narratives marks the ethical nature of traumatic memory itself:

> The accidental in trauma is a revelation of a basic, ethical dilemma at the heart of consciousness itself insofar as it is essentially related to death, and particularly to the death of others. Ultimately, then, the story of father and child [in Freud's account of a father's dream after the death of his son] is, for Lacan, the story of an impossible responsibility of consciousness in its own originating relation to others, and specifically to the death of others. As an awakening, the ethical relation to the real is the revelation of this impossible demand at the heart of human consciousness.[46]

This is what Lacan describes as the "ethical *relation* to the real,"[47] a mode of encounter that refuses salvific narratives insofar as they cover over the other's death and the accidental nature of one's own survival. At the heart of the individual's experience of the other's death, then, lies an ethical intuition about the social nature of existence.

Caruth argues that literary and philosophical accounts of trauma raise the question of whether trauma is an "encounter with death, or the ongoing experience of having survived it."[48] Caruth's account of trauma focuses on the onlooker, the one who encounters overwhelming events, unassimilable to consciousness, and hence always returned to in an attempt to make sense out of experience. In almost all of Caruth's examples, that onlooker remains physically untouched by the witnessed catastrophe. This understanding of trauma must be carefully differentiated from the understanding central to contemporary clinical literature like Herman's, which focuses on those who have themselves *undergone* extraordinary physical or psychic suffering.[49] This distinction between victims of physical and psychic violence and onlookers suggests a further distinction between trauma and catastrophe, that is, between the individual's encounter with violence and suffering (trauma) and such events as experienced within larger social, political, and historical networks (catastrophe). In his wartime texts, Bataille speaks not of trauma but of catastrophe. Yet at the same time, he demands that each onlooker take the catastrophe on as her own, thereby undermining the distinction between trauma and catastrophe on which his meditative practice rests.

Attention to the distinction between the one undergoing traumatic suffering and onlookers—no matter how meditatively invested in the other's suffering they may become—helps elucidate both Bataille's repetition, throughout the *Atheological Summa*, and particularly in the aptly named *Guilty*, of the themes of chance and ecstasy, and the relationship between these themes and Bataille's "ethics." At one point in *Guilty*, Bataille's reflection on chance and ecstasy takes the form of a fascination with the sturdy hooks he sees placed half way up a roof. (These hooks are used to hold in place poles that keep snow from falling off the roof.)

> I saw big, solid hooks on a roof, placed half way up. Suppose a man falls from the roof, perhaps [*par chance*] he could grab hold of one of them with his arm or leg. Precipitated from the roof of a house, I would crash into the ground. But if a hook were there, I could stop myself on the way down!

> A bit later I might say to myself: "One day an architect planned that hook without which I would be dead. I ought to be dead: it isn't so at all, I am alive, someone put a hook there."

> My presence and my life would be ineluctable: but I don't know what of the impossible, of the inconceivable, would be its principle.

> I understand now, imagining to myself the momentum of the fall, that nothing exists in the world without meeting a hook. (OC V 315; G 74)

This hook comes to represent the contingency of Bataille's survival; neither the war nor his illness kill him (although these issues are not raised explicitly by Bataille). There is no reason for him to be alive, nor can he make his life meaningful—all he can do is witness to life's contingency. In embracing chance, he stands outside of himself in ecstasy:

THE OBJECT OF ECSTASY IS THE ABSENCE OF RESPONSE FROM OUT-
SIDE. THE INEXPLICABLE PRESENCE OF MAN IS THE RESPONSE THAT
THE WILL GIVES ITSELF, SUSPENDED OVER THE VOID OF AN UNIN-
TELLIGIBLE NIGHT; THAT NIGHT, FROM ONE END TO THE OTHER,
HAS THE IMPUDENCE OF A HOOK. (OC V 320; G 78)

Chance is the hook on which existence falls. It is without meaning and offers
no answer to the question of human existence other than its own facticity. The
abruptness of this facticity, the absence of response in the response, is ecstasy.

Ecstasy is here engendered for Bataille through meditation on the absence
of a response to the "why" of his own survival. But this ecstasy is related to the
ecstasy brought on through Bataille's practice of meditating on photographs of
the Chinese man who suffers horrifying torture.

> I just looked at two photographs of torture. These
> images have become familiar to me; one of them, nevertheless,
> is so horrible that it makes my heart skip a beat.

> I must have had to stop writing. I was, as I often am,
> sitting before an open window; I had just sat down when I fell into
> a sort of ecstasy. This time, I no longer doubted, as I did painfully
> the previous night, that such a state was more intense than erotic
> pleasure. I see nothing: *that is neither visible nor sensible. That
> makes me sad and heavy not to die.* If I picture, in my anguish,
> all I have loved, I must imagine furtive realities to which my love
> attached itself like so many clouds behind which *what is there* hid
> itself. Ecstatic images betray. *What is there* comes entirely from fright.
> Fright makes it happen: a violent fracas is required for *it to be there.*
> (OC V 268–69; G 32)[50]

This ecstatic standing outside of the self is experienced as laceration, agony,
and anguish, a rendering of the self in the face of the real: "When an image
of torture falls before my eyes, I can, in my fright, turn away. But I am, if I
look at it, *outside of myself.* . . . The horrible sight of torture opens the sphere in
which is enclosed (is delimited) my personal particularity, it opens it violently,
it lacerates it" (OC V 272; G 35).

For Bataille, inner experience begins with dramatization and meditation on
"images of explosion and of being lacerated—ripped to pieces" (OC V 269;
G 32).[51] Meditation on the wounded body of the other lacerates the onlooker's

subjectivity; Bataille argues that woundedness and its recognition are necessary for opening one human being to the other. The greater this woundedness and laceration—the more the self is exploded and ripped apart—the fuller the communication that occurs between the nonself and the now ruined other.[52] Irigaray's work will raise the question of why openness to and communication with the other are understood as woundedness.[53] But the ways in which Bataille discusses his meditative practices in Guilty, a more anguished and personal text than Inner Experience, suggest that the question might be posed in another way: Is Bataille perhaps attempting to communicate a kind of experience unassimilable to traditional narrative forms and normal language use? It might help here to make a distinction between narrative memory and catastrophic memory. For Bataille the writings of the mystics (and of Nietzsche), like the photographs of the torture victim, communicate realities that stand outside of everyday experience, or at least outside what we like to believe about everyday experience. These texts and images force the onlooker/reader to recognize (to remember) the anguishing, catastrophic real hidden by narrative memory and the illusions of wholeness and unity on which it depends.[54] Inner Experience, Guilty, and On Nietzsche, written in the midst of the historical events of 1939–1944, attempt to find a way to communicate catastrophic suffering without succumbing either to salvific and compensatory narratives or to dissolution, silence, and death.

One might argue, however, that it is wrong to read Bataille's compulsion to witness the other's torture in light of historical catastrophe, for his texts elide history in its specificity. Though he writes during the war and the Nazi occupation, Bataille does not focus directly on contemporary European events, and he also bypasses the time, place, and context of the Chinese man's torture and death. He alludes only briefly to the circumstances of the execution, and they play no role in his meditative practices. Thus in Guilty Bataille is able to move rapidly from the traumatic dismemberment of the torture victim to the chance nature of human existence, reading the tortured body as emblematic of the human condition (this move reflects the one described in Inner Experience from ecstasy before an object to ecstasy before the void). Bataille ignores the stark differences between his own bodily experience and that of the dismembered Chinese man, and he conflates, far too rapidly, contingency with violence and horror.

It may be possible to save Bataille from this critique by arguing that he asks readers to look at this dismembered body, in all its unnamed specificity, and to recognize that only chance keeps that body from being their own. Bataille apprehends the radical otherness of the torture victim's suffering as itself the product of chance, and this recognition takes Bataille out of himself in an experience of ecstatic anguish and guilt. From this perspective, Bataille's move becomes less ethically dubious. Yet I still hesitate over the *only*, for while such horrors can befall any body, should we ignore the concrete ethical, political, and historical dimensions that engender many such events, including the persecution, torture, and murder of millions of Jews during the years Bataille was writing his books? The answer to this question seems obvious; but why, then, does Bataille refuse to address suffering at this level? He refuses, it seems, because to uncover these dimensions of experience—to ask why such events occur and how they can be stopped—is to provide a narrative for them that risks covering over their sheer horror.

Read in light of medieval meditative practices centered on the crucifixion, in which narrative memory plays a key role, Bataille's renunciation of such narratives becomes particularly stark. We can see what Bataille rejects in those practices, as well as the ramifications of his rejection. He offers guilt without redemption, anguish without salvation. Bataille implies that the specificity of the real (this body, in pieces, radically other in its suffering yet recognizably like mine in its very bodiliness) must take precedence over any narrative contextualization. To put the point more strongly, Bataille suggests that narrative and historical contextualization are (necessarily? can be if they take soteriological form?) ways of evading the real.[55] Given his understanding of reality, we can conclude that "history" has a double meaning within Bataille's text: on the one hand, it refers to those narratives that give meaning and direction to human action; but on the other, it names that which remains unassimilable to such narratives.

Patricia Yaeger cogently questions what is at stake for us in such apparently ventriloquizing moves.[56] In her discussion of contemporary academic attempts to speak for the dead victims of catastrophic events, she insists that we maintain a nervous vigilance against accepting too readily our ability to speak for the other. Nonetheless, she maintains a model of "speaking for." Bataille, on the contrary, never pretends to speak for the other; rather his texts demonstrate a compulsion *to see the speechless body*. Instead of providing the context in which demands for justice might be made, the sight of the speechless, fragmented body rejects meaning and any historical or soteriological framework in which the body might be turned into/read as a sign.[57] Bataille attempts to give an account of *communication* in and through the lacerating reality of the other's suffering that does not embrace any salvific narrative and does not reduce the suffering other to his or her "use" value (as heroic emblem, as call for political action, etc.).[58]

It is hard to see Bataille's meditative focus on the speechless body as a *sufficient* form of action, especially given his refusal to recognize the narrativizations through which suffering is itself often produced.[59] Furthermore, there is the real danger that with this rejection of soteriological narratives, historical and cultural memory will be annihilated. Yet his demand for radical communication may also be a necessary contestation of more immediately "useful" political projects. Just as there are two conceptions of history standing alongside each other in Bataille's text, perhaps we should distinguish two conceptions of political action: one that would contest power and injustice through narrativization, and one that would contest those very narrativizations themselves in the name of that which is unassimilable to redemptive political projects—the bodies of those who can never again be made whole.

Bataille himself suggests such a reading of his text in his 1947 review of John Hershey's *Hiroshima*, which recounts survivors' stories from the atomic bombing of that city. Bataille contrasts servile sentimentality with sovereign sensibility on the basis of their differing relationships toward the present, the future, and politics:

> The sensibility that looks for a way out and enters along the path of politics is always of cheap quality. It cheats, and it is clear that in *serving* political ends it is no more than a *servile*, or at least subordinated sensibility. The cheating is quite apparent. If the misfortunes of Hiroshima are faced up to freely from the perspective of a sensibility that is not faked, they cannot be isolated from other misfortunes. . . . One cannot deny the differences in age and in suffering, but origin and intensity change nothing: horror is everywhere the same. The point that, in principle, the one horror is preventable while the other is not is, in the last analysis, a matter of indifference. (OC XI 180; CA 228)[60]

To turn immediately to political questions about how suffering can be avoided, Bataille suggests, is to remain servile to precisely the forms of political project that brought about the suffering in the first place.

Even more damningly, Bataille insists that this servile attitude refuses to look the horror of suffering in the face and thereby refuses to recognize the reality and the particularity of the other's suffering. The person of sovereign sensibility, on the other hand, looking misfortune in the face, no longer immediately says, "At all costs let us do away with it," but first, "Let us live it." Let us lift, in the instant, a form of life to the level of the worst.

But no one, for all that, gives up doing away with what one can. (OC XI 185; CA 232)

For Bataille, this apprehension of suffering is the basis for a "morality of the instant" that refuses to subordinate the present to the future or to make suffering meaningful through any soteriological—be it religious or political—project.[61] Recognition of the essentially "nonsensical" nature of misfortune is the necessary preliminary to any real historical and political change.[62]

Reflecting his own sovereign sensibility, Bataille's wartime writing is sparked by an imperative to witness to the other's physical dissolution and to accept the dissolution of the self—the anguished ecstatic standing outside of oneself—that this witnessing demands. There is another reading of this imperative, however, as a desire to *escape* from the self by using the other's physical suffering as a means to this ecstatic end. Thus Sartre worries in a conversation with Bataille entitled "Discussion of Sin" that Bataille himself is engaged in a "project," that of apprehending "what is there" in the horror of traumatic suffering. Is not this desire to apprehend the suffering of others itself the product of a servile or subordinate sensibility, insofar as Bataille subordinates the other's suffering to his own ends? Does he not, in fact, use violent imagery for contemplative purposes and thereby appropriate others' real, bodily suffering for his own "ecstasy"?[63]

In the last chapter, I responded to Sartre's criticisms of Bataille by suggesting that Bataille's account of ecstasy might be understood in light of Lacan's theory of jouissance and its deployment by Jean Laplanche and Leo Bersani. One can thus read ecstasy in terms of Freud's late account of primary masochism, as a self-shattering that lies beyond the pleasure principle and yet is itself *desired*. In this chapter, I have offered an account of the ecstasy described in Bataille's wartime writings as one that is best framed in terms of an ethics of catastrophe. In both the masochistic and the catastrophic line of interpretation, Bataille's "compulsion to repeat" the encounter with extraordinary physical suffering has nothing to do with the obvious pleasure of mastering seemingly unmasterable horrors. Whatever ecstasy is, it is not mastery, and I take seriously Bataille's repeated claim that ecstasy is anguish (although an anguish accompanied by the joy of communication). Yet what is the relationship between masochistic desire and the ethical compulsion to confront the real?

For Bataille, ecstasy is anguish because behind the object that provokes ecstasy lurks catastrophe. War is the catastrophe to which Bataille, in a necessarily indirect fashion, bears witness; yet in a troubling way, the constant threat of death, like the death of Christ on the cross for Angela, leads to ecstatic communication and community:[64]

> Instead of avoiding laceration, I'll deepen it. The sight of torture/execution staggers me, but quickly enough I support it with indifference. Now I invoke innumerable tortures/executions of a multitude in agony. Finally (or maybe all at once) human immensity promises a horror without limit.
>
> Cruelly, I stretch out the laceration: at that moment, I attain the point of ecstasy.
>
> Compassion, suffering, and ecstasy mingle together [se composent]. (OC V 273–73; G 36)

Bataille is compelled to face catastrophe in order to communicate it, yet only the meditative embrace, even intensification, of catastrophe enables communication. The desire for "a horror without limit" in the early 1940s, when horror without limit was occurring throughout Europe, is profoundly troubling. Yet we must at least recognize that for Bataille the desire for horror is not a desire to escape the demands of history but to face them.

Bataille's insistence, throughout the wartime writings, on the necessity of communication points to his demand that the self not be fully dissolved (and that new forms of memorialization be established).[65] Regardless of his critics' claims, Bataille does not desire death. He recognizes that to speak of communication, one must have a self lingering on the edges of dissolution; the explosion cannot be literal, the catastrophe cannot be physically reenacted, if it is to be communicated. The torture victim cannot himself speak or write. Bataille does not purport to speak for him so much as to bear, subjectively and in writing, the consequences of witnessing his suffering. Yet what does it mean to communicate with another who is beyond speech? Does the other's dying body become a form of writing that communicates across the boundaries of mortality? And if so, does the radicality of the communication Bataille envisions demand the other's death, if not Bataille's own? These are questions with which Bataille would grapple throughout his life.

Bataille desires to live within death's breath; he is compelled to witness (to) the other's physical dissolution, through which the chance nature of existence is made known; he provides a model of dissolving subjectivity for others, one that witnesses to the void without reenacting physical dissolution. Yet we must ask again whether he desires to witness to the other's suffering, or simply to *witness* it as the spark for his own, less literal, dissolution? Bataille's texts here encapsulate the ambiguity of witnessing—what is the source of this desire? the ethical call of the other, whose suffering demands attention? or the desire for self-shattering anguish and ecstasy? For some late medieval women, like Angela of Foligno, Hadewijch, and Mechthild of Magdeburg, the two come together in Christ. The soul shattered in contemplation of Christ's suffering body attends, in and as Christ, to the suffering of others. Without that divine, salvific ground can we ever bring together love of the other and the desire for self-dissolution? Might communication provide a new ground for their convergence? Yet Bataille's work and the catastrophes to which it bears witness teach us to distrust promises of certainty and of salvation premised on the refusal of ambiguity. Bataille suggests that, at least among the onlookers, "pure" witnessing may not be possible.[66]

FROM IMAGE TO TEXT: PHOTOGRAPHY, WRITING, AND COMMUNICATION

....

It is perhaps unavoidable that, when a subject confronts the facti-
tiousness of object relation, when he stands at the place of the want
that founds it, the fetish becomes a life preserver, temporary and
slippery, but nonetheless indispensable. But is not exactly language
our ultimate and inseparable fetish? And language, precisely, is based
on fetishistic denial ("I know that, but just the same," "the sign is
the thing, but just the same," etc.) and defines us in our essence as
speaking beings. Because of its founding status, the fetishism of
"language" is perhaps the only one that is unanalyzable.

JULIA KRISTEVA, *Powers of Horror: An Essay on Abjection*

TRAUMA, PHOTOGRAPHY, AND THE SCANDAL OF THE
REAL   Sartre is astute in his reading of Bataille, recognizing—albeit in passing—what compels him to write and publish *Inner Experience*; "pressed to *witness*,
M. Bataille hands over to us his thoughts without any order and from very
different dates" (NM 156). Sartre argues that the force of Bataille's desire leads
to a confusion and disorder that undermines his powers of communication.
But for Bataille, that disorder is itself an aspect of his witnessing. One might
argue, then, that it is *what* Bataille communicates that Sartre rejects through
his dismissive comments about Bataille's inability to reach the reader. From
this perspective, the vehemence of Sartre's refusal itself seems to speak to the
performative power of Bataille's text.

Sartre aptly names the primary models for Bataille's writing practice and in doing so gives a further indication of the sources of his uneasiness with that practice. "Certain pages of *Inner Experience*," Sartre writes, "with their breathless disorder, their passionate symbolism, their tone of prophetic preaching, seem to have come out of [Nietzsche's] *Ecce Homo* or *The Will to Power*" (NM 144). The disdain that marks Nietzsche's texts is also, Sartre argues, continually present in Bataille's. Sartre also refers repeatedly to Bataille's text as mystical, thereby suggesting its ties to mystical modes of writing. The problem for Sartre is that Bataille writes only for "the apprentice mystic," that is, the one who will follow him on his journey into inner experience; yet he holds even that reader—as he does himself—in contempt. The result, Sartre argues, is a communication "without reciprocity" (NM 152).

Bataille's meditative practice emerges from the same testamentary desire as his writing practice. The photographs on which Bataille meditates witness to the silent suffering undergone by the torture victim, just as Bataille's texts are a witness to his anguish and ecstasy in the face of that suffering. Yet these photographs and the practices surrounding them heighten the sense of urgency in Sartre's critique of Bataillean communication, for the torture victim with whom Bataille claims to communicate is dead, making reciprocity seem impossible.[1] As I will argue in what follows, writing (understood either in a broadly Derridean or in a more specific sense) always points toward the possible death of the sender. Part of what we value in writing is precisely its ability to transcend limits of space and time and to enable communication across these barriers. Yet in the case of the photographs on which Bataille meditates, not only is the victim dead, but we are not at all sure who is transmitting the message, making the issue of reciprocity all the more acute.

In describing his meditative practice, Bataille discusses only the victim. The photographs themselves are not reprinted in the text; their provenance is never discussed; nor does Bataille give any attention to the historical and political context in which they were made. These omissions are, I think, deliberate.[2] Yet in eliding the photographer and the circumstances in which the photographs were taken, Bataille is able to avoid a crucial question concerning *who* is communicating through these images. Bataille implies that he communicates directly with the photographs' central subject, but this claim depends on his bypassing the photographer, the material conditions of the images' production, and the other people who appear in the photographs (torturers and onlookers). Who took the images? Was the photographer Chinese? European? Were the photographs produced to serve as warnings for other malefactors? As illustrated guides for would-be torturers? As "neutral" anthropological or historical reportage? As images of exotic horror for a Western audience?[3] Rather than attempting to respond to such questions, Bataille suggests that he can wrest the photographs from these various contexts and communicate directly with the man whose image appears within them.

Yet if one attains inner experience through dramatization, as Bataille argues, then the reliance on what appear to be genuine "snuff" photographs would seem to be the worst kind of exploitative appropriation. His use of the image of a Chinese man, moreover, participates in an orientalizing gaze that renders further suspect the simultaneous claim to absolute historicity and the elision of the historical. As Edward Said argues, European discussions of the Orient

> are all declarative and self-evident; the tense they employ is the timeless eternal; they convey an impression of repetition and strength. . . . For all these functions it is frequently enough to use the simple copula is. . . .
>
> Philosophically, then, the kind of language, thought, and vision that I have been calling Orientalism very generally is a form of radical realism; anyone employing Orientalism, which is the habit for dealing with questions, objects, qualities and regions deemed Oriental, will designate, name, point to, fix what he is talking or thinking about with a word or phrase, which then is considered either to have acquired, or more simply to be, reality. Rhetorically speaking, Orientalism is absolutely anatomical and enumerative: to use its vocabulary is to engage in the particularizing and dividing of things Oriental into manageable parts.[4]

Homi Bhabha sharpens and extends this analysis, arguing that when Westerners use the image of the Oriental to represent the real, the Oriental serves as a fetish through which loss (in classical psychoanalytic terms, the threat of castration) is both recognized and disavowed. This fetishization explains the Oriental's function both as castrated and feminized other (hence that which is lost) and as a sign of some timeless human reality, marking fullness and plenitude (because that loss is disavowed and made good by the other, who in his or her otherness stands in for the threatened penis).[5] Even in claiming to avow his own loss through meditation on the image of the torture victim, taken as emblematic of human laceration and finitude, Bataille maintains a distance—the chance that separates his experience from that of the other— that serves potentially as the continued basis for disavowal of this same loss.

The photographs raise again, then, and in particularly gruesome fashion, the problems of voyeurism, scopophilia, and the fetishization of the other discussed in chapter 1.

These issues render visible a crucial difference between Bataille's practice and that of Angela of Foligno. Angela describes her bodily and spiritual imitation of Christ's suffering; she lies on the ground in a cruciform pattern and experiences, physically and spiritually, ever-deepening torments. Bataille never suggests any participation in the bodily suffering of the tortured man on whose image he meditates.[6] Rather, the extremity of this man's physical suffering, his literal dismemberment, leads to Bataille's psychical laceration and the explosion of his subjectivity. In other words, the dramatization enacted by the torture victim is never literally reenacted by Bataille—a gap or abyss still lies between Bataille and the torture victim, a gap held in place by the vagaries of chance itself. Whereas Angela believes that she can expiate the guilt of her survival through a literal imitation of Christ's suffering, for Bataille chance and the resultant guilt of survival can never be fully overcome. Yet they do engender an ecstasy (a standing outside of oneself) in which the other's suffering is apprehended as radically other, and so disruptive of the psychic wholeness of the onlooker. Thus, Bataille would claim, his relationship to these images is not fetishistic, for it depends on the avowal of loss rather than on its elision.

Another apparent difference between medieval practices and those of Bataille is that the images Bataille uses to induce self-annihilation (or its simulacra) are tied to the real in a way that images of Christ crucified, it would seem, are not. Part of the horror of Bataille's practice lies in his use of photographs as the "object-point" for meditation, for we presume that what these pictures image was once real. As many prominent theorists of photography argue, photography's specificity lies in the fact that it "is part of, an extension of" its subject. This relationship between the subject and the photograph gives rise to what Walter Benjamin calls the photograph's "aura" and what Susan Sontag describes as photography's "primitive" or "magical" quality.[7] To describe this phenomenon, André Bazin makes use of the distinction, first introduced by Charles Sanders Peirce, between indexical and iconic signs; photographs are indexical because there is a material continuity between that which is photographed and the image that survives.[8] For Roland Barthes and Sontag, this continuity suggests the close relationship between photography and death. In the photograph, something of the dead remains, even as in taking the photograph, the subject's death is foreshadowed. Photography, according to these accounts, is a relic, a remnant of the subject through which it is present to the world even after destruction (in the case of inanimate physical objects) or death (in the case of living creatures); the photograph is the best of all possible fetishes.[9]

According to this view of photography, the photographic image itself bears the trace of the represented body. For Bataille, these photographic "traces of the real" appear to be what enables communication to occur between himself and the torture victim. It is precisely the indexical quality of the photographic image that enables him to elide the photographer (and the context in which the photograph was made) in order to communicate directly with the photograph's subject. In other words, communication seems to depend precisely on the fetishistic quality of the photographic representation. Yet if the photographs on which Bataille meditates have this relation to the real, then we are immediately led back to the questions asked earlier: Who took these pictures? To what end? For what audience? Who speaks through them?—the victim, the seemingly unmoved ring of observers who surround the tortured person and appear to present him to the viewer, the torturers (and Bataille may, at one point, suggest his horrified identification with them [OC V 276–77; G 38–39]), or the photographer through whose "eyes" we see? In other words, in these photographs a spectacle is being staged for the photographer—and through the photographer for us—but it is not at all clear that this spectacle is the same one to which Bataille invites his readers.[10] If the context in which the photographs were taken is one of sadism, injustice, and exploitation, can Bataille so easily divorce his interaction with their subject from that context?[11]

For many people the indexical nature of the photographs on which Bataille meditates—the reality of a human being's dismemberment and intense physical suffering—makes them an ethically impossible site for meditation. On this view, representations of the cross differ from photographic representations because the former are merely images, iconic signs that bear no material continuity with that which is represented. Yet for medieval viewers, the crucifixion was real both as historical event and as it was continually reenacted through the sacrifice of Christ on the altar in the Holy Eucharist. The eucharistic presence increasingly extended, at least on the level of popular belief, to certain images of Christ, which were then experienced as making present the living body of the suffering Godman. Although theologically understood as iconic rather than indexical (to use Peirce's terms), images of Christ are continually discussed by medieval people in ways that suggest continuity between Christ's suffering body and pictorial representations of it. Just as the thirteenth-century beguine Hadewijch sees a vision of the adult Christ in her reception of the Eucharist, so fourteenth-century Dominican nuns see the image of the crucified Christ come alive to embrace them.[12] In the same way, Julian of Norwich, a fourteenth-century English visionary and recluse, describes visions of Christ's bleeding and suffering flesh engendered through her meditation on the crucifix held over her sickbed.[13] Theologians might insist that representations of Christ do not share in his divine presence, but a host of medieval texts and images suggest otherwise; particularly for those to whom God wishes to grant special revelations and ecstasies, pictorial representations serve as a medium through which God becomes present in the world.[14]

These medieval understandings of the crucifix suggest that the real difference between medieval practices and those of Bataille lies less in the medium of meditation, or in the understanding of the "realness" of the suffering dramatized, than in the meanings attributed to that suffering. Hadewijch and Julian believe that Christ chose to suffer for humanity, just as the believer chooses to suffer with Christ on behalf of sinners. This is precisely the soteriological framework Bataille eschews. He refuses to make the torture victim's suffering meaningful. Without this meaning-giving framework, can we be sure that in his encounter with photographic images of suffering flesh Bataille communicates with the suffering other rather than with the sadistic-voyeuristic eye through which the photograph is made and disseminated? Can we ever fully separate the compassionate encounter with the other from that fetishistic and/or voyeuristic-sadistic look? Bataille argues that sight is shattered in this encounter, insisting on his masochistic identification with the torture victim—but his dependence on the look, and so his identification with the onlookers, torturers, and/or the photographer remains the necessary precondition for this shattering.[15] Moreover, the shattering is not literal, and hence Bataille maintains a distance between his experience and that of the torture victim on whom he gazes. What Said says of European discussions of the Orient applies to Bataille's discussion of the photographs of the torture victim: it is precisely the distance between Bataille and the victim that enables him both to particularize the suffering other (in ways that efface the historical and political grounds of his or her suffering) and to generalize from that individual to the suffering of any and all human beings.

Another way in which Bataille's practice differs fundamentally from that of most medieval mystical and contemplative writers is in the temporality of his meditation. Rather than pointing to the eternal presentness of the other's redemptive suffering, as do Christian relics and icons, photographs, according to theorists of photography, are radically contingent in their indexical relationship to reality. As Eduardo Cadava argues, following Siegfried Kracauer, the photograph both makes something present and tears the object out of its presentness, bringing it violently into the future. Responses to photography, then, move in two possible directions: toward a myth of total presence and immanence (tied, for Kracauer, to fascism and a culture of death) or toward recognition of the pastness of the past, and hence toward an encounter with mortality and with our own radical contingency.[16] In rejecting Christian soteriological narratives and finding in the object-point of meditation a visceral reminder of the radical contingency of human existence, Bataille seems to tend toward the latter response. In meditating on the other's suffering, he makes it viscerally present to himself, but only in order to shatter sight. For Bataille, then, the photograph depicts neither total presence nor simply the absence of the past; rather, by making the victim present through meditation, Bataille enacts a traumatic experience of absence—the absence of a lost, irrecoverably destroyed body. In other words, Bataille attempts to undermine the fetishistic and/or voyeuristic, potentially fascistic gaze by moving through that gaze to its dissolution in the shattering recognition of human mortality, contingency, and loss.

The photograph is always double, however, always capable of being read either as a support for the myth of total presence or as a sign of the past's "pastness." The photograph, not surprisingly, shares in the ambiguity of the fetish, marking both the reality of castration and loss *and* their disavowal. Moreover, this doubleness mirrors that which Bataille argues for within mysticism itself. Bataille wants to move through the fetish to embrace lack. As I argued in chapter 2, it is the way we encounter the photograph, according to Bataille, that determines its ability to communicate; yet instabilities and dangers remain, for the logic of fetishization, premised on the distance between viewer and object, seems relentless. For Bataille writing—in which the signatory and the addressee are always unstable and in which agency can never be fully determined—offers an alternative to the dangers of meditative practice.

FROM IMAGE TO TEXT

Bataille's meditative practice clearly differs from his medieval and early modern models in its rejection of salvific narratives within which suffering is made meaningful and redemptive. However, some late medieval mystical writers show an uneasiness with Christian valorizations of suffering and the potential fetishization of the suffering body not unlike the uneasiness I feel before Bataille's texts. Mystical writers like Hadewijch, Marguerite Porete, and Meister Eckhart turn to the interior realm of the spirit and to language as sites in which redemptive suffering and/or ascesis might occur. Looking at the ways in which they displace fetishism from the suffering human body to the exiled soul and language can shed light on the troubling interplay of suffering and desire within Bataille's work.

The location of the problem for medieval writers is slightly different than it is in Bataille. Within the late medieval context, the problem was less the valorization of Christ's suffering (understood as freely chosen and redemptive of all humanity, hence preeminently meaningful) than the valorization of the suffering of the mystic or holy woman herself, the believer who, through suffering identification with Christ, hoped to share in his redemptive activity and divine self-birth.[17] Bataille's practice is problematic in that he seems to use another human being's unchosen suffering as a means toward his own ecstatic anguish. Even if we read that ecstatic anguish as itself an ethical response to the meaninglessness of the other's radically contingent torment, problems remain, for it is not clear that who suffers is in fact so radically contingent. Rather, differences in race, class, gender, sexuality, and ethnicity make it more likely that members of one or another particular group will be the subject of physical torture and thus serve as the noncontingent means through which the contingency of human bodily experience finds expression.[18] Similarly, some late medieval men and women seem to have worried that Christian soteriology, and particularly the gendering of that redemptive narrative, demanded the intense physical suffering of women and made it the sole means by which women might share in Christ's work. Angela of Foligno continually wishes to suffer with Christ—and even more than Christ—in order to be worthy of salvation, to become one with him, and to participates in his saving work. As Caroline Walker Bynum shows, Angela's desire for suffering made perfect sense within the religious world in which she lived.[19] Women, associated with the body and hence with the body of Christ, took part in Christ's redemptive work by sharing in the body's suffering.

Texts produced by the beguine mystics of northern Europe make explicit this theological and practical agenda and at the same time contest the association of women with the body and, ultimately, with suffering. Hadewijch argues that one should be like Christ in his humanity in order to become like God in his divinity, and stresses, throughout her writing, the need to share in the endless suffering desire of divine Love.[20] Yet for Hadewijch, as for her near contemporaries Beatrice of Nazareth and Mechthild of Magdeburg, this suffering is described as predominantly spiritual.[21] Unlike thirteenth-century hagiographies of women (almost always written by men), which emphasize the physical suffering of women as a mark of sanctity, women's texts themselves, before the fourteenth-century, are remarkably silent about bodily asceticism and pain.[22] This silence suggests, as I have argued elsewhere, that thirteenth-century religious women writers sought to forge a religious ideal in which suffering—like sin—is located firmly in the will and, hence, spiritualized.[23]

The beguine Marguerite Porete and, following her lead, the German Dominican Meister Eckhart go a step further. Porete argues that the soul can become so free and unencumbered that suffering is no longer necessary, even on the spiritual level. The soul becomes as it was before creation, one with the divine, and as such is the place in which the divine itself works. Porete's book, *The Mirror of Simple Souls*, is an extended dialogue between Love, Reason, and the Soul (with various other interlocutors making occasional appearances) through which the annihilation of the soul is effected. In the book, Love elucidates her goal—to free souls from their servitude to works, asceticism, and suffering:

> *Love.*—When Love dwells in them [and] the Virtues serve them without any contradiction and without the work of such souls. Oh, without doubt, Reason, . . . such souls who have become free, have known for many days what Dominion usually does. And to the one who would ask them what was the greatest torment that a creature could suffer, they would say that it would be to dwell in Love and to be in obedience to the Virtues. For it is necessary to give to the Virtues all that they ask, whatever the cost to Nature. For it is thus that the Virtues demand honor and goods, heart and body and life. It is to be expected that such souls leave all things, and still the Virtues say to this Soul who has given all to them, retaining nothing in order to comfort Nature, that the just one is saved by great pain. And thus this exhausted Soul who still serves the Virtues says that she would be assaulted by Fear, and torn in hell until the judgment day, and after that she would be saved.[24]

For medieval people, suffering was a seemingly inescapable condition of human life. By embracing that suffering—even intensifying it through ascetic practice—certain men and women shared in the redemptive suffering through which Christ would overcome the pain and sorrow of human existence. Porete describes the outcome of this desire as a life of servitude, hellish torment, and exhaustion. Even the brief respite from anguish brought about by God's visionary or ecstatic presence engenders further suffering—either through visions of Christ's torment or the subsequent, and inevitable, loss of spiritual delights. In

Porete's dialogue, Love offers an end to this anguish through the annihilation of the will, reason, and desire. At the same time, the boundless goodness of God safeguards active forms of love, for Porete goes on to argue that the soul who is completely free and unencumbered becomes the place in which Love itself works in the world.

Eckhart systematizes the beguinal insights, arguing for a twofold interaction between the soul and the divine: the birth of the Son in the soul, through which the soul shares in the divine self-birth of the Godhead as justice, and the breakthrough to the divine ground in which the soul's ground and God's ground are one. Eckhart, again following insights first adumbrated by the beguines, brings together the active and the contemplative lives, for insofar as the soul becomes wholly detached and one with the uncreated ground of the Godhead, it shares in the work of the Godhead that is the birth of the Son as justice in the world. In a startling reversal of traditional readings of Mary and Martha, understood as the contemplative and active lives, Eckhart insists that Martha has chosen the better part, for she is so fully united to Christ that her work in the world is Christ's work.[25]

The movement away from suffering is tied to the particular form of religious language crucial to Porete and Eckhart. Both Porete and Eckhart downplay the importance of visionary and auditory experiences of the divine presence, as well as the images that give rise to and represent these experiences, and instead emphasize a language of unsaying or apophasis. Porete and Eckhart, in fact, eschew the extraordinary experiences and visionary, prophetic language on which the authority of so many medieval women's religious texts rests. Moreover, they associate this language and experience with asceticism and suffering. Porete and Eckhart transform bodily and spiritual asceticism into annihilation, detachment, and apophasis.[26] The connections between detachment and apophasis become clear in Eckhart's Sermon 2, where he argues that the soul must become absolutely virgin, free and empty of all images and desires, if it is to become a wife, and hence fruitful in God's work. Detachment involves "letting go" of images (hence, "unsaying" the names of God) and of the will and desire. Through "letting go" of all creaturely things, the soul becomes one with the divine ground, and so shares in the self-birth of the Godhead as justice. Asceticism is fully internalized as apophasis and detachment, and the valorization of physical and spiritual suffering on which visionary and ascetic spirituality depend is subverted.

I want to avoid, however, reasserting a simple opposition between visionary, imagistic texts and apophatic ones, with all of the gender implications such distinctions have carried in the modern study of mysticism. Highly visionary texts can also make use of apophasis, as we see, for example, in the writings of Hadewijch.[27] That which is "unsaid" is the visionary image itself. The most striking example of this double movement is, characteristically, Christological. While receiving the Eucharist, Hadewijch sees Christ in human form:

> Then he gave himself to me in the shape of the Sacrament, in its outward form, as the custom is; and then he gave me to drink from the chalice, in form and taste, as the custom is. After that he came himself to me, took me entirely in his arms, and pressed me to him; and all my members felt his in full felicity, in accordance with the desire of my heart and my humanity. So I was outwardly satisfied and fully transported. Also then, for a short while, I had the strength to bear this; but soon, after a short time, I lost that manly beauty outwardly in the sight of his form. I saw him completely come to nought and so fade and all at once dissolve that I could no longer recognize or perceive him outside me, and I could no longer distinguish him within me. Then it was to me as if we were one without difference.[28]

Here we see the movement from meditation on the object—the Eucharist and perhaps also an image of Christ—to the apprehension of that object in living experience. Yet this apprehension marks simply one moment in the mystical movement, for the vision itself is overcome, negated in a meditation before the void in which all distinctions between the soul and divine are erased.

Rather than marking a disjunction between female- and male-authored mystical texts, then, the distinction between visionary or cataphatic language and apophatic language occurs within mystical texts. Men, within medieval Christianity, had authority to interpret scripture; women did not. Thus, in naming the divine, male-authored texts tend to use language drawn from scripture rather than from visionary experience; scriptural language becomes the language unsaid through apophasis. On the other hand, for many medieval women, who were denied authority to interpret scripture, their visions, auditions, and ecstatic experiences of the divine become the texts that both name God and are "unsaid" in the process of mystical writing. Moreover, the rejection of visionary language associated with suffering and asceticism occurs first and perhaps most dramatically in a female-authored text, Marguerite Porete's The Mirror of Simple Souls.

Late medieval visionary imagination centers on the passion of Christ, on images of a mortally wounded, suffering human body.[29] When Hadewijch textualizes and "unsays" the visionary, she transposes suffering from the physical to the spiritual and textual level. Porete and Eckhart go further, eschewing the language of visionary imagination in favor of dialogic allegory and biblical exegesis.[30] Yet despite these differences, for all three the text itself become the site of divine presence and mystical experience. Hadewijch, Porete, and Eckhart each (re)enact through their writing the experience of divine presence and absence and attempt to engender such experience in their readers. Porete and Eckhart replace asceticism and suffering with apophasis, an unsaying of God and the soul through which the two become one while still on earth. Arguably, Porete and Eckhart enact precisely the move for which Sartre criticizes Bataille, namely, the attempt to escape history and temporality (which they see as the source of the suffering they wish to overcome). Hadewijch, on the other hand, replaces the image of the suffering Godman with the suffering, because always endlessly desiring, soul. This move to the soul marks less a rejection of history than an insistence on encountering that which is (the soul suffering in God's absence) and, through that reality, the possibilities of what might be (the joy of divine presence). Like Bataille, Hadewijch does not deny suffering but displaces it from the body to the soul or psyche. As I will show through a reading of Bataille's Guilty, writing—the move from image to text—is crucial to this transposition.

In situating Bataille's writing practice, Sartre places him within an essayistic tradition beginning with Montaigne and Pascal and more recently exemplified by Nietzsche and Breton. Despite his evident desire to label Bataille a mystic, Sartre ignores those texts that are arguably most similar to Bataille's and to which he is most indebted. This oversight contributes to Sartre's inability to understand the paradoxes engendered by Bataille's communicative practice, for it is grounded in his reading of mystical texts. In the *Atheological Summa*, Bataille himself repeatedly suggests that the primary models for his writing and experience are Nietzsche and the Christian and non-Western mystical traditions.[31] *Inner Experience* opens with evocations of Nietzsche, and the final volume of the trilogy, *On Nietzsche*, is "devoted"—albeit elliptically—to his work. References to mystical writings occur throughout *Inner Experience* and *Guilty*, and significant portions of both texts, as I have argued, can be read as "guides" for inner experience analogous to the "itineraries" of Angela of Foligno and Teresa of Avila (d. 1582), or as spiritual daybooks like that of Mechthild of Magdeburg. These models are, I think, the key to understanding not only Bataille's meditative practice (as I argued in chapter 2), but also his writing strategies in the *Atheological Summa*. Despite their apparent divergence, Bataille insists that mystical and Nietzschean texts reflect and are constitutive of the same experience and writing practice. Although Bataille acknowledges the oddity of his coupling the mystics and Nietzsche, he also rigorously defends it, arguing for a mystical and ecstatic experience in Nietzsche's work.[32] Bataille's experience of the failures of mysticism and of Nietzsche speak to each other and lead to Bataille's necessary apostasy as his true discipleship.

Commentators follow Bataille in resisting his identification with the mystics, whereas for Bataille and his readers Nietzsche is a less troubling model. In fact, however, what Bataille says of his debt to Nietzsche applies as well to his debt to the mystics, or at least what he says of Nietzsche can help us understand his relationship to mystical texts. The claim is made repeatedly—by Bataille and his interpreters—that Bataille does not comment on Nietzsche as a disciple or student might on the texts of a master; rather, Bataille attempts to live what Nietzsche himself lived, to experience that which gave rise to Nietzsche's writings. Nietzsche's texts embody a writing that is itself an experience.[33]

In *Beyond Good and Evil* and *Ecce Homo*, Nietzsche enjoins those who would understand him to read slowly, like philologists. Bataille attempts, in the preface to *On Nietzsche*, to specify how he reads Nietzsche and, by implication, how the reader should approach Bataille's own texts:

> *You shouldn't doubt it any longer for an instant:* you haven't understood a word of Nietzsche's work without living that dazzling dissolution into totality. Beyond that, this philosophy is just a maze of contradictions. Or worse, the pretext for lies of omission (if, as with the Fascists, certain passages are isolated for ends disavowed by the rest of the work). (OC VI 22; ON xxxi–xxxii)

Mystical works often open with similar instructions for reading. Mechthild of Magdeburg begins *The Flowing Light of the Godhead* with the claim that it must be read seven times if it is to be comprehended, and Marguerite Porete warns that those who approach her *Mirror of Simple Souls* armed with reason will fail to achieve the liberation that the book describes and enacts. In showing us how he reads Nietzsche (and thus how we should read him), Bataille echoes not only Nietzsche but mystical texts. Moreover, with his reference to the necessity of living what one reads in Nietzsche, I think Bataille gives us a picture of how he reads the mystics, again suggesting the interplay between the textual practices of these seemingly divergent figures.

The interplay between Nietzsche, the mystics, and Bataille is evidenced further in Bataille's "antigeneric" writing, which mixes genres and styles within and between texts.[34] His writing changes through the course of a career in which experience and writing are in a constant state of flux or chaos (to echo Bataille's self-description in On Nietzsche). Within what purport to be three unified books, the Atheological Summa encapsulates the diversity of genres and styles that runs throughout Bataille's corpus. These books contain ample quotations from Nietzsche's texts and from those of the mystics—undigested hunks and fragments of these allusive writings[35]—together with philosophical reflections, confessional meditations, diary fragments, letters, and, at the end of On Nietzsche, a set of six brief historical and theoretical appendixes. Anything broaching traditional textual commentary is reserved for the margins of these nonbooks. Like many mystics—particularly women who were denied access to the traditional genres of sermon, biblical commentary, and philosophical or theological treatise, and who, like Nietzsche, eschew and subvert traditional genre distinctions—Bataille comments and critiques through practice rather than exposition.

The parallel between Bataille's writing and that of mystics such as Mechthild of Magdeburg, Marguerite Porete, and Angela of Foligno is perhaps most marked in Guilty. Guilty is drawn from the journals or notebooks that Bataille kept from the opening of World War II (September 5, 1939) through October 1943. (To this text, first published in 1943, Bataille later added an introduction [1961] and a text from 1947, "Alleluia.") Although there are generic similarities between Mechthild's Flowing Light of the Godhead and Angela's Book, Guilty most closely resembles the former. There is no evidence that Bataille knew Mechthild's work—I doubt that he did, in fact—but a comparison between Bataille and Mechthild is enlightening because Mechthild displays in more marked form important, although obscured, features of Angela's book that Bataille (consciously or unconsciously) mimes. In other words, what fascinated Bataille about Angela are precisely those features of her text closest to Mechthild's work (and arguably, these features are less apparent in Angela's book because they were smoothed over by the mediating scribe).[36]

Both Mechthild and Angela wrote what are probably best called "confessions" in the tradition of Augustine.[37] However, radical differences between the nature of their experience and that of Augustine led them to a different set of writing and rhetorical practices. Confronted with these practices, many modern scholars have concluded that the women's texts are not "confessions." Instead, scholars have, until recently, insisted on reading the writings of Mechthild and Angela as diaries or journals, that is, as immediate outpourings of the woman author's experience.[38] This insistence is odd given the variety of formal genres that appear in a text like Mechthild's, which contains poems, dialogues, visions, prayers, and prose exposition. Moreover, *The Flowing Light of the Godhead* is not a journal or a diary in the common sense because it is written with the intention of influencing an audience. Indeed, it is precisely this intention, this projected relationship between writer and reader, that places Mechthild's text within the tradition of the *Confessions*, even as Mechthild's use of diverse genres distances her work from Augustine's relatively homogeneous text.

Like Mechthild's book, then, Bataille's wartime writings mix a variety of genres and are fragmentary in form ("Disorder is the condition of this book; it is unlimited in every sense" [OC V 264; G 28]).[39] Most importantly, however, like *The Flowing Light*, *Guilty* finds its unity in its confessional aim. Mechthild opens with the claim that the soul's experiences recounted within the book were given through her to all of Christendom. Bataille begins with similar clarity—soon to be effaced—about the pedagogical purpose of his writing: "As simply as I can, I will speak of the paths by which I found ecstasy, in the desire that others will find it in the same way" (OC V 264; G 28). This aim, however, is bound to sacrifice itself, for the pathless ecstasy he seeks cannot be given an itinerary. One side of the paradox enacted by Bataille's text can be located here, for although he envisions a reader on whom he wishes to act, the very desire to act is called into question by inner experience. Bataille is insistent on this point: "I hate sentences. . . . What I have affirmed, the convictions that I have shared, all of this is laughable and dead; I am only silence, the universe is silence" (OC V 277; G 40).

Later he makes a more characteristic claim about the reader, and with it about his text:

> What I write differs from a diary/journal in this: I imagine a man, neither too young nor too old, neither too subtle nor too sensible/practical, pissing and shitting, simply (cheerfully). I imagine him (having read me) reflecting on eroticism and the putting into question of nature. He would see then what care I have taken to lead him to the decision. There's no use giving an analysis: he evokes the moment of arousal—naive, but ambiguous, unconfessable. He is putting nature into question. (OC V 355; G 109)[40]

Only a writing that puts itself, the writer, and the reader into question can lead to inner experience. This point becomes clearer when we look to the other major interlocutor within the confessional tradition (and the other noninterlocutor of Bataille's communications).

Augustine's *Confessions* and Mechthild of Magdeburg's *Flowing Light* are addressed not only to the human reader on whom the texts hope to work a transformation, but also to God before whom the human authors stand "confessing" their sinful lives and the glory of God reflected in them. The role God plays in Augustine's and Mechthild's confessions seems to mark the point of greatest divergence between their work and Bataille's, and on one level it clearly does, particularly in the case of Augustine, who throughout the *Confessions* speaks as a human being to a transcendent God. Mechthild's use of voice, however, is more complex. When in the first person, the text speaks more often *as* God than to God. Furthermore, when Mechthild does portray the soul speaking to God (and God to the soul), she does so in the third person and in allegorical or dramatic form, thereby achieving a distancing effect and undercutting the text's autobiographical character. These rhetorical strategies are a function of Mechthild's lack of traditional authority as a woman within medieval Christianity. She takes her subordination to its limit, negating herself so fully that the self is lost and becomes the place in and through which God speaks. Paradoxically, Mechthild's work attains divine authority in her very act of self-denial. There are moments in the text, moreover, where Mechthild pushes this self-negation to the point of denying personal salvation. Other women, like Angela of Foligno and Marguerite Porete, will go even further, implicitly negating the divine being itself.

Bataille's relationship to a divine or sacred other within *Guilty* is equally complex. Nietzsche argues in *On the Genealogy of Morals* that there is no simple atheism, or that simple atheism is really a kind of idealism in that the atheist still believes in truth. Bataille's relationship to God and to the sacred must be located within this paradox, which Bataille himself describes in his 1961 introduction to *Guilty*:

> It seemed to me that human thought had two terms: God and the sentiment of the absence of God. But God being the confusion of the sacred (the religious aspect) and reason (the instrumental aspect), he has a place only in a world where the confusion of the instrumental and the sacred becomes the basis for reassurance. God terrifies if he is no longer the same thing as reason (Pascal, Kierkegaard). But if he is no longer the same thing as reason, I am before the absence of God. (OC V 240; G 6)

Bataille attempts to extricate himself from Nietzsche's paradox by freeing the sacred from God. The sacred is nothing, it is the absence of God, insofar as God is understood as that which gives reason, order, coherence, and meaning to human existence. The sacred is that which lies beyond meaning, instrumentality, and reason, and hence beyond God. It lies beyond salvation. When Mechthild, Angela, Porete, and Eckhart claim that the soul no longer cares for heaven or for hell, they seek this same beyond. According to Bataille, however, when Christian mystics move beyond God, they do so without knowing it. Yet what does it mean to know that you are in the realm of the unknowable? Here the crucial distinction Bataille tries to make between himself and the mystics seems to collapse.

Elsewhere, Bataille calls the absence of God "the impossible," thereby indicating clearly the extent to which Nietzsche's paradox structures Guilty. What does it mean to write (to) the impossible, especially when, for Bataille, human beings are themselves this impossible paradox, when, that is, human beings and "the impossible" and so the human and divine are one and the same? Bataille first undermines the distinction between himself and his human and divine addressees through the correlation of the writing self and chance. In a passage cited already in chapter 2, but that we are now in a better position to understand, Bataille returns to the question of the "object" of desire and of ecstasy:

THE OBJECT OF ECSTASY IS THE ABSENCE OF RESPONSE FROM OUT-
SIDE. THE INEXPLICABLE PRESENCE OF MAN IS THE RESPONSE THAT
THE WILL GIVES ITSELF, SUSPENDED OVER THE VOID OF AN UNIN-
TELLIGIBLE NIGHT; THAT NIGHT, FROM ONE END TO THE OTHER,
HAS THE IMPUDENCE OF A HOOK. (OC V 320; G 78)

We have seen Bataille's fascination with this hook, which he associates with chance. The philosophical reference—one that runs throughout Bataille's writings—is to the question articulated by Nietzsche at the end of On the Genealogy of Morals: "Why man at all?" Guilty's meditations on chance particularize this question. As Surya notes, Bataille not only questions the meaning of his own existence in the context of human existence generally (why live in the face of death) but also continually brings himself face to face with the sheer contingency of his own existence as the individual he himself is.[41]

Bataille continually plays on the relationship between the absence of God and the contingency of the self. He insists that religion is that place in which everything is put into question. God, the confusion of the sacred and reason, represents an attempt to answer the question of existence and to elude the hook.

But, Bataille claims: "I don't believe in God: from an inability to believe in myself" (OC V 282; G 45). Or conversely: "God is dead: he is so to the point that I can't make his death understood without killing myself" (OC V 327; G 85). For Bataille, the death of God brings the self face to face with the inevitability of its own death. However, the self cannot understand or experience the death of God without apprehending its own death, which, of course, it cannot do. Because one cannot experience one's own death, then, Bataille suggests that God will never be entirely dead. Yet the self must be put into question in order to move toward an experience of the absence of God. Moreover, Bataille claims that the self has always already put itself into question insofar as it attempts to communicate. Whereas "the God of theology and reason never puts himself into play," Bataille insists that "without end, the unbearable me, that we are, plays itself; without end, 'communication' puts it into play" (OC V 328; G 85). We return, then, to the imaginary, "impossible" other to whom Bataille writes. The attempt to communicate to another the way to ecstasy puts the self into play, destabilizes the sacred, and leads to the lacerations of ecstasy.

The question now becomes why communication puts the self into play or into question and engenders the experience of the absence or death of the self and the absence or death of God. Here Bataille evokes the paradoxes of writing elaborated further by Maurice Blanchot and Jacques Derrida.[42] "History," Bataille writes, "is unfinished. When this book will be read, the smallest schoolchild will know how the war turned out. At this moment when I write, nothing can give me the knowledge of that schoolchild" (OC V 261–62; G 26). Here, like Nietzsche, Bataille claims to love his ignorance of the future— and, even more, its fundamental unknowability. By thus invoking the absent, yet to be born, and hence fundamentally mortal other, Bataille evokes his own death. Writing is an attempt to inscribe presence (transparence) that is always predicated on absence: the absence of the other to whom one writes and the absence of the self to that addressee. This interplay of presence and absence within writing makes it, like the photograph, fetishistic in structure; writing is founded on the gap between the writing self and his or her projected audience. The one who writes and the other whom she addresses both are and are not present to and in writing. Yet writing like Bataille's, which foregrounds the fetishistic nature of writing, holds before our eyes the absence at the root of fetishism, rather than claiming an ultimate presence through a purported indexical relationship to the real.

In the penultimate section of the main body of Guilty, "La Volonté" ("Will/ Willpower"), Bataille ties the problem of death to the paradox engendered by human beings' desire to write so as to transform the other, even as this transformation itself denies all intentionality. Here, as in "The King of the Wood," *Guilty's* final section before a series of appendixes, Bataille condenses the paradoxes that have been enacted throughout the text. After evoking the radical nothingness and unthinkableness of his own death, Bataille argues that "to write is to go elsewhere. The bird who sings and the man who writes deliver themselves" (OC V 359; G 113). The man who writes delivers himself to death in the going elsewhere and yet also attempts to escape death through the act of writing, the inscription of an always already absent presence. The one who will receive this writing is no longer a man who can be imagined (pissing and shitting):

> I do not write for this world (surviving—intentionally—that world from which war has emerged), I write for a different world, a world without respect. I don't desire to impose myself on it, I imagine myself being silent there, as if absent. The necessity of efface- ment to the point of transparency. I do not oppose real strengths or necessary connections: idealism alone (hypocrisy, lies) has the virtue to condemn the real world—to ignore its physical truth. (OC V 360; G 113)

Bataille is caught here in his own paradox: how to reject idealism, which refuses the real world and its physical truth, while speaking to a world different from that one full of idealism, lies, and hypocrisy in which world war is inevitable (according to Bataille's political analysis throughout the 1930s). Bataille's strat- egy, like that of the mystics, is not to avoid the paradox, nor to attempt to resolve it, but to embrace it and force the reader to think it in all its contradiction. Only in this way, the text suggests, can the physical world be that other world to which Bataille speaks silence.

Furthermore, if to write is to go elsewhere and to encounter death (to speak *silence*), it is also an attempt to stay alive (to *speak*). "The King of the Wood" refers to Dianus (the priest of Diana), under whose name Bataille first signed fragments of *Guilty*. According to legend, Orestes is the first Dianus, a criminal who gains power over the woods (of *nemo*—nothing) through a second crime, the murder of his predecessor; he then rules awaiting his own murder. This is the place from which Bataille writes:

> I am inhabited by a mania to speak, and a mania for exactitude.
> I imagine myself to be precise, capable, ambitious. I should have

been silent and I spoke. I laugh at the fear of death: it keeps me awake! Battling against it (against fear and death).

I write, I do not want to die.
For me, the words "I will be dead" aren't breathable. My absence is the wind from outside. It is comical: pain is comical. I am, for my protection, in my room. But the tomb? already so near, the thought of it envelopes me from head to toe.

Immense contradiction of my attitude!
Has anyone ever had, so gaily, this simplicity of death?
But ink changes absence into intention. (OC V 365; G 118)

When Bataille says that he does not write for this world but for a different one in which he imagines being silent, he stresses the absence that always already haunts writing; here he emphasizes the other side of the paradox encompassed in writing. To write a book, Bataille repeatedly reminds us in *Guilty*, is to participate in instrumentality; to use language in the attempt to accomplish an end; "to change absence into intention."

The paradox of *Guilty* is how to write (a) desire (without object) aimlessly or how to write without end and without a why:

I couldn't find what I am looking for in a book, still less put it in a book. I fear courting poetry. Poetry is a drawn arrow. If I have aimed well, what counts—what I want—is neither the arrow nor the target (but), but the moment when the arrow is lost, dissolves into the air of the night; until the memory of the arrow is lost. (OC V 340; G 95)

The significance of this paradox becomes clear when we juxtapose Bataille's critique of the Christian mystics with his insistence on Nietzsche's failure. Whereas the mystics err insofar as they refuse to err—to do without an end for their speech and experience—Nietzsche's fault lies in his abrogation of communication. If the great prophet of aimlessness seeks an ideal with which to overcome the ascetic, as some argue (and as is constantly suggested and then subverted in *Zarathustra*), then he capitulates to the ascetic ideal. For Bataille, however, greater danger lies in Nietzsche's suggestion that any attempt at communication is in service to the ascetic ideal. Bataille insists on his communion with Nietzsche in the writing of *On Nietzsche*, thereby pointing to other modes of communication possible through writing and reading.[43] Only through this writing practice is the sacred released from the ideal and the God to which it is still in part held captive within Nietzsche's work. Taken as an answer to the question of the meaning of being, Nietzsche's writing capitulates to the ideal. Taken as a process of writing (and reading) and as a putting into question of the self (both that of the writer and the reader), it communicates.[44]

WRITING TRAUMA, WRITING DESIRE

In an important essay on Bataille, Jean-Luc Nancy argues that Bataille does not completely reject the language of asceticism. Bataille's writing, Nancy argues, is "a sacrifice of writing, by writing, which redeems writing."[45] Nancy, like Bataille, tends toward the hyperbolic; given Bataille's persistent rejection of salvific narratives, the language of redemption is particularly problematic. Yet Nancy's description of Bataille's writing is evocative, especially when Bataille is placed in the context of his mystical models. I think Nancy is right to suggest that Bataille does not completely reject the language of asceticism; rather he moves asceticism into writing through apophasis, an unsaying of both the divine and the self. The contradictions of Bataille's texts work as apophatic negations of substantive notions of God and the self, eliciting inner experience in the reader who thinks these contradictions. As the site of endless deferral and difference, writing contains asceticism without capitulating to idealistic totalization and the effacement of history. Yet as a present trace through which communication occurs, writing engenders community without necessitating the fetishization of the other.

Nancy coins a term to describe Bataille's writing practice—*exscription*—through which he attempts to describe the mechanisms by which Bataille's texts point outside of themselves to an experience that is constituted in the very act of writing. The parallels with Eric Blondel's work on Nietzsche and with contemporary studies of the linguistic strategies of apophatic mysticism are striking.[46] As does Nancy's work, these analyses demonstrate how insistence on the materiality of the text through which the practice of writing is inscribed leads not to a stultifying idealism, as some people oddly insist, but to a recognition of the interpenetration of world and writing in the production of a textual experience of desire without limit, without end, and without aim. By exacerbating the paradoxes of writing a desire without object and without aim, Bataille creates a performative text in which inner experience is (for him and perhaps for the reader who thinks the contradictions of his text) "realized." Through writing, Bataille does not attempt to escape history and the constant interplay of presence and absence, ecstasy and anguish on which both writing and history are grounded; rather he embraces history as that which is and as the unknown future.[47]

To put this point in terms of my earlier discussion of trauma, Bataille moves traumatic memory and its compulsive repetitions into writing. Unlike contemporary therapies, however, Bataille does not bring trauma and catastrophe into language in order to give them meaning, shape, or coherence, but in order to traumatize writing itself—and through this traumatized writing to communicate the writer's self-shattering apprehension of catastrophe to the reader. Bataille displaces trauma from the body to language; this displacement does not, Bataille insists, redeem that experience, but it does offer limited transcendence and prevention of further bodily trauma.[48] Bataille's move from visionary imagination to writing enables him to communicate the ecstatic anguish of inner experience without the dangers of sadistic voyeurism or masochistic literalization of the suffering body (to which, one might argue, Angela succumbs). Language becomes the fetish, permanently undecidable and unstable, through which the trauma of loss is both enacted and provisionally denied—the questions of whose trauma and of how to distinguish between victims of physical and psychological violence and onlookers, however, remain.

Language is a realm of relative transcendence of the body's limitations and hence of the body's pain; but language is still material, and hence tied to the body and its desires. As Derrida shows, language partakes in both materiality and ideality. In Barthes's terms, writing is always, in a sense, fictional, and hence enables a move away from "reality" without denying the "real." Bataille's textually generated, always moving, desirous, anguished, and annihilated subjectivity replaces the lacerated body as the site of communication, suffering, desire, and identification. The danger then becomes that the physical suffering to which Bataille's experience responds may be lost in the fictive movements of language. In addition, writing, like all fetishism, participates in a generalizing movement that both acknowledges and elides ("I know, but even so") the specificities of race, class, gender, and other historically salient differences that, in part, engender acts of torture like those on which Bataille meditates. Bataille both participates in this fetishization—arguing that human mortality must be acknowledged in its absolute specificity and absolute generality before the challenges of historically specific forms of oppression can be met—and recognizes the potential and danger of writing as a site of fetishization. Bataille's reinscription within Guilty of his meditative practice suggests that the dangers of voyeurism and its reification of the fetish may be necessary in order to fix the real as the site of ethical challenge.[49]

Here desire and the catastrophic, masochism and trauma, come together. Freud's theories of childhood fantasy, sexuality, and masochism can help to uncover the complexities of traumatization when it is perpetrated by someone the victim loves. Similarly, Bataille's writing is a record of what it means both to love and to be traumatized by history, to desire without reason and without limits that which is, while fully recognizing its horror. Like his contemporary Simone Weil, Bataille insists that only through this encounter with the real can historical change occur. Yet unlike Weil, Bataille refuses to believe in a loving, torturer God through whose sacrifice history will be redeemed.[50] Only ecstatic attention to the real and its catastrophes can serve as the basis for contestation and change—and that change will always be incomplete, unfinished, and without limit.

2

FROM WOUNDEDNESS TO CASTRATION;

OR, ON THE GENDER OF MYSTICISM

Sartre struggles, in 1943, to assert his difference from Bataille. Most importantly, Sartre insists that one must recognize and accept the limitations of historical existence and yet continue to strive toward transcendent subjectivity through historical projects. Bataille's mistake, according to Sartre, is that he desires to "be all"; refusing to abjure this desire for totality, Sartre claims, Bataille can offer only a simulacrum of success through claims to escape history in instantaneous experience. I have argued in the previous chapters that this critique rests on a misapprehension—one that serves to obscure another source of Sartre's disagreement with Bataille; for what Bataille effects through inner experience is not the eradication of history but an encounter with "what is there" in all of its inescapable beauty and fatality. Bataille encounters precisely the givenness of existence that Sartre wishes to escape through project.

My reading of the relationship between Bataille and Sartre relies on two different conceptions of mysticism and its relationship to history. Sartre understands mysticism as a desire for and experience of wholeness and unity in which all distinctions between the self and the divine other—even if that other is nothingness, as in Bataille—are effaced. To become all, one must escape the constraints of time and space, and hence of history itself. The mystic, according to Sartre, seeks an eternal now in which reality is unified and becomes forever present. Bataille, on the other hand, through his reading of Angela of Foligno's meditations on Christ and the "darkness" within Christ's eyes, suggests that mysticism can be an unassuageable desire for "what is there" in its historical particularity. Inner experience occurs in the present not through either an effacement of past and future or their apotheosis in an "eternal now," but through the refusal of those projects through which one attempts to contain the endless deferrals of history.[1] Only in this way, Bataille suggests, can one encounter history and the historical other. The present (like the past and the future) is always in excess of the projects through which human beings attempt to constrain it.

Bataille articulates this alternative conception of mysticism in part through his analysis of the traditions of Christian mysticism, yet he remains ambivalent toward those traditions, implicitly arguing for their doubleness. Angela both desires to be all through redemptive identification with Christ's suffering and, in her apprehension of that suffering, negates all salvific projects. The ambivalence of her text—and of Christian mystical traditions themselves—gives rise to Bataille's simultaneous refusal and appropriation of the term "mysticism." Although Bataille openly acknowledges his debt to Angela, he also implies that he surpasses her. By distancing himself from Angela and at the same time claiming to occupy her position with regard to "that which is," Bataille can be read as appropriating her mystical position, thereby raising questions about the gender politics embedded within his account of inner experience.

Bataille himself does not explicitly gender mysticism in the *Atheological Summa*, yet a number of factors suggest an implicit and complex gender dynamic operating within these texts. Most obviously, Bataille focuses on the work of a woman mystic. He reads and takes with utmost seriousness a woman's text; yet in that he claims to surpass her experience, this attention might be seen as another instance of the male appropriation of women's experience.[2] Even more tellingly, Bataille suggests that inner experience's superiority to Christian mysticism is a mark of its virility, thereby explicitly gendering his relationship to more traditional forms of Christian mysticism.

Susan Suleiman shows the centrality of the language of virility to Bataille's work in the 1930s.[3] Although the metaphor drops out almost completely in the *Atheological Summa*, it makes at least one crucial appearance. In a discussion of poetry, which Bataille both allies with and wishes to distance from inner experience, he argues that

> to go to the end of man, it is necessary, to a certain point, no longer
> to submit to fate but to force it. The contrary attitude, poetic non-
> chalance, passivity, the disgust for a virile reaction that decides: this
> is literary decadence (beautiful pessimism). Rimbaud's damnation:

he had to turn his back on the possible that he attained, in order to rediscover a force of decision intact within himself. Access to the extreme has, for its condition, the hatred, not of poetry, but of poetic femininity (absence of decision, the poet is woman, invention, words violate him). I oppose to poetry the experience of the possible. It has to do less with contemplation than with laceration. Yet this is the "mystical experience" of which I speak (Rimbaud practiced it, but without the tenacity that he later put into attempting to win his fortune. To his experience, he gave a poetic end; in general, he did not know that simplicity which affirms—desires without a future, in some of the letters—he chose feminine evasiveness, aesthetics, uncertain and involuntary expressions.) (OC V 53; IE 40)

Rimbaud fascinates Bataille precisely because he gives up poetry for action.[4] Yet Bataille ultimately wishes to negate the apparent gap between feminine, passive poetry and the virility of decision and action, a rift that he thinks is upheld by surrealism's emphasis on automatism, which demands that writing become completely passive.[5] Rimbaud's mistake, Bataille argues, is to believe that the only way to escape passivity is through the rejection of poetry itself. Instead, Bataille claims that through poetry, understood in a new way, a self-lacerating encounter with "what is there" becomes possible. Bataille's emphasis on encounter and laceration might seem to render poetry passive once again. However, the difference between Bataille's experience of "inner sundering" and poetic femininity, as Suleiman notes astutely, "is that the hero of inner experience *actively engages himself* in 'la déchirure.' He is dominant and virile (Bataille will later say, 'sovereign') because he actively chooses his sundering."[6] In thus making a project out of submission, Bataille seems significantly closer to Sartre than either would like to have admitted.

Here mysticism is on the side of virility. Bataille will insist that Angela of Foligno attains "sovereignty" and actively engages in her own self-laceration through meditation on the cross. We might speculate, moreover, that Bataille's fascination with Angela is connected to his move away from the explicitly gendered language of virility (itself already potentially subverted—albeit inadequately, as I will argue—by the language of laceration and headlessness so crucial to his writings of the 1930s).[7] If we were to transpose Bataille's gendered account of poetry onto his understanding of mysticism, "feminine evasiveness" would be associated with the desire for salvation and for a passive relationship to a suffering savior through whom humanity is made whole. In a move that on first sight seems counterintuitive, this reading would render the desire to be everything feminine and passive, whereas virility and decisiveness would be associated with laceration and an anguished recognition of the limitations of being.[8] Inner experience occurs not in the former but in the latter experience.

Bataille does not make these genderings explicit in his account of inner experience. Instead, he finds in Angela and other Christian mystics both a decisive embrace of "what is there" and an evasion of the real through appeals to salvation. Yet again, if we read Bataille as claiming a more "authentic" experience than that of Angela, we might easily criticize his usurpation of a feminine position in the name of a certain understanding of virility—virility as, paradoxically, an embrace of castration. Even when Bataille tries to undermine phallic masculinity, he does so within its terms. The wounds of the torture victim on which Bataille meditates are marks not simply of mortality and bodily limitation but also of castration. The man is not only dismembered (a standard displacement of castration from the penis to the arms and legs), but a large, oblong wound covers his side, exposing the ribs. The wound is reminiscent of Christ's, and like that injury the opening on the tortured man's side looks distinctly vaginal, suggesting a conflation of the wound with the female sex.[9] When Bataille writes that he hopes the reader will fall into his text as "into a hole," he associates his own writing practice with that side wound and with the "castrated" female body.

For Bataille, the female sex is a wound, a terrifying and beautiful mark of castration and of the emergence of life out of laceration. The connection between the photographic images of a torture victim and the female sex are made even more explicit if we follow Bataille's advice and read Inner Experience alongside his short fiction Madame Edwarda: "I wrote this little book in September and October of 1941, just before 'The Torment/Torture,' which forms the second part of Inner Experience. The two texts, to my mind, are closely allied and one cannot understand the one without the other" (OC III 491).[10] Central to this brief narrative is a scene in which a prostitute, Madame Edwarda, exposes her genitals to the unnamed narrator:

—You want to see my rags? she said.
My two hands gripping the table, I turned toward her. Seated, she lifted her leg up high: to open her slit better, she pulled the skin apart with her two hands. Thus the "rags" of Edwarda looked at

me, hairy and pink, full of life like a repugnant spider. I stammered softly:

—Why are you doing that?

—You see, she said, I am GOD . . .

—I am mad . . .

—But no, you have to look: look!

Her harsh voice softened, she became almost childlike, saying for me, with lassitude, with the infinite smile of abandon: "Oh, how I come [joui]!" (OC III 20–21)[11]

Madame Edwarda's genitals are the site of woundedness and castration, inscribing her body fully within a phallic logic in which the female sex is experienced and represented only as an absence. Understood as "the all," God does not exist. But in the recognition and active embrace of that absence, another God emerges. Madame Edwarda's genitals are the present absence, the laceration or wound in which men apprehend human finitude, contingency, and lack. Like Angela of Foligno pressing her lips to the wound on Christ's side, *Madame Edwarda*'s unnamed narrator kisses Edwarda's genitals: "Finally, I knelt, I trembled, and put my lips on the living wound" (OC III 20).[12] This homage leads not, Bataille insists, to nihilism but to a celebration of life and the sacred.[13]

Yet this crucial scene in Madame Edwarda looks like a classic moment of fetishization—a man confronts the "fact" of woman's castration only to disavow any possible threat to his own penis. Freud argues that when the boy child sees a woman's or girl's body, he immediately understands that she does not have a penis and assumes that she has been castrated. This induces his own fear of castration; what could happen to her could also happen to him. Fetishization is one response to this apparent threat; the boy or man objectifies the woman's body (or, more commonly, parts of that body and/or clothing and other adornments associated with it), which then becomes a substitute phallus with which he can replace his own penis if it is lost or threatened. Seen from this perspective, and in light of Bataille's later writing on eroticism, the prostitute is the ultimate fetish because, as "infinitely available," she is a "dead object" (OC VIII 124).[14] In Bataille's postwar writings, the prostitute is the "erotic object" through which men attain the sacred. In these texts, the objectification of the corpselike other is explicit, giving rise to "a fiction of death" through which both mortality and the sacred can be apprehended by men.[15] Read in light of Bataille's *Theory of Religion*, the prostitute is the sacrificial object through whose death (through abjection and objectification) the sacred is made present.

Bataille claims in the *Atheological Summa* to refuse the fetishization of the female sex and its concomitant shoring up of the fantasy of male phallicism. He calls on male subjects to take that lack on as their own. Yet if women continue to represent lack for men—and if that lack leads to an ecstatic experience of the sacred—the distance between the male subject and the other who signifies lack both depends on and perpetuates the logic of fetishization. (This problem may in part explain Bataille's move to a male figure in the *Atheological Summa*. But the distance and its potential for fetishization remain, as I have argued, in the fact that the man represented is Chinese.) Put another way, the more Bataille focuses attention on the sacrality that emerges through meditation on lack and woundedness, the more the death or the deathlike state of the other, no matter how fictional, seems necessitated by the onlooker's desire to attain the sacred.[16] In the postwar writings in which this move occurs most starkly, moreover, that other is usually feminine. During the war, Bataille tends to emphasize the encounter as one with a suffering other, justifying ethical readings of his text.[17] After the war, however, he increasingly focuses on the sacred that emerges through that encounter, and so objectifies and fetishizes precisely that wounded other encountered in the experience of communication.

As Irigaray will argue with regard to Lacan, to the extent that Bataille continues to read the human condition in terms of castration and lack, the phallic economy of Western culture, no matter how severely undermined, remains in place. The penis/phallus—whether in its presence or absence—will continue to determine subjectivity, and women (and/or the prostitute) will become emblematic figures of contingency, mortality, and death (and perhaps also, as in Bataille, of a vaguely repugnant life). Before we can fully appreciate the force of Irigaray's critique, however, we need to turn to Beauvoir and Lacan who both, albeit in different ways, bring together explicitly the questions of mysticism, history, and sexual difference.

Beauvoir recognizes that mysticism has been a site of female agency within the Christian tradition, and she attempts to explain why this has been the case. She claims that mysticism is an inadequate justification for women's existence and the site of an illusory desire "to be everything" through the agency of another (a phantom other in this case—God). Yet at the same time, Beauvoir catches glimpses within the Christian mystical tradition of modes of intersubjectivity freed from the constrictions of gender. For Beauvoir, mysticism is primarily about the human desire to be everything, a desire shared by both men and women. Lacan will argue, on the contrary, that the desire to be everything—and the illusion that one *is* everything—are marks of masculine subjectivity.

Femininity for Lacan is on the side of the "not all"; to speak from that side is to accept one's position as lacking, split, or—in Bataille's terms—lacerated. For Lacan, this position is the site of mysticism, and it is by definition feminine. But as we will see, these gender categories are only loosely tied to bodily differences; to say that the site of mysticism is feminine does not mean that men cannot go there.

"MYSTICISM IS TEMPTING": SIMONE DE BEAUVOIR ON MYSTICISM, METAPHYSICS, AND SEXUAL DIFFERENCE

....

It is probable that free from both the anguish of passion and biological anguish—since nature always takes her revenge and compen-
sates for one change by another and since everything in life balances
out mysteriously—women will know another form of anguish, the one
you feel so strongly, Sir, and which was your exclusive luxury: metaphysical anguish. It is then and only then that genius can flourish.

FRANÇOISE PARTURIER, *Lettre ouverte aux hommes*

"SHE WANTED TO BE EVERYTHING"

In the third volume of her memoirs, *Force of Circumstance*, Beauvoir acknowledges
an apparent convergence between her early writing and Bataille's: "'How can
one consent not to be everything [tout]?' Georges Bataille asks in *Inner Experience*.
This phrase had struck me because in *She Came to Stay* that was Françoise's de-
vouring hope: she wanted to be everything [tout]."[1] Beauvoir goes on to read
not only her first published novel, *She Came to Stay*, but also the subsequent two in
light of this desire "to be all." As in her deployment of Bataille's understanding
of the festival to explain their wartime fetes, Beauvoir cites Bataille and at the
same time subtly misreads him; for Bataille both names a desire "to be all" and
asks what happens when one realizes one is not and cannot be everything. *Inner
Experience* is, according to Bataille, the result of this abdication of the attempt
to be everything in the face of "what is there." Communication becomes possible only through inner experience, which demands that one live "in death's
breath," recognizing one's own radical contingency without succumbing to it.

120

On the other hand, Françoise, the central character in *She Came to Stay*, refuses to accept the impossibility of her desire to be everything. Françoise is guilty of what Edward and Kate Fullbrook call the "bad faith of transcendence";[2] she denies her own immanence and bodiliness, wanting to be only a transcendent and free consciousness. This characterization of Françoise depends on a philosophical distinction, crucial to *She Came to Stay*, between conscious being (being-for-itself) and nonconscious being (being-in-itself).[3] Humans are both conscious and become the object of consciousness for others. To be an object of consciousness for another is to be reduced to being-in-itself; hence transcendent, conscious subjectivity is threatened by the advent of the other as a conscious subject. When Françoise recognizes Xavière as a conscious subject who encounters her as a being-in-itself, she experiences Xavière as a threat to her own transcendent subjectivity.[4] The meaning of this conflict becomes clear at the end of the novel. Françoise's thoughts before she murders Xavière reveal the metaphysical stakes of their rivalry:

> Annihilate a consciousness. How can I? thought Françoise. But how could it be that a consciousness existed that was not her own? In that case, it was she who did not exist. She repeated. She or I.[5]

Commenting on the novel, Beauvoir explains that it is an account of an illusion and its collapse—one cannot be pure transcendence (or pure immanence). Beauvoir struggles in her novels and philosophical essays to formulate a mode of reciprocity between conscious beings in which autonomy does not depend on the destruction of the other, one in which the desire to be is not threatened by the mere existence of the other who signals the reality of one's own death. But in *She Came to Stay*, this alternative vision is not articulated; the collapse of Françoise's illusions ends not in ecstatic anguish and communication, but in denial and murder. Françoise never renounces her desire to be all but instead annihilates the other who threatens her supremacy.

She Came to Stay does not deal explicitly with religious mysticism but with the love between men and women (itself understood as a kind of mystical union in which all divisions between two beings are overcome). Françoise desires to be fully united with her lover, Pierre—to be everything to and with him—and it is Xavière's intrusion into that relationship that ultimately leads to her death. For Beauvoir, as for Bataille, eroticism and mysticism are linked in that both express human beings' desire to be everything. Beauvoir insists, however, on the gendered ways in which erotic love and love for God are experienced. Whereas men can justify their existences through a multitude of endeavors, eroticism and mysticism are among the few modes of self-justification for women and therefore are more important features of women's lives than of men's. Yet these modes of self-justification, insofar as they mask a woman's love for her self in an ineffectual attempt to shore up her narcissism through relationships with illusory others, will always fail.

Beauvoir most directly discusses women's religiosity, particularly the mystical experiences of women within the Christian tradition, in two closely connected sections of The Second Sex, her landmark text on women and femininity. In both "Situation and Character" and "The Mystic" Beauvoir reads women's religiosity in terms of their identification as man's other.[6] Man's desire to be the one, to be all, gives rise to his positing woman as the other, the inessential, the not-all. For Beauvoir, this othering is an essential aspect of human consciousness, although its deployment in terms of sexual difference is not. In The Second Sex's long and complex analyses of women's experience, Beauvoir moves uneasily between claims about the essentially hierarchizing nature of this othering, in which the other is always reduced to object-like status, and its possible reconfiguration in less inherently oppressive ways through the mutual recognition of free conscious beings.

In The Second Sex, as in her novels, Beauvoir insists that women, like men, desire to be everything. Whereas men are empowered to project themselves onto the world through action, objectifying and effacing the other in an assertion of their own unity and wholeness, women's actions, and hence their desires, are constrained by their role as man's other. Within male-dominant society, there is no support for women's desire to be everything. The desire, however, does not disappear; rather it emerges through those activities open to women—most crucially, according to Beauvoir, love, whether of the self, man, or God.[7] The three justifications for women's existence, then, are narcissism, romantic love, and mysticism.[8] Understood as love for man or God, women's desire to be all becomes their desire to be everything for, to, or with another (so Françoise, in She Came to Stay, desires to be everything to and with Pierre, a desire thwarted by Xavière). Unable to act directly on the world, women can only seek transcendence and the justification of their existences through others (although as we will see, these others are ultimately effaced in women's love for themselves).

The political and the metaphysical here converge,[9] for Beauvoir insists both that women are systematically thwarted in their desire to be all, able only to approximate transcendent subjectivity through their immanence, and that this desire for absolute transcendence and totality is itself a mark of inauthenticity.

The particular political problems faced by women, then, are both complicated by and lead to potential resolutions of profound metaphysical problems concerning the relationship between body and consciousness and the existence of other conscious beings. Most crucially, Beauvoir asks how it might be possible to conceive of subjects as both autonomous and situated, and how such situated agents might interact with each other in a mode of reciprocity rather than of objectification and denial. Such reciprocity depends on the recognition of the bodiliness, finitude, and interdependence of human subjectivity. In ways that Beauvoir herself does not articulate fully, mysticism partakes in both the desire for inauthentic totalization and the encounter with others as conscious, free, yet situated subjects. For Beauvoir, the rare great mystic, like Teresa of Avila, encounters death and the possibility of annihilation, and so is able to grapple with the world and engage in real projects within it. Yet Beauvoir effaces the intersubjective and divine relationships that make Teresa's projects possible. As we will see, despite suggesting an account of human subjects as both situated and free, without God or the absolute death remains a problem for Beauvoir. The death of others and the projected death of the self both enable and threaten the meaningfulness of all projects in ways Beauvoir never fully resolves.[10] As I will show, Beauvoir's early fascination with mysticism is tied to her continued uneasiness in the face of limitation and mortality (both of which are made apparent to the subject in part through his or her relationships with others).

LOVE OF MAN, LOVE OF GOD

Much of the recent philosophical work on Beauvoir emphasizes the way in which she uses her own experience as the material for philosophy, reworking and constantly revising the story of her life as the experimental basis for her philosophical inquiries.[11] Beauvoir insists, moreover, on the primacy of metaphysical issues to her developing consciousness, writing the story of her childhood and adolescence as a narrative of childhood faith in the beliefs handed down by her parents, followed by growing metaphysical questions, doubts, and anguish, and the gradual resolution of some of those questions through study, thought, and action.[12] The philosophical work Beauvoir accomplishes in her autobiographies and fictions (often themselves closely tied to autobiographical sources) requires that we treat these texts as carefully constructed narratives through which Beauvoir explores the manifold meanings of her experience. Unlike Bataille, who sought always to shatter experience through writing, Beauvoir's narratives are a way of constructing the self as an autonomous and free, yet always also situated, agent.[13] Her depictions of various selves, then, are crucial self-presentations through which she describes and analyzes the pitfalls and possibilities of female subjectivity. As many commentators have noted, much of Beauvoir's own experience (as well as that of the women about whom she had read and to whom she spoke) serves as the basis for the phenomenological account of female subjectivity found in *The Second Sex*.

Beauvoir received a strict bourgeois Catholic upbringing and education; her father respected Catholicism as essential to French nationalism and the family but did not himself practice the faith, relegating the spiritual to the realm of women.[14] Beauvoir's mother, Françoise, on the other hand, was educated in a convent school.[15] Despite the family's financial difficulties after the First World War, Françoise de Beauvoir insisted that Simone and her sister Hélène attend a private institution for the education of Catholic girls (the Institut Adéline Désir) rather than a secular and publicly funded lycée (such institutions were made widely available by reforms instituted in 1880).[16] Run by lay women with loose ties to the Jesuit order, the Cours Désir provided moral and religious instruction, with some attention to academics (although apparently not of a very high quality). Beauvoir recalls the centrality of the philosophy of Thomas Aquinas in her theological and philosophical education.

In addition, Beauvoir pursued a course of daily reading in *The Imitation of Christ* and *The Golden Legend*, supplemented by copious late nineteenth- and early twentieth-century sentimental and melodramatic religious narratives. These included novels about the life of Christ that served as the basis for a series of semi-erotic childhood fantasies (MJF 101; MDD 73). As Beauvoir explains, among middle-class Catholics girls of her generation, the body was not to be seen uncovered or to be discussed; the ideal girl was completely innocent and spiritual, or, in practical terms, ignorant about the body and sexuality. Yet in her reading of saint's lives and martyrdom accounts, Beauvoir found scenes of mortification and abjection that turned her attention to the body. She imitated these practices during various "holy periods," sleeping on the floor, rubbing her thighs with a pumice stone, and engaging in other ascetic activities.[17] This masochistic asceticism was heavily eroticized, involving tearful submission before a male leader (in the case of the martyrdom accounts) or deity. Simone's religious reading, then, served as the basis for an intense erotic and masochistic fantasy life during her early adolescence.[18]

Beauvoir describes herself as an obedient and pious child, although always more interested in the eroticized excesses of extreme sanctity than in the "every-day" sanctity preached by her teachers and many of the children's authors she was given to read. This extremism both provided a space for the body and allowed free reign to early metaphysical queries centering on the fear of death. Beauvoir writes that she decided early to choose the infinite over the world of finite things and so to become, like Teresa of Avila, a Carmelite:

> I was more and more persuaded that there was no place in the profane world for the supernatural life. And yet, it was the latter alone that counted: it alone. I suddenly received certainty, one morning, that a Christian convinced of a future beatitude should not attach the least importance to ephemeral things. How could the majority of people accept to remain in the present world? The more I reflected, the more I was astonished. I concluded that, in any case, I would not imitate them: between the infinite and the finite, my choice was made. "I will enter a convent," I decided. The activities of the sisters of charity seemed to me to be entirely futile; there was no other reasonable occupation than to contemplate to the end of my days the glory of God. I would be a Carmelite. (MJF 103–4; MDD 75)

The young Simone rejects the religious world of her teachers for one dedicated solely to the infinite. Yet the gap between the profane and the supernatural worlds (which, no doubt, was loosely, if not quite accurately, grounded in the Thomistic distinction between the natural and supernatural that played such a large role in her education) leads to Beauvoir's loss of faith at the age of fourteen. When her confessor—to whom she had spoken only of lukewarmness in the fervor of her faith and of her desire for mortification and religious ecstasy— reproaches her with the reports made by her teachers that she had become disobedient and noisy, Simone suddenly realizes that the God of her fantasies (and of the supernatural, absolute realm) and that of her rule-giving, seemingly petty school teachers (and hence of the natural, this-worldly realm) might in fact be the same (MJF 187–88; MDD 134–35).

According to Beauvoir, her childhood self eventually recognized that she was living a double life. Eating forbidden apples and reading forbidden books (Balzac!) are, according to the terms set by her mother and teachers, sins:

> It was impossible to deceive myself any longer: deliberate and sys-
> tematic disobedience, lies, impure fantasies were not the conduct
> of the innocent. I plunged my hands in the freshness of the cherry
> laurels, I heard the gurgling of the water, and I understood that
> nothing could make me renounce earthly joys. "I no longer believe

in God," I said to myself, without any great astonishment. There was evidence: if I had believed in him, I would not have consented to offend him with a gay heart. I had always thought that, at the price of eternity, this world counted for nothing; it counted, because I loved it, and it was God suddenly who didn't count. (MJF 191; MDD 137)

Because God no longer intervened in her life in any meaningful way, God had ceased to exist. She chose the natural over the supernatural. Beauvoir claims, moreover, not to have experienced this loss of faith as traumatic. Rather, following the example of her father's skepticism, she felt, as she puts it, "freed from my childhood and from my sex, in accord with the free spirits that I admired" (MJF 191; MDD 137).

Just after describing her adolescent loss of faith, Beauvoir turns to the question of love; the young Simone begins to look for another being through whom she can justify her existence (although without diminishing her freedom, she claims retrospectively). Her hopes to be a writer emerge at the same time; yet they continually vie with her desire to find another to take the place of the now absent God. Her best friend, Zaza, with whom she discusses the possibility of such a lover, is never considered as serving this function, nor is her sister and confidant, Hélène. Beauvoir (both the adolescent Simone and the narrator) assumes that only a man can serve this role: first and only briefly, the leftist Catholic professor of literature, Robert Garric; then her cousin Jacques; and finally Jean-Paul Sartre (with whom she maintained a lifelong bond).

Beauvoir describes her own development, then, as one from dependence on God to the search for a man's love as a justification for her existence. Constantly disrupting and in tension with that narrative is her desire for work. She sees men around her fully immersed in projects, yet these activities always fall short of her own desire for the absolute. The inadequacy of even men's work is most apparent in the case of Robert Garric, her literature professor at the Institut Sainte-Marie at Neuilly (where she studied for the Sorbonne exams that would qualify her as a teacher). Garric was the founder of a movement known as *Équipes sociales* that hoped to undermine the class divisions in French society through education and social action. Simone's intense interest in Garric (whom, by the way, she first pursued as a way to catch the eye of her handsome cousin Jacques) led her to participate in the movement, but she rapidly became disenchanted. Although she continued to serve as a group leader for a time (primarily, she will imply later, as an excuse to get out of the house at night), the adult Beauvoir claims to have seen immediately that the interests of the bourgeois leaders of the movement and those of the workers who participated in it were radically at odds, undermining the very unity the groups were meant to forge.[19] At this point in her life, then, the glamour of work pales beside the possibility of a man's love.

When in *The Second Sex* Beauvoir argues that women attempt to justify their existences through an other, whether human or divine, she echoes these accounts of her own early adolescent experience (found in *When Things of the Spirit Come First* as well as in *Memoirs of a Dutiful Daughter*).[20] In her autobiographical writings, the movement is from love of God to love of man; in *The Second Sex*, she reverses this trajectory: "Love has been assigned to woman as her supreme vocation, and when she directs it toward a man, she seeks God in him; if circumstances deny her human love, if she is disappointed or demanding, it is in God himself that she will choose to adore the divinity [*la divinité*]" (DS II 582; SS 743). Here, Beauvoir points to the conflation of the erotic and the spiritual, which, she argues, underlies all mystical texts. In both forms of experience, women attempt to justify their existence through another. Erotic love and mysticism are not solely the domain of women, but, unlike women, men have other paths open to them for attaining a transcendent subjectivity (in the political, economic, intellectual, artistic, and—as ecclesiasts, missionaries, theologians, etc.—religious realms).

In *The Second Sex*, Beauvoir's reading of mysticism suggests that even those women who seem to have transcended men's positioning of them in the place of the other are in fact still living out the romantic fantasy assigned to them because of their sex. Women do not transcend their nature or their sex in the mystical; rather, the mystical is an extension of their gendered identity. Since women are deemed incapable of achieving transcendence except through men, in men's absence they turn to the male God:

> Human love, divine love commingle, not because the latter would be a sublimation of the former, but because the first is also a movement toward a transcendent, toward the absolute. In any case, it is a matter for the loving woman of saving her contingent existence by uniting it to the All incarnated in a sovereign Person [*une Personne souveraine*]." (DS II 582–83; SS 744)

Beauvoir insists that this divine Person is male.[21] Whereas in a pathological case of erotomania, a woman explains that "each time I seek God, I find a man" (DS II 584; SS 745), the mystic sees God both in men and in their absence. The seventeenth-century French mystic, Madame Guyon (1648–1717), for example, loves her confessor, Pere LaCombe, in a divine manner, for "he was in her eyes something other than himself" (DS II 584; SS 745). Denied transcendence by man, who assures women that they are his other and as such are always tied to the immanent, women receive illusory transcendence through their relationship to his transcendence; they seek in men and in the male God the source of all value and meaning.[22]

Beauvoir insists on the continuity between erotic love and mystical love; yet she also argues that this continuity does not commit her to the conclusion that mystics are hysterics. Reinforcing Beauvoir's desire to distinguish at least some manifestations of mysticism from hysteria is her ambivalent attitude toward psychoanalysis. Early in *The Second Sex*, she repudiates Freud's insistence on the sexual etiology of character, claiming that Freud's account focuses on only one aspect of women's situation to the detriment of their full humanity (DS I 87–95; SS 50–58). In addition, she rejects Freud's theory of the unconscious, wishing to maintain the viability of transcendence through action that she believes such a theory vitiates. In denying that the association of eroticism and mysticism involves the pathologization of mystical states (i.e., a reading of them as necessarily hysterical), Beauvoir seems to hold open the possibility, against her own earlier claims, that erotic mysticism can be the site through which the body transcends itself and women transcend their sex.[23]

Beauvoir is at pains, then, to show that her reading of mystics as erotomaniacs does not denigrate all women mystics' experiences. Furthermore, she claims that in accepting the bodily nature of much mystical experience (for it is bodily insofar as it is sexual, not platonic), she is not being reductionistic: "the body is never the *cause* of subjective experiences, since it is under its objective aspect the subject itself: the subject lives his attitudes in the unity of his existence" (DS II 586; SS 747). The meaning of the mystics' experience cannot be reduced to either physiological or psychoanalytic terms, according to Beauvoir, for at least some mystics have mastery over their bodies. Whereas the hysteric is degraded by the fact that her body signifies without her conscious consent and without her knowledge of its meanings, the mystic—at least the great Teresa of Avila—despite the movements of her body, possesses "a sane, free consciousness": "The writings of St. Teresa hardly lend themselves to equivocation and they justify Bernini's statue" (DS II 586–87; SS 747). Bernini's statue, which represents Teresa's ecstatic encounter with an angelic dart, makes visible the eroticism of her experiences, an eroticism that, according to Beauvoir, Teresa's writings justify. Yet at the same time, perhaps because these texts are Teresa's own, the result of her active agency, Beauvoir sees her as controlling rather than succumbing to that eroticism (hence she is not hysterical). Here we seem to have, in Bataille's terms, a more "virile" relationship to the divine other than the passive submission Beauvoir associates with hysteria and erotomania.[24]

For Beauvoir, Teresa's agency is expressed through her active and self-conscious sexual response to and desire for her lover, who is God. Beauvoir claims admiration for the intensity of Teresa's faith, in which the absent object is made present on the body.[25] Unlike the hysteric, Teresa "is not the slave of her nerves and her hormones: it is necessary, rather, to admire in her the intensity of a faith that penetrates to the most intimate regions of her flesh" (DS II 587; SS 747). Unlike the hysteric whose flesh is passively inscribed by her disorder, Teresa writes the body in the intensity of her mystical experience. Yet despite her admiration for Teresa's faith, Beauvoir insists that the value of mystical experience lies not in the pleasure with which it is subjectively experienced, but in the objective influence it allows its subject to wield. Beauvoir insists that in the absence of criteria for determining the authenticity of mystical experience (she will go further and claim that mystical experience cannot be genuine, as there is no God), its value lies in its outcome.[26]

METAPHYSICS AND ACTION

Beauvoir distinguishes the "objective outcome" of Teresa's experience from that of her "minor sisters" in two ways: metaphysically and practically. At the level of metaphysics, Beauvoir argues that Teresa's erotic mystical experiences lead her to pose the central problems of religion concerning the relationship between the individual and the absolute:

> The phenomena of ecstasy are almost the same in Saint Teresa and in Marie Alacoque: the interest of their message is entirely different. St. Teresa poses in an entirely intellectual fashion the dramatic problem of the relationship between the individual and the transcendent Being; she lived, as a woman, an experience whose meaning surpasses every sexual specification; it is necessary to put her on the side of St. John of the Cross. But she is a striking exception. What her minor sisters give us is an essentially feminine vision of the world and of salvation; it is not a transcendence that they seek: it is the redemption of their femininity. (DS II 587; SS 747–48)

Thus Teresa transcends her femininity to ask questions of universal significance (regardless of how falsely posed and answered) concerning life, death, and the nature of human existence. Madame Guyon, Marie Alacoque (1647–1690), and hosts of "lesser" women, on the other hand, do not transcend femininity, Beauvoir argues, but attempt to redeem it through mystical experience (DS II 587, 592; SS 748, 752).[27]

The "essentially feminine vision of the world" provided by the "minor sisters" offers women the illusion that they can justify their existence and attain transcendence through their very immanence and bodiliness (both, of course, associated with femininity). In an analysis surprisingly close to that made so persuasively in the 1980s by Caroline Walker Bynum, Beauvoir argues that Christian women's asceticism, self-denial, and self-torture are grounded in their imitation of the passion of Christ, whose suffering body saves humanity. "One has seen how woman's attitude with regard to her body is ambiguous: it is through humiliation and suffering that she transforms it in glory. . . . The mystic will torture her flesh to have the right to claim it; reducing it to abjection, she exalts it as the instrument of her salvation" (DS II 589; SS 749). Salvation through bodily humiliation and suffering is possible because the savior himself operates through the body—he himself is a feminine figure, achieving transcendence through the immanence of the body:

> In the humiliation of God, she marvels at the dethronement [déché-ance] of Man; inert, passive, covered with wounds, the crucified is the reversed image of the white and bloody martyr exposed to wild beasts, to daggers, to men, with whom the little girl has so often identified herself; she is overwhelmed in seeing that Man, the Man-God has assumed her role. It is she who is hanging on the tree, promised the splendor of the Resurrection. (DS II 590–91; SS 751)

Here Beauvoir discovers a divine feminine person through whom women's existence might be justified. In Christianity, she argues, the divine Father takes on feminine abjection in the figure of his suffering, bleeding, and wounded Son.

Yet rather than finding in this feminized Son a resource within Christianity through which women might attain subjectivity, agency, and power, Beauvoir insists that the mystic is doomed insofar as she seeks transcendence in and through immanence. Femininity in its abject bodiliness is not transcended but glorified.[28] Beauvoir, in fact, frames her entire discussion of the justifications for women's existence with the claim that they are always inadequate. Transcendence, she argues, cannot be realized in and through immanence but only through its rejection (DS II 522; SS 698). This claim seems to suggest that the body—at least as it is configured within patriarchy—cannot be the site through which transcendent agency is attained. Yet Beauvoir has already argued that not every mystic is a hysteric and that the difference between the "authentic" mystic and the hysteric lies in the former's conscious control of the erotic movements of her body. She thereby suggests that other configurations of bodily subjectivity are possible. Similarly, through just such an eroticized relationship with Christ, Beauvoir claims, Teresa of Avila is able to transcend sexual difference and attain the metaphysical. Thus we encounter a deep ambiguity in Beauvoir's text, for as she only fleetingly acknowledges, Teresa comes to these metaphysical speculations precisely through her eroticized, sexualized, and hence feminized relationship with Christ.

Beauvoir insists that Teresa is an "intellectual" figure who is somehow able to transcend femininity and sexual difference. But given, as Beauvoir admits, that Teresa's experience of ecstasy is "almost the same" as that of her "minor sisters," in other words, that her mysticism remains bodily and thus sexualized, her intellectual transcendence of femininity is not sufficient to distinguish her from "lesser" mystics. Beauvoir thus makes an additional distinction by considering the practical outcomes of mystical experience. Among women mystics, Beauvoir argues,

> the connection between action and contemplation takes two very different forms. There are women of action like St. Catherine, St. Teresa, Joan of Arc, who know very well what ends they have in mind and who lucidly invent means of attaining them: their revelations merely give an objective aspect to their certitudes; they encourage them to follow the paths they have traced out for themselves with precision. There are narcissistic women, like Madame Guyon, Mme Krüdener, who, at the end of a silent fervor, suddenly feel themselves in "an apostolic state." They are not very precise about their tasks; and—just like the ladies-of-good-works [les dames d'oeuvres] in a fever of agitation—they care little what they do provided they do something. (DS II 592; SS 752)

Teresa, Catherine of Siena, and Joan of Arc, in other words, engage actively in human society—they have projects through which they express their transcendent subjectivity, even if they must rely on the support of a divine being to enable them to enact these projects. Narcissistic women like Madame Guyon, on the other hand, have no definite ideas or goals other than to affirm themselves as beings inspired and chosen by God. Action serves only to enhance their own narcissism.[29]

In the accusation of narcissism, we see another reason—perhaps the crucial one—for Beauvoir's rejection of mysticism as a justification of women's existence. Beauvoir argues that justification occurs not only through love of man and love of God, but also through narcissism or the love of self. Moreover, Beauvoir at times seems to assert that erotic and mystical love can be reduced to narcissism (Teresa is the great exception). Beauvoir recognizes that narcissism is not found only among women—nor is it found among all women. Furthermore, it may mark a necessary stage in the subject's development. Yet she argues that women are more prone to narcissism because their subjectivities are thwarted by their (biologically and culturally imposed) femininity.[30] In one of the more anatomically based arguments in The Second Sex, Beauvoir claims that because women do not have penises, they lack a readily available alter ego through which they can externalize their own desires (DS II 26–27; SS 313). More importantly, girls are not allowed to engage actively with the world: as a result, Beauvoir argues, woman "gives herself a sovereign importance because no important object is accessible to her" (DS II 526; SS 700). Women are objects for others and hence become objects for themselves. Not allowed to work on objects in the world, they take themselves as objects through which to express their subjectivities. Yet this process of self-love and self-creation is not deployed toward some greater end, but only in order to make a pleasing object for that other being through whom woman's existence is justified. So woman's narcissism is dependent on her love of man and of God, just as her love of man and of God can (often) be reduced to love of self. Women (or at least narcissistic women) turn to men and to God not as objects of desire but as beings who might be compelled to desire them. Beauvoir implies that the recognition of the other as a conscious, free, and autonomous being is needed to break this circular relationship between self and nonexistent other (i.e., God); only in this way can the real existence of other human beings be experienced.

This slippage between love of God and love of self runs throughout Beauvoir's discussion of religion. Even when she most strongly asserts religion's power to justify women's existence, the charge of narcissism lurks not far behind. For example, in "Situation and Character," Beauvoir argues that through religion women can escape the primacy of sexual difference and hence their subservience to femininity and immanence:

> This is why the little girl and the female adolescent throw themselves into devotion with a fervor infinitely greater than that of their

brothers; the eye [*regard*] of God, which transcends the boy's transcendence, humiliates him: he will remain a child forever under this powerful guardianship, it is castration more radical than that by which he feels himself menaced through his father's existence. In as much as the female "eternal child" finds her salvation in this eye [*regard*] that transforms her into a sister of the angels it cancels the privilege of the penis. A sincere faith greatly helps the little girl in avoiding any inferiority complex: she is neither male nor female, but a creature of God. (DS II 515; SS 692)

Religion would seem, then, to be the one place where women have been able, historically, to exist as subjects not reduced to their sex, for in "the heavenly absent One" women find support for their subjectivities and their projects.

Yet this very escape from femininity is dependent on femininity and on the primacy of the masculine, for God is the phallus in the face of which all humans are lacking or castrated. Woman, always already castrated within male-dominant society, gives up nothing in her relationship to the divine. In fact, the divine safeguards her if she accepts that lack. The more she accedes to the nothingness of the creature, moreover, the more fully united she becomes with the divine. Mysticism, then, becomes narcissism. According to Beauvoir, women ultimately make "religion a pretext for satisfying [their] own desires" (DS II 516; SS 693). The divine, all-encompassing other with whom the mystic relates and who supports her subjectivity is a mirage; what she sees in that mirroring other is only herself.

For Beauvoir, the narcissist, the lover, and the mystic all seek "to transform [their] prison into a heaven of glory, [their] servitude into sovereign liberty" (DS II 522; SS 698). The problem for Beauvoir is that these women have no object outside of themselves—even the human or divine being whom they love serves only as a mirror for their own narcissistic cravings:

But in themselves these attempts at individual salvation can end only in failure: either woman puts herself into relation with an unreality: her double, or God; or she creates an unreal relation with a real being [i.e., she absolutizes a man]; in either case, she has not taken hold of the world; she does not escape her subjectivity; her liberty remains mystified. (DS II 593; SS 752–53)

For Beauvoir there is only one way for women to use their freedom authentically—"to project it by a positive action into human society" (DS II 593; SS

753). Only a handful of exceptional women, like the mystics Teresa of Avila and Catherine of Siena, have yet come close. According to Beauvoir, what marks Teresa off from other mystics is that the divine supports her in projects that go beyond the self and involve active engagement with the world and other beings in the world. Teresa founded an order, the reformed or Discalced Carmelites, and actively engaged in establishing convents throughout Castille. Her writings were an essential part of this work. So despite Beauvoir's predominantly negative attitude toward mysticism, she claims that, for Teresa, mysticism served as a support not for narcissism but for a transcendent and active form of subjectivity.

What remains to be clarified is why some women's actions count as authentic when others are deemed narcissistic. Beauvoir's explicit answer, which grounds Teresa's transcendent and autonomous subjectivity in her encounter with death, seems inadequate given the philosophical revisioning of subjectivity as necessarily intersubjective provided in *The Second Sex*. As I will show below, only when we understand the context out of which Teresa lived and worked can we account adequately for her free and autonomous, yet situated and reciprocal, subjectivity.

THE TRANSFORMATION OF THE WORLD AND THE REC-
OGNITION OF THE OTHER AS A CONSCIOUS BEING   Beauvoir's emphasis in *The Second Sex* on projects and engagement with reality as the expression of authentic freedom is grounded in her deployment of an existentialist ethic. Central to this ethic is the claim that the subject achieves being and liberty only through choice and action—in other words, transcendence. If we do not strive against the material constraints and contingent facts of our human condition, we lose transcendence, fall into immanence and stagnation, and become subject to those very conditions and contingencies that it is our moral duty to contest (DS I 31–32; SS xxxiii–xxxiv). On this reading, Beauvoir's ethic seems to maintain and reinforce the dualistic hierarchies on which male privilege has traditionally rested: reason/unreason, culture/nature, subject/object, mind/body, self/other, transcendence/immanence. The task for women is not to disrupt this series of hierarchies but to reposition themselves on the side previously occupied only by men. The mysticism of Teresa of Avila and Catherine of Siena, the two mystics Beauvoir most admires, might then be read as masculine in contrast to the feminine, narcissistic, and hysterical mysticism of Madame Guyon and Angela of Foligno (DS II 587; SS 747–48). There is no need for Beauvoir to explain how Teresa and Catherine's actions were possible given the constricted circumstances in which women lived in their societies, for strength of will alone

can explain action. (Teresa, of course, ascribes this inexplicable freedom of the will to God: "The Lord gave me the freedom and strength to perform the task [of cutting all social ties and devoting herself totally to God's service]. . . . He gave the freedom that I with all the efforts of many years could not attain by myself.")[31]

A countertext runs throughout *The Second Sex*, however, in which Beauvoir suggests that women with the strength to act do not simply appropriate these dualistic hierarchies but call them into question. The countertext begins with Beauvoir's divergence from Sartre on the issues of freedom, responsibility, and situatedness. Whereas the Sartre of *Being and Nothingness* views all people as equally capable of freedom despite differing degrees of external constraint on their being, Beauvoir argues that this conception of freedom is incapable of recognizing the reality and effects of oppression. If external constraints do not limit freedom, they are not genuinely oppressive. Women, like other oppressed groups, are subject to systematic forms of oppression in which "transcendence is condemned to fall uselessly back on itself because it is cut off from its goals."[32] From the moment Sartre began to develop his existentialist ethic, Beauvoir argued this point with him, insisting that subjects are always situated, and that these circumstances, in their very contingency, shape ethics.[33] Once this situatedness and subjection to circumstances are acknowledged, the possibility of pure transcendence is undermined (and begins, in fact, to look like inauthenticity).

Yet at the same time, recognition of the interdependence and situatedness of human subjectivity raises particular problems for women, as becomes most evident in Beauvoir's discussion of sexuality. Here Beauvoir argues that a relationship of true respect and mutuality between men and women is possible, and she claims a kind of authenticity for such relationships that seems unattainable in relationships between women (or between men).[34] True reciprocity, she argues, becomes possible when women refuse to be the other to the male subject.[35] By claiming their own autonomy and limited transcendence, women foster in men an appreciation both of alterity without hierarchical subordination and of the necessity of recognizing the other as a conscious being. Women thereby force men to recognize that they contain the other within themselves, that is, that they, too, are subject to the constraints of the flesh, the necessities of nature, and to contingency and change. By acknowledging his own embodiment, therefore, man frees woman from her role as the other. The possibility of such relationships between men and women, however, lies in men's recognition of women's autonomy. Women, although apparently freed through their own actions, are still dependent on men for recognition of their subjectivities (DS II 658–59;

SS 810). The Hegelian master/slave relation that frames and shapes Beauvoir's discussion cannot be escaped.[36] Alterity and struggle are necessary, even if only to be sublated through the movement of the dialectic. Women are thus in the impossible position of being able to gain freedom only through men's recognition of the very autonomy that women have yet to attain.[37]

Beauvoir asserts, then, both that women have been incapable of creating a solid "counter-universe" to men's, one that would provide a space for freedom, action, and subjectivity, and that entrance into the male universe is dependent on men's recognition of women's subjectivity. Yet Beauvoir also argues that Teresa overcomes her femininity (apparently, in Beauvoir's version, without the help or recognition of men) to the extent that she acts in the world, confronting and shaping reality out of her own freedom. Moreover, Beauvoir insists that in overcoming femininity, Teresa overcomes sexual difference itself. Against those critics who assert that The Second Sex fails because it reinscribes a masculine subject in an illusory site of neutrality, one might argue that Beauvoir holds open a utopic site in which sexual difference is not fundamentally constitutive of human identity. Beauvoir suggests, like Françoise Parturier, that only when women arrive at this site will they confront those metaphysical questions about the nature of human subjectivity that until now have been available only to men—and to a few outstanding women like Teresa.[38]

The problem with this defense of Beauvoir is that her account of Teresa's transcendence of sexual difference is itself masculinized. Beauvoir insists that Teresa transcends gender simply through the force of her will ("One finds in many of the great female saints an entirely virile firmness" that "recognized no masculine authority" [DS II 515; SS 692]). We see, then, in Beauvoir's account of Teresa the reemergence of a concept of absolute freedom, despite Beauvoir's concern for situatedness and the necessity of mutual recognition. Because she effaces the complex context out of which Teresa emerges, Beauvoir is unable to account for the fact that, as she herself acknowledges, Teresa moves through an eroticized and sexualized mysticism to get to the site of supposed metaphysical neutrality.

In fact, the actions through which Teresa supposedly transcended sexual difference were dependent on male authorization and legitimation, both divine and human. Even authorization by God is insufficient without the approval of male church leaders.[39] Moreover, in the process of self-legitimation, Teresa worked with many of the same theological arguments deployed by her "minor sisters," who were, as Beauvoir reads them, trapped within the immanence of femininity. In her rhetoric of humility and her emphasis on an erotic, loving relationship between the soul and the divine, Teresa deploys widely shared cultural expectations about femininity, with the aim of justifying her role as God's mouthpiece. Teresa, like her "minor sisters"—although for a variety of reasons, more successfully than they—was forced to work both with and against contemporary ideologies of gender in order to attain voice and authority.[40] By obscuring the importance of this context, Beauvoir is in danger of making Teresa a lone individual, both unmarked by and unable to fight against the institutional, societal, and cultural oppression to which women are subject.[41] In other words, although demanding engagement with the world as the mark of free subjectivity, Beauvoir refuses to acknowledge the way in which Teresa's activities were both engendered and enabled by the world in which she lived— in particular by her deployment of claims to divine authorization with and against human, male-dominant institutions. Teresa's situation not only limited or denied her freedom, but also provided the means by which she was able to transcend at least some of its constraints. (In a similar way, the body— in its limitations and mortality—not only serves as a constraint to human transcendence and autonomy but also is the means through which we attain consciousness and subjectivity.)

Beauvoir's inability fully to contextualize Teresa emerges from her con- tinued—albeit ambivalent—allegiance to a conception of absolute freedom and transcendence as constitutive of authentic subjectivity. Even when, in *The Second Sex*, she acknowledges that human beings are always situated, Beauvoir reads the material conditions of existence primarily as constraining rather than as the context out of which possibilities for transcendence and action emerge. (In part, this view is rooted in her understanding of femininity as a patriarchal construct that cannot be redeemed; Beauvoir's distrust of the female body as lived within male-dominant culture and society, however, seems in danger of undermining her insights into the ambivalence of bodily experience itself.) Yet Beauvoir's fascination with Teresa suggests a way out of the very impasse generated by her existentialist ethic. As I argued above, for Beauvoir, the difference between Teresa and Guyon lies in the degree to which they engage actively with the world and with others. Madame Guyon, according to Beauvoir, is a narcissist for whom action serves only as a sign of her chosenness by the divine. She has no concrete goals, no real projects for improving the lives of others or the religious world of her day—her desire for action is merely a desire for self- assertion (a kind of thwarted Nietzschean will-to-power). Without object or aim, her desire inevitably flounders. Guyon wants to be all for God and because of this is unable to acknowledge the subjectivity of any other—including, ultimately, the subjectivity of God himself, who exists only as a mirror for her own subjectivity.

Teresa, on the other hand, through her active engagement with the world, has projects external to herself through which she can actualize her freedom and relate to others as conscious beings. If we look beyond Beauvoir to recent studies of Teresa, we see that Teresa engages in the religious reform of the Carmelite order in an explicit attempt to safeguard women's religious roles within a Counter Reformation church hostile to visionary experience and mysticism.[42] Her writing emerges out of the same desire. In response to the Valdez Index, which outlawed most vernacular translations of mystical treatises and guidebooks, Teresa undertook to write from her own experience in order to provide support for other women's mystical pursuits.[43] Teresa's concern to safeguard women's ability to pursue a mystical relationship with the divine, moreover, leads her to what Alison Weber calls a "metaphysical pragmatism" not unlike Beauvoir's own position:

> What I find fascinating is the manner in which Teresa has moved from an essentialism that assumes notions of women's inferiority ("self-love in us is great") to a difference feminism (women are more intuitive than men), to a kind of metaphysical pragmatism that looks beyond gender (what matters is not the sex of the believer or the discerner, but the effects of the believer on the community).[44]

For Teresa, as finally for Beauvoir, one's ability to engage meaningfully with others, both women and men, determines the efficacy of one's experience.

Although I would contest Beauvoir's characterization of Guyon, who also wished to participate in the reform and missionizing movements of her day but was barred from such activities by her enemies, Beauvoir's understanding of the importance of Teresa's activities opens up new conceptions of subjectivity never completely worked out in *The Second Sex* (perhaps in part because, as the example of Guyon shows, such subjects remain painfully vulnerable to the other, who can enable or thwart their projects by refusing to recognize them). According to Beauvoir, Teresa, through her activities, escapes both the dangerous solipsism of masculine subjectivity, which in its desire to be all denies any conscious existence to the other, and the narcissism of feminine subjectivity, in which the desire to be all for the other collapses into an embrace of the self as object of desire. Teresa's recognition of the other as a conscious being—her engagement with the world of religious women and men out of which and to which she speaks—disrupts the solipsistic and (for Beauvoir) illusory relationship between Teresa and God. Unlike the childhood Beauvoir who admires the Carmelite's embrace of the infinite, the Beauvoir of The Second Sex admires Teresa as a powerful example of genuine action. This action, moreover, was supported by and helped create and maintain communities of women (and men)—women who, like Teresa, in their lives and activities shaped and created the world.[45]

We are now in a position to see that Beauvoir's critique of femininity contains within it an implicit critique of masculinity (despite her continuing admiration for precisely those features of masculinity that she simultaneously denigrates).[46] In their desire for absolute transcendence and totality, men make women the repository of all bodiliness and immanence and thus efface the other as a conscious being. Masculinity in its pure form is a kind of "bad faith of transcendence," in which immanence and the body are denied and projected onto women, who become consciousless beings on whom men can assert their freedom. Men's desire to be all and women's desire to be all for the other, then, mirror each other and ultimately collapse into similarly vain attempts to assert oneself at the expense of conscious alterity. Mysticism only rarely serves as the ground for free subjectivity—not simply because the God encountered within it does not exist, nor because it is a vain attempt to seek transcendence through immanence; rather, to the extent that mysticism is associated with the desire to be everything even God is effaced by the solipsism and narcissism of human desire. Human beings desire God, Beauvoir suggests, primarily in their desire to be God. On the other hand, to the extent that it is through her mystical relationship to the absolute that Teresa comes to work with and in the world to create new institutions, mysticism makes possible her freedom. My account reads her mysticism in terms of an encounter with other conscious beings. In the closing chapter of The Second Sex, Beauvoir emphasizes Teresa's encounter with the possibility of her own death. Teresa's mysticism, then, offers possibilities for articulating the intersubjectivity of human existence that Beauvoir tends to cover over rather than exploit. We need now to explain why this might be the case.

DEATH AND RESPONSIBILITY

As I have suggested, recent scholarship on Beauvoir insists on crucial points of divergence between her work and that of her companion and friend Jean-Paul Sartre. Margaret Simons argues that these differences are apparent in Beauvoir's earliest philosophical work. These recently uncovered journals predate Beauvoir's relationship with Sartre and suggest the independent roots of certain aspects of her thinking. For the Sartre of *Being and Nothingness* (as for Beauvoir in *She Came to Stay*), the conscious subject or being-for-itself exists in solipsistic isolation. Any encounter with an other is experienced by that consciousness as an assault on its freedom and autonomy, for in the eyes of the other the subject must recognize its objectification as being-for-others. Intersubjectivity is a constant oscillation between sadism and masochism in which there seems to be no possibility of mutual "recognition," independence, and autonomy.[47] For Beauvoir, this account of intersubjectivity describes the masculine subject in his desire to be everything, a desire that depends on the othering of woman.

Women, on the other hand, consigned culturally to this secondary position, can justify their existence only through (or in mystical union with) another (the lover, the child, God). The desire to be all, as I have argued, finds expression in a desire to be everything to or with another. Hence, as Simons argues, for Beauvoir subjectivity is always already involved with others. The central ethical problem for women, then, is not solipsism but what Simons calls "selflessness, or the temptation to self-abdication."[48] In *The Second Sex*, Beauvoir makes another, more Nietzschean argument, claiming that selflessness is itself a thwarted expression of the desire to be everything that lies at the root, for Beauvoir, of inauthentic subjectivity. Men are privileged because they are able to pursue their desire in the world; yet their desire to be everything, when pursued, leads them to efface the world itself as other.

The challenge for Beauvoir is to articulate another conception of intersubjectivity in which the other is not effaced and true interaction between free agents occurs. *The Second Sex* can be read as a text that moves between an acceptance of paradigms of transcendent subjectivity as normative and desirable, and a resistance to masculine subjectivity in the name of an account of the intersubjectively defined subject for whom sexual difference is not definitive of identity. In recent scholarship on Beauvoir, this ambivalence in her thought is often framed in terms of the extent of Sartre's influence—her emphasis on transcendence, autonomy, and freedom is associated with a Sartrean existentialist ethic and contrasted to her own work on situatedness and reciprocity.[49] In terms of mysticism, Beauvoir's ambivalence is apparent in the distinction between the narcissist's recreation of the world in his or her own image and Teresa of Avila's more intersubjectively oriented practice. Yet Beauvoir leaves out precisely this aspect of Teresa's life, emphasizing instead her creation of a free consciousness through the strength of her will alone. Here, where she might radically depart from Sartre, she sounds most like him. Moreover, Beauvoir's account of her own childhood and adolescence, taken together with evidence provided by the recently accessible student journals, suggests that the desire to be everything and the lure of transcendence were central to Beauvoir's philosophical and subjective formation even before she met Sartre. In other words, perhaps Beauvoir's "Sartreanism" predates Sartre.

Beauvoir's early attitude toward mysticism displays a desire for transcendence and the absolute unconstrained by situation. Beauvoir's early diaries suggest that mysticism, understood as unconstrained pursuit of the desire to be everything, is the great temptation against which she must fight in order to articulate an alternative conception of subjectivity and freedom. As a young student of philosophy, Beauvoir finds herself adrift, shorn of all her previous convictions and supports:

> I know nothing, nothing: not only no answers but no presentable manner of posing the question. Scepticism, indifference are impossible, a religion is impossible for the moment—mysticism is tempting: but how will I know the value of a thought which leaves no place for thought? what can I lean on to reject or accept it, agree to spend two years in reading, conversations, fragmentary meditations. I am going to work like a brute: I don't have a minute to lose. And neglect nothing: link up with Baruzi, do my homework, endeavor to know, to know.[50]

As Simons shows, when Beauvoir writes these lines in 1927, all of those things that previously served to support her subjectivity—her family, religious faith, and love—are lost. She turns to philosophy as a new form of intellectual discipline through which she might justify her existence. (This is also the time when she is engaged with leftist Catholic movements for social change but finds their goals misguided and petty and so without real justificatory power.) For the young Beauvoir, mysticism marks a rejection of reason through which faith in one's being might be restored against reason's onslaught. Poised over the "void" of a life without meaning, mysticism is a temptation.[51]

Yet Beauvoir insists that mysticism is a temptation she must resist. Despite reason's self-corrosive quality—the study of philosophy, she argues, leads only to a recognition of the powerlessness of reason—Beauvoir eschews the certainties of faith.

> I cannot stop myself from envying them because it seems that there is something more complete in faith and happiness than there is in doubt, disquietude. But I know well, however, that their God

is not. . . . No, truly; that which I love above all, is not ardent faith. . . . It's the broken élans, the searches, the desires, it is the ideas above all, the intelligence and criticism, the weariness, the flaws, those beings who cannot allow themselves to be duped and who struggle to live despite their lucidity.[52]

This lucidity, it would seem, demands recognition that the self cannot be everything; we live in a world that conditions and determines us even as we have a limited freedom to act within it. The roots of Beauvoir's career-long struggle to maintain a balance between situatedness and freedom, then, can be glimpsed in notebooks she kept at nineteen:

> I know myself that there is only one problem and that it does not have a solution, because it has no sense. . . . I would like to believe in something—to encounter total exigency—to justify life; in brief, I would like God. Once this is said, I will not forget it. But knowing that this unattainable noumenal world exists where alone could be explained to me why I live, in the phenomenal world which is not for all that so negligible, I will construct my life. I will take myself as an end.[53]

All we can know is the phenomenal world in which we are determined by forces beyond our control. In the face of that world, Beauvoir rejects God and the desire to be everything (to oneself or for the other) with which she associates the divine. And yet without these supports for her subjectivity, her only recourse is to take herself as the source of ultimate value. She must create and so justify her life.

Beauvoir's rejection of mysticism is grounded not only in her analysis of the merely compensatory pleasures it offers women within male-dominant society, but also in her metaphysically based rejection of the claims to totality on which, she believes, it rests. Nonetheless, she admires Teresa; in emphasizing Teresa's relationship to others as conscious beings, I have uncovered one possible explanation for this admiration. Yet at the end of *The Second Sex*, Beauvoir suggests another. She writes that it is precisely Teresa's totalizing autonomous subjectivity that both enables her to work in the world and that elicits Beauvoir's admiration. Teresa shares in the greatness of those men who "in one fashion or another— have taken the weight of the world on their shoulders. They have been more or less pulled down, they have succeeded in recreating the world or they have foundered. But first of all they have assumed the enormous burden. This is what no woman has ever done, what no woman ever *could* do" (DS II 639; SS 793). Most women, Beauvoir insists, are unable to take responsibility for the world precisely because they are denied responsibility for themselves. To the extent that their justification for existence come from an other (child, God, or man), they cannot be responsible for the universe. Women have been kept from the privileged position in which one takes responsibility for the world and for one's own self-justification. Teresa is, for Beauvoir, the great exception:

> There is hardly any woman other than St. Teresa who has lived on her own account, in a total abandonment, the situation of human-ity: we have seen why. Taking her stand beyond the earthly hier-archies, she did not feel, any more than did St. John of the Cross, a reassuring ceiling over her head. There was for both the same night, the same flashes of light, in the self the same nothingness, in God the same plenitude. When at last it will be possible for every human being to set his pride beyond the sexual differentiation, in the difficult glory of his free existence, then only will woman be able to identify her history, her problems, her doubts, her hopes, with those of humanity; then only will she be able to seek in her life and her works to reveal the whole of reality and not merely her personal self. As long as she still has to struggle to become a human being, she cannot become a creator. (DS II 640; SS 794)

What is crucial here for Beauvoir is neither Teresa's erotic encounter with God nor her relationship to communities of women and men through and with whom she justifies her actions and creates new institutions; what is crucial is Teresa's ability to live without "a reassuring ceiling over her head." The force of character that enabled Teresa to embrace freedom rather than to flee its vertiginous demands reemerges at the end of *The Second Sex* as the focal point for Beauvoir's admiration and as the necessary basis for the authenticity of Teresa's actions. Mysticism is thus a site of absolute freedom from and transcendence of the limitations of situatedness. In its ideal form, it is the place where one faces death (and implicitly rejects it), and so becomes capable of encountering the world as project. Implied here is a return to that (male) narcissistic subject who relates to others only as objects for manipulation and world-creation.

For Beauvoir, metaphysical anguish will remain even after women come to occupy positions of privilege in which they can and must take responsibility for the world. Moreover, the encounter with the potential meaninglessness of existence is essential to attaining such responsibility. Yet this reading of Teresa elides the central role she ascribes to God and that we might ascribe to a conjunction of faith, genius, and supportive community structures that enabled Teresa to engage in meaningful projects. Beauvoir, on the contrary, re-creates Teresa as an existentialist hero for whom the force of her will in the face of death is sufficient to generate meaning, value, and projects. Yet Beauvoir herself, despite the proclamation of faith in the meaning-generating power of projects with which she ends *The Second Sex*, often seems to question the self-legitimating value of work in the face of death's threat.[54]

In the famous lines with which Beauvoir closes the third volume of her memoirs (the same volume in which she recalls her affinities with Bataille), she expresses an intense dissatisfaction with her life. Despite the fulfillment of many dreams, death still threatens the value of life:

> All the things I've talked about, others about which I have said nothing—there is no place where they will live again. If at least it had enriched the earth; if it had given birth to . . . what? A hill? A rocket? But no. Nothing will have taken place. I see again the hedge of hazel trees that the wind rustles and the promises with which I threw my heart into a turmoil when I contemplated the gold-mine at my feet: a whole life to live. The promises have been kept. And yet, turning an incredulous gaze toward that credulous adolescent girl, I realize with stupor how much I have been swindled.[55]

Her books, she argues, are not creations, but at best a record of never-to-be repeated experiences. Beauvoir holds open the possibility that the swindle lies in her inability to leave a lasting monument on earth—she will later claim that these lines were written in a state of intense depression caused by French responses to the war in Algeria. This assertion suggests another reading of the difference between Teresa of Avila and Madame Guyon, one that leads us to ask how clearly we can distinguish Beauvoir's lifelong project—to create and justify her own life—from the narcissistic projects of apparently inauthentic men and women. Beauvoir's despair emerges when the world refuses to comply with her projects, just as Guyon's desire to share in the apostolic life is thwarted by her religious enemies. Beauvoir recognizes that human subjectivity depends on interactions between conscious beings and that the success of human projects depends on cooperation with, compliance from, and recognition by others. Yet she simultaneously desires to assert herself as a free and autonomous human subject in the face of a male-dominant world's refusal of that cooperation, compliance, and recognition. By effacing the context in and out of which Teresa's free subjectivity emerges, Beauvoir keeps alive the (potentially enabling) myth that subjects can successfully assert themselves independently of the world's recognition. Yet in distinguishing between Teresa's success and Madame Guyon's failure, Beauvoir also suggests the situatedness of freedom and its dependence on recognition by other conscious beings.

Yet one continues to wonder whether any achievement could stand up to the corrosive sense of time, contingency, and meaninglessness inscribed within the final lines of Force of Circumstance. The swindle is not simply to do with her sex but is a sign of the metaphysical anguish out of which, Beauvoir argues, greatness comes. Even if our political projects succeed, death continues to undermine claims to ultimate meaning or value. Only the one who can withstand this threat, who exalts in "the difficult glory of free existence," can act. Beauvoir's companion Jean-Paul Sartre argues that value can only be constructed—one must accept contingency and relativity in the face of death and give up the idealism that demands absolutes.[56] (Beauvoir, in her philosophical essays, seems to agree with this claim.) Bataille's practice of inner experience implicitly accuses Sartrean projects of making the subject and his or her freedom absolute and so denying the reality of death (an assessment of the younger Sartre with which the older Sartre might agree). For Bataille, communication occurs through an embrace of death's possibility and a radical realization of the absence of the absolute (what is communicated, finally, are the affects engendered by that absence).

Beauvoir's often anguished encounters with the thought of her own death stand curiously between these two positions in ways that are, I think, tied to sexual difference. Perhaps it is the relative stability of their privileged subject positions, as white, educated, European men, that enable Sartre and Bataille to flirt with death and deny the absolute. Beauvoir the philosopher adopts a similar stance, arguing that we must accept mortality, contingency, and the relativity of human values in order to create meaningful human worlds. Yet her novels, memoirs, and—perhaps mostly tellingly—The Second Sex suggest that women, with their still tenuous hold on claims to human subjectivity, autonomy, freedom, and transcendence often continue to strive for an absolute, whether in the form of religious belief, political projects, or, as is sometimes the case with Beauvoir, unfulfilled metaphysical desire.[57] This desire for the absolute uneasily grounds Beauvoir's subjectivity and frees her from dependence on the contingent recognition of others, others who, all too often, fail her.

JACQUES LACAN, *ENCORE:* FEMININE JOUISSANCE, THE REAL, AND THE GOAL OF PSYCHOANALYSIS

. . . .

That which is written [*l'écrit*] is not to be understood.

It is for this reason that you are not compelled to understand my writings. If you don't understand them, it's all the better—that will give you just the opportunity to explain them.

JACQUES LACAN, *Seminar XX*

Knowledge is access to the unknown. Nonsense is the outcome of each possible meaning [*sens*].

GEORGES BATAILLE, *Inner Experience*

MYSTICAL ECSTASY: FULLNESS OR LACK?

The word "mysticism" comes from the ancient Greek μύω, to close (the eyes). It is used both as a noun, denoting things hidden or veiled and as an adjective. Early Christian thinkers borrow the word from the Greek mystery religions in order to designate the hidden reality underlying scripture and liturgy, namely, Jesus Christ, believed to be the referent of even the most obscure and seemingly mundane biblical texts and the constant underlying presence in the ritual life of the Christian community. According to Louis Bouyer, who offers the most detailed account of early uses of the term, only with Origen do we begin to get an understanding of the mystical as a particular mode of theologizing or of spiritual practice. Origen designates as "mystical" the spiritual knowledge produced through allegorical interpretation of the Bible (the uncovering of its hidden meanings). This usage marks a shift toward the experiential: the process by which one comes to know hidden things is designated as mystical rather than the things themselves.[1] In Origen, the primary mode of contemplation through which the hidden becomes manifest is exegetical; the allegorical interpretation of biblical texts is at the center of his religious practice and experience. Yet within the early Christian and medieval periods, women were generally not allowed to interpret the Bible. For those women who wished to offer religious teaching, visions and other extraordinary experiences of divine presence both legitimated their claims to religious authority and became the text on which they extended their own allegorical and exegetical skills.[2] The experiential base of the mystical, then, widens and intensifies in the later Middle Ages, when significant numbers of women first begin to write about their religious lives.

Yet the term "mysticism" itself emerges as a substantive only in the seventeenth century, when it designates a specific mode of theologizing that is grounded in individual experience rather than in scripture, in the Holy Spirit's revelations to the Catholic Church, or in the rational exposition and elaboration of such revelatory truths.[3] Michel de Certeau argues that this shift in the meaning of "mysticism" was the result of the breakdown of medieval theological hierarchies prevalent through the sixteenth century. Late medieval theology, expressed most systematically in the Franciscan tradition, distinguishes between symbolic theology, in which sensible things lead to knowledge of the divine; scholastic theology, which makes use of intelligible things to come to God; and mystical theology, understood as the perfection of divine knowledge in contemplation. Certain people of extraordinary ability thus move through the sensible and the intelligible to a fuller spiritual apprehension of God. In the sixteenth and seventeenth centuries, Certeau argues, this hierarchy breaks down and is superseded by three competing methods of doing theology: positive or historical, scholastic, and mystical. The first method relies on the Bible and the revelations of the church, the second on philosophical and analytic elaborations of those revealed truths, and the third on experience. Mysticism is no longer the most perfect form of theological apprehension but merely an alternative method for attaining that knowledge also made available by other means. (Again, experience as an alternative source for divine knowledge is particularly prominent among late medieval women, whose visionary, auditory, and unitive experiences both legitimate and provide the subject matter for their teachings.)

With the emergence of the substantive, as Certeau shows, a mystical tradition is retroactively created. Sixteenth- and seventeenth-century authors and compilers look back on the Christian tradition and qualify as mystical those texts whose exegetical techniques, spiritual practices, or experiential accounts legitimate and reinforce developing understandings of mysticism.[4] The modern study of mysticism emerges out of this specifically Christian context.[5] As modern epistemologies increasingly focus on experience as the ground for knowledge, scholars turn to mysticism as the aspect of religion most conducive to rational analysis and debate.[6] So despite the diversity of interpretations and evaluations given to mysticism, almost all modern scholarly accounts agree that mysticism has to do with experience, in particular the experience of divine presence or union.

Modern accounts of mysticism generally claim that in mystical experience one encounters the putative source of wholeness and plenitude in which (or in whom) the individual actively participates. According to the terms elaborated by Bataille and Beauvoir, the mystic is one whose desire to be everything is met, paradoxically, through her experience of the one who is all. Yet Bataille insists that within Angela of Foligno's text and within his own experience, there is another kind of ecstasy, one sparked by the realization that one is not and cannot be everything. This realization comes about not through participation in the one who is all, but in an encounter with the radical contingency and partialness of a human other, whether it be the crucified Christ or the victim of more recent tortures (or, even more controversially, the genitals of a prostitute, as Bataille suggests in *Madame Edwarda*).[7] Both Bataille and Beauvoir find within the mystics' texts traces of this other form of ecstatic anguish, one that seems antithetical to union with the all. Both forms of mystical experience are literally ecstatic: the subject stands outside of herself, encountering and communicating with another. Yet whereas in the standard conception of mysticism, that other is an all-encompassing divine being through whom the fragmented self achieves wholeness and plenitude, Bataille insists that ecstasy can also be the experience of an other who is radically contingent, partial, and incomplete.

There are two ways to pose the question that emerges from the juxtaposition of these divergent conceptions of mystical ecstasy. We might ask, adopting a nominalist stance, how two seemingly antithetical experiences come to be associated with the term "mysticism." We might then argue that Bataille simply wrests the term from its theistic context and replaces it with an atheological anguish that is, in fact, alien to the texts themselves. Yet to make this argument is, I think, to miss the power of Bataille's reading of Angela (as well as the enormous suggestiveness of Beauvoir's attraction to Teresa of Avila). If we take Bataille's reading seriously, we see that in Angela's text the two experiences overlap. Although always framed within a larger salvific narrative, Angela's experience of the suffering Godman leads her willingly to give up all hope of and desire for personal salvation. Angela's ecstatic encounter with the tortured Christ is always in danger of taking precedence over either personal or universal redemption. The desire for (divine) wholeness and plenitude and the ecstatic anguish of the realization that one cannot be everything stand side by side in Angela's text. Bataille suggests, furthermore, that these two conceptions of mysticism can be found together throughout the Christian tradition. This possibility leads to the second, more difficult, and more pressing formulation of our question: why do these two seemingly antithetical experiences so often emerge in such close proximity to each other?[8]

Jacques Lacan's *Seminar XX: Encore* suggests an answer to this question. He describes two tendencies in language; the first attempts to fix meaning by positing a transcendental signifier. Understood to be seamlessly united with its signified, the transcendental signifier assures the stability of language. Yet there is another movement in language away from the stability of meaning, for Lacan argues that the transcendental signifier is always, in fact, empty; its putative wholeness and fixity is an illusion that psychoanalysis aims to expose. The very site meant to fix meaning becomes the place where it is destabilized. He argues, even more pointedly, that signification—marked by the transcendental signifier—becomes possible only because of this constitutive instability. Hence mysticism, as a quest for the absolute, for that which would ensure meaning, stability, and being, encounters instead that which radically destabilizes subjectivity and meaning—mysticism seeks the transcendental signifier but discovers the paradoxical interplay of presence and absence through which signification is made possible. Ecstasy occurs in both moments (what Lacan refers to as phallic jouissance and the jouissance that goes beyond); and as he argues in the seminar, if this does not quite make for two Gods, "nor does it make for one alone."[9]

I suggested in chapter 2 that *Encore*, or at least those portions of it dealing with mysticism and feminine jouissance, can be read as a defense of Bataille's mysticism against Sartre's charge that Bataille's mystical turn was an evasion of politics in the face of world war.[10] I will extend that reading here, arguing that Lacan's conception of the doubleness of language, the body, and woman can be read as a theoretical articulation of the ambiguities deployed by Bataille throughout his wartime writings. Elisabeth Roudinesco asserts that Lacan's notion of the real, particularly as it is elaborated in his later seminars, is indebted to Bataille's conception of heterogeneity, reinforcing my sense of the close relationship between Bataille's work and *Encore*.[11]

In *Seminar XX*, Lacan takes the concept of heterogeneity that emerges in Bataille's writing out of a particular political context (the left-wing tumult of the 1930s, in which Bataille always insisted on giving voice to the unassimilable) and places it within a generalized psychoanalytic theory. Lacan insists that feminine jouissance and the mystical are the site of the heterogeneous real's emergence and that the goal of analytic discourse is to engender mystical jouissance. According to Lacan, to open oneself to the emergence of the real as feminine jouissance demands that one eschew the masculine subject position of (always in part illusory) power in order to stand on the side of the "not all" or femininity.[12] Lacan never explicitly associates his account of the man who seeks this path with Bataille, and we can never know if he had Bataille in mind when he gave the 1972–1973 seminars. Yet I think that Lacan's theories of the doubleness of language, mysticism, and jouissance help explain, even if they do not fully resolve, the contradictions in Bataille's texts. In the process, Lacan makes explicit (and perhaps unnecessarily reifies) the gender dynamics of Bataille's mystical turn.

Lacan gave *Seminar XX* within a different historical and political context than that out of which Bataille's and Sartre's writings emerged. Bataille's wartime writings respond indirectly to the political failures of the 1930s and to the devastation of World War II. Lacan's conception of the real (that in human experience resistant to representation and symbolization)[13] insistently displaces history, just as his reading of mysticism is decontextualized (and if we take it as a reading of Bataille, the particular historical moment in which Bataille's mysticism appears is completely effaced). Moreover, the only politics with which Lacan shows overt concern are the politics of psychoanalysis and, to a lesser extent, of feminism.[14] So although it is useful to read Bataille and Lacan side by side, it is important to remember that their works emerged out of different historical and political contexts and that they display differing conceptions of history and politics. Bataille contests the claims to unity and wholeness of a broadly Hegelian conception of history and/or of Sartrean engagement (which he sees as still implicated within that idealist project). Lacan shifts the site of contestation from theology and history to psychoanalysis (and, in part, feminist politics). Moreover, in claiming the necessarily double nature of language, Lacan always contests psychoanalysis from within, holding together cataphatic claims to meaning and their apophatic unsaying more closely than does Bataille (perhaps because psychoanalysis is established less firmly than the kinds of historical, theological, and philosophical claims unsaid and/or contested by Bataille).

For Lacan, mysticism is linked closely to the issues of sexual difference and the unconscious, and particularly to the ramifications of Freud's radical understanding of the unconscious for psychoanalysis's claims to scientific status and knowledge. *Seminar XX* not only suggests ways of understanding Bataille's mysticism and its relationship to the salvific mystical narratives of the Christian tradition, but also relates these issues to the two fundamental tenets of psychoanalysis rejected by Simone de Beauvoir (explicitly, if not always in practice).[15] Beauvoir criticizes psychoanalytic accounts of sexuality because she believes that they ground human subjectivity too thoroughly in an unchanging and unchangeable body. Similarly, she fears that Freud's conception of the unconscious vitiates existentialist claims to freedom and agency.[16] Lacan offers another account of freedom, however, in which psychoanalysis as the study of the unconscious and a discourse of desire makes a limited form of freedom possible against scientific determinism.[17] Bataille was hesitant during the war to equate the mystical and the feminine, but for Lacan there are close ties between mysticism, the body, sexual difference, and the unconscious. Lacan will suggest, as does my brief historical sketch of the emergence of mysticism within Christianity, that there is something about women's position within a phallic symbolic order that gives them particularly good access to the two-sided nature of mysticism, the body, and God.

Lacan's arguments are emphatically not grounded in a conception of women's "nature" and its greater proximity to the "mystical." Rather Lacan argues that sexual difference, like subjectivity itself, is a function of language. In *Encore*, he shows how male-dominant culture has invested a particular bodily difference with enormous symbolic power by associating the phallus with the transcendental signifier through which meaning is stabilized. Lacan at times even seems attuned to the real force this symbolic power carries within male-dominant institutions and discourses. He suggests that only by loosening the illusory hold of the body over language can other, more egalitarian symbolic systems be formed. With this suggestion, Lacan does not claim that the subject can ever attain the wholeness and unity it desires—the gap in being that is fundamental to the speaking subject is, for Lacan, ineradicable. Yet the phallus as the symbol for that lost wholeness and plenitude, a symbol always in danger of being mistaken for that on which its iconicity rests (the penis), is historically contingent. Women, symbolically effaced by the primacy of the phallus (although they can still "take it on" and speak from the side of the masculine subject), are in a particularly apt position to see the emptiness of its claims and to experience the jouissance that emerges in and through that recognition.

IS AND IS NOT THE PENIS   *Encore* focuses on the issues of feminine sexuality, knowledge, and the scientific character of psychoanalytic discourse.[18] The latter issue frames the seminar as a whole, subverting the claims for knowledge found within it; for, Lacan asks, if the unconscious is truly unconscious, how can we ever claim to know anything about it? Lacan not only repudiates claims to the transparency and knowability of the Cartesian subject, but questions the extent to which the Freudian subject can ever be anything other than a mystery to itself.[19] Freud, Lacan argues, was revolutionary in that he radically decentered the subject through his discovery of the unconscious: "The Copernican revolution is not really a revolution. If the center of a sphere is supposed to constitute the master point in a discourse that works only by analogy, the fact of changing the master point, to make the earth occupy it, or the sun, has nothing in it which would subvert that which the signifier *center* conserves of itself" (E 43; S XX 43).[20] According to Lacan, Kepler and Newton brought about the real revolution. In showing that the planets moved in an elliptical path Kepler questioned the function of the center itself and with it the concept of totality.[21] Newton switched the relevant metaphor from revolving, which always involves a return to that which existed before, to falling. Freud is revolutionary (if we can even continue to use that term) in this radical way, for the very foundation of knowledge is undermined by the unconscious. The problem, of course, is to stay true to that discovery and that decentering. Any attempt to know the unconscious, any science of the unconscious, implicitly undercuts the radicality of its own claims. To the question "Why engage in analysis at all?" Lacan suggests that something other than or in addition to knowledge is at stake.

The issue linking this epistemological problem with that of female sexuality is raised by the title of the seminar itself, *encore* (again, more), but also *en-corps* (in the body). The question of female sexuality is one of knowledge, and for Freud it is always tied to the unconscious. Throughout *Encore*, Lacan raises doubts about Freud's attempts to "conquer" woman and the unconscious, those "dark continents." Lacan questions the status of the body in psychoanalytic teaching and the extent to which both Freud's analyses of the woman issue and the scientific character of analysis depend on the body, despite (in Lacan's view) Freud's better judgment.[22] At times, Lacan suggests that Freud's reversion to the body results from his desire to reassert an organic base for his theory, thereby consolidating its claims to scientific status. And yet there is another appeal to the body in Freud through which the gap in being constitutive of subjectivity is made known—the body, like woman, jouissance, and God is always already double, not quite two and yet clearly not one (E 104; S XX 114–15). In this case the appeal is to the body as the site of an affect—a bodily, psychic, and emotive response—irreducible to the referential terms of language and representation. Here, Lacan suggests, psychoanalysis does its real work.

Like God, the body, woman, and jouissance, psychoanalysis is double. It is both a scientific discourse, one "supposed to know," and the site of a bodily affect that goes beyond knowledge and can never be reduced to its terms. In its twofold status, psychoanalysis is like mysticism, which is both a language and an experience of divine presence, and the subversion of that unity through the emergence of a mystical affect that goes beyond "the all," or perhaps better, that marks its always unassimilable remainder. Just as the Christian mystical tradition moves between cataphatic attempts to name the divine and apophatic "unsayings" of those divine appellations, so Lacanian psychoanalysis both purports to know the unconscious and apophatically unsays that knowledge through a language in which affect takes precedence over reference. This unsaying and its effects, according to Lacan, are the fundamental goal of psychoanalysis. Yet it is a goal that, paradoxically, depends for its articulation on a host of scientific (some would say pseudoscientific) claims.[23] Hence Lacan's insistence on diagrams, Borromean knots, and logical notation, as, for example, in the following diagram through which he purports to demonstrate the "logic" of psychoanalytic views of sexual difference.

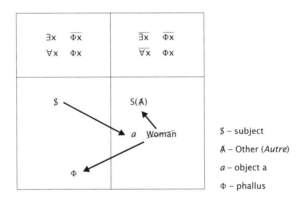

According to Lacan, the goal of his teaching is rendered visible through this diagram; his work,

> inasmuch as it pursues that aspect of analytic discourse that can be
> said and enunciated, is to dissociate the *a* and the *A*, by reducing the

former to that which is of the imaginary and the latter to that which is of the symbolic. That the symbolic is the support of that which was made God, is beyond doubt. That the imaginary supports itself by the reflection of like to like, is certain. And yet, *a* lends itself to confusion with the S($\cancel{A}$) beneath which it is written on the board, and it has done so by means of the function of being. It is here that a split, a detachment remains to be made. And it is in this that psychoanalysis is something other than psychology. For psychology is this unachieved split. (E 77; S XX 83)

This formulation of the goal of Lacan's teaching depends on his understanding of sexual difference, for the diagram schematizes the two gendered subject positions available within our current linguistic system and the ways in which they relate (or, as Lacan will argue, do not relate) to each other. Lacan claims that the position one occupies in language is not dependent on the kind of body one has. Anatomically or genetically defined male and female human beings can occupy either the position of the masculine speaking subject or that of the feminine speaking subject (this flexibility is most clear, however, with regard to men). The difference between the two positions, as Lacan's notations show, is in the relationship they take toward the phallus, the transcendental signifier within male-dominant society through which meaning is fixed and grounded (although, as Lacan will go on to argue, the transcendental signifier is always empty and hence meaning always loosed once again). As the transcendental signifier, the phallus takes the place of God or truth, that which ensures that the reality signified by language and language itself always coincide. The notations on the upper register of the diagram denote the different relationships that subjects can have with the phallus. On the left, "for every *x*, the property ϕ applies to *x*" denotes the masculine speaking subject, who is thereby said to have a phallus. On the upper right, we find "for every *x*, the property ϕ does not apply to *x*"; thus the feminine speaking subject is defined as one who does not have a phallus.[24]

In a crucial move away from Freud, Lacan insists that sexual difference is a function of language (although in his later work he does come to see that the kind of body one has matters, given the cultural determinants put on different kinds of bodies).[25] Language makes us subjects (as opposed to simply animal organisms). Lacan insists that Freud needs language in order to explain the move from body to psyche, for the shared worlds into which we are born as human subjects cannot be conveyed through the body (this would be to remain at the level of animal, bodily existence) nor through some kind of unmediated shared unconscious (such as Jung's collective unconscious, whose transmission from generation to generation can never be adequately accounted for), but only through language. We are born as subjects in and through language, and subjectivity itself is a function of language. So Lacan insists that for human subjects *as* human subjects, there is no prediscursive reality; rather "men, women and infants, these are only signifiers" (E 34; S XX 33). Despite, and in part because of, the fact that there is no subjectivity outside language, there are important differences between the signifiers "man" and "woman." Whereas man is fully encapsulated within symbolic discourse and the signifier, woman is "not all" (or "not everything") within the symbolic, and thus "there is always something in her which escapes discourse" (E 34; S XX 33).

Lacan's privileging of the phallic signifier raises questions about the relationship between the phallus and the penis.[26] Despite the repeated protestations by Lacan and his followers that the phallus is not the penis, it remains the case that for Lacan the phallus is not merely an arbitrary signifier; it is also iconic and so dependent for its significance on the anatomical part.[27] The understanding of woman as "not all" within the phallic economy is dependent, at least metaphorically, on her apparently absent penis. This conflation of the imaginary and symbolic phallus, Kaja Silverman argues, creates an impossible political situation for women:

> If primal repression is effected through the paternal metaphor, then the subject must be understood as entering language only through the inscription of the phallus in a privileged position within the unconscious, and the Name-of-the-Father in the place of meaning above the bar of repression. All attempts to alter this state of affairs, and the system of sexual differentiation which it secures, would have as their consequence the ruination of subjectivity.[28]

If subjectivity depends on the Name-of-the-Father and the primacy of the phallus, then any challenge to the phallic order is destructive of subjectivity itself. Feminism would then be the enemy of human sociality and culture (and Lacan sometimes seems to offer just this reading of feminism and its putatively destructive capacities).

Yet this privileging of the phallus as penis contradicts Lacan's claim that anyone, regardless of their bodies, can occupy either side with regard to the phallic function—he insists that you do not have to be literally castrated in order to occupy the side of the "not all" (E 70; S XX 76). This claim suggests, by extension, that you do not need to have a penis in order to occupy the position of the male speaking subject.[29] Silverman argues that beginning with *Seminar VII* Lacan moves away from the centrality given to the phallus and the Name-of-the-Father in his discourse on the subject. Silverman is able, then, to criticize Lacan's early work, which is based on an inappropriate privileging of the phallus, with the apparent approval of Lacan's later seminars. The phallus and the Name-of-the-Father suffer a "theoretical diminution"; they no longer define the subject but become one of many signifiers that retroactively give significance to the lack inhabiting the speaking subject.[30] Whether one accepts this assessment of the movement of Lacan's work as a whole, *Encore* clearly interrogates and undermines the phallic function as constitutive of sexual identity and as privileged in symbolic discourse, for Lacan insists on the contingency of the phallic and paternal functions and, therefore, of the configuration of sexual difference created within any discourse governed by them (E 87; S XX 94).[31]

Throughout *Seminar XX*, as Jane Gallop points out, Lacan insists on using "old words" whose meanings are problematized by analytic discourse: God, the soul (l'âme), love (l'amour), being (l'être), woman (la femme).[32] The problematization of these terms involves, in each case, questioning male privilege that derives from an illusory identification between the penis and the phallus. In *Encore*, Lacan analyzes patriarchal culture and exposes the fantasy of fullness and plenitude on which male power is based. He argues that the aim of psychoanalysis is to undo precisely this conflation (between the *a* and the *A*, arguably the phallus and the Name-of-the-Father as the site of castration). In making this argument, Lacan clearly does not ignore the *reality* of male power (or of the slippage between the penis and the phallus that, in a sense, consolidates this power); rather, by characterizing woman as "not all" within the phallic economy he clarifies both her powerlessness with regard to the symbolic *and* the source of the illusion of terrifying female power that in part fuels men's desire to dominate and oppress women (through the confusion of *la femme* with the object *a*, with the phallus, and with the *A*).[33]

THE LITTLE *a* AND THE BIG *A*

The goal of analytic discourse and teaching, then, is to expose and maintain the distinction between *a* and *A* and so to reveal the lack of relation between the sexes. Male subjects (Ꞩ in the diagram) only relate to the object *a*, not to woman herself (la femme), and this lack of relation becomes emblematic, for Lacan, of the illusory nature of male claims to wholeness and plenitude. Lacan suggests, moreover, that only when the fantasmatic nature of relationships between the sexes is recognized, does love of the Other becomes possible.

Lacan's theory of the imaginary, the symbolic, and the real is crucial to his account of the goal of analytic discourse in *Encore*.[34] The symbolic can best be understood as the network of signifying systems in which we live—most crucially language, but also human practices and social institutions insofar as they carry meaning.[35] Lacan argues in an early and widely influential paper, "The Mirror Stage," that in order to enter into language the child must be constituted as a subject in relationship to the world.[36] The child's apprehension of its image in the mirror becomes emblematic, for Lacan, of that moment in which it first recognizes itself as a subject with fixed boundaries. Yet in recognizing the mirror image as itself, the subject apprehends itself as other. The gap between the subject's experiential body and its image in the mirror marks the gap or split constitutive of subjectivity. In the moment that makes language acquisition possible, the subject is formed as other than itself, and its desire for a lost, imaginary plenitude is born. The endless movement of desire mimics the open play of signification made possible, for Lacan, by the gap between subject and object, body and psyche, signifier and referent. The signifying function of language depends on this gap, and yet because of the gap meaning can never be fully stabilized, nor the subject's desire completely fulfilled. For Lacan, the desire for plenitude is both imaginary in the sense of "make believe"—Lacan insists that for the speaking subject as speaking subject there is no access to a prediscursive reality—and the source of the imaginary register, that aspect of the psyche that always desires wholeness and plenitude.[37] The real, on the other hand, emerges only with the detachment of the imaginary from the symbolic, effected by the rupturing of the conflated a and A.

The relationship with the object a, then, is an imaginary relationship in which the split subject attempts to stop up the lack in its being made (apparent) by entry into language. In another early account of the subject's constitution and entry into language, Lacan associates the taking on of the patronym (the father's name) within male-dominant cultures and the paternal prohibition central to Freud's account of the castration complex.[38] For Freud, the threat of castration is central to the development of the male child, who resolves his Oedipal complex (the desire to possess the mother and kill the father) through recognition and internalization of the mother's castration and the threat to his own penis posed by the father. Lacan, as we might expect, is significantly less interested in this literal account of castration anxiety than was Freud. Instead he argues that in being named by the father, we are always already constituted as lacking, split, and, hence, symbolically castrated. Lacan's formulation, Nom-du-père, brings together the Name and the No of the Father, uniting the symbolic and the prohibition through which castration anxiety emerges in Freud. Again we see how Lacan takes a Freudian theory that is not immediately applicable to female infants and argues for a symbolic reading that both recognizes the reality of male-dominant culture and is able to account for the female child's entry into language. Yet Lacan maintains the gendering of Freud's account, for he asserts the masculinity of the split subject who puts himself on the side of the phallus and in relation to the object *a*. This move enables him to describe male privilege even as he denaturalizes it.[39]

According to this reading of subjectivity, to speak requires that one relate to the phallus as one's own. Although the subject is always already castrated in that it exists in language, it is haunted by the fantasy of fullness (because it seems to have the phallus in the form of the penis) and the continued threat of its loss (a loss that, according to Lacan, has always already occurred). Together, this fantasy and threat give rise to the subject's ceaseless desire for the object *a* through which it believes it can fill in the gap in its being. Whether seen as the mother's breast (the original lost object), "the representation of the object of lack," or "the metonymic object of desire,"[40] the object *a* is never radically other than the subject but is that which the subject believes it has lost/will lose, an image of itself that would unify it/ensure its unity, if such unity could be attained.[41]

So within the phallic economy, according to Lacan, the subject that defines itself as male can "only ever relate as a partner of the object *a*" that is seen to be "on the other side of the bar" (E 75; S XX 80), the side of woman. The necessity of man's relation to the object *a* is a result of the subject's identification with the phallus, which creates a fantasy of totality by threatening the subject with castration if it should attempt to situate itself on the side of the woman (*la femme*), defined as "not all" within phallic discourse. Yet Lacan shows that this fantasy of totality exists only if the object *a* is confused with the Other (*Autre*); if the subject recognizes that the object *a* as object of desire is merely a fantasy of its desire for unification and totality, then it can attain the "truth" of its being, namely, that it is split and lacking in being. The phallus, according to Lacan, is not a signifier of the mastery of meaning, the transcendental signifier, as he claims in earlier texts—or it is not only that;[42] it is also "the signifier for which there is no signified, and which, in relation to meaning, symbolizes its failing" (E 74; S XX 80). In this sense, the phallus merely duplicates the inevitable split in the subject and leads it to the object *a* in an always impossible attempt to reach the Other through the mediation of this object. The object *a*, then, in its confusion with the Other (*Autre*), renders the phallus transcendent; or perhaps better, in that the penis becomes confused with the phallus, and the illusion of the fullness of being is maintained by its possession, the penis is the part object par excellence, one that is rendered transcendent by the apparent unity between symbol and material reality.[43] Yet, Lacan insists, despite this illusion of unity, the gap between the penis and the phallus remains. As the transcendental signifier of a male-dominant symbolic, the phallus simultaneously supports and undermines the male speaking subject: it generates and maintains the fantasy of male plenitude and the sexual relation and at the same time signifies their impossibility.

In arguing that the Other and the object *a* must be separated by psychoanalytic discourse, Lacan points to the necessity of recognizing the fantasmatic character of any claim to phallic mastery and totality. "By means of the function of being," of a being that continually desires to "return" to the fantasmatic totality and unification of the imaginary, the always partial and inadequate object of desire is elevated and confused with the Other (*Autre*), the unknowable locus and source of signification. This myth of male totality and mastery (only the claim to complete mastery is mythic, it should be noted, since within male-dominant society a great deal of male power is real), Lacan argues, is the source of knowledge and of the fantasy of genuine relations between the sexes. Thus in the realm of sexuality, the male believes that the object *a* is woman (*la femme*) and, therefore, that woman is subject to him. Lacan insists throughout the seminar, moreover, that from the standpoint of the masculine speaking subject, woman is always maternal, for she is always that lost object to which the infant subject wishes to return. As imaginary locus of plenitude, the mother is also phallic, and hence a source of both desire and fear.

ON THE OTHER SIDE

The attempt to recover this lost object of desire (and fear) is displayed in the psychoanalytic debates on feminine sexuality (by both male and female analysts), which attempt to discover the locus and source of feminine jouissance within the anatomy of woman. Lacan dismisses these debates in a characteristically high-handed fashion. He insists that feminine jouissance cannot be located (and cannot therefore be constrained by analytic discourse), and that women themselves experience it but "know nothing about it" (E 71; S XX 76). This claim sounds like—and was probably intended to be—another male attempt to silence women, yet we miss something crucial if we dismiss Lacan too quickly.

Lacan argues that if we associate feminine jouissance with the body, we are in danger of making the same error as the masculine speaking subject who confuses the phallus with the penis. Phallic jouissance rests, it would seem, on the imaginary conflation of penis and phallus; feminine jouissance—that ecstatic pleasure experienced by subjects who refuse to stand on the side of the phallus and instead relate to that which is "not all/not whole/not everything"—can be experienced but not known (and although bodily, is not tied to any particular bodily organ). Lacan both contests feminist claims to knowledge in order to reassert his own, and undermines any claim to the value and possibility of knowledge.[44] Lacan's discourse, not surprisingly, is double-edged. On the one hand, he upholds a position of male psychoanalytic mastery, reinscribing the phallic father who is supposed to know against the claims of feminists; yet at the same time, this position of mastery claims its own emptiness, a self-subversion Lacan reads in terms of femininity.[45]

In articulating what it means to reject the masculine speaking position and occupy the side of the "not all," Lacan makes his (in)famous statement that within phallic discourse "woman [la femme] can only be written with the [la] crossed through. There is no such thing as woman [la femme] since of her essence—I've already risked the term, so why should I think twice about it?—of her essence she is not all [pas toute]" (E 68; S XX 72). Within phallic discourse, woman is "not all" insofar as she does not have the phallus; she is partial and always lacking from the standpoint of an imaginary male totality. On the other hand, woman marks the "truth" of psychoanalytic discourse, and of the phallus itself; every speaking subject is always already partial, split, and separated from the object of desire.[46] The phallus, when unveiled, reveals a lack, just as the phallic mother in Freud's (imaginary) discourse reveals a lack when exposed to the eyes of the child. Once again, when Lacan puts the la in la femme under erasure, he indicates the nonrelation between the sexes and the tenuous nature of the feminine speaking position from within a discourse governed by the phallus. Man relates not to woman but merely to the a, the la in la femme, and as such he relates not to an Other (Autre) but to himself (or his image, the phallus, or the object a).[47]

Whereas the male subject is supported and duplicated by the phallus, woman has no support within the phallic economy. This instability is reflected in the doubleness of woman's position: "Woman relates to the $S(\cancel{A})$, and it is in this that she is already doubled, that she is not all, since, on the one hand, she can also relate to Φ (E 75; S XX 81). In other words, woman can relate to that which is within the phallic economy, the phallus, or she can relate to that which is "beyond the phallus." This double relation raises the question of the difference between occupying the male side and relating to the object *a* and occupying the female side and relating to the phallus. From the standpoint of the theory of the subject, the two positions are analogous; but whereas the male speaking subject believes he *has* the phallus, female subjects can make this claim only through a kind of masquerade. Although the male claim to have the phallus is also illusory, it is upheld by the culturally sanctioned slide between the phallus and the penis. All of this suggests that within a male-dominant symbolic, men may be able to occupy either side of the divide, but women are relegated to the side of the "not all," even if they choose, from that site, to relate to the phallus. Despite Lacan's overt claims, within a symbolic governed by the phallus, women are defined by their bodies in ways that men are not.

There are many ways in which women can take on the phallus for themselves. In an earlier text, "The Meaning of the Phallus," Lacan argues that women can become the phallus through a masquerade in which they become "the signifier of the desire of the Other."[48] In this way, women support the male fantasy of sexual relation by renouncing the "attributes of femininity," of a sexuality that is other than male.[49] By taking on the phallus, women accept the male definition of being as that which has or is the phallus, and so support the male fantasy of totality (hence the close relationship between women's role as the object *a* and the phallus). On the other hand, as that which is "not all" within the phallic economy, woman has a supplementary jouissance that cannot be contained within the phallic realm and that, by virtue of its existence, reveals the partial and fragmentary character of that realm. For this reason, feminine jouissance is frightening and threatening to male subjectivity—or, to be more exact, to the male ego created by the coalescing of *a* and *A*.

Lacan insists on the unknowable character of feminine jouissance (although at the same time maintaining his right to explain the "something more" insofar as it has to do with God). If feminine jouissance could be known, circumscribed, and reduced to the terms of the phallic economy, it would no longer be in excess of those terms. Lacan therefore undermines his own allusion to Bernini's statue of St. Teresa of Avila (a picture of which appears on the cover of the French edition of the seminar). He begins with an apparent reduction of the experience of jouissance to biological terms ("you only have to go and look at Bernini's statue of St. Teresa in Rome to understand immediately that she's coming [jouit], there is no doubt about it" [E 70; S XX 76]) but then adds something more. Charcot and his circle, Lacan writes, attempted to "reduce the mystical to questions of fucking. If you look carefully, it's not that at all. This jouissance that one experiences and about which one knows nothing, might this not be that which puts us on the path of ex-istence? And why not interpret one face of the Other, the God face, as supported by feminine jouissance?" (E 71; S XX 77). Charcot, it should be added, attempted to provide a pictorial (and highly eroticized) representation of feminine hysteria in order to reduce it to that which could be seen.[50] Through his allusion to Charcot, Lacan undermines the "simple" male solution to the phenomenon of feminine jouissance and raises questions about the allied attempt to reduce it to that which can be captured in an image.

Yet characteristically, Lacan does not simply dismiss the visual—and with it the body and its representations. Rather he allies his own style with the baroque—of which Bernini's statue is one of the great exemplars—and argues that it does not offer images of "copulation" but "is the regulation of the soul by corporal radioscopy" (E 105; S XX 116). Providing an X-ray vision of the soul through its representations of bodily excesses, the baroque unleashes affects that go beyond genital sexuality, to which earlier psychiatric and psychoanalytic researchers reduced the mystical.[51] The baroque saints that fill churches throughout Europe are "martyrs," Lacan writes, witnesses of "a more or less pure suffering" that is at the same time a jouissance (E 105; S XX 116). This jouissance exceeds "copulation"—and hence normative, heterosexual, genital intercourse—and as such, Lacan says, is obscene.[52]

Two things are important here. First, Lacan's discussion of the baroque makes clear that his notion of jouissance cannot be reduced to genital sexuality and that, like Bataille's inner experience, it brings together anguish and ecstasy.[53] Second, the baroque, as a seventeenth-century style of artistic expression, is an art of excess in which the materiality of the signifier and/or of representation constantly threatens to supersede signification and mimesis. Similarly, Lacan's baroque style impedes interpretation, suggesting that what is crucial in his work is not signification but that which goes beyond. Lacan here makes clear that the ultimate goal of psychoanalysis is not scientific knowledge but the eruption of affect in and through language. ("'I ask you to refuse what I offer you because that is not it.' That formulation is carefully designed to have an effect, like all those I proffer" [E 101; S XX 111].) The issue of the scientific status of psychoanalysis leads Lacan to Christianity and to the baroque (a return to the sources of Christianity, he says), for Christianity, like psychoanalysis, deals with that which cannot be fully known; hence the discourses and representations of Christianity, like those of psychoanalysis, work toward some other end.

Within psychoanalysis, these effects are engendered primarily through a language that Lacan associates with the mystics. Commentators continually complain that Lacan ignores the evidence of the mystics themselves, but in fact he points his listeners and readers to mystical writings, arguing that his own texts share some crucial quality with them:

> Even so, there is a small connection when you read certain serious people, by chance certain women. I am going to give you a bit of information, that I owe to a very nice person who read it and who brought it to me. I pounced on it. I must write it on the board, otherwise you won't buy it. It's Hadewijch of Anvers, a beguine, what one so quaintly calls a mystic. (E 70; S XX 76)[54]

> These mystical ejaculations are neither idle gossip nor mere verbiage, they are in sum the best thing you can read—note right at the bottom of the page—*Add there the Écrits of Jacques Lacan*, because it is of the same order. (E 71; S XX 76)

Lacan not only wants his audience to read mystical texts, but counts his own writings among them, partaking in what Certeau calls the mystic's *modus loquendi*.[55]

Lacan's association of his own linguistic practice with mysticism is related, I think, to his distinction between the goal of analytic discourse, which is capable of being formulated, and an aspect of his teaching that cannot be articulated. The unarticulated aspect of his teaching is, most obviously, the practice of psychoanalysis and the discourse between the analyst and the analysand (arguably restaged through the seminars themselves).[56] Yet Lacan also points here to an aspect of his writing and performing practice that resists the very terms of analytic discourse. Lacan argues that language not only refers but also has effects irreducible to the terms of referential communication (E 126; S XX 138).[57] Lacan's discourse communicates an effect that is an affect—jouissance—brought about by the dissociation of the *a* and the *A*.

Throughout *Seminar XX*, Lacan insists on the inadequacy of analytic discourse in the face of feminine jouissance and the *Ⱥ*. This symbol marks, in Jacqueline Rose's formulation, the "place of *signifiance*, Lacan's term for this very movement in language against, or away from, the positions of coherence which language simultaneously constructs."[58] As Bruce Fink shows, this movement in language against meaning is also the site that makes meaning possible. *Signifier* means "to mean" or to "signify"; *signifiant* can be either an adjective, "meaningful," or a noun, "signifier." For Lacan, signifiers both carry meaning and are non-sensical, for they exist "apart from any possible meaning or signification that they might have." They are nonsensical, moreover, in that they are material. When the materiality of the sign takes precedence over its signifying function, the communication of meaning is endangered. *Signifiance*, then, refers both to the fact of having meaning and to the fact that signifiers exceed meaning and have effects other than meaning effects (S XX 19). Woman, always herself double, relates to this doubled place that both enables signification and resists it.[59]

In disarticulating the object *a* and the *A*/Other, analytic discourse functions like a negative theology and sets the stage for the emergence of feminine jouissance within and through language. Analytic discourse works to expose the "false" images (object *a*) that have become attached to the place of the Other, and through these negations it generates an effect irreducible to knowledge. The place of the Other within any symbolic system, like that of woman within a phallic, male-dominant symbolic, is always double:

> Since all of this comes about thanks to the being of *signifiance*, and since this being has no place other than the place of the Other (*Autre*) that I designate with a capital *A*, one can see the cockeyed-ness of what happens. And since it is there too that the function of the father is inscribed in so far as it is this which relates to castration, one sees that while this doesn't make two Gods, it doesn't make for one alone either. (E 71; S XX 77)

The doubleness of God is the source of the doubleness of mysticism. The split subject desires an other through which it might become whole, and it conflates that desire with the very operation of language through which subjects are constituted as split and other than themselves. Mysticism and psychoanalysis are allied discourses that attempt to speak that desire and strive incessantly after an absolute other through whom it might be fulfilled. Yet this unstinting quest for the absolute exposes the subject's own lack and the always absent and unattainable other through which it is brought into existence. Christians, like psychoanalysts, Lacan argues, "are horrified by what was revealed to them"; thus the suffering soul exposed by baroque excesses always attempts to cover over its theft of being and the lack from which its ecstatic anguish emerges (E 103; S XX 114). In the same way, the pretensions of psychoanalysis to scientific status are both an ineluctable movement toward oneness and fixed meaning and an evasion of the real.

The subject's lack is grounded, paradoxically, in the body—for the disarticulation of the *a* and the *A* (and hence of the penis and the phallus) exposes the gap between the body and its speech. The jouissance that goes beyond the phallus is described by Lacan as a jouissance of the body, as the bodily affect that emerges through the exposure of the rift in the body that enables it to speak:[60]

> The gap inscribed in the very status of jouissance as dit-mension
> of the body, in the speaking being, that is what reemerges in Freud
> by the test—and I am not saying anything more—that is the ex-
> istence of speech. There where it speaks, it comes. [*Là où ça parle,
> ça jouit.*] And that doesn't mean that it knows anything, because,
> even now in the new order, the unconscious has revealed nothing
> to us about the physiology of the nervous system, nor about the
> process of getting an erection, nor about early ejaculation. (E 104;
> S XX 114–15)

In the mirror stage, the gap between the subject and its imago makes possible the split between thing and sign that is necessary for language acquisition. Yet at the same time, that gap opens up the endless deferrals through which language signifies and that require language always to operate at a remove from the material realities to which it refers. In other words, precisely that distance between body and sign that makes signification possible irrevocably splits the signifier from the body and its referents. Desire for the One, the transcendental signifier in which signifier and signified are united, marks our desire to bring language together with the world of bodies to which it refers. The gap in our being will always lend itself to the coalescing of the signifier and signified and to the fantasy of totality on which this coalescence is based. In language itself, Lacan argues, "there is something of the One," a striving after the point that would fix meaning.

Lacan insists on the impossibility of this desire but at the same time suggests that language can bring the body and signification together in another way: through the affect that it communicates performatively. Psychoanalysis and mysticism, by separating the object *a* from the site of the Other, allows the jouissance of speech itself to emerge. Lest this promise of a relationship between signifier and signified be mistaken for a new fantasmatic union of the subject with its Other, Lacan insists that only the subject who recognizes the function of the father as an obstacle and as the place of castration is able to renounce the fantasy of totality and sexual relation and so move to the place of the woman and feminine jouissance. The "goal of satisfying the thought of being" is accomplished only "at the price of castration" and, hence, through relinquishing the goal itself (E 104; S XX 115).

The place of feminine jouissance is both within and beyond language, for it is the effect of language—or at least of a certain kind of language—on the speaking body. This jouissance of the body belongs neither to the imaginary nor to the symbolic, but to the real, which is both the source and result of the tension between these two registers. The coalescing of *a* and *A* is an attempt to reduce this tension; it is, according to Lacan, the foundation of both the reality and pleasure principles, which, despite their opposition in Freud's text, are seen to work together in the construction of a "reality" always under the shadow of the imaginary. In dissociating the object *a* and *A*, Lacanian psychoanalysis heightens the tension between the symbolic and imaginary and creates a space for the emergence of the real in and through language, the emergence of a nonphallic jouissance. When it/*ça* speaks, the speaking body experiences jouissance, an anguished ecstasy in which the real, the recognition of the endless gap in being and the ceaselessness of desire, emerges.

In his wartime writings, Bataille shows how the reader's or viewer's encounter with representations of self-dissolution can elicit the shattering of the psychic subject, experienced both as anguish and ecstasy. Lacan's allusions to mystical texts and to the baroque, together with his account of the goal of psychoanalytic practice, suggest that in his work jouissance is elicited through the engulfing of representation by the materiality of the sign. The baroque is an art of excess in which that represented is always in danger of being overwhelmed by ornamentation (for example, on Bernini's statue, the folds of Teresa's gown overtake her figure); yet this excess, Lacan tells us, is a witness to the "more or less pure suffering" of the subject. In other words, when the materiality of the sign (whether pictorial or linguistic) takes precedence over representation and signification, meaning is effaced, and the subject, as a linguistic, meaning-communicating being, is shattered. The collapse of the distance between the sign and its referent, rather than effecting the unity or plenitude of being, effaces meaning, signification, and subjectivity.[61]

Like Bataille's account of inner experience, Lacan's account of the subject and its jouissance is poised between masochism and trauma, for he describes an originary trauma, endemic to speaking beings and productive of both suffering and pleasure.[62] There is a difference, however, between this originary trauma, in which we are constituted as split, and the power of traumatic events to shatter the subject despite its bodily survival.[63] Whereas Bataille's account of the real associates it explicitly with the traumatic violence of history, Lacan, one might argue, dehistoricizes and depoliticizes Bataille's inner experience, positing it as a universal "truth" of subjectivity.[64] For Lacan, this universal truth is, in the end, bodily. The body is the support of the subject, yet when the subject begins to speak it is always already at a remove from its own body. The body is always already ec-centric to the subject itself. Psychoanalysis, like mysticism, by exposing the fantasmatic quality of all appeals to unity and wholeness, engenders linguistic effects that are, Lacan tells us, affects; they are bodily and so return us through language to the body (E 127; S XX 139).[65] Ec-static subjects can never be fully united with themselves or with the Other, but through psychoanalytic and mystical practices, the real emerges, "the mystery of the speaking body, the mystery of the unconscious" (E 118; S XX 131).

BEYOND THE FATHER: LACAN AND FEMINISM

Within the present male-dominant, phallic symbolic and imaginary the work of psychoanalysis is necessarily—and curiously, given Lacan's antifeminism—allied with feminism. Lacan insists that the separation of the *a* from the *A* has crucial implications for women, for the fantasizing movement through which the object *a* and the Other are conflated occurs at the expense of woman: "For the soul to come into being, she, the woman, is differentiated from it, and this from the beginning. Called woman (*dit-femme*) and defamed (*diffame*)" (E 79; S XX 85). In other words, woman is reduced to nothing while also serving as the foundation and substance of male immortality, being, the soul (*l'âme*), and love (*l'amour*).[66] The terms "passive" and "active," with which Freud attempts to replace the suspect (because essentialist and biological) "masculine" and "feminine," like all concepts tied to the acquisition of knowledge, share in the fantasy of creating a sexual relationship.[67] Lacan argues that in this gross polarity "that makes matter passive and form the agency which animates it, something, but something ambiguous, occurs at the same time; that is that this animation is nothing other than that *a* whose agency animates what?—it animates nothing, it takes the other for its soul" (E 76; S XX 82). The soul, then, which secures man's immortality, comes out of the *hommosexual* and the a-sexual. Man takes the *a* (and hence *la femme*) as his soul, denying woman's existence and agency in the very movement through which he secures his own being. Lacan argues, moreover, that for male subjects, woman is always ultimately reducible to the mother; the male child negates the phallic mother and takes her phallus as his own, even as it is constantly threatened by the paternal function. The God of this male economy, who both threatens and supports male subjectivity, is in the image of man. By separating the object *a*, which is supported by the image of like to like, from the Other, the unknowable source and locus of signification and of the paternal metaphor, the identification of man with God is, Lacan argues, no longer possible (although I will argue below that in continuing to associate the *A* with the paternal, Lacan fails to fulfill completely his own injunctions). Thus Lacan gives an account of the aims of psychoanalysis that demands it be feminist in its subversion of the fantasy of masculine plenitude. (Psychoanalysis strives against *any* fantasy of plenitude, however, and as such is critical of any feminism that replaces the fantasy of phallic wholeness with an account of woman as "all.")[68]

In an earlier seminar, Lacan makes the enigmatic claim that "in a certain register it is not God who is not anthropomorphic, it is man who is begged not to be so."[69] The goal of analytic discourse is not to strip God of certain attributes but to show man that he himself has never really possessed them. By separating the imaginary and the symbolic registers and exposing the fantasmatic character of the male relationship with the object *a*, Lacan lays bare the character of the paternal metaphor as an obstacle to the imaginary unity of like to like; yet he still calls that "castrating" principle paternal and so is in danger of perpetuating the fantasy of male totality that he sets out to undermine. Lacan insists on the contingency of both the phallic and paternal functions. He argues that the gap or lack at the root of subjectivity will always remain, that it is endemic to language insofar as language implies a movement away from the body toward the psychic and symbolic; nonetheless, the male privilege with regard to the fantasy of wholeness and mastery that is inscribed within the patriarchal symbolic is not necessary to the symbolic's operation. Everything in Lacan's seminar leads to the conclusion that another symbolic, one not governed by the phallus and so not privileging male subjects, is possible. Yet as long as Lacan continues to use the language of castration, lack, and paternity to name the gap in the subject, he continues to privilege masculinity and to uphold the very fantasy his work sets out to subvert.

At the same time, in making woman emblematic of the "truth" of psychoanalysis, Lacan makes it too easy to confuse woman with the Other, and so to generate new fantasies of fullness and plenitude: hence the return of the phallic mother, whether for male speaking subjects who stand castrated before her or for female speaking subjects who wish to identify with her. In other words, feminists are not the only ones in danger of propagating fantasies of female wholeness.

Fantasies of either masculine or feminine wholeness are dangerous, for Lacan, because they render love and hate impossible. Hence despite my earlier suggestion that Lacan dehistoricizes and depoliticizes the mystical, history and politics ineluctably return at the site of the relation between the sexes: "So that one could say that the more man is able to lend woman in confusion with God, that is to say that which she joys [jouit], the less he hates [hait], the less he is [est]—the two spellings should be used here—and, since after all there is no love without hate, the less he loves" (E 82; S XX 89). Man takes his being from woman (la femme, the object a who gives man his soul, l'âme), yet if he merely reverses this movement and ascribes to woman that which he associates with God (again confusing the a with the A), he once again renders love impossible.

Mark Taylor's readings of Lacan are emblematic of the problems that can emerge when one refuses to separate fully the a and the A, for Taylor confuses woman with God, going to the point of finding a goddess in Lacan's text.[70] Taylor takes Lacan's comments in Encore as an approbation of the confusion between woman and God, and hence as a call for detachment rather than love. Yet Lacan does not repudiate love; rather, he speaks against that in the phallic economy that makes real love between the sexes—and between human beings—impossible. He claims that la femme does not exist and is not all; one of the reasons he insists on this point is that for men, woman always becomes a fantasmatic object of desire, an object a. Taylor's goddess is just such a fantasy, one that involves him in the very confusion between the object a and the Other that Lacan's discourse attempts to subvert (although by calling the jouissance of the body feminine, Lacan helps generate the confusion).[71] The difference between Lacan and Taylor is the same as that which exists, according to Lacan, between John of the Cross and Angelus Silesius—between the man who becomes la femme, subverting his own subject position within the symbolic, and the man who, while remaining male, confuses la femme and God. In this confusion, the always contingent phallic function and the privilege it accords seem necessary (E 132–33; S XX 145–46), although they are ascribed here not to man, or to the paternal function, but to the goddess as phallic mother.

This figure, the Other/woman/mother endowed with phallic wholeness, is one response to the subject's recognition of its own lack or castration. Rather than simply submitting to that lack, the subject fantasizes a god/dess in which plenitude and unity exist—even as this god/dess threatens the unity of the subject itself. The specter of the phallic mother in Taylor's texts marks both the return of a phallic fantasy of wholeness and the fear of woman as the other who threatens male claims to totality. Lacan describes woman as castrated and hence as emblematic of the lack endemic to subjectivity; yet as Taylor's (mis)readings of Lacan show, the fantasy of the phallic mother, who both guarantees and threatens the subject's plenitude, lies embedded within the figure of the castrated mother. The same double figure can be seen throughout Bataille's work, from *Story of the Eye* through the wartime writings and his postwar theories of religion and society. Although Bataille, like Lacan and Taylor, insists that we are all always already castrated, lacking, lacerated, and split, a fantasy of fullness and phallic plenitude is inscribed within this very account of subjectivity. What is required is a symbolic system in which the site of the transcendental signifier/*signifiance* is not symbolically associated with either sex—one in which the privileging of particular kinds of bodies is no longer made viable by their symbolic association with that which tends to wholeness in language.

FEMINISM, MYSTICISM, AND BELIEF

3

FEMINISM AND PSYCHOANALYSIS IN FRANCE

In 1974, the Belgian-born psychoanalyst, philosopher, and linguist Luce Irigaray published *Speculum of the Other Woman*, a radical rereading of Freudian psychoanalysis and selected texts from the Western philosophical tradition. In
Speculum, Irigaray repeatedly demonstrates that these theories of the "subject"
have "always been appropriated by the 'masculine'" (SA 165; SO 133).[1] Although the book does not analyze Lacan directly, it is both dependent on and
marks a crucial shift away from Lacanian psychoanalysis. Irigaray both accepts
Lacan's dictum that within the Western tradition "woman" does not exist and
challenges the inevitability of her absence. Like Lacan, she points to mysticism
as "the only place in the history of the West in which woman speaks, acts, so
publicly" (SA 238; SO 191). Irigaray mimes mystical texts in order to hear what
is said within them and in order to uncover the outlines of another imaginary
that begins to emerge through the feminization of Christ. Lacan, too, insists
on the importance of mystical texts, comparing his own writings to those of
the mystics and declaring that the jouissance of the body effected by the operations of these texts is the goal of psychoanalysis itself. For Lacan, however,
this jouissance cannot be reduced to the imaginary or to the specificities of the
sexed body; it is feminine only in that it is not phallic. This is the key point
on which Irigaray challenges Lacan, although in *Speculum* her critique remains
implicit.

When, in 1974, Irigaray proposed to teach a course based on *Speculum*
at the Lacanian-controlled department of psychoanalysis at Vincennes, with
which she was affiliated at the time, Lacan refused.[2] The only rebellions Lacan

tolerated, apparently, were his own.[3] The following year Irigaray published an essay in which she responded directly to the theories of femininity and sexual difference in *Encore*. In "Così fan tutti" (reprinted in *This Sex Which Is Not One*), Irigaray makes explicit and accentuates her divergences from Lacan. Whereas in *Speculum* she concedes that both women and men can go to the place of mystical jouissance, at least within the terms of a still phallogocentric order, in "Così fan tutti" Irigaray insists on the links between the kind of body that one has and one's ability to speak "from the other side." This move makes explicit what was implied in *Speculum*—in the mystic's writings an imaginary grounded in the form of the female body emerges, one that can serve as the support for feminine subjectivity just as the phallus has upheld the illusion of a whole, unfragmented subjectivity for men. Irigaray insists that this imaginary does not involve either a complementarity between male and female, or the phallicization of women; rather, it is a supplementary imaginary that will forever alter the logic of the psyche. At issue between Lacan and Irigaray, then, are unsettled questions of central concern to psychoanalysis concerning the relationship between the body, the psyche, and sexual difference. A brief account of debates concerning feminine sexuality within Freudian psychoanalysis, particular in France, will help clarify what is at stake in the struggle between Lacan and Irigaray.

Between 1905 and 1932, Freud repeatedly argues that there is only one libido. This argument puts him in the paradoxical position of denying any close connection between anatomy and libido in the development of sexual difference, while also asserting the role of the penis—or at the very least of our unconscious representations of it—in sexual development. Freud argues that in early childhood, the penis and the clitoris play parallel roles, to the detriment of girls who think that they bear castrated organs. The results of this purported deficiency are wide-reaching. Both boys and girls, according to Freud, take their mothers as the first love object and resent the intrusion of the father between themselves and the mother. For boys, this Oedipal configuration is resolved by the threat of castration: the boy discovers—in a startling visual moment—that girls and women lack a penis; he then fears that the father, who does have one, will castrate the boy as punishment for his attempted theft of the mother and usurpation of the father's position. The paternal prohibition and concomitant threat (or imagined threat) of castration are then internalized by the boy and serve as the foundation for the superego. For the girl child, on the other hand, who is already castrated, the Oedipal complex is much more difficult to resolve. As a result, most women do not develop as potent a superego as do most men, accounting, Freud argues, for their moral and cultural deficiencies.[4]

Freud insists that the girl's move from her initial maternal love object and privileged erotic zone (i.e., from the clitoris to the vagina) occurs not through some natural instinct that determines the site of pleasure and object choice, but through a psychically organized reappraisal of the best way to attain a penis for herself (unless she refuses to recognize that she does not have a penis, in which case, according to Freud, she has a "masculinity complex" that will lead, typically, to either lesbianism or feminism).[5] Thus girls turn from their mother, who they come to hate as castrated and to blame for their own deficiency, and toward their father, who, they believe, can provide them with a boy child and hence with a surrogate penis. If you cannot be a boy, the logic of the unconscious posits, you can at least have one. In this way, Freud both removes sexual difference and sexuality from anatomy, arguing that they are functions of desire and its unconscious representations, and centers this sexual romance on the primacy—particularly the visual primacy—of the penis.

This contradiction, together with the lack of fit between clinical evidence and Freud's arguments (namely, with regard to the girl's apprehension of the vagina and hence of her own anatomical specificity) gave rise early on in the psychoanalytic movement to competing accounts of sexuality and sexual difference. What came to be known as the Viennese position (Freud's view, supported by early psychoanalysts like Jeanne Lampl de Groot, Hélène Deutsch, and Marie Bonaparte) was challenged by Karen Horney in Berlin and by the so-called British school, represented by Ernest Jones and Melanie Klein. Horney argued that the idea of penis envy was rooted in masculine narcissism. She was particularly troubled by Freud's claim that the desire for motherhood was only compensatory, insisting instead that women's sexuality, which included the drive toward motherhood, was a "primal, biological principle."[6] Ernest Jones, one of the few "men analysts with feminist views," also argued for a specifically feminine libido or sexual drive and claimed that the girl child could apprehend the vagina (presumably not through vision, but through touch). Bisexuality, for Jones, results not from a single libido's dual possibilities in its object choice, but from the existence of two distinct libidos within each individual. The prevalence of one or the other—usually but not always tied to anatomical sex—determines object choice. In addition, Jones reconfigures the threat of castration as a fear that the inappropriate deployment of sexuality will be punished by its disappearance (aphanisis).[7]

In France, the Viennese school of Freudian orthodoxy held sway throughout the first half of the century, in large part due to Marie Bonaparte's influence, and little new work on the issue of sexuality and femininity was produced by French psychoanalysts.[8] Elisabeth Roudinesco argues that because of Bonaparte's extreme Freudian orthodoxy and the nationalistic conservatism of her opponents (in a Maurrassian tradition that upheld Catholic ideals of marriage, family, patriarchy, and virginity), "the first coherent book to take female sexuality for its subject could not have been written by a member of the French psychoanalytic community."[9] Instead, as we have seen, it was the work of Simone de Beauvoir, whose book *The Second Sex* appeared in 1949. For the first time in France, the feminist project of emancipation and equality was connected explicitly to the issue of sexuality. Although critical of psychoanalysis, Beauvoir's account of women's political and cultural destiny is thoroughly sexualized, using the terms that psychoanalysis made available. At the same time, she struggles against the constraints of existing psychoanalytic explanations for femininity and argues that one is not born a woman but becomes one. Beauvoir thereby, as Roudinesco notes, offers a third alternative to "Freudian phallicism" and "Jonesian naturalism," what Roudinesco calls "Beauvoirian culturalism."[10]

Lacan's first contributions to the psychoanalytic theory of female sexuality emerges out of this context. His early work, in which he insists on the centrality of the phallus only if it is carefully distinguished from the penis, is an attempt to resolve the dilemmas of Freud's position. Phallic power is not about anatomy, Lacan argues, but about desire—even the maternal desire that brings the subject into being is read, by Lacan, as phallic.[11] For Lacan, desire itself is phallic, and yet, paradoxically, it is a sign of lack and hence marks the split inherent to subjectivity. Subjects are constituted through the desire of the other, and are thus subjected to the other—yet at the same time, the conflation of the penis (as object *a*) with the Other as the site of prohibition and desire enables men to identify with the other through whose desire they are constituted. As a result, they cover over the lack in their being (the sign of desire itself) and assert a mastery and fullness of being that, while fantasmatic, has real material consequences.[12]

Encore responds not only to the psychoanalytic debates surrounding female sexuality, but also to the feminist appropriation of psychoanalysis tentatively begun by Beauvoir and more actively pursued by feminists in the wake of the French student rebellions of May 1968. Almost immediately, some women brought the ideologies and practices of this emancipatory political struggle together with a desire for sexual liberation inspired by *The Second Sex*. Roudinesco argues that the mainstream of this post-May radical feminism oscillated between Beauvoirian culturalism and Jonesian naturalism, that is, it held both that one becomes a woman and that there is an innately given feminine libido.[13] A minority view soon emerged, however, that contested Beauvoirian culturalism in favor of a position closer to Lacan's; the debates central to this group appear in the margins of Lacan's 1972–1973 seminar.

The term "feminism" was itself the subject of intense criticism in the France of the late 1960s and 1970s. Some women within what the press came to call the "Mouvement de libération des femmes" (MLF) rejected the label "feminist," arguing that in its desire for equality with men, mainstream feminism participated in the idealization of masculinity and the denigration of femininity.[14] In essence, these women repeated, although in the service of a radically different political agenda, the arguments made earlier by culturally conservative psychoanalysts like Édouard Pichon, who claimed that the feminist movement was deeply phallocentric (and hence would be better called "hoministe").[15] In one form or another, this is the line that would be adopted by the most famous so-called "French feminists"—Hélène Cixous, Julia Kristeva, and, although less categorically, Luce Irigaray. Whereas Cixous forthrightly asserts "I am not a feminist" and Kristeva argues that feminists evince a wrong-headed desire to take over "phallic power," Irigaray recognizes that feminism may at times be a necessary term, but she prefers to speak of women's struggles or liberation movements (in the plural).[16]

For our purposes, the most important group within the MLF was *Psychanalyse et Politique*, headed by Antoinette Fouque. (In 1979, under Fouque's leadership, the group attempted to appropriate legally the name *Mouvement de Libération des Femmes*, much to the consternation of other groups and nonaffiliated members of the MLF.) *Psych et Po*'s activities were similar to those of the consciousness-raising groups found among U.S. feminists and included sponsorship of informal groups in which women could "speak out" about their sexual oppression.[17] Psychoanalytic terminology was widely, if not always rigorously, used, in large part due to the influence of Fouque, who was in analysis with both Lacan and Irigaray.[18]

Fouque produced little written work, making it difficult to uncover the full extent of her tremendous influence on this period of French feminism. But as Roudinesco argues, through "a multitude of tracts, slogans, posters, and mimeographed sheets," the MLF, under the leadership of Fouque, "implemented . . . a new mythology of the feminine articulated with a doctrine of sexuality."[19] Women, according to Fouque, were innately homosexual. *Psych et Po*'s goal was to rediscover women's homosexuated sex, understood as a second libido that was activated in the girl's relationship with the mother. As Roudinesco puts it: "For [Fouque] one did not become a woman; one *was* a woman.

But one also rediscovered oneself as a woman by moving beyond the phallic, or feminist, phase of sexuality conceived in the image of the paternal phallus. It was then that access to a genital phase of reunion with 'homosexuation' loomed."[20] One of the main tasks of the women's liberation movement was to create the space in which this feminine, homosexuated libido, grounded in female anatomy, might express itself—hence the importance of writing (*écriture* in the broad sense, derived from Derrida, of any signifying practice) in which the specificity of feminine sexual difference might be voiced.[21]

Lacan knew of this antifeminist feminist work through a variety of channels. Fouque was in analysis with Lacan from 1969 to 1975.[22] The idea of an *écriture féminine* was also brought directly into Lacanian circles by another of his analysands, Michèle Montrelay. In an article published in *Critique* (the journal founded by Bataille in 1946 and at the time edited by Jacques Derrida) and later republished in *L'ombre et le nom* (1977), Montrelay moves beyond the Lacanian position on phallocentrism and argues for a transformation of female sexual pleasure into writing. Through a reading of Marguerite Duras's *The Ravishing of Lol V. Stein*, Montrelay defines primary femininity as a shadow, an ineffable dimension of the psyche repressed by psychoanalysis itself. Unlike Fouque, however, Montrelay argues that this primary femininity exists within the psyches of both men and women and that both should seek to uncover this lost and primary site of eroticism.[23]

Through various connections, then, Lacan was, as Roudinesco puts it, "caught up in the feminist blaze":

> He had heard Antoinette's message, and although he had taken up none of her affirmations, he showed himself to be sensitive to the new rhetoric of *écriture féminine*. He reaffirmed the primacy of phallocentrism, defined supplementarity once again, and denounced the error of the naturalist prejudice: *La femme*—woman—existed only if the *la* were barred. In other words, there were *des femmes*—women— and a specifically female mode of sexual bliss whose impossibility to be articulated was revealed by the mystics.[24]

What Roudinesco misses in this summary of Lacan's encounter with feminism is his insistence that the mystics do articulate something; as I have shown, Lacan argues that at least some mystical texts communicate affects that psychoanalysis also seeks to engender.

Lacan refuses Fouque's claim that there are two sexualities grounded in male and female anatomy; however, what Lacan says of mysticism suggests that he does subscribe to something like Montrelay's notion of a female eroticism that is supplementary (and irreducible) to the phallic economy. Lacan insists that this feminine jouissance cannot be tied to anatomy. Feminine jouissance does not depend on a relationship to representations of the vagina or the uterus that would replace or supplement the masculine subject's relationship to the phallus. To posit this kind of complementary jouissance, Lacan suggests, would merely reduplicate the terms of the phallic order for women; women might then conflate the little *a* (the vagina, for example) with the big *A* (some iconic representation of the vagina taken to be a transcendental signifier) in ways parallel to men's fantasmatic claims to unity and identity with the phallus as transcendental signifier. For Lacan, this conflation would simply repeat and reinforce the fantasmatic situation that he wishes psychoanalysis to disrupt—a disruption he believes is enabled by the feminine position as "not all." Lacan also refuses to posit two libidos, if we take the libido to be an innate sexual drive. Instead, he argues that in a symbolic and imaginary governed by the phallus, desire can inscribe itself in relationship to the phallus or in relationship to that which lies beyond the phallus (the Other/*Autre* that is only fantasmatically confused with the phallus and/as the object *a*). Desire, brought into being by the gaze of the Other/*Autre*, can move in two directions (not reducible to the sex of one's object choice), a doubleness that points to a way out of phallicism (although we still need to ask, for whom?).

In calling the seminars of 1972–1973 Encore, Roudinesco argues, Lacan indicates "that he was still present, he the *maître*."[25] In *Encore*, Lacan claims that psychoanalysis is the discourse through which feminine jouissance speaks; thus he displaces the MLF as the site of *écriture féminine*. (This displacement becomes most explicit when Lacan tells his audience that "a lady from the MLF" objected to his claim that there was no sexual relation and that it was necessary for him to explain to her "what it is all about" [E 54; S XX 57].) What can be known about this other desire and jouissance, moreover, is specified by psychoanalysis—Lacan is both the one who knows and the one who, in subverting the discourse of knowledge and mastery, brings about the jouissance of a speech that goes beyond the phallic. The doubleness of discourse then becomes an alibi for the doubleness of Lacan's own position as the one who both masters discourse—the one supposed to know—and inevitably experiences and generates knowledge's dissolution in affect.

Both Irigaray's *Speculum of the Other Woman* and *This Sex Which Is Not One* (1977) are deeply influenced by Antoinette Fouque and the MLF. Roudinesco, for example, characterizes Irigaray's project as an attempt to bring together the MLF's concern for the liberation of female sexuality with a more explicitly egalitarian political agenda derived from Beauvoir.[26] In addition, Irigaray brings together a Derridean attack on the logocentrism of Western metaphysics and its subordination of the other with a reading of Freudian and Lacanian phallocentrism as grounded in the suppression of femininity and of women. Her critique of Lacanian psychoanalysis becomes most explicit in "Così fan tutti," where Irigaray argues that within the phallogocentric symbolic and imaginary, femininity as a psychic construction and as anatomical femaleness are linked more closely than Lacan admits. Whereas Lacan claims that language splits the subject from his or her body, thereby making bodies largely irrelevant to the formation of subjects as sexed, Irigaray demonstrates that the slide between the penis and the phallus supports male subjectivity and, of necessity, weakens female claims to occupy the position of the masterful, meaning-producing speaking subject.

"Così fan tutti" poses a major challenge to Lacan's claim that his psychoanalytic discourse effects feminine jouissance in ways parallel to the writings of Hadewijch or Teresa of Avila. If, Irigaray argues, the kind of body you have matters within a symbolic and imaginary order dominated by the phallus, then one's ability to speak from the side of the "not all" is compromised by the possession of a penis, regardless of its ultimate inadequacy. More importantly, Irigaray insists that Lacan never names or acknowledges the specificity of the female body. In fact, he explicitly refuses women the possibility of developing an imaginary (and, through its slippage into the A, a symbolic) grounded in the specificity of their own bodies, one that would provide a fantasmatic support for women's subjectivities parallel to that provided by the phallus within male-dominant society. All of this leads to Irigaray's central charge: Lacan makes woman emblematic of the situation of human beings, thereby lifting feminine jouissance from genital specificity (although not, I would argue, away from the body itself as the site of speech) and, thus, away from male dominance. Yet in articulating the truth of human subjectivity in terms of lack and castration, the phallus continues to be privileged. "The problem is that they pretend to make a law of this impotence itself and continue to submit women to it" (CS 101; TS 105).[27] As I will show in more detail in chapter 6, Irigaray insists that by reading subjectivity and desire in terms of lack, Lacan maintains the centrality of the phallus and castration to the formation of human subjectivity.

According to Irigaray, the tasks of a feminist philosophy are twofold. It must subvert the privilege accorded to the phallus and masculinity, through a feminine miming and mirroring of phallogocentric discourse that subtly displaces its claims to mastery, totality, and wholeness. As I have suggested, this remains a profoundly Lacanian project. Yet Irigaray insists that feminist philosophy must also articulate a new symbolic and a new imaginary grounded in the morphology of the body marked as female within male-dominant discourse.[28] In other words, Irigaray pursues the project explicitly rejected by Lacan in *Encore*. So, as I will show in chapter 6, the reading of Christian mysticism she offers in *Speculum* sees in the feminized figure of Christ the emergence—within a still male-dominant discourse—of a powerful feminine imaginary and of a transcendental signifier reconfigured in woman's image (and therefore affording a conflation of *a* and *A* that supports female subjectivity). Already in *Speculum*, however, Irigaray insists that this feminized male figure, who becomes woman through being wounded, remains grounded in phallogocentrism. Any reading of subjectivity in terms of lack, Irigaray argues after *Speculum*, participates in the logic of castration and so valorizes the phallus even if the claim is made that no human subject ever actually possesses it. This critique, applicable, as I will show, to both Bataille and Lacan, extends to an analysis of the logic of sacrifice that subtends Christianity (as well as other religious traditions). In rejecting phallogocentrism, Irigaray argues, feminist philosophy must also reject the sacrificial logic to which, she claims, it inevitably gives rise.

Following her more decisive break with Lacan, signaled by "Così fan tutti," Irigaray rejects the claims to gender fluidity on which her reading of Christ as a feminized divinity are based. As chapter 7 shows, she then calls for more completely feminine avatars of the divine, arguing that divine women are required if women are to achieve full autonomy and freedom. This move is tied both to a rejection of the logic of the "all" and the "not all" that Irigaray sees as endemic to phallogocentrism, and to her insistence on the close relationship between the kinds of bodies we possess, the imaginary representations of those bodies made available through the psychic imaginary, and the possibilities for autonomous subjectivity made possible through the conflation of the imaginary and symbolic. In other words, the slide between the phallus and the penis that supports male subjectivity within cultures centered on the phallus must be mirrored, Irigaray suggests, by a slide between the vagina, the lips, and the mucous membrane and their psychically and culturally valorized representations (although the term "representation," with its emphasis on the visual, is inadequate to express the range of sensory apprehension Irigaray wishes to articulate within the feminine imaginary and symbolic registers).[29]

In all of her work, then, Irigaray attempts to articulate feminine imaginary and symbolic realms that will replace psychoanalysis as the master discourse through which subjects are constituted.[30] One might argue, from a Lacanian perspective, that her feminist philosophy becomes the site of both fantasmatic mastery and of its unsaying or deconstruction through the separation of the imaginary and the symbolic, the *a* and the *A*. Yet against Lacan's insistence that the *A* (the Other through which meaning is generated and always already destabilized) should not be confused with the *a* (the part objects that serve as the illusory basis for human claims to fullness and mastery), Irigaray suggests that when the imaginary is feminized, it operates in different ways than do the supports of masculine subjectivity within phallogocentric societies. By reconfiguring subjectivity through a female morphology, the seemingly inescapable movement between "the all" and the "not all" will be surpassed in a subjectivity of fluidity and openness to the other. Irigaray insists, in other words, that feminism will not be a new phallicism in which the penis is simply replaced with the vagina (or the clitoris, or some other body part) as the site of plenitude, for with the rejection of the penis goes the emphasis on wholeness and lack. Thus feminism will transform not only the imaginary but also the symbolic, and with it the very configuration of the symbolic order as premised on lack and its denial.[31]

In part 1 and part 2, I argued that two divergent conceptions of the mystical operate within the texts of Bataille, Beauvoir, and Lacan: the desire to be all and the recognition that one is not everything converge in the mystical. Lacan argues that this convergence is the result of the fact that the transcendental signifier through which meaning is fixed is always empty; it is the site both of meaning's production and of *signifiance*, the place where the gap between signifier and signified that is necessary to the operation of language becomes apparent. In other words, that which makes meaning possible also renders it forever unstable, and that instability is experienced, Lacan argues, as the jouissance of the speaking body. Bataille emphasizes the emergence of something like this anguished ecstasy through the encounter with "what is there": the broken body in all of its meaninglessness and/or the erotic body in ecstasy. In both cases, something occurs in the experience of ecstasy or jouissance that cannot be reduced to meaning, an experience that occurs through language but is not reducible to its generally acknowledged functions.

In part 3, I examine Irigaray's fear that in associating the real with lack and castration, the real as possibility—as "a *physical reality* that continues to resist adequate symbolization" and as the "sensuous pleasures of ecstatic human interaction"—will be lost (CS 105; TS 106).[32] In other words, as Patricia Huntington argues, Irigaray differentiates between "(a) fantasies which lapse into fetishizing the real and (b) those which open productive pathways to richer forms of sociality or a richer eros binding human beings together."[33] For Huntington, Irigaray's reading of the real as the realm of physicality and possibility "marks the substantial difference between static and dynamic, masculinist and feminist, substitutive and critical forms of utopianism."[34] Irigaray thus subverts the rigid distinction between imaginary and symbolic and binds together more closely the body and the body imago, arguing that Lacan underestimates the extent to which the form in which bodies are represented within the imaginary supports the subjectivities of certain kinds of bodies while denying that of others. In this way, Irigaray argues for the necessity of elaborating a feminine imaginary and symbolic, grounded in the specificity of the female body, if women are to achieve subjectivity. This conflation of imaginary and symbolic is not a fetishization and/or phallicization of women, Irigaray argues, because it is premised on the recognition, rather than the denial, of the partiality and openness (both temporal and figural) of subjectivity.

Yet the real is the site both of possibility and of the potential foreclosure of possibility in experiences of limitation, mortality, and loss. The utopic fantasies that, Irigaray argues, are necessary to the formation of subjectivity are always in danger of foreclosing these realities in that they conflate lack with loss, thereby repressing affective responses to the latter.[35] In *Speculum* Irigaray does argue for the traumatic effects of feminine subject formation under patriarchy. Yet loss and its affective outcome are not simply the result of political and social injustice. Rather, loss is endemic to our experience as embodied, mortal beings for whom the body is the site of both possibility and limitation.

According to Freud, primal loss (or its threat) evokes two kinds of response: fetishism, in which the idea that the (boy) child might lose his penis is disavowed; and hysteria, in which desire (presumably, in Freud's account, desire for the father and, hence, for a penis) is repressed. We can read Irigaray and the responses to her work as dephallicized renderings of these mirroring neuroses. We can take her problematic insistence on the primacy of sexual difference as a fetishization of the categories of "woman" and "sexual difference" that refuses to acknowledge the reality of loss and thereby effaces other differences constitutive of embodied subjects and, with them, the deeply ambiguous nature of embodied being. On the other hand, the insistent reading of Irigaray as a biological essentialist can easily be understood as a return of the repressed (the emotion generated by loss) in the form of a hysterical female body (this reading will be taken up in chapter 8).

Analysis of Irigaray's work and the responses to her work in terms of fetishism and hysteria, then, enables us to understand the close relationship between these two interpretive possibilities. However, as chapter 7 shows, there is a counternarrative in Irigaray's work, in which she implicitly recognizes these problems and insists on the necessity of both belief (allied with fetishism and hysteria) and its deconstruction. There are, arguably, two accounts of belief in Irigaray's work. In the first, belief is portrayed as a fetishistic disavowal of lack and of the loss of the mother('s body). To this understanding of belief, Irigaray opposes belief as risk, as an openness toward the other and the possibilities inherent in the real. Given these two accounts of belief, confusion emerges about how to understand the belief that Irigaray demands for women. At times, she suggests that the positing of "divine women" partakes in the fetishistic logic of belief and must ultimately be deconstructed, just as Lacan argues for the deconstruction of the male divine of Western monotheism and philosophy. Elsewhere, however, she seems to argue that the positing of a feminine divine necessarily involves a movement from fetishization to risk.

Despite her criticism of Freud and Lacan, Irigaray remains deeply indebted to them, and the role of belief in her work cannot be sorted out without reference to their thought. She continues to look to psychical representations of the physical body as the support for subject formation (because the bodily imago that emerges through the mirror stage is the basis of the subject) and insists that subjects are constituted primarily in terms of dual sex difference (because she insists that the human body is always and primarily sexed). If the mirror image is the first object of belief (and thus the first fetish), the problems of belief and of sexual difference are closely related. In other words, the central terms of the psychoanalytic debates concerning subjectivity and female sexuality remain in place within Irigaray's work, despite her critique of Lacan's phallicism and his valorization of lack and sacrifice. Irigaray thus maintains one crucial aspect of the logic of belief articulated by Freud and Lacan, in which the subject is constituted through his or her imaginary identification with a bodily imago always to some extent other than the body itself (although also always tied to the body). Thus for Irigaray, the subject is still a believing subject, and that in which she believes makes subjectivity possible. Although she attempts to overcome the alienating gap between the subject and her imaginary other, Irigaray cannot completely elide this gap without undermining the very external supports for subjectivity (in language, culture, and society) required by women if they are to become subjects. As I will argue in chapter 7, Irigaray ultimately succumbs to fetishism and demands belief in sexual difference itself (even as she continues, in other places, to demand the deconstruction of belief, arguing for its essentially fetishistic—and hence, in Irigaray's view, phallic—structure).

It may be that fetishism is not the problem and that in our fragility and finitude we require fetishistic (or alternatively, as I will argue in chapter 8, melancholic) supports for subjectivity, especially if we hold open the possibility of reconfiguring fetishism, melancholic incorporation, and belief in more mobile and multiple ways. Yet Irigaray's claim to the primacy of sexual difference, by effacing the multiple differences of bodies and subjects, is fetishistic in ways that risk dangerous exclusions. Moreover, the very claim that we cannot think the body without thinking sexual difference leads Irigaray to evade the specificity of bodies and of history that, ostensibly, she wishes to embrace. By reducing difference to sex, Irigaray both provides something in which one can believe, so advancing the cause of feminism, and potentially undermines her own political projects. Moreover, the repressed body, in all of its intractable specificity, will return.

As I will argue in the opening of chapter 6, the common critique of Irigaray as a biological essentialist is inapt and does not take sufficiently seriously either the psychoanalytic framework of her theory or the future-oriented and open-ended nature of her understanding of the imaginary. Yet, as I have outlined briefly here, Irigaray's attempt to generate an imaginary that will enable the slide between the symbolic, the imaginary, and the body perhaps inevitably gives rise to—even demands—precisely the misreadings to which her work has been subjected. Although the registers of the symbolic, the imaginary, and the body may be analytically distinct—and many of Irigaray's early critics, as I will argue, are surely mistaken in confusing them—at least part of the work of Irigaray's feminist philosophy is to undermine rigid boundaries between them. From the perspective of Irigaray's early work, in particular, the problem then would not be that her readers have confused the imaginary with the body, but that they have *rejected* this association.

An analogous misreading of women's lives and texts occurs in the later Middle Ages. When Beatrice of Nazareth's hagiographer set out to write her life, he based part of his work on her short treatise "The Seven Manners of Loving God." Translating this text from Flemish into Latin, he engaged in a series of misreadings that accented Beatrice's mystical body as the site of sanctity. As I will show in chapter 8, Beatrice's hagiographer merely follows a predominant strand of thirteenth-century hagiography that both hystericizes and fetishizes women's bodies, making them the object of belief for male hagiographers and their readers. Male hagiographers thus misread these women's lives and writings in ways both enabled and, if they are read carefully, resisted by women's own texts. A comparison of Beatrice's situation with that of Irigaray enables us to see that the misreadings of their work are symptomatic—motivated by the desires, fears, and beliefs generated by their texts and by the gender dynamics in which they are embedded. Both Beatrice and Irigaray, although in different ways, ultimately repress the body in its historicity, specificity, and ambiguity (as the site of both possibility and limitation) in favor of an ideal, future-oriented object of belief: the fully interiorized soul in the case of Beatrice; sexual difference or "woman" in the case of Irigaray.

Although Irigaray claims to ground subjectivity in the body, her increasingly insistent emphasis on sexual difference maintains an ideality through which she seems to hope to evade loss and mortality (and their association with the female body). Her critics are similarly unable to grapple with the body as the site of both pleasure and loss and fear the debilitating effects the cultural association of women with the body, and hence with death and limitation, has had on women.[36] These critics reject Irigaray (and her supposed essentialism) in an attempt to deny the body to which her work (poised between the body and the imaginary) always inevitably returns. Simply to refuse the association between the body, death, femininity, and women, however, cannot break the metaphorical link between them. What is required is a resolute attempt to think the body otherwise, as the site of possibility and limitation, pleasure and suffering, natality and death, for all human beings in all of our multiplicity and diversity.

FROM LACK TO FLUIDITY:

LUCE IRIGARAY, *LA MYSTÉRIQUE*

....

The Word became flesh so that I might become God.

ANGELA OF FOLIGNO

And if one objected to her that the Good being thus in her, she then
has no longer to receive it, she would respond in her ateleological way
that, for her, the one doesn't preclude the other.

LUCE IRIGARAY, *Speculum of the Other Woman*

MYSTICISM AND THE PRIMACY OF SEXUAL DIFFERENCE

In a 1990 essay on the philosophical writings of Emmanuel Levinas, Luce
Irigaray remarks that Levinas "has little taste for mysticism." She goes on to
speculate on the connection between "this lack of attraction and his conception
of sexual difference," asking: "Is mysticism not linked to the flesh in its sexual
dimension [*comme sexuée*]? But outside of mysticism, who is God? What is God?
What is the point of flesh without mysticism?"[1] Irigaray links mysticism, God,
the flesh, and sexual difference, implying that any viable conception of the
divine must be tied to the body and that the body cannot be thought without
sexual difference. Her questions to Levinas suggest that mysticism is the site
on which the divine becomes flesh, and, conversely, that without mysticism's
divinization of the body, flesh and sexual difference are without meaning.

According to Irigaray, mysticism disrupts the borders between body and
soul, immanence and transcendence, sensible and intelligible, and in doing
so is always marked by sexual difference. Moreover, unsettling the boundaries

between bodies requires recognition of "the irreducible difference of sex" (leaving one boundary, it seems, untouched). Levinas rejects mysticism because of his refusal to acknowledge woman as truly other than man:

> The transcendence of the other that becomes im-mediate ecstasy [*exstase instante, en-stase*] in me and with him (or her), Levinas appears never to have experienced. For him, the distance is always maintained with the other in love. The other is "near" to him (or her) in "duality." This autistic, egological, solitary love does not correspond to the shared [*à deux*] outpouring, to the loss of boundaries of the one and of the other by the passage of skin into the mucous membrane of the body, from the circle of my solitude to a shared space, a shared breath, by the abandonment of the relatively dry and precise contours of the exterior volumes of our bodies for a fluid universe where the perception of duality [*de la dualité*] becomes indistinct, and above all, by access to another energy, neither that of the one nor that of the other, but that produced together and as a result of the irreducible difference of sex. Pleasure between the same sex does not result in that immediate ecstasy between the other and myself.[2]

Irigaray here assumes that there are or should be two (at least, she sometimes adds) sexes and that these two sexes must be fully articulated in their difference before the dissolution of that difference in ecstatic unity can be attained. In order for women to exist as truly other than men—not only "biologically," but also socially, culturally, and symbolically (and to some extent the former depends on the latter)—Irigaray claims that they must find, rediscover, or invent a female divine. The mystical is both dependent on the existence of a female deity and the site on which she can be apprehended.

Irigaray's thought is defined by this complex intertwining of mysticism, belief, the body, and sexual difference. Moreover, these topics are the major source of conflict within and around her work. The most well-known debate concerns the issue of biological essentialism: the claim that there is an essential difference between men and women that is somehow grounded in the body.[3] The early reception of Irigaray in the United States and England tended to focus on this issue, one that defenders of Irigaray insist emerges more from the expectations and presuppositions of her readers than from her texts. Irigaray herself has been perplexed by the charges of biological essentialism, for *Speculum* and *This Sex Which Is Not One*, the early pieces that gave rise to these charges, do not make claims about real empirical women, but deal with woman as a philosophical construct both absent from and in excess of male discourse.[4] Although I will argue in chapter 8 that these misreadings are symptomatic of larger issues submerged within Irigaray's work and within feminist theory in general, I do think that, in part, the problem results from the confrontation between an empirically oriented readership and texts that talk about female bodies within a psychoanalytic and philosophical framework. More pointedly, as Tina Chanter argues, early Anglo-American readers of Irigaray interpreted her work through a particular deployment of the sex–gender distinction, in which sex is equated with the body and gender with culture and society. Within this version of the distinction between sex and gender, sex and the body are taken to be the unchanging ground onto which changing cultural and societal models of gender are erected.[5]

For Irigaray, as for many recent Anglo-American feminists, however, nothing is simply "given"; there is no such thing as an unchanging, ahistorical ground: neither the body, nor sex, nor nature itself.[6] Appeals to sex and to the body need not be essentializing, since the body itself is—at least in part—a historical artifact.[7] The ways in which bodies are sexed, moreover, has a history and hence is subject to change. Irigaray argues that ahistorical formulations of the body as the unchanging ground of subjectivity are the result of male-dominant forms of rationality in which men are associated with culture, reason, and transcendence, and women with the unchanging materiality, formless and inert, that grounds masculine subjectivity. Irigaray's appeals to female morphology, the form and image of women's bodies, must be understood within the framework of her historicizing presumptions, in which nothing exists outside of the discourses and practices that shape human experience.

As Margaret Whitford argues, since women are often culturally identified with the body, they must move through these reinterpreted and reevaluated bodies in order to attain subjectivity.[8] They must, in other words, change not only conceptions of femininity, but also understandings of nature, sex, and the body. In showing the possibilities for change within these apparently static categories, Irigaray undermines male-dominant philosophy's grounding metaphors and presumptions. Thus Irigaray's references to the specificity of the female body—the lips and mucous membrane, for example—are meant to offer imaginary and symbolic support for feminine subjectivity.[9] By creating a new imaginary based on the form of the female body rather than on that of the male, Irigaray hopes to generate the necessary conditions for a specifically feminine subjectivity. She insists that the transcendental conditions of subjectivity are bodily, that the body is sexed in a twofold way, and that even the psychic operations through which subjectivity is constituted are grounded in bodily morphologies. Whether as sensorially experienced or psychically configured, the body is the very site and support of human transcendence and subjectivity. Men have been able to ignore the bodily base of subjectivity through their projection of fleshliness and its limitations on to women. The transcendence of bodily limitations afforded human beings by their bodies, on the other hand, is disembodied and associated solely with masculinity. As women take on subjectivity as embodied beings, what Irigaray calls the sensible transcendental—a recognition that the body is the site both of limitations and of the transcendence of some of those limitations—radically reconfigures the conditions and possibilities of subjectivity itself.[10]

Another problem lurks within the charge of essentialism, however, one that neither Irigaray nor her defenders have yet addressed adequately. Within the context of American feminism, essentialism has been a term of abuse not only because of its apparent appeals to a body that lies outside of discourse, a mute realm of factuality that can supposedly ground female identity. Many critics of "essentialism" have also attacked very sophisticated psychological, cultural, and even historically informed accounts of female identity (one thinks of debates surrounding the work of Nancy Chodorow, for example, and some of the more recent critiques of Irigaray's work), for their apparent claim that all women share some essential psychological, sociological, or cultural features.[11] Although the suspicion may be that these forms of psychological, sociological, or cultural essentialism ultimately rest on biological claims, essentialism does not necessarily depend on such a move. (In the contemporary discourses surrounding transsexuality, for example, the claim is often made that an individual is essentially female despite having a male body. Recent surgical procedures allow the body to be altered when, so the argument goes, psychology or some other immaterial essence cannot be.)[12]

To avoid the confusion and rancor that have surrounded the debates around essentialism and to increase the precision of the discussions about Irigaray, the issue might usefully be recast in terms of the primacy of sexual difference. Thus many feminist theories agree that those identified as "women" within a given culture can be and in fact routinely *are* differentiated from those defined as "men" (although it is not at all clear, cross-culturally, that these are the only options).[13] However, how femininity and masculinity are inculcated and lived is not only historically variable, but also intertwined with the other differences salient within any particular culture. In the contemporary United States race, ethnicity, sexuality, and class are particularly conspicuous and powerful features of subjectivity.[14]

Irigaray's recent work shows that she is aware of this critique of claims to the primacy of sexual difference and rejects it. In language that should be read in light of her earlier reappraisal of nature and the body, Irigaray argues that

> sexual difference is an immediate natural given and it is a real and irreducible component of the universal. The whole of human kind is composed of women and men and it is not composed of anything else. The problem of races is, in fact, a secondary problem—save from the geographical point of view?—which means we cannot see the wood for the trees, and the same goes for other cultural diversities—religious, economic and political. (JAT 84–85; ILTY 47)

Irigaray here argues that sexual difference is the one universally experienced form of bodily difference and that bodies cannot be thought or apprehended without sexual difference.

A generous reading of Irigaray would interpret race as secondary not because it occupies a less prominent and constitutive role in the subjectivities of those whose lives are effected by it, but because racial differences are not always and everywhere accorded the same (if any) significance. To the argument that sexual differences, no less than those of race, are not always and everywhere accorded the same significance, Irigaray would counter that they are always recognized and accorded *some* significance. (Yet is not this also true of ethnicity? And of sexuality? And how would we go about verifying or falsifying such universalizing claims?) Irigaray's defenders argue, moreover, that no content is implied in Irigaray's assertion of the universality of sexual difference; thus she may be read as opening a space for the complexities of particular experiences of sexual difference as they are complicated by race, class, sexuality, or other salient markers.[15]

Yet Irigaray shows little active interest in theorizing those differences and their multiple ramifications on subjectivity. Moreover, her assertion of a sexual binary—male and female—as universal and irreducible seems at odds with her consistent deconstruction of the metaphysical binaries that underlie male-dominant culture. As critics have pointed out, her conception of the "becoming female" of the divine is increasingly premised on a model of male–female relationships that seems patently heterosexist (hence her claim, cited above, that "pleasure between the same sex does not result in that immediate ecstasy between the other and myself").[16] Others defend Irigaray, arguing that without fostering new forms of heterosociality, women can never hope to have the autonomy and subjectivity required for them to love themselves and each other.[17] Yet it is not clear how an emphasis on heterosociality can avoid reinscribing normative heterosexuality, however redefined and reimagined, and effacing the multiplicities of difference (sexual and other).

In "Questions to Levinas," Irigaray asserts that bodies in their sexual difference are the site both for recognition of the other and for mystical union with that other, leading, it would seem, to the dissolution of difference itself. Yet she insists that mysticism leads to and/or requires recognition of sexual difference; in mystical experience the divine becomes flesh, and for Irigaray it is impossible to think the flesh without sexual difference. Yet Irigaray's earliest text on mysticism pulls against any such simplistic identification of bodily difference with sexual difference, particularly if understood in binary terms. In *Speculum of the Other Woman*, Irigaray follows Lacan in seeing mysticism as the site of a jouissance that goes beyond the phallus. This feminine jouissance is tied to the speaking body, but without reference to any privileged site of sexuality or sexuation. Lacan argues that both men and women can occupy the position of the masculine speaking subject (who relates to the phallus) and of the feminine speaking subject (who occupies the site of the "not all" and thus engenders linguistic bodily effects that go beyond signification and beyond the conflation of the penis with the phallus on which male claims to mastery over signification rest). In *Speculum*, Irigaray follows Lacan, claiming that although women, because of the ways in which their bodies are inscribed within a phallic symbolic (as "not all"), have easier access to this feminine site, men can follow women there.

In *Speculum*, Irigaray argues that it is the feminized figure of the Godman, Jesus Christ, on whose body the feminine imaginary is inscribed and given symbolic value. Like many medieval and early modern Christian mystics, Irigaray posits a fluidity of gender differences that enables a series of complex cross-identifications and desires. Only in the 1975 essay "Così fan tutti" does Irigaray begin to insist that the language one uses is determined by the kind of culturally and genitally constituted body one has. In the same text, Irigaray argues that Lacan's reading of human subjectivity as lacking and "not all" is a result of the tyrannical hold of the phallic economy and its "law of impotence." On these grounds, Irigaray now rejects the wounded body of Christ as a figure of the feminine imaginary and demands that women need their own divine beings in order to achieve subjectivity.[18] A subjectivity grounded in the female morphology of the two lips, the mucous membrane, or the placenta, she argues, will be fluid and open—both imagistically and temporally—to the (sexual) other and will not experience the other's reality as a wound to its being (as masculine subjectivity has traditionally experienced femininity). Yet with this new fluid feminine subjectivity comes a reification of sexual difference—and, paradoxically, an idealizing movement away from the complexity and ambiguity of the body—foreign to at least some medieval and early modern Christian mystical texts and to Irigaray's early reading of them in *Speculum*.

Speculum offers deconstructive readings of the Western philosophical tradition, beginning with Freud ("The Blind Spot of an Old Dream of Symmetry") and ending with Plato ("Plato's *Hystera*"). The long central section of the book is made up of a series of chapters dealing with Plato, Aristotle, Plotinus, Descartes, Kant, and Hegel. These essays are framed by two chapters in which Irigaray argues that the subject of Western philosophy is always masculine ("Any Theory of the 'Subject'") and suggests the possibility of another subjective economy grounded in female morphology ("Volume-Fluidity"). Tucked in the midst of all this, between discussions of Descartes and Kant, lies "La Mystérique";[19] here Irigaray both analyzes and mimes mystical discourse, suggesting that within the Christian mystical tradition a feminine subject emerges, if only in provisionary form.

Speculum is shaped by Irigaray's debates with Lacan, with the feminism of equality she associates with Beauvoir, and with the deconstructive projects she will come increasingly to criticize as nihilistic (although she does not name them, one might see here a certain reading of Bataille and Derrida). She argues throughout *Speculum* for the existence of a "feminine imaginary," the repressed underside of masculine subjectivity and rationality, and demonstrates the ways in which uncovering this alternative imaginary radically decenters masculine subjectivity. The feminine imaginary is (at least) twofold: woman as the unspoken material support for male identity, and as the possibility for a new subjectivity grounded in another relationship to language. Like her contemporaries in the MLF, Irigaray explicitly rejects the male standpoint; at the same time, she argues that insofar as one asserts or assumes any theory of subjectivity one occupies this position (SA 165–82; SO 133–46). This quandary leaves Irigaray with the task of having to discover another way of writing and inscribing "femininity" within a discourse governed by the phallic desire for identity and sameness, a desire legitimated and seemingly fulfilled by the phallic masculine imaginary and its conflation with the symbolic (as the paternal metaphor or

Name-of-the-Father).[20] One can read *"La Mystérique"* as a response to Lacan's suggestion that mystical writings attest to a supplementary jouissance, made possible when one separates the imaginary and the symbolic and comes to recognize the split nature of all subjectivity.

Irigaray uses Lacanian psychoanalysis against itself, demonstrating the unconscious drives and desires that bring about its phallocentrism.[21] Woman occupies that place where consciousness "is no longer master" and so has access to the unconscious, the cave that provides the lining, backing, or foundation for (male) subjectivity. As the repressed other of male mastery, reason, and consciousness, the unconscious is feminized; rather than rejecting this association, Irigaray interrogates its significance. She therefore reads the mystic as embracing her otherness and finding a fantasmatic support for a new, feminine subjectivity in the figure of the feminized Son (SA 238–39; SO 191–92).[22]

Irigaray's subversion of Lacanian psychoanalysis can be seen already in the placement of *"La Mystérique."* Given the chronological ordering followed in the second part of *Speculum,* the mysticism chapter should precede the chapter on Descartes and hence occupy the structural center of the work as a whole; instead *"La Mystérique"* comes after Descartes. This chronological displacement both highlights the chapter's importance and raises questions about the relationship between the feminine imaginary and the origins of the modern symbolic subject in Descartes. Irigaray questions Lacan's claim that the imaginary is a retroactive creation of the symbolic; she thus reopens the possibility of a presymbolic realm to which the subject might have access. For Lacan, mysticism and feminine jouissance provide access to the real; they are shattering and ecstatic encounters with "that which is." Irigaray suggests that what constitutes the real for the masculine speaking subject is, in fact, the feminine imaginary (so for Bataille, Madame Edwarda's female sex and its analogue in the torture victims gaping wounds). For the masculine speaking subject, the female sex is a lack and a wound, the site of fascination and horror in which human mortality and death are encountered, the unknowable and indecipherable other that disrupts male fantasies of totality and mastery. For the feminine subject, Irigaray argues, representations of the female sex might, if they were to be reflected within a new symbolic order, serve as the fantasmatic support for her subjectivity.

This reflection of a feminine bodily morphology and hence of a feminine imaginary in the symbolic occurs, if only in compromised form, within the mystical writings of some medieval men and women. According to Irigaray, mysticism is that place "within a still theological onto-logical perspective" where

"she" speaks—or he, but only through "her"—about the bedazzle-
ment by the source of light, logically repressed, about the flowing
out of the "subject" and "Other" into an embrace of fire that con-
founds them as terms, about contempt for form as such, about mis-
trust for understanding as an obstacle to perseverance in jouissance,
about the dry desolation of reason. And, again, about a "burning
glass" ["*miroir ardent*"]. (SA 238; SO 191)

Irigaray thus finds the image of the mirror, so central to her analysis of women's
place within Western philosophy, within the Christian mystical tradition itself.
She argues both that women have served as the empty, passive surface in which
men have seen themselves reflected, and that this mirror, in its representation
and repetition of male subjectivity, can reflect men's words and images back
with a difference. This subtle subversion marks the difference that is femininity
within male-dominant society; Irigaray's mirroring and miming of male voices
and texts seeks to mark this difference textually.

In medieval thought, the enflamed/enflaming mirror represents the soul
when she empties and purifies herself in order to become the perfect reflective
surface for the divine. The French-speaking beguine, Marguerite Porete, for
example, calls her treatise *The Mirror of Simple Souls*. The soul becomes a mirror
of the divine and unites with "the all" that is God by emptying herself of all
createdness and hence of all being. Porete's use of the mirror image would seem,
then, still to be inscribed within a masculine discourse that reduces alterity to
the same. Yet if the self becomes nothing in order to reflect the divine, God is
also nothing. The mirror image, then, is both central to masculine discourse
and a source of its subversion. In the same way, Irigaray uses the image of
the enflamed mirror to spark her meditation on the multiple meanings of the
speculum—both identity-creating and destroying, support of male subjectivity
and cause of its subversion.

Irigaray's text alludes to and elaborates on other central metaphors of the
Christian mystical tradition, from the paradoxical interplay of darkness and
light to the mystic "touch."[23] As is often the case in Irigaray's work, it is not
always easy to decide what status she accords to these "metaphors."[24] She begins
by claiming that the men who attempt to follow women into this place that
supports and is repressed by consciousness and subjectivity take a "detour
through metaphors that hardly have the status of figures" (SA 239; SO 192).
Thus she follows the mystic's claim that the metaphors of mystical discourse are
inadequate to their object and are attempts to name an "experience" that shares

in an "immediacy of the all" (*immédiaté de tout*) (SA 244; SO 196). Language can only point beyond itself; anyone who attempts to follow the mystical way loses her/himself in this "a-typical, a-topical mysteria" (SA 239; SO 192). Here, Irigaray tells us, the lowliest are the most "eloquent."

It is not immediately clear if this eloquence is primarily linguistic or bodily. "*La Mystérique*" participates in the fluidity of sexual difference so central to Lacan in *Encore*; the mystic is generally female, but "he" also can follow her into this place, suggesting some freedom of movement between the side of the masculine speaking subject and that of the feminine. Yet at the same time, Irigaray focuses on the body, marked as feminine, and its role within Christian mysticism, thereby foreshadowing her later critique of Lacan's insistence on a sharp split between sexual difference and the body. Two things are operative here—on the one hand, Irigaray distrusts Lacan's claim that femininity is merely a matter of discourse and that anyone, no matter what kind of body he or she has, can occupy the site of femininity or the "not all." She therefore highlights the bodies of women mystics, going to the point of suggesting that their eloquence is less a feature of language than of the inscription of their bodies. (The mystic's eloquence is not unlike that of the hysteric, whose symptoms, according to Lacan, are a kind of unconscious writing on the body.) On the other hand, and reinforcing this move, Irigaray distrusts language as the domain of the masculine speaking subject; she understands language as caught within a logic of vision and representation that rests on the repression of touch, embodiment, and so, she argues, of women. Freud's (and Lacan's, Irigaray would argue) valorization of the penis rests on its visibility; the vagina, on the other hand, is more easily apprehended through touch.

Although female-authored mystical texts may seem to be the site of female autonomy, for Irigaray language is always implicated in the masculinity of the speaking subject. Irigaray's distinction between the linguistic text and the body does not, then, mirror that between mysticism and hysteria or between freedom and constraint. Just as Beauvoir reads God's/Teresa's inscriptions on Teresa's body as a sign of her autonomy, Irigaray even more pointedly seems to favor the marked body and the sense of touch as the site of feminine jouissance and subjectivity; she claims that the experiential or lived body better evades the phallogocentrism of language and its emphasis on the visual and representation, both of which reinscribe the (woman) mystic within a male specular economy.[25]

As I have suggested, Irigaray's emphasis on the mystic's body is related to her insistence that the efficacy of speech is limited in the face of mystical experience. When the "soul" escapes her confines within male discourse and representation, she loses identity, the support of certain "truths," and with them the ability to name herself and her desires.[26] Moving from the objectifying logic of the gaze to that of the touch, in which distinctions between subject and object, self and other, are more fluid, she/the soul loses her grasp on language, which is rooted in these distinctions:

> But without the power to specify what she wants. Failing in her words. Sensing a *remains to be said* that resists all speech, that one can hardly stammer out. All the terms are over used, or too weak, to translate in a sensible manner. For it is no longer a matter there of sighing after some determinable attribute, some mode of essence, some face of presence. What is expected is neither a *this* nor a *that*, not even a *here*, nor a *there*. Without being, neither time nor places designatible. Better to refuse all discourse, to keep quiet, or to utter only a sound so inarticulate that it hardly forms a *song*. Also keeping an ear toward any shuddering announcing a return. (SA 241; SO 193)

Responding to Lacan's claim that "woman" cannot name what she wants, Irigaray underlines the coincidence between the mystery of feminine desire and the unspeakability of the mystic's God. Irigaray reduces mystical language to pure affect—a barely articulated song that conveys emotion with little if any signifying power.

    Yet in repeating Lacan's suggestion that the unknowability of women and of the divine are linked, Irigaray elides the specificity of women's texts in a way that Lacan does not. Having said that woman does not know what she wants, Lacan goes on to make clear that she inscribes her desire within texts that work according to a different logic. He does not cite these writings, instead claiming to mime them through his own rhetorical and linguistic practice. For Lacan, remember, mystical language produces an effect—an affect or bodily anguish and ecstasy that goes beyond that made available in the realm of the phallus. Irigaray both follows and subverts Lacan's appropriative move, for her language, too, seems to share in the effects of mystical discourse. The elision of the subject in Irigaray's fragmented sentences, the confusion of pronouns, and her almost ejaculatory and incantatory style mirror the dispersal of the subject as knowing agent, in control of his or her discourse, just as for the mystic such linguistic performances serve as an analogue of the union between subject and object, soul and divine.[27] Yet because she mimes rather than directly cites women's texts, and because she so often focuses on the bodily figure of the mystic as she is overcome by jouissance, it might seem that the female body, and not the mystical text, becomes the primary site of mystical inscription.

In fact, I have argued elsewhere that Irigaray moves from mystical writing to mystical experience and thence to the mystical body.[28] Despite her desire not to repeat a male emphasis on the visual and its reduction of the other to the identical or the same, Irigaray moves from stating the unrepresentability of "God" to seeing his self-inscription on the mystic's body: "And maybe it is in her body that he inscribed his 'desires' even if she is less able to read them, poorer in language, 'crazier' in her speech, more shackled by an excess of matter(s) that one has historically deposited in her, more fixed in/by the speculative plans that paralyze her desire" (SA 246–47; SO 198). This slide from language to the body risks reasserting the logic of specularity precisely where Irigaray is most at pains to subvert it. Yet, against my own earlier argument, I now see that Irigaray argues carefully that God's inscription occurs not on but in the mystic's body; the touch blurs distinctions between inside and outside, opening women's bodies to the jouissance of the divine. It is the emotional effect of mystical experience that mystical language—and Irigaray's language following it—engenders or performs. Just as Lacan argues that psychoanalysis generates the jouissance of the speaking body, thereby uncovering the bodily effects engendered by language and subverting the absolute distinction between language and the body so central to his earlier work, Irigaray insists that mystical language emerges out of and gives rise to effects felt within, on, and through the mystical body. The mystical metaphors that are most important for her in "La Mystérique" are those that subvert the boundaries between inside and outside, body and language, masculine and feminine. Although as we will see in chapter 8, the emphasis on the mystic's lived body may open the door to an objectification and externalization of her experience onto the visible body, Irigaray's own text pushes back from the visual to the felt body and its dissolution into the other.

CHRIST AND THE FEMININE IMAGINARY

Like Beauvoir, Irigaray recognizes that within the history of Christianity, the Incarnation leads to the recognition of the salvific power of the body and of femininity insofar as it is identified with human beings' bodily nature. Drawing on the centrality of the Incarnation within Christian theologies, medieval interpreters understand the female visionary and ecstatic as capable, like Christ, of redeeming her own physicality and that of those around her.[29] The body is not negated but transformed—its limitations destroyed. Beauvoir's and Irigaray's differing attitudes toward and ability to understand the meaning of this form of self-creation and overcoming rest on their competing claims with regard to transcendence, subjectivity, and the body. Beauvoir argues that a transcendence mediated by the immanent body is feminized, and hence inadequate, whereas one that surpasses the body entirely is always false and illusory. Her attempt to resolve this dilemma depends on a radical reconfiguration of bodily experience, but one that still emphasizes the centrality of the will and consciousness to subjectivity. Irigaray wants to redeem femininity and immanence more explicitly, creating what she will later call a "sensible transcendental," transcendence within and through immanence (EDS 111; AE 115). She tries to uncover a new conception of subjectivity in which transcendence is rooted explicitly in immanence, rather than posited as antithetical to it (although as I will argue in chapter 7, increasingly a certain ideality takes over within her work).

In that they understand the mystic's experience as marked primarily by embodiment, Beauvoir and Irigaray share in prevalent modern readings of female spirituality; their differing valuations of women's mysticism mirror the differing valuations placed on female piety and mysticism in reputedly more "neutral" historiography. In 1949, Beauvoir took a "masculine," denigratory attitude toward women's mysticism (at least in the main lines of her argument), thereby offering further evidence for many later feminists' claims that Beauvoir's account of subjectivity is masculine. Irigaray's more positive assessment of women's mysticism is an attempt to embrace immanence and embodiment, thereby disrupting male systems of valuation. Yet at the same time, she insists that mystical disruptions still occur within the framework of a phallocentric system.

For Beauvoir, Christ as a feminized aspect of the divine serves only to justify an always inferior femininity. The free subjectivity unconstrained by sexual difference for which Beauvoir hopes can be glimpsed only in mystics like Teresa, who seem to move beyond narcissistic identification with the fleshly, suffering, and feminized Christ. In *Speculum*, on the other hand, Irigaray embraces the valorization of femininity made possible in the Incarnation. God become human makes possible women's divinization *as women*, for when God becomes flesh, women's jouissance can be recognized. "The Son," according to Irigaray, is "the most feminine of all men"; the mystic soul

> does not cease to contemplate his nudity offered up to inspection, the gashes of his virginal flesh, the suffering extension of

his crucified body, the wounds made by the nails that pierced him, his hanging, his passion and his abandon. Inundated by love for him/herself. Model who, in his crucifixion, opens for her a way of redemption from the degeneration [*déchéance*] in which she existed. (SA 249; SO 199–200)

For Irigaray, femininity's fallenness is tied to the specificity of the female body, known to women through touch rather than sight. Christ's body is not only intellectually linked to femininity, but itself takes on the features of the female flesh: "Thus might every wound not be unavowable, every tear not shameful? A wound could be *sacred*? Ecstasies in that glorious cleft where she coils up as if in her residence, where she reposes as if at home—and He is in her as well. Bathing in a warm blood and purifying in his generous flood" (SA 248; SO 200). The wound in Christ's side sacralizes the wound that is woman's lack from the standpoint of a male specular economy; his blood mimes and redeems women's menstrual flow.[30] Christ's feminized body offers an iconic figuration of feminine bodily specificity. Because this feminized body is also said to be divine (hence aligned with the Other, or *A*), in it the *a* and the *A*, the imaginary and the symbolic, are potentially conflated for women, thereby providing a fantasmatic support for a specifically feminine subjectivity.

Irigaray recognizes that it is impossible entirely to escape representation, and hence the logic of the mirror in which difference is reduced to identity and sameness. Her strategies of miming and mirroring rest on the Derridean premise that repetition always involves sameness *and* difference—the subtle alterations effected by the movement across space and across time. The mystic takes this disruption of the specular further, however, for in her self-emptying, which reflects the self-emptying of the divine, vision shatters the visual. "Authorized to be silent" about her secret embrace with the divine, the soul

> *sees* (herself) that which she cannot say. There where she sees nothing and where she sees everything [*tout*]. . . . Thus I see you, you see me in order to see you, in that depthless wound that is the source of our marvelous comprehension and of our drunkenness. And to know myself, I hardly have need of a "soul"; it is sufficient to contemplate the gap of your loving body. Every other instrument, no matter how untheoretical, separates me from myself in separating—and/or sewing up again—artificially the lips of that cleft where I re-cognize myself, re-touching myself there (as if immediately. (SA 249–50; SO 200)

For Irigaray, as for Bataille, through the contemplation of Christ's wounds, vision itself is shattered into affect, an autoaffection and jouissance grounded in the laceration of bodily existence itself. Irigaray describes a movement from vision to touch and autoaffection. Women's "soul-lessness," posited by Lacan as the result of the relationship between the sexes in which man takes the woman (the part object or *a*) as his soul, does not hinder her relationship to the divine. Rather, in his wounded (and hence symbolically castrated) body, Christ valorizes the lack that is femininity. In doing so, masculine pretensions to totality are subverted.

For Irigaray, as for Beauvoir and Lacan, this ravishing ecstasy, which occurs through contemplation of Christ's suffering body, is explicitly feminized and so carries enormous implications for women:

> And if in this contemplation of the Son's pierced body, I drink
> a joy concerning which it is impossible for me to speak a single
> word, one should not judge too quickly that I take pleasure in his
> sufferings. But that the Word thus and to this extent was made
> flesh, this could only be so that I might become God in my finally
> recognized jouissance. (SA 250; SO 200)

No longer split between the absolute transcendence of heaven and the depths of her own sinfulness, the feminine soul recognizes the cleft or slit between heaven and hell in which they come together—the sensible transcendental in which the boundaries between height and depth, inside and outside, immanence and transcendence are subverted through ec-stasy. The power of this moment is marked by Irigaray's switch from third-person evocations of "the soul/she" to a first-person appropriation of the divine jouissance; Irigaray directly mimes the mystic in her divinization. This is a moment in which bodies in their openness, woundedness, and mortality are recognized to be the site of divinity, and hence the limitations of human existence are sacralized. "The more distant in her ecstasy and more soaring in her soul, the further she moves inside of that lack of soul that she is" (SA 251; SO 201). Her very lack, fallenness, or emptiness serves as the site of her union with the nothingness that is the divine.[31]

In this valorization of the wounded body, Irigaray wishes to affirm an order of touch and of language in which the boundaries between inside and outside, and hence between body and spirit, are continually undermined:

> In her and/or outside of her, for in her jouissance her entrails open
> up and pour out indefinitely. . . .

> Strange economy of the specula(riza)tion of woman, who in her
> "mirror" seems always to refer back to a transcendence. Who moves
> away (for) who comes near, who groans to be separated from the
> one who holds her closest in his embrace. But who also calls for
> the dart which, piercing through her, will with the same stroke
> tear out her stomach/womb [ventre]. (SA 250–251; SO 201)

The allusion is to Teresa of Avila, although Irigaray does not name her. The passages mimed by Irigaray concern the experience sculpted by Bernini, ones thus judged amenable to representation (and, no doubt, attractive to male viewers).[32] Like Lacan, Irigaray intensifies the moment's visual and visionary quality, and so explodes it, for that which Irigaray names cannot be seen in the baroque excesses of Bernini's statue. By reasserting the violence of Teresa's experience and by emphasizing the site of the transverberation as the viscera (stomach or womb) rather than the heart (Teresa describes the arrow as piercing the heart so deeply it reaches into her entrails and pulls them out), Irigaray upsets the boundaries between inside and outside, moving beyond even Bernini's baroque excesses to the improper entrails of the saint. Teresa's insides literally create her interiority as other than and unrepresentable (by man). Violence disrupts subjectivity, yet, as I argue in chapter 8, subjects are also formed in pain. Teresa's pleasure partakes in both. Although this pleasure is still constrained by male representations and prescriptions (in that it is contained by an onto-theological discourse), its violence constantly disrupts male norms and creates, according to Irigaray, Teresa's own interior space.[33]

"And if she does not feel raped by 'God,' even in her fantasies of rape, this is because He never limits her orgasm (even if) hysterical. Understanding all its violence" (SA 251; SO 201). Rather than being dependent on men to recognize her autonomy, the mystic finds her freedom in the divine; not the "good old God," the father God of Christianity, still conflated with the phallus, but his feminine and feminizing son. Only this divine being understands the radicality of a desire whose violence, experienced as ec-static jouissance, generates the shattering of boundaries between inside and outside, subject and other. Irigaray seems to see the two mystical moments outlined by Bataille and Lacan—the desire to be all and the recognition that one is not all and that one's desire is always excessive and shattering—as occurring in and through this feminized divine being. Christ serves both as the fantasmatic support for a feminine subjectivity, defined as "not all" within the terms of a phallic symbolic but here valorized through the suffering cleft in Christ's side, and as the suffering other through whom women might encounter the limitations of bodily existence. Through Christ, the mystic is both constituted as a subject and overcomes the boundaries between subject and other in loving desire and identification. For the Irigaray of *Speculum*, femininity is defined as an openness and fluidity to the other that both upholds subjectivity and enables women to experience the other, not as a threat to their own being, totality, and mastery, but as the site of an ec-static movement out of subjectivity and into alterity.

AGAINST SACRIFICE

For Lacan, the possibility of sexual relations—and the communication between persons that this relationship symbolizes—depends on the refusal of the fantasy of lost wholeness, yet the refusal of that fantasy itself depends on the recognition that the sexual relation never occurs (E 82; S XX 89). Like many Christian mystics, Lacan, through the deployment of this double paradigm, attempts to subvert the laws of noncontradiction in order to point to or bring into being a new form of consciousness in which the real is manifested. The only possibility for human communication lies in living and writing this contradiction—and what is communicated in this way is not meaning but affect. Lacan's references to mystical texts, including his own, may thus point to a way through this logical and experiential impasse, but Irigaray argues in "Così fan tutti" that Lacan usurps women's voices through his claims to speak from the side of the "not all." As Lacan himself sometimes glimpses, when women and men speak from one or the other side of that divide between masculinity and femininity created by male-dominant discourse, their relation to the penis/phallus—their having or not having it—makes an essential difference. Yet in "Così fan tutti" Irigaray goes even further, suggesting that men, as constituted through a phallic economy, can never really occupy the site of the "not all."

In addition, Irigaray argues that Lacan's (and implicitly also Bataille's) emphasis on castration, lack, and wounding creates a rhetoric of impotence that a feminine imaginary must challenge. She here implicitly critiques her own earlier reading of Christian mysticism as a discourse that offers glimpses of a feminine imaginary in the feminized body of Christ and the jouissance elicited by the encounter with him.[34] By reading Christ's side wound as vaginal, the Irigaray of *Speculum* participates in a phallic rhetoric that sees the vagina as a wound, the mark of castration. Like Bataille's association of Madame Edwarda's genitals with the bodily laceration of the torture victim on whose image he meditates, Irigaray's reading of Christian mysticism in "La Mystérique" participates in a logic that can read femininity only as the other of masculinity. Irigaray's subsequent work takes up the challenge of *Encore* in a more radical vein, attempting to demonstrate how an imaginary grounded in a nonphallic morphology might empower women—serving as a support for their subjectivities—and/or might free all humans from the illusory plenitude (and all too real power) of a symbolic governed by the phallus. Irigaray argues that for Lacan (and, by implication, for Bataille), women have no unconscious but are themselves the unconscious of the male symbolic—they serve as voiceless and unknowing emblems for the "truth" of male subjectivity. Thus an encounter with woman is itself, for the masculine subject, an encounter with the real. In giving voice to women's own imaginary and (potential) symbolic, Irigaray seeks to challenge women's emblematic status and the powerlessness to which it consigns them. Moreover, she hopes to provide an imaginary and symbolic grounded in female morphology, one in which openness can be reconfigured not as lack, woundedness, or castration, but as fluidity and receptivity to the other.

The shifts between *Speculum* and "Così fan tutti" are played out even more dramatically in Irigaray's subsequent work. Her interpretation of Nietzsche reads like a direct response to Bataille's *On Nietzsche*, particularly in her rejection of the sacrificial logic of Christianity and in her suggestions about the relationship between that logic and phallocentrism.[35] Whereas my reading of the *Atheological Summa* in chapters 2 and 3 focuses on the ethical call of the other, which demands that we submit to a lacerating encounter with "what is" in order to witness to the suffering mortal body, in *On Nietzsche*, Bataille underlines the necessity of woundedness and sacrifice to communication. He does so, in part, by meditating on the meaning of the crucifixion, which he claims is a crime, but one without which communication would be impossible (OC V 42–44; ON 17–19). The "wounding" of Christ on the cross is emblematic of the laceration demanded by communication. In other words, for Bataille the logic of communication is encapsulated by the crucifixion (although Christianity is hypocritical in its refusal to recognize the necessity of crime and hence the inapplicability of moralism to the realm of sacrifice and the sacred).[36] Yet it is a logic about which Bataille himself seems increasingly uncomfortable. Thus in his postwar work he is both fascinated and horrified by the proliferating violence to which, he argues, Christianity gives rise, and he attempts to differentiate his own position from those who would call for literal sacrifice and murder.[37] He insists, for example, that Sade ultimately fails to communicate because he denies the reality of the other and claims that "abuse, exploitation are what break communication," whereas "sacrifice reestablishes it."[38]

Bataille seems torn between an understanding of communication dependent on woundedness, laceration, and sacrifice (however fictionalized they may be) and his recognition that this sacrificial logic and the desires it engenders are in danger of affirming sadism, unrestrained violence, and oppression (indeed, Bataille spent his life fighting against the totalitarian display of the latter). This doubleness, Lacan suggests, reflects the instability of the subject itself, always poised between the desire to be all and the recognition of its constitutive lack. For Bataille and Lacan, ultimately, sacrifice and the sacrality or jouissance to which it gives rise take precedence over concerns about the violence sacrifice requires.[39] Irigaray insists, however, that this valorization of sacrifice and laceration is grounded in phallocentrism and that both—together with the ambivalence to which they give rise—can be avoided through a reconfiguration of subjectivity in terms of openness, fluidity, and a temporality rooted in becoming rather than in being.

Irigaray argues that although the Incarnation may be the grounds for a new relation to language, the Christ of traditional Christianity does not save women, but usurps their power, creativity, and bodiliness through his feminized body, which, when sacrificed on the cross, serves to hide the primordial death of the mother on which entry into the masculine economy depends.[40] In other words, as I show in chapter 7, the loss of the mother('s body) that is mourned by each human child is effaced under the valorized—and apparently redemptive—sacrifice of the Godman. Irigaray insists in her later work, as she suggests already in *Speculum*, that the Christian mystical tradition inadequately disrupts the hom(m)osexual economy of Western patriarchy and cannot create or make room for a new female imaginary or symbolic. Irigaray rejects both Christianity's masculine God and its sacrificial nature (SP 89–102; SG 75–88). She calls for an alternative to sacrifice as the ground of community and for female images of the divine, reflections of the good that lies within women and women's bodies (SP 69–85; SG 57–92). In doing so, Irigaray returns to that female divinity implicit in Beauvoir's text (but in whom Beauvoir herself refuses to believe), that "whole embodied in a supreme Person," who would give meaning to women's contingent existence (DS II 582–83; SS 744). Irigaray insists, however, that this being should not be understood as "whole." As I will show in chapter 7, Irigaray is careful to dephallicize female divinity; yet her insistence on the primacy of sexual difference suggests that the push toward wholeness is not completely effaced. In order to evade the violence and mortality to which bodies are subject, Irigaray reasserts an ideality that potentially forecloses the inevitability of loss (and hence participates in the logic of fetishization she wishes to avoid).

This problem emerges most clearly in the tension between Irigaray's call for a feminine divine (paralleling the call for a feminine imaginary and symbolic) in "Divine Women" and her deconstruction of belief and its object in "Belief Itself."[41] Again, in Lacanian terms, one is led to ask whether Irigaray's call for the divinization of women does not rest on a denial of the gap between the imaginary and the symbolic similar to that effected by men within patriarchy. As Patricia Huntington argues, on one reading the overcoming of this gap is precisely what Irigaray intends. Moreover, Irigaray claims that the violence of sacrifice will also be overcome through such a reimagining of subjectivity, and she rejects entirely Lacan's "law of impotence," that is, his claim that subjectivity is grounded in lack. However, having offered this account of the feminine divine, in which she asks women to believe, Irigaray nonetheless insists, as we will see in chapter 7, that belief must always also be deconstructed.

This tension in Irigaray's work is displayed further in her argument that although feminine subjectivity is always partial, contingent, and finite, finitude should be understood primarily in terms of openness and possibilities, and not, as for Lacan, in terms of mortality, woundedness, illness, and pain. The more Irigaray confuses the latter instances of finitude with Lacanian lack, thus rendering them mere adjuncts to phallocentrism and/or secondary to the human condition (at least as redefined through a feminine morphology), the more she may be in danger of eliding fundamental aspects of human experience as embodied beings—and of positing a fantasmatic unity of the imaginary and the symbolic that gives rise to the fetishism against which many mystical texts strive. In her shift between a mystical and a Feuerbachean logic, as I will show in chapter 7, Irigaray risks leaving one boundary between bodies and between subjects unchallenged, allowing it to serve as the unquestioned support for subjectivity—and hence she is in danger of claiming a kind of infinitude and universality for sexual difference that obscures the multiplicities of bodies and desires made visible in some mystical texts.[42]

THE PROBLEM OF BELIEF; OR, IF CHRIST IS THE LITTLE *a*, WHO IS THE BIG *A* ? In *Speculum*, Irigaray suggests that in the encounter with the feminized body of Christ, Christ—as the object *a*—subverts the association of the other with the phallus and the Name-of-the-Father through his explicit feminization. Thus the mystic's relationship to the feminized Godman serves both to support her subjectivity (because a feminine imaginary is associated with the divine, hence with the symbolic) and to undermine (although not sufficiently) the prevalent phallic symbolic, eliciting a jouissance that goes beyond, precisely through the feminization of its mortal human avatar. Many medieval women mystics take this process even further, however, for the love that Christ embodies and with which the mystic strives to achieve union is, in the vernaculars of medieval Europe, feminine. For many women, this love is the central name of God. In the thirteenth-century beguine writers Mechthild of Magdeburg, Hadewijch, and Marguerite Porete, God in her immanence is female, for love serves as the bridge between human and divine. Love is the *sensible transcendental*, to use Irigaray's term (EDS 111; AE 115), the support of that dialectic between transcendence and immanence in which their apparent opposition is overcome. Through bodily affects God is radically immanent to humanity. Yet at the same time, even as the body and emotions provide the conditions for subjectivity, love allows one to transcend one's own particular body and opens one to the other.

To the extent that reality is grounded in love, according to Mechthild, it is one with the divine from before its existence. Likewise, Hadewijch's soul, masculinized as the knight errant of love, seeks union with Lady Love, in whose existence his own is grounded. Such linguistic turns, working with and against grammatical gendering, demonstrate that these women sought to disrupt, subvert, and move beyond traditional sex and gender categories. This disruption and subversion is most apparent in the writings of Marguerite Porete, who moves through such gendered language—in which God as Love, in her immanence, feminizes both the soul and the divine—to a language of philosophical abstraction in which she collapses sex and gender distinctions, just as she collapses distinctions between the soul and the divine. Many mystical texts from the later Middle Ages move through the human incarnate Christ (imagistically both male and female) to God as radically immanent within humanity in its uncreated ground (which is neither male nor female).

Attention to these thirteenth-century women's texts reveals a radicality of vision suggested by Irigaray's evocations of Angela and Teresa. Like Bataille, Lacan, and the Irigaray of "*La Mystérique*," Mechthild of Magdeburg, Hadewijch, and Marguerite Porete treat sexuality and gender as fluid entities, disrupting the ideological constraints within which their texts are constructed.[43] In medieval Christian culture, the hierarchy between male and female generally remains firm, as does the identification of the former with spirit and the latter with flesh. Moreover, within most male-authored and many female-authored texts, the redeemability of the flesh and of femininity depends on sacrificial suffering. Yet the culture's incarnational theologies allow room for differing relations to femininity and embodiment. Thus some texts undermine the hierarchy between male and female and reject the association of redemption with sacrifice in order to posit another mode of access to the sacred through a feminine divine Love.[44]

Medieval women not only find a feminine bodily morphology reflected in the suffering body and humanity of Christ (whereby Christ functions as the object *a*, the part object or fantasmatic object of desire that serves as a support for female subjectivity), but also feminize *A*, the Other as the locus of signification and *signifiance*. For Mechthild, Hadewijch, Beatrice of Nazareth, and Marguerite Porete, Love, an endless outpouring toward the other, occupies the site of the Name/No-of-the-Father. Much of the power of their discourse, moreover, rests on their passionate belief in this Other/Love in whom they both see themselves reflected (as feminine) and forever find themselves lacking. The more they lack, the more they see themselves in that Love, which is a boundless and ceaseless desire. Yet because Love always desires more, it occupies the site both of the transcendental signifier, which fixes meaning and insures wholeness and stability, and of *signifiance*, in which meaning is always unmoored and put in motion. The beguine mystics hold together the mystical apprehension of the all and the not all, but in terms no longer governed strictly by a "law of impotence."

Simone de Beauvoir noted astutely that Teresa of Avila's ability to engage in meaningful projects in the world was facilitated by the power of her belief. Teresa's relationship to the divine was essential for her freedom to act within and against the male symbolic, even in the face of crushing opposition. Irigaray's careful attention in *"La Mystérique"* to the lived experience of the body serves in part to elide the vexing question of belief and its object. Rather than following mystical texts in their attempts to name the unnameable divine, Irigaray emphasizes the embodied subjectivity created in relationship to the other; she thus potentially makes the mystic's body both the source and the site of discourse. As Kathryn Bond Stockton argues, Irigaray replaces God with the body as the always unattainable and unnameable other toward which language tends.[45] Here again she follows Lacan, who replaces the other encountered in the mystical moment (Bataille's wounded and suffering torture victim, for example) with the speaking—and hence split and yet joying—body. Yet Irigaray also criticizes Lacan for his association of the real with the body. Lacan, she argues, remains at the level of the imaginary and the object *a*, conflating the real with the feminine imaginary. Lacan mistakes the feminine imaginary for the real because within the male-dominant discourses and institutions of the West, women have consistently come to stand in for the body—in its pleasures and pains, possibilities and, more often, limitations. Yet insofar as Irigaray continues to associate the feminine imaginary with the body, her texts remain open to just the debilitating association of women, the body, and death that she wants to challenge, hence the charges of bodily essentialism continually leveled against her (however inadequate these critiques are to the details of her texts).

At best, Lacan and Irigaray transform the imaginary; yet among medieval women, the transformation of the imaginary—even its subversion of the male symbolic through the conflation of a feminized body with the male father God—is not enough. Instead they achieve a potentially radical revision of the symbolic through a relationship to an other figured not as paternal prohibition and threat but as divine Love. In doing so, they preserve the tension between the other as the One and the other as the dispersal of unity, while also refusing to read this doubleness solely in terms of lack and woundedness.

Yet this transformation—in conceptions of the divine and in female subjectivity—demands belief in the other, both in its power and in its dispersal through all of creation as divine Love. Whether one accepts the reality of the mystics' God, one cannot help but be aware of the power this God invests in them. This power incites the admiration of Beauvoir and Irigaray, who recognize in Teresa a female subjectivity not grounded in or subservient to men, a female subjectivity that simultaneously is located within and transcends the body. In Teresa, Beauvoir and Irigaray see a female subject who thinks of herself as other to no one, except to that other who is the divine.

Unlike Beauvoir, however, Irigaray recognizes the importance of belief. Thus she argues in "Divine Women" and subsequent essays that religion is important to women because it remains a central means through which society is constituted and subjectivities are grounded. Until there are new gods, she claims, there can be no new social, political, and sexual order. Irigaray, as we will see, suggests that women must *pass through* belief *and* deconstruct it; they must be accorded an independent subjectivity, even if such a subjectivity will always overflow rigid boundaries and demarcations. This is the movement Irigaray intuits and imitates in the texts of Angela of Foligno and Meister Eckhart. She argues for the importance of women's subjectivity and transcendence in a way reminiscent of Beauvoir, yet insists against Beauvoir that religion is central to both the attainment of such autonomy and the recognition of human (inter)dependence.[46] Yet Irigaray still at times risks forgetting that without belief and its deconstruction the fragile interplay of immanence and transcendence constitutive of free subjects is lost.[47] She claims to recognize the necessity of an other against Lacan's reading of the body as itself other, yet at the same time she remains uncomfortable with theistic claims in that they refer to a being radically other than woman. Here she follows Feuerbach, as I will show, but with a crucial difference; whereas for Feuerbach, "man" or the species being becomes the site onto which beliefs are projected and from which they are reappropriated by and for humanity, for Irigaray this site is sexual difference. Indeed, Irigaray reifies sexual difference and insists on its primacy in the constitution of human subjects.

SEXUAL DIFFERENCE

AND THE PROBLEM OF BELIEF

. . . .

Divinity is that which we need in order to be free, autonomous, sovereign. No constitution of subjectivity or of human society has ever been elaborated without divine assistance. There is a time for destruction. But, to be destroyed, it is necessary that God or the gods exist.

LUCE IRIGARAY, *Sexes and Genealogies*

No one ought to believe.

LUCE IRIGARAY, *je, tu, nous: Toward a Culture of Difference*

So therefore let us pray to god that we may be free of god.

MEISTER ECKHART, *Essential Sermons*

Just as commentators have worried about the intended reference of Irigaray's bodily language, they have been uneasy with her assertion that the creation of a new feminine imaginary and symbolic depends on the discovery and creation of a female divine; their concern is with the meaning and intended reference of Irigaray's religious language. There is an impasse evident in recent feminist readings of Irigaray's work on religion, particularly with regard to her apparently uncritical acceptance of the Feuerbachean claim that religion is a projection and reflection of the ego ideals of its human creators. Elizabeth Grosz takes Irigaray's dependence on Feuerbach's constructivism as a reassurance that Irigaray is not calling for a "leap of faith," a return to belief, or a seemingly apolitical religiosity.[1] Serene Jones, however, points to the difficulties that arise for Irigaray if Grosz's interpretation is correct.[2] For Jones, a Christian theologian, Irigaray's concern to protect the incommensurability of the "other" sex against its inscription within a "logic of the same" makes any claim that she is willing to reduce the divine to a newly projected "ego ideal" for women suspect. The rejection of the alterity of God, Jones argues, suggests an inability to accept the alterity of the other sex.

For Irigaray, men and women exist tangibly in the world and are available to human sensory perception. God, as an absolutely transcendent entity, is not. In response to Jones, then, Irigaray might argue that the human other is real in a way that God, as normally understood, is not. Penelope Deutscher argues, furthermore, that Irigaray recasts the divine as that which is experienced when men and women recognize each other in their difference. The divine is not a supernatural being with whom we relate independently, but rather the outcome of true relations between the sexes.[3] Thus sexual difference itself becomes the site of one's own and the other's divinization. In her more recent work, Irigaray expands this understanding of heterosociality, arguing that sexual difference offers a horizontal transcendence through which the subject recognizes itself as partial and finite, hence open to the reality of the other (see JAT; ILTY). Through this mutual experience of recognition, embodied spiritual subjects are born. The divine is not outside but within the subject, Irigaray argues; and she goes on to repeat her claim that conceptions of an absolutely transcendent, immaterial God result from man's forgetting of the other as other (see EDS 97–111, 127–41, 173–99; AE 97–115, 133–50, 185–217; SA 225–37; SO 180–90; SP 37–65; SG 25–3).

Yet against this reading stands Irigaray's claim that women must also reach toward infinity (SP 69–85; SG 57–72) and her insistence that the transcendence of "'God' can help in the discovery of the other as other, a locus where expectation and hope hold themselves in reserve" (EDS 188; AE 204). Even in her most recent work, which emphasizes sexual difference as the source of the negativity necessary to openness and subjectivity, Irigaray repeats her call for a refiguration of the mother–daughter relationship through which a new feminine divine might become culturally available.[4] Irigaray argues that daughters have the potential for radically different kinds of relationships with mothers, ones that have been denied within male-dominant culture. The little girl, because she identifies with the mother('s body), is capable of communication and openness to the other in a way the little boy is not. Mothers, trained by patriarchy to the suppression of such bonds, refuse their daughters' gestures of communication and identification. To achieve the communication between women of which daughters are capable, Irigaray argues, we need a cultural valorization of the bonds between mothers and daughters through figures of female divinity or divine women.[5]

We can bring Irigaray's claims about immanence and transcendence together in terms of her discussion of vertical and horizontal relations and the problems of subjectivity and intersubjectivity. Deutscher stresses that Irigaray deconstructs vertical relation between the divine and human by focusing on horizontal transcendence between the sexes. Thus desire itself both makes possible intersubjectivity and becomes the locus of the divine. This divinized desire, however, which is the source of sexual relations, cannot come into being without the full articulation of women's subjectivity. Yet feminine subjectivity depends on a process of identification with the mother and with a projected divine that is best understood as a refiguring of the vertical relation between divinity and humanity. Communication between the divine and the human must move in both directions, destabilizing the hierarchies implied by verticality. Eventually, women will become divine, thereby overcoming the gap between humanity and divinity and making possible an intersubjective horizontal transcendence between men and women, which itself then creates a new kind of divinity.

If Irigaray's argument for the destruction of hierarchy and the creation of new divinities seems paradoxical, or at least circular, it is because she insists that before they can be destroyed "it is necessary that God or the gods exist" (SP 74; SG 62). This claim leaves us with the seemingly paradoxical task of both positing and deconstructing a feminine divine. The paradox becomes most apparent when we look at two crucial essays from the early 1980s, "Divine Women" and "Belief Itself," which appear side by side in *Sexes and Genealogies*. The positioning of these two essays, together with the juxtaposition of claims for horizontal and transcendental conceptions of divinity in texts like *An Ethics of Sexual Difference* and *I Love to You*, necessitate that we read the two sets of apparently contradictory claims together. As I will show in this chapter, sexual difference is the site of their convergence. God or the gods may be destroyed, but sexual difference, Irigaray claims, can never be. As such, sexual difference (and/or "woman") becomes the site of an undeconstructed and fetishized ideality on which Irigaray's utopian visions rest.

DIVINITY AND SUBJECTIVITY

Irigaray's 1984 text "Divine Women" startled many readers with its claim that women need a divine in order to attain political, social, and economic power.[6]

As Deutscher notes astutely, with this claim Irigaray moves beyond the feminist notion that religious belief and practice must be reshaped by feminist analysis to the more radical assertion that "no substantial modification of women's subjectivity and identity could be achieved without the cultivation of a 'feminine divine.'"[7] Appealing to psychoanalytic theory and to Ludwig Feuerbach's *The Essence of Christianity*, Irigaray insists that human beings require identificatory structures in order to uphold their subjectivity. The God of monotheism has been such a structure for men, but within Western culture no corresponding ideal exists for women. Women's lack of subjectivity is not only reflected in but also at least in part caused by the absence of a female divine.

Irigaray's brief analysis of the Melusine story, with which "Divine Women" opens, shows that this new female divine cannot be a mere complement to the masculine God. Melusine is a "lady of the spring," one of three sisters condemned by their mother to be half human and half nymph. Melusine is part water serpent and part woman and she can lift this curse only by finding a man who will marry her without attempting to discover the secret (serpent) half of her identity. If she can find such a man, she will become fully human and thus able to receive a Christian burial (and with it, Christian salvation). Melusine appears to find such a faithful husband, a nobleman with whom she has seven sons who will be the founders of a great political dynasty. Yet her humanization and salvation depend on her husband's ability to keep his promise not to pursue her secret identity. When he first breaks the promise, she forgives him. But prompted by intriguers at the court, he breaks the promise again and spies on Melusine in her bath. Cursing her as a serpent—a demonized, inhuman other—the husband releases Melusine to her fate. She sprouts wings and flees out the castle window, lingering in popular memory as a "white lady" who appears on the ramparts in the form of a bird. Melusine never achieves Christian salvation and, hence, is cursed, yet her continued existence as a benevolent bird-like figure suggests other readings of her fate, ones effaced only partially by the Christianization of the folk narrative.[8]

For Irigaray this is a story about man's relationship to the mother; the value placed on vision marks "his victory over the maternal power and his possible mastery of the mother whom he experiences as amorphous, formless, chasm and dangerous abyss for his form" (SP 71; SG 59). Melusine makes explicit the mother's place within society as a changeling whose movement from the womb (water) to the air (the realm of speech and culture) is at best provisional. She makes that movement possible for her children, bringing them from the womb into language and subjectivity, and yet is denied access to full subjectivity herself. The mother's mixed status—as both womb and independent being, water and air, nature and culture—is experienced by men as a threat to their own subjectivity, a threat they stave off through visual mastery and through their relationship to a transcendent and immaterial divine denied to women. Because men fear that their own transcendent subjectivity is threatened by the mother's continued association with the womb, they relegate her to that space in an attempt to differentiate themselves fully and clearly from her.

Despite her fascination with the elemental (water, earth, fire, air) and her insistence that we must recover contact with the elements that constitute our natural being,[9] Irigaray warns against relegating the feminine to the womb, and so accepting the identification of women with the body, an identification perpetrated by male-dominant culture. Thus she does not call simply for the redivinization or appropriation of Melusine as a goddess of water and air:

> To resist the hierarchies—the man-woman hierarchy, State-woman, a certain God-woman, machine-woman—only to fall back under the *power* [*pouvoir*] of nature-woman, animal-woman, even matriarchs-women, women-women, doesn't hold a great interest. Respecting the universe as one of our vital and cultural dimensions, as one of the macrocosmic keys to our microcosm, we have to become women more, and not again more alien to ourselves than we were, more in exile than we were. (SP 73; SG 60)

Simply to embrace male-dominant society's identification of women with nature, animals, and the untamed, amorphous realm of the womb will lead to the further estrangement of women from subjectivity. Women require access to both the realm of nature, cut off and denied by male-dominant culture, and to divinity. Only in this way, Irigaray argues, will they attain full humanity.[10]

According to Irigaray, Melusine's story shows that women have not yet attained either this full humanity or the divinity that enables it. Melusine is paradoxically both a lost divine figure (as a powerful water nymph and protective bird-like being) and insufficiently divinized (hence her demonization as a serpent by her mother and husband). Her loss or suppression is a function of her insufficient divinization, for the figure who *should* be divine, who marks the movement from the womb to the air made possible by the maternal, is denounced as a demon (although she is also remembered as the "white lady" flitting around her ancestral battlements). In demonizing Melusine, male-dominant culture refuses both divinity and humanity to women. So, Irigaray argues, women share with the diabolical only their absence from God and the fact that, deprived of God, they find themselves bent to models that do not suit them, that exile them, double them, mask them, cut them from themselves and in themselves, taking away their progress into love, art, thought, the ideal and divine fulfillment of her/themselves. (SP 76; SG 64)

This demonized other, moreover, serves as the support for male subjectivity, the obverse of that divine ideal in whom he sees himself. Irigaray struggles to articulate a new feminine divine that will not be similarly dependent on a demonized other; at the same time, she hopes to create a continuity between nature and the divine, rather than a reassertion of the discontinuity intrinsic to male subjectivity. The problem Irigaray faces is how to articulate women's subjectivity and divinity without repeating the mistakes of male-dominant culture.

Irigaray insists not only that women require a female divine in order to attain subjectivity, but, as Deutscher argues aptly, that such a divine can be brought into existence only through a "reshaping of philosophical conceptions of divinity."[11] A female divine cannot simply mirror "the good old God" of Western monotheism; rather the very articulation of that female divine works to recast divinity itself. The God of Western monotheism, in his absolute transcendence to nature and the human, serves as a support for male subjectivity but at the same time posits men as lacking in the face of the divine. This awareness of lack leads man to turn to woman as an additional support—the silent, lacking ground—for his subjectivity. To avoid the hierarchization between the sexes perpetrated by male-dominant culture, Irigaray calls for a female divine that will exist in continuity with the natural realm while still allowing women autonomy and freedom. Continuity is central to Irigaray's conception of divinity—continuity between divine and human and between the projected ideal and the subjectivity of the believer—yet she does not completely deny the importance of transcendence.[12] Irigaray both accepts the need for overcoming the gap between man and God found within male-dominant traditions like Christianity and insists that the process of projection and divine support that generates this gap is necessary to the formation of human subjects. Women must articulate the qualities of a female divine if they are to become women, fully free and autonomous.

The female divine makes autonomous female subjectivity possible because in projecting their own values, ideals, and goals onto the divine, women understand themselves independently of familial and other communal roles: "If there is to be consciousness of self on the feminine side, it is necessary for each woman to situate herself freely in relationship to herself, and not only communally, or in the couple or the family" (SP 82; SG 69). To recognize oneself in the divine, according to Irigaray, is to recognize the divine as incarnate in female flesh. Therefore, becoming woman and becoming divine are inextricably entwined for Irigaray. Two sets of interrelated problems arise from this move—the first is related to Irigaray's understanding of gendered symbols and their deployment, and the second to the Feuerbachean presumptions of her account of belief.

First, then, Irigaray insists on the need to establish a female divine because she believes that a mirroring of like to like is required for women to achieve subjectivity. Her account of identification explicitly rejects the possibility of cross-identification as the ground for women's subjective becoming. In order to become women, understood as other than men, women must identify with specifically female projections. Yet Irigaray's understanding of identification is overly simplistic. As Caroline Walker Bynum argues cogently, attention to the history of religious traditions and to women's place within those traditions raises important questions about whether symbolic identification works in the way that Irigaray, like many feminist theologians, assumes.[13] Bynum's essay responds directly to feminist theological debates about the appropriateness for women of male divine symbols, particularly in the context of feminist struggles for subjectivity, autonomy, and freedom. Those people who claim that such imagery must be discarded and replaced by female imagery for the divine assume that symbols reflect and shape social realities and that human beings use symbols in fairly straightforward identificatory ways. Bynum argues, conversely, that symbols are polysemic and multivalent and that there are many ways in which human beings use the symbols available to them. Symbols not only reflect and shape reality but also invert, question, reject, and transcend it; moreover, given the numerous ways in which symbols can be used, one cannot predict from a given symbol what its effects on human lives and institutions will be. We can clearly see the complexities of desire and identification as they play themselves out in late medieval Christian women's texts.

Irigaray presumes not only that women will achieve subjectivity through the articulation of a female divinity, but also that this articulation will be accompanied by an increase in the cultural, economic, and political status of women. Thus she argues that the female divinities of India and the suppressed matriarchal traditions of Greece and the ancient Near East represent indigenous traditions in which women have their own cultural identity and value.

She seems to imply that in these societies, women have greater access to subjectivity, autonomy, and freedom.[14] Yet recent work on the traditions of the ancient Mediterranean world and the ancient Near East show that there is little or no correlation between female images of the divine and the actual political, social, economic, or even religious power of women.[15]

Again, we can look to the history of Christianity to see the lack of historical substance to Irigaray's assumptions. Within the medieval Catholic Church, in which the figure of Mary approached divinization, women had only meager access to political, cultural, and economic autonomy. The rise of the cult of Mary, in fact, coincided with a diminution of women's religious autonomy. Moreover, those women who showed signs of remarkable religious subjectivity generally did so not under the aegis of Mary but in relationship to Christ and the Trinity. Many women understood themselves as female souls supported by a love relationship to a male divine (the reading of women's mysticism denigrated by Beauvoir). The few remaining texts produced by medieval religious women contain a host of complex patterns of identification, cross-identification, and desire. Their use of the symbols made available to them by the Christian tradition and their own experience is tremendously complex, undermining any simple assertion of the primacy of sexual difference and of same-sex models of identification.[16]

The second and related set of problems that arise from Irigaray's understanding of the relationship between becoming woman and becoming divine concerns the Feuerbachean presumptions of her account of belief. Feuerbach's work on religion shows sensitivity to the complexity of identification and desire operative within religious traditions. Yet, according to Feuerbach, religion is subject to philosophical analysis and critique precisely because it tends toward the occlusion of human subjectivity as the source of the divine. The problem with religion, Feuerbach argues, is that humanity *does not* recognize itself in the divine, and he often seems to argue that projection itself creates this alienation. The more firmly we establish God as a supernatural object of belief, the more alienated we become from our own best qualities, ideals, and projects. As Feuerbach writes, "To enrich God, man must become poor; that God may be all, man must be nothing."[17] In *The Essence of Christianity*, Feuerbach operates with the assumption that exposing the mechanism of projection through which the object of belief is generated will destroy belief in that entity (God) as something other than ourselves. Philosophical analysis and critique, by exposing the human origins of belief, will overcome alienation and turn belief in a divine being into belief in the divinity of humanity. Thus *The Essence of Christianity* can be read as a call for a new form of religion in which human beings reappropriate divinity and thus make themselves divine.

Irigaray begins with the presumption of a successful Feuerbachean project in which women recognize themselves in the divine. She seems to assert, moreover, that such projections can occur without faith and without any alienation between the believer and projected deities:

> Only a God can save us, keep us safe. The feeling or experience of a positive, objective, glorious existence, of our subjectivity is necessary for us. Such a God who assists us and leads us in our becoming, who keeps measure of our limits—women—and of our rapport with the infinite, who inspires our projects [qui inspire nos projets]. . . . To have a goal is essentially religious (according to Feuerbach's analysis). (SP 80; SG 67)

To posit new values grounded in the feminine is, according to Irigaray, to posit a divine, and to recognize these new ideals and values as divine, she argues, is the work of reason. Supernatural belief is not required: "This utterance is still only a statement of *reason*. So far it demands no faith other than faith in the possibility of our autonomy, of our salvation, of our not only redemptive, but glorifying love, conscious of self: thought toward oneself and of oneself that does not renounce love without being, for all that, subject to it" (SP 80; SG 68). Here Irigaray seems to speak to a skeptical, atheistic, or agnostic audience, reassuring them of the rationality of her project. If one believes in the possibility of a future for women, she argues, one believes in the divine woman required for that realization.

"Divine Women," then, calls for the articulation and projection of a female divine and at the same time evinces a sharp distrust of belief. This distrust is rooted in Feuerbach's understanding of traditional religious belief as something that alienates humanity from its own divinity. Insofar as human beings believe in a transcendent deity possessing infinite perfection, they are unable to recognize those perfections as their own. Feuerbach does not eschew belief in the divine but relocates it; humanity is divine, not God, and Feuerbach's critique works to bring about this de-alienating recognition. Irigaray, following Feuerbach, hopes to rearticulate the divine as the projects, ideals, and open-ended becoming of women. Yet in the 1980 essay "Belief Itself," which, as I have said, appears alongside "Divine Women" in *Sexes and Genealogies*, we find another critique of belief. Here Irigaray argues that belief, as it has been articulated within male-dominant culture, effaces the sacrifice of the mother('s body) on which Western religion and male subjectivity have been erected. As such, belief is the denial of what the senses know, and it must be deconstructed in order to free new forms of divinity. This deconstruction demands a risk that eschews projects themselves, thereby suggesting an alternative conception of belief deeply in tension with the projection of divinity Irigaray calls for in "Divine Women."

In "Belief Itself," Irigaray argues that both the structure and the object of belief in Western discourse are male, and as such in need of deconstruction. The central texts in Irigaray's analysis—Freud's *Beyond the Pleasure Principle* and Derrida's "To Speculate—On Freud"—seem, on first sight, to have little to do with the question of belief, particularly religious belief. They are concerned with the scientific status of psychoanalysis, the nature of Freud's speculative hypothesis surrounding the repetition compulsion, and the related issue of priority. As we will see, however, these issues all lead, for Irigaray (as for Lacan), to the question of belief.

Irigaray's reading of *Beyond the Pleasure Principle* focuses on its most famous episode: the game played by Ernst, Freud's grandson. For Irigaray, little Ernst's game becomes an allegory of belief itself. Freud introduces the story as an example of the compulsion to repeat. He is perplexed by Ernst's favorite activity, playing "gone" with his toys by throwing them away from himself while making a long, drawn out "o-o-o-o" sound, which Freud and his daughter (referred to in the text as the child's mother) interpret as *fort* ("gone" in German). The meaning of this simple childhood game is revealed one day when Freud sees what he understands to be its full expression:

> The child had a wooden reel with a piece of string tied round it. It never occurred to him to pull it along the floor behind him, for instance, and play at its being a carriage. What he did was to hold the reel by the string and very skillfully throw it over the edge of his curtained cot, so that it disappeared into it, at the same time uttering his expressive "o-o-o-o." He then pulled the reel out of the cot again by the string and hailed its reappearance with a joyful "*da*" [there].[18]

In *Beyond the Pleasure Principle*, Freud argues that the repetition compulsion necessitates the hypothesis that something lies beyond the pleasure principle, namely the death drive (which is not in opposition to the pleasure principle, but its "master"). Yet Freud's account of Ernst's game undermines the stated intentions of the text itself, for he argues that both Ernst's game with the wooden reel and string and his making toys "gone" *can* be explained by the pleasure principle. On the one hand, Ernst is able to take mastery of a situation—the absence of his mother Sophie—over which he has no overt control. On the other, according to Freud, Ernst is able to revenge himself against the mother whose absence causes him pain. In both cases, Freud interprets Ernst's action as identifying his mother with his toys and then reenacting his experiences with her in a field he can control (fort and da).[19]

Irigaray responds to this story and to Freud's analysis of it by asserting that as a woman and as an analyst, she has access to a place obscured from Freud's view, that "still dark, oneiric experience" in which the drives that make us human have not yet been fully bound or cathected. Freud spoke from the place of the ego, the secondary processes, and bound energy; Irigaray argues that from this place certain stories or messages cannot be heard or understood, namely, those of Ernst's mother and Freud's daughter, "Sophie, the Sunday daughter."[20]

To clarify what Freud misses in the story of little Ernst and to suggest why Freud cannot hear Sophie's story, Irigaray tells the story of another woman, one of her own analysands. This patient tells Irigaray: "When they, the (spiritual) father and son, recite together the ritual words of the consecration, saying, 'This is my body, this is my blood,' I bleed" (SP 38; SG 25–26). The relationship between the father, son, and bleeding woman is ambiguous, even more so than the relationship between Ernst, Freud, and Sophie in *Beyond the Pleasure Principle*. For Irigaray, the mother/daughter/wife's bleeding body, cast as it is in a relationship with the body of the father and the son and with the words of the mass, knots together the questions of embodiment, belief, and sexual difference and demonstrates what is at stake for Freud beyond the pleasure principle. Where Freud sees a drive toward death, Irigaray sees the mother's body and the child's ambivalent relationship to her and to it.[21]

The bleeding woman does not "believe" the doctrines of the Catholic Church, Irigaray tells us, although she is not "alien to a divine who, apparently, formulates itself and accomplishes itself badly in their celebrations—coming like blood that flows *over and above*" (SP 38; SG 26). Here Irigaray introduces a split between the divine object of (a certain kind of) belief and some other conception of the sacred that may be "unbound" or "released" from it. She claims that we forget the real "for belief" (SP 38; SG 26). Irigaray's use of the term "real," which must be read against its Freudian (the reality principle) and Lacanian usages, is clearly tied to factuality, to what is or is not the case. Her evaluation of belief is thus tied to her assertion of the inadequacy of the idea of the divine as the "object" of perception, experience, or belief. Irigaray argues that belief is dependent on concealment:

> If this is exposed, no need to believe, at least according to a certain mode of adherence. But truth, any truth throughout the centuries, assumes a belief that undermines it and that captivates and lulls to sleep the one who believes. That this belief affirms and unveils itself in the form of myths, dogmas, figures, or religious rites, doesn't this reveal that metaphysics keeps watch over the crypt? (SP 39; SG 27)

Irigaray seems to begin her analysis of belief, then, by saying that it is false by definition; belief depends on the concealment of its object and yet, in the end, posits an apparently unconcealed but invisible object—God, Truth—in which to believe. As Irigaray will argue throughout the essay, truth in fact lies in communication and mediation. The "demons" that thwart this to and fro movement between persons, that reify communicated and communicating truths into a single Truth that is to be unreflectively accepted, are, curiously, allied with belief (just as they are associated with the repetition compulsion by Freud). Theology (the popular theology of the Roman Catholic Church lies behind Irigaray's generalizations here) and metaphysics join together in their attempt to hide that which founds the "monocratic, patriarchal truth . . . its order, its word, its logic" (SP 39; SG 27)—the concealment and implicit sacrifice of the mother('s body). The constitution of the normative subject of Western philosophy and theology, whose elucidation is the necessary preliminary to any account of sexual difference, is dependent on an act of faith (in the absent mother's presence), which is itself an act both of mastery (the child holds the string) and concealment (he makes the toy absent in order to control its return).

The bleeding woman's story and Ernst's come together here, for they both tell, from different sides, what occurs and what is at stake in that constituting act. Whereas Lacanian psychoanalysis posits the mirror stage (the moment when the subject sees itself, experienced as fluid and fragmented, as whole, unified, and yet other in its own mirror image) as the pivotal moment in the constitution of the subject preceding the Oedipal complex (for Lacan interpreted as the entrance into language), Irigaray looks to the realm prior to either of these moments. Before Ernst learns to play "gone" with his own image in the mirror, he plays gone with his toys and, symbolically, with his mother. Just as, in *Speculum*, Irigaray modifies Lacan by demonstrating the association of woman with the mirror that serves as the reflective surface in which man constitutes his identity, so in her reading of *Beyond the Pleasure Principle* she highlights an element brought to the fore by neither Freud nor Derrida. The veil (of the bed onto which Ernst throws his reel) stands between Ernst and his toys/his mother, allowing him to master their/her presence and absence. Although censored by the father (of psychoanalysis—the pleasure principle/PP or grandfather, Freud), the veil is the necessary prop for the game of presence and absence, concealedness and unconcealedness enacted by Ernst.[22]

Here the paradoxical relationship between belief and mastery is made apparent, for in fact, as Irigaray remarks, the reel is not the mother:

> He believes, this little angel, that to come into the world or to go out of the world can thus be made into a game. He *believes* it because it is not the truth. This event remains without mastery in its expiration, obeying a necessity with which it is impossible to play so easily, except by killing, and fasting to death. . . . Then, when he thinks he can control her appearance-disappearance, it is then that he believes the most. (SP 43–44; SG 31)[23]

Through the game Ernst comes to believe not only in himself and his power, but also in his mother and the fact that despite her apparent absence, she is there.

Again, Irigaray's analysis must be read against its Lacanian background. For Irigaray, following Lacan, when the move is made into the mirror stage (the necessary preliminary to entrance into language), the other in whom the male subject believes becomes a reflection of himself, and the male god is born. Presumably, the little girl sees her own reflection in the mirror, yet what she sees is in the image of that which must be denied. The little boy, on the other hand, is affirmed within male-dominant systems, where "the phallus" (i.e., that which represents masculinity as the locus of meaning and power) is given ascendancy as the transcendental signifier and the Name/No-of-the-Father serves to unify and constitute the subject. The subject is always lacking before the power of the phallus, of the father, and of God, and this lack is then projected onto woman, defined as constitutively lacking and other. Against Lacan, however, Irigaray insists that the relationship between the divine Father and the believing son is not a quest for the phallus (or at least not merely or initially) but rather for the "first crypt, a first dwelling to which he longs to return" (SP 44; SG 32). What is lost is not the plenitude of being promised by the phallus, but the mother('s body) itself. Through the assertion of a transcendent divine phallus and the denial of the mother('s body) as that which has been lost, men articulate an uncertain, always nostalgic subjectivity for themselves and deny any subjectivity to women. In other words, the mother('s body) is lost twice—first in the child's necessary movement away from the mother and then again when he denies that loss, covering it over with the phallus.

There are two steps to Irigaray's deconstruction of Ernst's and his grandfather's belief. First, the string of his toy reel is not the hollow thread of the umbilical cord through which the gift of life is given to the child by the mother('s body). Second, the mother cannot be equated simply with the first dwelling, for this equation conflates the mother with her body, denies her independent and transcendent subjectivity, and thereby precludes the possibility of any relationship with her (other than as an object). This association of the mother with the first dwelling is, it seems, the mistake committed by patriarchal thought and religion, with dire consequences for women.[24] As Irigaray argues, with implicit reference to Heidegger, the attempt to reconstruct the first dwelling is impossible, for the placental veil that stands between the child and the mother from the beginning has been destroyed and cannot be reconstructed. Irigaray extends Derrida's critique of the nostalgia implicit in Heidegger's evocation of the primal dwelling (and thus also responds to the Derridean charge that Irigaray herself, in reinscribing sexual difference at the (non)origin of subjectivity, evinces a nostalgic desire for return to the maternal womb):

> To have access to her—woman—would come after the nostalgia for this return to her, for that regression to the lost paradise where she shelters him and feeds him with and through her/their envelope. To have access to her demands another threshold than that approach where she always stands behind the veil. The veil has served the life between them one time only and without possible repetition. (SP 46; SG 34)

The subject attempts to recreate the first dwelling and the primal veil or placenta that must remain intact if that dwelling is to be reconstituted. Desire not for the father's power but for this primal home leads the boy to conflate the destroyed veil or placenta with the mirror in which he sees himself whole and intact. His own illusory wholeness, then, replaces and conceals the mother. Conversely, when he sees the mother, he does not recognize her as other but as his own lost wholeness. According to Irigaray, for real difference to be recognized, the conditions for a face-to-face encounter must be met; the boy must renounce his desire for wholeness (and with it the illusion of an absolutely transcendent deity), recognize the inevitable loss (to him) of the mother('s body), and acknowledge the mother as an other.

In Freud's account, the son can relate to the mother only through the strings (of the reel) and veils (of the bed) that divide space into horizontal and vertical relations. The possibility of a face-to-face encounter is lost, and "everything is in place for [the mother] never to arrive at the destination, never to come face to face with him" (SP 46; SG 34). The only way the son and the mother can communicate is through a scar or wound that the son opens "in her womb so that he can close up the navel, the heart, or the mouth over the wound of her absence, of her disappearance from him" (SP 47; SG 34). The placenta is both his and hers, pointing to the ambiguity of their identity(ies), neither fully two nor clearly one (i.e., before birth).[25]

For the son, then, the mother's absence is experienced as a wound or gap in his own being. His desire to heal that wound, to suture that gap, leads him to conflate the mother with her womb, thereby denying her independent subjectivity. The child's desire to heal his own fractured body and his inability to accept the openness and fluidity of embodied existence lead him to equate femininity and bodiliness, and therefore to claim mastery and transcendence as his own. Although here Irigaray downplays the role of the phallus, it is only in the face of this ideal of (masculine) totality and unity that the normatively defined subject struggles toward wholeness and mastery. The ideal denies openness, fluidity, and partiality, and it is here that Irigaray locates the God of Western monotheism.[26]

In "Belief Itself," Irigaray points to other possibilities, other futures, other conceptions of the sacred, and other articulations of sexual difference and of the space between persons necessary to communication. These gestures are effected through Irigaray's transposition of the veil from Ernst's bed and the placenta to angels, who have been "misunderstood, forgotten, as the nature of that first veil. Except in the work of poets, and in religious iconography" (SP 47; SG 35). Evoking Rilke and Heidegger's reading of Rilke in "What Are Poets For?" Irigaray suggests that the angel communicates from that place beyond the veil (beyond the pleasure principle and its implication in the desire for mastery over death and for death itself). Paradoxically it is the seemingly transparent, disembodied, and sexless angel who foreshadows the possibility of a communication between two bodies in the face-to-face encounter.[27] Through her allusions to angels, Irigaray points to the continued necessity of a limited transcendence in the articulation of human subjectivity, while denying the reification and absolutizing of that transcendence.

Moreover, angels can serve their mediating and salvific function only if there are two or more, one coming from God to Mary and one from Mary to God. To thwart hierarchical relations, the vertical relationship must run in at least two directions. The ambiguity of the Virgin Mary lies here, for despite the overt dogma,

> when the angel goes toward her, is it not possible that he already comes from her? Isn't it from her that the angel takes off? Almost imperceptible skin or membrane, almost transparent whiteness, almost indecipherable mediation, always at work in every operation of language, of representation, ensuring the connection between the most earthly and the most heavenly, the first dwelling place in her, from which he makes and remakes his bed, and works out the transcendence of the Lord. (SP 50–51; SG 38–39)

By "angelicizing" (hence divinizing) Mary, Irigaray suggests that the divine can be brought to earth. Mary is made transcendent with the Father and the Son, and they become embodied, leading to "a new conception of flesh" and a self-transcending embodiment. Rather than serving as the fleshy surface onto which male transcendence is inscribed, mothers/women might then become free subjects in a face-to-face encounter.[28]

The significance of all of this for our understanding of belief is suggested by Irigaray's warning against the domestication of the angel. Irigaray here points to the dangers of the Western ideology of woman as the angel in the house and also of attempts to take the angelic literally: "They light up sight and all the senses on condition that we perceive the instant when they pass by, hear their word and fulfill it, without wanting to show, demonstrate, prove, argue about their coming, their speaking, or appearance" (SP 55; SG 42–43). Irigaray asks not that we "believe" in angels, who are not literally there in the shape of apprehensible entities, but that we take the risk they symbolize: the possibility of relations between beings who share in both immanence and transcendence.

The attempt to master absence (the concealment or transcendence of the other) gives rise to the objectification and, ultimately, denial of the (m)other('s transcendence). She is rendered voiceless (in the first move of the fort-da) and then effaced (in the mirror stage) so that the son might see himself in his own image. Irigaray reverts to an analysis of Roman Catholic ritual to augment her point, arguing that the eucharistic sacrifice masks that of the mother and the other woman, the woman as lover, on which it rests. The effaced sacrifice of the mother and the lover is the "truth" of the analysand's bleeding body. Who, Irigaray asks, is this father who demands that sexuality, sexual difference, and the flesh be abolished? Irigaray continues her questioning, asking whether the effacement and denial of sexual difference is the real meaning of religion. Does the mother('s body) lie in

> the crypt of an order put in place by a sole sex that claims to make the law on truth at the price of life? Aren't the sons henceforth not led to some occult *fort-da* between very exceptionally virginal mothers and mysteriously absent fathers? How can the spirit weave itself in these estrangements, these beliefs, these paralyses, these negations and denials of life? (SP 59; SG 47)

Only badly, Irigaray suggests, although the possibilities of another economy and other forms of relation (and with them other conceptions of religion) emerge from the chaos of the old. "But there are still flowers," she writes, in an indirect allusion to the story of Demeter, who is willing to sacrifice herself for her daughter, although not unto death. In the image of the rose, Irigaray again evokes the possibility of "a risk that risks life itself" without embracing death (SP 61; SG 50).

Here Irigaray mimes Heidegger's language in "What Are Poets For?" making explicit the role of breath and air in a movement of immanent transcendence suggested by the image of the rose that lives without a why. Breath gives life, yet it cannot be seen. It is the concealed but still material source of a human transcendence that is horizontal and nonhierarchical, a movement out toward the other rather than of mastery over her. The silent, moving source of existence, the air requires that we take the risk of opening ourselves to the other if we are to experience presence within language. Rather than attempting to master and deny the other's absence/transcendence, experienced as a gap or wound in one's being, the poets trust in language as the means of human communication:

> Beyond go one to the other those who renounce their own will. Invoking themselves under every speech already articulated, every word already spoken, every conversation already exchanged, every rhythm already beaten out, they are drawn into the mystery of a word that seeks its incarnation. Trusting beyond measure in that which makes flesh of every word: air, breath, song, they receive themselves and give themselves in a senseless abandon, in which they are reborn one by the other invested with a speech of forgotten

inspiration, buried beneath logic, over and above any existing language. (SP 64; SG 52)

In the heavily allusive final pages of the essay, Irigaray suggests that the poets' trust in language requires forgoing traditional belief and embracing risk. By renouncing the protection of god (and of "that age-old citadel of man—being"), the poets from the future and of the future discover "the trace of gods who have fled" (SP 64; SG 52–53).[29]

> These prophets are aware that, if something of the divine can still come to us, it is in the abandonment of all calculation, of all language and every meaning already produced, in risk, only risk, no one knowing where it leads, of what future it is the message, of what past, the secret commemoration. No project here. [*Aucun projet, ici.*] Only this refusal to refuse what is perceived, whatever the distress or wretchedness that may come of it. (SP 65; SG 53)[30]

These lines not only echo Heidegger but also, in the refusal of project and the demand for attention to "what is perceived," evoke Bataille. Like Bataille, Irigaray calls on every subject to take the risk of encountering what is and what might be.[31] This risk entails the rejection not only of belief understood as the refusal to acknowledge perception but also of belief as project, precisely the form of "rational" projection that, elsewhere, Irigaray claims is necessary for women.

Given the context of "Belief Itself"—it was written for an academic conference dedicated to the work of Jacques Derrida (aptly entitled "The ends of man" ["*Les fins de l'homme*"])—perhaps we should read the essay as addressed to male subjects, asking them to take the "risk" of difference, to put aside their own projects in order to open a space for those of women. Yet is not this risk also required of women? Irigaray argues that the boy, longing for the lost body of the mother, asserts himself as whole to protect against that loss. In doing so, he projects a phallic God and effaces the mother as an independent subject who might be encountered face to face. Yet does not the female child also suffer the loss of the mother('s body)? And is not Irigaray's call for a female divine in fact an attempt to provide symbolic representations capable of mediating that loss (even if ultimately these representations will be incorporated into the subject)?

Irigaray argues that "woman" is constitutively open to the other and hence able to accept herself as finite without positing woundedness and lack as the basis of subjectivity. Yet the primordial home that was the mother('s body) is lost by both boys and girls. Why should not women mourn this loss as much as men? And even if that loss is reconfigured in ways that stress the survival of the mother as a possible interlocutor in a face-to-face encounter, we should remember that Sophie, Freud's daughter and little Ernst's mother, died. Loss may not be constitutive of subjectivity in the ways Freud argued (for the primordial loss of the mother['s body] is not absolute), but the fact of human mortality remains something with which the subject must eventually grapple. There are real limits to the openness and possibilities of the real. In what follows, I suggest that it is precisely Irigaray's reluctance to acknowledge the emotional effects of such losses that leads to her fetishistic belief in sexual difference.

FROM SPECIES BEING TO SEXUAL DIFFERENCE

Irigaray asserts both that women require a female divine, one onto whom they project their ideals, values, and projects, *and* that such projections must be deconstructed. Are Irigaray's demands contradictory? Insofar as belief involves projects, it seems clear that they are (although this might still be a fruitful, rather than a debilitating, contradiction). In the face of our deconstructive proclivities, moreover, how is belief possible? Certainly it lies outside the rational control within which Irigaray seems to hope to encase it ("rational" here understood, with Irigaray, as assent to that which is there). Irigaray attempts to resolve this dilemma by claiming that the "object" of belief does not lie outside the subject, but within: "God ought rather to be that which contributes to the becoming of that subjectivity, in being already posed by me, or in me, as the blind source of my conscious, of my project, of my becoming, of my horizon."[32] But what is this blind source? What ontological status does it have, and whence does it emerge? And does not Irigaray's assertion that this source is "blind" seem at odds with the claim she makes in "Divine Women" for the rationality of belief? Feuerbach solves the problem of the ontological status of the object of belief by arguing, in *The Essence of Christianity*, that the perfections and ideals of human beings have objective existence in the species concept or species being of humanity. Unlike Feuerbach, Irigaray does not articulate clearly the mechanism by which religious ideals emerge and by which they might be appropriated as one's own.

Grace Jantzen argues that because Irigaray calls for conscious projection of a female divine, projection does not involve alienation.[33] For Feuerbach, objectification—the projection of one's own ideals and values onto another—involves alienation only if that other is divorced from the self. In his Hegelian inspired terminology, as long as human beings recognize that they contain all of these ideals, attributes, and values (or have the possibility of doing so) in their humanity or species being, projection does not involve alienation. No finite individual, according to Feuerbach, can contain within herself the perfections of the species. This gap between the mortal, limited, and finite individual and the species gives rise to the process of projection itself. Only when those attributes are projected onto a radically other being, one whose possession of goodness, justice, or love deprive human beings of their claims to these same attributes, blinding them to the real source of these human values and qualities, does alienation occur.

Feuerbach derives his understanding of the species concept from Hegel, transposing Hegel's notion of absolute spirit to humanity understood in its totality. Outside of this ontological context—one that few contemporary readers accept—Feuerbach's notion of the species being makes little sense. Yet Irigaray's account of religion becomes coherent only in light of a modified version of the species concept. Thus, she takes Feuerbach's notion of "humanity" as the site of infinitude and perfection and argues, in keeping with her insistence on the centrality of sexual difference, that humanity is at least two. Sexual difference, then, silently occupies the space of Feuerbach's species concept. Because Irigaray does not make this move explicit, it is difficult to understand how we can both reasonably project female values, qualities, and projects and avoid reifying those ideals in a divinity that lies outside the individual. Thus Irigaray seems both to denounce and to demand belief. Irigaray's claims cohere, however, if we supply the missing ontological foundation, reading woman or sexual difference as the locus of female projection (although there may be other ways to make these contradictions fruitful, they will require beginning with that which we do, already, believe). Irigaray calls on women to believe not in a divine being transcendent to women, or in the limited potentialities and perfections of individual, empirically existing women, but in the (always only potential? or is it actual?) divinity of "woman" as a gender.

Thus Irigaray's problematic hypostatization of gender binaries and of claims to the primacy of sexual difference are tied to and partially resolve the difficulties in her understanding of religion and belief. "Woman as a gender" provides the universal site of projection and appropriation; it is the locus of divinity through which individual women can attain subjectivity. In Feuerbachean terms, this projection and appropriation might not require a belief that goes beyond the demands of reason, for in believing in women as a gender and in the reality of sexual difference, women merely believe in the possibility of their own value, projects, and goals. Yet insofar as Irigaray insists, in "Belief Itself," that the subject must risk even her own projects if she is to open herself to the encounter with the other, contradictions remain. Irigaray might well argue that women cannot risk their projects until they have them. Yet in arguing for the universality and necessity of sexual difference, grounded in and grounding the difference between men and women, Irigaray implies that women must never take the risks demanded by "Belief Itself" (as well as by much of *An Ethics of Sexual Difference*).

How much sense can we make of woman as a gender? Again, the elucidation of Feuerbach's parallel notion of the species being is helpful. Commentators on Feuerbach have demonstrated convincingly that the notion of the species being is crucial to the theory of religion he provides in *The Essence of Christianity*. In the words of Marx Wartofsky: "The fundamental distinction in his work is that between the existing individual man as the finite and incomplete instance of the species, and human nature as such, which is the infinite character of the species, its essence, or that unlimited potentiality or capacity humanity has for being 'truly' human."[34] So, as Van Harvey argues, alienation refers either to the gap between the individual and the species or "to the failure of an individual to be 'truly human,' that is, to realize in his/her own life those distinctive potentialities which define him/her as human."[35]

Having given these two possible readings of Feuerbach's claim, Harvey goes on to argue that without endorsing an outmoded Hegelian anthropology, we cannot make sense of the idea of a species concept in which the infinite resides. Some idea of the infinite might be defended, however, in terms of human potentialities and possibilities. The primary philosophical objection to this move is its essentialism, which seems to assert that humanity can be universally defined. Harvey argues, however, that any appeal to the notion of alienation *must* depend on some account of the human essence or potentiality that one fails to achieve. He offers Kierkegaard and Heidegger as examples of philosophers who have eschewed talk of human essences while maintaining notions of inauthenticity and human potentiality.[36] They can maintain these notions, Harvey argues, because of the minimal content they ascribe to "humanity," which makes their conceptions of human nature both plausible and potentially less exclusionary than more robust accounts. Similar claims have been made about Irigaray's notions of sexual difference and woman. Drucilla Cornell and Patricia Huntington argue that for Irigaray woman is a purely formal signifier, governed by a reiterative rather than substitutional logic; it therefore "gains substance only through the manifold ways that specific women interpret their actual and dissimilar lives."[37] According to Elizabeth Grosz and Pheng Cheah, Irigaray leaves the concept of sexual difference open and so avoids the charge of essentialism—she insists that there must be men and women but does not tell us what men and women are.[38]

Yet however open the concepts of woman, man, and sexual difference within her work, Irigaray reifies sexual difference as the essential difference that replaces the universal human possibility or actuality represented by Feuerbach's notion of the species being.[39] Sexual difference not only marks the finitude of each sex in its relationship to the other, but the infinity of the species made up of these (at least) two sexes. Sexual difference is the locus for finite human beings' desire for infinite possibility. Irigaray may safeguard against the reification of female (or male) divinities, but in order to accomplish this task she must put sexual difference in the place once occupied by God. It is, she argues, the universal and objective difference through which subjectivity can be discovered, and without it, she claims, humanity as a species will perish (JTNP 14; JTN 12).

Irigaray's account in I Love to You of a horizontal transcendence made possible through the bodily encounter with the other, a movement through which we recognize our finitude and our human potential, offers a compelling account of intersubjectivity, one whose power is undermined by her reification of sexual difference. Through a recognition of the other in his or her difference, Irigaray argues, transcendence is reconfigured as "enstasy" rather than "ecstasy": "Transcendence is thus no longer ecstasy, going out of the self toward an inaccessible, extra-sensible, extra-earthly entirely-other. It is respect for the other whom I will never be, who is transcendent to me and to whom I am transcendent" (JAT 163; ILTY 104).[40] This is an attractive portrait of bodily spirituality (or a sensible transcendental), yet it is not clear how Irigaray can justify (ontologically or politically) reducing such intersubjectivity to the encounter between men and women. Moreover, despite Irigaray's own explicit antiessentialism, it is not clear how one can recognize the other as other without some defining characteristics of alterity.[41] If those defining characteristics are to be created and imagined, why reduce them to sexual difference? And why reduce this difference to the difference between only two entities, when we have seen that such binaries offer an inadequate account of the multiplicity of sexed bodily experience and, thus, are potentially exclusionary? If, on the other hand, Irigaray asserts that sexual difference is not created and imagined but ontological (whether as something bodily or psychic), then we return to the charges of essentialism with which we began.[42]

The biggest problem with Irigaray's insistence on the primacy of sexual difference, however, is not a lurking biological or psychological essentialism, but rather an idealism that bypasses the specificity and complexity of real human bodies. Irigaray claims that we cannot think the body without thinking sexual difference, but in fact (dual) sexual difference is an ideal category that is incapable of encapsulating the complexity, ambiguity, and multiplicity of bodily experience. Human bodies may always be sexed, but, as both biological science and cultural theories of intersecting identities show, human bodies are not only nor simply sexed. When sexual difference becomes the site of human becoming and divinity, bodies and the multiplicity of differences grounded in bodies that are and/or can be constitutive of human identity are effaced. Thus I wonder if Irigaray's project in I Love to You—to reconfigure subjectivity in terms of bodily encounters with others—might not be rethought in terms that recognize the alterity and similarity of each bodily subject to the other. Rich possibilities can be found within Irigaray's own work. For example, her discussions of language in The Forgetting of Air in Martin Heidegger, An Ethics of Sexual Difference, and Sexes and Genealogies suggest a reading of the speaking body as the site of the sensible transcendental—the place where materiality and ideality are inextricably linked through the repetition of bodily signs.[43] This speaking body is sexed, but not only—nor perhaps inevitably (at least in terms of dual sex difference)—sexed, rendering it both ontologically and politically a more defensible basis for reconfiguring subjectivity, intersubjectivity, situatedness, and freedom.

Irigaray herself seems increasingly to fear multiplicity, claiming that it diffuses political energies and vitiates women's claims to autonomy and subjectivity. She argues that stultifying disagreements between feminists are engendered by "the lack of objective determinations proper to the female gender" (JAT 15; ILTY 4) and that without such determinations, grounded in and/or creating the distinction between male and female, we will be left in a world without value and meaning, hopelessly fragmented and nihilistic. Yet Irigaray's reification of sexual difference is in constant danger of eliding the differences among women (as well as between women, men, and others not defined so easily in these dualistic terms). We need to find ways to negotiate multiplicity without succumbing to the nihilism and quietism Irigaray fears. Again, Irigaray's own appeals to mysticism offer possible alternatives. Read in light of the mystically inflected conclusions of "Belief Itself," Irigaray's Feuerbachean project seems to stop short of risking it all. The projects, plans, and ideals through which female subjectivity is to be engendered, while open to the other and self-subverting insofar as they imply divine transcendence of humans, never fully undo themselves. The gods may ultimately be destroyed, but sexual difference and woman as a gender, Irigaray insists, must remain.

From the standpoint of certain mystical texts, Irigaray makes an idol of sexual difference. The thirteenth-century German mystic Meister Eckhart once prayed to God to free him from God—a prayer that both posits and subverts the divine. I have suggested here that the body in its complexity and multiplicity might be a more apt site for the divine and its subversion than is sexual difference. To speak of the body in these terms, however, requires recognizing the body as the site both of human possibility and transcendence of limitation, and of limitation, mortality, and loss. Irigaray's fear of multiplicity reflects her reluctance to grapple with these aspects of human bodily existence. In eschewing Lacan's "law of castration" and its emphasis on lack, Irigaray is in danger of disavowing the reality of loss as both constitutive and destructive of human embodied subjects.

Feuerbach's account of religion helps clarify why "Divine Women" seems profoundly dangerous to those who distrust Irigaray's turn to religion and yet remains inadequate as a religious project. For Feuerbach, religion is not simply an operation of consciousness or reason. Rather, the will and imagination are central to the process of projection and alienation, for it is human *desire* that motivates projection. Van Harvey offers a useful summary of Feuerbach's complex account. The encounter with another being engenders the process of self-differentiation, in which

> the individual I experiences a powerful inrush of two types of feeling: on the one hand, a painful feeling of limitation and inadequacy over against the unlimitedness of the species and, on the other, an ecstatic sense of the attractiveness of the species, an attractiveness grounded in the individual's joy in the exercise of his/her own distinctive powers. But because the idea of the species is an abstraction and as such has very little emotional power, it is seized upon by the imagination and transformed into the idea of a single being. The individual, driven by his/her desire to live and his/her sense of finitude, finds in the perfection of the divine being a substitute for the true bearer of these predicates, the species, as well as an assurance of his/her own worthiness and immortality as an individual.[44]

In his account of Christianity, Feuerbach suggests that human egotism, desiring the immortality of the individual over against that of the species, lies behind the movement of alienating projection. However, as Harvey indicates, Feuerbach also argues that it is the abstraction and emotional barrenness of the species concept that causes the imagination, driven by desire, to concretize the species being in a divine being.

To cast the issues in Feuerbach's terms, we can say that those who distrust Irigaray's turn to religion do so because when she claims that women *need* religious projection, she acknowledges the power and the necessity of desire and imagination, and thus seems in danger of thwarting reason. On the other hand, Irigaray's turn to religion remains inadequate as a religious project because even as she recognizes the importance of desire and imagination, she attempts to keep them under rational control. Yet Feuerbach's argument shows convincingly that desire, the source and motivation of the religious imagination, cannot be programmatically and rationally generated and deployed. Feuerbach's argument also shows us something else, something more crucial, about the problems endemic to Irigaray's turn to religion. I have already suggested that political and religious projects, grounded in understandings of alienation or suppression, depend on some projected, free, and autonomous goal against which current experience is found lacking. Yet as Harvey explains, that goal also requires emotional and imaginative appeal. According to Feuerbach, God gives emotional power to human beings' desire to escape mortality, finitude, and limitation—God provides human beings with imaginatively concrete and emotionally salient dreams of the possibility of immortality, and so enables them to evade the harsher realities of the flesh. Similarly, I will argue in the next chapter that Irigaray claims to embrace finitude and mortality and yet bypasses their bodily effects. In other words, through her fetishistic belief in sexual difference, she both acknowledges and disavows the fears and desires evoked by human finitude, limitation, and loss—the mortality of the human body.

VENTRILOQUIZING HYSTERIA: FETISHISM, TRAUMA, AND SEXUAL DIFFERENCE

....

My argument has been that the erection of the phallus as a privileged symbol, as the transcendental signifier—the establishment of the male subject as the figure for wholeness to which the female and her body are compared—is not a universal fact of culture. It rather occurs in the philosophical tradition at the moment when women's humanity is conceded, when they are named as defective, partial men. The "symbolic pre-eminence of the male organ" is a historical fact, not a universal description of culture. To historicize is to see differently.
PAGE DUBOIS, *Sowing the Body: Psychoanalysis and Ancient Representations of Women*

In working from psychoanalytic theory, however, it is easy to fixate on the figure of the phallus and to slide into viewing the physical loss of the penis as a generalized lack. Freud's text, in fact, slips between loss and lack as if they are equivalent. There is, however, a significant difference between loss and lack, and one should not be too hasty in discarding loss in favor of lack.
E. L. MCCALLUM, *Object Lessons: How to Do Things with Fetishism*

FETISHISM AND BELIEF

In "Belief Itself," Irigaray suggests that man's belief—in himself as an autonomous subject and in the father God who serves to uphold his being—is premised on the sacrifice of the mother.[1] Irigaray's psychoanalytic account posits God as the site of the transcendental signifier or, in Lacanian terms, the phallus that secures meaning and subjectivity. If we place Irigaray's articulation of the logic of belief in the context of Freud's arguments about fetishization, we see that for Irigaray the God of Christianity—whether it be the Father, the Son, or the Son's sacramental instantiation in the Eucharist—is a fetish, an overvalued part object filling in for the mother's lost phallus (although for Irigaray, what is lost is, more simply, the mother['s body]).[2] In other words, as I suggested in my reading of Lacan's *Encore*, the phallus (and with the it the penis, which is always secondary to the phallus for Lacan) is itself a fetish.[3]

Whereas for Freud the fetish is always a substitute for the penis, Lacan insists on reading fetishization in terms of the phallus, which, he argues, cannot be reduced to the penis. Although, as I argued in chapter 5, there are problems with this claim, Lacan does make the logic of the fetish basic to human subjectivity in a way that potentially undermines the centrality of the phallus and the primacy of sexual difference. In Lacanian theory, the bodily ego that emerges in the mirror stage is itself always already a fetish, for it posits a whole subject who is always also distanced or split from itself. In other words, this imaginary fullness covers over an essential lack at the heart of subjectivity, and so, although providing a necessary support for subjectivity, it is also a fetishistic object of belief. Irigaray claims that Lacan's insistence on lack demonstrates the phallic nature of his thinking—either you have one, or you do not. She suggests that in articulating a feminine imaginary and symbolic not premised on lack but on fluidity, doubleness, viscosity, openness to the other, and a forward moving temporality, women will no longer be subject to the logic of fetishism. Her mimicking of hysteria can, in fact, be read as an attempt to speak from the site of the fetish, thereby disrupting its objectifying power. From the standpoint of women, Irigaray argues, hysteria depends on the repression of affects engendered by traumatic forms of subjectification. She attempts to speak these symptoms, thereby uncovering their close ties to man's disavowal of (traumatic) loss through the fetishization of the penis, the phallus, and/or women.[4]

Irigaray's Feuerbachean premises depend on recognizing oneself in the divine. For Feuerbach, humanity itself contains the plenitude and potential for immortality posited of God. Feuerbach recognizes that there is a gap between the individual and the ideal that leads to the latter's alienating projection onto a divine other. To counter this move, Feuerbach replaces God with humanity. The debates surrounding Feuerbach's theory of religion can be recast in terms of fetishism; for insofar as the species being becomes an overvalued and empirically unavailable site of plenitude, humanity becomes God and, thus, an object of fetishized belief. Irigaray's insistence on the primacy of sexual difference and its inscription in the philosophical position occupied, in Feuerbach, by the species being seems to posit plenitude at the site of the couple, thereby potentially fetishizing the male–female pair. Hence Irigaray is in danger of returning to the logic of fetishization engendered by experiences of limitation and loss.

Irigaray attempts to forestall such a charge, arguing that the sexual other is radically unknowable and that this negativity demands recognition of human limitation: "The negative in sexual difference is the acceptance of the limits of my gender and recognition of the irreducibility of the other. It is insurmountable, but it gives a positive access, neither instinctual nor drive-related, to the other" (JAT 32–33; ILTY 13). In other words, only recognition of our own limits, derived through an encounter with the sexual other, renders communication and relationship possible. Here Irigaray suggests that human beings can recognize and accept mortality and limitation without the need for the fetishizing substitutions through which one's own immortality is posited. Yet as I asked near the end of chapter 7, why only the sexual other? Would not experience of any other bodily being mark my limits as a bodily subject, and so my need for the other? Again, by insisting on sexual difference, Irigaray seems to privilege the centrality of heterosexual bonds to the discovery of mortality and suggests implicitly that procreation (whether biological or metaphorical) enables an immortality that surpasses the mortality of finite individual beings. In so doing, she conflates loss with Lacanian lack and so repeats precisely the fetishistic disavowal ("I know, but even so") of which both she and Lacan are critical.

Although Irigaray acknowledges the need to embrace one's own mortality (an easier thing to do cognitively, I think, than affectively), she elsewhere denies loss—arguably the primordial experience lying behind fetishization, mourning, and melancholia—a constitutive role in the formation of feminine subjectivity. Yet, as I asked in chapter 7, does not the girl child also mourn the loss of the mother('s body), of the first home, and the placental veil that ties mother and child, for a period of time, together? And even if we can acknowledge that loss and so reconfigure this experience in ways that enable a face-to-face encounter between mother and child, what if the mother, or another loved one, dies (as did Sophie, little Ernst's mother)? By conflating loss and lack, Irigaray is unable to account for the role of loss and its foreclosure of the possibilities of the real in the formation of subjectivity. Her fetishization of the heterosexual pair as the site of mortality and limitation for each gender works implicitly to uphold belief in the potential immortality of sexual difference itself, thereby enabling this disavowal of loss.[5] At the very least, Irigaray's fetishization of the heterosexual pair maintains the association of death and mortality with sexual difference in ways potentially dangerous for women, who often seem to bear the weight of that difference.

For Freud, fetishism is a response to sexual difference—a refusal to acknowledge the other's difference and hence a refusal of that other's subjectivity (because she becomes objectified through the fetish). Irigaray argues that the refusal to acknowledge the other is premised on the primordial loss of the mother('s body) and the disavowal of that loss. Moreover, for both Freud and Irigaray, the refusal to acknowledge the other involves an obsession with sexual difference as the single most salient form of difference—only through sexual differentiation (a sexual differentiation Freud both posits and denies) can subjects come to be. One effect of the explicit restriction of difference to sex is the naturalization, depoliticization, and dehistoricization of sexual difference and of the other forms of difference that are both reinforced and hidden from view by claims to the primacy of sex. Because sexual difference is seen as unassailably "natural," it becomes the alibi and cover for other forms of difference that are effectively "naturalized" through their metaphorical inscription in terms of sexual difference.[6]

In light of such critiques of the monological explanatory system of psychoanalysis, Anne McClintock calls for a rereading of the fetish as "the displacement of a host of social contradictions onto impassioned objects" that defies "reduction to a single originary trauma or the psychopathology of the individual subject."[7] Psychoanalysis's attempt to reduce all difference to sexual difference is part of a larger cultural project. Freud's psychoanalytic theories articulate a crucial aspect of the culture in which he lived and wrote, a culture in which ethnic, racial, religious, and other differences were consistently read in terms of sexual difference and sexuality. Moreover, by making sexual difference primary, these cultural formations of thought, practice, and the unconscious attempted to naturalize the multiple forms of power and oppression on which white, propertied, Christian, European men grounded their supremacy.[8] Thus I would amend McClintock's project slightly and suggest that we not only uncover the specific social contradictions that give rise to particular forms of fetishization, but also pay attention to the way these contradictions are often collapsed into naturalized categories of sexual difference, which, in turn, naturalize and hide other forms of difference. We need both to historicize and to politicize our reading of fetishization.

Freud's model of sexual differentiation is, as Irigaray argues cogently, a dualism that always collapses into a monism. Irigaray critiques Freud's refusal of femininity as genuine difference, but she never asks whether the problem might not be with the focus on sexual difference (and its implicitly binary structure) itself. Irigaray's failure to address this question gives rise, I think, to the endless controversies surrounding her work, for as long as sexual difference remains primary, the danger of fetishizing that difference (and thereby participating in an imperialistic erasure of other differences) remains. Irigaray may not intend to fetishize either woman or sexual difference, and I have argued that some of the criticisms of her work, especially with regard to the issue of essentialism, are mistaken. Yet I think these mistakes are symptomatic, marking a return of crucial issues repressed by Irigaray's work.

I would like to explore this possibility by returning to late medieval mysticism and to the complex interaction of the body, belief, and sexual difference within it. By reading Beatrice of Nazareth's "On the Seven Manners of Loving God" with and against its translation—or perhaps more aptly, mistranslation—by her male hagiographer and in the context of the thirteenth-century hagiographical tradition in which he writes, we can see how the fetishized body of the mystical holy woman is produced and carefully controlled by cultural authorities. This hysterical and/or fetishized female body becomes the site on which differences—particularly those between clergy and laity and between orthodox and heretic—are naturalized. Yet this saintly female body, as attention to Beatrice's text will show, is the product of a series of fetishizing misreadings of Beatrice's spirituality, misreadings that effectively erase her resistance to culturally dominant models of female sanctity and their dependence on bodily suffering.

What I hope to show is that these mistranslations, like the misreadings of Irigaray's work, are highly motivated and symptomatic of unresolved issues concerning the body, loss, and mortality both within Beatrice's text and within the highly gendered context in which it is translated. Reading Beatrice with and against contemporary hagiographical works demonstrates the ways in which she resists the fetishization and hystericization of the female saintly body through a melancholic incorporation of the suffering Godman that attempts to foreclose loss. Yet her own hagiographer fetishizes Beatrice's body in an attempt to make it stand in for his own bodily mortality and hopes for immortality. Like Beatrice, Irigaray deploys utopic belief—here sexual difference itself—as a way to avoid the loss that is endemic to bodily experience. And like Beatrice's hagiographer, both Irigaray's critics and her defenders engage in a fetishization of Irigaray: in the first case, by finding within her theory an essentialized body that must be abjected (in part because of fears of just the kind of fetishization of women's bodies that occurs in the case of Beatrice); in the latter case, through a narrow emphasis on the letter of the text and the complexities of its theoretical context that refuses to acknowledge contradictions within the work itself.[9]

Some feminist and queer theorists want to rehabilitate fetishism as a vital and mobile way to deal with loss.[10] However, the history of the fetishization of women and of women's bodies within Western culture suggests that the fetish, as external to the self, is susceptible to fixation and reification. For the potential subject to be the object of this fetishistic logic is profoundly debilitating. This danger becomes evident when we compare Beatrice's text to her hagiography and see the move from something like hysteria as a feminine subject position, to the fetishization (and hence objectivization) of that female subject, to, finally, her/its abjection. Similarly, I will argue that the fetishization of Irigaray('s texts and theories), like her own fetishization of sexual difference, has profoundly debilitating political and philosophical consequences.

FETISHISM AND HYSTERIA: READING THE LIVES OF THIRTEENTH-CENTURY HOLY WOMEN   In the famous prologue to his *Life of Marie of Oignies* (1176–1213), the first of a series of mystical hagiographies produced in the Low Countries and Belgium during the thirteenth-century, James of Vitry, the Augustinian canon and soon to be bishop of Acre, describes groups of virgins, widows, and matrons who, having dedicated themselves to poverty and devotion, are constantly overwhelmed by the divine. In the *Life of Marie*, and in other hagiographies that will follow, sanctity is grounded in claims to spiritual experiences (visions, auditions, and other manifestations of the spiritual senses) and rapture. These women, for example, with bodies wasting away from divine love, "would faint from desire and they were only rarely able to rise from their beds over the course of many years. There is no other cause for their infirmity than he, desire for whom liquefies their souls. . . . The more they were comforted in spirit, the more infirm their bodies became" (VMO "Prologue" 6, 637; LMO 20).[11] One woman wept until her cheeks were permanently marked by the tracks of her tears.[12] Another was able to do without food for forty days.[13] Others "were rapt outside of themselves with such inebriation of spirit that while they rested in that holy silence for almost an entire day and the King was in their chamber, they had no voice and no senses for any external things."[14]

Perhaps the most startling behavior was exhibited by a woman who ultimately merited a hagiography of her own, *The Life of Christina the Astonishing*, written by the Dominican Thomas of Cantimpré. According to James (who does not name her), "the Lord worked so wondrously" in Christina (1150–1224)

> that after she had lain dead for a long time but before her body was buried in the ground, her soul returning to her body, she lived again. She obtained from the Lord that, living in the body, she would sustain purgatory. Therefore she was afflicted for a long time by the Lord so that she sometimes rolled herself in fire, and sometimes in winter she remained for lengthy periods in icy water, and at other times she was driven to enter the tombs of the dead. After having undergone penance in so many things, she lived in peace and merited so much grace from the Lord that many times, rapt in spirit, she led the souls of the dead as far as purgatory, or through the ends of purgatory as far as the Kingdom of heaven, without any injury to herself. (VMO "Prologue" 8, 638; LMO 23)

Robert Sweetman has argued that Thomas of Cantimpré depicts Christina's "postresurrection" life as a long exemplum through which she instructs others while also freeing souls from purgatory. She provides a theatrical depiction of both purgatorial suffering and postresurrection bodily lightness and joy, thereby teaching through her deeds (as she will eventually come to preach through her words).[15]

Yet for Barbara Newman, this explanation of The Life of Christina the Astonishing remains insufficient, for Newman wants to understand the person behind the vita, a person whose extreme actions and bodily symptoms seem pathological to modern readers.[16] Thus in her analysis of Thomas's detailed and extraordinary version of Christina's Life,[17] Newman argues that there is good reason to understand Christina's behavior in terms of hysteria.[18] Like James, Thomas describes Christina as engaging in a host of activities similar to those found in nineteenth- and early twentieth-century cases of hysteria: deathlike trances, levitations, extreme asceticism (Christina throws herself in boiling vats of water and roaring fires), self-exorcisms, screams, tears, and bodily contortions (in grief over the damnation of sinners, Christina "wept and twisted herself and bent herself backwards and bent and rebent her arms and fingers as if they were pliable and had no bones" and "cried out as if in childbirth and twisted her limbs and rolled about on the ground with great wailing" [VCM 26, 37]).[19] Not surprisingly, Christina is a figure of fear and consternation to the townspeople of St. Trond, who assume that she is mad or possessed by demons (as the Middle English version of the Life puts it).[20] Casting the issue in terms of modern notions of mental illness, Newman insists that we need to ask why "Thomas of Cantimpré took the risk of representing the village lunatic as a saint."[21]

But what is at stake for modern historians in accepting nineteenth- and twentieth-century evaluations of Christina and other holy women as mentally ill, and in particular, as hysterical? The association of medieval women's sanctity and of the forms of mysticism most often found among women with hysteria runs throughout the modern literature on both phenomena. The neurologist Jean-Martin Charcot (1825–1893)—so important in the modern medical study of hysteria because of his insistence that hysteria is a disease of the nerves rather than a sign of moral degeneration, malingering, and laziness—first introduced the reading of mysticism as hysteria in "La foi qui guérit," written shortly before his death. There he argues that Francis of Assisi and Teresa of Avila were "undeniable hysterics" with the ability, nonetheless, to cure hysteria in others.[22] The association of mysticism—particularly the visionary and somatic forms of mysticism most often associated with women—and hysteria was used throughout the early twentieth century (and beyond) to disparage and denigrate women's experience and writing.[23]

We have seen, for example, that Beauvoir distinguishes between the mysticism of Saint Teresa, the product of "a sane, free consciousness," and that of her "minor sisters." Beauvoir interprets the mysticism of Angela of Foligno, Madame Guyon, and others as a form of erotomania and hysteria (the two are often indistinguishable in the psychoanalytic literature), with hysteria understood in a broadly Freudian sense. The hysteric, for Freud, is one who suffers bodily symptoms she (or he) does not know how to interpret. These symptoms mark the return of traumas and/or desires that, due to the force of repression, can appear only in veiled form (and so are not immediately legible). Thus for Beauvoir, whereas Teresa controls her bodily, sexualized experiences of the divine (a claim Teresa would find surprising), the bodies of other women signify without their conscious consent and without their knowledge of the body's meanings (a sign of degradation for Beauvoir).

Beauvoir's feminist analysis leaves room for a distinction between hysteria and mysticism; nonetheless, she assimilates most examples of female mysticism to the former, degraded category. Most scholars who have wanted to take mysticism seriously have, as a result of such dismissive diagnoses, either avoided the term "hysteria" entirely or have reserved it for those figures seen as somehow marginal, excessive, or troubling to standard religious categories.[24] Not surprisingly, the term has recently reemerged around women who display a particularly somatic and/or erotic mysticism, namely, Christina the Astonishing (for whom we have, it should be emphasized, only a hagiography written by a man who did not know her) and Margery Kempe.[25] Yet as attention to other vita produced in Belgium and the Low Countries during the thirteenth century shows, the forms of divine possession seen in *The Life of Christina the Astonishing* differ only in degree from that ascribed to other women (and those differences are grounded, theologically, in the claim that Christina already possesses a resurrected body). What I want to ask here, through both an analysis of aspects of a few of these hagiographies and a comparison of them with a treatise produced by one of these women (Beatrice of Nazareth), is whether hysteria is the best category through which to explain these vita and make them accessible to modern audiences (a crucial concern, I think, for Newman) and, if so, *whose* hysteria is being described in the hagiographical texts.

Newman hypothesizes that Christina, having survived an unknown illness and deathlike coma, shows signs of severe mental disturbance: "antisocial behavior, violent self-mutilation, peculiar and repellent choices in food and dress."[26] The people of St. Trond, judging her to be ill or possessed, attempt to restrain her, make her a public spectacle, and have her exorcized, all to no avail. She remains an unassimilable mad woman, reduced to begging to stay alive (an act that, according to Newman, would have had no religious significance for Christina or her neighbors). "Into this wretched existence," Newman continues,

> came a cleric. . . . Seeing Christina's extravagant sufferings, he assimilated them to the mortifications offered by women like Marie of Oignies for the benefit of souls and devised a new interpretation of her state. Christina was indeed tormented—but her torments now had meaning: she was a madwoman with a mission. . . . Under the tutelage of this priest and his circle, Christina became increasingly pious and began to model her behavior, insofar as she could control it, on the devotions of lay *mulieres sanctae.*[27]

Thus by a "stroke of pastoral genius," the bodily pathologies of a hysterical woman are transformed into a theologically coherent glimpse of the next world. Newman argues that a male advisor superimposes theological value on Christina's hysterical experience, and only then does it take on religious significance (and hence become something other than hysteria).

Newman's argument, if valid, has ramifications for the study of thirteenth-century women's religiosity, for although extreme, Christina's actions are remarkably similar to those of the other women discussed in James of Vitry's prologue. There were also, however, contemporary theological, philosophical, and medical discourses available to explain these women's experiences, ones with which James himself was familiar. The question then becomes what relationship, if any, exists between medieval and modern categories of analysis. As Dyan Elliott shows, thirteenth-century philosophers like Alexander of Hales (d. 1245), William of Auvergne (d. 1249), and Thomas Aquinas (d. 1274) frequently use the terms "rapture," "ecstasy," and "alienation" or "departure of the mind" (*alienatio mentis* or *excessus mentis*) "to connote the alienation from the senses that occurs during an encounter with a higher spirit."[28] Early Christian and medieval debates about the nature of such experiences focused on Paul's description of being caught up into the third heaven (2 Corinthians 12:2–4). Following Augustine's distinction between corporeal, spiritual, and intellectual vision, most scholars agreed that Paul describes an unmediated experience of intellectual vision, one that does not depend on images. The general belief was that such intellectual vision, and even the lesser experience of spiritual vision, depended on an alienation from the body, certainly from the sensitive faculty of the soul (the senses), if not from the vegetative faculty (the animating principle itself). For thirteenth-century commentators, then, alienation of the mind or the senses gives rise to trance-like states or a deathlike bodily appearance. As Bernard McGinn points out, James of Vitry's *Life of Marie* (c. 1213) is the first text to use language traditionally associated with the heights of monastic contemplation (*separatus a corpore, a sensibilibus abstracta, in excessu rapta*) for those trance-like states. Moreover, whereas earlier monastic literature emphasized the brevity of this moment, James depicts Marie and other women remaining in trance-like states for hours, even days, on end.[29]

In thirteenth-century philosophical, medical, and theological literature, women's bodies are depicted as particularly suited to such rapture in that they are judged to be more porous, permeable, and weak than men's. In addition, according to these texts, the great humidity and softness of women's bodies makes them more impressionable and so more imaginative. Although often a source of problems for women, this imaginative capacity can also make them more open to spiritual vision. However, medieval thinkers also understood hysteria or suffocation of the womb as a pathological condition almost indistinguishable from rapture and demonic possession in its bodily effects. It was widely believed that "the absence of sex permits corrupted humours to build up so that the womb actually rises and presses against the heart," giving rise to a deathlike appearance.[30] Even Thomas of Cantimpré (author of five mystical hagiographies as well as a collection of marvels, *De apibus*) recognized that deathlike trances might be the sign of bodily illness rather than of rapture.[31] Moreover, for Thomas, and increasingly, as we will see, for others, demonic possession becomes another possibility almost completely indistinguishable physically from divine rapture or ecstasy. Therefore, theologians and spiritual advisors needed to be adept at interpreting bodily signs in order to determine if they were caused by rapture, demonic possession, or disease.

The use of hysteria, as a medieval and a modern category for explaining apparent cases of demonic possession and at least some examples of mystical experience, raises the question of who is authorized to interpret these bodily phenomena.[32] One of the commentators on pseudo-Albert the Great's *De secretis mulierum* (*Women's secrets*) shows that conflicts of interpretation were already at work in the medieval period: women who suffer from "suffocation of the womb"

> lie down as if they were dead. Old women who have recovered from it say that it was caused by an ecstasy during which they were snatched out of their bodies and borne to heaven or to hell, but this is ridiculous. The illness happens from natural causes, however they think that they have been snatched out of their bodies because vapors rise to the brain. If these vapors are very thick and cloudy, it appears to them that they are in hell and they see black demons; if the vapors are light, it seems to them that they are in heaven and that they see God and his angels shining brightly.[33]

Here we see a male authority rejecting women's own theological interpretations of their bodily experience. The obvious question with regard to Newman's reading of *The Life of Christina* is why we should suppose, given the absence of any account of a mediating influence, that Christina did not herself interpret her experience theologically.[34] She may have needed male clerical approbation to sanction her interpretation, but there is no evidence within either *The Life of Christina* or *The Life of Marie of Oignies* to suggest that Christina did not develop this interpretation of her experience on her own. The only figure Thomas depicts influencing Christina is a woman recluse, Ivetta of Huy.[35]

Newman's reading seems to rest on assumptions like those of Freud and Beauvoir—what is most salient about hysteria is less its symptomology than the lack of consciousness the "victim" has with regard to the cause of her symptoms. To label Christina (and the demoniacs Newman also analyzes in her essay) as hysterical seems to presume that she has no available interpretative frame for her experience. When one is provided by a priest, Newman argues, her hysteria takes on meaning, becomes theologized, and is transformed into religious activity. The hysteric, then, is one who cannot read her symptoms or, as the author of *Women's Secrets* shows, is judged to have interpreted them incorrectly. Yet available evidence contradicts Newman's thesis, suggesting that women both desired and were often able to interpret their own symptoms, even if at times in the face of male resistance.[36]

Beauvoir asks whether the mystic submits to bodily symptoms or controls them with a "sane, free consciousness"; for medieval women and men, however, this question poses far too stark a contrast. Women like Christina presumably understood themselves as overpowered by an experience beyond their control (this is the way thirteenth- and fourteenth-century texts by women talk about such raptures), yet there is evidence that they struggled to maintain the authority to interpret that experience against the competing claims of male medical and ecclesial authorities. Moreover, analysis of a female-authored mystical text, Beatrice of Nazareth's "Seven Manners of Loving," alongside its "translation" in a male-authored hagiography suggests that to some extent these visibly symptomatic women's bodies were constructed by men. In other words, hagiographers constructed the mystical body—read as hysterical by many modern readers—through their interpretation of women's words and actions.

These mystical bodies authorized both women's claims to sanctity and the clerical voice who interpreted these bodies correctly. Beatrice's hagiographer, like many of his contemporaries, displaced his own and the larger culture's fears about bodily limitation, suffering, and mortality onto the body of a woman. He ventriloquized his culture's spiritual dilemmas and its conflicts over materiality and religious authority through the mystical female body.[37] If we want to maintain the validity of hysteria as a psychoanalytic category, one that points to the operation of unconscious desires and motivations, it is essential to recognize that the hagiographical construction of medieval women's bodies was undertaken by men. By ventriloquizing their own hysteria through women's bodies, hagiographers created the women's body as a fetish (a place where belief is both asserted and denied) always in danger of abjection. Fetishism, then, emerges here as the masculine correlate to hysteria—it is hysteria ventriloquized through the body of the other.

BEATRICE OF NAZARETH AND THE MYSTICAL BODY

Beatrice spent most of her life in one or another of the three Cistercian monasteries founded by her father in the Low Countries; within these houses she assiduously followed *The Rule of Benedict*, copied book manuscripts, prayed, meditated, studied, and later served as prioress. She also wrote religious works in the vernacular, although only a short treatise, "Seven Manners of Loving God," survives.[38] Taught by beguines before entering the Cistercian order and in close contact with a number of other women noted for their sanctity and extraordinary experiences of the divine, Beatrice participated in what historians call the "women's religious movement" (Frauenbewegung) of the later Middle Ages. In the north, this enormous upsurge of women religious and semi-religious (beguines) originated and was centered in the diocese of Liège. The vitae of Marie of Oignies, Christina the Astonishing, and a host of other holy women emerge in this diocese over the course of the thirteenth century. Within the context of this literature, Beatrice's external life within an established order was unexceptional; her treatise, however, suggests that her inner life boiled and teemed with waves of violent love and insane desire. Within the religious world of thirteenth-century northern Europe, at least some people revered the ecstatic experiences described by Beatrice in her treatise and understood them as marks of extreme sanctity.[39] Most likely her reputation for sanctity led the abbess of the monastery at Nazareth, or someone else close to Beatrice, shortly after her death, to commission a book about her life. The hagiographer had at his disposal Beatrice's own "book"; in fact he claims that The Life of Beatrice is merely a translation of Beatrice's mystical journal into Latin.[40] Although the mystical journal itself appears now to be lost, Beatrice's one remaining treatise, "Seven Manners of Loving," is the source for much of the vita's third book. Only for the account of Beatrice's death does he acknowledge that he must turn to the evidence of other "reliable people," including Beatrice's sister Catherine.[41]

The hagiographer consistently portrays Beatrice as undergoing intense interior experiences that mark themselves externally on her body and in her behavior: "Therefore it frequently happened that, whether she willed it or not, her interior jubilation of mind would break out in some manifestation, and the mind's inner jubilation would betray itself outwardly either in laughing or dancing a gesture or some other sign."[42] Throughout the text, Beatrice's interior state makes itself manifest in tears, fainting spells, trance-like states, laughing, and dancing.[43] She is frequently depicted as attempting to hide these external signs from her companions,[44] or as feigning illness as a mask for her inner jubilation.[45] At other times, illness is itself described as a sign of her interior state.[46] According to Beatrice's hagiographer, "even if she could not explain in words what and how much spiritual delight she received, or what she sensed and tasted in this melting, it was to some extent apparent outwardly by the fainting of her bodily senses" (LBN 238–39). The crucial difference between

Freud's hysteric and the mystic, as represented in *The Life of Beatrice*, is that whereas the hysteric's symptoms are rooted in her unconscious desires and so unknown to her, Beatrice is presumed to be aware of her interior state even if she cannot control it or express it fully to others.

Elsewhere I have shown in detail that the hagiographer both personalizes (what she ascribes to "the soul," he ascribes to her) and externalizes Beatrice's account of the loving soul.[47] We can see this double interpretive move in Beatrice's and the hagiographer's descriptions of the fourth manner of loving, where Beatrice describes a passing away of the body that is in strict accordance with contemporary theories of rapture. She also makes use of a mystical commonplace to express the overwhelming nature of love's presence to the soul, and here we begin to see a crucial gap emerge between Beatrice's text and that of her hagiographer:

> TREATISE: When the soul feels itself to be thus filled full of riches and in such fullness of heart, the spirit sinks away down into love, the body passes away, the heart melts, every faculty fails; and the soul is so utterly conquered by love that often it cannot support itself, often the limbs and the senses lose their powers. And just as a vessel filled up to the brim will run over and spill if it is touched, so at times the soul is so touched and overpowered by this great fullness of the heart that in spite of itself it spills and overflows. (SMM 15–16; SML 202; translation modified)
>
> VITA: In this stage the holy woman's affection was so tender that she was often soaked with the flood of tears from her melted heart, and sometimes because of the excessive abundance of spiritual delight, she lay languishing and sick in bed, deprived of all her strength. . . . Just as a vessel filled with liquid spills what it contains when it is only slightly pushed, so it happened frequently that Beatrice, pushed as it were, would let spill out by many signs of holy love what she felt inside; or else she would undergo a kind of paralyzed trembling, or would be burdened with some other discomfort of langour [illness]. (LBN 304–7)[48]

Beatrice describes a trance-like state in which the body and its faculties are quieted. Medieval medical and theological discussions of such experiences make use of language remarkably close to Beatrice's, suggesting that it is right to read her account in terms of claims about the soul being rapt from the body and the body's subsequent failure. There is, then, some indication of a "hysterical" body in Beatrice's treatise.[49] But the vita not only reads her experience of alienation from the senses in terms of a languishing body (which is how it would appear to outsiders), but also literalizes her mystical metaphors. Beatrice describes the passing away of the body's faculties in the soul's ecstasy; the hagiographer, by rendering the vessel Beatrice uses to describe her overflowing soul as her *body* overflowing in tears and other physical signs, underlines the signs on the body that such an experience is occurring.

A similar externalization of the bodily aspects of Beatrice's text can be seen in her hagiographer's descriptions of the fifth stage of loving, in which Beatrice's own writing achieves an intensity and fervor meant to evoke the madness and violence of love. The strength of divine love is felt in both body and soul, the lines between the two becoming increasingly difficult to decipher:

> TREATISE: And at times love becomes so boundless and so over-flowing in the soul, when it itself is so mightily and violently moved in the heart, that it seems [*dunct*] to the soul that the heart is wounded again and again, and that these wounds increase every day in bitter pain and in fresh intensity. It seems [*dunct*] to the soul that the veins are bursting, the blood spilling, the marrow wither-ing, the bones softening, the bosom burning, the throat parching, so that her visage and her body in its every part feels this inward [*van binnen*] heat, and this is the fever of love. (SMM 19–20; SML 203; translation modified)[50]

Here Beatrice uses bodily metaphors to express the intensity of her experience, its significance, and its divine referent; the hagiographer, characteristically, fo-cuses on her sensibly marked body:[51]

> VITA: Indeed her heart, deprived of strength by this invasion, often gave off a sound like that of a shattering vessel, while she both felt the same and heard it exteriorly. Also the blood diffused through her bodily members boiled over through her open veins. Her bones contracted and the marrow disappeared; the dryness of her chest produced hoarseness of throat. And to make a long story short, the very fervor of her holy longing and love blazed up as a fire in all her bodily members, making her perceptibly [*sensibiliter*] hot in a wondrous way. (LBN 308–11)

In the hagiographer's account, Beatrice possesses a hysterical, divinely marked body, uncommonly like those found in the hagiographies of other thirteenth-century women. (Beatrice's enlarged heart and open veins, moreover, are found elsewhere in the vita, suggesting the influence of the treatise's metaphors on the text as a whole.)[52]

According to Beatrice, when the soul has passed through the six manners of loving, having become love itself and returned to her own nature, which is love, she laments her misery on this earth and desires to be freed from the body. Yet this very sorrow, and the internally experienced fissuring of the body that her desire brings about, becomes a part of the union between the soul and God. The hagiographer, although emphasizing the suffering body in his rendition of Beatrice's text, feels called on to soften her expressions of desire and their vehemence. He both literalizes and fears the audacity of Beatrice's desire to be with God:

> VITA: The vehemence of this desire was so excessive that she sometimes thought she would lose her mind for its grievousness, or would shorten the days of her life because of her anguish of heart and great damage to her vital bodily organs. (LBN 324–25)

Fearing for her health, the hagiographer tells us, Beatrice avoided thinking about heaven and her future bliss when such thoughts affected her body in this way. The hagiographer has struggled with Beatrice's desire for death since book 2, chapter 16, when the theme is first introduced. For the hagiographer, this desire is an affliction, and he wishes to depict Beatrice overcoming it. Yet despite his claims to resolution, the desire continually recurs.[53]

For Beatrice, the desire for death and its attendant internally experienced suffering are central to the movement of ascent to the divine:

> TREATISE: So the soul refuses every consolation, often from God himself and from his creatures, for every consolation which could come to it only strengthens its love and draws it up towards a higher life; and this renews the soul's longing to live in love and to delight in love, its determination to live uncomforted in this present misery. And so there is no gift which can appease or comfort it, for the soul's one need is to be in the presence of its love. (SMM 34–35; SML 205; translation modified)

This portion of the text is not included in the vita, the hagiographer having lost the meaning of the treatise at this point; thus he writes that Beatrice's experiences "can be conceived only by [mental] experience, not by a flood of words" (LBN 324–25). His literalizing tendencies make it impossible, theologically and narratively, to follow Beatrice in the soul's mad desire for death.[54] As for her contemporaries Hadewijch, Mechthild of Magdeburg, and Marguerite Porete, for Beatrice the will is the locus of the conflict that leads to the experience of union and exile. The body is not the focus of battle, nor is it said to be externally marked by this struggle (through ascetic practices, tears, fevers, or paramystical phenomena—although it is marked by languishing trance-like states); rather, the internal disposition of the will and the affections define the field of battle. Thus the desire for death does not threaten death directly, as it does within the hagiography, in which internal dispositions threaten literally to tear Beatrice's body apart.

For the hagiographer, Beatrice's body is the visible site of her sanctity—it suffers, weeps, groans, grows hot and glows, in its progression from its first aspirations for divine love to its final achievement of union with that God who is love. Representations of Beatrice's hysterical body transform her into a fetish for the hagiographer and his audience. Beatrice's body, in its tears, dancing, laughter, trances, and illnesses, marks the presence of the divine in the world. Through this body, the gap between belief (in a salvific God) and knowledge (the apparent unavailability of that God to the senses) is overcome. The hagiographer cannot sanction her desire for death, for it would deny him access to that body through which he apprehends the divine.

Hagiography tends to represent the internal disposition of the soul through external narrative devices. This mode of representation becomes most pronounced in texts describing women's lives.[55] Various factors might contribute to the greater emphasis on the mystically marked body in hagiographies of holy women. In the Middle Ages, women were identified with the body, and this identification seemed to demand that their sanctification occur in and through that body.[56] Furthermore, women's access to religious authority was, in the thirteenth century, primarily (if not solely) through visionary/auditory/spiritual imaginative and mystical experience.[57] Linked to embodiment through its ties to the imagination, and often described using bodily images and metaphors, such visionary and auditory experience was also at times described in terms of its interiorly apprehended effects on the bodily experience of the holy woman. But women mystics in the thirteenth century seem to take up these associations in ways subtly different from their hagiographers. As we have seen in the case of Beatrice, the alienation of the senses brought about by experiences of rapture appear in both mystical and hagiographical texts, although they are described in different ways (i.e., from the "inside" in terms of what the soul experiences or from the "outside" in terms of the trance-like appearance of the body). More importantly, the impressionability that gives rise to spiritual vision and audition and to the use of intensely bodily metaphors is literalized and externalized by hagiographers, in spite of the fact, at least in the case of Beatrice, that this interpretive move requires that the hagiographer ignore the mystic's careful attention to the metaphorical nature of her language and hence to the distinction between the corporeal and spiritual senses.[58] This literalizing tendency radically increases the symptomatic quality and hence "hysteria" of the mystic, whose externally visible body is seen to be the direct site of impressionability. Medieval hagiographers want externally sensible signs in order to verify both the woman saint's claims to sanctity and the presence of divinity in the world. Beatrice's hagiographer provides these signs by transposing accounts of internal experience onto the externally visible body. The ecstatic woman becomes a vision, a divinely marked body, a spectacle for the viewing pleasure of her contemporaries.[59] The internal mystical life of Beatrice is transformed into a series of bodily practices and struggles, of battles represented and enacted on the body of the holy woman.

Beatrice's languishing and shattered body never attains the theatricality and excess attributed to Christina's body (nor do the bodies of any other mystics described in thirteenth-century vita). Yet the divergences between Beatrice's treatise and the vita's translation of that text demonstrate tendencies toward externalization and theatricality within male-authored hagiographies that raise suspicions about the *Life of Christina the Astonishing*. After all, Beatrice's moments of greatest hysteria are, in fact, created by the hagiographer himself through his literalistic reading of Beatrice's own bodily metaphors. In other words, whereas Newman participates in the hystericization of Christina's body by arguing that its theological reinterpretation comes from the outside, in Beatrice's case we see a move from her own theological accounts of bodily interiority to the hagiographer's emphasis on—in some sense creation of—a hystericized body. This mystical body becomes the site of belief and theological value for the hagiographer and his audience—although one that will continually challenge the limits of the very orthodoxy it is meant, symbolically, to uphold.[60]

VENTRILOQUIZING ORTHODOXY

There is evidence that the hagiographer's dramatization and intensification of Beatrice's incipient hysteria is a response to larger religious and cultural crises; in the face of heresy, the hysterical mystical body marks a return of the repressed and an attempt to disavow potential loss. In other words, through the female mystical body the hagiographer both ventriloquizes his own hysteria and/or creates a fetish through which loss is forestalled and belief reinstated. Beatrice's hagiographer gives little indication of what kind of crisis or trauma might lie behind his depiction of the saint. Yet, as I have said, *The Life of Beatrice* is just one of a group of hagiographical texts produced during the thirteenth century about the holy women of Liège and the new forms of sanctity and mystical piety emerging among them. If we look to the slightly earlier hagiographies by James of Vitry and Thomas of Cantimpré, texts that were foundational for the emerging genre of mystical hagiography, we can begin to get a clearer picture of what might have been at stake for Beatrice's hagiographer in undertaking her *Life* (although by the later thirteenth century, Beatrice's hagiographer may have been more interested in writing within existing models than in the precise theological and ecclesial struggles that shape James's text).

In the prologue to his *Life of Marie of Oignies*, James articulates the reasons for his decision to recount her life. The hagiography is addressed to Fulk, the Bishop of Toulouse. According to James, when Fulk was driven from Toulouse by the Cathar heretics, he came to the diocese of Liège, where he marveled at the virtue and sanctity of its holy women.[61] In response to Fulk's request, James (who himself preached against the Cathars) writes the life of one of these women as an incitement to the virtuous and as an argument against heresy.[62] Central to the debates between Cathars and Catholics was the place of the body, both of Christ and of the believer. The Cathars were radical dualists who denied the resurrection and redemption of the body, as well as the role of Christ's body and, with it, the sacraments in human salvation. Their teachings posed an enormous challenge to the authority of the priesthood, understood as an office handed down by and controlling sacramental power (the manifestation of God in the material). The Cathar heresy precipitated a crisis in the sacramental and priestly authority of the church, a crisis that was crucially centered on issues of materiality and embodiment (both associated, in the Middle Ages, with women). For the Cathars, moreover, the perfect were those (men *and* women) who rigorously rejected this world as they moved toward purely spiritual status.[63]

Some scholars suggest that it was because the Cathars allowed women to enter into the bands of the perfect that James and other orthodox prelates in the thirteenth century highlighted the sanctity of orthodox women. They wanted to demonstrate that there was a place for women's religious authority and power within the Catholic Church, even if this authority was always depicted in the writings of male ecclesiastics as willingly subordinated to priestly authority.[64] James's response to the Cathar heresy in his *Life of Marie of Oignies* is complex. On the most obvious doctrinal level, the holy women's bodily asceticism and sanctity demonstrate that, for orthodox Christianity, asceticism is not a rejection but a transformation of the body. The centrality of the imitation of Christ, of eucharistic piety, and of visible signs of the body's redemption (through oozing salvific substances, inscription by stigmata, bouts of joyous singing, etc.) demonstrates the corresponding centrality of the human body and the body of Christ to thirteenth-century orthodoxy, thereby safeguarding the sacramental system and priestly authority.[65] At the same time, this emphasis on the body serves another function, for, as I have shown, the late medieval "hysterical" body could be read in a number of different ways—as rapt by the spirit, possessed by demons, or diseased. In the hagiographical tradition, it is the writer (and sometimes other priestly authorities) who interprets and thus authenticates as divinely inspired the bodily experiences depicted within the text.[66] The elevation of women's saintly mystical bodies, then, participates in and enables the abjection of the heretic (although it is difficult to know, as I have shown, to what extent women participated in this process).[67] The bodies of these holy women serve as a fetishistic site onto which conflict with the Cathars and its threat to priestly authority are symbolically projected and provisionally resolved.

James and Thomas of Cantimpré (who added an important supplement to James's *Life of Marie of Oignies*) also suggest the fetishistic quality of Marie's body for individual men. Women's bodies can save others—particularly men—both in life and death, from both physical ills and purgatorial flames.[68] According to Thomas, one man was healed from an illness simply by touching a hank of Marie's hair that she obligingly pulled from her head for him. When his son later arrived home with a terrible head injury, the man pushed Marie's hair into the gaping wound, which miraculously closed up. James of Vitry describes himself as overcoming vacillations in his faith and cementing his religious commitment through his relationship with Marie. She is thus instrumental in his decision to become a priest, and so in instituting and safeguarding his priestly authority. Through her apt words and the example of her life, moreover, she endows James with preaching skills he hitherto lacked. In an extraordinarily complex ventriloquizing move, James depicts Marie on her deathbed proclaiming him her mouthpiece to the world against heresy and disbelief (VMO 53, 650; LMO 69). Marie fetishistically safeguards not only James's faith and his priestly authority, but also his body. After Marie's death, according to Thomas of Cantimpré, James obtained a finger from her corpse, which he wore around his neck in a reliquary. Crossing the Mediterranean from the Holy Land to Rome, James's ship encountered a storm and he was prepared to die at sea. Remembering the relic he always carried with him, he prayed for

Marie's intercession, swooned, saw a vision of Marie in which she predicted his future, and awoke to find the sea tranquil and all on board saved.

As depicted within the hagiographical tradition, Marie's body—like the bodies of other holy women from Liège, such as Christina the Astonishing and Beatrice of Nazareth—contains (both in the sense of holding and holding in check) intense cultural conflicts concerning the body and authority. These women's "hysteria" reveals less about their own concerns and practices than about those of men. They are figures through whom male subjects ventriloquize their own hysteria. Men's desire for the salvation of the body, a desire perhaps partially repressed by the claim that men are closer to reason and the higher faculties of the soul, reemerges in the suffering and ecstatic bodies of women through which men's bodies are redeemed. Against the Cathar's denial of the body and, thus, of the sacramental system through which priestly authority is maintained within orthodox Catholicism, the (repressed) body reasserts its value, although only as redeemed through asceticism and paramystical phenomena and as interpreted and controlled by male religious leaders (whose authority, paradoxically, these very bodies serve to uphold). These bodies, then, can be seen as fetishes, as objects in which what the senses proclaim to be true and what one wishes to believe coincide. Just as the Eucharist is both bread and the body of Christ (transubstantiation is arguably the theological authorization of fetishization), so the bodies of Marie of Oignies, Christina, and Beatrice are both weak, mortal women's flesh and immortal spiritual bodies. Of course, the hagiographers always push against that doubleness or ambiguity to claim the complete transformation of the body, but limitations generally remain.

The doubleness or ambiguity of the fetish presents dangers to the desiring subject, for it both creates an object worthy of desire, in which the subject's own internal conflicts are resolved, and has the potential to expose the lack in the subject, threatening it with powerlessness in the face of an omnipotent other. So the hysterical and fetishized mystical saint is a divinely possessed, ecstatic figure who provides a powerful and visible safeguard of male priestly authority; but this very same power and charismatic authority potentially undermines clerical supremacy. In the fourteenth and fifteenth centuries, after the Cathar threat (symbolically displaced by Marie's and Christina's sanctity) has been violently subdued, these ambiguities give rise to heightened interpretative conflicts around the fetishized bodies of possessed women. Increasingly, it becomes difficult to differentiate by external signs holy women from ones possessed by demons.

The issue is already raised in the thirteenth century by Thomas of Cantimpré, whose work becomes crucial in the following centuries, when a large literature appears instructing clerics in a hermeneutics of the (possessed) body.[69] In the thirteenth century and the first half of the fourteenth, as Dyan Elliott shows, "rapture was frequently so effective a shorthand for denoting sanctity that it was essentially freestanding, requiring little, if any, theological commentary regarding its meaning or ultimate source" (again, at least in part because these rapt female bodies were needed to help uphold sacramental and priestly authority and orthodox teachings about the body).[70] However, by the end of the fourteenth century, "suspicion surrounding rapture could no longer be resolved by reference to more rapture."[71] The growing inability to discern between possession by God and by demons leads, as Elliott argues convincingly, to "an eventual slippage into the diabolical."[72] The more the possessed woman threatens male subjectivity and authority (in the face of new conflicts and debates), the more likely she is to be abjected as a witch or demoniac.

Thus the seeds for the late medieval and early modern witch hunts can be found in thirteenth-century mystical hagiography (itself complexly related, as I have shown, to women-authored mystical texts).[73] The rules for discernment or interpretation of bodily signs rest squarely in the hands of the clergy. The potentially self-authenticating nature of women's ecstatic and visionary experience, which men used to help shore up sacramental and priestly authority against the Cathars, increasingly becomes itself a threat. Male control over female sanctity and mysticism, at first often left implicit in male-authored hagiographies (again, because these same men in part depended on the holy woman's body for their own authority), becomes increasingly explicit. As women's claims to authority begin to seem dangerous to male religious leaders, that same male leadership becomes increasingly dangerous to women.

TRAUMATIC REPETITION, MELANCHOLIC INCORPORATION, AND INTERIORITY   At this point, I would like to extend the interpretation of Beatrice's treatise that is implicit in my comparisons between the treatise and the *Life*, for I think that Beatrice's discussion of the soul in "Seven Manners" actively resists the hysterization and fetishization of women's saintly bodies effected by hagiographers. In contrast to my reading of the relationship between Beatrice's text and that of her hagiographer, Caroline Bynum argues that distinctions between external and internal are fluid in the medieval period, making the move from "inner, glorious, wordless moment" to "vision, apparition" or paramystical phenomenon unexceptional and not in need of elaborate explanation.⁷⁴ Yet this argument begs several questions. Why are certain forms of exteriority highlighted so persistently within medieval texts about women? Why, more importantly, does Beatrice insist both on the interiority of that which she sees, hears, and tastes and on the spiritual nature of her absorption into the divine? What is at stake for Beatrice in insisting on this interiority against the externalizing tendencies of hagiography, with which she was no doubt familiar?

These questions become even more pressing when we recall what is present in the *Life of Beatrice* but absent from Beatrice's own text. Her hagiographer stresses the role of external practices in the formation of a sanctified subjectivity. Like Angela of Foligno's intense meditation on and imitation of Christ's passion, these exercises center on the cross. Beatrice's treatise, on the other hand, names Christ explicitly only once (although in a very telling instance, as I will show) and never mentions the cross. Bodily asceticism and meditative practices involving Christ's cross, so crucial to the depiction of Beatrice in the hagiography, simply do not appear in the treatise. The *Life*, on the other hand, insists that it is the ordering of her spiritual life through meditative practice that leads Beatrice to experience the presence of God. This insistence is apparent in the structure of the narrative itself: the hagiographer first discusses the external life, then spends three chapters on the ordering and exercise of Beatrice's meditations, her profession into the religious life with its monastic regulation, and her friendship with Ida of Nivelles. Ida prays that Beatrice might receive special grace and has visions promising this grace to Beatrice. Only after providing this background, which highlights Beatrice's preparation through corporal and spiritual exercises, does the hagiographer describe her first rapture. That rapture, moreover, occurs during compline: Beatrice first "quieted herself" and "with a great effort . . . raised her heart to the Lord," meditating on the text of the antiphon. She raised herself up, through meditation, to the Father's presence and only then did "she immediately leap up there, seized in an ecstasy of mind" (LBN 66–69). Without preparation through spiritual exercise, the hagiographer implies, Beatrice would never have come to experience the presence of God and absorption into divine love.

After describing this first rapture, the hagiographer returns to Beatrice's spiritual exercises, emphasizing their importance for her continued pursuit of union with God. Late in book 1, the hagiographer describes methods Beatrice uses against forgetfulness:

> Day and night she wore on her breast a wooden cross, about a
> palm in length, tightly tied with a knotted string. On it was written

the Lord's passion, the horror of the last judgment, the severity of the judge and other things she wanted always to keep in mind. Besides this she also carried tied to her arm another image of the Lord's cross painted on a piece of parchment. She had a third, painted on a piece of wood, set before her when she was writing, so that wherever she went, or whatever exterior work she did, all forgetfulness would be banished, and by means of the image of the cross she would keep [firmly] impressed on her heart and memory whatever she feared to lose. (LBN 88–91)

The subsequent chapter describes Beatrice's habit of prostrating herself before "the feet of the crucified Lord, before his image" (LBN 90–91) whenever troubled inwardly by a harmful thought or by misfortune. Eventually the presence of external reminders becomes unnecessary:

Thereafter for about five unbroken years she had the mental image of the Lord's passion so firmly impressed in her memory that she scarcely ever quit this sweet meditation, but clung from the bottom of her heart with wonderful devotion to everything he deigned to suffer for the salvation of the human race. (LBN 92–93)

The external practice of prostration before images and meditation on them leads to their internal appropriation and the transformation of the self. By the end of the vita, Beatrice no longer carries images of Christ, or even sees them continually in her mind's eye, but has herself become the image of Christ on earth for others.[75]

Beatrice's hagiography, like Angela's Book discussed in chapter 2, depicts the literal incorporation of bodily and spiritual dispositions through meditative practices. In other words, external bodily practices inculcate and form certain kinds of interior subjectivity. Yet Beatrice herself does not mention ascetic practices or spiritual exercises such as the use of texts, images, and meditative techniques so crucial to the picture of her development given in the vita. In this way, her work is similar to that of other medieval women's texts, particularly those of her beguine contemporaries.[76] Nonetheless, the practices described in the vita are not completely unrelated to Beatrice's emphasis on interiority (and on suffering interiority in particular), as will become apparent if we consider contemporary psychoanalytic accounts of the construction of interiority through bodily practices and intersubjective relations. By understanding how bodily and meditative practices enable human beings to deal with loss and construct an interiorized subjectivity, psychoanalysis can help us understand how Beatrice's emphasis on interiority both emerges from and resists the kinds of meditative and bodily practices discussed in the vita.

The forms of traumatic repetition meant to induce bodily memories of Christ's suffering and death so central to Angela's spirituality and to the *Life of Beatrice* bear an uncanny resemblance to Freud's account of melancholic incorporation. As Judith Butler explains, melancholy is one response to the loss of another, a response in which loss is disavowed through the incorporation of the other into one's own psyche. Butler, following Freud, argues that this process of melancholic incorporation is constitutive of (gendered) identity.[77] The connection between meditative practices like those of Angela and melancholic incorporation is strengthened when we remember that for Freud, psychic trauma is experienced by the one who escapes bodily harm as well as by (if not even more often than) the one who suffers physically. Even more crucially, Freud's central example of traumatic repetition compulsion is the game played by his grandson as a response to the mother's absence. When Freud wrote his account of Ernst's game in *Beyond the Pleasure Principle*, moreover, Freud's daughter, his grandson's mother, Sophie, was no longer just provisionally absent, but dead. Thus Freud's repetition of Ernst's game marks his own attempt to incorporate the lost object of desire, his daughter Sophie, within his text. Traumatic repetition, then, might itself be one of the mechanisms through which lost objects are melancholically incorporated. The attempt to inculcate bodily memories of Christ's traumatic suffering and death through meditation enables the subject to incorporate melancholically the lost figure of Christ and to repeat his suffering on earth. Internalization is the goal and sign of successful incorporation. Hence Beatrice's emphasis on interiority in "Seven Manners of Loving" marks her successful incorporation of a new subjectivity grounded in Christ.

Butler places loss and the melancholic response to loss through which the subject incorporates the idealized other in the context of Freud's understanding of the role of pain in the formation of the bodily ego. Freud argues that the ego itself is primarily a bodily ego, an imaginary construct in which the limits and boundaries of the body are defined through its experiences of pleasure and pain: "Pain seems to play a part in the process, and the way in which we gain new knowledge of our organs during painful illness is perhaps a model of the way by which in general we arrive at the idea of our own body."[78] Butler uses Freud, then, to argue that our subjectivities are constructed by bodily practices and by the body's experience when it encounters the world, with pain (together with, and often inseparable from, pleasure) playing a crucial role in the formation of the bodily ego and, thus, of subjectivity. In support of both Freud and Butler, phenomenologists argue that we become most conscious of ourselves as embodied beings through those experiences (predominantly of limitation and suffering) in which corporeality intrudes itself on our attention. Through these experiences, the boundaries of the body are established both as "my" boundaries and as other than "me," for in experiences of pain we both become conscious of the body and attempt to distance ourselves from it.[79]

The challenge, then, is to recognize that both physical and psychic pain (experiences of loss) are integral to the formation of the bodily ego.[80] For Lacan in *Encore* what is lost most primordially is the body itself—in pain we move away from the body in an attempt to distance ourselves from suffering. Thus the image we form of the body, an image that serves as the foundation for the ego, is other than and split from the body itself. Because of this split in subjectivity and because of the subject's dependence on another (that image in and through which it [mis]recognizes itself), the subject is constituted and its existence threatened in the same moment.

For Lacan, then, as I interpret him, the subject is constituted in a fetishistic moment of identification with an imaginary ego ideal. The doubleness of the fetish ("I know, but even so") reflects the instability at the center of subjectivity. In contrast to this reading of Lacan, E. L. McCallum argues that as an internalized, psychic image, the imaginary ego ideal is not a fetish but marks a moment of melancholic incorporation. I think, however, that McCallum may make too sharp a distinction between interiority and exteriority, especially given women's tendency, within a Freudian scenario, to fetishize themselves and their adornments rather than external objects. In other words, what is incorporated melancholically is an internalized fetish. In melancholy, the lost other (be it the body, the mother, or another lost object of desire) is incorporated into the (now split) subject in an attempt to keep it alive and present.

My pairing of melancholic incorporation with fetishism helps make sense of the relationship between bodily practices and spiritual exercises centered on imagery, for the contemplation of images of divine suffering become internalized and then enacted in and on the bodies of those represented within these texts. By internalizing the cross of Christ through meditation and bodily reenactment, the hagiographer's Beatrice attempts to overcome the gap between her own subjectivity and that of the divine other through which it is (re)constituted. She wants fully to incorporate the divine and so to move from identification with a fetishized other to its melancholic incorporation.

With regard to the another medieval text, a rule addressed to women anchorites entitled *Ancrene Wisse*, Sarah Beckwith argues that "just as in Lacan's mirror stage, the anchoress encounters the crucified Christ as the Other, who is at the same time the internal condition of her identity; she meets him, in Lacan's terms, in *affairement jubilatoire* and *connaissance paranoiaque*, or, in theological terms, in a perpetual oscillation between presumption and despair."[81] Beckwith thus shows how the subjectivity formed through the practice of the *Ancrene Wisse* involves the formation of an imaginary bodily ego experienced in and as a fantasmatic identification with the suffering body of Christ. This imaginary bodily ego, like the figure of Christ with which it identifies, is a fetish, for it posits a plenitude that is never really there. The subjectivity constituted through this fantasmatic identification is always at odds with itself, for the bodily ego and Christ are "at once the guarantor[s] of . . . identity and the annihilator[s] of it."[82]

A crucial passage in "Seven Manners of Loving God" suggests that Beatrice has internalized her identification with the divine so as to experience melancholically and, thus, internally what was first learned in relationship to images of the cross. Throughout the treatise she has spoken of the divine as love, lord, and God; only in the seventh manner of loving does she name Christ:

> Therefore the soul is filled with great longing to be set free from this misery, to be loosed from this body; and sometimes it says with sorrowing heart, as the apostle said: *Cupio dissolvi et esse cum christo*, that is "I long to be set free and to be with Christ." So it longs greatly and with a tormenting impatience for death to this world and for life with Christ. (SMM 33; SML 205; translation modified)

The soul's desire for life with Christ makes this life one of unbearable torture, "a blessed martyrdom, a cruel suffering, a long torment, a murderous death and an expiring life" (SMM 34; SML 205). The scriptural citation suggests meditative practice. The image of Christ has been so thoroughly internalized that the soul itself is formed and constituted in that image, although, as I will show below, it is important that Beatrice identifies this suffering only obliquely with Christ, reserving the phrase "life in Christ" for future bliss rather than present suffering. In following her invocation of Christ with a statement of the soul's spiritual martyrdom, however, Beatrice leads the reader to understand the soul as reliving Christ's passion. Through its practice, the soul so internalizes Christ as to share in an imaginary identification with his suffering exile. Meditative and bodily practices have been so successful that the soul created through them feels trapped within the body and desires to burst the limits of the body itself.[83] The fissure in the self described by Lacan remains, then, but is experienced now as the alterity of the body itself. In order to keep alive the soul's endless desire, the soul, in the seventh stage of love, rejects the (earthly) body.[84]

Reading Beatrice's text against her hagiography suggests an important supplement to this reading, one that acknowledges Beatrice's agency and resistance to prevalent cultural norms. As I have shown, the hagiographer insists on externalizing Beatrice's experience. Whereas in the treatise, Beatrice's soul becomes absorbed in love through love, in the hagiography, Beatrice's suffering flesh—its expanding heart and bursting veins—itself becomes a sign of Christ's presence on earth. This hysterical/fetishistic externalization is demanded by the hagiographical genre and by cultural prescriptions about women, sanctity, and the body. Presumably, Beatrice herself was familiar with these same presuppositions; hagiographical texts were routinely read within convents, and many of the thirteenth-century examples of the genre appear to have been written for this purpose.[85] In rejecting the externalizing movements of hagiography, both in relation to the road to the divine and in the account of the nature of one's identification with Christ, Beatrice implicitly rejects precisely the association of women with the body, and hence with bodily suffering, so crucial to the hagiographer. She refuses hagiographical depictions of women's hysterical and fetishized bodies as the site of their sanctity.

Beatrice's desire for freedom can be understood as a desire to free suffering women's bodies from their literalistic identification with the suffering body of Christ. She crucially displaces typical understandings of the "life in Christ," arguing that it is not the present life of suffering imprisonment but the life of internal and eternal rapturous identification with divine love. For Beatrice, however, the formation of the free soul still occurs through suffering, suggesting that her displacement of identification with Christ from suffering to ecstasy is only partial—rather than identifying with the suffering flesh, she emphasizes the interiority of her passion. As long as one is on this earth, it is the soul not the body that suffers in an internal anguish that is itself one with the ascent to the divine. The further movement toward freedom, and the claim that the soul can be uncreated, free, and without suffering in this life, will occur in the work of Marguerite Porete and Meister Eckhart (and is dependent on the sacrifice of desire).

Beatrice's treatise shows some evidence of an imaginary bodily ego formed out of ascetic practice and identification with the suffering Christ, yet Beatrice refuses to externalize her imaginary suffering body and only obliquely acknowledges its source in images of the suffering Christ. Her reticence about bodily asceticism and meditative practices centered on Christ's passion suggests that she challenges the prescriptions for the suffering self found in the hagiography produced after her death.[86] For Beatrice, sparing the body demands breaking the fluidity between internal and external, thereby marking off interiority as the site of suffering and ecstasy. Paradoxically, her refusal to occupy a hysterical and fetishized body gives rise to her melancholic formation of an internalized self and to her disdain for the body.

Sarah Beckwith offers us a way to understand the ambiguity of Beatrice's language and the paradoxical nature of her relationship to the body. Beckwith suggests that ascesis creates an imaginary ego that incarnates the ambiguities of embodiment. Following Judith Butler, she argues that the imaginary ego generated within the *Ancrene Wisse* is an object "neither interior nor exterior to the subject, but the permanently unstable site where that spatialized distinction is permanently negotiated."[87] The imaginary ego is the very oscillation between interior and exterior, bodily and spiritual, material and imaginary—thus the ambiguity of Beatrice's language, which uses sensual imagery to describe the movements of the soul. It is just this ambiguity that the hagiographer refuses by externalizing Beatrice's experiences and fetishizing her body. On the other hand, we should not lose sight of the fact that by insisting on the interiority of the soul's experience, Beatrice, too, refuses this ambiguity.

For Beckwith, Beatrice's refusal of bodily ambiguity is a mark of her asceticism. Beckwith argues that the aim of asceticism is to transcend ambiguity; it is, she writes, "indeed an impossible, defiant, and hopelessly blighted attempt to move beyond the subject's permeability to history and to transience; it ends up producing the spectacle of that historically marked transience."[88] Asceticism is the attempt to attain a redeemed and redeeming body by overcoming corporal limitations, to attain the always already lost unity of the mirror image through a denial of the split within subjectivity. Asceticism disavows the ambiguity of bodily experience—which involves both possibility and limitation—through the rejection of the body in its mortality. Yet as Beckwith shows, this disavowal of ambiguity is always doomed and leaves behind it a record of its failure in depictions of suffering women's bodies.

The portrayal of fissured, bleeding, and suffering women's bodies in and through which others see the divine occurs, however, in male clerics' descriptions of and prescriptions for female asceticism. Through the suffering of women's bodies, the transience, historicity, and ambiguity of the reader's subjectivity is, perhaps, provisionally overcome. Beatrice does not describe bodily asceticism, but, to use her language, a spiritual one. We might also think of it as a linguistic asceticism, in which Beatrice desires to regulate the ambiguity of language, firmly locating her experience within. Beatrice implicitly attempts to avoid the fate described by Beckwith, attempting to forestall the hysterization/fetishization of her body as a spectacle of ambiguity, transience, and bodiliness through which her contemporaries can find their wholeness (through healing miracles, intercessory prayers, or simply the experience of reading). Yet the (earthly) body Beatrice's soul hopes to escape insistently returns after her death, and in precisely the hysterical and fetishized form she rejected. Beatrice's desire to foreclose this constant oscillation (and its persistent association with women) appears doomed to failure, although it remains important to acknowledge both the subtle shift in her understanding of asceticism and her defiance of predominant prescriptions and norms.

The shift from the body to the soul in Beatrice's treatise is crucial historically, insofar as it suggests that women's texts and the problems that emerge around women's mysticism and sanctity gave rise to an emphasis on interiority usually associated with men and with the early modern period (as is melancholy). Beatrice's "Seven Manners of Loving God" and Marguerite Porete's *Mirror of Simple Souls* not only reject asceticism and the hysterical/fetishized female saintly body, but also eschew visionary experience and suggest a tension between it and ecstatic and apophatic forms of mysticism. In these texts, external works and signs are sublated, and, as the soul moves further inward in its experience of the divine, so too do the spiritual senses. After the condemnations of Marguerite Porete, Eckhart, and the so-called heresy of the Free Spirit at the beginning of the fourteenth century, and with the increased persecution of the beguines following these events, this alternative movement inward is complicated by an emphasis on autohagiographical gestures within women-authored texts.[89] Yet a revised genealogy of mysticism suggests that women's mystical texts are one of the places in which the interiority of the subject emerges.

In forging this interiority, medieval women's texts are an important source for modern conceptions of the internalized self—conceptions that are currently under attack by many feminists. Through the melancholic incorporation of Christ's suffering body, Beatrice claims the autonomy of the internal self, thereby freeing herself, paradoxically, from cultural demands for a visibly suffering female body. Marguerite Porete will go farther, attempting to free the soul from all suffering, internal and external (although she will be burned at the stake, rejected and rendered abject by a world that has no place for a fully interiorized, nonsuffering, female subject).[90] These women's resistance to male prescriptions for a hysterical, fetishized, and suffering female body generated an early version of that interiorized, disembodied subject associated by both Beauvoir and Irigaray with masculinity. Yet without the political and institutional authority to control the interpretation of their bodies, lives, and texts, Beatrice and Marguerite were powerless to effect more long-lasting changes in women's sanctity and subjectivities.

For Irigaray, the central problem with Freud and Lacan (and by implication, with Bataille) is their insistence on the primacy of the penis/phallus and of lack as constitutive of human subjectivity. She suggests that a fetishistic logic is one result of this phallogocentrism, for the subject will always disavow difference, understood as lack, in an attempt to fill up the lack in its own being and thus render itself phallic. The fetish, moreover, is always created at the expense of the other, who is objectified (i.e., treated as a part object through which the subject can be made whole). Women, in other words, exist only as fetishized objects, never as fully recognized autonomous subjects, within phallocentric cultures. Despite Beauvoir's and Irigaray's different attitudes toward the question of sexual difference, Irigaray's position, as I have formulated it, closely parallels Beauvoir's critique of man's desire to be everything, a desire that objectifies woman as other.

Despite this commonality, there is a crucial limitation in Irigaray's position, insofar as she tends to insist, unlike Beauvoir, that woman has no subjectivity within phallogocentrism. At her best, Beauvoir speaks in terms of greater or lesser autonomy and freedom. Irigaray's argument is grounded in her belief that as long as subjectivity is constructed phallically, women occupy subject positions only with extreme difficulty and only at the expense of their difference. Yet this argument erases any sign of women's resistance to male dominance.[91] Following her more radical critique of Lacan in "Così fan tutti," Irigaray turns away from readings such as the one presented in "La Mystérique," where she shows women working both with and against male-dominant imaginary and symbolic systems. Beauvoir at least concedes that one or two women managed to live as free and autonomous subjects within predominantly male-dominant societies. And if we pay attention to the aspect of Beauvoir's thought in which she recognizes the embodied—and hence limited—nature of all subjectivity, we can offer even more nuanced readings of women's varying positions within male-dominant cultures. In other words, we can understand women as more or less free, more or less subjected by—and at times benefiting from—debilitating and oppressive structures of domination, rather than simply as either denied or attaining a distinct subjectivity.

Irigaray differs from Beauvoir in her claim that women must articulate a form of subjectivity grounded in relationships to new imaginary and symbolic realms; this feminine subject will not depend on the (fictional and substitutionary) presence of that which is absent but on a forward-looking embrace of that which might be. Risk then becomes constitutive of feminine subjectivity and replaces (or, following McCallum, subtly reconfigures) fetishism as the stance toward the unknown. The utopian quality of Irigaray's project seems to demand her radical break with the past—including the past of women. Even in those places where, historically, women have spoken publicly, she suggests, they have done so within the terms of a phallogocentrism that reads femininity as castration and lack. The feminine imaginary, she argues, enables one to see that only from the standpoint of the one who is supposed to be everything does the encounter with "that which is" represent sacrifice and accession to lack. Thus by recognizing the sexually different other as the horizon of one's own being, she argues, desire is reread as openness (both figural and temporal) rather than as a lack wishing to fill itself, to become everything. In this way, Irigaray reconfigures women's desire to be all—a desire clearly visible in Beatrice and still present in Beauvoir—in terms of an infinite openness to the always distinct other and the possibilities of the real.[92]

I have already argued that the one thing Irigaray is not willing to risk is sexual difference. Claiming that historically sexual difference has always been erased, Irigaray increasingly has to assert the obviousness, the givenness of sexual difference (at odds with her own assertions that it is to be created) in order to avoid the charge of fetishization; for, as I have shown, the fetish is a substitute for that which is not there (Freud's analysis) or for anxieties generated by what is there (a possible analysis of Freud's fetishization of the penis). Irigaray's critique of belief is premised on the boy child's refusal to accept a loss (that of the first home, the primal womb) and to encounter that which is (the mother as a subject to be recognized as other). A similar critique can be leveled at Irigaray: she fetishizes sexual difference in response to the absence of women's autonomy and freedom. At the same time, sexual difference becomes the means through which the losses women (and others) will continue to sustain, even if all women and men were to attain meaningful autonomy, can be evaded.

An emphasis on openness, risk, and the real as possibility is always in danger of refusing to grapple with the effects of loss—the loss of self implied by our own mortality; the loss of bodily abilities brought about by accident, illness, and age; the loss of others, signified psychoanalytically by the loss of the mother('s body), that first primal home, but including losses grounded in political and social oppression and victimization. Neither Irigaray nor any of the feminist philosophers who have taken up her interest in reconfiguring subjectivity deny the reality of human mortality. Yet the deep bodily affects that result from loss—affects that we must confront with viable therapeutic means and not simply with rational acceptance—are often evaded in favor of an emphasis on natality, openness, and possibility. This evasion of loss repeats a posture with which women have been associated historically. Whereas Freud reads fetishism and the process of melancholic incorporation through which interiority is shaped as masculine, he consistently interprets hysteria as feminine.[93] The melancholic internalizes loss and trauma; the hysteric represses affective responses to traumatic loss, which then reemerge as marks on the external body. Beatrice, in her insistence on interiority through melancholic incorporation of Christ, takes over a subject position that will, by the Renaissance, be firmly encoded as masculine.[94] Irigaray and many of her followers, on the other hand, repeat the repression of affective responses to loss and prepare the way for the (perhaps inevitable) reappearance of the hysterical female body.

Thus the conflict-laden reception of Irigaray's work can be elucidated through comparison with Beatrice's work and its reception. Like Beatrice, Irigaray is continuously misconstrued by her critics (and by some of her fans), who insist on seeing a hysterical and fetishized female body within her text. Rather than interpreting this critical reception as a simple misreading (although it is that), I think we can perhaps see something like the return of the repressed operating in the reception of both Beatrice and Irigaray. For although Beatrice and Irigaray do not fetishize the female body, they do posit fetishistic objects of belief, ones meant to deflect attention away from the fetishized female body and its association with suffering and death. These repressed elements—the body, suffering, and death—are precisely what return, although with different valuations, in the reception of their work.

Beatrice rejects externality and the (earthly) body in order to overcome death in a never-ending desirous relationship with the divine other. Presumably, the body will return after death in a new, spiritually vibrant form. Yet her hagiographer brings back the external body, making it the site of her suffering and sanctity. Her body becomes a prosthesis for the male hagiographer, a way for him to encounter the suffering, death, and promised resurrection of the body without having to confront (or even acknowledge) his own bodily existence. In other words, the female body becomes the fetishized object of belief through which the male hagiographer—and presumably his male and female audience—encounters and resolves the threat posed by death.

In their readings of Irigaray as a biological essentialist, Anglo-American feminists repeat the move of Beatrice's hagiographer, finding a fetishized female body within her early works. Yet whereas Beatrice herself rejects the body, Irigaray's call for a new imaginary and symbolic grounded in the morphology of the female body—one that would enable the slide between body, imaginary, and symbolic rigidly resisted by Lacan—seems to demand a reconfiguration of bodily experience rather than its rejection. The crucial difference between Irigaray and her critics, then, seems to be that while Irigaray believes in the historicity and malleability of bodily experience, her critics fear the body as the site of the natural, the given, and so of unavoidable limitation. What differentiates Irigaray's critics from Beatrice's hagiographer, of course, is that the hagiographer embraces Beatrice's fetishized body as an object of belief through which his own and his culture's anxieties about authority and death can be resolved. Irigaray's feminist critics, on the other hand, fear and reject this fetishization of the female body.

In response to charges of bodily essentialism, Irigaray and her commentators have insisted repeatedly that her early work is not about the body, but about bodily morphology and its psychic deployment. In other words, Irigaray and her followers insist on the interiority—arguably even the ideality—of her references. Irigaray resists the very slide between the body and the imaginary that her work apparently demands. Thus, like Beatrice, Irigaray remains deeply ambivalent about the body and its doubleness. Beatrice rejects the body as a way of rejecting her culture's construction of female sanctity in terms of suffering women's flesh. Through the melancholic incorporation of Christ's suffering body, she constructs an interiority that ensures her soul's immortality, and so she overcomes the mortality, limitation, and loss associated with bodily existence. Irigaray's repeated and explicit demand for a philosophy grounded in embodied experience makes it difficult to argue that she rejects the body, yet her insistence on an open reconfiguration of woman and on the primacy of sexual difference do seem premised, as I have argued, on a refusal to acknowledge the suffering body—the ineluctably mortal body—and the losses it continually undergoes and experiences emotionally and viscerally. In this way, I think, we can see that Irigaray denies much of the particularity, specificity, and multiplicity of bodily experience, which includes both pleasure and suffering, possibility and loss, natality and mortality.

Although I embrace Irigaray's (and many of her most astute readers') desire to bring pleasure, possibility, and natality into philosophy and psychoanalysis, I think there is a danger in refusing to think, at the same time, the realities of loss and limitation.[95] In supposing that we can unproblematically embrace mortality in our relationships with each other, Irigaray potentially forecloses death as a meaningful subject for feminist philosophy. (Similarly, in refusing to recognize the contradictions within Irigaray's work, many of her most faithful commentators foreclose discussion of the issues that give rise to them.) In doing so, Irigaray rejects mourning, melancholy (themselves ultimately indistinguishable for Freud), and fetishism as means for dealing with loss. What she provides in their place is a celebration of sexual difference that is itself always in danger of ignoring the fragility of human lives and human bonds and the multiple differences by which human beings are constituted. Not surprisingly, Irigaray reconfigures these multiple differences as themselves dangerous to the project of feminist philosophy, posing, perhaps, the unresolved specters of loss, limitation, and death.[96]

As the reception of Irigaray's work shows, the repressed will return, and it will do so in dangerous ways that reinscribe the association of women with the body and with death. Irigaray's feminist critics fear just this move and so preempt it in their (mis)readings of Irigaray's work and their rejection of the fetishized female body that they find—and that they fear others without feminist agendas will find—within it. Yet if we refuse to think about death in ways that actively challenge its association with women and sexual difference, metaphorical links between women and death will remain in place. Irigaray's fetishization of sexual difference itself seems in danger of reinscribing the association of women with the body and death. Her emphasis on a metaphorics of reproduction and natality and her location of the recognition of mortality and limitation in sexual difference in fact reinforce the association of death solely with (dual) sexual difference—and so with the sexual other. (And sexual difference, in turn, is in danger of continuing to serve as the "naturalizing" camouflage for the association of other differences with death.)

Irigaray rejects phallocentrism and, with it, she seems to claim, the logic of fetishization. Yet perhaps fetishization is not caused by phallocentrism; rather, phallocentrism itself might be a result of the logic of fetishization—in which case Irigaray's rejection of phallocentrism not only fails to solve the problem, but fully succumbs to it. Indeed, Irigaray's disavowal of loss as problematic—a way of dealing with loss that is not unrelated, I have argued, to melancholic incorporation—ineluctably gives rise to fetishization, in this case, of sexual difference itself.[97] In this way, Irigaray remains deeply embedded within the terms and the operations of psychoanalysis, which arguably is the theorization of the modern West's preoccupation—even fetishization—of sexual difference and of the processes of substitution through which sexual difference covers over and resolves other, unacknowledged conflicts and losses, including those engendered by the ambiguity of embodied existence.

Psychoanalysis both limits Irigaray and provides the means for understanding and thinking past her fetishization of sexual difference. The bodily ego, that first support for subjectivity associated both with primary identification and primary narcissism, is, according to Freud, formed through the infant's pleasurable and painful interactions with the world. Through these interactions—visual, tactile, kinetic, auditory, etc.—the child first begins to generate a mental map of his or her body and its borders. This psychic bodily configuration, like Lacan's mirror imago, to which it can be assimilated, provides a sense of interiority and exteriority, of boundaries between the child and the world, and hence serves as the first articulation of subjectivity. It is not quite the body itself, but a psychic representation of the body generated through the senses and the child's proprioceptive being in the world (as well as, Lacan would insist, on his or her losses and desires). The gap in the bodily ego that is the subject remains, yet the child always attempts to overcome this gap and to identify itself with the relatively unified sense of self provided by that psychic map.

Because the bodily ego is generated through pleasurable and painful interactions with the world, pleasure—and hence sexuality—is crucial to the constitution of the subject, yet so is pain—hence the extraordinary difficulty in separating pleasure and pain in the understanding of trauma and masochism. One of the ethical insights of the feminist movement is its call for the extrication of pain from the constitutive moments of sexuality (although it is not yet clear how far this is possible). Freud insisted that early childhood sexuality could not be articulated in terms of binary sexual difference (despite his own unfortunate tendency to reduce this multiplicity back to a single male model). Moreover, the emphasis on genital sexuality occurs relatively late in a child's development, certainly well after the first emergence of the bodily ego. Although sexual difference is an important factor in subjectivization, then, fetishization precedes sexuation (if not sexualization, which can be kept distinct from sexuation analytically—and perhaps in some future configuration of identity, more definitively)[98] and so should not be conflated with it. Fetishization precedes the so-called castration complex and emerges first around the bodily ego itself, which, as Lacan allows us to see, is itself a fetish. "I am a body in pieces, but even so, I am that whole, unified bodily imago." The body experiences itself as drive and potentiality, but also as limited, suffering, and mortal. The bodily ego, on this reading, is both the first psychic recognition and the first attempt to create a safeguard against mortality.

According to Irigaray, one recognizes one's limitations (as a gender) in an encounter with the sexual other.[99] Although in a culture in which bodies are rigorously defined according to gender binaries this experience of mortality will always be gendered, I would argue against Irigaray that the experiences of loss and pain that give rise to the recognition of mortality can be analytically (and perhaps genetically) distinguished from binary sexual difference. Mortality and fetishization come together, and if we insist, with Irigaray, that we recognize our mortality in the sexually different other, we fall into the danger of making sexual difference itself the sign of mortality. This is precisely the fetishistic move made by Beatrice of Nazareth's hagiographer, who can encounter mortality only through the fetishized body of the female (or feminized) saint (through whom mortality is simultaneously disavowed). The sexual other becomes the repository for precisely those limitations one wishes to disavow (and in male-dominant cultures, men have been able to control this movement almost entirely).

Even in a world in which gender binaries (and other oppressive modes of differentiation) have been overcome or radically transformed, we will still experience bodily limitation and pain; and no matter how long life might extend, we will most certainly die (and no doubt, the experiences of pain and death will continue to be sexualized in various and complex ways). Subjects are always constituted in ambivalent recognition and disavowal of this fragility. Irigaray offers a particularly stark example of how the late twentieth-century return to the body tends to disavow this constitutive fragility through its utopian political projects. The widespread contemporary interest in the Middle Ages can be read as a nostalgia not simply, I think, for a lost wholeness or plenitude, as Françoise Meltzer argues (although that is certainly part of it),[100] but for a cultural world that provided ritual, emotive, and intellectual resources for thinking about death, loss, and limitation.[101] The Christian Middle Ages had a utopia, of course, that included the restored, whole, and unlimited body. Yet as Bataille showed in the 1930s and 1940s, women like Angela of Foligno were not afraid to risk everything in their encounter with "what is there," to eschew the soteriological in response to the real, in its possibilities and its limitations. Although, with Irigaray, we must question Bataille's (and Angela's) emphasis on guilt, sacrifice, suffering, and the abjected, femi-nized body, with Bataille we must also acknowledge that Angela encountered the real, in ecstasy and anguish, in ways that Irigaray approaches only at her most mystical—hence most audacious, desirous, and least programmatic—moments.

In the closing pages of *An Ethics of Sexual Difference,* Irigaray brings together the loss of the mother('s body) and death: "The distance, infinitesimal but impassable, in the relationship to death, would it not be, from then on, that which would take place in the touching again of the feminine sex? From which comes the assimilation of the one to the other? And the forgetting of the threshold of life— the tactile" (EDS 196; AE 214). Women are associated with death, according to Irigaray, because the loss of the mother's body is experienced as the loss of the mother herself—hence the child's separation from the mother becomes dependent on her double sacrifice.[1] Within Christianity, the sacrifice of the Son covers over that originary death and promises a return to the primordial dwelling, reimagined apart from the maternal body. Irigaray argues that we need "architects of beauty who fashion jouissance" and who will create another relationship to touch and to the mother (EDS 197; AE 214). She rejects "the preciosity of the fetish or of the celebratory perfume of some sacrifice," for both the fetish and sacrifice depend on a logic of substitution in which the loss of the mother('s body) is redeemed by another. For Irigaray, as for Bataille, "the other is not transformable into discourse, fantasies, or dreams; I cannot substitute the other for any other, for any thing, for any god, because of this touching of and by him/her whose memory my body keeps" (EDS 198; AE 216).

Irigaray does not deny the reality of separation but refuses to allow any consoling substitutions to erase the memory of what has been lost:

To each wound of separation, I would respond by the refusal of the holocaust, attesting silently, for myself and for the other, that the most intimate perception of the flesh escapes every sacrificial substitution, every taking up into discourse, every abandonment to God. Smell or presentiment between me and the other, this memory of the flesh as a place of approach is ethical fidelity to the incarnation. To destroy it is to risk suppressing the alterity of God and of the other. Dissolving, thus, every possibility of access to transcendence. (EDS 199; AE 216)

Here Irigaray deploys a conception of bodily memory reminiscent of that found in discussions of trauma.[2] Yet for Irigaray, what is remembered is not pain, loss, or catastrophe but the pleasures of two bodies together. In other words, she reconfigures bodily memory as a commemoration of the joys of the flesh rather than of its agonies, of the other's presence rather than of her loss.[3]

Women are associated with death, Irigaray argues, when the lost mother('s body) is remembered only in terms of loss and limitation and the pleasures of the flesh are forgotten. Irigaray hopes to resurrect bodily memories in which the mother is the site of jouissance and ecstasy, thereby opening imaginary and symbolic supports for feminine subjectivity that are grounded in the body and its pleasures, rather than in its suffering and loss. Yet, as I have argued, the body is the site of both pleasure and pain, possibility and limitation, natality and death—and it is often difficult fully to distinguish the two sides of each of these pairs from each other. Angela of Foligno screams out when Christ leaves her, not only because she lives within the terms of a salvific economy that stresses the redemptive power of suffering, but, perhaps more importantly, because the joys of her experience of God lead to intense suffering in his absence. What Irigaray is in danger of forgetting is that the body experiences loss itself as suffering, not only the loss of the mother('s body), but the more definitive losses by which our mortal bodies are continually touched.

Irigaray's resistance to thinking the body only, or even primarily, in terms of laceration and suffering is understandable, given the proliferation of death and its representations in contemporary Western society. For many people in the contemporary West, the real seems to be configured only in terms of trauma. As the writings of both Angela and Bataille display, repeated exposure to violence gives rise to a desensitization that demands even more intense representations of suffering if some semblance of that which the body undergoes is to be apprehended. So Angela, in trying to elicit a sense of the torments by which her soul is inflicted, describes an image of absolute and unending abandonment: "Concerning the torments of the soul that demons inflicted on her, she found herself incapable of finding any other comparison than that of a man hanged by the neck who, with his hands tied behind him and his eyes blindfolded, remains dangling on the gallows and yet lives, with no help, no support, no remedy, swinging in the empty air."[4] In such passages, Angela's soul is described as absolutely abject, defined by its apparently unending suffering and irredeemable guilt and loss. When, in contemporary feminist discourse, identity is defined primarily (if not solely) in terms of traumatic suffering, there is the danger that "woman" will signify only "victim" and that feminist politics will be reduced to reactionary forms of *ressentiment*. Irigaray's attempt to reconceive bodily memory in nontraumatic terms works against just this limitation of the categories of "woman" and "femininity."[5]

Bataille is even more explicit about the need to invoke increasingly intense images of torture in order to communicate suffering and ecstasy:

> Instead of avoiding laceration, I'll deepen it. The sight of torture/ execution staggers me, but quickly enough I support it with indif- ference. Now I invoke innumerable tortures/executions of a mul- titude in agony. Finally (or maybe all at once) human immensity promises a horror without limit.
>
> Cruelly, I stretch out the laceration: at that moment, I attain the point of ecstasy.
>
> *Compassion*, suffering, and ecstasy mingle together [*se composent*]. (OC V 273–74; G 36)

Bataille evokes another risk in the tendency to understand suffering as the sole site of the real, for his logic seems dangerously close to that of the serial killer (among whom we might count Gilles de Rais), that contemporary figure of horror, fantasy, and speculation. As Mark Seltzer argues, the serial killer is described within the contemporary United States as someone who kills in order to sustain his fantasies, blurring once again the lines between fantasy, the real, and reality.[6] When and if the pursuit of ecstasy takes precedence over compassion, there seems to be no remaining constraint on human action (just as Sartre feared). The ethical demand that one respond imaginatively and affectively to violence seems in danger of leading to proliferating fantasies (and ultimately, perhaps, even enactments—or at least fantasies of enactments) of violence. If the victims of violence are consistently feminized, the outcome for women and others associated with them is particularly dire.[7]

The problem is not only that women will become the objects of violence and violent fantasies, but also that they will remain without resources for countering these traumas. As Juliana Schiesari shows, in *Speculum* Irigaray demonstrates the unrepresentability of women's loss within a discourse governed by the phallus. The phallus, whose lack is signified by the female sex, not only enables men to deny their losses but also gives them a way to *symbolize* loss—as castration, woundedness, and femininity. Women, then, are disabled within phallic discourse by their inability to symbolize their own losses, including those constitutive of subjectivity itself (and so they are unable, Irigaray argues, to be constituted fully as subjects). When Irigaray later rejects the Lacanian discourse of lack as itself phallic, she conflates lack with loss and so forgets this crucial insight. The question of how women might symbolize and so mediate their own losses, both those suffered under patriarchy and those that will come about even after its end, remains unposed (perhaps even unposable) and so unanswered.

We are left, then, with the problem of how to acknowledge trauma and loss and allow for mourning and recognition of its bodily effects without forcing women and other oppressed people to bear the weight of this work through their symbolic association with the mortal body, and without succumbing to a valorization of trauma as the sole site of the real.[8] We need, first, to reject claims to the primacy of (dual) sex difference in the constitution of the human subject (although without losing site of gender and sexuality as crucial axes of subject formation). Only in this way do we have a chance of breaking the association of women and femininity with the body in its pleasure and pain. We also need to find ways to acknowledge loss and its ineradicable bodily and psychic effects without allowing these effects to define human embodiment. Rather than attempting to disavow or repress the ambiguities of bodily existence in new forms of fetishism or hysteria, feminists need to *use* these ambiguities politically and metaphysically.[9] Although our experiences of loss, limitation, and death are always embedded in the social, and hence in the ethical and political, they are not reducible to these realms.[10] So we need, finally, to recognize that politics cannot do away with every loss and that it probably cannot perform all of the affective work demanded by our lives as embodied beings.[11]

Recognizing the limits of politics can help us begin to understand the fascination among many contemporary feminist thinkers with religion and mysticism.[12] Julia Kristeva, for example, argues that religion was once the site in which the emotional work of love and mourning was enacted; today, she suggests, art and psychoanalysis must take over that role.[13] Both art (particularly literature) and psychoanalysis, however, are generally understood to be located—

at least at the point of reception—in the private realm. As such, they are often accused of being sites of privilege in which politics can be ignored. Perhaps more importantly, they involve little bodily ritual. Irigaray's work suggests that women need publicly recognized processes of identification and mourning. Attention to late medieval women's mysticism and the ways in which it performs its affective work suggests that we may also need sites for more fully embodied practices. What is still unclear is what forms of ritual might allow us to negotiate the dangers of irrationalism and emotionalism lurking, for many, within any public "return" to religion.[14] If we disavow or repress these dangers through appeals to a purely rational political discourse and practice, however, they will inevitably return in unexamined and, thus, more politically and ethically dangerous forms.

Feminist philosophy can learn from the doubleness of mystical discourse and practice, which reflects and speaks to the deep ambiguities within bodily existence. Poised between the desire to transcend the body's limitations and the recognition that transcendence occurs only through the body, women like Beatrice of Nazareth, Mechthild of Magdeburg, Hadewijch, and Angela of Foligno hold out the possibility that endless, ceaseless, illimitable desire might be thought and lived outside of a phallic law of impotence. For this, neither politics nor religion will suffice. Read critically, then, these exorbitant mystical writings and others like them may help us devise new ways to negotiate the often fraught relationship between the political, the religious, and the mystical. At the very least, feminist philosophy should follow these women in opening itself to the messiness, multiplicity, and pain—as well as to the pleasure, beauty, and joy—of embodied subjectivity.

NOTES

INTRODUCTION

1   *Il Libro della Beata Angela da Foligno*, ed. Ludger Thier and Abele Calufetti (Grottaferrata: Editiones Collegii S. Bonaventurae ad Claras Aquas, 1985), 168–70; and Angela of Foligno, *Complete Works*, trans. Paul Lachance (New York: Paulist Press, 1993), 136. I have used Lachance's translations.

2   Angela, *Libro*, 184; and Angela, *Works*, 141–42. For more on Angela, see chapter 2.

3   See Pierre Janet, *De l'angoisse à l'exstase: Études sur les croyances et les sentiments*, 2 vols. (Paris: Alcan, 1926–28), 1:166; cited in Cristina Mazzoni, *Saint Hysteria: Neurosis, Mysticism, and Gender in European Culture* (Ithaca, N.Y.: Cornell University Press, 1996), 199. Also see Henri F. Ellenberger, *The Discovery of the Unconscious: The History and Evolution of Dynamic Psychiatry* (New York: Basic Books, 1970), 395–96; George Frederick Drinka, *The Birth of Neurosis: Myth, Malady, and the Victorians* (New York: Simon and Schuster, 1984), 347–56; and Catherine Clément and Sudhir Kakar, *La folle et le saint* (Paris: Seuil, 1993), esp. 23–105.

4   On Charcot and the difference between Charcot's and Janet's attitudes toward mysticism, see Mazzoni, *Saint Hysteria*, 19–30, 199–200.

5   Janet and Madeleine's religious confessor seemed curiously to double each other; Madeleine called Janet "*mon Père*" just as she would a Catholic priest. See Ellenberger, *Discovery of the Unconscious*, 397–98. With Janet, as with some of his more religiously sympathetic contemporaries (one thinks of William James), the religious and pathological interpretations of certain phenomena exist in a subtle and often not fully resolved state of equilibrium— not unlike Madeleine's own state on her departure from the Salpêtrière.

6   Janet, *De l'angoisse*, 1:181; cited in Mazzoni, *Saint Hysteria*, 200.

7   Ellenberger, *Discovery of the Unconscious*, 396. This is Ellenberger's description of the views expressed by the Catholic theologian Father Bruno de Jésus-Marie in his account of Madeleine's case. The very phrasing, of course, maintains the sharp distinction between pathology and religion, which will be used by other theologians, together with Christian mystics' own distinctions between lower and higher forms of the spiritual life, in order to

279

downplay those aspects of mysticism deemed potentially pathological. Usually, the term "pathological" refers to the forms of affective, erotic, and bodily mysticism associated, in the medieval and modern periods, with women. Thus, proponents of the mystical life like the Jesuit Augustin-François Poulain (1836–1919) will distinguish true mystical union from more extraordinary experiences, although he does not deny the reality of the latter. See the discussions of Madeleine in *Etudes Carmélitaines* 16 (1931), especially Bruno de Jésus-Marie, "A propos de la Madeleine de Pierre Janet," *Etudes Carmélitaines* 16, no. 1 (1931): 20–61; see also, Augustin-François Poulain, *The Graces of Interior Prayer: A Treatise on Mystical Theology*, trans. Leonora L. Yorke Smith (Westminster, Vt.: Celtic Cross Books, 1978), chaps. 5–6. On the extraordinarily intense interest in mysticism among theologians and philosophers in France before the Second World War, much of which shares in these attitudes, see Bernard McGinn, *The Foundations of Mysticism: Origins to the Fifth Century* (New York: Crossroads, 1991), 278–80, 297–310.

8 Traces of Madeleine's own words remain, however, both within Charcot's book and in letters published by Bruno de Jésus-Marie. Further study might yield significant revisions of the standard narrative. Janet used Madeleine's failed prophecies and own doubts, occasioned by periods of darkness in which she feared her ecstasies were really from the devil, to inculcate "his sense of reality," as Drinka puts it. Drinka takes Madeleine's later state of equilibrium, which lasted from 1904 to her death in 1918, as a sign of Janet's success. See Janet, *De l'angoisse*; Bruno de Jésus-Marie, "A propos"; and Drinka, *Birth of Neurosis*, 354–55.

9 Hélène Cixous and Catherine Clément, *La Jeune Née* (Paris: U.G.E., 1975), 183; Hélène Cixous and Catherine Clément, *The Newly Born Woman*, trans. Betsy Wing (Minneapolis: University of Minnesota Press, 1986), 99; translation modified. The title of Clément's essay, "*La Coupable*"/"The Guilty Woman," evokes Georges Bataille's *Le Coupable*, translated as *Guilty* but rendered more accurately as *The Guilty Man*.

10 Cixous and Clément, *La Jeune Née*, 284; Cixous and Clément, *Newly Born*, 155; translation modified. Allusions to a desire for everything or the all, a "restricted little economy," and the destruction of calculation once again evoke Bataille.

11 Cixous and Clément, *La Jeune Née*, 289; Cixous and Clément, *Newly Born*, 157; translation modified.

12 Cixous and Clément, *La Jeune Née*, 290; Cixous and Clément, *Newly Born*, 157. Cixous appeals explicitly here to Bataille. Clément can understand Cixous's comments only "poetically"; otherwise she is unable to make sense of the idea of a "a people that doesn't communicate." On Bataille's understanding of communication, see chapters 2 and 3.

13 Cixous and Clément, *La Jeune Née*, 289–90; Cixous and Clément, *Newly Born*, 157; translation modified.

14 Cixous and Clément, like Georges Bataille, Simone de Beauvoir, Jacques Lacan, and Luce Irigaray, tend to essentialize mysticism, extrapolating a generalized figure or group—"the mystic" or "mystics"—without giving careful attention to the varieties of Christian and non-Christian mystical texts. As I will show, however, specific texts ground each of their accounts of mysticism. Thus although I will sometimes follow Cixous, Clément, and others in writing of "the mystic" or "mystics," I will continually disrupt this essentializing gesture through attention to the historical particularity of Christian mystical traditions.

15 For more on the association of mysticism and hysteria, see chapter 8.

16 Cixous engages in little direct, theoretical reflection on religion or mysticism, yet religious and mystical language recurs throughout her work. Clément, the skeptic in *The Newly Born Woman*, has become increasingly interested in religion in recent years. See Amy Hollywood, "Mysticism, Death, and Desire in the Work of Hélène Cixous and Catherine Clément," in *Religion in French Feminist Thought*, ed. Judith Poxon, Kathleen O'Grady, and Morny Joy (London: Routledge, forthcoming). See also Julia Kristeva, *Powers of Horror: An Essay on Abjection*, trans. Leon S. Roudiez (New York: Columbia University Press, 1982); and Julia Kristeva, *Tales of Love*, trans. Leon Roudiez (New York: Columbia University Press, 1987). The relevant work of Luce Irigaray will be discussed at length in part 3. For a study of medieval women's mysticism that is heavily influenced by Irigaray, see Luisa Muraro, *Lingua materna, scienza divina: scritti sulla filosofia mistica di Margherita Porete* (Naples: D'Auria, 1995).

17 Irigaray uses the terms "imaginary" and "symbolic" in their broadly Lacanian senses to refer to the two central registers or levels of the psychic life, both of which are crucial to the emergence and perdurability of the subject. Because for Lacan the unconscious is structured like a language and the subject emerges in language, both also have transpsychical, cultural resonances.

18 What is meant by the senses in medieval texts and in their modern rereadings can be quite different. See chapter 8.

19 Some scholars also argue for a mystical element in the work of Emmanuel Levinas, but I think Irigaray is right to note that his thought is at root deeply antimystical, at least in the sense in which that term emerges within the Christian tradition. Suzanne Guerlac argues for Bergson's importance to Bataille, and Kevin Hart explores the relationship between Bataille and Blanchot, particularly with regard to the mystical. Foucault is, I think, the direct heir of certain mystical tendencies in Bataille and Blanchot, although in elliptical and complex ways. Finally, Derrida's relationship to mysticism has been the subject of extensive commentary both by Derrida and by others. What is lacking in all of this work is explicit attention to the relationship between mysticism and sexual difference. The narrative I tell here will, I hope, transform the ways in which we read the work of these thinkers. See Suzanne Guerlac, *Literary Polemics: Bataille, Sartre, Valéry, Breton* (Stanford, Calif.: Stanford University Press, 1997), esp. 89–94; Kevin Hart, *The Trespass of the Sign: Deconstruction, Theology, and Philosophy* (Cambridge: Cambridge University Press, 1989), as well as his forthcoming study of Blanchot; James Bernauer, "The Prisons of Man: An Introduction to Foucault's Negative Theology," *International Philosophical Quarterly* 27 (1987): 365–80; and Jeremy R. Carrette, *Foucault and Religion: Spiritual Corporeality and Political Spirituality* (New York: Routledge, 2000), 85–108. For an introduction to the literature on Derrida and mysticism, including important essays by Derrida and Mark Taylor, see *Derrida and Negative Theology*, ed. Harold Coward and Toby Foshay (Albany: State University of New York Press, 1992). For an important articulation of the analogy between the object of apophatic discourse in Dionysius and death in the thinking of Derrida and Jean-Luc Marion, see Thomas Carlson, *Indiscretions* (Chicago: University of Chicago Press, 1999), esp. 190–236.

In addition, as Bernard McGinn has argued, France before the Second World War was experiencing an unprecedented period of theological, philosophical, and, I would add, political and nationalistic reflection on the mystical. This period is also in need of detailed historical study. See McGinn, *Foundations*, 278–80, 297–313; see also Michel de Certeau, "Mysticism," *Diacritics* 22 (1992): 11–25.

20 There are also, of course, Christian apologetic authors who are interested in these kinds of phenomena, but increasingly even they feel the need to explain away the more seemingly "pathological" excesses of medieval and early modern mysticism. For an attempt to distinguish the pathological from seemingly similar mystical phenomena, see Auguste Saudreau, L'état mystique (Paris: Charles Amat, 1921), 143–44. For an earlier important piece of apologetic dealing with somatic phenomena, see Antoine Imbert-Gourbeyre, La Stigmatisation: L'Extase divine et les miracles de Lourdes: Réponse aux libre–penseurs, 2 vols. (Clermont-Ferrand: Librairie Catholique, 1894).

21 The account of Christian mysticism and its gendering offered here is both dependent on and differs fundamentally from the pioneering genealogical work of Michel de Certeau. In a series of studies culminating in The Mystic Fable (first published in French in 1982), Certeau shows that the substantive term la mystique emerges only in the sixteenth and seventeenth centuries, together with the development and systematization of a "mystical science" or "science of mystics." Certeau associates "mystics" both with a mode of speaking and a mode of making the body speak, without reflecting on the sometimes contradictory nature of these two aspects of mysticism. The centrality of women's situation and of their desire for religious voice to the development of certain forms of mysticism is covered over by Certeau's privileging of sixteenth- and seventeenth-century material and by his relative inattention to gender. See Michel de Certeau, The Mystic Fable, vol. 1, The Sixteenth and Seventeenth Centuries, trans. Michael B. Smith (Chicago: University of Chicago Press, 1992). For more on the history of the word "mysticism" and changing conceptions of its meaning, see chapter 5.

22 See Amy Hollywood, "Ca. 1147: Hildegard of Bingen Writes to Bernard of Clairvaux" and "Ca. 1265: The Beguine Mechthild von Magdeburg Defends Herself against an Unnamed Critic," in The New History of German Literature, ed. David E. Wellbery (Cambridge, Mass.: Harvard University Press, forthcoming).

23 See Herbert Grundmann, Religiöse Bewegungen im Mittelalter: Untersuchungen über die geschichtlichen Zusammenhänge zwischen der Ketzerei, Den Bettelorden und der religiösen Frauenbegegung im 12. Und 13. Jahrhundert (1935; reprint, Hildescheim: Georg Olms Verlagsbuchhandlung, 1961), esp. 430–31. There have been challenges to the idea of a beguinal spirituality. Although I would be happy to talk about the beguinal-Cistercian milieu of the Low Countries, I think that some evidence for specifically beguinal contributions exists. See Ursula Peters, Religiöse Erfahrung als literarisches Faktum: Zur Vorgeschichte und Genese frauenmysticher Texte des 13. And 14. Jahrhunderts (Tübingen: Niemeyer, 1988); see also the discussion of these debates in Amy Hollywood, The Soul as Virgin Wife: Mechthild of Magdeburg, Marguerite Porete, and Meister Eckhart (Notre Dame, Ind.: University of Notre Dame Press, 1995), 26–56; and Bernard McGinn, The Flowering of Mysticism: Men and Women in the New Mysticism, 1200–1350 (New York: Crossroad, 1998), 153–98.

24 See Hollywood, Virgin Wife; and Meister Eckhart and the Beguine Mystics, ed. Bernard McGinn (New York: Continuum, 1994).

25 Cited in Karma Lochrie, Margery Kempe and Translations of the Flesh (Philadelphia: University of Pennsylvania Press, 1991), 2.

26 Partly at issue here was a potential slippage between the spiritual and the bodily senses. For more on this issue, see chapter 8.

27 See the references in Caroline Walker Bynum, Jesus as Mother: Studies in the Spirituality of the High

Middle Ages (Berkeley: University of California Press, 1982), 172, n. 9, and 182–84. Bynum has worked to disseminate a similar distinction between male and female spirituality, although without the negative valuations. She offers a more historically grounded version, then, of the revaluation of values effected by Cixous. See, for example, Bynum's characterization of the distinction in *Fragmentation and Redemption: Essays on Gender and the Human Body in Medieval Religion* (New York: Zone Books, 1991), 194.

28 See, for example, the highly influential work of W. T. Stace, *Mysticism and Philosophy* (Los Angeles: Jeremy P. Tarcher, 1960).

29 Hadewijch, *Complete Works*, trans. Mother Columba Hart (New York: Paulist Press, 1980), Vision 7, 280–82.

30 Angela, *Libro*, 362; and Angela, *Works*, 205.

31 Dionysius the Areopagite is the apostle Paul's Athenian convert, named in Acts 17:34. The probably Syrian monastic author of the texts known under this name was part of a religious circle, many members of which took pseudonymous names from the New Testament. Throughout the Middle Ages, however, his work was believed to be that of Paul's convert and therefore to date from the first century. For this information and an introduction to Dionysius, see McGinn, *Foundations*, 157–82. For the relevant texts, see Pseudo-Dionysius, *The Complete Works*, trans. Colm Luibheid (New York: Paulist Press, 1987).

32 For Aquinas on women, holy orders, and prophecy, see *Summa Theologica* II–II, q. 177, a. 2, concl.; III, q. 27, a. 5; III, supplement, q. 39, a. 1; Kari Elisabeth Børresen, *Subordination et équivalence: Nature et rôle de la femme d'après Augustin et Thomas d'Aquin*, 2d ed. (Oslo: Universitetsforlaget, 1968), 183–88; and Eleanor Commo McLaughlin, "Equality of Souls, Inequality of Sexes: Woman in Medieval Theology," in *Religion and Sexism: Images of Women in the Jewish and Christian Traditions*, ed. Rosemary Radford Ruether (New York: Simon and Schuster, 1974), 235–36.

33 Certeau reads mystical modes of speaking and writing as grounded in a promise "whose affirmative force," Tom Carlson argues, "opens the groundless ground of the subject capable of writing and reading that text." Carlson goes on to show how Derrida elaborates on Certeau's notion of mystic speech; Derrida argues that there is absolute performativity at its root, which opens the possibility of any engagement or communication. This basic affirmative risk opens up every possibility, even that of radical evil. Certeau, Derrida, and Carlson are echoed in fundamental ways by both Bataille and Irigaray, as I will show in chapters 3 and 7. See Michel de Certeau, "Mystic Speech," in *Heterologies: Discourse on the Other*, trans. Brian Massumi (Minneapolis: University of Minnesota Press, 1986), 80–100; Certeau, *Mystic Fable*, 113–200; Jacques Derrida, "Nombre de Oui," in *Psyché: Inventions de l'autre* (Paris: Galilée, 1987), esp. 647–48; and Thomas Carlson, "Remarks on Derrida and the Mystical Logic of Self-Creation" (paper presented as the annual meeting of the American Academy of Religion, Nashville, Tenn., November 2000).

34 See D. A. Csányi, "'Optima Pars': Die Auslegungsgeschichte von Lk. 10, 38–42 bei den Kirchenvätern der ersten vier Jahrhunderte," *Studia Monastica* 2 (1960): 5–78. The issue of contemplation versus action is central to Bernard of Clairvaux's *Sermon on the Song of Songs*. See Jean Leclercq, *Saint Bernard mystique* (Bruges: De Brouwes, 1948), 393–94; Bernard McGinn, *The Growth of Mysticism: Gregory the Great through the 12th Century* (New York: Crossroad, 1994), 218–23; and Bernard of Clairvaux, *On the Song of Songs*, vol. 3, trans. Kilian Walsh and Irene

Edmunds (Kalamazoo, Mich.: Cistercian Publications, 1979), Ser. 49–51, pp. 21–48. On the theme in the beguine hagiographies, see Hollywood, *Virgin Wife*, 39–50.

35 Even when they owned property, many beguines continued to support themselves with manual labor. On the beguines, see Walter Simons, "The Beguine Movement in the Southern Low Countries: A Reassessment," *Bulletin de l'Institut Historique Belge de Rome* (1990): 63–105; and the literature cited in Hollywood, *Virgin Wife*, 207–8, n. 1.

36 Marguerite Porete, *Le Mirouer des simples ames anienties et qui seulement demourent en vouloir et desir d'amour*, ed. Romana Guarnieri and Paul Verdeyen, Corpus Christianorum: Continuatio Mediaevalis, vol. 69 (Turnhout: Brepols, 1986), chap. 118, p. 322. There are two useful modern English translations of this text. Marguerite Porete, *The Mirror of Simple Souls*, trans. Ellen Babinsky (New York: Paulist Press, 1993); and Marguerite Porette, *The Mirror of Simple Souls*, trans. Edmund Colledge, J. C. Marler, and Judith Grant (Notre Dame, Ind.: University of Notre Dame Press, 1999).

37 Eckhart, although he discusses rapturous or ecstatic states in a few places, warns against such experiences and stresses the importance of detachment over sensible experiences of the divine. See Hollywood, *Virgin Wife*, 288, n. 51.

38 The fifteenth- and sixteenth-century development of mysticism is traced most persuasively by Certeau, *Mystic Fable*.

39 See Hollywood, *Virgin Wife*, 201–6.

40 Porete, *Le Mirouer*, chap. 131, p. 384. For a reading of the trial of Love as a retelling and subtle recasting of the story of patient Griselda, see Nicholas Watson, "'If wommen be double naturelly': Remaking 'Woman' in Julian of Norwich's Revelation of Love," *Exemplaria* 8 (1996): 2–3.

41 For more on the changing understandings of mysticism in the sixteenth and seventeenth centuries, shifts that might usefully be rethought in terms of feminization and its resistance, see Certeau, *Mystic Fable*.

42 Despite recent objections to the term, I continue to find the concept of gender useful to name the purportedly cultural articulation of masculinity and femininity, particularly if it is remembered that "sex" is no more given or natural than is gender. Irigaray's use of the concept of sexual difference is equally problematic, depending, as does psychoanalytic theory in general, on a slide between sex difference, subjective formation as sexed/gendered, and sexuality. The conflation of sex/gender/sexual difference and sexuality is crucial to the working of normative heterosexuality; all of these terms, then, are simultaneously necessary and deeply problematic. On the relationship between sex, sexuality, and gender, see Eve Kosofsky Sedgwick, *Epistemology of the Closet* (Berkeley: University of California Press, 1990), 27–35.

43 Ludwig Feuerbach, *The Essence of Christianity*, trans. George Eliot (New York: Harper Torchbooks, 1957), 126.

44 Sharon Farmer has complicated the picture of gender and the body in the Christian Middle Ages by giving attention to social status and ethnic or religious differences. Celtic men and women associated the poor, both men and women, with the body. See Sharon Farmer, "The Beggar's Body: Intersections of Gender and Social Status in High Medieval Paris," in *Monks and Nuns, Saints and Outcasts: Religion in Medieval Society*, ed. Sharon Farmer and Barbara H. Rosenwein (Ithaca, N.Y.: Cornell University Press, 2000), 153–71.

45 A complex issue underlies this question concerning the relationship between politics,

reason, the emotions, and the perceived threat of fascism when the emotions enter the political sphere. These are the same issues that give rise to many of the controversies surrounding Bataille's work, for Bataille resolutely undermines the very distinctions between reason and the emotions, politics and the sacred, that many feel are necessary to protect against fascism. Irigaray's continued deployment of philosophical and psychoanalytic discourses suggests her similar attempt to undermine clear-cut distinctions between reason and the emotions, although as I argue in chapter 7, she shows some worries in her more programmatic texts about unleashing "belief" or the "sacred" from reason within the political sphere.

INTRODUCTION TO PART ONE

1   Beauvoir mentions two texts, Roger Caillois, *Le mythe de la fête*, and Georges Bataille, *La part du diable*. The latter is, in fact, by Denis de Rougemont. See Denis de Rougemont, *La part du diable* (New York: Brentano's, 1942). On the text and its relationship to the College of Sociology, see Jeffrey Mehlman, *Émigré New York: French Intellectuals in Wartime Manhattan, 1940–44* (Baltimore: Johns Hopkins University Press, 2000), 74–84. Beauvoir's mistake here may be in part responsible for her misinterpretation of Bataille, who differs in crucial ways from both Caillois and Rougemont.

2   Cited in Philip Watts, *Allegories of the Purge: How Literature Responded to the Postwar Trials of Writers and Intellectuals in France* (Stanford, Calif.: Stanford University Press, 1998), 34.

3   For Bataille's complex and ambivalent relationship to surrealism, see the introduction by Michael Richardson and the texts collected in Georges Bataille, *The Absence of Myth: Writings on Surrealism*, trans. Michael Richardson (London: Verso, 1994). Bataille's most important prewar writing was done for various avant-garde and left-wing journals, among them *Documents* (which he edited), *La Critique sociale* (edited by Boris Souvarine), and *Acéphale* (also edited by Bataille). Most of Bataille's essays from these journals are collected in OC I. For a chronology and useful biographical information, see Michel Surya, *Georges Bataille, la mort à l'oeuvre* (Paris: Gallimard, 1992).

4   Although Sartre's "denunciatory" comment is not usually cited, I wonder how much it has fueled the repeated claim that Bataille "flirts with" or is "attracted to" fascism, a claim that persists despite Bataille's explicitly avowed antifascism. The charges were no doubt further fueled by Boris Souvarine's damning critique of Bataille in the introduction to a reissue of *La Critique Sociale*. Souvarine's personal animosity toward Bataille, who had "stolen" his girlfriend, Colette Peignot, needs to be taken into account in assessing this account.

It is true that Bataille studied fascism and wanted to understand its methods in order to make use of them for the left. Jürgen Habermas is perhaps the most careful of Bataille's critics when he argues that despite Bataille's antifascist position, he does not make clear how subversive deployments of the heterogeneous differ from "the fascist canalizing of them." One clear difference is Bataille's persistent demand for a radically democratic, "headless" society. As I will show in the following chapters, moreover, Bataille's appeal to experience over or beyond reason—an appeal that many find politically dangerous and that was explicitly associated with the fascist threat in the 1930s and 1940s—is increasingly delimited by his concern for communication. At least some of the ethical dilemmas posed by his work are responded to through this insistence. See Boris Souvarine,

"Prologue," La Critique sociale (Paris: Éditions de la Différence, 1983); and Jürgen Habermas, The Philosophical Discourse of Modernity, trans. Frederick Lawrence (Cambridge, Mass.: MIT Press, 1987), 221.

5   Peter Connor suggests, however, that in 1943, the reading of Bataille as a mystic would itself have carried implications of fascism, or at the very least of the irrationalism that leads to fascism. Connor also shapes his reading of Bataille in large part against Sartre's critique, with particular attention to the apparent gap between philosophy and mysticism. For the association of mysticism with fascism, see Peter Tracey Connor, Georges Bataille and the Mysticism of Sin (Baltimore: Johns Hopkins University Press, 2000), 127–30.

6   For Bataille's essay "Formless" and important commentaries, see Yve-Alain Bois and Rosalind E. Krauss, Formless: A User's Guide (New York: Zone Books, 1997). Krauss also uses the notion of the formless brilliantly in her reading of surrealist photography. See Rosalind Krauss, "Corpus Delicti," in L'Amour Fou: Photography and Surrealism, ed. Rosalind Krauss and Jane Livingston (New York: Abbeville Press, 1985), 56–112. For a reading of "Formless" and Bataille's other early texts from the journal Documents in light of the historical context in which they were written, see Georges Didi-Huberman, La ressemblance informe ou le gai savoir visuel selon Georges Bataille (Paris: Macula, 1995).

7   Sartre's comments about the "softness" and "unformed" quality of Bataille's ideas are rendered ironic by comparison with the U.S. reception of Sartre's own work. As Ann Fulton argues, early responses to Sartre's work generally considered it to be philosophically muddled and incoherent. These responses in part arose from a misapprehension of the philosophical methodology central to Sartre's work. U.S. philosophers, trained either in naturalism and empiricism or some version of philosophical idealism, were generally unfamiliar with the continental tradition of phenomenology crucial to Sartre's philosophical project. For Sartre, phenomenology offered a way between empiricism and idealism, one that enabled him to provide a descriptive ontology grounded in human experience and consciousness. Sartre argues that only this method can offer a general analysis of consciousness; hence the incoherence of Bataille's thought without such phenomenological grounding. See Ann Fulton, Apostles of Sartre: Existentialism in America, 1945–1963 (Evanston, Ill.: Northwestern University Press, 1999). For the distinction between Sartre's deployment of phenomenology and Husserl's founding work, see Robert D. Cummings, "Roleplaying: Sartre's Transformation of Husserl's Phenomenology," in The Cambridge Companion to Sartre, ed. Christina Howells (Cambridge: Cambridge University Press, 1992), 39–66.

8   See Jean-François Louette, "Existence, dépense: Bataille, Sartre," Les Temps modernes 602 (1999): 23. For other discussions of the relationship between Sartre and Bataille, see Michele H. Richman, Reading Georges Bataille: Beyond the Gift (Baltimore: Johns Hopkins University Press, 1982), 112–37; Jean-François Fourny, "La communication impossible: Georges Bataille and Jean-Paul Sartre," Stanford French Review 12 (1988): 149–60; Rebecca Comay, "Gifts without Presents: Economies of 'Experience' in Bataille and Heidegger," Yale French Studies 78 (1990): 66–89; Jean-Michel Heimonet, "The Modernity of Mysticism: Bataille and Sartre," Diacritics 26 (1996): 59–73; and Connor, Mysticism of Sin, 7–15, 32–38, 119–27.

9   Bataille became a Christian as a young man (1914) and seems to have been devout; he even considered the priesthood or life as a monk. Although he abandoned all plans for the latter in 1920, Michel Surya argues that his loss of faith was not decisive until 1922 or

1923, when he began to read Nietzsche and Freud and, through the friendship of Leon Chestov, the work of Dostoevsky. See Surya, *Bataille*, 28–77. The evidence is not, however, decisive, as Connor argues. On this issue and the importance of Chestov for Bataille's thought, see Connor, *Mysticism of Sin*, 24, 28–30, 45, 165–66.

10 After World War II, Bataille's writing shows a new respect for surrealism, one that marks his alliance with surrealism against Sartre and existentialism. Crucial to this debate are the different conceptions of freedom found in surrealism and existentialism. See, for example, Georges Bataille, "Surrealism and How It Differs from Existentialism," in *The Absence of Myth*, 57–67.

11 A fundamental problem is broached here, for it is impossible to separate form and content in Bataille's work. Sartre, at times, intuits this.

12 This aspect of Sartre's critique emerges most clearly in a debate between Bataille, Sartre, and others following Bataille's presentation of a lecture in March 1944. Subsequently published in modified form as the "Summit and Decline" section of *On Nietzsche*, the lecture offers an early formulation of Bataille's complex account of interdiction and transgression and of the relationship between crime and communication. As Peter Connor cogently explains: "From Sartre's viewpoint, Bataille's quest for ecstasy is itself a form of project, and that, ipso facto, makes it into a value. And his values are less than clear: 'What's to prevent one from raping human beings, for you? I don't see why, according to your principles, one wouldn't rape human beings as one drinks a cup of coffee'" (*Mysticism of Sin*, 123). Many people would say the same thing about Sartre's existentialist philosophy, which perhaps explains the vehemence of Sartre's attack. I will return to these ethical issues, especially in chapter 2. For the entire debate, see OC VI 315–58; and Connor, *Mysticism of Sin*, 119–27.

13 Jean-François Louette argues that in distinguishing himself from Bataille, Sartre engages in an "auto-criticism" through which he distances his wartime and postwar positions from those found in *Nausea*. Louette's argument is important, although I think he brings *Nausea* and *Inner Experience* closer together than the texts themselves warrant. On my reading, Sartre's narrator may desire to "be all"—and hence his imputation of this desire to Bataille—but the Bataille of *Inner Experience* relates to an excess beyond this desire for totality. See Louette, "Bataille, Sartre."

Suzanne Guerlac, on the other hand, argues that Bataille and Sartre were closer than either of them could see, in part because of a shared Bergsonian heritage that they were both loath to admit. As Guerlac argues, contra Bataille, Sartrean action is not utilitarian and involves "a notion of action as free invention" that brings Sartre closer to Bataille "than the polemic rhetoric of the exchanges between them would suggest." Suzanne Guerlac, *Literary Polemics: Bataille, Sartre, Valéry, Breton* (Stanford, Calif.: Stanford University Press, 1997), 91. Sartre's and Bataille's conceptions of temporality are, however, quite different. For more on the relationship between reason, consciousness, and desire in Sartre, see Judith Butler, *Subjects of Desire: Hegelian Reflections in Twentieth-Century France* (New York: Columbia University Press, 1987), 101–74.

14 Some critics see Sartre's critique of Bataille continued in the *Roads to Freedom* trilogy, in particular through the character Daniel. One problem with this reading is that *The Age of Reason* was completed before the publication of *Inner Experience*, suggesting that the character was conceived without reference to Bataille. Despite this problem, I find the association

of Bataille with the character compelling; particularly compelling is Louette's suggestion that Sartre parodies *Inner Experience* through Daniel's speeches in *The Reprieve*. Through Daniel, Sartre also associates religious excess with homosexuality. See Ronald Hayman, *Sartre: A Life* (New York: Simon and Schuster, 1987), 198–99; Louette, "Bataille, Sartre"; Jean-Paul Sartre, *The Age of Reason*, trans. Eric Sutton (New York: Knopf, 1947); and Jean-Paul Sartre, *The Reprieve*, trans. Eric Sutton (New York: Knopf, 1947).

15 The exchange between Sartre and Bataille continued through the 1940s and 1950s, ending only with Bataille's death in 1962. It was, at least explicitly, a one-sided debate, with Bataille responding to Sartre's texts. Bataille appears explicitly (as the one who desires all) in Sartre's *Cahiers pour une morale* (1947–1948) and implicitly in *What Is Literature?* but there is no further extended commentary by Sartre on Bataille's work. He does continue to read him, however. In Sartre's *Critique of Dialectical Reason* he makes positive reference to Bataille's commentary on the potlatch in *The Accursed Share*. See Jean-Paul Sartre, *Notebooks for an Ethics*, trans. David Pellauer (Chicago: University of Chicago Press, 1992), 34–36, 96, 148, 492–93; and Jean-Paul Sartre, *Critique of Dialectical Reason*, trans. Alan Sheridan-Smith (London: NLB, 1976), 1:106. In a moment of great historical irony, Benny Lévy appeals to Bataille's understanding of rupture in a conversation with Sartre about insurrection and the student revolts of 1968. See Jean-Paul Sartre and Benny Lévy, *Hope Now: The 1980 Interviews*, trans. Adrian van den Hoven (Chicago: University of Chicago Press, 1996), 97.

For Bataille's continuing engagement with and critique of Sartre, see Georges Bataille, "Sartre," review of Jean-Paul Sartre, *Réflexions sur la question juive*, *Critique* (1947); "De l'existentialisme au primat de l'économie," *Critique* (1948); "L'existentialisme," *Critique* (1950); "Le temps de la révolte," *Critique* (1952); "L'affaire de 'L'Homme révolté,'" *Critique* (1952). These texts are collected in OC XI and XII. See also Georges Bataille, *Literature and Evil*, trans. Alistair Hamilton (London: Marion Boyars, 1985), 31–61, 173–208, which first appeared in *Critique* as reviews of Sartre's *Baudelaire* and *Saint Genet*.

CHAPTER ONE

1 Georges Bataille, *Erotism*, trans. Mary Dalwood (San Francisco: City Lights, 1986), 35.

2 Ibid., 34–35. It is clear what bodily response eroticism elicits if it "works"; it is less clear what response is elicited by religious writings and practices, although Bataille's insistence on their relationship with eroticism suggests that "inner experience" is also something bodily and visceral. As I hope to show, Bataille ultimately subverts the very distinction between "physical" eroticism and "religious" eroticism, between the "bodily" and the "spiritual."

3 Bataille's texts are concerned with experience, but experience as associated with the Lacanian "real" rather than with a "reality" that can be unproblematically represented through traditional autobiographical narratives. For related work on this issue, see Peter Tracey Connor, *Georges Bataille and the Mysticism of Sin* (Baltimore: Johns Hopkins University Press, 2000), 58–66; and Gilles Ernst, *Georges Bataille: analyse du récit de mort* (Paris: Presses Universitaires de France, 1993), 144.

4 This effect of Bataille's texts on the reader may account for the often profoundly Bataillean narratives his writings inspire, as well as for the vehement rejection of Bataille's writings by those who dislike his work: one is either like Bataille, and therefore reads and writes like him, or one hastily denies any association with the kinds of experience he purportedly

records and elicits. For an interesting account of divergent scholarly responses to Bataille's writing, see Connor, *Mysticism of Sin*, 42–45.

5   Martin Jay, "The Limits of Limit-Experience: Bataille and Foucault," in *Cultural Semantics: Keywords of Our Time* (Amherst: University of Massachusetts Press, 1998), 64. For other readings of "experience" in Bataille's work, see Julia Kristeva, "Bataille, L'expérience et la pratique," in *Bataille*, ed. Philippe Sollers (Paris: Union Générale d'Éditions, 1973), 267–301; Jacques Derrida, "From Restricted to General Economy: A Hegelianism without Reserve," in *Writing and Difference*, trans. Alan Bass (Chicago: University of Chicago Press, 1978), 251–77; and Rebecca Comay, "Gifts without Presents: Economies of 'Experience' in Bataille and Heidegger," *Yale French Studies* 78 (1990): 66–89.

6   Jay, "Limit-Experience," 64.

7   Jay is thinking primarily of Joan Scott, whose work he criticizes for making experience discursive. I think he misunderstands Scott's project, which is less at odds with his own than he seems to believe. See Joan Scott, "The Evidence of Experience," *Critical Inquiry* 17, no. 4 (1991): 773–97.

8   Derrida, "From Restricted to General Economy," 267.

9   Ibid., 272.

10 For another suggestive reading of the relationship between these two parts of the text, see Carolyn Dean, *The Self and Its Pleasures: Bataille, Lacan, and the History of the Decentered Subject* (Ithaca, N.Y.: Cornell University Press, 1992), 235–42.

11 Linda Williams, *Hard Core: Power, Pleasure, and the "Frenzy of the Visible"* (Berkeley: University of California Press, 1989), 191–92.

12 Ibid., 190.

13 Williams, however, argues that those who have seen the film (as she has) and are familiar with horror movie violence, editing techniques, and special effects recognize the action to be staged. According to Williams, the pleasures of "snuff" operate according to the same fetishistic logic—"I know (it is not real), but even so"—that runs throughout the horror genre. In this way, she seeks to distinguish "snuff" from pornography. I have not seen the movie, but I wonder whether these reality effects would have been obvious, even to sophisticated viewers, in 1976. For more on this phenomenon, also see Roland Barthes, "The Reality Effect," in *The Rustle of Language*, trans. Richard Howard (New York: Hill and Wang, 1986), 141–48.

14 For questions about this claim, see *Wide Angle* 19, no. 3 (1997). This special issue is devoted to pornography.

15 With new digital technologies, of course, anything can be faked. Or so a new set of conventions tells us.

16 Similarly, because Troppman, the narrator of *Blue of Noon*, is read as fascinated with fascism, Bataille is read as being a fascist. See the review by John Sturrock in the *Times Literary Supplement* 4964 (May 22, 1998): 30. On the complex debates surrounding Bataille's work and its relationship to fascism, see Francis Marmande, *Georges Bataille politique* (Lyon: Presses Universitaires de Lyon, 1985), 43–46, 167–69; Jean-Michel Besnier, *La politique de l'impossible: L'intellectuel entre révolte et engagement* (Paris: La Découverte, 1988); Jean-Michel Besnier, "Georges Bataille in the 1930s: A Politics of the Impossible," *Yale French Studies* 78 (1990): 169–80; Allan Stoekl, "Truman's Apotheosis: Bataille, 'Planisme,' and Headlessness," *Yale French Studies* 78 (1990): 181–205; Michel Surya, *Georges Bataille: la mort à l'oeuvre*

(Paris: Gallimard, 1992), 291–308; Carolyn Dean, *The Self and Its Pleasures*, pp. 222–31; Susan Suleiman, "Bataille in the Streets: The Search for Virility in the 1930s," in *Bataille: Writing the Sacred*, 26–45; Jean-Michel Besnier, "Bataille, the Emotive Intellectual," in *Writing the Sacred*, 12–25; and Denis Hollier, *Absent without Leave: French Literature under the Threat of War*, trans. Catherine Porter (Cambridge, Mass.: Harvard University Press, 1997), 76–93.

17 See Surya, *Bataille*, 11–37.

18 For the interview, see Madeleine Chapsal, *Envoyez la Petite Musique* . . . (Paris: Grasset, 1984), 227–39. For the information on Martial Bataille's reaction to this interview, see OC I 644.

19 See Susan Suleiman, "Transgression and the Avant-Garde: Bataille's *Histoire de l'oeil*," in *On Bataille: Critical Essays*, ed. Leslie Anne Boldt (Albany: State University of New York Press, 1995), 313–33. This essay is reprinted from Susan Suleiman, *Subversive Intent: Gender, Politics, and the Avant-Garde* (Cambridge, Mass.: Harvard University Press, 1990).

20 See Lucette Finas, "Reading Bataille: The Invention of the Foot," *Diacritics* 26, no. 2 (1996): 97–106.

21 Cited in Derrida, "From Restricted to General Economy," 258. See Georges Bataille, "Hegel, Death, and Sacrifice," trans. Jonathan Strauss, *Yale French Studies* 78 (1990): 9–28.

22 Derrida, "From Restricted to General Economy," 263.

23 Jacques Lacan similarly describes his psychoanalytic project as a displacing of the subject through which the "real" emerges (S XX 77; E 83).

24 Bataille later revised the final line, omitting the references to "a crew of blacks" (OC I 605).

25 Photographs, moreover, are described as sparking these autobiographical reflections on the meaning of "The Tale." In chapter 3, I will explore the role of photography as the mark of the "real" in Bataille's fictional and mystical texts.

26 See Jean Dragon, "The Work of Alterity: Bataille and Lacan," *Diacritics* 26, no. 2 (1996): 31–48; and, on the mobility of the Freudian narrative, Leo Bersani, *The Freudian Body: Psychoanalysis and Art* (New York: Columbia University Press, 1986).

27 See Dragon, "Bataille and Lacan."

28 See Roland Barthes, "The Metaphor of the Eye," in *Critical Essays*, trans. Richard Howard (Evanston, Ill.: Northwestern University Press, 1972), 239–47.

29 Within classical psychoanalysis, the child assumes that the mother, whom the child experiences as all powerful, has a penis. Her power is thus rendered potentially visible and is sexualized. When the child discovers that the mother does not, in fact, have a penis, the trauma of this discovery can engender various responses. The child can refuse to acknowledge the mother's lack, rendering her forever phallic, sexualized, and threatening, and the child potentially psychotic. He can simultaneously acknowledge and deny the mother's lack through fetishization. Or, finally, he can recognize the mother's lack, the potential threat it poses to his own penis (if she can lose hers, perhaps I, too, can lose mine), and so internalize the incest prohibition represented by the father's law. (The situation is, needless to say, significantly more complex for girls. See chapter 8.) See also the introduction to part 3.

30 See Laura Mulvey, "Visual Pleasure and Narrative Cinema," in *Visual and Other Pleasures* (Bloomington: Indiana University Press, 1989), 14–26.

31 Although this reading is problematized by Simone, who seems to triumph in her sexualization and violence.

32 Carol Clover, *Men, Women, and Chain Saws: Gender in the Modern Horror Film* (Princeton, N.J.: Princeton University Press, 1992), 206.

33 For more on the distinction between a one-sex and two-sex model, see Thomas Laqueur, *Making Sex: Body and Gender from the Greeks to Freud* (Cambridge, Mass.: Harvard University Press, 1990). Lacqueur's historical thesis has been subjected to some debate and criticism, but the basic point seems to hold. For an interesting theoretical critique of Lacqueur, see Mark Seltzer, *Serial Killers: Death and Life in America's Wound Culture* (New York: Routledge, 1998), 78–79.

34 Cross-identification might be more difficult in written narratives, in which the first-person voice predominates, than in film. As Clover argues, even in those moments in horror films in which the first-person perspective of the killer is given, instabilities in that perspective may blur the viewer's identification with it.

35 Despite this claim, I think it is important to ask which selves are shattered and how they are gendered. Again, the textual evidence is not as clear as many readers assume, for Marcelle and Don Aminado (as a priest, perhaps a feminized man, but still a man and a figure of authority) mirror each other in the position of victimized, shattered subject, just as N1 and Simone mirror each other as sadistic-voyeurs. The lines between victim and persecutor are further undermined by each character's divergent reactions to violence.

36 This subversion, as I will argue in chapter 3, calls into question any simplistic condemnation of Bataille as voyeuristic or scopophiliac. For the critique of vision in Bataille, see also Martin Jay, *Downcast Eyes: The Denigration of Vision in Twentieth-Century French Thought* (Berkeley: University of California Press, 1993), 216–36.

37 See Jonathan Crary, *Techniques of the Observer: On Vision and Modernity in the Nineteenth Century* (Cambridge, Mass.: MIT Press, 1990), 143; Crary suggests that the blinding vision of the sun, for nineteenth-century scientists, itself becomes a paradoxical guarantor of the bodily nature of vision.

38 As I will argue in part 2 (chapter 6) and in part 3, it would be precipitous to read this masculine masochism as feminist or even as compatible with feminism. Rather, one could argue with Irigaray that Bataille usurps and appropriates the feminine position, thereby reestablishing the ubiquity of men. At the same time, I think it is important to see that a certain crisis of masculinity is being enacted by Bataille. See also Suzanne R. Stewart, *Sublime Surrender: Male Masochism at the Fin-de-Siècle* (Ithaca, N.Y.: Cornell University Press, 1998), esp. 164–93.

39 Bersani shows that Freud at one point argues that sadism is nothing but an identification with the suffering of the victim, hence masochism. The interplay between sadism and masochism will be a point of contention throughout Bataille's work, as I will show further in chapter 2.

40 On the Freudian conception of masochism, see Sigmund Freud, *Three Essays on the Theory of Sexuality*, in *The Standard Edition of the Complete Psychological Works of Sigmund Freud*, ed. and trans. James Strachey (London: Hogarth Press, 1953–74), 7:123–45; "Instincts and Their Vicissitudes," in *Complete Psychological Works*, 14:109–40; "A Child Is Being Beaten," in *Complete Psychological Works*, 17:175–204; and "The Economic Problem of Masochism," in *Complete Psychological Works*, 19:157–70; see also Jean Laplanche, *Life and Death in Psychoanalysis*, trans. Jeffrey Mehlman (Baltimore: Johns Hopkins University Press, 1976), 85–139; Jean Laplanche, *Essays on Otherness*, trans. John Fletcher (New York: Routledge, 1999), 197–213;

Margaret Ann Fitzpatrick Hanly, *Essential Papers on Masochism* (New York: New York University Press, 1995); and Bersani, *Freudian Body*.

41 Bersani, *Freudian Body*, 38.

42 For a reading of the novel in terms of visuality and Bataille's notion of the "formless," see Patrick ffrench, *The Cut/Reading Bataille's Histoire de l'oeil* (Oxford: Oxford University Press, 1999).

43 The desire to associate sexuality with the father and hence to protect the child's sexual innocence fits with contemporary accounts of recovered memory and sexual abuse. One is led both to consider the possibility that these texts point to early childhood trauma *and* to ask why Bataille so consistently both makes and problematizes this move.

44 Sigmund Freud, *The Ego and the Id*, in *Complete Psychological Works*, 19:33; cited in Bersani, *Freudian Body*, 99–100.

45 For more on Freud's various models of masochism and the subversive potential of his account of primary masochism, particularly with regard to biological essentialism, see John K. Noyes, *The Mastery of Submission: Inventions of Masochism* (Ithaca, N.Y.: Cornell University Press, 1997), 145–54. Noyes shows the constant movement between biologism and its subversion in accounts of sadomasochism. Attention to this movement in Bataille would demand careful attention to the cultural contexts of primary masochism and jouissance that I cannot fully elaborate here.

46 Judith Surkis claims that the male narrator continues to see and lives, and that a castrating woman is the agent—either directly or indirectly—of Granero's and Don Aminado's blinding. Yet N1 is also implicated in both acts, as perpetrator and victim. See Judith Surkis, "No Fun and Games until Someone Loses an Eye: Transgression and Masculinity in Bataille and Foucault," *Diacritics* 26, no. 2 (1996): 18–30.

47 John Noyes reminds us that sadomasochistic practice and imagery always plays with reality and depends on this play for its instantiation. Although I would insist on the centrality of primary masochism in Bataille and on the need to distinguish primary masochism analytically from its secondary formations, the movement from one to the other is always a possibility; moreover, sadomasochism's "play with reality" is clearly crucial for Bataille. See Noyes, *Mastery of Submission*, 34.

48 Bataille often contradicts himself on this point, however, arguing during the war both for the near identity of eroticism and religion and for their difference. Only in the 1950s does he make conclusive arguments about their relationship. See Bataille, *Erotism*; and Georges Bataille, *The Tears of Eros*, trans. Peter Connor (San Francisco: City Lights, 1989).

49 The other crucial ethical question posed by Bataille's texts is that which asks who experiences the shattering of the self as a jouissance that goes beyond the phallic (to use Lacan's formulation). There is significant evidence, contra Bataille and Bersani, that for subjects denied access to a phallic (and white, European) symbolic, shattered subjectivity is a constant source of pain. Although Bataille also insists on the anguish and torture of these ecstatic moments, his texts might usefully be compared with Frantz Fanon's analysis of black, male subjectivity in *Black Skin, White Masks*, in order to clarify and critique the political stakes of Bataille's account of self-shattering subjectivity. See Franz Fanon, *Black Skin, White Masks*, trans. Charles Lam Markmann (New York: Grove Weidenfeld, 1967). See also Diana Fuss, *Identification Papers* (New York: Routledge, 1995), 141–65; and Kaja Silverman, *The Threshold of the Visible World* (New York: Routledge, 1996), 9–37.

50 See the texts translated in Georges Bataille, *Visions of Excess: Selected Writings, 1927–1939*, ed. Allan Stoekl (Minneapolis: University of Minnesota Press, 1985); and *The College of Sociology* (1937–1939), ed. Denis Hollier, trans. Betsy Wing (Minneapolis: University of Minnesota Press, 1988).

51 Many, often contradictory, claims have been made about Bataille's (and Acéphale's?—it is not clearly how widely shared the desire was) supposed desire to perform a human sacrifice. For discussion of the topic, see Surya, *Bataille*, 303.

52 The torture victim on whose image Bataille describes meditating in *Inner Experience* and *Guilty* does not voluntarily submit to torture but is its passive victim, and Bataille seems fully aware of the difference.

53 Suzanne Guerlac argues that in *Erotism*, Bataille substitutes interdiction for Hegelian negation "and by placing the woman, as 'living cadaver,' in the position of the slave . . . appears to have elided the scene of recognition altogether. But he has only postponed it. His version of the scene of recognition—eroticism as relation to the erotic object—occurs in a second moment, a *reprise* of the dialectical turn that yields the experience of the sacred." The erotic object, according to Bataille, is the female prostitute, a living object through whom the "fiction of death" is enacted for the male reader and writer. Guerlac's analysis points directly to the problems of fetishization that I will address in chapter 3; fetishization occurs, I will argue, when sacrality takes prominence over the relationship to the other. In his insistence on communication, and so on the necessity that the other be recognized (as, for example, in his postwar reservations about Sade), Bataille continually contests this fetishizing movement, even as his texts continually make it. See Suzanne Guerlac, *Literary Polemics: Bataille, Sartre, Valéry, Breton* (Stanford, Calif.: Stanford University Press, 1997), 28.

54 Although I focus here on the "operation" of his texts, Bataille insists on the gap between meditative practice and its "ends." No technique, according to Bataille's ateleological practice, necessarily gives rise to the chance encounter with nonmeaning. This paradox is also central to many Christian mystical texts.

55 Georges Bataille, *Theory of Religion*, trans. Robert Hurley (New York: Zone Books, 1989), 53.

56 OC VI 373. Bataille refers here not to the desire to perform a sacrifice, a desire to which he never admitted, but the desire to found a religion.

57 Although Bataille, as I have argued, made use of writing, and particularly fiction, as a vehicle for self-dissolution from the 1920s on, his explicit *attitudes* toward writing, fictionality, and poetry changed decisively during the war. This change can be seen most explicitly through comparison of his prewar and postwar writings on the Marquis de Sade. Whereas before the war, Bataille chides those who make a hero of Sade but refuse to follow his criminality beyond "poetry" (a clear dig at the surrealists), after the war Bataille's fascination with Sade centers around his writing practice. Compare, for example, the prewar "The Use Value of D. A. F. de Sade," in *Visions*, esp. 93, and *Blue of Noon*, trans. Harry Matthews (London: Marion Boyars, 1986), 68; and the postwar *Literature and Evil*, trans. Alastair Hamilton (London: Marion Boyars, 1985), 105–29, and *Erotism*, 164–96. Jean-Michel Heimonet notes these two divergent readings and argues for their dialectical relationship. See Jean-Michel Heimonet, "Recoil in order to Leap Forward: Two Values of Sade in Bataille's Text," *Yale French Studies* 78 (1990): 227–36.

58 Jay, "Limit-Experience," 78. Also see Jürgen Habermas, *The Philosophical Discourse of Modernity*, trans. Frederick Lawrence (Cambridge, Mass.: MIT Press, 1987), 235–36.

CHAPTER TWO

1   Angela is the most extensively cited mystic in the wartime writings. Teresa of Avila and John of the Cross are also mentioned frequently, particularly in the postwar texts. For a suggestion of the range of Bataille's reading in mysticism during the war, see the list of books Bataille borrowed during that period from the Bibliothèque Nationale, in Pierre Prévost, *Georges Bataille, René Guénon: L'expérience souveraine* (Paris: Jean-Michel Place, 1992), 15–16; also cited in Peter Tracey Connor, *Georges Bataille and the Mysticism of Sin* (Baltimore: Johns Hopkins University Press, 2000), 172–73, n. 7. As Michel Surya points out, Bataille also made use of collections of mystical and religious texts, in particular Rémy de Gourmont's *Le Latin mystique*, which, according to André Masson, Bataille read continually in 1918–1919. See Michel Surya, *Georges Bataille: la mort à l'oeuvre* (Paris: Gallimard, 1992), 41–44.

2   For Bataille's isolation, his movements during 1939–1942, and the diagnosis of tuberculosis, see Surya, *Bataille*, 363–65.

3   Susan Suleiman, "Bataille in the Street: The Search for Virility in the 1930s," in *Bataille: Writing the Sacred*, ed. Carolyn Bailey Gill (New York: Routledge, 1995), 44, n. 23. On the exigencies of publishing during the Occupation, see Gisele Sapiro, *La guerre des écrivains: 1940–1953* (Paris: Fayard, 1999).

4   Sarah Wilson, "Fêting the Wound: Georges Bataille and Jean Fautrier in the 1940s," in *Bataille: Writing the Sacred*, 172–92.

5   For recent debates about Bataille's political commitments before, during, and after the war, see Suleiman, "Bataille in the Street"; Jean-Michel Besnier, *La politique de l'impossible: L'intellectuel entre révolte et engagement* (Paris: La Découverte, 1988); Allan Stoekl, "Truman's Apotheosis: Bataille, 'Planisme,' and Headlessness," *Yale French Studies* 78 (1990): 181–205; Carolyn Dean, *The Self and Its Pleasures: Bataille, Lacan, and the History of the Decentered Subject* (Ithaca, N.Y.: Cornell University Press, 1992), 221–45; Surya, *Bataille*, 291–308; and Denis Hollier, *Absent without Leave: French Literature under the Threat of War*, trans. Catherine Porter (Cambridge, Mass.: Harvard University Press, 1997), esp. ch. 4 and 5.

6   Jan Patočka argues that mysticism and orgiastic mystery are antithetical to responsibility, a distinction that Derrida, in his commentary on Patočka's text, troubles and potentially subverts. Bataille argues in the *Atheological Summa* that responsibility has its roots in the ecstatic. See Jan Patočka, *Essais hérétiques sur la philosophie de l'histoire*, trans. Erika Abrams (Lagrasse: Verdier, 1981); and Jacques Derrida, *The Gift of Death*, trans. David Wills (Chicago: University of Chicago Press, 1995).

7   Other early dismissive comments were made by Gabriel Marcel and Antonin Artaud, who thought that conversion would solve all of Bataille's problems, and by Nicholas Calas, who lamented Bataille's egocentrism. For Marcel's and Artaud's comments, see Connor, *Mysticism of Sin*, 25, 44; see also Nicolas Calas, "Acephalic Mysticism," *Hémisphères* 2, no. 6 (1945): 3–13.

8   Francis Marmande, *Georges Bataille politique* (Lyon: Presses Universitaires de Lyon, 1985), 8. Marmande reads the guilt of these texts in relationship to the death of Colette Peignot (Laure) in 1938. Guilt at surviving Laure (as well as his father) is certainly a crucial part of the situation out of which Bataille writes from 1939 through the early 1940s. In an

unpublished biographical note, he writes that "a dead woman tore him apart in 1938." Yet Bataille purposely effaced this "third party" in the published text of *Guilty*. As Bataille himself notes, Peignot's posthumous writings show marked affinities with his own, particularly with regard to the sacred and communication. I hope to take up her work and its relationship to Bataille's in a future study. See Laure, *Écrits*, ed. Jérôme Peignot (Paris: Pauvert, 1977), 288–302, 311; and Laure, *The Collected Writings*, trans. Jeanine Herman (San Francisco: City Lights, 1995), esp. 246–64, 273.

9 This definition follows Jacques Lacan's conception of the real in terms of trauma in his 1964 seminar, *The Four Fundamental Concepts of Psychoanalysis*. As Hal Foster succinctly describes it: "Lacan defines the traumatic as a missed encounter with the real. As missed, the real cannot be represented; it can only be repeated, indeed it *must* be repeated." See Jacques Lacan, *The Four Fundamental Concepts of Psychoanalysis*, trans. Alan Sheridan (New York: Norton, 1978), 17–64; and Hal Foster, *The Return of the Real* (Cambridge, Mass.: MIT Press, 1996), 132. For Lacan's changing conception of the real, see chapter 5.

10 Bataille's understanding of history is influenced by Alexander Kojève's reading of Hegel, against whose dialectical and progressivist narratives Bataille continually pushes. Bataille seemed to take only half seriously Kojève's contention that history ends with the advent of revolutionary communism. Regardless, for Bataille the question is what happens to negativity in history and/or if history ends. As Mikkel Borch-Jacobsen argues, Kojève's "most attentive" listening and reading audience—"Bataille, Blanchot, and Lacan, each in his own way . . . would also repeat: the complete fulfillment of desire (that is, of history, of philosophy), far from satisfying desire once and for all, exacerbates it instead, beyond all limit, for then and only then does the desperate question arise of what one can possibly desire once *everything* has been accomplished." This is the site of what Blanchot calls Bataille's "limit experience." What is thereby exposed is a logic of desire and negativity that radically disrupts teleological conceptions of history, whether "complete" or not. Mikkel Borch-Jacobsen, *Lacan: The Absolute Master*, trans. Douglas Brick (Stanford, Calif.: Stanford University Press, 1991), 7. See also Maurice Blanchot, *The Infinite Conversation*, trans. Susan Hanson (Minneapolis: University of Minnesota Press, 1993), 202–11; and, for Bataille's response to Kojève, OC V 369–71; G 123–25.

Bataille's emphasis on "what is there" divorced from its recuperation by any salvific or progressive account seems to me a key precursor of Foucault's return to Nietzschean forms of genealogy. Contemporary ethical accounts of history as the uncovering of "what has been" in its concrete particularity, then, are in part indebted to Bataille's concerns. For an excellent recent account of this ethical historiography, see Carolyn Dinshaw, *Getting Medieval: Sexualities and Communities, Pre- and Postmodern* (Durham, N.C.: Duke University Press, 1999), esp. 1–54.

11 Bataille himself calls inner experience a "hypermorality." See Georges Bataille, *Literature and Evil*, trans. Alastair Hamilton (London: Marion Boyars, 1985), ix. For a recent repetition of the necessity of distinguishing inner experience and mysticism, see Jeremy Carrette, "Prologue to a Confession of the Flesh," in Michel Foucault, *Religion and Culture*, ed. Jeremy Carrette (New York: Routledge, 1999), 18–25.

12 This move parallels Bataille's earlier attempt to differentiate a sovereign community without authority from totalitarian demands that one sacrifice individual autonomy before the authority of the state. For Bataille, community must involve a dissolution of the self *and*

his or her sovereignty with and as the whole. See Georges Bataille, *Visions of Excess: Selected Writings, 1927–1939*, ed. Allan Stoekl (Minneapolis: University of Minnesota Press, 1985), 116–29, 137–60.

13 Three other dissenting voices, who insist on historically contextualizing Bataille's work, have been influential on the reading I offer here. Suleiman, "Bataille in the Street"; Hollier, *Absent without Leave*; and Alexander Irwin, "Saints of the Impossible: Politics, Violence, and the Sacred in Georges Bataille and Simone Weil" (Ph.D. diss., Harvard University, 1997).

14 Lacan no doubt alludes to Péguy's line from *Notre Jeunesse* (1910): "Tout commence en mystique et finit en politique," which was, according to Peter Connor, a popular bit of graffiti in May 1968. The line, whether taken as denunciatory or hopefully prophetic, seems to pose an opposition between mysticism and politics that Lacan challenges. Or conversely, we might read Lacan as challenging Péguy's association of mysticism with French nationalism. In his reading of this line, Peter Connor goes on to cite Julien Benda's denunciation of the link between mysticism and politics, one he associates with Péguy as well as with Barrès and Maurras. As Connor notes, for Benda in 1927, as for many other European intellectuals, mysticism marks the abandonment of reason and a dangerous submission to the passions that lead to war and violence. For Lacan, on the other hand, the association of mysticism and politics is an explicitly ethical move. See Connor, *Mysticism of Sin*, 20–21. For more on the ambivalent legacy of Charles Péguy, "socialist, republican, Dreyfusard, severe critic of anti-Semitism, Catholic mystic" and yet read as a forebear by French fascists before and during the Second World War, see David Carroll, *French Literary Fascism: Nationalism, Anti-Semitism, and the Ideology of Culture* (Princeton, N.J.: Princeton University Press, 1995), 42–70. For this characterization of Péguy, see 44.

15 Lacan argues in *Encore* that the work of analytic practice, insofar as it can be formulated, is to separate the imaginary and symbolic realms, the object "a" and the Other, so that the "real" can emerge. In this, his writings are like those of the mystics. For more on this subject, see chapter 5.

16 The real is also tied to the symptom and hence to hysteria. From Charcot to Irigaray, hysteria and mysticism are linked by this convergence in the real. See chapter 8.

17 Since this *Book* is so central to Bataille's wartime writing, it is worth briefly highlighting its tremendous complexity. Modern editors divide Angela's *Book* into two texts, the *Memorial*, which is a relatively coherent narrative of Angela's religious experience from the time of her conversion, organized into a series of steps or "transformations" of the soul; and the *Instructions*, a group of visions, letters, and hagiographical accounts emanating from Angela and her circle. Bataille focuses his attention on the *Memorial*, although he also discusses the *Instructions'* account of Angela's final words. The *Memorial* raises central textual and authorial problems, as well as problems of translation, for it is the work of a scribe, Brother A., who tells us that he took down Angela's Umbrian dialect, translating rapidly into Latin. When he reads portions of this text back to Angela, she invariably complains about its brevity, dryness, and lack of accuracy, at times claiming not to recognize her own words in his (it is not clear whether he read to her in Latin or translated her words back into her original Umbrian dialect). The importance of Brother A. to the production of the *Memorial* is still hotly contested, with some scholars going so far as to argue that we cannot posit Angela's authorship and that the text is so mediated as to offer little concrete information about

Angela herself. For Bataille, however, Angela was the author of her *Book*, and I will proceed with my discussion on Bataille's terms.

For the critical edition and a modern English translation, see Angela of Foligno, *Il Libro della Beata Angela da Foligno*, ed. Ludger Thier and Abele Calufetti (Grottaferrata: Collegii S. Bonaventurae ad Claras Aquas, 1985); Angela of Foligno, *Complete Works*, trans. Paul Lachance (New York: Paulist Press, 1993). Bataille generally cites the *Book* through the 1927 edition and translation of M. J. Ferré, which gives the Latin text facing a French translation. In the portions cited by Bataille, this edition and translation do not substantively differ from the critical edition of Ludger Thier and Abele Calufetti on which Paul Lachance's recent English translation is based.

18 Bataille suggests in his preface to *Inner Experience* that readers should focus on part 2, "The Torment/Torture," and on the final brief section, which contains two poems ("Gloria in excelsis mihi" and "God"); only these sections were "written with necessity" rather than with "the laudable concern of creating a book" (OC V 9–10; IE xxxi). "The Torment/Torture" offers an account of inner experience, and "Post-Scriptum to the Torment/Torture (or the New Mystical Theology)" describes the methods used to attain it (although Bataille insists that no method alone can promise inner experience). Given the more explicit debt to Angela in the latter section, I will focus my attention here. I believe, however, that Angela is crucial to all of *Inner Experience* and *Guilty*.

19 The passages cited are *Libro*, 354, 358; *Works*, 202, 204. Bataille's English translator, Leslie Anne Boldt, makes some telling alterations and mistakes (e.g., "Nothingness" for *néant* and "above" for *au-dessous*) in just these passages, all designed to stress their "atheism" and hence to remove from Bataille all taint of Christianity. Bataille substantializes "nihil," and Boldt further reifies the concept with her decision to capitalize Nothingness.

20 For the passage in Angela's work, see *Libro*, 734; *Works*, 315–16.

21 The "partly-failed" experience reads like a kind of nature mysticism—ecstasy before scenery, if you will. Bataille's digressions are an attempt to clarify the distinction between contemplation of the point and this kind of more amorphous experience.

22 See also Georges Bataille, *Méthode de méditation* (1947), in OC V 191–234. On Bataille's techniques, see Jean Bruno, "Les techniques d'illumination chez Georges Bataille," *Critique* 195–196 (1963): 706–20; and Catherine Cusset "Technique de l'impossible," in *Georges Bataille après tout*, ed. Denis Hollier (Paris: Belin, 1995), 171–89.

23 *Libro*, 362; *Works*, 205; translation modified.

24 Peter Connor argues that Bataille had already begun to practice something like this meditative technique in 1922. In a letter to his cousin Marie-Louise Bataille, written from Madrid in 1922, Bataille describes a method he uses to make himself "dream." It involves staring at an "absolutely inexpressive visage" to induce a dream that "flows in a night of moon." As Connor notes, however, Bataille never says this method induces ecstasy. See Connor, *Mysticism of Sin*, 167, n. 3; Surya, *Bataille*, 54; and Georges Bataille, *Choix de Lettres, 1917–1962*, ed. Michel Surya (Paris: Gallimard, 1997), 27. The letter, which I have cited here, differs from Connor's description.

25 This account of contemplation suggests further the importance for Bataille of thinking about God as a projection of human desire. The point is not that God is "merely" humanity, but that this process of projection is necessary to attain inner experience.

26 Denise Despres, *Ghostly Sights: Visual Meditation in Late Medieval Literature* (Norman, Okla.: Pilgrim

Books, 1989), 9. For a brief history of meditative texts, see Thomas Bestul, *Texts of the Passion: Latin Devotional Literature and Medieval Society* (Philadelphia: University of Pennsylvania Press, 1996), 26–95.

27 Although grounded in the life of Francis of Assisi, this mode of affective meditative practice and the claim that it was itself a form of action was particularly important for women. As I argued in the introduction, moreover, the beguine movement that emerged in northern Europe at the same time as the mendicant orders in the south emphasized the interplay between action and contemplation in meditative practice, ecstasy, and prayer for souls on earth and in purgatory. Arguably, since women were generally denied access to other forms of action, their texts and those written about them conflate the two modes of life in order to provide actions in which women could participate. See Amy Hollywood, *The Soul as Virgin Wife: Mechthild of Magdeburg, Marguerite Porete, and Meister Eckhart* (Notre Dame, Ind.: University of Notre Dame Press, 1995), 39–52.

28 Robyn O'Sullivan, "Mimesis, Exegesis, and the Deconstruction of the Self" (paper presented at the 33d International Conference on Medieval Studies, Kalamazoo, Mich., 1998).

29 In the Middle Ages, visual images were routinely used for meditative purposes. See Mary Carruthers, *The Craft of Thought: Meditation, Rhetoric, and the Making of Images, 400–1200* (Cambridge: Cambridge University Press, 1998); Jeffrey Hamburger, *The Rothschild Canticles: Art and Mysticism in Flanders and the Rhineland circa 1300* (New Haven, Conn.: Yale University Press, 1990); Jeffrey Hamburger, *Nuns as Artists: The Visual Culture of a Medieval Convent* (Berkeley: University of California Press, 1997); and Jeffrey Hamburger, *The Visual and the Visionary* (New York: Zone Books, 1998).

30 *Libro*, 192–94; *Works*, 145–46.

31 On the significance of the fact that these images are photographs, see chapter 3.

32 Bataille claims that he does not identify with the sadistic torturer (God, in at least one understanding of the Passion). Yet if we take the passage to be disavowing sadism alone, not every pleasure (as the claim that the young Chinese man is "seductive" suggests we must), then his response might still be read as a masochistic identification with and eroticization of the tortured person. This interpretation suggests that to disavow God is to disavow sadistic pleasure. Yet Bataille himself raises doubts about the possibility of clearly differentiating between sadism and masochism. Later, moreover, he will claim that there is a link between sadism and ecstasy. See Georges Bataille, *The Tears of Eros*, trans. Peter Connor (San Francisco: City Lights, 1989), 205–6. I will return to the ethical problems of Bataille's aestheticization and eroticization of the torture victim later in this chapter and in the conclusion.

33 For suggestive comments about the distinction between dramatization and narrativization, see Mieke Bal, introduction to *Acts of Memory: Cultural Recall in the Present*, ed. Mieke Bal, Jonathan Crewe, and Leo Spitzer (Hanover, N.H.: University Press of New England, 1999), vii–xvii.

34 This practice is related to Bataille's claim, cited in chapter 1, that "without private experience we could discuss neither eroticism nor religion." Arguably, the chief reason for Bataille's association of eroticism with religion is that it works to render visible the bodily nature of religious experience. Whether the bodily effects of eroticism and religion are the same, however, remains open to debate, leaving still unresolved questions about the ethical consequences of Bataille's apparent eroticization of the figure on which he contemplates.

See Georges Bataille, *Erotism*, trans. Mary Dalwood (San Francisco: City Lights, 1986), 35. I will argue in chapter 8 that Bataille and Freud describe an association of sexuality and suffering typical of subject formation but perhaps not necessary to it. Feminist attempts to reenvision and offer possibilities for new forms of subjectivity hinge on the possible gap between sexuality and suffering.

35 This criticism is related to the claim that Freud never adequately distinguishes between repression and dissociation. See Bessel A. Van Der Volk and Onno Van Der Hart, "The Intrusive Past: The Flexibility of Memory and the Engraving of Trauma," in *Trauma: Explorations in Memory*, ed. Cathy Caruth (Baltimore: Johns Hopkins University Press, 1995), 168–69.

36 Pierre Janet, *Psychological Healing*, trans. E. Paul and C. Paul (New York: Macmillan, 1925), 1:661–63. Cited in Judith Herman, *Trauma and Recovery* (New York: Basic Books, 1992), 37.

37 As Herman reports, researchers suggest possible neurophysiological causes for such memories; further research would be needed to determine whether meditative practices might elicit a similar set of neurophsyiological responses. Yet the intrusive and repetitious nature of traumatic memory is precisely what is induced through meditative practices. On the mimetic aspects of trauma and a critique of the neurophysiological hypothesis, see Ruth Leys, *Trauma: A Genealogy* (Chicago: University of Chicago Press, 2000), esp. 229–65.

38 Herman, *Trauma and Recovery*, 41.

39 Ibid., 177.

40 Ibid., 178.

41 *Libro*, 144; *Works*, 128. See also *Libro*, 206–8; *Works*, 150–51.

42 *Libro*, 338; *Works*, 197. This is just one of many similar images of abjection found throughout *Angela's Memorial*. See *Libro*, 144, 206–8, 242, 302–4; *Works*, 128, 150–51, 162–63, 184–85.

43 We should not forget, however, that Angela's book was recorded by a scribe who translated her words into Latin. Similar translations by male scribes of women's texts suggest that emphasis on the external suffering and asceticism of medieval women may be a hagiographical trope rather than an accurate reflection of mystical experience. In this reading, Angela's suffering body might be seen as an "object" onto which her readers can project themselves. See Amy Hollywood, "Inside Out: Beatrice of Nazareth and Her Hagiographers," in *Gendered Voices: Medieval Saints and Their Interpreters*, ed. Catherine Mooney (Philadelphia: University of Pennsylvania Press, 1999), 78–98; also see chapter 8.

44 On the dangers of over-identification and retraumatization, see Dominick LaCapra, *Representing the Holocaust: History, Theory, Trauma* (Ithaca, N.Y.: Cornell University Press, 1994), 198–200.

45 For powerful examples among Holocaust survivors, and an examination of the ethical ramifications of this refusal, see Lawrence Langer, *Holocaust Testimonies: The Ruins of Memory* (New Haven, Conn.: Yale University Press, 1991). The work of memorialization surrounding the Holocaust is specific to that event; yet a similar refusal to accept meaning-giving narratives can be found among victims of less historically overdetermined forms of trauma.

46 Cathy Caruth, *Unclaimed Experience: Trauma, Narrative, and History* (Baltimore: Johns Hopkins University Press, 1996), 104.

47 Ibid., 102.

48 Ibid., 7.

49 The distinction between onlooker and victim probably cannot be made too sharply, how-
    ever, since witnessing violent crimes often seems to give rise to PTSD, and the lines be-
    tween psychological and physical violence can be difficult to determine. On the related
    shift from the use of the term "trauma" to designate physical injury to its use for invisi-
    ble injuries inflicted on the mind, psyche, or soul, see Ian Hacking, "Memory Sciences,
    Memory Politics," in *Tense Past: Cultural Essays in Trauma and Theory*, ed. Paul Antze and Michael
    Lambek (New York: Routledge, 1996), 67–88; and Ian Hacking, *Rewriting the Soul: Multiple
    Personality and the Sciences of Memory* (Princeton, N.J.: Princeton University Press, 1995), 183–
    97, 210–20. For a cogent critique of Caruth and of the negative ethical consequences of
    her ascription of trauma to both victims and onlookers—perhaps even to perpetrators—
    see Leys, *Trauma*, 266–97. My hope is that the distinction between trauma and catastro-
    phe will help guard against some of these problems while recognizing the real—often
    bodily—consequences of witnessing death and other catastrophic events.
50 Connor suggests that Bataille's conception of "what is" derives from the vision at Ostia in
    Augustine's *Confessions*: "And thus, with the flash of one hurried glance, [my mind] attained
    to the vision of that which is." Augustine, *Confessions*, bk. 7, chap. 17; Connor, *Mysticism of
    Sin*, 6, 167, n. 2.
51 Here I have used Bruce Boone's evocative translation. The slide between image and reality
    is, I think, intentional, as is that between physical and subjective dissolution. These moves
    point to crucial issues concerning fictionality and writing in Bataille's approach to catastro-
    phe that I will explore in chapter 3.
52 The link between laceration and communication is explicit: "Communication demands
    a flaw, a 'fault': it enters, like death, by a chink in the armor. It demands a coincidence
    between two lacerations, in me and in the other" (OC V 266; G 30). I stress this point
    against Jean-Luc Nancy's insistence that "what makes singularities communicate is not to
    be confused with what Bataille calls their lacerations. . . . What is lacerated in this way is
    not the singular being: on the contrary, this is where the singular being compears. Rather,
    it is the communal fabric, it is immanence that is lacerated. And yet this laceration does
    not happen to anything, for this fabric does not exist. There is no tissue, no flesh, no
    subject or substance of common being, and consequently there is no laceration of this
    being. But there is sharing out." Jean-Luc Nancy, *The Inoperative Community*, ed. Peter Connor
    (Minneapolis: University of Minnesota Press, 1991), 30. Although this is inadequate
    as a reading of Bataille, it may provide a better way to think about communication and
    laceration, one to which Bataille, in making laceration a matter of language and textuality,
    may point. For more on this issue, see chapter 3.
53 The ethical problems of Bataille's position are heightened when we remember that for
    some people, bodily memories in PTSD are of events in which they perpetrated violence.
    See, for example, Allan Young, "Bodily Memory and Traumatic Memory," in *Tense Past*, 89–
    102; for a critique of such possible extensions of conceptions of trauma, see Leys, *Trauma*,
    292–97.
54 The American Psychiatric Association's *Diagnostic and Statistical Manual of Mental Disorder*, 3d
    ed., rev. (Washington, D.C.: APA, 1987) designates trauma as an event that lies "outside
    the range of human experience" (250), despite the fact that this is clearly not the case.
    See also Laura S. Brown, "Not Outside the Range: One Feminist Perspective on Psychic
    Trauma," in *Trauma: Explorations in Memory*, ed. Cathy Caruth (Baltimore: Johns Hopkins

University Press, 1995), 100–112. This specification is dropped in the fourth edition of *Diagnostic and Statistical Manual of Mental Disorder.*

55 My hesitations again point to the two different conceptions of history and contextualization that emerge in and around Bataille's work, as well as to the complex relationship between post-Foucaultian conceptions of history and anonymity.

56 Patricia Yaeger, "Consuming Trauma; or, The Pleasures of Merely Circulating," *Journal x* (1997): 225–51.

57 The danger that political narrativization trivializes human suffering is the source of Bataille's uneasiness with Sartre's *Anti-Semite and Jew*, in which Auschwitz is not discussed and "the critique of anti-semitism" becomes "above all the critique of rationalism." Bataille, who opens his review with an evocation of the horrors of Auschwitz, continues: "I am not saying that Sartre's critique is without worth (there is a flight at the base of the universal), but there is an epoch of reason, of which the Jews wrote authentic pages, and doesn't Jewish authenticity consist in just this, that up to Auschwitz it was reason that suffered in their flesh?" (OC XI 227–28). See Jean-Paul Sartre, *Anti-Semite and Jew*, trans. Georges J. Becker (New York: Schocken Books, 1965).

58 Of course, this body *communicates* only through the mediation of the photographer, raising crucial issues about agency, fictionality, and the real.

59 John Berger argues, for example, in the context of the Vietnam War, that the proliferation of photographic images of torture and physical agony work to universalize—and so depoliticize—suffering. See John Berger, "Photographs of Agony," in *About Looking* (New York: Pantheon Books, 1980), 37–40. There is now a growing literature on photography and the Holocaust that raises questions relevant to my project. See in particular, Andrea Liss's use of Levinas's notion of alterity to describe the ethical stakes of contemporary displays and artistic deployments of Holocaust photography. Andrea Liss, *Trespassing through Shadows: Memory, Photography, and the Holocaust* (Minneapolis: University of Minnesota Press, 1998); also see Barbie Zelizer, *Remembering to Forget: Holocaust Memory through the Camera's Eye* (Chicago: University of Chicago Press, 1998); Marianne Hirsch, *Family Frames: Photography, Narrative, and Postmemory* (Cambridge, Mass.: Harvard University Press, 1997); and Marianne Hirsch, "Projected Memory: Holocaust Photographs in Personal and Public Fantasy," in *Acts of Memory*, 3–23.

60 Many people would strenuously contest this claim, insisting that trauma is an ethical category and occurs only or primarily when a moral agent causes the event. Against this view, I would argue that trauma is a diagnostic category that should not be moralized, although where there are perpetrators, any ethical evaluation of the event demands that they be named and judged. Another telling problem is Bataille's assertion that the difference in sheer numbers of those killed is unimportant to the traumatic ramifications of an event (either for the victim or the onlooker). This problem becomes particularly clear when he goes on to argue that the apprehension that once occurred before "the suffering of Christ nailed to the Cross" now occurs before the victims of Hiroshima: "Not because any given horror should by itself grip me more than another that is less striking, but because the horror of Hiroshima holds, in fact, the attention of my fellowmen, like a lamp attracts a swarm of insects" (OC XI 184–85; CA 232). Yet surely there is an ineradicable difference between the suffering of one man and that of the millions injured, tortured, and killed in Hiroshima and the death camps of Europe. This is a significant failure in

Bataille's essay, even if we concede that the horror of suffering must be apprehended in its particularity in order for large-scale slaughter ever to be thought. The question after World War II is precisely whether this is possible. On the need to rethink death philosophically after the experience of man-made mass death, see Edith Wyschogrod, *Spirit in Ashes: Hegel, Heidegger, and Man-Made Mass Death* (New Haven, Conn.: Yale University Press, 1985).

61 As Suzanne Guerlac argues, for Bataille "the moment of '*se saisir*'—the *se saisir* (bringing to consciousness) of a *désaisissement* (loss of consciousness)—is the experience common to eroticism, laughter, sacrifice, and poetry. It is what Bataille calls the 'being in the instant.' It is in this sense that poetry, for Bataille, is event. . . . Poetry, Bataille writes, 'is a cry that gives to visibility [*un cri qui donne à voir*].'" It gives visibility to, according to Bataille, "what is." As Guerlac notes, this articulation of a poetry of the event is meant to counter Sartrean engagement. Suzanne Guerlac, *Literary Polemics: Bataille, Sartre, Valéry, Breton* (Stanford, Calif.: Stanford University Press, 1997), 37. The citations are from Georges Bataille, "From the Stone Age to Jacques Prévert," in *The Absence of Myth: Writings on Surrealism*, trans. Michael Richardson (London: Verso, 1994), esp. 148–53; OC XI 87–106.

62 As Peter Connor shows, Bataille ties this moment of sovereign sensibility to the birth of the atomic bomb, moving lexically beyond his medieval sources to a language of "shock," "force," and "charge" derived from that specific historical moment. See Connor, *Mysticism of Sin*, 92–93.

63 This reading of Bataille seems to emerge the more closely one associates "ecstasy" with a simplistic notion of either erotic or aesthetic pleasure, which is the tendency of many critics. See, for example, Jill Robbins, *Altered Reading: Levinas and Literature* (Chicago: University of Chicago Press, 1999), 97; and Edith Wyschogrod, *An Ethics of Remembering: History, Heterology, and the Nameless Others* (Chicago: University of Chicago Press, 1998), 235, 247. These critiques echo earlier work by Jean-Luc Nancy in "The Unsacrificeable," *Yale French Studies* (1991): 34–38; and in *The Inoperative Community*. See also Mark C. Taylor, "Politics of Theory," in *About Religion: Economies of Faith in Virtual Culture* (Chicago: University of Chicago Press, 1999), 48–79. Dominick LaCapra recently warns against a position in which "trauma (including the induced trauma of the *mise en abîme* of the text) is transvalued in an aesthetic of the sublime into an occasion for ecstasy and exhilaration." Dominick LaCapra, *History and Reading: Tocqueville, Foucault, French Studies* (Toronto: University of Toronto Press, 2000), 50–51. For more on this issue, see my conclusion.

64 The horror of the images produced by the war draw these problems out much more explicitly for many readers. What would Bataille do with photographs of holocaust victims? What do we do, as a culture and as individuals, with such images? I will explore the problem of Bataille's use of photographic images more fully in chapter 3.

65 I would contest Leo Bersani's otherwise astute reading of Bataille. Bersani claims that Bataille's understanding of "communication" seems to describe "an experience in which the very terms of a communication are abolished" and "thus lends itself to a dangerous confusion if we allow it to keep any of its ordinary connotations." Leo Bersani, "Is the Rectum a Grave?" in *AIDS: Cultural Analysis/Cultural Activism*, ed. Douglas Crimp (Cambridge, Mass.: MIT Press, 1988), 218, n. 25.

66 Edith Wyschogrod argues that Bataille's ecstatic mysticism is unacceptable as a way to think exteriority because in it, the pursuit of ecstasy is "unconstrained by the responsibility of

one for the other." She suggests instead a language of "the cataclysm, a power that over-powers, constrained by language so as to resist mythologization as sheer will to power" (*Ethics*, 247). Yet as I have argued, for Bataille catastrophe and ecstasy—at least for the onlooker—are inextricably mingled. We might hope for more restrained ways to meet the excesses of history—or ones less suspect of themselves inducing the excesses they encounter. Bataille, however, again casts doubt on the possibility of such a pure witness.

CHAPTER THREE

1   Recall that photographs also play a crucial role as a "marker of the real"—although one that will be subverted—in *Story of the Eye*. Photographs also figure in *Ma mère*, the second part of Bataille's posthumously published novel, *Divinus Deus*. See OC III 94–96; Georges Bataille, *My Mother/Madame Edwarda/The Dead Man*, trans. Austryn Wainhouse (London: Marion Boyars, 1989), 40–42.

2   Bataille gives more information about the photographs in his last book, *Tears of Eros*: "These texts were published in part by Dumas and Carpeaux. Carpeaux claims to have witnessed the torture on April 10, 1905. On March 25th, 1905, the 'Cheng Pao' published the following imperial decree: 'The Mongolian Princes demand that the aforesaid Fou-Tchou-Li, guilty of the murder of Prince Ao-Han-Ouan, be burned alive, but the Emperor finds this torture too cruel and condemns Fou-Tchou-Li to slow death by *Leng-Tch'e* (cutting into pieces). Respect this!' This torture dates from the Manchu dynasty (1644–1911)." Georges Bataille, *The Tears of Eros*, trans. Peter Connor (San Francisco: City Lights, 1989), 204.

The claim is often made that Bataille insists on the victim's ecstasy; see, for example, Peter Tracey Connor, *Georges Bataille and the Mysticism of Sin* (Baltimore: Johns Hopkins University Press, 2000), 3–4. There is no evidence of this insistence in the wartime writings. The claim does appear in Bataille's last book, *Tears of Eros*, but is attributed to Dumas and only reluctantly taken up by Bataille, despite his investment in the claim for the conjunction of anguish and ecstasy: "Dumas insists on the ecstatic appearance of the victim's expression. There is, of course, something undeniable in his expression, no doubt due at least in part to the opium, which augments what is most anguishing about this photograph. I have owned one of these pictures. . . . It was given to me by Dr. Borel, one of the first French psychoanalysts. This photograph had a decisive role in my life. I have never stopped being obsessed by this image of pain, at once ecstatic (?) and intolerable" (*Tears of Eros*, 205–6). He then goes on to ask what kind of "voluptuous effect" the image would have had on the Marquis de Sade and insists on the close tie between ecstasy and eroticism, particularly sadism. But of course, the victim cannot be accused of sadism, suggesting that here Bataille either critiques the sadism of his own meditative practice or dangerously elides the distinction between torturer and tortured. For more on this issue, particularly as it is reflected in Bataille's changing attitudes toward Christ and Christianity, see chapter 6. The question of who took the picture, and why, remains unexplored.

3   The Chinese writer Lu Xun describes his decision to abandon medicine for writing as one that was sparked by a film recording a similar event: "It was a long time since I had seen any compatriots, but one day I saw a film showing some Chinese, one of whom was bound, while many others stood around him. They were all strong fellows but appeared completely apathetic. According to the commentary, the one with his hands bound was a spy working for the Russians, who was to have his head cut off by the Japanese military as

a *public demonstration*, while the Chinese beside him had come to *appreciate this spectacular event.*"
Here Lu Xun's reading of the reactions of his compatriots within the film image plays a
direct role in the effect that image has on him.

As Rey Chow argues, what is demonstrated here is both the "direct, cruel, and *crude*
power of the film medium itself" and the ability of that medium—like torture itself—to
reduce spectators to "a passive collective mesmerized in spectatorship"; "faced with the
monstrous vision of the execution, these other men act as if what is in front of them is
some *final* meaning that requires absolute submission." For Chow, the power of film points
to a fundamental affinity between film and execution, and ultimately, between film and
fascism. As she argues in a later essay, liberal multiculturalism shares in this "desire for
a pure-otherness-in-pristine-luminosity . . . a longing for a transparent, idealized image
and an identifying submission to such an image. . . . This fascism seeks empowerment
through a surrender to the other as film—as the film that overcomes me in the spell of an
unmediated 'experience.'" Although I wonder if Chow does not dangerously overextend
the term "fascism," her critique is compelling. Bataille's call for an ethics of attention to
horror seems dangerously close to a submission to such seemingly raw displays of power.
See Rey Chow, *Primitive Passions: Visuality, Sexuality, Ethnography, and Contemporary Chinese Cinema*
(New York: Columbia University Press, 1995), 4, 8–9; and Rey Chow, *Ethics after Idealism:
Theory-Culture-Ethnicity-Reading* (Bloomington: Indiana University Press, 1998), 32.

On radical passivity as an ethic (with reference to Bataille's meditative practices), see
Thomas Carl Wall, *Radical Passivity: Levinas, Blanchot, and Agamben* (Albany: State University of
New York Press, 1999). The claim central to my account of Bataille is that he demands
both passivity and contestation, as can be seen, for example, in his deeply ambivalent response to the work of Simone Weil, which he criticizes for its emphasis on submission
to an all-powerful other. See Georges Bataille, *Blue of Noon*, trans. Harry Matthews (London: Marion Boyars, 1986); Georges Bataille, "La victoire militaire et la banqueroute de la
morale qui maudit," OC XI 532–48; and Connor, *Mysticism of Sin*, 72–79. The point where
Bataille most merits critique is in his inability to recognize that where one stands in relationship to power crucially effects one's ability to experience sovereignty through the
interplay of submission and contestation. See the introduction to part 2.

4   Edward Said, *Orientalism* (New York: Vintage, 1978), 72. For similar problems with regard
to gender in Bataille's meditative practice, see the introduction to part 2.

5   See Homi Bhabha, "The Other Question: Stereotype, Discrimination, and the Discourse
of Colonialism," in *The Location of Culture* (New York: Routledge, 1994), 66–84. Also see
Kobena Mercer, *Welcome to the Jungle: New Positions in Black Cultural Studies* (New York: Routledge,
1994), 171–219. For a critique of such extensions of the Freudian notion of fetishism,
see Whitney Davis, "HomoVision: A Reading of Freud's 'Fetishism,'" *Genders* 15 (1992):
86–118.

The logic of Orientalism may also be evident within representations of the crucifixion, for Jesus was, of course, a Jew. On the ways in which Jesus' Jewishness is disavowed
through the representation of the bad thief as stereotypically Jewish, see Mitchell Merback,
The Thief, the Cross, and the Wheel: Pain and the Spectacle of Punishment in Medieval and Renaissance Europe
(Chicago: University of Chicago Press, 1999).

6   I am grateful to Ann Mongoven for pointing out this crucial difference between Bataille
and Angela. Other women mystics from the thirteenth and early fourteenth century seem

to have resisted the cultural identification of women with bodiliness and of women's
sanctity with bodily pain and suffering. Women like Mechthild of Magdeburg, Beatrice
of Nazareth, and Marguerite Porete, then, may here be closer to Bataille than is Angela of
Foligno.

7 Susan Sontag, On Photography (New York: Anchor Books, 1977), 155. Also see Walter Benjamin, Illuminations, ed. Hannah Arendt, trans. Harry Zohn (New York: Schocken Books,
1968), 217–51; and "Little History of Photography," in Walter Benjamin: Selected Writings: Volume 2, 1927–34, ed. Michael W. Jennings, Howard Eiland, and Gary Smith (Cambridge,
Mass.: Harvard University Press, 1999), 507–30.

8 See André Bazin, "The Ontology of the Photographic Image," in The Camera Viewed: Writings on Twentieth-Century Photography, ed. Peninah R. Petruck (New York: Dutton, 1979),
2:140–46.

9 See Roland Barthes, Camera Lucida: Reflections on Photography, trans. Richard Howard (New York:
Hill and Wang, 1981); and Christian Metz, "Photography and Fetish," October 34 (1985):
81–90. Barthes's account of the "that has been" quality of photography seems to parallel
Bataille's insistence on "what is there." As Carolyn Dinshaw suggests, the photographic
punctum "wounds" the spectator. On these aspects of Barthes's text, see Carolyn Dinshaw,
Getting Medieval: Sexualities and Communities, Pre- and Postmodern (Durham, N.C.: Duke University
Press, 1999), 51–52.

10 For similar problems in medieval images of the crucifixion, see Merback, The Thief, the Cross,
and the Wheel. Merback shows how Calvary images carried significant ideological messages
(particularly with regard to Judaism) generally not discussed in mystical texts grounded in
meditative practice.

11 This question might simply indicate a desire for a kind of ethical purity that Bataille
suggests is impossible. Yet as I will show, the question has a source in Bataille's own
practice.

12 Hadewijch, Complete Works, trans. Mother Columba Hart (New York: Paulist Press, 1980),
Vision 7, 280–82; David Freedberg, The Power of Images: Studies in the History and Theory of Response
(Chicago: University of Chicago Press, 1989), 199–303. Freedberg gives examples of
images of Mary also coming to life and speaking.

13 See Julian of Norwich, Showings, trans. Edmund Colledge and James Walsh (New York:
Paulist Press, 1978).

14 For evidence of how visionaries discuss their experience, see Jeffrey Hamburger, Nuns as
Artists: The Visual Culture of a Medieval Convent (Berkeley: University of California Press, 1997);
and Jeffrey Hamburger, The Visual and the Visionary: Art and Female Spirituality in Late Medieval Germany (New York: Zone Books, 1998). For the role of the visionary imagination and meditation in mysticism, see Amy Hollywood, The Soul as Virgin Wife: Mechthild of Magdeburg, Marguerite Porete, and Meister Eckhart (Notre Dame, Ind.: University of Notre Dame Press, 1995),
16–25; and Amy Hollywood, "Inside Out: Beatrice of Nazareth and Her Hagiographer,"
in Gendered Voices: Medieval Saints and Their Interpreters, ed. Catherine M. Mooney (Philadelphia:
University of Pennsylvania Press, 1999), 78–98. Similarly, icons, panels, frescoes, and
predellas of saints, rather than the relics of saints, were sometimes the site of miracles.
See Michael Goodich, Violence and Miracle in the Fourteenth Century: Private Grief and Public Salvation
(Chicago: University of Chicago Press, 1995), 2.

For the theological arguments, which clearly assert that the body of Christ is in heaven and only "spiritually" present to the visionary, see Dyan Elliott, "True Presence, False Christ: Antinomies of Embodiment in Medieval Spirituality" (paper presented at the Fifth Annual Conference in Comparative Religion, New York University, March 2001).

15 This same problem, it should be noted, exists for the Christian viewer of the cross and is arguably compounded by the fact that God is the ultimate agent of Christ's suffering.

16 Eduardo Cadava, *Words of Light: Theses on the Photography of History* (Princeton, N.J.: Princeton University Press, 1997), xxviii.

17 The problem seems to be one of masochism rather than voyeurism. Yet the larger Christian culture often "used" saintly figures as models and means of intercession, so arguably voyeurism remains an issue. For the particularly gendered nature of this emphasis on the saint's suffering body, see Hollywood, *Virgin Wife*, 180–93.

18 One might argue that the denigration of one group over another on the basis of such differences is itself ultimately contingent. Yet even if we want to assert with Bataille that it is necessary to recognize this ultimate contingency, there are also crucial reasons to insist on the historical and critical exposure and explanation of patterns of distinction and discrimination.

19 See Caroline Walker Bynum, *Holy Feast and Holy Fast: The Religious Significance of Food to Medieval Women* (Berkeley: University of California Press, 1987), esp. 260–76. For a critique of Bynum's refusal to question this emphasis on suffering, see Julie B. Miller, "Eroticized Violence in Medieval Women's Mystical Literature," *Journal for Feminist Studies in Religion* 15, no. 2 (1999): 25–49. For a complicating account of medieval views of the body and gender, see Sharon Farmer, "The Beggar's Body: Intersections of Gender and Social Status in High Medieval Paris," in *Monks and Nuns, Saints and Outcasts: Religion in Medieval Society*, ed. Sharon Farmer and Barbara H. Rosenwein (Ithaca, N.Y.: Cornell University Press, 2000), 153–71.

20 Hadewijch, *Works*, Letter 6, 56–63.

21 See Hollywood, *Virgin Wife*, 57–86; and Hollywood, "Inside Out."

22 On this issue, see Hollywood, *Virgin Wife*, 173–206; and Hollywood, "Inside Out." Angela's book is one of the earliest exceptions and clearly mixes mystical and hagiographical elements, as will many subsequent religious works by women.

23 This movement toward the spiritualization of suffering comes together with a spiritualizing of the ideal of "work"; in the latter case, the spiritualizing tendency is clearly tied to gender expectations and to what was possible for men and women in late medieval Europe. The emphasis on virginity and enclosure for women's sanctity made it difficult for them to follow an apostolic life in the world, despite evidence that some women wished to pursue such ideals. See Hollywood, *Virgin Wife*, 39–50.

24 Marguerite Porete, *Le Mirouer des simples ames anienties et qui seulement demourent en vouloir et desir d'amour*, ed. Romana Guarnieri and Paul Verdeyen, Corpus Christianorum: Continuatio Mediaevalis, vol. 69 (Turnhout: Brepols, 1986), chap. 8, pp. 28–30. The crucial distinction here is between those souls who dwell in Love with the virtues serving them and those who dwell in Love while still themselves serving virtue.

25 For an earlier instance in which Martha is given primacy over Mary, see André Vauchez's brief description of Anselm of Harelberg's exegesis of the Lukan passage; André Vauchez, *The Spirituality of the Medieval West: From the Eighth to the Twelfth Century*, trans. Colette Friedlander (Kalamazoo, Mich.: Cistercian Publications, 1993), 125.

26 Eckhart's explicit teachings on suffering are complex, demonstrating his desire both to downplay the role of suffering in spiritual formation and to comfort suffering human beings. He writes to Queen Agnes of Hungary, perhaps after the murder of her father: "But if my suffering is in God and God is suffering with me, how then can suffering be sorrow to me, if suffering loses its sorrow, and my sorrow is in God, and my sorrow is God?" *Meister Eckhart: The Essential Sermons, Commentaries, Treatises, and Defense,* trans. Edmund Colledge and Bernard McGinn (New York: Paulist Press, 1981), 235. For more on Porete and Eckhart on suffering and apophasis, and on the crucial differences between them, see Amy Hollywood, "Eckhart's Apophatic Ethics," *Eckhart Review* 10 (2001): 35–46.

27 For more on the complexities involved in the "visionary," which in fact often includes the whole range of spiritual senses, see chapter 8.

28 Hadewijch, *Works,* 281.

29 Of course, in this period, images of the suffering Christ were not the only kind of vision, and so visions were not always explicitly associated with suffering. However, there is some evidence to suggest that the reception of visions was tied to suffering and asceticism. See Hollywood, *Virgin Wife,* 1–25.

30 In Porete's case, however, suffering does arguably still play a crucial role in the soul's path to God. Toward the end of the *Mirror,* the soul undergoes a "trial of love," modeled, Nicholas Watson argues, on that of patient Griselda. Yet as Watson shows, Porete uses this gendered story of submission in order to attain radically new ends. See Nicholas Watson, "'If wommen be double naturelly': Remaking 'Woman' in Julian of Norwich's Revelation of Love," *Exemplaria* 8 (1996): 2–7; and Hollywood, "Eckhart's Apophatic Ethics."

31 Nietzsche's work had been important for Bataille since the 1920s and was part of his movement away from Christianity. Although Bataille seems to have read ascetic, medita-tive, and mystical works during his Christian period and after, the word "mystic" or "mys-tical" does not appear regularly in his work until the late 1930s. For this information, see Michel Surya, *Georges Bataille, la mort à l'oeuvre* (Paris: Gallimard, 1992), 334, 366–77, 466.

32 For more on the mystical aspect of Nietzsche's writing, see Tyler T. Roberts, *Contesting Spirit: Nietzsche, Affirmation, Religion* (Princeton, N.J.: Princeton University Press, 1998), 103–201. Roberts has not been able to locate some of the passages concerning mysticism that Bataille attributes to Nietzsche (and neither have I), in particular: "The definition of a mystic: someone with enough happiness of his own, maybe too much, seeking a language for his happiness because he wants to *give away* that happiness." See OC VI 261; and Roberts, *Contesting Spirit,* 104, n. 1.

33 Here we hear echoes of Bataille's response to Sartre—most explicitly in *Thus Spoke Zarathustra,* which, like the Gospels of the New Testament and many mystical treatises, is a transforma-tive text meant to bring about the experience of conversion described within it. Yet this account of *Zarathustra* implies that the text has an aim, as all practices and acts do according to Bataille; Zarathustra's fifth gospel thereby subtly misses the pure aimlessness of inner experience. This might be read as a response to Sartre's claim that *Inner Experience* is a gospel spoken from "on high" and hence without reciprocity (NM 152).

34 For an account of how Bataille's work resists generic constraints, see Philippe Sollers, "De grandes irrégularités de langage," *Critique* 195–196 (1963): 795–802.

35 A later text, *The Memorandum,* is made up only of citations from Nietzsche's work, almost like a florilegium of Nietzschean writings. See OC VI 209–72.

36 I concede Peter Connor's point that there is potentially something odd in reading Bataille against a text that he did not know, but the close ties between the types of mysticism found in Mechthild and Angela and the relatively unmediated form of Mechthild's text justify the comparison. For the critique of an earlier paper of mine in which I first introduce the comparison, see Connor, Mysticism of Sin, 10–11.

37 Surya includes the Confessions in his list of possible models for Bataille's work. Of course, it is precisely the confessional aspect of mysticism that Bataille abjures, insofar as it is tied to dogmatics (OC V 15; IE 3).

38 This claim goes together with a number of standard assertions about the nature of women's writings—namely, that it is more spontaneous, immediate, more often in the first person and hence autobiographical—almost all of which are false. See Hollywood, Virgin Wife; and for how this issue plays out in the modern novel, Susan Sniader Lanser, Fictions of Authority: Women Writers and Narrative Voice (Ithaca, N.Y.: Cornell University Press, 1992).

39 The closest thing to a structuring paradigm for Mechthild's Flowing Light is the constant interplay of presence and absence in the Song of Songs. Through this interplay of alienation and ecstasy, the joyful experience of divine presence and the anguish engendered by divine absence, Mechthild depicts the suffering, desiring soul that, like Hadewijch's, shares spiritually in the suffering of Christ. Similarly, Bataille's "Alleluia," the final appended section of Guilty, is described by Denis Hollier as Bataille's rewriting of the Song of Songs. See Denis Hollier, "A Tale of Unsatisfied Desire," in Guilty, vii–xiii.

40 Early in the text, Bataille makes it clear that it is not addressed to his friends or intimates but to those whom he does not know and who will be alive after his death.

41 In her articulation of a birth-focused metaphysics, Christine Battersby argues for the oddity of just such claims. See Christine Battersby, The Phenomenal Woman: Feminist Metaphysics and the Patterns of Identity (New York: Routledge, 1998), 2–3.

42 See, for example, Maurice Blanchot, The Madness of the Day, trans. Lydia Davis (Barrytown, N.Y.: Station Hill Press, 1981). For Blanchot on Bataille, see Maurice Blanchot, The Infinite Conversation, trans. Susan Hanson (Minneapolis: University of Minnesota Press, 1993), 202–15; Maurice Blanchot, Friendship, trans. Elizabeth Rottenberg (Stanford, Calif.: Stanford University Press, 1997), 289–92; and Maurice Blanchot, The Unavowable Community, trans. Pierre Joris (Barrytown, N.Y.: Station Hill Press, 1988). For an early and important formulation of the paradox of writing by Jacques Derrida, see "Signature, Event, Context," in Margins of Philosophy, trans. Alan Bass (Chicago: University of Chicago Press, 1982), 307–30.

43 Eric Blondel begins to demonstrate a similar twofold movement within Nietzsche's texts. See Eric Blondel, Nietzsche, the Body and Culture: Philosophy as a Philological Genealogy, trans. Seán Hand (Stanford, Calif.: Stanford University Press, 1991).

44 Whether the reduction of Nietzsche to a truth that can be communicated is the fault of Nietzsche or of those commentators who insist on reducing his work to a discourse and a doctrine can be decided only by a comparison of Nietzsche's and Bataille's writing practices.

45 Jean-Luc Nancy, The Birth to Presence, trans. Brian Holmes et al. (Stanford, Calif.: Stanford University Press, 1993), 334.

46 See Blondel, Nietzsche; Michel de Certeau, "Mystic Speech," in Heterologies: Discourse on the Other, trans. Brian Massumi (Minneapolis: University of Minnesota Press, 1986), 80–

100; Michel de Certeau, *The Mystic Fable*, vol. 1, *The Sixteenth and Seventeenth Centuries*, trans. Michael B. Smith (Chicago: University of Chicago Press, 1992); and Michael Sells, *Mystical Languages of Unsaying* (Chicago: University of Chicago Press, 1994).

47 At stake here, as often between Sartre and Bataille, is the question of history's rationality or irrationality. Bataille does not want to do away with reason entirely but to subvert reason by pushing against its limits—which for him are marked by that in history that is irreducible to human projects. For more on the relationship between reason and irrationality in Bataille, see Connor, *Mysticism of Sin*, esp. 127–53.

48 On the complex interplay between violence, representation, and the technologies of writing in late twentieth-century culture, see Mark Seltzer, *Serial Killers: Death and Life in America's Wound Culture* (New York: Routledge, 1998). Seltzer's work suggests the dangers of Bataille's obsession with wounds (to be explored further in parts 2 and 3). Seltzer sees in contemporary culture a continual collapse of the distinction between sign and thing, writing and bodies, whereas I think there is something to Bataille's attempt to differentiate the two, despite their perhaps inevitable complicity. For a related discussion of death and representation in Bataille and Lacan, see Mikkel Borch-Jacobsen, *Lacan: The Absolute Master*, trans. Douglas Brick (Stanford, Calif.: Stanford University Press, 1991), esp. 91–96.

49 The use of images is again crucial in Bataille's final book, *Tears of Eros*, although perhaps this time with a subtle critique of the ethical implications of this practice. See my conclusions to this book.

50 Bataille's 1935 novel *Blue of Noon* (not published until 1957) can be read as an extended response to and critique of Weil's understanding of God and as a parody of that God's sadistic hypermasculinity. For Weil's understanding of God, see, for example, Simone Weil, *Waiting for God*, trans. Emma Craufurd (New York: Harper and Row, 1951), 117–36. Despite their differences, Bataille and Weil are extremely close in their emphasis on the necessity of encountering, with love and horror, that which is. For more on the relationship between Bataille and Weil, see Alexander Irwin, "Saints of the Impossible: Politics, Violence, and the Sacred in Georges Bataille and Simone Weil" (Ph.D. diss., Harvard University, 1997).

INTRODUCTION TO PART TWO

1 My understanding of history is indebted to Derrida's reflections on the difference between history as the repetition of the same and as the rupture of *différance*. According to Derrida, language, as citational, operates through difference and deferral. This operation opens language, experience, and history to the other. Meaning and experience are never completely recoverable (although communication can and does occur), nor can they ever be completely contained. Rather than a cause for lament, this loss makes change possible. See Jacques Derrida, "Signature, Event, Context," in *Margins of Philosophy*, trans. Alan Bass (Chicago: University of Chicago Press, 1982), 307–30.

2 Bataille's relationship to Laure and to her experience and writing is similarly ambivalent. See chapter 2, n. 8; also see Sarah Wilson, "Fêting the Wound: Georges Bataille and Jean Fautrier in the 1940s," in *Bataille: Writing the Sacred*, ed. Carolyn Bailey Gill (New York: Routledge, 1995), 179, 190, n. 32.

3 Susan Suleiman, "Bataille in the Street: The Search for Virility in the 1930s," in *Bataille: Writing the Sacred*, ed. Carolyn Bailey Gill (New York: Routledge, 1995), 26–45.

4   During the war, Bataille borrowed the work of Rolland de Renéville from the Bibliothèque Nationale. Renéville wrote about poetry and mysticism, particularly in the work of Rimbaud. See Pierre Prévost, *Georges Bataille, René Guénon: L'expérience souveraine* (Paris: Jean-Michel Place, 1992), 15–16. Cited in Peter Tracey Connor, *Georges Bataille and the Mysticism of Sin* (Baltimore: Johns Hopkins University Press, 2000), 172–73, n. 7.

5   Whereas medieval women, who were not permitted to act in the world, chose to emphasize the active nature of writing and contemplation (although it was God writing through them in their complete passivity to the divine agent), the surrealists (and in the early circle they were all men) abjured action through writing understood as passive automatism. Or at least this is how Bataille characterizes the movement in *Inner Experience*. After the Second World War, he engages in a major reevaluation of the surrealist movement, premised in part on a rejection of this binary opposition between action and contemplation. See the essays collected in Georges Bataille, *The Absence of Myth: Writings on Surrealism*, trans. Michael Richardson (London: Verso, 1994).

6   Suleiman, "Bataille in the Street," 41. Freud and Lacan both persist in using "active" and "passive" to denote masculinity and femininity, respectively.

7   On the complexities of Bataille's sexual identity, see Calvin Thomas, *Male Matters: Masculinity, Anxiety, and the Male Body on the Line* (Urbana: University of Illinois Press, 1996). Despite the reservations I express here and in the following chapters, Bataille's powers of subversion are manifest in the ways in which he has been taken up by gay and queer theorists. Much of what is useful to such thinkers in Lacan is also grounded in Bataille's work. See, for example, Leo Bersani, *The Culture of Redemption* (Cambridge, Mass.: Harvard University Press, 1990), 102–23.

8   This move may be less counterintuitive than it appears in that it associates Christianity with feminine passivity, and the rejection of Christianity and salvation with masculinity. As we will see, this gendering of religion is central for Simone de Beauvoir, both in her life and in her writing. Beauvoir will insist, however, that both men and women desire to "be everything," although the illusion of attaining this wholeness is more readily available to women through Christianity than through other, more active means.

9   In an essay on the relationship between Bataille and the painter Jean Fautrier, Sarah Wilson shows that within their work there is a similar association of the human form with woundedness and a conflation of woundedness with the female sex (see Fautrier's *L'homme ouvert*, 1928–1929, remarkably reminiscent of the torture victim and his side wound). Jean Fautrier is perhaps best known for his *Otages* (Hostages) series (first shown in 1945), which was sparked by the intensified Nazi hostage taking and reprisal shootings of September and October 1941 (also the catalyst for *Madame Edwarda* and "The Torment"). The images in the series, like Bataille's writings, mix horror and eroticism in profoundly troubling ways. Although Francis Ponge notes the connection with *Story of the Eye* in his "Note sur les Otages" of 1945, Wilson is the first person to trace the link between Fautrier and Bataille's wartime writings. As she shows, Fautrier first met Bataille in 1942 and was a close associate until 1947. Fautrier did illustrations for two of Bataille's texts from the 1940s, *Madame Edwarda* and *Alleluiah, Catechism of Dianus*. See Wilson, "Fêting the Wound." On vaginal images of Christ's side wound in the Middle Ages, see Karma Lochrie, "Mystical Acts, Queer Tendencies," *Constructing Medieval Sexuality*, ed. Karma Lochrie, Peggy McCracken,

and James A. Schultz (Minneapolis: University of Minnesota Press, 1997), 180–200; and my discussion of Irigaray in chapter 6.

10 These remarks are from a preface to *Madame Edwarda* that, prior to its inclusion in Bataille's collected works, was never published.

11 For more on the image of the spider in Bataille, see Yve-Alain Bois and Rosalind E. Krauss, *Formless: A User's Guide* (New York: Zone Books, 1997), in particular the translation of Bataille's brief text of that name. The scene in *Madame Edwarda* is remarkably reminiscent of Courbet's *L'Origine du monde* (Origin of the World), a painting owned by Lacan. For the painting and its significance to Lacan's thought, see Shuli Barzilai, *Lacan and the Matter of Origins* (Stanford, Calif.: Stanford University Press, 1999), 8–18. For an interpretation of the painting as "the forbidden site of specularity and ultimate object of male desire" as well as "the very source of artistic creation itself," see Linda Nochlin, "Courbet's *L'Origine du monde*: The Origin without an Original," in *Spectacles of Realism: Body, Gender, Genre*, ed. Margaret Cohen and Christopher Prendergast (Minneapolis: University of Minnesota Press, 1995), 339. At the time Nochlin wrote her essay, the painting was believed to be lost. Only after Lacan's death in 1987 did it become known publicly that he had owned the painting. Hence Nochlin's closing comments about Lacan are uncannily prescient.

12 For the association of *Madame Edwarda* and Angela's kissing Christ's side wound, and also for the evocative phrase "fêting the wound," see Wilson, "Fêting the Wound," 179, 181, 190, n. 39. For more on this aspect of Angela's text, see chapter 6.

13 We can also see here a fear of the female sex as that apparent absence from which all life emerges. This scene can be read, as can *Story of the Eye*, simply in terms of castration anxiety and the disavowal of that lack through the fetishization of the woman's body. Yet Bataille claims not only to fear but to embrace castration. Similarly, he claims to embrace blindness, despite Peter Kussel's claim that Bataille feared blindness. See Peter B. Kussel, "From the Anus to the Mouth to the Eye," *Semiotext(e)* 2, no. 2 (1976): 105–19.

14 Cited in Suzanne Guerlac, *Literary Polemics: Bataille, Sartre, Valéry, Breton* (Stanford, Calif.: Stanford University Press, 1997), 25. Guerlac goes on to explain that Bataille argues that autonomous women may be equally, even more, desirable than prostitutes, but with them one could not "avoid struggle which would lead to destruction." This clarification is important in terms of the charge of misogyny, for Bataille explicitly does *not* equate the prostitute with femininity. The position of the prostitute as sacred object depends on her (or his? it seems possible, at least, for the prostitute to be male) putative lack of autonomy. Bataille thereby begins with the assumption of women's freedom and full subjectivity, which is then given up and/or taken away through prostitution. Bataille's whole account is written, however, from a heterosexual male perspective and without raising any questions about whether the sacred would have to be made available in other ways for differently situated subjects. There is a deep contradiction, moreover, between Bataille's desire for radical democracy and his claims for the necessity of subordination or sacrifice.

As Guerlac shows, what is at stake for Bataille here is a recasting of the Hegelian master/slave scene in which the relationship to the erotic object gives rise to the sacred: "In this corrected, second-order version of the master/slave dialectic, it is not a question of real struggle to the death, as in Hegel's scenario, but of a fiction of death—a philosophical equivalent of *la petite mort* of erotic jouissance. Recognition operates through a fiction of death. But it is not a question of fictive death, as in the case of the dialectically suppressed slave according to Hegel. It is rather a matter of a fiction, or illusion of death as absolute recognition, or recognition of the absolute. The fiction does not occur by default, for want of the real thing. It is the positive result—the meaning—of this dialectic. The *figure figée* of the prostitute, the beautiful erotic object, is essential to the staging of this fiction" (Guerlac, *Literary Polemics*, 32).

15   Ibid., 32.

16   Mark Seltzer comments about a putative shift in "the spectacle of the wounded body" that he argues occurs around 1900: "The wound, for one thing, is by now no longer the mark, the stigmata, of the sacred or heroic: it is the icon, or stigma, of the everyday openness of the body." Mark Seltzer, *Serial Killers: Death and Life in America's Wound Culture* (New York: Routledge, 1998), 2. In Bataille, we see the opposite move. During the war, he focuses on the "everyday" nature of mortality and bodily horror, whereas after the war he shifts to a reading of that woundedness as the mark of the sacred.

17   In the *Atheological Summa* both language itself and the "I" of these texts are sacrificed and thus are the object through whose sacrifice the sacred becomes manifest. To locate sacrifice *in writing* rather than to represent it through a description of some sacred object seems to mitigate some of the dangers of the later, more descriptive texts discussed by Guerlac, although this mitigation depends on a logic of substitution whereby Bataille is able to erase his relatively privileged status and become a self-sacrificing (textual) victim.

CHAPTER FOUR

1   Simone de Beauvoir, *La forces des choses* (Paris: Gallimard, 1963), 75; *Force of Circumstance*, trans. Richard Howard (Harmondsworth: Penguin, 1968), 70–71. See also Simone de Beauvoir, *Pour une morale de l'ambiguïté* (Paris: Gallimard, 1947), 101; *The Ethics of Ambiguity*, trans. Bernard Frechtman (Secaucus, N.J.: Citadel Press, 1970), 70.

2   Edward Fullbrook and Kate Fullbrook, *Simone de Beauvoir: A Critical Introduction* (Cambridge: Polity Press, 1998), 78. Eva Lundgren-Gothlin also notes that there should be a distinction made between authentic and inauthentic transcendence, but Beauvoir only occasionally makes this clear in *The Second Sex*. See Eva Lundgren-Gothlin, *Sex and Existence: Simone de Beauvoir's "The Second Sex,"* trans. Linda Schenck (Hanover, N.H.: Wesleyan/University Press of New England, 1996), 241.

3   The philosophical terminology of being-in-itself and being-for-itself is developed by Jean-Paul Sartre in *Being and Nothingness* and is rarely used by Beauvoir. For the philosophical importance of *She Came to Stay* and its influence on Sartre's philosophical project, see Edward Fullbrook and Kate Fullbrook, *Simone de Beauvoir and Jean-Paul Sartre: The Remaking of a Twentieth-Century Legend* (New York: Basic Books, 1994), 97–127. For Beauvoir's use of and divergences from Sartre's philosophical vocabulary, see Lundgren-Gothlin, *Sex and Existence*, 127–65.

4   The situation is complicated by the fact that Françoise believed herself to be fully united as one consciousness with Pierre. Xavière disrupts that illusion of unity and reveals that Pierre also encounters Françoise as a being-in-itself. On the philosophical positions developed in the novel, see Toril Moi, *Simone de Beauvoir: The Making of an Intellectual Woman* (Oxford: Blackwell, 1994), 95–124; and Fullbrook and Fullbrook, *Critical Introduction*, 78–79. The Fullbrooks distinguish two kinds of "bad faith" in Beauvoir, that of transcendence and that

of immanence. In the former, the subject denies his or her immanence and in the latter his or her transcendence. They read Françoise as guilty of the bad faith of transcendence and Xavière as guilty of the bad faith of immanence. Although the latter may be more typical of women, Beauvoir insists that women demonstrate both types of bad faith. For the distinction, see Fullbrook and Fullbrook, *Critical Introduction*, 67–70.

5   Simone de Beauvoir, *L'Invitée* (Paris: Gallimard, 1943), 440; *She Came to Stay* (New York: Norton, 1954), 404.

6   I am skirting an enormous problematic within Beauvoir's text: the question of why women submit to being the other for men. As Beauvoir argues in her introduction, if women are acquiescent, they are morally culpable, whereas if they are forced to acquiesce they are the victims of oppression. In making this distinction and pointing to the role of oppression, Beauvoir rejects Sartre's early formulation of the existentialist ethic. See Simone de Beauvoir, *Pyrrhus et Cinéas* (Paris: Gallimard, 1944); Beauvoir, *Pour une morale*; Deirdre Bair, *Simone de Beauvoir: A Biography* (New York: Summit Books, 1990), 270–71; Sonia Kruks, *Situation and Human Existence: Freedom, Subjectivity, and Society* (London: Unwin Hyman, 1990), 83–112; Sonia Kruks, "Simone de Beauvoir: Teaching Sartre about Freedom," in *Sartre Alive*, ed. Ronald Aronson and Adrien van den Hoven (Detroit: Wayne State University Press, 1991), 285–300; Sonia Kruks, "Gender and Subjectivity: Simone de Beauvoir and Contemporary Feminism," *Signs* 18, no. 1 (1992): 89–110; Debra Bergoffen, *The Philosophy of Simone de Beauvoir: Gendered Phenomenologies, Erotic Generosities* (Albany: State University of New York Press, 1997), esp. 141–81; and Margaret Simons, *Beauvoir and the Second Sex: Feminism, Race, and the Origins of Existentialism* (Lanham, Md.: Rowman and Littlefield, 1999), esp. 185–243.

     Feminists influenced by Foucault have found his work useful for bridging this apparent dichotomy and theorizing power in such a way that we can understand women as oppressed by dominant power structures and as implicated in the process of their own oppression. By arguing that power is not possessed by individuals but is systemic, creative, and regulatory, Foucault helps explain how human needs and desires are created and maintained through ideologies and practices. For an extremely useful critical and constructive account of power, which makes use of Foucault, Judith Butler, and Hannah Arendt, see Amy Allen, *The Power of Feminist Theory: Domination, Resistance, Solidarity* (Boulder, Colo.: Westview Press, 1999).

7   This shifting of desire suggests a danger in giving too much primacy to the Fullbrooks' analytic distinction between the bad faith of transcendence and that of immanence. Beauvoir argues in *The Second Sex*, as I will show, that immanence can itself become a route to transcendence, but one that is always inadequate, hence the difficulty of determining if the narcissist, the lover, and the mystic are guilty of the bad faith of transcendence (denying the immanence of existence) or that of immanence (denying transcendence). For Beauvoir, they are, paradoxically, guilty of both. It should be mentioned, however, that bad faith is not always a matter for moral censure, according to Beauvoir. Bad faith acquires an ethical dimension only when the subject has the freedom to choose. On this issue, see Beauvoir, *Ethics of Ambiguity*, 35–40; Beauvoir, *Pour une morale*, 51–60; Fullbrook and Fullbrook, *Critical Introduction*, 69–70; and Moi, *Beauvoir*, 103–5.

8   The other crucial mode of justification, of course, is motherhood. Beauvoir discusses motherhood at length in her description of women's situation, perhaps because she takes

it to be so fundamental to her culture's understanding of what it means to be a woman (DS II 330–91; SS 540–88).

9   Metaphysical issues include those about the nature of consciousness, the relationship between body and mind or consciousness, and the existence of other minds or centers of consciousness.

10 On the problem of death in Beauvoir's work and her inability ever fully to resolve the challenge to meaning that death poses, see Elaine Marks, *Simone de Beauvoir: Encounters with Death* (New Brunswick, N.J.: Rutgers University Press, 1973).

11 For the philosophical importance of Beauvoir's fictions and autobiographies, see Jo-Ann Pilardi, "Philosophy Becomes Autobiography: The Development of the Self in the Writings of Simone de Beauvoir," in *Writing the Politics of Difference*, ed. Hugh J. Silverman (Albany: State University of New York Press, 1991), 145–62; Fullbrook and Fullbrook, *Critical Introduction*, 37–51, 63–67; Jo-Ann Pilardi, *Simone de Beauvoir Writing the Self: Philosophy Becomes Autobiography* (Westport, Conn.: Greenwood Publishing Company, 1999); and Ursula Tidd, *Simone de Beauvoir, Gender and Testimony* (Cambridge: Cambridge University Press, 1999). On the necessary concreteness of her philosophical work, see Toril Moi, *What Is a Woman? and Other Essays* (Oxford: Oxford University Press, 1999), 121–250.

12 This narrative pattern is philosophically articulated in Beauvoir, *Ethics of Ambiguity*, 35–40; Beauvoir, *Pour une morale*, 51–60.

13 For more on Beauvoir's autobiographical practice, see Leah D. Hewitt, *Autobiographical Tightropes* (Lincoln: University of Nebraska Press, 1990), 13–52; and Mary Evans, *Missing Persons: The Impossibility of Auto/biography* (New York: Routledge, 1999), 26–51.

14 According to Beauvoir, her father thought the monarchy a dream, but felt only disgust for the Republic (and presumably for democracy as practiced within it). He did not subscribe to the monarchical *L'Action Française* but had friends among its subscribers and admired its grand theoretician, Charles Maurras. This conservative patriotism stayed with Beauvoir even after her loss of religious faith (MJF 50; MDD 35). For more on Charles Maurras and his relationship to the later emergence of fascism in France, see David Carroll, *French Literary Fascism: Nationalism, Anti-Semitism, and the Ideology of Culture* (Princeton, N.J.: Princeton University Press, 1995), 71–96.

15 Beauvoir's account of the gendering of her family life and religious training falls into line with a prevalent thesis, derived from Michelet, concerning the feminization and repressed eroticism of nineteenth-century French religion. On the Michelet thesis and its limitations, see Ruth Harris, *Lourdes: Body and Spirit in the Secular Age* (London: Penguin, 1999), 213–14, 234–35, 244.

16 On Beauvoir's education, see Moi, *Beauvoir*, 38–72; and Fullbrook and Fullbrook, *Critical Introduction*, 7–29. For more general information about the education of women in the Third Republic, see Françoise Mayeur, *L'enseignement secondaire des jeunes filles sous la Troisième République* (Paris: Presses de la fondation nationale des science politiques, 1977).

17 For example, Beauvoir recounts reading the lives of the saints and being happy to have a room to herself so that she could sleep on the bare floor during her periods of holiness (MJF 112; MDD 81).

18 Arguably the interplay of heroic sanctity and submissive humility within saints' lives and martyrologies continues to play a role in Beauvoir's desire to justify her existence through autonomous action and in her insistence on the dangers of narcissism. I will point to a

potential resolution of this dilemma in what follows, although one so dependent on the recognition of others as to perhaps be itself a danger for women within male-dominant society.

19 Simons, *Beauvoir*, 191. In *When Things of the Spirit Come First*, Marcelle and Marguerite work for a similar group, with which they become disillusioned. The character Marguerite repeats much of the material found in *Memoirs of a Dutiful Daughter* concerning Beauvoir's childhood faith, loss of faith, and involvement with *Équipes sociales* and her cousin Jacques (Dénis in the story). See Simone de Beauvoir, *Quand prime le spirituel* (Paris: Gallimard, 1979); *When Things of the Spirit Come First*, trans. Patrick O'Brian (New York: Pantheon Books, 1982).

20 *Memoirs of a Dutiful Daughter* is particularly marked by Beauvoir's sense of chosenness and vocation, first expressed in terms of religion, then, after her abrupt and apparently untraumatic loss of faith, in terms of writing (MDD 29–31, 57–59, 73–75, 125–27, 133–42); see Karen Vintges, *Philosophy as Passion: The Thinking of Simone de Beauvoir* (Bloomington: Indiana University Press, 1996), 112.

21 In using the feminine *personne*, Beauvoir may open the possibility of another, feminized transcendence. On the other hand, the other meaning of *personne*—"no one"—may come to the fore here, suggesting the emptiness of the divine other, particularly in its feminine manifestation.

22 The materiality of this desire, its embodied nature, varies, according to Beauvoir. Just as erotomania can take either platonic or sexual form, the mystic's desire has varying degrees of bodily expression. Beauvoir insists, however, that if bodily, this desire is sexual. She wishes to escape the constraints of Freudian theory, which she believes reads subjectivity solely in terms of sexuality (and hence of the body). As Beauvoir reads him, Freud is a biological essentialist. For Beauvoir, on the other hand, embodiment and sexuality are continuous, but both can and must be transcended, or at least put in their subordinate place, in order for human freedom to be attained by women.

23 In *Memoirs*, however, she argues that her loss of faith freed her from her sex, which suggests that religion will always be associated with femininity. Zaza's father, for example, is religious and hence feminized in the eyes of Simone (MJF 160; MDD 114).

24 Beauvoir posits a conscious and controlled eroticism in Teresa that is markedly different from that described by either Lacan or Irigaray, both of whom emphasize the loss of consciousness and control in such moments of jouissance. See chapters 5 and 6.

25 For an elaboration of how the absent God is made present, particularly through pain and wounding, see Elaine Scarry, *The Body in Pain: The Making and Unmaking of the World* (Oxford: Oxford University Press, 1985); and Amy Hollywood, *The Soul as Virgin Wife: Mechthild of Magdeburg, Marguerite Porete, and Meister Eckhart* (Notre Dame, Ind.: University of Notre Dame Press, 1995), 13–16.

26 Here Beauvoir holds a position similar to that put forward by William James in his *Varieties of Religious Experience*. Margaret Simons argues for the possible influence of James on Beauvoir, although not with regard to this issue. See William James, *The Varieties of Religious Experience* (1902; reprint, New York: Modern Library, 1929), 19; and Simons, *Beauvoir*, 196–98. Teresa herself makes this kind of argument in her attempt to safeguard the validity of mystical experience and to offer criteria for judging its authenticity. In fact, her work can be read as an attempt to provide such guidelines in the face of Counter Reformation unease

with appeals to experience. For this argument, see Gillian T. W. Ahlgren, *Teresa of Avila and the Politics of Sanctity* (Ithaca, N.Y.: Cornell University Press, 1996), 29.

27 This denigration of women's creative activity is paralleled by Beauvoir's discussion of literature in *The Second Sex* (DS II 627–41; SS 783–95).

28 The glorification of abjection and suffering goes to the point that some women mystics seem to posit their suffering as itself eternal, although this idea is usually balanced by more orthodox claims. See for example, Hadewijch, *Complete Works*, trans. Mother Columba Hart (New York: Paulist Press, 1980), 356–57; and SML.

29 Here we can perhaps see echoes of the young Simone's attitude toward the "sisters of charity," her "busy body" teachers, and Garric's *Équipes sociales*, whose projects seem without any purpose other than self-justification and narcissism. As I will show below, we can clarify Beauvoir's distinction between real projects and ones that are simply assertions of self with reference to the quality of the relationship to the other on which they are based. If the other is treated as an unconscious, fully immanent being rather than as a conscious one, then narcissism renders these actions inauthentic.

30 Beauvoir's philosophical views on the body and its relationship to femininity are complex. Although I tend to agree with those who argue that for Beauvoir sexual difference, even in its bodily nature, is historically and ideologically shaped, there are places in *The Second Sex* where she seems to posit a certain "givenness" and ahistoricism to the sexed body. Ultimately, I think that Toril Moi is right when she argues that many of the apparent ambiguities of Beauvoir's position arise from her tendency to overvalue masculinity. Moi is also right, I think, to emphasize that the distinction between sex and gender often does more to obscure than to clarify Beauvoir's positions. See Arleen B. Dallery, "Sexual Embodiment: Beauvoir and French Feminism," in *Hypatia Reborn: Essays in Feminist Philosophy*, ed. Azizah al-Hibri and Margaret A. Simons (Bloomington: Indiana University Press, 1990), 270–79; Judith Butler, "Sex and Gender in Simone de Beauvoir's *Second Sex*," *Yale French Studies* 72 (1986): 35–49; Judith Butler, "Gendering the Body: Beauvoir's Philosophical Contribution," in *Women, Knowledge, and Reality*, ed. A. Garry and M. Pearsall (Boston: Unwin Hyman, 1989), 253–62; Kristana Arp, "Beauvoir's Concept of Bodily Alienation," in *Feminist Interpretations of Simone de Beauvoir*, ed. Margaret A. Simons (University Park: Pennsylvania State University Press, 1995), 161–77; Julie K. Ward, "Beauvoir's Two Senses of "Body" in *The Second Sex*," in *Feminist Interpretations*, 223–42; Moi, *Beauvoir*, 148–78; and Moi, *What Is a Woman?* 3–120.

31 Teresa of Avila, *The Collected Works of St. Teresa of Avila*, vol. 1, *The Book of Her Life*, trans. Kieran Kavanaugh, O.C.D., and Otilio Rodriguez, O.C.D. (Washington, D.C.: Institute of Carmelite Studies, 1987), chap. 24, nn. 7–8, 212. Cited in Jodi Bilinkoff, *The Avila of Saint Teresa: Religious Reform in a Sixteenth-Century City* (Ithaca, N.Y.: Cornell University Press, 1989), 121.

32 Beauvoir, *Pour une morale*, 117–18; Beauvoir, *Ethics of Ambiguity*, 81.

33 As Kruks points out, Sartre's later philosophical position is much closer to Beauvoir's, although Sartre credits Merleau-Ponty with showing him the importance of embodied and situated subjectivity. Kruks, "Teaching Sartre."

34 Beauvoir's own sexuality, her relationship with Sartre, and her views of sexuality have been the subject of an enormous amount of study. Most importantly here, she consistently denies any sexual component in her relationships with women and denies real oppositional power to such relationships. Yet the existence and importance of such relationships in her

life is becoming clear. See Margaret Simons, "Lesbian Connections: Simone de Beauvoir and Feminism," in *Beauvoir and the Second Sex*, 115–44. Beauvoir's discussion of lesbianism is ambivalent. She begins by claiming that it is neither biological nor a mark of arrested development but an attempt to reconcile autonomy with the passivity of the flesh (DS II 194–96; SS 453–54). She then goes on, however, to claim lesbianism represents a masculine inferiority complex (DS II 216–17; SS 472). This ambivalence runs throughout *The Second Sex*. In one sense, Beauvoir thinks that women are inferior and should have an inferiority complex, in that their culture constitutes them as inferior. Yet she is caught in the dilemma of having no clear way to contest this inferiority if it is so culturally pervasive. For an exploration of the unsettling effects of bisexuality in representations of Beauvoir, see Mariam Fraser, *Identity without Selfhood: Simone de Beauvoir and Bisexuality* (Cambridge: Cambridge University Press, 1999). On the general issue of sexuality in Beauvoir's work, see Melanie C. Hawthorne, *Contingent Loves: Simone de Beauvoir and Sexuality* (Charlottesville: University of Virginia Press, 2000).

35 Debra Bergoffen and Edward and Kate Fullbrook argue for a fully articulated philosophy of reciprocity that emerges first in *Pyrrhus et Cinéas* (1944) and *Ethics of Ambiguity* (1947). See Bergoffen, *Philosophy of Simone de Beauvoir*; and Fullbrook and Fullbrook, *Critical Introduction*, 85–115. Also see Linda Singer, "Interpretation and Retrieval: Rereading Beauvoir," in *Hypatia Reborn*, 323–35. What I am interested in exploring here is both how that philosophy of reciprocity can be derived from a reading of Teresa and why Beauvoir quite pointedly *does* not provide this kind of reading.

36 For the Hegelian context, see Lundgren-Gothlin, *Sex and Existence*, 56–82; and Tina Chanter, *Ethics of Eros: Irigaray's Rewriting of the Philosophers* (New York: Routledge, 1995), 47–79. Beauvoir's use of the Hegelian master/slave dialectic might be compared usefully to Bataille's.

37 In *Pyrrhus and Cineas* and *Ethics of Ambiguity*, Beauvoir argues that human freedom itself demands that we acknowledge the freedom of others. "Only the freedom of the other keeps each of us from hardening in the absurdity of facticity." Beauvoir, *Pour une morale*, 102–3; *Ethics of Ambiguity*, 71. Yet if we refuse to acknowledge the objectifying gaze of the other, might not his or her freedom also be denied without any detriment to our own sense of freedom as conscious beings?

38 As we will see, Beauvoir's argument is circular, for it is only when Teresa confronts these metaphysical issues—the reality of death and the contingency of human existence—that she becomes a free subject.

39 For comments on Teresa and her dependence on the approval of male church leaders, as well as for illuminating comparisons with other Spanish religious women who did not fare as well as Teresa, see Alison Weber, *Teresa of Avila and the Rhetoric of Femininity* (Princeton, N.J.: Princeton University Press, 1990), 17–41; Ahlgren, *Politics of Sanctity*, 6–31, 67–84; and Mary Giles, "Spanish Visionary Women and the Paradox of Performance," in *Performance and Transformation: New Approaches to Late Medieval Spirituality*, ed. Mary A. Suydam and Joanna E. Ziegler (New York: St. Martin's, 1999), 273–97.

40 On Teresa's subversive use of a rhetoric of humility and femininity, see Weber, *Rhetoric of Femininity*. Madame Guyon's relationship to a male divine is also the source for her visionary and mystical teachings. She moves beyond this gendered relation into one of pure love, which in many ways is reminiscent of Teresa's advice with regard to the highest stages of prayer. Like Teresa, furthermore, Guyon attempts to use her experiences as the base for

action in society. Her failure to succeed in active engagement with the world probably had as much to do with her inability to find sufficiently powerful male supporters as with the paucity of her creative vision. See Madame Guyon, *La Vie de Mme J. M. B. de la Mothe Guyon écrite par elle-même*, 3 vols., ed. Jean-Philippe Dutoit (Paris: Libraires associés, 1791).

41 Beauvoir repeats the same move as those who canonized Teresa after her death. She grounds her claims for Teresa's singularity, as I will show, on Teresa's confrontation with the dark night of the soul. Guyon, while to most a less attractive figure than Teresa, follows a similar mystical movement, as have others not discussed by Beauvoir.

42 With the threat of Lutheranism in the sixteenth century, the distrust of extraordinary religious experience and the necessity of priestly control over that experience becomes particularly intense. For the situation in Tridentine Spain and its impact on Teresa's writing, see Ahlgren, *Politics of Sanctity*, esp. 6–31.

43 Ibid., 29.

44 Alison Weber, "The Fortunes of Ecstasy: Teresa of Avila and the Discalced Carmelite Reform," *Harvard Divinity Bulletin* 28 (1999): 15.

45 Jodi Bilinkoff establishes the importance of the sixteenth-century reform movements in Spain, as well as of the emerging merchant classes, for Teresa's reform movement. See Bilinkoff, *The Avila of Saint Teresa*, 78–151. There is a sad historical irony concerning Teresa's reform movement, for Teresa's goal was to found fully enclosed convents in order to insure women's spiritual freedom. Enclosure effectively cut off women's familial, political, and economic ties to the outside world. As religion became more and more secondary— even obsolete—within the public realm of western Europe, these enclosed institutions were seen to have little value and were often closed down. In many cases, only those orders with some public mission, such as teaching, were able to survive. The very teachers and "women of good works" whom Beauvoir describes as engaged in narcissistic and meaningless activity alone have a clearly justifiable role within modern European society. On the fate of convents in western Europe, see, for example, Ulrike Strasser's account of nunneries in Catholic Bavaria. Ulrike Strasser, *States of Virginity* (Ann Arbor: University of Michigan Press, forthcoming).

46 On Beauvoir's overvaluation of masculinity, see Moi, *Beauvoir*, 161–78, 195–96. As I argue in what follows, Beauvoir offers an *ethical* critique of autonomous masculine subjectivity in that it takes others as nonconscious beings subject to manipulation. This critique leads to her arguments about the necessity of reciprocal recognition between conscious beings. Yet from the *political* standpoint, she hopes for women to be able to move out of immanence (the realm of nonconscious beings) into the realm of free, autonomous, conscious being. But if this move is dependent on the recognition of others, how are women to accomplish it? From this perspective, the "bad" transcendence of traditional masculinity begins to look tempting.

47 This description of Sartrean intersubjectivity is primarily a recounting of Simons's negative views. See Jean-Paul Sartre, *Being and Nothingness*, trans. Hazel Barnes (New York: Washington Square Press, 1966), 328, 474, 529, 531, 536, 549–51; and Simons, *Beauvoir*, 217–18.

48 Simons, *Beauvoir*, 231.

49 In the scholarship, claims diverge about the ultimate supremacy of situatedness and reciprocity within *The Second Sex*. Against early readings that insist on Beauvoir's dependence on Sartre, Edward and Kate Fullbrook argue for *Beauvoir's* early influence on Sartre. Debra

Bergoffen, Karen Vintges, Eva Lundgren-Gothlin, and Margaret Simons argue for her philosophical independence from Sartre, with important attention to other philosophical and literary sources for her thinking. Michèle Le Doeuff and Toril Moi also work to uncover the sources of Beauvoir's theoretical and philosophical insights, but they make more temperate claims about her originality and her possible influence on Sartre. See Fullbrook and Fullbrook, *Remaking of a Legend*; Fullbrook and Fullbrook, *Critical Introduction*; Bergoffen, *Philosophy of Simone de Beauvoir*; Vintges, *Philosophy as Passion*; Lundgren-Gothlin, *Sex and Existence*; Simons, *Beauvoir*, esp. 41–54, 185–243; Michèle Le Doeuff, *Hipparchia's Choice: An Essay Concerning Women, Philosophy, etc.* (Oxford: Blackwell, 1991); and Moi, *Beauvoir*.

50 Simons, *Beauvoir*, 198–99. The reference is to Jean Baruzi, who held the history of religion chair at the Collège de France from 1933 to 1951 and taught a course at the Sorbonne in 1926–1927 and 1927–1928. Baruzi was a Catholic philosopher and historian of religion who had been a student of Bergson's and who was heavily influence by William James's psychology of religion. He may have played a role in introducing phenomenology into France in the mid-1920s. His dissertation, *St. John of the Cross and the Problem of Mystical Experience* (1924) was controversial and condemned by French Thomists. In it, he attempts to offer an account of the mystic's lived experience, which might then serve as the basis for religious truth claims. Beauvoir wrote a thesis on Leibniz with Baruzi, who appears as a mentor throughout the 1927 diaries. Earlier, Baruzi taught the young Jacques Lacan philosophy at the Collège Stanislas in 1917–1918. Bataille also knew Baruzi and his work. See Simons, *Beauvoir*, 198–200; Elisabeth Roudinesco, *Jacques Lacan*, trans. Barbara Bray (New York: Columbia University Press, 1997), 11–12; Jean Baruzi, *Saint Jean de la Croix et le problème de l'expérience mystique* (Paris: Librairie Félix Alcan, 1924); and Jean Baruzi, "Introduction à des recherches sur la langage mystique," *Recherches philosophiques* 1 (1931–1932): 66–82.

51 In *Memoirs of a Dutiful Daughter*, Beauvoir describes her cultivation of mystical states, in which she "embraced everything [tout]." She claims that she gave up these "vertigous notions" because "one could not erect one's life" on them (MJF 370–71; MDD 267–68).

52 Simons, *Beauvoir*, 210.

53 Ibid., 214.

54 It should be noted that even attention to the intersubjectively defined context out of which Teresa's work emerges does not mitigate the threat death poses to the value of her projects. In fact, the encounter with the other as a conscious being, a free subject with the power to thwart one's goals and a mortal being whose loss is beyond one's control, may itself be a harbinger of one's own limitation and death. Only the absolute—for Teresa, God—can provide an ultimate safeguard against these threats.

55 Beauvoir, *La force des choses*, 696; Beauvoir, *Force of Circumstance*, 674.

56 In *The Words*, Sartre admits that it took him almost thirty years to overcome the idealism he inherited from Christianity. Despite fleeing religion, he remained in a "lucid blindness" in which he believed in his own power to save himself through the word. "For a long time, to write was to ask Death and my masked Religion to preserve my life from chance." Even recognizing the illusion, Sartre admits "I still write. What else can I do?" Jean-Paul Sartre, *The Words*, trans. Bernard Frechtman (New York: Fawcett, 1964), 157, 159.

57 The philosophical context for this existentialist dilemma is provided most pointedly in the closing section of Nietzsche's *On the Genealogy of Morals*, where he asserts that humanity would rather suffer than not have a meaning for its existence. Nietzsche sought a culture

that would affirm and justify its own existence. Like Sartre, Beauvoir follows Nietzsche in this desire for an affirmation of the self in the face of death, yet death retains for her its power to cast the meaningfulness of all projects into doubt. The problem is exacerbated by Beauvoir's fear of narcissism. She seems to distinguish feminine narcissism, in which women take only themselves as projects, from masculine projects in the world. Yet her critique of masculinity suggests that it is also deeply narcissistic in its refusal to recognize the independent reality of the other. As Elaine Marks argues, the more Beauvoir stresses the uniqueness of the self, the more that self will be utterly annihilated by death. See Marks, *Encounters with Death*, 127.

CHAPTER FIVE

1   See Louis Bouyer, "Mysticism: An Essay on the History of the Word," in *Understanding Mysticism*, ed. Richard Woods (Garden City, N.J.: Doubleday Image Books, 1980), 42–55. My account here goes against the argument, recently made by Denys Turner, that premodern mysticism cannot be understood through the category of experience. Turner discusses central figures within the apophatic or negative theological tradition, such as Meister Eckhart, in articulating his distinction between an experience of absence and the absence of experience. But Eckhart's turn away from extraordinary experiences emerges out of a specific context, in particular, the highly experiential mysticism of women monastics, mendicants, and beguines. By ignoring the women mystics among whom Eckhart lived and worked, Turner provides a partial picture of late medieval mysticism. See Denys Turner, *The Darkness of God: Negativity in Christian Mysticism* (Cambridge: Cambridge University Press, 1995), 262. Bernard McGinn cautions against a potential overstatement of the distinction between an experience of absence and the absence of experience in his review of *The Darkness of God*, *Journal of Religion* 77 (1997): 309–11. For more on the extent to which experience is a viable term for understanding medieval mysticism, see Michael Sells, *Mystical Languages of Unsaying* (Chicago: University of Chicago Press, 1994), 214; and Thomas Carlson, *Indiscretion: Finitude and the Naming of God* (Chicago: University of Chicago Press, 1999), 256–57.

2   Visionary experience is important not only for women, of course. Also of note is the visionary exegesis of figures like Rupert of Deutz (ca. 1070–1135) and Joachim of Fiore (d. 1202). For these authors, as for Hildegard of Bingen (1098–1179), visions offer direct insight into the interpretation of the Bible. See Bernard McGinn, "Apocalyptic Traditions and Spiritual Identity in Thirteenth-Century Religious Life," in *The Roots of the Modern Christian Tradition*, ed. E. Rozanne Elder (Kalamazoo, Mich.: Cistercian Publications, 1984), 1–26, 293–300; and Bernard McGinn, *The Growth of Mysticism: Gregory the Great through the Twelfth Century* (New York: Crossroads, 1994), 325–41.

3   For the historical argument locating the emergence of the substantive in the seventeenth century, see Michel de Certeau, "'Mystique' au XVIIe siècle: Le problème de langage 'mystique,'" in *L'Homme devant Dieu: Mélanges offerts au Père Henri de Lubac* (Paris: Aubier, 1964), 2:267–91; Michel de Certeau, "Mystic Speech," in *Heterologies: Discourse on the Other*, trans. Brian Massumi (Minneapolis: University of Minnesota Press, 1986), 80–100; Michel de Certeau, "Mysticism," *Diacritics* 22 (1992): 11–25; and Michel de Certeau, *The Mystic Fable*, vol. 1, *The Sixteenth and Seventeenth Centuries*, trans. Michael B. Smith (Chicago: University of Chicago Press, 1992), 75–112. Lacan also reflects on the substantive in *Encore*, which in

one sense can be read as waging a battle against the substantive, particularly that of being (E 24; S XX 20–21).

4   See Certeau, "'Mystique' au XVIIe siècle."

5   The modern philosophical degradation of mysticism as irrationalism emerges out of this same context. For more on this issue, see Michel de Certeau, "Mysticism." For the importance of mysticism in the development of the study of religion and for the problematic politics of the isolation of mysticism as a particular form of religiosity (often then described as "irrational" and imputed to "the other"), see Steven M. Wasserstrom, *Religion after Religion: Gershom Scholem, Mircea Eliade, and Henry Corbin at Eranos* (Princeton, N.J.: Princeton University Press, 1999); Grace Jantzen, "Mysticism and Experience," *Religious Studies* 25 (1989): 295–315; and Richard King, *Orientalism and Religion: Postcolonial Theory, India, and "The Mystic East"* (New York: Routledge, 1999), 7–34.

6   For a useful overview of modern studies of mysticism, see Bernard McGinn, *The Foundations of Mysticism: Origins to the Fifth Century* (New York: Crossroads, 1991), 265–343, 420–41. For debates about the claimed justificatory potential of mystical experience, see Wayne Proudfoot, *Religious Experience* (Berkeley: University of California Press, 1985); William Alston, *Perceiving God: The Epistemology of Religious Experience* (Ithaca, N.Y.: Cornell University Press, 1991); and Matthew Bagger, *Religious Experience, Justification, and History* (Cambridge: Cambridge University Press, 1999).

7   Lacan makes interesting comments on the baroque, with which he associates his own style, and obscenity (E 95–105; S XX 104–17).

8   A reading somewhere between these two might argue that Bataille mistakes the "dark night of the soul" for the end of the mystical life itself. This reading is suggested by those who criticize Bataille for accepting something like the cross (in the image of the torture victim on which he meditates) and rejecting the solution of the resurrection. See, for example, the remarks made by Gabriel Marcel, cited in Peter Tracey Connor, *Georges Bataille and the Mysticism of Sin* (Baltimore: Johns Hopkins University Press, 2000), 25.

9   Lacan, like Beauvoir, was raised in a conservative Catholic family, with particularly strong signs of piety in his mother and on her side of the family. Lacan rejected Catholicism and any religious faith as a young man and was reported to be horrified when his younger brother entered a Benedictine monastery. Despite this rejection of Catholicism, however, his first marriage was officiated by a priest. Only with the breakup of this marriage and his attachment to Sylvia Maklès Bataille did Lacan give up the traditional markers of bourgeois respectability. See Elisabeth Roudinesco, *Jacques Lacan*, trans. Barbara Bray (New York: Columbia University Press, 1997), 12–13, 91, 134, 146, 173–74.

10   Lacan's biographer Elisabeth Roudinesco insists that Lacan was resolutely apolitical throughout the thirties, forties, and fifties. He became somewhat involved in leftist politics only during the sixties, partially at the instigation of his daughter and son-in-law, Judith and Jacques-Alain Miller, and his stepdaughter, Laurence Bataille. During the occupation, Lacan neither collaborated nor engaged in resistance activities. See Roudinesco, *Lacan*, 158, 160–70, 187–88, 334–35.

11   Lacan and Bataille knew each other and shared more than intellectual interests. Lacan's second wife, the actress Sylvia Maklès, had first been married to Bataille. Sylvia and Georges Bataille had one child, Laurence Bataille (1930–1986), who grew up close to her stepfather, Lacan, and later become a psychoanalyst. A child was born to Sylvia Bataille and

Lacan before she was divorced from Georges Bataille. (Georges and Sylvia remained married through the occupation to protect Sylvia, who was Jewish.) As a result of French law, the child's name was Judith Bataille (1941—). Lacan did not have it legally changed to "Lacan" until after Bataille's death in 1962. Roudinesco argues that Lacan's emphasis on the paternal metaphor is rooted in this complex familial scene, a suggestive but perhaps too narrowly psychobiographical reading. See Roudinesco, *Lacan*, 163–64; and Elisabeth Roudinesco, "Bataille Entre Freud et Lacan: Une Expérience Cachée," in *Georges Bataille après tout*, ed. Denis Hollier (Paris: Belin, 1995), 191–212. For an encounter with Sylvia Lacan, see James Hunt, "The Mirrored Stages: Reflections on the Presence of Sylvia [Bataille] Lacan," in *The Ends of Performance*, ed. Peggy Phelan and Jill Lane (New York: New York University Press, 1998), 236–46. For a glimpse at the daughters' views of the fathers, see Laurence Bataille, *L'Ombilic du rêve* (Paris: Seuil, 1987); and the very different book by Lacan's last daughter from his first marriage, Sybille Lacan, *Un père: puzzle* (Paris: Gallimard, 1994).

12 In fact, François Perrier and David Macey both argue for Bataille's influence on Lacan's later use of the term jouissance. Although his initial use of the term in his Kojèvean readings of Hegel can easily be translated as "pleasure," after 1956 he shifts toward more sexual and ecstatic connotations and toward assertions of a gap between pleasure and jouissance. See François Perrier, "Démoïsation," in *La Chausée d'Antin*, vol. 2 (Paris: Christian Bourgeois, 1979), 163–78; David Macey, *Lacan in Contexts* (London: Verso, 1988), 204–5; and Dylan Evans, "From Kantian Ethics to Mystical Experience: An Exploration of Jouissance," in *Key Concepts of Lacanian Psychoanalysis*, ed. Dany Nobus (New York: Other Press, 1999), 4. As Evans points out, Lacan cites Bataille only two times in the published work, once in *Écrits* and again in the seventh seminar, *The Ethics of Psychoanalysis* (and there to disagree with him about Sade). See Jacques Lacan, *Écrits*, trans. Alan Sheridan (New York: Norton, 1977), 225, n. 40; and Jacques Lacan, *The Seminar. Book VII: The Ethics of Psychoanalysis* (1959–60), trans. Dennis Porter (New York: Norton, 1992), 201.

Roudinesco shows that Bataille encouraged Lacan to publish and that there is little evidence that Bataille was influenced by Lacan's work. Lacan, on the other hand, was clearly influenced by Bataille, both personally and intellectually. Roudinesco argues most convincingly for the importance of Bataille's early notion of heterogeneity for Lacan's understanding of the real. See Roudinesco, *Lacan*, 121–39, 217. For a different reading of the relationship between the two men, see Carolyn Dean, *The Self and Its Pleasures: Bataille, Lacan, and the History of the Decentered Subject* (Ithaca, N.Y.: Cornell University Press, 1992); and, much more briefly, Mikkel Borch-Jacobsen, *Lacan: The Absolute Master*, trans. Douglas Brick (Stanford, Calif.: Stanford University Press, 1991), 1–12.

13 The notion of the real in Lacan's work is complex and its meanings shift throughout his career. The literature on this and other issues in Lacan is voluminous. In the notes that follow, I have cited those discussions I have found most useful for my own work. On the shifting meanings of the real, see Jonathan Lee, *Jacques Lacan* (Amherst: University of Massachusetts Press, 1990), 135–70; Malcolm Bowie, *Lacan* (Cambridge, Mass.: Harvard University Press, 1991), 94–110; Borch-Jacobsen, *Lacan*, 123–67; and Richard Boothby, "The Psychical Meaning of Life and Death: Reflections on the Lacanian Imaginary, Symbolic, and Real," in *Disseminating Lacan*, ed. David Pettigrew and François Raffoul (Albany: State University of New York Press, 1996), 337–63. On the real and history, see Joan Copjec, *Read My Desire: Lacan against the Historicists* (Cambridge, Mass.: MIT Press, 1994); Slavoj Žižek,

The Metastases of Enjoyment: Six Essays on Women and Causality (London: Verso, 1994), esp. 116; and Charles Shepherdson, Vital Signs: Nature, Culture, Psychoanalysis (New York: Routledge, 2000), 153–85.

14 Jacques Derrida suggests similarly that Lacan's writings are political but only provincially so, in that they are concerned only with subverting the institutions of psychoanalysis. See Jacques Derrida, Positions, trans. Alan Bass (Chicago: University of Chicago Press, 1981), 109–10; and David Fisher, introduction to Lacan and Theological Discourse, ed. Edith Wyschogrod, David Crownfield, and Carl Raschke (Albany: State University of New York Press, 1989), 14.

15 Lacan knew Beauvoir and Sartre during the war and participated in the festivals that took place in the spring and summer of 1944. While researching The Second Sex, Beauvoir appreciatively read Lacan's early essay on the family and contacted him with questions about psychoanalytic views on female sexuality. Lacan replied that it would take five or six months to work through the relevant issues; Beauvoir suggested four interviews and Lacan declined. See Roudinesco, Lacan, 169. For the commonalities between their work, see Toril Moi, Simone de Beauvoir: The Making of an Intellectual Woman (Oxford: Blackwell, 1994), 157–58, 161, 164, 280–81, 293.

16 As Roudinesco shows, aspects of Lacan's work can be seen as an attempt to articulate a concept of freedom different from that of Sartre. See Roudinesco, Lacan, esp. 171–78.

17 Roudinesco insists that Lacan stayed true to Freud's desire to establish a science of the unconscious. She seems to view his later subversion of these claims through the topological theories and other practices as an aberration. I think that Lacan wants both to maintain the claims to scientific status and to show how the science of the unconscious subverts science itself. Without claims to scientific status, the ramifications of the later move for other sciences would never be taken seriously. See Roudinesco, Lacan, 263–90, 334, 337, 360–61; and Bruce Fink, The Lacanian Subject: Between Language and Jouissance (Princeton, N.J.: Princeton University Press, 1995), 138–52.

18 Lacan was an active psychiatrist, psychoanalyst, and teacher for almost fifty years, making it impossible to summarize his thinking in any simple form. Moreover, other than scattered journal articles and his Écrits, published in 1966, the bulk of his teaching was passed down through his yearly seminars (conducted in various sites around Paris from 1951 to 1979). Notes and recordings of these seminars were shared among Lacan's students and followers. In 1972, his son-in-law, Jacques-Alain Miller, began the difficult work of transcribing the seminars and establishing an "official" text. The project has become increasingly controversial, particularly given Miller's attempt to consolidate an official Lacanian school just before and subsequent to Lacan's death. For the controversies and the textual problems with the existing versions of the seminars, see Roudinesco, Lacan, 413–27.

Given the ongoing nature of the establishment of Lacan's oeuvre, any reading of individual texts remains provisional. I focus here on one late text, making use of earlier theories as they seem assumed and/or are subverted by that seminar. I agree with David Macey and Roudinesco on the need to historicize Lacan's work (particularly against the systematizing tendencies of Miller and other early commentators) and would argue that Lacan himself was moving toward such a position in the later seminars. See Macey, Lacan in Context, 1–25; and Roudinesco, Lacan, 305–6, 414–15.

19   The critique of the Cartesian subject is central to Lacan's early work on the mirror stage and the split subject, despite the presence in the text of phenomenological and developmental explanatory models Lacan will later repudiate. See "The Mirror Stage," in Jacques Lacan, Écrits, trans. Alan Sheridan (New York: Norton, 1977), 1–7. For later formulations of the issue, see Jacques Lacan, The Four Fundamental Concepts of Psychoanalysis, trans. Alan Sheridan (New York: Norton, 1978). See also Lee, Lacan, 22–23, 146–54; and Alain Juranville, Lacan et la philosophie (Paris: Presses Universitaires de France, 1984). Roudinesco shows how Lacan revises rather than rejects Cartesianism. See Roudinesco, Lacan, 91, 105, 195; and Elisabeth Roudinesco, Jacques Lacan and Co.: A History of Psychoanalysis in France, 1925–1985, trans. Jeffrey Mehlman (Chicago: University of Chicago Press, 1990), 303–4.

20   Also see Jean Laplanche, Essays on Otherness, trans. John Fletcher (New York: Routledge, 1999), 52–83. We can see the ties here with Derrida. For an early (and perhaps less radical) formulation from the early Derrida, see his remarks in The Structuralist Controversy: The Language of Criticism and the Sciences of Man, ed. Richard Macksey and Eugenio Donato (Baltimore: Johns Hopkins University Press, 1970), 271–72.

21   See Lee, Lacan, 191–92.

22   The most obvious example of this problematic is penis envy—a not so subtle return to anatomy. See Sigmund Freud, "Some Psychical Consequences of the Anatomical Distinction between the Sexes," in The Standard Edition of the Complete Psychological Works of Sigmund Freud, ed. and trans. James Strachey (London: Hogarth Press, 1953–74), 19:243–58; Sigmund Freud, "Female Sexuality," in Complete Psychological Works, 21:223–43; and "Femininity," in Complete Psychological Works, 22:112–35.

      On the complex question of how to read Lacan's "return" to Freud, see Roudinesco, Lacan, 340–41; Richard Boothby, Death and Desire: Psychoanalytic Theory in Lacan's Return to Freud (New York: Routledge, 1991); and Philippe Julien, Jacques Lacan's Return to Freud: The Real, the Symbolic, and the Imaginary (New York: New York University Press, 1994).

23   See, for example, Alan Sokal and Jean Bricmont, Fashionable Nonsense: Postmodern Intellectuals' Abuse of Science (New York: Picador, 1998), 18–37. The most persistent claims for the seriousness of Lacan's scientific and mathematical pretensions come from his son-in-law, Jacques-Alain Miller, who is crucial in the dissemination of a formally coherent, systematic, dehistoricized Lacan. See Roudinesco, Lacan, 304–6; and Sherry Turkle, Psychoanalytic Politics: Freud's French Revolution (Cambridge, Mass.: MIT Press, 1978). For a fuller articulation and defense of such a view, see Jean-Claude Milner, L'oeuvre claire: Lacan, la science, la philosophie (Paris: Seuil, 1995). As I argue here, Lacan both makes and contests scientific and mathematical claims; the question then becomes to what extent these claims are coherent, illuminative, and/or empirically grounded and to what extent, given his ultimate subversion of the scientific, these claims matter. The affective power of contestation depends, in large part, on one's prior apprehension of and belief in that which is unsaid.

24   See Roudinesco, Lacan, 369.

25   See Lacan, Écrits, 151–52, for an early version of the view that suggests that the kind of body one has lacks any significance. For useful commentary, see Jacqueline Rose, "Introduction II," in Feminine Sexuality: Jacques Lacan and the École Freudienne, ed. Juliet Mitchell and Jacqueline Rose (New York: Norton, 1985), 41–42.

26   See, for example, Jane Gallop, Reading Lacan (Ithaca, N.Y.: Cornell University Press, 1985);

Jane Gallop, *Thinking through the Body* (New York: Columbia University Press, 1988); Diana Fuss, *Essentially Speaking: Feminism, Nature, and Difference* (New York: Routledge, 1989); Kaja Silverman, "The Lacanian Phallus," *Differences* 4 (1992): 83–115; and Charles Bernheimer, "Penile Reference in Phallic Theory," *Differences* 4 (1992): 116–32.

27 Silverman, "Lacanian Phallus," 85–97.

28 Ibid., 105.

29 For an important argument suggesting the potentially subversive deployment of the gap between the penis and the phallus, see Judith Butler, "The Lesbian Phallus," in *Bodies That Matter: On the Discursive Limits of "Sex"* (New York: Routledge, 1993), 57–91.

30 Silverman, "Lacanian Phallus," 112.

31 Drawing on the structuralist context of Lacan's work, particularly Claude Levi-Strauss's work on kinship, Judith Butler argues that this contingency does not undermine the claims to the universality of the phallic and paternal functions. I will argue here that in *Encore* Lacan calls for, if he does not completely effect, the separation of the symbolic position of the transcendental signifier from that of the father and the phallus. The separation of the *a* and the *A*, the imaginary and the symbolic, might be read, in Butler's terms, as a demand for a separation of the social from the symbolic. See Judith Butler, *Antigone's Claim: Kinship between Life and Death* (New York: Columbia University Press, 2000), 19–20.

32 Jane Gallop, *The Daughter's Seduction: Feminism and Psychoanalysis* (Ithaca, N.Y.: Cornell University Press, 1982), 54.

33 At the same time, Lacan offers a theory that enables us to recognize and account for the power that some women have been able to attain in Western patriarchal society. All of this is obviously in sharp contrast to those critics who claim that Lacan's thinking is radically ahistorical and apolitical—an argument that begins, at least, with Luce Irigaray in her reading of *Encore* (CS 99; TS 103).

34 For the complex development of the theory of the registers in Lacan's work, see Roudinesco, *Lacan*, 216–17; Lee, *Lacan*, 31–99; Bowie, *Lacan*, 88–121; and Julien, *Lacan's Return to Freud*. For an excellent introduction to the concept of the imaginary, see Jacqueline Rose, "The Imaginary," in *The Talking Cure: Essays in Psychoanalysis and Language*, ed. Colin MacCabe (New York: St. Martin's, 1986), 132–61.

35 To say that the symbolic is the network of signifying systems in which we live does not entail, as Charles Shepherdson suggests, reducing the symbolic to history, understood in a humanistic sense as the realm of human action, consciousness, and agency. On the contrary, for Lacan the symbolic—and hence language and history—are always in part unconscious and constitute us as subjects in ways beyond the control of consciousness. History, as Bataille shows, cannot be reduced to reason and consciousness. He tends to associate history, in fact, with that which is irreducible to reason, although that also is probably too one-sided a view. For the need to distinguish between psychoanalytic conceptions of the symbolic and historical contextualization, insofar as it implies a kind of humanism, see Charles Sheperdson, "On Fate: Psychoanalysis and the Desire to Know," in *Dialectic and Narrative*, ed. Tom Flynn and Dalia Judovitz (Albany: State University of New York Press, 1993), 271–302; and Sheperdson, *Vital Signs*, 44–47.

36 On the complex history of this idea, which Lacan takes over from Henri Wallon, see Roudinesco, *Lacan*, 111–17. For other useful discussions, see Gallop, *Reading Lacan*, 74–92; Fink, *The Lacanian Subject*, 35–48; and Dany Nobus, "Life and Death in the Glass: A New

Look at the Mirror Stage," in *Key Concepts of Lacanian Psychoanalysis*, ed. Dany Nobus (New York: Other Press, 1999), 101–38.

37 Crucial here is Lacan's early distinction between the subject and the ego, and later between the ego ideal and the ideal ego. See Lacan, *Écrits*, 1–7; Jacques Lacan, *The Seminar of Jacques Lacan, Book III: The Psychoses, 1955–1956*, trans. Russell Grigg (New York: Norton, 1993), 144–45; Fink, *The Lacanian Subject*, 35–48; and Roudineso, *Lacan*, 110–17, 145–46, 283–84.

38 *Seminar II* is a crucial text, for in it Lacan introduces both his distinction between *a* and *A* and the Name-of-the-Father. He elaborates these notions in the following year's seminar, which focuses on a rereading of the case of Judge Daniel Schreber. See Jacques Lacan, *The Seminar of Jacques Lacan, Book II: The Ego in Freud's Theory and in the Technique of Psychoanalysis, 1954–1955*, trans. Sylvana Tomaselli, with notes by John Forrester (New York: Norton, 1988); Lacan, *Seminar III*; and Roudinesco, *Lacan*, 283–84.

39 To say that Lacan denaturalizes male privilege is not necessarily to say that he contests it. On the contrary, Roudinesco reads Lacan as responding to a crisis in masculinity, which he both records and contests through his own claims to psychoanalytic mastery. On the need to distinguish between denaturalization and contestation, see Penelope Deutscher, *Yielding Gender: Feminism, Deconstruction, and the History of Philosophy* (New York: Routledge, 1997), esp. 11–33.

40 Anika Lemaire, *Jacques Lacan*, trans. David Macey (London: Routledge, 1977), 174.

41 On another level, the object *a* is the site of the phallic mother whose power threatens the child and whose loss of phallic power presages the child's own. In relating to the object *a* in the place of woman, Lacan suggests, man constantly repeats his conflicted relationship to the phallic and/or castrated mother.

42 For the phallus as the *point de capiton* that fixes meaning within the signifying chain, see Lacan, *Écrits*, 281–91.

43 For a reading of the *la* as phallic, see Gallop, *Reading Lacan*, 138–41.

44 And as we will see, the silence is only apparent. On the problems with Lacan's "tone" here and elsewhere, see Gallop, *Daughter's Seduction*, 33–55; and Lisa Jardine, "The Politics of Impenetrability," in *Between Feminism and Psychoanalysis*, ed. Teresa Brennan (New York: Routledge, 1989), 63–72.

45 Like Bataille's "active" and "virile" self-laceration, this self-subversion can be read as a male attempt to control his own powerlessness and castration.

46 As Fuss argues, Lacan here paradoxically reuniversalizes woman precisely as that which resists universalization. See Fuss, *Essentially Speaking*, 11.

47 The terms are similar to those Beauvoir uses to analyze the relationship between men and women under patriarchy, no doubt due to a shared Hegelian context. On this context for Lacan, see Judith Butler, *Subjects of Desire: Hegelian Reflections in Twentieth-Century France* (New York: Columbia University Press, 1987), 186–204; and Borch-Jacobsen, *Lacan*, 1–20.

48 Lacan, *Feminine Sexuality*, 84.

49 This claim is the source for Luce Irigaray's critique of the male homosexual economy, in which women are merely reflections of male subjectivity—hence her call for the full elaboration of two sexes, which I will discuss in chapter 6.

50 See Stephen Heath, "Difference," *Screen* 19 (1978): 51–112. Heath discusses the relationship to Charcot (57) and critiques Lacan on this point (51–78). See also TS 90–91; and Macey, *Lacan in Context*, 66–74, 177–209.

51 Although Charcot is reported to have said that hysteria was all about sex, his published writings point in other directions. See Cristina Mazzoni, *Saint Hysteria: Neurosis, Mysticism, and Gender in European Culture* (Ithaca, N.Y.: Cornell University Press, 1996), 17–30.

52 As Bataille argues: "Obscenity is our name for the uneasiness which upsets the physical state associated with self-possession, with the possession of a recognized and stable individuality." Georges Bataille, *Erotism*, trans. Mary Dalwood (San Francisco: City Lights, 1986), 17–18.

53 Like all of Lacan's central concepts, the meaning of jouissance changes across texts. See Evans, "Jouissance," 28; and Nestor Braunstein, *La Jouissance: un concept lacanien* (Paris: Point Hors Ligne, 1992).

54 Many commentators on this text miss the reference to Hadewijch. See Alice Jardine, *Gynesis: Configurations of Woman and Modernity* (Ithaca, N.Y.: Cornell University Press, 1985), 162, where she lists the women mentioned in the seminars and leaves out Hadewijch d'Anvers. See also Elizabeth Grosz, *Jacques Lacan: A Feminist Introduction* (New York: Routledge, 1990), 146. For useful readings of Lacan's relationship to mysticism, see Kathryn Bond Stockton, *God between Their Lips: Desire between Women in Irigaray, Brontë, and Eliot* (Stanford, Calif.: Stanford University Press, 1994), 40–49; and Mazzoni, *Saint Hysteria*, 44–50, 150–52, 180–89.

55 See Certeau, "Mystic Speech"; and Certeau, *Mystic Fable*, esp. 113–56. On the relationship between psychoanalysis and mystic speech, see Certeau, *Mystic Fable*, 6–9.

56 See the discussion earlier in the seminar of the thing said, stupidity, and free association (E 17–20, 24–25; S XX 12–16, 21–22).

57 Lacan speaks simply of "communication," but I think he confuses communication with its *referential* function, even though he argues that affects as well as meanings are communicated through language. Following Bataille, I will take communication to include effects that go beyond descriptive and referential language. In other words, some aspects of language may not be referential, but that does not mean that they have nothing to do with communication.

58 Lacan, *Feminine Sexuality*, 51. See also Fink's note on the translation of the term (S XX 18–19, n. 12).

59 One of Lacan's early biographers and commentators, Catherine Clément, argues that "from the impasse he himself describes, Lacan holds out one hope of exit, doubtless the only one: mysticism, the only legitimate means of transgressing boundaries." See Catherine Clément, *The Lives and Legends of Jacques Lacan*, trans. Arthur Goldhammer (New York: Columbia University Press, 1983), 174. As the abundance of mystical writings attests, mysticism offers a means of transgression (by no means always legitimate) through language—a language operating according to another logic. What Clément and others miss is that this language is not concerned primarily with reference but with affect.

60 For the place of the body in performative language, see Shoshana Felman, *The Literary Speech Act: Don Juan with J. L. Austin, or Seduction in Two Languages*, trans. Catherine Porter (Ithaca, N.Y.: Cornell University Press, 1983); Judith Butler, *Excitable Speech: A Politics of the Performative* (New York: Routledge, 1997), esp. 127–63; and Amy Hollywood, "Performativity, Citationality, Ritualization," in *Bodily Citations: Religionists Engage Judith Butler*, ed. Ellen Armour and Susan St. Ville (Bloomington: Indiana University Press, manuscript under consideration).

61 We might, then, read the baroque as a cataphatic excess through which, paradoxically, apophatic unsaying (the negation of meaning) occurs. In other words, either one can

deny that the penis is the phallus and that the phallus is the transcendental signifier or one can represent the penis in such excessively material terms as to render it meaningless. Hence Lacan's posturing as the absolute master might be read as a subversion of that very mastery. See Gallop, *Daughter's Seduction*, 33–42.

62 Given the constant, if often covered over, repetition of this originary trauma in art, religion, and psychoanalysis, it seems that it gives rise to pleasure. Or is it repeated only in order to cover over the rupture and, hence, to find pleasure not in dissolution but in mastery? Perhaps the two movements are inseparable.

63 Elisabeth Roudinesco contrasts Lacan's situation between the wars with that of his analyst, Rudolph Loewenstein, a Jew who suffered repeated exile throughout his life; she seems almost to deride Lacan for the lack of trauma in his life: "Lacan, then, had come to man's estate after suffering only the typical kinds of bourgeois tribulation: the pains of perpetual dissatisfaction, of impatience driven to the limit, of not yet being master of the universe. Imaginary suffering, in short, accompanied by the more ordinary neuroses. He had never known real privation: hunger, poverty, lack of freedom, persecution. Too young to have had to waste his best years under fire at Verdun, he had watched the war from the gardens of the Collège Stanislas, his only whiff of its epic madness brought to him in glimpses of shattered limbs and eyes awaiting death. He had never been choked by the stench of blood on a battlefield; he had never had to fight against real oppression. Pampered from the cradle by generations of comfortable merchants, he had inherited only the hardships of family constraints, and they had made him anything but a hero. But his lack of heroism came with a defiant refusal to conform in any way. Lacan was a kind of antihero, not at all cut out for a normal life, destined to eccentricity and incapable of knuckling under to the countless commonplace rules of behavior—hence his excessive interest in the discourse of madness, as the only key to understanding a crazy world" (Roudinesco, *Lacan*, 71).

64 Another way to put the difference between Bataille and Lacan would be to say that for Lacan the Other is unnameable and unknowable (the speaking body), whereas for Bataille, in the wartime writings, the other is a lacerated human subject (through whom the sacred is made manifest).

65 For a similar reading of Lacan see Boothby, *Death and Desire*, 223–28.

66 Lacan engages in a series of elaborate wordplays here, all dependent on the *a*. Another is developed around the words for mastery and being. These wordplays could be related to the central role of Antigone in *Seminar VII*. See also the endless ramifications of the "a" and of Antigone in Jacques Derrida, "Différance," in *Margins of Philosophy*, trans. Alan Bass (Chicago: University of Chicago Press, 1982), 1–28.

67 On knowledge as paranoic and as tied to the sexual relation, see Lee, *Lacan*, 28–29.

68 For more on the implications of this critique of feminism in France, see the introduction to part 3.

69 Lacan, *Four Fundamental Concepts*, 113.

70 See Mark Taylor, *Altarity* (Chicago: University of Chicago Press, 1987), 109; and Mark Taylor, "Refusal of the Bar," in *Lacan and Theological Discourse*, 48. Not surprisingly, perhaps, Taylor's discovery of a goddess within Lacan depends on reading *Seminar XX* in light of *Seminar XI, The Four Fundamental Concepts of Psychoanalysis*, in which Lacan analyzes the story of his grandson, Ernst, and his game of *fort-da*. There the real is read as that trauma—the loss of the mother—that cannot be apprehended and so is endlessly repeated. The boy child,

in believing that he can make the mother present again through his game, participates in precisely the conflation of the imaginary and the symbolic that Lacan argues against in *Seminar XX*. Yet it should be noted that for Lacan the real is both the site of trauma and of jouissance, replicating Bataille's anguished ecstasy. For both Lacan and Bataille, the experience of the real is premised on lack, loss, and their conflation. For a critique of Slavoj Žižek's deployment of the "real" that is similar to my critique of Taylor, see Judith Butler, "Arguing with the Real," in *Bodies That Matter*, 187–222.

71 Taylor's goddess seems related to the problem that emerges when Bataille focuses attention more on the sacred that emerges through laceration and communication than on suffering itself. Taylor takes the additional step of reifying this feminized sacrality. See Taylor, *Altarity*, esp. 83–183.

INTRODUCTION TO PART THREE

1 For Irigaray's complaints about this translation of *Speculum de l'autre femme*, beginning with the title, see Elizabeth Hirsch and Gary A. Olson, "Je—Luce Irigaray: A Meeting with Luce Irigaray," *Hypatia* 10 (1995): 93–114.

2 On the incident, see Sherry Turkle, *Psychoanalytic Politics: Freud's French Revolution* (Cambridge, Mass.: MIT Press, 1978), 181.

3 For the history of Lacan's rebellions within the psychoanalytic establishments of Europe and France, see Elisabeth Roudinesco, *Jacques Lacan and Co.: A History of Psychoanalysis in France, 1925–1985*, trans. Jeffrey Mehlman (Chicago: University of Chicago Press, 1990); and Elisabeth Roudinesco, *Jacques Lacan*, trans. Barbara Bray (New York: Columbia University Press, 1997).

4 See Sigmund Freud, "Some Psychical Consequences of the Anatomical Distinction between the Sexes," in *The Standard Edition of the Complete Psychological Works of Sigmund Freud*, ed. and trans. James Strachey (London: Hogarth Press, 1953–74), 19:243–58; Sigmund Freud, "Female Sexuality," in *Complete Psychological Works*, 21:223–43; and "Femininity," in *Complete Psychological Works*, 22:112–35.

5 Karl Abraham was the first to trace feminism to penis envy, a suggestion soon followed up by Freud. See Karl Abraham, "Manifestations of the Female Castration Complex," in *Selected Papers of Karl Abraham*, trans. Douglas Bryan and Alix Strachey (London: Hogarth Press and the Institute of Psycho-analysis, 1927), 336–69; Sigmund Freud, "The Psychogenesis of a Case of Female Homosexuality," in *Complete Psychological Works*, 18:145–72; and Mary Jo Buhle, *Feminism and Its Discontents: A Century of Struggle with Psychoanalysis* (Cambridge, Mass.: Harvard University Press, 1998), 67–69.

6 See Karen Horney, "Flight from Womanhood: The Masculinity Complex in Women, as Viewed by Men and by Women," in *Feminine Psychology*, ed. Harold Kelman (New York: Norton, 1973), 54–70; Buhle, *Feminism and Its Discontents*, 74–77. Buhle articulates the close ties between this position and maternal feminism, particularly that associated with the Swedish educator Ellen Key (1849–1926).

7 See Ernest Jones, "Early Development of Female Sexuality," in *Papers on Psycho-analysis* (London: Baillière, Tindall, and Cox, 1950), 438–51; and Ernest Jones, "Early Female Sexuality," in *Papers on Psycho-analysis*, 485–95. Mari Jo Buhle rightly objects to the tendency to label these discussions "The Freud-Jones debate," pointing out the centrality of female analysts like Horney and Deutsch as catalysts for Freud's own thinking. See Buhle, *Feminism*

and *Its Discontents*, 53–84. Also see Lisa Appignanesi and John Forrester, *Freud's Women* (New York: Basic Books, 1992), 397–454.

8   Marie Bonaparte was resolutely Freudian in her views, particularly concerning femininity. She attempted to cure her own self-diagnosed frigidity by undergoing surgery to move her clitoris closer to her vagina. On Bonaparte, her relationship to Freud, and her views on femininity, see Marie Bonaparte, *Female Sexuality* (New York: International Universities Press, 1953); Appignanesi and Forrester, *Freud's Women*, 329–51; and Roudinesco, *Lacan and Co.*, 510–11.

9   Roudinesco, *Lacan and Co.*, 511.

10 Ibid., 512. As I showed in chapter 4, Beauvoir in fact remains ambivalent about the body. At times she seems to assert the superiority of the male body and the penis; at other times, such assertions can clearly be read as her assessment of the cultural valorization given to the male body within male-dominant society. For more on these issues, see Toril Moi, *What Is a Woman? and Other Essays* (Oxford: Oxford University Press, 1999), 3–120.

11 See Jacques Lacan, *Feminine Sexuality: Jacques Lacan and the École Freudienne*, ed. Juliet Mitchell and Jacqueline Rose (New York: Norton, 1985), 74–98; and Roudinesco, *Lacan and Co.*, 513–15. For other psychoanalytic work in France outside of Lacan's circle, see Roudinesco, *Lacan and Co.*, 515–16.

12 This formulation suggests that the fantasy gives rise to and enables the material conditions for male dominance. One could argue just as easily that the material conditions of male dominance put the phallus in the site of the transcendental signifier and facilitate fantasmatic claims to absolute power, mastery, and self-identity.

13 Roudinesco, *Lacan and Co.*, 517.

14 The term "feminism" came to English from the French "feminisme," first used in the 1890s by Hubertine Auclert, the founder of the first French suffrage society. For the history of the term, see Nancy F. Cott, *The Grounding of Modern Feminism* (New Haven, Conn.: Yale University Press, 1987), 14–15. As Mari Jo Buhle argues cogently, many groups that modern historians might easily label as feminist did not themselves make use of the term, either because it had not yet been devised or because they believed it carried ideological connotations at odds with their own enterprises. See Buhle, *Feminism and Its Discontents*, 11–16.

15 Roudinesco, *Lacan and Co.*, 511.

16 "I don't particularly care for the term *feminism*. It is the word by which the social system designates the struggle of women. I am completely willing to abandon this word, namely because it is formed on the same model as the other great words of the culture that oppress us." Luce Irigaray, "Interview," in *Women Analyze Women*, ed. Elaine Baruch and Lucienne Serrano (New York: New York University Press, 1980), 150. Also see Hélène Cixous, "Entretien avec Françoise van Rossum-Guyon," *Revue des sciences humaines* 168 (1977): 482; and Julia Kristeva, "Woman Can Never Be Defined," in *New French Feminisms*, ed. Elaine Marks and Isabelle de Courtivron (Amherst: University of Massachusetts Press, 1980), 141; cited in Kelly Oliver, *Reading Kristeva: Unraveling the Double-bind* (New York: Routledge, 1993), 164–65. For more on the problematic American production of "French feminism," see Christine Delphy, "The Invention of French Feminism: An Essential Move," *Yale French Studies* 87 (1995): 190–221. I think both Kristeva and Irigaray work toward the liberation of women and so would be called feminists by most contemporary scholars,

despite their objections to the term as it is sometimes narrowly conceived, particularly within France.

17 As Rey Chow points out, the feminist movements of the 1960s and 1970s "drew on the Chinese Communists' practice of encouraging peasants, especially peasant women, to 'speak bitterness' (suku) against an oppressive patriarchal system." Consciousness-raising finds its origins, then, in "the Chinese 'revolution' as described by William Hinton's *Fanshen*." Rey Chow, *Writing Diaspora: Tactics of Intervention in Contemporary Cultural Studies* (Bloomington: Indiana University Press, 1993), 18.

18 See Claire Duchen, *Feminism in France: From May '68 to Mitterrand* (London: Routledge, 1986), 32–39.

19 Roudinesco, *Lacan and Co.*, 519. In the early years, all MLF/Psych et Po publications appeared anonymously.

20 Roudinesco, *Lacan and Co.*, 519.

21 Fouque and the MLF thus created a publishing house, Éditions des femmes, in 1974.

22 Roudinesco, *Lacan and Co.*, 422–23.

23 See Michèle Montrelay, "Inquiry into Femininity," trans. Parveen Adams, m/f 1 (1978): 83–101; reprinted in *French Feminist Thought*, ed. Toril Moi (Oxford: Basil Blackwell, 1987), 227–49; and Michèle Montrelay, "Recherches sur la fémininité," in *L'Ombre et le nom: Sur la fémininité* (Paris: Minuit, 1977), 57–81.

24 Roudinesco, *Lacan and Co.*, 524. Roudinesco also recognizes the importance of Bataille, calling the seminar "an act of homage to the Bataille of *Madame Edwarda*, to the absolute figure of the hatred and love of God."

25 Ibid.

26 Ibid.

27 This point is similar to my argument in chapter 5: when Lacan claims that the symbolic is governed by the paternal function, he confuses the imaginary and the symbolic (the *a* and the *A*), even though it is precisely such confusion that, according to Lacan, psychoanalysis must subvert. In other words, Lacan inadequately dephallicizes the symbolic, both in terms of the explicit language he uses to describe it and in terms of the metaphors that govern his account of the subject.

28 See, for example, Hirsch and Olson, "Je—Luce Irigaray." In other interviews, Irigaray stresses the importance of the first project to *Speculum of the Other Woman*, and yet the second also plays a part within the book, particularly in the central section and its displaced center, the essay "La Mystèrique." As I will show in chapter 6, here Irigaray reads Western Christian mysticism, following Lacan in *Encore*, as one moment in which women have spoken from "the other side." Still caught, she argues, within a phallocentric, theological order, nevertheless, the mystic offers glimpses into other possible imaginary and symbolic domains.

29 Like many medieval women mystics, Irigaray is interested not only in vision but also in touch, taste, smell, and hearing as sensory modes that can participate in the psychical as well as the physical realm (medieval women write in terms of spiritual and bodily senses and so often mark a break between the two, whereas Irigaray pushes for the close ties between these different registers). See, for example, Constance Classen, *The Color of Angels: Cosmology, Gender, and the Aesthetic Imagination* (New York: Routledge, 1998).

30 For feminine subjects only? If so, what happens to masculine subjectivity?

31 Ewa Plonowska Ziarek argues that Irigaray insists on "the discontinuous temporality of the body" and so "theorizes the interminable becoming of women's bodies" in ways that work against phallic claims to totality and mastery. I think this description is apt, yet as I will argue in chapter 7, sexual difference remains the reified horizon against which this future must be thought. Huntington argues similarly for a temporal dimension to Irigaray's reconception of the imaginary, the symbolic, and their relationship, while also recognizing that Irigaray's category of "Woman" is not as empty as some of her commentators claim (Drucilla Cornell, to whom Huntington refers, has commented more recently on the problematic nature of Irigaray's insistence on the primacy of sexual difference). See Ewa Plonowska Ziarek, "Toward a Radical Female Imaginary: Temporality and Embodiment in Irigaray's Ethics," *Diacritics* 28 (1998): 64; Patricia Huntington, *Ecstatic Subjects, Utopia, and Recognition: Kristeva, Heidegger, Irigaray* (Albany: State University of New York Press, 1998), 134–40, 264–66; Drucilla Cornell, *Beyond Accommodation: Ethical Feminism, Deconstruction, and the Law* (New York: Routledge, 1991), 77–78, 166–72; and Judith Butler and Drucilla Cornell, with Pheng Cheah and Elizabeth Grosz, "The Future of Sexual Difference: An Interview with Judith Butler and Drucilla Cornell," *Diacritics* 28 (1998): 19–42.

32 Cited in Huntington, *Ecstatic Subjects*, 136.

33 Ibid., 137.

34 Ibid.

35 Ellen McCallum, in contrasting fetishism with melancholic incorporation as a method for managing loss, insists on recognizing that lack and loss are distinct phenomena, despite Freud's and Lacan's (and, I would add, Irigaray's) tendency to conflate them. The lack engendered by recognition of one's (real or potential) castration is premised on a fetishistic logic of wholeness and plenitude, whereas loss has to do with "a singular sense of being without something one once had (or at least believed in)." Loss does not necessarily imply a normative standard of wholeness or plenitude against which the subject is found lacking, yet it enables us to take seriously the (often) negative quality of experiences such as the separation from the mother that are constitutive of individuation. E. L. McCallum, *Object Lessons: How to Do Things with Fetishism* (Albany: State University of New York Press, 1999), 111.

36 Death is not always, however, associated with femininity and women. For the complex gendering of death within Western culture, see Karl S. Guthke, *The Gender of Death: A Cultural History in Art and Literature* (Cambridge: Cambridge University Press, 1999).

CHAPTER SIX

1 Luce Irigaray, "Questions à Emmanuel Lévinas sur la divinité de l'amour," *Critique* 522 (1990): 919; Luce Irigaray, "Questions to Emmanuel Levinas," in *The Irigaray Reader*, ed. Margaret Whitford (Oxford: Basil Blackwell, 1991), 186–87; translation modified.

2 Irigaray, "Questions," 913; *Reader*, 180; translation modified.

3 For examples of the early charge of essentialism, which comes in widely varying degrees of subtlety, see Toril Moi, *Sexual/Textual Politics: Feminist Literary Theory* (London: Methuen, 1985), 127–49; Iris Marion Young, "Humanism, Gynocentrism, and Feminist Politics," *Women's Studies International Forum* 8, no. 3 (1985): 231–48; Ann Rosalind Jones, "Writing the Body: Towards an Understanding of l'écriture féminine," in *The New Feminist Criticism: Essays on Women, Literature and Theory*, ed. Elaine Showalter (New York: Pantheon, 1985), 361–

77; and Diana Fuss, *Essentially Speaking: Feminism, Nature, and Difference* (New York: Routledge, 1989), 55–72 (it should be noted that Fuss defends Irigaray's strategic essentialism). For defenses of Irigaray against this charge, see Monique Plaza, "'Phallomorphic Power' and the Psychology of 'Woman,'" trans. Miriam David and Jill Hodges, *Ideology and Consciousness* 4 (1978): 4–36; Elizabeth Grosz, *Sexual Subversions: Three French Feminists* (Sydney: Allen and Unwin, 1989), 110–19; Jane Gallop, *Thinking through the Body* (New York: Columbia University Press, 1988), 92–99; Margaret Whitford, *Luce Irigaray: Philosophy in the Feminine* (New York: Routledge, 1991), 41–45, 116–17; Tina Chanter, *Ethics of Eros: Irigaray's Rewriting of the Philosophers* (New York: Routledge, 1995), 3–5, 41–49; Naomi Schor, "The Essentialism Which Is Not One: Coming to Grips with Irigaray," in *Engaging with Irigaray: Feminist Philosophy and Modern European Thought*, ed. Carolyn Burke, Naomi Schor, and Margaret Whitford (New York: Columbia University Press, 1994), 57–78; Moira Gatens, *Imaginary Bodies: Ethics, Power, and Corporeality* (New York: Routledge, 1996), 60–75; and Ellen Armour, *Deconstruction, Feminist Theology, and the Problem of Difference: Subverting the Race/Gender Divide* (Chicago: University of Chicago Press, 1999), 106–35. For the larger discussion of essentialism, see "The Essential Difference: Another Look at Essentialism," *Differences* 1 (1989); and Cressida J. Heyes, *Line Drawings: Defining Women through Feminist Practice* (Ithaca, N.Y.: Cornell University Press, 2000).

4   For Irigaray's most explicit statements against essentialism, see Luce Irigaray, *Amante marine, de Friedrich Nietzsche* (Paris: Minuit, 1980), 92; Luce Irigaray, *Marine Lover of Friedrich Nietzsche*, trans. Gillian C. Gill (New York: Columbia University Press, 1991), 86. For her dismay at English-language feminists' responses to *Speculum*, see JTN 58–59; JTNP 67–69; and Elizabeth Hirsch and Gary A. Olson, "Je—Luce Irigaray: A Meeting with Luce Irigaray," *Hypatia* 10 (1995): 93–114. Also see Penelope Deutscher, *Yielding Gender: Feminism, Deconstruction, and the History of Philosophy* (New York: Routledge, 1997), 77–88.

5   See Chanter, *Ethics of Eros*, 44–49.

6   For English-language feminists' critique of the sex–gender distinction, see Gatens, *Imaginary Bodies*, 3–20; Elizabeth Grosz, "A Note on Essentialism and Difference," in *Feminist Knowledge: Critique and Construct*, ed. S. Gunew (New York: Routledge, 1990), 332–44; Judith Butler, *Gender Trouble: Feminism and the Subversion of Identity* (New York: Routledge, 1990), esp. 1–34; Judith Butler, *Bodies That Matter: On the Discursive Limits of "Sex"* (New York: Routledge, 1993), esp. 1–23; Suzanne Kessler, *Lessons from the Intersexed* (New Brunswick, N.J.: Rutgers University Press, 1998), 134, n. 2; and Toril Moi, *What Is a Woman? and Other Essays* (Oxford: Oxford University Press, 1999), 3–120. For the history and use of the term "gender," see Linda Nicholson, "Interpreting 'Gender,'" in *The Play of Reason: From the Modern to the Postmodern* (Ithaca, N.Y.: Cornell University Press, 1999), 53–76; and Barbara L. Marshall, *Configuring Gender: Explorations in Theory and Politics* (Peterborough, Ontario: Broadview, 2000). Kessler argues that the term "sex" ought to be dropped, as it implies that there is something "given" in the body. Grosz suggests that we not use the term "gender," as it implies that there is a given, namely, sex. Yet it seems to me that we live in a culture that operates with the distinction between the "bodily" and the psychological, cultural, or social. Thus we may need to maintain the use of both terms even as we insist that both sex and gender are constructed categories and must be thoroughly historicized.

7   For further discussion of the historicity of the body and citation of some important texts, see Amy Hollywood, "Transcending Bodies," *Religious Studies Review* 25 (1999): 13–18.

8   See Margaret Whitford, "Irigaray, Utopia, and the Death Drive," in *Engaging with Irigaray*, 379–400.

9   As Whitford argues, and I will show later in this chapter, Irigaray hopes to replace a culture grounded in sacrifice and an understanding of finitude as lack and woundedness with a culture in which finitude is experienced as an openness to the other. See Whitford, "Irigaray, Utopia, and the Death Drive," 379–400.

10   Irigaray's fullest articulations of the sensible transcendental appear in *An Ethics of Sexual Difference* and *Sexes and Genealogies*. For a full explication of this idea and its ramifications for Irigaray's philosophy of the body, see Tamsin Lorraine, *Irigaray and Deleuze: Experiments in Visceral Philosophy* (Ithaca, N.Y.: Cornell University Press, 1999), 67–89. Margaret Whitford aptly characterizes the sensible transcendental as the "flesh made word"; in other words, the flesh is the necessary base for the intelligible that exceeds, to some extent, the limitations normally associated with fleshliness itself. See Whitford, *Irigaray*, 48; and Hollywood, "Transcending Bodies."

11   Henry Louis Gates, for example, writes that he worries about an implicit "*social essentialism*" in Irigaray's thought. See Henry Louis Gates, "Significant Others," *Contemporary Literature* 29 (1988): 606–22.

12   See, for example, Jay Prosser, *Second Skins: The Body Narratives of Transsexuality* (New York: Columbia University Press, 1998). Arguably similar claims might be made about premodern Western conceptions of sex and gender distinctions. According to Thomas Laqueur, premodern medicine and popular thought held that there was one kind of body that was either male or female depending on the disposition of organs and humors. Although the body was fungible, however, conceptions of masculinity and femininity (i.e., gender?) were not. See Thomas Laqueur, *Making Sex: Body and Gender from the Greeks to Freud* (Cambridge, Mass.: Harvard University Press, 1990); and Amy Hollywood, *The Soul as Virgin Wife: Mechthild of Magdeburg, Marguerite Porete, and Meister Eckhart* (Notre Dame, Ind.: University of Notre Dame Press, 1995), 224–25.

13   For the cross-cultural data, see Gilbert Herbert, *Third Sex, Third Gender: Beyond Sexual Dimorphism in Culture and History* (New York: Zone Books, 1994). For the great complexity of bodies when it comes to distinguishing sex, see Kessler, *Lessons from the Intersexed*; and Anne Fausto-Sterling, *Sexing the Body: Gender Politics and the Construction of Sexuality* (New York: Basic Books, 2000).

14   See, for example, Audre Lorde, "Age, Race, Class, and Sex: Women Redefining Difference," in *Sister/Outsider* (Trumansburg, N.Y.: The Crossing Press, 1984); Elizabeth Spelman, *Inessential Woman: Problems of Exclusion in Feminist Thought* (Boston: Beacon, 1988); Chandra Talpade Mohanty, "Under Western Eyes: Feminist Scholarship and Colonial Discourses," in *Third World Women and the Politics of Feminism*, ed. Chandra Talpade Mohanty, Ann Russo, and Lourdes Torres (Bloomington: University of Indiana Press, 1991); Kimberlé Crenshaw, "Demarginalizing the Intersection of Race and Sex: A Black Feminist Critique of Antidiscrimination Doctrine, Feminist Theory, and Antiracist Politics," in *Feminist Legal Theory*, ed. Katharine T. Bartlett and Rosanne Kennedy (Boulder, Colo.: Westview Press, 1991); Kimberlé Crenshaw, "Mapping the Margins: Intersectionality, Identity, and Violence against Women of Color," *Stanford Law Review* 43 (1993): 1241–99; and Lisa Lowe, *Immigrant Acts* (Durham, N.C.: Duke University Press, 1996), esp. chap. 3.

15   Elizabeth Grosz and Pheng Cheah make this claim forcefully and persistently, although

without convincing their interlocutors, Judith Butler and Drucilla Cornell. See Judith Butler and Drucilla Cornell, with Pheng Cheah and Elizabeth Grosz, "The Future of Sexual Difference: An Interview with Judith Butler and Drucilla Cornell," *Diacritics* 28 (1998): 27–34. For a less successful defense of Irigaray's claim to the primacy of sexual difference, see Gail Schwab, "Sexual Difference as Model: An Ethics for the Global Future," *Diacritics* 28 (1998): 78–80.

16 For the charge of heterosexism, see Annamarie Jagose, *Lesbian Utopics* (New York: Routledge, 1994), 25–42; and Butler and Cornell, "The Future of Sexual Difference," 19–42. Jagose argues that this heterosexism is already apparent in Irigaray's early work and cites others who make this claim.

17 For this defense, see Pheng Cheah and Elizabeth Grosz's comments in Butler and Cornell, "The Future of Sexual Difference," 19–42; and Elizabeth Grosz, "The Hetero and the Homo: The Sexual Ethics of Luce Irigaray," in *Engaging with Irigaray*, 335–50. Pheng Cheah and Grosz note correctly that Irigaray does not privilege reproductive sexuality, for she argues that true creativity between men and women can occur only when reproduction is secondary to the meeting of sexually different human beings. She argues, in fact, that human sexuality focused on reproduction is more animal than human—hence her arguments against reproductive technologies. Yet her insistence that creative or spiritual bonds occur (first? only? she is ambiguous on this issue) between men and women leans, at least metaphorically, on the idea of sexual reproduction. Moreover, her claim that without such relations between the sexes we will die as a species, although perhaps meant as an utterance about distinctive human becoming, borrows its rhetorical power from the allusion to sexual reproduction. Daniel Boyarin follows Jean-Joseph Goux in reading these apocalyptic utterances as statements about the genocide of the female sex not the human species as a whole, but Irigaray argues quite explicitly that the "neutralization" of sexual difference, "if it were possible, would correspond with the end of the human species" (JTNP 10; JTN 12). See Daniel Boyarin, "Gender," in *Critical Terms for Religious Studies*, ed. Mark C. Taylor (Chicago: University of Chicago Press, 1998), 129–30; and Jean-Joseph Goux, "Luce Irigaray versus the Utopia of the Neutral Sex," in *Engaging with Irigaray*, 181–82.

18 See Irigaray, *Amante marine*, 175–203; Irigaray, *Marine Lover of Friedrich Nietzsche*, 164–90; SP 89–102; SG 75–88.

19 The title of Irigaray's chapter on mysticism, "La Mystérique," with its allusions to mysticism, hysteria, mystery, and femininity, leads back to Beauvoir as well as Lacan. Just as Beauvoir reads the Christian mystics as occupying the cusp between mysticism and hysteria, so Irigaray points to the relationship between these two "feminine" cultural phenomena. For more on this issue, see chapter 8. For Irigaray on mysticism, see Moi, *Sexual/Textual Politics*, 135–37; Sarah Beckwith, "A Very Material Mysticism: The Medieval Mysticism of Margery Kempe," in *Medieval Literature: Criticism, Ideology, and History*, ed. David Aers (New York: St. Martin's, 1986), 34–57; Elizabeth Robertson, *Early English Devotional Prose and the Female Audience* (Knoxville: University of Tennessee Press, 1990), 74–75, 193–94; Anna Antonopoulos, "Writing the Mystic Body: Sexuality and Textuality in the *écriture féminine* of Saint Catherine of Genoa," *Hypatia* 6 (1991): 185–207; Kathryn Bond Stockton, "'God' between Their Lips: Desire between Women in Irigaray and Eliot," *Novel* 25 (1992): 348–59; Kathryn Bond Stockton, "Bodies and God: Poststructuralist Feminists Return to the Fold of Spiritual Materialism," *Boundary 2* 19 (1992): 113–49; Kathryn Bond Stockton, *God between Their Lips*:

Desire between Women in Irigaray, Brontë, and Eliot (Stanford, Calif.: Stanford University Press, 1994), 27–29, 32–37, 39, 46–50; Joyce Lorraine Beck, "Negative Subjectivity in Luce Irigaray's 'La Mystérique,' Donne's 'A Nocturnall Upon S Lucies Day,' and Crashaw's 'Glorious Epiphanie,'" *Studia Mystica* 15 (1992): 3–17; Philippa Berry, "The Burning Glass: Paradoxes of Feminist Revelation in Speculum," in *Engaging with Irigaray*, 229–46; Carole Slade, *St. Teresa of Avila: Author of a Heroic Life* (Berkeley: University of California Press, 1995), 133–38; Sharon Hackett, "Looking into the Mystic Mirror," *Intertexts* 2 (1998): 104–18; Cristina Mazzoni, *Saint Hysteria: Neurosis, Mysticism, and Gender in European Culture* (Ithaca, N.Y.: Cornell University Press, 1996), 150–58, 184–85; and Lorraine, *Irigaray and Deleuze*, 70–75. Beauvoir herself refers to the work of Irigaray and others as a "mysticism of the body." See Arleen Dallery, "Sexual Embodiment: Beauvoir and French Feminism," in *Hypatia Reborn: Essays in Feminist Philosophy*, ed. Azizah Y. Al-Hibri and Margaret A. Simons (Bloomington: Indiana University Press, 1989), 53.

20 Many commentators disagree with Irigaray's assessment of the (necessarily) phallogocentric tenor of philosophical discourse. See, for example, Michèle Le Doeuff, *Hipparchia's Choice: An Essay Concerning Women, Philosophy, Etc.*, trans. Trista Selous (Oxford: Basil Blackwell, 1991). For the way in which Irigaray's all-or-nothing logic tends to efface the history of women's participation within and resistance to male-dominant culture and society, see chapter 8.

21 For a counterreading of Freud on women, see Sarah Kofman, *The Enigma of Woman*, trans. Catherine Porter (Ithaca, N.Y.: Cornell University Press, 1985). For an interpretation of Kofman's reading of Irigaray as symptomatic, see Ranita Chatterjee, "Of Footnotes and Fathers: Reading Irigaray with Kofman," in *Psychoanalyses/Feminisms*, ed. Peter L Rudnytsky and Andrew M. Gordon (Albany: State University of New York Press, 2000), 55–68.

22 What, then, is unconscious for woman? What would disrupt her fantasmatic wholeness? Irigaray suggests both that woman's consciousness will be structured differently, so that there is no fantasy of wholeness, and that the deconstruction of belief will be necessary for women as well as for men. Hence the deep tensions that run throughout her work.

23 For the centrality of the touch in Irigaray's project and its relationship to a new feminine imaginary grounded in the morphology of women's bodies, see Irigaray, CS 23–32; TS 23–33; and Cathryn Vasseleu, *Textures of Light: Vision and Touch in Irigaray, Levinas, and Merleau-Ponty* (New York: Routledge, 1998), 3–18, 66–67.

24 This interpretative problem is, of course, tied to the problem of essentialism discussed above. For a similar issue with regard to medieval women's texts, see chapter 8.

25 For discussion of Irigaray's views of vision, see Martin Jay, *Downcast Eyes: The Denigration of Vision in Twentieth-Century French Thought* (Berkeley: University of California Press, 1993), 526–41. For more on this issue, see chapter 8.

26 On the centrality of the dialectics of all and nothing and named and nameless in Marguerite Porete and Meister Eckhart, see Michael Sells, *Mystical Languages of Unsaying* (Chicago: University of Chicago Press, 1994), chaps. 5–7; and Hollywood, *Virgin Wife*, chaps. 4 and 6.

27 See especially Sells, *Mystical Languages of Unsaying*, 1–13.

28 Amy Hollywood, "Beauvoir, Irigaray, and the Mystical," *Hypatia* 9 (1994): 158–85. I argue in chapter 8 that this final focus on the body is precisely the fetishizing move that occurs in certain readings of medieval women's texts, and in certain readings of Irigaray herself, including, as I suggest below, my own reading in the article cited here.

29 See especially Caroline Walker Bynum, *Holy Feast and Holy Fast: The Religious Significance of Food to Medieval Women* (Berkeley: University of California Press, 1987); and Caroline Walker Bynum, *Fragmentation and Redemption: Essays on Gender and the Human Body in Medieval Religion* (New York: Zone Books, 1991). For arguments critiquing and nuancing this position, see chapter 8.

30 The passage seems dependent on Angela of Foligno, who writes of entering into Christ's side and of Christ's spiritual sons entering into his side and their lips becoming red with his blood. See Angela of Foligno, *Complete Works*, trans. Paul Lachance (New York: Paulist Press, 1993), 128, 176, 246. The imagery emerges in the tradition of commentaries on the Song of Songs, where the cleft in the rock in which a dove rests is interpreted as the side wound of Christ in which the soul rests. See, for example, Aelred of Rievaulx (d. 1167): "From the rock streams have flowed for you, wounds have been made in his limbs, holes in the wall of his body, in which, like a dove, you may hide while you kiss them one by one. Your lips, stained with his blood, will become like a scarlet ribbon and your word sweet." Aelred of Rievaulx, *Treatises and Pastoral Prayer*, trans. Theodore Berkeley, Mary Paul Macpherson, R. Penelope Lawson (Kalamazoo, Mich.: Cistercian Publications, 1971), 90–91. Cited in Thomas Bestul, *Texts of the Passion: Latin Devotional Literature and Medieval Society* (Philadelphia: University of Pennsylvania Press, 1996), 39.

For the association of Christ's side wound, Mary's breast, blood, and milk, see Bynum, *Fragmentation*, 79–117; and Charles T. Wood, "The Doctors' Dilemma: Sin, Salvation, and the Menstrual Cycle in Medieval Thought," *Speculum* 56 (1981): 710–27. On the association of the side wound and the vulva, see Karma Lochrie, "Mystical Acts, Queer Tendencies," in *Constructing Medieval Sexuality*, ed. Karma Lochrie, Peggy McCracken, and James A. Schultz (Minneapolis: University of Minnesota Press, 1997), 180–200; and Wolfgang Riehle, *The Middle English Mystics*, trans. Bernard Standring (London: Routledge and Kegan Paul, 1981).

31 For a similar logic as it is enacted in Marguerite Porete's work, see Sells, *Mystical Languages of Unsaying*, 127–31.

32 Teresa of Avila, *The Life of Teresa of Jesus*, trans. E. Allison Peers (Garden City, N.J.: Image Books, 1960), 273–75.

33 It remains an open question whether the violence of Teresa's experience is required only because of the patriarchal constraints under which she labors or whether violence and pain are, to some degree, endemic to subjectivity.

34 See also Irigaray's rejection of suffering as an end in "Divine Women." "To suffer does not in any way constitute a perfection, but a means of restoration. As such, suffering doesn't correspond to any sanctity, but to the installation of human nature in perversity. An experience of suffering, unless it is a redemptive passage, is a denial of the divine" (SP 79; SG 66–67). The line between suffering as an end and as a moment in the redemptive process is often difficult to determine.

35 Also see SP 89–102; SG 75–88; and Nancy Jay's social scientifically grounded argument for the close relationship between sacrifice and patriarchal structures. Jay argues that sacrifice is used to establish paternity as opposed to the bodily base of maternal ties. Nancy Jay, *Throughout Your Generations Forever: Sacrifice, Religion, and Paternity* (Chicago: University of Chicago Press, 1992).

36 See OC VII 324–29; and Georges Bataille, *Theory of Religion*, trans. Robert Hurley (New York: Zone Books, 1989), 69–77.

37 Although some scholars read Bataille's text on Gilles de Rais as simply an affirmation of Gilles's violence, such interpretations are clearly inadequate. Bataille's stance is one of both fascination and horror. See Georges Bataille, *Le Procès de Gilles de Rais*, in OC X; and Georges Bataille, *The Trial of Gilles de Rais*, trans. Richard Robinson (Los Angeles: Amok, 1991).

38 See OC IX 239–58; Georges Bataille, *Literature and Evil*, trans. Alistair Hamilton (London: Marion Boyars, 1985), 105–25; OC V 455; IE 208.

39 See, for example, the closing section of Bataille's *The Tears of Eros*, trans. Peter Connor (San Francisco: City Lights, 1989), 205–7; OC X 626–27.

40 Irigaray, *Amante marine*, 175–203; Irigaray, *Marine Lover of Friedrich Nietzsche*, 164–90.

41 The same tension can be described in terms of that between wonder and self-love as they are described in Iriagray, *An Ethics of Sexual Difference*. See Serene Jones, "Divining Women: Irigaray and Feminist Theologies," *Yale French Studies* 87 (1995): 42–67.

42 Although Irigaray's utopic drive runs this risk, one might argue that there is a difference between the "male" desire to fill a gaping wound in being through the death and fetishization of the mother, and the openness to communication symbolized by the fluidity of the mucous membrane. The feminine imaginary opens the subject to the possibility of risk without demanding faith in the closure of a life-threatening wound. Moreover, it might be necessary to risk belief in order to create a new imaginary and symbolic. Perhaps the fantasy of wholeness is *necessary* to women's full subjectivities (even if this belief is subject to eventual deconstruction, as in "Belief Itself"). As I have suggested, a central question is whether there is something in the feminine imaginary that *invites* such deconstruction more readily than does the male imaginary—and whether the feminine imaginary is able to function without the subjugation of the other seemingly so necessary to the phallic economy. To pose the question from another angle, we might ask with Lacan whether the new imaginary and symbolic will generate a single divine woman or rather god(s) who are not quite double and yet also not one.

43 On this issue, see Caroline Walker Bynum, *Jesus as Mother: Studies in the Spirituality of the High Middle Ages* (Berkeley: University of California Press, 1982); Bynum, *Holy Feast*; Ulrike Wiethaus, "Sexuality, Gender, and the Body in Late Medieval Women's Spirituality: Cases from Germany and the Netherlands," *Journal of Feminist Studies in Religion* 7 (1991): 35–52; Sells, *Mystical Languages of Unsaying*, chap. 5; Hollywood, *Virgin Wife*, chaps. 3 and 4; Barbara Newman, "La mystique courtoise: Thirteenth-Century Beguines and the Art of Love," in *From Virile Woman to WomanChrist: Studies in Medieval Religion and Literature* (Philadelphia: University of Pennsylvania Press, 1995), 137–67; and Lochrie, "Mystical Acts, Queer Tendencies."

44 See Hollywood, *Virgin Wife*, 173–203, for this argument and the relevant literature.

45 Stockton, "'God between Their Lips'"; and Stockton, "Bodies and God." Tom Carlson's work suggests that the mediating term between the two may in fact be death. See Thomas Carlson, *Indiscretion: Finitude and the Naming of God* (Chicago: University of Chicago Press, 1999), esp. 239–62.

46 Implicit here is the assumption that the gap between God and man is the source of an alienating tension that causes man to use woman as another support for his subjectivity. I will discuss this assumption further in chapter 7.

47 Kristeva points to this potential problem within feminism: "The trap that is set for this demystifying force, a force that the women's movement can be, is that we will identify with the power principle that we think we are fighting: the hysterical saint plays her pleasure

against social order, but in the name of God. The question is: 'Who plays God in present-day feminism?' Man? Or Woman—his substitute? As long as any libertarian movement, feminism included, does not analyze its own relationship to power and does not renounce belief in its own identity, it remains capable of being co-opted both by power and an overtly religious or lay spiritualism." Julia Kristeva, "Warnings," in *New French Feminisms*, ed. Elaine Marks and Isabelle de Courtivron (Amherst: University of Massachusetts Press, 1980), 141.

The problem, I think, is not simply the relationship to power, about which Irigaray is astute, but also the relationship to mortality, loss, and limitation. Simply to claim acceptance of these realities is insufficient. We need philosophical, theoretical, and practical means for dealing with their bodily effects.

CHAPTER SEVEN

1   Elizabeth Grosz, "Irigaray and the Divine," in *Transfigurations: Theology and the French Feminists*, ed. C. W. Maggie Kim, Susan M. St. Ville, and Susan M. Simonaitis (Minneapolis: Fortress Press, 1993), 214. Grosz also points to another, "cosmic," dimension of the divine more in line with my readings. See Elizabeth Grosz, *Sexual Subversions: Three French Feminists* (Sydney: Allen and Unwin, 1989), 180–81.

2   Serene Jones, "This God Which Is Not One: Irigaray and Barth on the Divine," in *Transfigurations: Theology and the French Feminists*, 138.

3   See Penelope Deutscher, "'The Only Diabolical Thing about Woman . . .': Luce Irigaray on Divinity," *Hypatia* 9 (1994): 88–111; and Penelope Deutscher, *Yielding Gender: Feminism, Deconstruction, and the History of Philosophy* (New York: Routledge, 1997), 81–86.

4   Irigaray's argument that one needs religious models of mother–daughter relationships makes it clear that her call for a female divine and for a reconfiguration of the mother–daughter bond are closely related. See EDS 70–71; AE 68–69; SP 84; SG 71; LTD 26–31; TD 9–14.

5   See, for example, LTD 26–31, 71, 121–23; TD 9–14, 56, 110–12; JTNP 29–31, 57–61, 159–62; JTN 25–26, 47–50, 133–36; JAT 201–4; ILTY 130–31.

6   See Grosz, "Irigaray and the Divine," 199. Irigaray herself discusses responses to the essay and the complex personal and political context out of which it emerged in Luce Irigaray et al., *Le souffle des femmes* (Paris: ACGF, 1996), 215–18. The volume as a whole marks the much more positive response to Irigaray's work on religion among some feminists.

7   Deutscher, "Luce Irigaray on Divinity," 89. For further discussion of Irigaray's work on religion, see the discussions of Irigaray and mysticism cited in chapter 6, and also Grosz, "Irigaray and the Divine"; Grosz, *Sexual Subversions*, 151–83; Margaret Whitford, *Luce Irigaray: Philosophy in the Feminine* (New York: Routledge, 1991), 140–47; Ellen Armour, *Deconstruction, Feminist Theology, and the Problem of Difference: Subverting the Race/Gender Divide* (Chicago: University of Chicago Press, 1999), 130–32, 180–81; Morny Joy, "Equality or Divinity—A False Dichotomy?" *Journal of Feminist Studies of Religion* 6 (1990): 9–24; Philippa Berry, "Women and Space according to Kristeva and Irigaray," in *Shadow of Spirit: Postmodernism and Religion*, ed. Philippa Berry and Andrew Wernick (London: Routledge, 1992), 229–46; Philippa Berry, "The Burning Glass: Paradoxes of Feminist Revelation in *Speculum*," in *Engaging with Irigaray: Feminist Philosophy and Modern European Thought*, ed. Carolyn Burke, Naomi Schor, and Margaret

Whitford (New York: Columbia University Press, 1994), 229–46; Jones, "This God"; Serene Jones, "Divining Women: Irigaray and Feminist Theologies," *Yale French Studies* 89 (1995): 42–67; Kathryn Bond Stockton, *God between Their Lips: Desire between Women in Irigaray, Brontë, and Eliot* (Stanford, Calif.: Stanford University Press, 1994), 3–91; Graham Ward, *Theology and Contemporary Critical Theory* (New York: St. Martin's Press, 1996), 29–37; Graham Ward, "Divinity and Sexuality: Luce Irigaray and Christology," *Modern Theology* 12 (1996): 221–37; Grace Jantzen, "Feminism and Pantheism," *The Monist* 80 (1997): 266–85; Jenny Daggers, "Luce Irigaray and 'Divine Women': A Resource for Postmodern Feminist Theology?" *Feminist Theology* 14 (1997): 35–50; Anne-Claire Mulder, "Thinking about the Imago Dei—Minimalizing or Maximalizing the Difference between the Sexes," *Feminist Theology* 14 (1997): 9–33; Alison Ainley, "Luce Irigaray: Divine Spirit and Feminine Space," *Post-Secular Philosophy: Between Philosophy and Theology*, ed. Philip Blond (London: Routledge, 1998), 334–45; Ree Boddé, "A God of Her Own," *Feminist Theology* 19 (1998): 48–62; Marsha Hewitt, "Do Women Really Need a 'God/ess' to Save Them? An Inquiry into Notions of the Divine Feminine," *Method and Theory in the Study of Religion* 10 (1998): 149–56; and Tamsin Lorraine, *Irigaray and Deleuze: Experiments in Visceral Philosophy* (Ithaca, N.Y.: Cornell University Press, 1999), 49–89. For an extended Irigarayan analysis of the gendering of early trinitarian language, see Virginia Burrus, *"Begotten, Not Made": Conceiving Manhood in Late Antiquity* (Stanford, Calif.: Stanford University Press, 2000). In addition, many recent works of feminist philosophy of religion are heavily dependent on Irigaray. See Daphne Hampson, *After Christianity* (Valley Forge, Pa.: Trinity Press International, 1996); Pamela Sue Anderson, *A Feminist Philosophy of Religion: The Rationality and Myths of Religious Belief* (Oxford: Blackwell, 1998); and Grace Jantzen, *Becoming Divine: Towards a Feminist Philosophy of Religion* (Bloomington: Indiana University Press, 1999).

8 See Jean d'Arras, *Mélusine. Roman du XIVe siècle*, ed. Louis Stouff (Dijon: Imprimerie Bernigaud et Privat, 1932; reprinted, Geneva: Statkine, 1974). For a modern French translation, see Jean d'Arras, *Le Roman de Mélusine ou l'Histoire des Lusignan*, trans. Michèle Perret (Paris: Stock, 1979). My thanks to Katharine Conley for information and ideas about the Melusine story.

9 See Irigaray's reading of central modern philosophers in light of the elements suppressed and forgotten in their work, as well as her more poetic evocation of the elements, in Luce Irigaray, *Elemental Passions*, trans. Joanne Collie and Judith Still (New York: Routledge, 1992). Irigaray describes the planned tetralogy (one volume for each of the elements), of which only three volumes were written, in Luce Irigaray, *Le corps-à-corps avec la mère* (Montreal: Les éditions de la pleine lune, 1981), 43–44.

10 I find this formulation of the problem extremely troubling. Surely we do not want to deny humanity to oppressed and suppressed women but to acknowledge the severe limitations placed on their freedom and autonomy? For this reason, Beauvoir's formulations seem both much more apt and politically useful. See also Toril Moi, *What Is a Woman? and Other Essays* (Oxford: Oxford University Press, 1999), 3–120.

11 Deutscher, "Luce Irigaray on Divinity," 89.

12 Deutscher offers the most sustained and convincing version of this reading. See Deutscher, "Luce Irigaray on Divinity."

13 For Irigaray's views of identification and the necessity of the divine, see, in addition to "Divine Woman," Luce Irigaray, "Equal to Whom?" in *Differences* 1 (1989): 59–76;

Irigaray, *Souffle*, 185–249; and Luce Irigaray, *Être Deux* (Paris: Grasset, 1997), 153–68. For Bynum's account of symbols and gender, see Caroline Walker Bynum, "Introduction: The Complexity of Symbols," in *Gender and Religion: On the Complexity of Symbols*, ed. Caroline Walker Bynum, Stevan Harrell, and Paula Richman (Boston: Beacon Press, 1986), 1–20.

14 On matriarchal traditions, see Irigaray, LTD 26–31; TD 8–14; Irigaray, *Souffle*, 243–45; Irigaray, *Entre Orient et Occident* (Paris: Grasset, 1999).

15 See, for example, Carole R. Fontaine, "A Heifer from Thy Stable: On Goddesses and the Status of Women in the Ancient Near East," *Union Seminary Quarterly Review* 43 (1989): 67–91; Jo Ann Hackett, "Can a Sexist Model Liberate Us? Ancient Near Eastern 'Fertility' Goddesses," *Journal of Feminist Studies in Religion* 5 (1989): 65–76; Helene Foley, "A Question of Origins," *Women's Studies* 23 (1994): 193–219; and Ruth Tringham and Margaret Conkey, "Rethinking Figurines: A Critical View from Archaeology of Gimbutas, the 'Goddess' and Popular Culture," in *Ancient Goddesses: The Myths and the Evidence*, ed. Lucy Goodison and Christine Morris (London: British Museum Press, 1998), 22–45. On the history of the idea of matriarchy, and on its limitations for feminist theory, see Cynthia Eller, *Living in the Lap of the Goddess: The Feminist Spirituality Movement in America* (Boston: Beacon Press, 1993); and Cynthia Eller, *The Myth of Matriarchal Prehistory: Why an Invented Past Won't Give Women a Future* (Boston: Beacon, 2000).

16 See Caroline Walker Bynum, *Jesus as Mother: Studies in the Spirituality of the High Middle Ages* (Berkeley: University of California Press, 1982).

17 Ludwig Feuerbach, *The Essence of Christianity*, trans. George Eliot (New York: Harper, 1957), 26.

18 Sigmund Freud, *Beyond the Pleasure Principle*, in *On Metapsychology*, trans. James Strachey (New York: Penguin Books, 1984), 284. Irigaray's interpretation of the episode should also be read against that of Lacan in *Seminar XI*, in which he defines the traumatic as a missed encounter with the real and links trauma and the real to God and the supposed death of God. See Jacques Lacan, *The Four Fundamental Concepts of Psychoanalysis*, trans. Alan Sheridan (New York: Norton, 1978), esp. 17–64.

19 As Derrida points out, Freud himself, by constantly circling around the repetition compulsion, explaining it in terms of pleasure and then refusing these explanations, himself enacts the scene of writing as one of repetition.

20 Irigaray describes this "other place": "Bound and chained in and under the secondary processes? 'Poste-restante,' if that signifies the place where are gathered messages for unknown persons, who lack an address, remain unreceivable according to the usual, already coded, telecommanded, circuits" (SP 37; SG 25). The illusion is to Derrida's *The Post Card*, in which woman seems to be the (non)recipient of the "Envoie." Irigaray is also making implicit reference to Lacan's claim that there is no sexual relation. See Jacques Derrida, *The Post Card: From Socrates to Freud and Beyond*, trans. Alan Bass (Chicago: University of Chicago Press, 1987).

21 Thus for Freud the mother is associated with the death drive. Irigaray hopes to show one way in which this association might be deconstructed.

22 Irigaray here brings in language from Heidegger, also deployed by Derrida throughout *The Post Card*.

23 There is the suggestion here that Ernst's game marks a sublimation of destructive impulses that would lead to the murder of the mother or the suicide of the son. Belief, then, saves

the mother('s body) in her literality, but always at her expense as an active agent within the symbolic.

24 I follow Irigaray here in her use of the term "patriarchal," although I find its universalizing application problematic.

25 For more on the placenta, see JTNP 45–54; JTN 37–44.

26 As Irigaray argues elsewhere, the constitution of the subject and its relation to a male other becomes dependent on the primordial concealment and sacrifice of the mother's independent subjectivity, a sacrifice simultaneously revealed and concealed within (Catholic) Christianity by the sacrifice of the Son (SP 21–33; SG 9–21).

27 Before exploring this possibility, Irigaray offers warning reflections on the story of little Ernst and the traditional Catholic account of the annunciation, in which the angel works for the male subject and the male God. In both cases, woman is relegated to the status of a supporting structure on or through which the presence of the divine is represented. Yet the terror of the angel lies in its power to evoke the sacrifice of the mother on which this inscription of male subjectivity and divinity depends.

28 Irigaray also discusses the devils who block communication by insisting on the repetition of the same and thereby evoking the "demonic" force of the repetition compulsion discussed by Freud in *Beyond the Pleasure Principle*. But the angel, according to Irigaray, has priority (contra Freud and Derrida), offering the hope for difference and a future. Otherwise, "the stage is in the hands of the devil, the devils, who turn everything upside down to leap and make leap into a dark, hidden, sulfurous beyond. Unless the whole thing goes suddenly up in flames?" (SP 53; SG 41). The devil blocks movement and change, yet Irigaray suggests that giving into the demonic completely may be the move that sets the whole system of repetitions and denial in flames. She is not clear about how passing through the demonic might allow "an irreducible difference to befall us" (SP 53; SG 41), although it could be, as Derrida would argue, that repetition is never really of the same and hence contains difference already within it. The leap, then, would be the attempt to push that difference to the fore, thereby giving voice to the other.

29 These pages appear in slightly different form in Luce Irigaray, *L'Oubli de l'air chez Martin Heidegger* (Paris: Minuit, 1983). The futurity of Irigaray's prophets suggests her desire for a "first, last word" in the debates about priority underlying her interchange with Freud and Derrida. For Irigaray, Derrida's concern with priority seems to be at the expense of any really new future.

30 The Heideggerian heritage of the text heightens the danger one might hear in Irigaray's evocation of risk, although I suspect she would argue that Heidegger fell short in his risk-taking. In her call for "risk" rather than "detachment," however, Irigaray may be more Bataillean than Heideggerian. On Irigaray's relationship to Heidegger, see Ellen Mortensen, *The Feminine and Nihilism: Luce Irigaray with Nietzsche and Heidegger* (Oslo: Scandinavian University Press, 1994); Joanna Hodge, "Irigaray Reading Heidegger," in *Engaging with Irigaray*, 191–209; Tina Chanter, *Ethics of Eros: Irigaray's Rewriting of the Philosophers* (New York: Routledge, 1995), 127–69; Ellen Armour, "Questions of Proximity: 'Woman's Place' in Derrida and Irigaray," *Hypatia* 12 (1997): 63–78; and Patricia Huntington, *Ecstatic Subjects, Utopia, and Recognition: Kristeva, Heidegger, Irigaray* (Albany: State University of New York Press, 1998).

31 Just as belief and its objects have different implications (and perhaps even different

structures) for differently positioned people, so also might the call for risk. Irigaray is describing the normative subject, who is not only male—as she explicitly argues—but also white, Western, heterosexual, and economically privileged.

32 Irigaray, Être Deux, 155.

33 Jantzen, Becoming Divine, 88–95. Similarly, Pamela Sue Anderson raises important questions about the variety of meanings that might be given to the term "exist" in the claim "God or the gods exist." See Anderson, A Feminist Philosophy of Religion, esp. 118.

34 Marx Wartofsky, Feuerbach (Cambridge: Cambridge University Press, 1977), 209. Cited in Van Harvey, Feuerbach and the Interpretation of Religion (Cambridge: Cambridge University Press, 1995), 115.

35 Harvey, Feuerbach, 115.

36 Ibid., 115–16.

37 Huntington, Ecstatic Subjects, 140; and Drucilla Cornell, Beyond Accommodation: Ethical Feminism, Deconstruction, and the Law (New York: Routledge, 1991), 87. Huntington worries, however, about just how open Irigaray leaves the concept.

38 See Judith Butler and Drucilla Cornell, with Pheng Cheah and Elizabeth Grosz, "The Future of Sexual Difference: An Interview with Judith Butler and Drucilla Cornell," Diacritics 28 (1998): 27–34. Margaret Whitford also points to Irigaray's ambivalence with regard to the category "woman." On the one hand, Irigaray wants to keep the term radically open; on the other she seems to argue that woman can be/must be defined. See Whitford, Irigaray, 49–52.

39 Grosz denies that sexual difference is the only fundamental difference for Irigaray; but Irigaray quite clearly posits it as primary, as I show in chapter 6. See Butler and Cornell, "The Future of Sexual Difference," 34.

40 Irigaray argues that through this mutual recognition, grounded in irreducible sexual difference, the Hegelian dialectic between master and slave will be overcome. There will be no final totalization, moreover, for the continued existence of the two sexes protects against this move. Irigaray thus sees herself as resolving the dilemma posed by Beauvoir in the opening of The Second Sex (and, implicitly, by Bataille and Lacan as well). I would like to explore these competing Hegelianisms and anti-Hegelianisms in another place. For now, suffice it to say that it leads Irigaray to this revision of Beauvoir: "It is not, as Simone de Beauvoir said: one is not born a woman, one becomes one (through culture), but rather: I am born woman, but I must still become this woman that I am by nature" (JAT 168; ILTY 107).

41 In addition, Irigaray's claim that our sexed natures are potentially infinite seems based on an implicit understanding of sexual binaries as complements creating a final plenitude.

42 Irigaray talks about sexual difference in terms of the encounter between men and women. Although Irigaray's use of the concept probably signifies both differences of sex/gender (what I focus on here) and sexuality, we need to distinguish between the two (despite the fact that they are inextricably entwined within our current sexual economy). The multiplicity of forms of bodies and desires renders unstable any claim to the dual nature of sexual difference. Moreover, as I will argue below, although it is clear that we are always formed as sexual subjects—pleasure playing a key role in subject formation—it is less clear that we are necessarily sexed or gendered as male and female. Thus although sex difference and sexuality are currently inextricably tied together, they can and should be analytically

separated; only through this kind of separation can we begin to understand the multiplicity of actual bodies and desires. On ways in which sexuality destabilizes prescribed gender dualisms, see Judith Butler, *Gender Trouble: Feminism and the Subversion of Identity* (New York: Routledge, 1990); Judith Butler, *Bodies That Matter: On the Discursive Limits of "Sex"* (New York: Routledge, 1993); Eve Kosofsky Sedgwick, *Epistemology of the Closet* (Berkeley: University of California Press, 1990), 27–35; and Biddy Martin, "Sexualities without Genders and Other Queer Utopias," *Diacritics* 24 (1994): 104–21. Martin rightly warns against allowing gender to stand as the stable core against which sexuality pulls. Yet at the same time, Irigaray's conflation of sex/gender and sexuality works to normalize associations that can be disrupted by recognition of the multiplicity of bodies and desires.

43   In this way, one could also make use of Irigaray's incredibly rich work on embodied subjectivity and the senses, particularly in *An Ethics of Sexual Difference*. I will turn briefly to this text in the conclusion. For a helpful analysis of Irigaray on beauty, see Hilary Robinson, "Whose Beauty? Women, Art, and Intersubjectivity in Luce Irigaray's Writing," in *Beauty Matters*, ed. Peg Zeglin Brand (Bloomington: Indiana University Press, 2000), 224–51.

44   Harvey, *Feuerbach*, 110.

CHAPTER EIGHT

1   In "Divine Women" Irigaray suggests that other kinds of belief are possible. Thus she argues that women, "who have not had a God to sublimate their hysteria" or "to accomplish their *genre*," need "to be God *for ourselves* in order to be divine for the other, not an already outlined and determined idol, fetish, or symbol" (SP 83–84; SG 70–71).

2   Freud distinguishes between calling religious claims illusions and asserting that they are untrue. Illusions are wish fulfillments and cannot be verified or falsified, and so Freud suggests that there are strong rational and moral grounds for giving them up. This move, not surprisingly, is gendered. As Judith Van Herick shows, Freud associates Christianity with femininity and illusion, whereas he sees Judaism as masculine and as grounded less in wish fulfillment than in subjection to the Law; hence it is a moral religion. See Judith Van Herick, *Freud on Femininity and Faith* (Berkeley: University of California Press, 1982).

3   See Marjorie Garber, *Vested Interests: Cross Dressing and Cultural Anxiety* (New York: Routledge, 1992), 125.

4   Freud associates fetishism and hysteria by describing both as neuroses grounded in something like traumatic amnesia. At first Freud holds that for the hysteric the trauma is infantile sexual experience inflicted on a not yet sexualized child by an adult; later he says that it is the unfulfillable nature of the child's desire. Of fetishism, on the other hand, Freud argues that "the fright of castration at the sight of the female genital" results in a disorder that "reminds" him of "the stopping of memory in traumatic amnesia." Freud differentiates between the two conditions by positing hysteria as the repression of affect, found primarily among women, and fetishism as the disavowal of an idea, found primarily among men (a primacy dependent on Freud's grounding of neurosis on the presence or absence of the penis). The most crucial distinction between fetishism and hysteria is in the affects they engender; the displacement and overvaluation of nongenital body parts that the hysteric experiences as pathological suffering are intensely pleasurable for the fetishist (because he disavows originary trauma and thus consolidates his subjectivity and his sexual pleasure). The fetishist, then, gets to enjoy his symptom in a way the hysteric does not

(at least according to Freud). Similarly, for Freud, the presence of a superego or internally regulating agency of repression in women is perceived as being pathological, whereas its absence in men, although pathologized by the psychoanalyst, provides only pleasure for the subject.

The ties between fetishism and pleasure may help explain the curious fact, noted in our reading of Bataille and inscribed within Freud's own essay, that the very representation of women's lack or woundedness can itself be a source of fetishistic desire and pleasure for men. Bataille's narrator in *Madame Edwarda* stands before the naked genitals of the prostitute, in a gesture that many read as fetishistic. Similarly, I have suggested that Bataille's meditation on the body of a tortured Chinese man recalls the fetishization of the wounded and feminized other endemic to Orientalist discourses. Freud attempts to explain such practices, in particular "the Chinese custom of mutilating the female foot and then revering it like a fetish after it has been mutilated." "It seems," he observes, "as though the Chinese male wants to thank the woman for having submitted to being castrated." In other words, it is precisely the fact of women's castration that here gives rise to adulation and desire, presumably because her castration is taken as a substitute for man's own. Sigmund Freud, "Fetishism," in *The Standard Edition of the Complete Psychological Works of Sigmund Freud*, ed. and trans. James Strachey (London: Hogarth Press, 1953–74), 21:157.

5 I agree with Margaret Whitford and Gail Schwab that at times Irigaray is fully cognizant of the power of the death drive and of loss, yet I also think there is a strong—often contradictory—counternarrative in her work: "Yes, but even so. . . ." Sexual difference as fetish marks the site of that tension and its attempted resolution. See Margaret Whitford, *Luce Irigaray: Philosophy in the Feminine* (New York: Routledge, 1991); Margaret Whitford, "Irigaray, Utopia, and the Death Drive," in *Engaging with Irigaray: Feminist Philosophy and Modern European Thought*, ed. Carolyn Burke, Naomi Schor, and Margaret Whitford (New York: Columbia University Press, 1994), 379–400; and Gail M. Schwab, "Mother's Body, Father's Tongue: Mediation and the Symbolic Order," in *Engaging with Irigaray*, 351–78.

6 Here there are parallels with contemporary discourses of trauma, where the primacy given to sexual trauma gives rise to an inability to see and name other forms of trauma. On this issue, see Janice Haaken, "The Recovery of Memory, Fantasy, and Desire: Feminist Approaches to Sexual Abuse and Psychic Trauma," *Signs* 21 (1996): 1069–94; and Janice Haaken, *Pillar of Salt: Gender, Memory, and the Perils of Looking Back* (New Brunswick, N.J.: Rutgers University Press, 1998).

7 Anne McClintock, *Imperial Leather: Race, Gender, and Sexuality in the Colonial Context* (New York: Routledge, 1995), 202–3.

8 As an example of the way sexual difference hides other differences, see Daniel Boyarin's argument that Freud fetishizes the penis because of his simultaneous avowal and disavowal of Christian culture's subordination of him as a Jew. Daniel Boyarin, "Épater l'embourgeoisement: Freud, Gender, and the (De)Colonized Psyche," *Diacritics* 24 (1994): 17–42; and also Sander Gilman, *Freud, Race, and Gender* (Princeton, N.J.: Princeton University Press, 1993).

9 The flip side of adulation before the fetishized other—and the danger (or for Bataille, the opportunity) lurking within fetishism—is what Bataille calls "abjection." Julia Kristeva first introduces the term into psychoanalytic theory, describing abjection as the originary moment of subjectivity in which the nascent subject differentiates itself from a still

not fully objectified or externalized other. Kristeva also uses the term in verb form to denote the action whereby the infant expels or casts out that which is other than itself. I thus follow English translations of Kristeva in resurrecting the obsolete verb form "to abject," which implies both expulsion and the abjection—humiliation, wretchedness, and miserableness—of that which has been so expelled.

In articulating herself as a subject, the infant must create borders between the self and the world by expelling or abjecting—both rejecting and rendering miserable or degraded—that which is extraneous to the self or that which might threaten its newly formed borders. Freud argued in *Civilization and Its Discontents* that the subject constitutes itself as a social being through repression and the incest taboo. Kristeva takes this analysis further, showing how negation and abjection are crucial to subjectivity and form the ever-present borders of the self. Kristeva provides visceral descriptions of the process of abjection and its remains: spit, vomit, feces, tears, all the dirt and detritus rejected by civilized domesticity. Yet central to Kristeva's account of abjection is the figure of the abject mother. As the primary caretaker within most societies, the mother exists in bodily symbiosis with the infant. This symbiosis of drives and bodily affects must be disrupted if the child is to attain subjectivity. The very closeness of mother and child gives rise to the mother's abjection as that which is not-self and yet also not recognized as a fully other subjectivity (although Kristeva suggests an alternative path to subjectivity in *Tales of Love*).

Kristeva does not unpack the gender dynamics inherent in traditional psychoanalytic accounts of fetishization, and hence in the possible slide from fetishization to abjection. But if the fetish simultaneously marks and disavows the reality of castration—both one's own and the mother's—then it also poses a double threat to the subject. By endowing the mother with a phallus, the fetish is in danger of erasing the subject before an all-powerful and all-encompassing other. This phallic mother must then be abjected (both rejected and degraded) if the subject is to survive without slipping into psychosis. The imagistic potential for this abjection is, curiously, already present in the fetish itself: insofar as it marks the mother's castration, the fetish participates in the abjection of the mother as that incomplete, not-quite other from whom the subject must separate itself.

For the relevant texts from Bataille and for critical discussion, see *More & Less*, ed. Sylvère Lotringer (Pasadena, Calif.: Art Center College of Design, 1999). Also see Julia Kristeva, *Powers of Horror: An Essay on Abjection*, trans. Leon S. Roudiez (New York: Columbia University Press, 1982); and Julia Kristeva, *Tales of Love*, trans. Leon S. Roudiez (New York: Columbia University Press, 1987).

10 See especially E. L. McCallum, *Object Lessons: How to Do Things with Fetishism* (Albany: State University of New York Press, 1999).

11 On Marie of Oignies, see Bernard McGinn, *The Flowering of Mysticism: Men and Women in the New Mysticism, 1200–1350* (New York: Crossroad, 1998), 32–41; Michel Lauwers, "Expérience Béguinale et récit hagiographique: A propos de la 'Vitae Mariae Oigniacensis' de Jacques de Vitry (vers 1215)" *Journal des Savants* (1989): 61–103; and Michel Lauwers, "Entre Beguinisme et Mysticisme: La Vie de Marie d'Oignies (d. 1213) de Jacques de Vitry ou la définition d'une sainteté féminine," *Ons geestelijk Erf* 66 (1992): 46–69.

12 VMO "Prologue" 6, 637; LMO 21.

13 VMO "Prologue" 8, 638; LMO 23.

14 VMO "Prologue" 7, 637; LMO 21. The reference to the king in the chamber is to a standard mystical reading of the Song of Songs.

15 See Robert Sweetman, "Christine of St. Trond's Preaching Apostolate," *Vox Benedictina* 9 (1992): 67–97; and McGinn, *Flowering*, 161–62.

16 This understanding of Newman's project was suggested to me by Lyndal Roper's arguments for the usefulness of psychoanalysis for historical work, although the nature of the texts with which Roper works and the quality of her analysis differ considerably from Newman's. See Lyndal Roper, *Oedipus and the Devil: Witchcraft, Sexuality, and Religion in Early Modern Europe* (New York: Routledge, 1994), 1–4.

17 Thomas's account of Christina's life is more detailed, and more extraordinary, than James's. The broad appeal and influence of both of these vitae is suggested by the manuscript traditions. James's *Life of Marie of Oignies* survives in twenty-six Latin manuscripts, one French, and one English version; Thomas's *Life of Christina* in twelve Latin, one English, and three Dutch manuscript versions. For this information, see Barbara Newman, "Hildegard and Her Hagiographers: The Remaking of Female Sainthood," in *Gendered Voices: Medieval Saints and Their Hagiographers*, ed. Catherine M. Mooney (Philadelphia: University of Pennsylvania Press, 1999), 32.

18 See Barbara Newman, "Possessed by the Spirit: Devout Women, Demoniacs, and the Apostolic Life in the Thirteenth Century," *Speculum* 73 (1998): 733–70. Newman does not explicitly extend this diagnosis to other women represented in thirteenth-century hagiography, but given the commonality of their "symptoms"—catatonia and trances, paralysis, inability to speak or involuntary locutions, coughing and production of excessive phlegm, the proliferation of other bodily fluids, etc.—such an extension is implied.

19 Cited in Newman, "Possessed," 764. There are striking parallels between these descriptions and Charcot's photographs of hysterics in extreme bodily contortions and spasms.

20 It is probably worthy of note that Thomas *does not* put it that way. For the reference, see Newman, "Possessed," 765.

21 Ibid., 763.

22 Charcot remained puzzled by these curative skills. Also, in another text, cowritten with Paul Richer in 1886, Charcot retroactively diagnosed demonic possession as hysteria. See Jean-Martin Charcot and Paul Richer, *Les démoniaques dans l'art suivi de "La foi qui guérit"* (Paris: Macula, 1984); and Cristina Mazzoni, *Saint Hysteria: Neurosis, Mysticism, and Gender in European Culture* (Ithaca, N.Y.: Cornell University Press, 1996), 21–22. For Freud on the parallels between hysteria and possession, see Carlo Ginzburg, "Freud, the Wolf-Man, and the Were-Wolves," in *Myths, Emblems, Clues*, trans. John and Anne Tedeschi (London: Hutchinson Radius, 1990), 150–51. For the links between hysteria, modern anorexia nervosa, and medieval inedia, see Rudolph Bell, *Holy Anorexia* (Chicago: University of Chicago Press, 1985); and Éric Bidaud, *Anorexie mentale, ascèse, mystique: Une approche psychanalytique* (Paris: Denoël, 1997). In his book on hysteria, Christopher Bollas reads Francis of Assisi as an ascetic hysteric. See Christopher Bollas, *Hysteria* (New York: Routledge, 2000), 80–81.

23 See, for example, the debate between Oskar Pfister and Martin Grabmann with regard to Margaret Ebner—discussed by Gertrud Jaron Lewis in *By Women, for Women, about Women: The Sister-Books of Fourteenth-Century Germany* (Toronto: Pontifical Institute of Medieval Studies,

1996), 70. Nancy Partner argues for the viability of hysteria as an explanation of medieval mysticism. See Nancy Partner, "Reading *The Book of Margery Kempe*," *Exemplaria* 3 (1991): 29–66; and Nancy Partner, "Did Mystics Have Sex?" in *Desire and Discipline: Sex and Sexuality in the Premodern West*, ed. Jacqueline Murray and Konrad Eisenbichler (Toronto: University of Toronto Press, 1996), 296–311. For a more nuanced approach, see Hope Phyllis Weissman, "Margery Kempe in Jerusalem: *Hysterica Compassio* in the Late Middle Ages," in *Acts of Interpretation: The Text in Its Contexts, 700–1600*, ed. Mary J. Carruthers and Elizabeth D. Kirk (Norman, Okla.: Pilgrim Books, 1982), 201–17.

24 My own tendency has been to distinguish mysticism from hagiography, in which, before the fourteenth century, most of the hysterical symptoms occur, and then to read the fourteenth- and fifteenth-century texts as autohagiographical. I will both extend and problematize that argument here.

25 On an alternative reading of Margery Kempe as "queer," see Carolyn Dinshaw, *Getting Medieval: Sexualities and Communities, Pre- and Postmodern* (Durham, N.C.: Duke University Press, 1999), 143–83. I think that Kempe's queerness in part emerges from her insistence on her own interpretations of her experience.

26 Newman, "Possessed," 766.

27 Ibid., 766–67.

28 Dyan Elliott, "The Physiology of Rapture and Female Spirituality," in *Medieval Theology and the Natural Body*, ed. Peter Biller and A. J. Minnis (Woodbridge, Suffolk: York Medieval Press, 1997), 142.

29 McGinn, *Flowering*, 37–38. Also see Mary Wack on William of Auvergne's assimilation of the languages of lovesickness and mystical rapture. Mary F. Wack, *Lovesickness in the Middle Ages: The "Viaticum" and Its Commentaries* (Philadelphia: University of Pennsylvania Press, 1990), 23–24.

30 Elliott, "Physiology," 159–60.

31 Elliott cites William of Auvergne and Albert the Great as well as Thomas of Cantimpré on the issue. See Elliott, "Physiology," 159–60.

32 The relationship between medieval and modern conceptions of hysteria requires further elaboration. My concern here is with the hermeneutical questions raised by the deployment of both understandings of hysteria.

33 Commentator B in H. R. Lemay, *Women's Secrets: A Translation of Pseudo-Albertus Magnus's 'De Secretis Mulierum' with Commentaries* (Albany: State University of New York Press, 1992), 134. Jacquart and Thomasset tend to use the terms interchangeably. See Danielle Jacquart and Claude Thomasset, *Sexuality and Medicine in the Middle Ages*, trans. Matthew Adamson (Princeton, N.J.: Princeton University Press, 1988).

34 In one of the few cases where we have letters between a woman and her spiritual advisor or collaborator, the beguine Christina of Stommeln tends to read her experiences as demonic attacks, whereas the Dominican Peter of Dacia provides the mystical reading. See McGinn, *Flowering*, 179; and John Coakley, "A Marriage and Its Observer: Christine of Stommeln, the Heavenly Bridegroom, and Friar Peter of Dacia," in *Gendered Voices*, 99–117.

35 It is worth noting that in his *Life of Margaret of Ypres*, Thomas does depict the collaboration between a male confessor and a beguine; thus we have at least some reason to think that had a male advisor influenced Christina's interpretation of her experience, Thomas would have recorded it.

36 The medieval situation also raises new questions about modern hysteria, accounts of which are primarily supplied by male doctors and analysts. Perhaps some of these women and men, like Janet's Madeleine, had different interpretations of their symptoms.

37 The term "ventriloquism" itself emerges from demonology. It literally means speaking from the belly and was used to denote demonic possession. See Janet Beizer, *Ventriloquized Bodies: Narratives of Hysteria in Nineteenth-Century France* (Ithaca, N.Y.: Cornell University Press, 1994), 47.

38 For this information and the text of the vita in Latin and English, see LBN.

39 On mystical hagiographies, see Simone Roisin, "L'efflorescence cistercienne et le courant féminin de piété au XIIIe siècle," *Revue d'histoire ecclésiastique* 39 (1943): 342–78; Simone Roisin, *L'hagiographie cistercienne dans le diocèse de Liège au XIIIe siècle* (Louvain: Bibliothèque de l'Université, 1947); Caroline Walker Bynum, *Holy Feast and Holy Fast: The Religious Significance of Food to Medieval Women* (Berkeley: University of California Press, 1987); and Caroline Walker Bynum, *Fragmentation and Redemption: Essays on Gender and the Human Body in Medieval Religion* (New York: Zone Books, 1991).

40 LBN bk. 3, chap. 16. Ursula Peters questions the attestation of "Seven Manners" to Beatrice of Nazareth, arguing that the differences between this text and book 3, chapter 14 of *The Life of Beatrice* are too great for the latter to be a translation of the former. Yet the similarities in structure, metaphors, and images are exceptionally strong and clearly override their divergences. See Ursula Peters, *Religiöse Erfahrung als literarisches Faktum: Zur Vorgeschichte und Genese frauenmystischer Texte des 13. und 14. Jahrhunderts* (Tübingen: Niemeyer, 1988), 32–33. For additional comparisons of the two texts, see Amy Hollywood, "Inside Out: Beatrice of Nazareth and Her Hagiographer," in *Gendered Voices*, 78–98; Else Marie Wiberg Pedersen, "The In-Carnation of Beatrice of Nazareth's Theology," in *New Trends in Feminine Spirituality: The Holy Women of Liège and Their Impact*, ed. Juliette Dor, Lesley Johnson, and Jocelyn Wogan-Browne (Turnhout: Brepols, 1999), 61–80; and Nicholas Watson, "Desire for the Past," *Studies in the Age of Chaucer* 21 (1999): 82–83.

41 LBN bk. 3, chap. 15.

42 LBN bk. 1, chap. 16.

43 LBN bk. 1, chaps. 11, 13–18; bk. 2, chap. 16; bk. 3, chaps. 2, 4–5, 14.

44 LBN bk. 1, chap. 18; bk. 3, chap. 5.

45 LBN bk. 3, chap. 8.

46 See LBN bk. 1, chap. 11; bk. 2, chap. 18; bk. 3, chaps. 1, 18.

47 Hollywood, "Inside Out."

48 The hagiographer here also follows a familiar topos of the genre, tears as a mark of compunction and mystical fervor. See, for example, VMO n. 18.

49 Here, of course, I refer to the modern sense of "hysterical," since Beatrice's medieval interpreters did not read her body as hysterical in their sense of the term. I differ here slightly from my own earlier reading of the text. See Hollywood, "Inside Out."

50 My thanks to Walter Simons for help with this difficult passage and for other suggestions about reading the Dutch text.

51 This movement can be traced in texts involving the stigmata. Although in the early texts describing this phenomenon, the visibility of the markings was unimportant, in later texts it takes precedence. On this phenomenon, see Herbert Thurston, *The Physical Phenomena of Mysticism* (Chicago: Regnery, 1952); and Antoine Imbert-Gourbeyre, *La Stigmatisation: L'Extase*

divine et les miracles de Lourdes: Réponse aux libres-penseurs, 2 vols. (Clermont-Ferrand: Librairie Catholique, 1894).

52 See LBN bk. 2, chap. 16; bk. 3, chap. 2.

53 LBN bk. 2, chap. 16; bk. 3, chap. 8.

54 Christina the Astonishing, unlike Beatrice, is represented as enacting the most extreme forms of bodily asceticism and self-inflicted suffering. This is possible because her body was said to be untouched by her trials (hence its quasi-resurrected quality). Newman is unable to account for this aspect of Christina's vita. Although a certain lack of feeling is associated with some modern forms of hysteria, Christina is said to feel the pain without her body being marked in any way.

55 Although there are important exceptions, asceticism and paramystical phenomena are more prominent in the hagiographies of women than in those of men. See, for example, Bynum, Holy Feast, 82–87, 103–4, 237–44; André Vauchez, La Sainteté en Occident aux derniers siècles du moyen âge d'après les procès de canonisation et les documents hagiographiques (Paris: Ecole Française de Rome, 1981), 450–55; and Donald Weinstein and Rudolph M. Bell, Saints and Society: The Two Worlds of Western Christendom, 1000–1700 (Chicago: University of Chicago Press, 1982), 123–27, 153–57, 236–37. Francis of Assisi and Henry Suso are two famous exceptions. Others include male conversi within the Cistercian order, suggesting the importance of social status as well as gender in determining patterns of sanctity. The importance of suffering and extreme asceticism in late medieval female sanctity can be seen in Brenda Bolton's reading of the hagiographies of the mulieres sanctae as "desert mothers"— early Christian male models of ascetic heroism are transformed in the later Middle Ages into women. It is precisely the gap between the desert fathers and Beatrice's life and text that creates difficulties for her hagiographer. See Brenda Bolton, "Mulieres Sanctae," in Women in Medieval Society, ed. Susan Mosher Stuard (Philadelphia: University of Pennsylvania Press, 1976), 141–58.

56 On the identification of women with the body, see Joan Ferrante, Woman as Image in Medieval Literature (New York: Columbia University Press, 1975), 17–35; Vern Bullough, "Medieval Medical and Scientific Views of Women," Viator 4 (1973): 485–501; and Bynum, Fragmentation, 181–238.

57 See Elizabeth Alvilda Petroff, "The Visionary Tradition in Women's Writing: Dialogue and Autobiography," in Medieval Women's Visionary Literature, ed. Elizabeth Alvilda Petroff (Oxford: Oxford University Press, 1986), 3–86; and Caroline Walker Bynum, Jesus as Mother: Studies in the Spirituality of the High Middle Ages (Berkeley: University of California Press, 1982), 247–62. For the authorizing function of visionary experience, see Thomas Aquinas, Summa Theologiae, ed. Blackfriars (New York: McGraw Hill, 1964–81), pt. 3, supplement, q. 39, a. 1; and Barbara Newman, Sister of Wisdom: Saint Hildegard's Theology of the Feminine (Berkeley: University of California Press, 1987), 34–41.

58 Karen Scott and Barbara Newman suggest other reasons for the differences between women's writings and male-authored hagiography. Scott suggests, in the case of Catherine of Siena, that modesty might play a role. Yet Beatrice makes astonishing claims for the soul that raise doubts about this possible motivation. Newman suggests more plausibly that Beatrice's hagiographer might have been worried about accusations of heresy and so "sanitized" and "dumbed down" her claims. See Karen Scott, "Mystical Death, Bodily Death: Catherine of Siena and Raymond of Capua on the Mystic's Encounter with God," in Gendered

Voices, 136–67; and Barbara Newman, "Hildegard." For an account of suspicions about beguines in the diocese of Cambrai, in which Beatrice lived, see Newman, "Hildegard," 28–29.

59 Elizabeth Castelli's comments about the movement between the visionary and object of vision in *The Martyrdom of Perpetua and Felicitas* helped me to clarify this point. See Elizabeth Castelli, "Mortifying the Body, Curing the Soul: Beyond Ascetic Dualism in *The Life of Saint Syncletica*," *Differences* 4 (1992): 151, n. 17.

60 Newman, on the other hand, implicitly maintains the split posited by Beauvoir between that which happens *to* a subject and that which is controlled by a sane, free consciousness, although Newman does acknowledge that Christina might eventually have internalized the interpretations of her bodily and psychic experience provided by male leaders. There are aspects of the quite anomalous *Life of Christina the Astonishing* (perhaps particularly its roots in the brief, and more "believable," description of Christina's life in James of Vitry's *Life of Marie of Oignies*) that suggest her experience may have been more radically somatic than Beatrice's. Yet I hesitate to foreclose the possibility that (1) Christina herself interpreted her bodily and psychic states religiously and (2) she may have talked about these states in a way quite different from their depiction by either James or Thomas (who never knew her).

61 Archbishop Fulk of Toulouse was instrumental in campaigns against the Cathars, supporting the rise of the Dominicans as an antiheretical preaching order and going north himself to preach and gather money and men for the crusade against the heretics instituted by Pope Innocent III in 1208. It was while he was on this preaching tour that he came to Liège and met James of Vitry, Marie of Oignies, and other holy women. He was also the sponsor of a Dominican convent for women founded by Dominic in Prouille as a refuge for converts from Catharism and as a place to educate women in an orthodox fashion. See McGinn, *Flowering*, 35–36; and Brenda Bolton, "Fulk of Toulouse: The Escape that Failed," in *Church, Society, and Politics*, ed. Derek Baker (Oxford: Blackwell, 1975), 83–93.

62 On the antiheretical thrust of the *Life of Marie of Oignies*, see Iris Geyer, *Marie von Oignies: Eine hochmittelalterliche Mystikerin zwischen Ketzerei und Rechtgläubigkeit* (Frankfurt: Peter Lang, 1992), esp. 221–24.

63 On the Cathar heresy, see *Heresies of the High Middle Ages*, ed. Walter Wakefield and Austin Evans (New York: Columbia University Press, 1969); and Malcolm Lambert, *The Cathars* (Cambridge: Basil Blackwell, 1998). For its appeal to women, see R. Abels and E. Harrison, "The Participation of Women in Languedocian Catharism," *Mediaeval Studies* 41 (1979): 215–51. Abels and Harrison estimate that up to a third of the *perfecti* may have been women and show that women *perfectae* could preach and administer the *consolamentum* (the laying on of hands by which the perfect were ordained), although probably mostly in emergency situations. See Abels and Harrison, "Participation," 227, n. 61. These perfect women were probably seen as becoming male or sexless through asceticism.

64 We should not let this subordination of women to priestly authority obscure the enormous prestige that Marie had in the eyes of James, or Lutgard of Aywières in those of Thomas, both of whom used women's bodily sanctity to shore up their own troubled authority. For an argument, in a similar vein, about the dual authorization of hagiographer and subject, see Dyan Elliott, "Authorizing a Life: The Collaboration of Dorothea of Montau and John Marienwerder," in *Gendered Voices*, 168–91.

65 Certain mystical texts by women challenge this priestly supremacy in limited ways. See, for example, Mechthild of Magdeburg's vision in which John the Baptist gives her the Eucharist, and her defense of that vision. Mechthild of Magdeburg, *The Flowing Light of the Godhead*, trans. Frank Tobin (New York: Paulist Press, 1998), bk. 2. chap. 4; bk. 6, chap. 36.

66 In his supplement to the *Life of Marie of Oignies*, Thomas of Cantimpré insists that Marie was the only holy woman in the area who possessed discretion of spirits and so was never deceived by a demon in any way. Thomas of Cantimpré, *Vita Mariae Oigniacensis Supplementum*, in *Acta Sanctorum*, ed. J. Bolland and G. Henschenius (Brussels: Culture et civilisation, 1965–70): vol. 23, chap. 2.

67 For a critique of Bynum's inattention to the ways in which women's sanctity and authority were premised on the suppression of others, see Kathleen Biddick, "Genders, Bodies, Borders: Technologies of the Visible," in *The Shock of Medievalism* (Durham, N.C.: Duke University Press, 1998), 135–62. Also see David Aers, "The Humanity of Christ: Reflections on Orthodox Late Medieval Representations," in David Aers and Lynn Staley, *The Powers of the Holy: Religion, Politics, and Gender in Late Medieval English Culture* (University Park: Pennsylvania State University Press, 1996), 15–42; and Richard Rambuss, *Closet Devotions* (Durham, N.C.: Duke University Press, 1998), 16–18, 42–49. For arguments that Bynum offers a redemptive model of history, see Dominick LaCapra, *Representing the Holocaust: History, Theory, Trauma* (Ithaca, N.Y.: Cornell University Press, 1994), 178–83; and, in a different and more sympathetic light, Watson, "Desire for the Past."

68 As Bynum argues, women are more likely to be shown enduring physical illness, and men being physically healed. There are a number of women cured of demonic possession within the hagiographical tradition, no doubt reflecting the cultural perception of their greater susceptibility to that problem. See Bynum, *Holy Feast*, 199–200.

69 As Elliott shows, Thomas of Cantimpré's *De apibus* was a key source for John Nider's *Formicarium*, which in turn was a central resource for the *Malleus Maleficarum*. See Elliott, "Physiology," 154–55.

70 Ibid., 162.

71 Ibid., 164.

72 Ibid., 167. Also see also Nancy Caciola, "Discerning Spirits: Sanctity and Possession in the Later Middle Ages" (Ph.D. diss., University of Michigan, 1994); Peter Dinzelbacher, *Heilige oder Hexen? Schicksale auffälliger Frauen in Mittelalter und Frühneuzeit* (Zurich: Artemis and Winker, 1995); Richard Kieckhefer, "The Holy and the Unholy: Sainthood, Witchcraft, and Magic in Late Medieval Europe," in *Christendom and Its Discontents: Exclusion, Persecution, and Rebellion, 1000–1500*, ed. Scott L. Waugh and Peter Diehl (Cambridge: Cambridge University Press, 1996); Newman, "Possessed"; and Dyan Elliott, *Fallen Bodies: Pollution, Sexuality, and Demonology in the Middle Ages* (Philadelphia: University of Pennsylvania Press, 1999), esp. 127–63.

73 See Elliott, *Fallen Bodies*, esp. 127–63.

74 Bynum, *Holy Feast*, 151.

75 The hagiographer does not explicitly compare Beatrice's suffering to that of Christ on the cross, yet the increasing emphasis on her suffering, bloody, and wrenched body suggests the identification. See, for example, LBN bk. 3, chaps. 1, 2, 3, 4, 14. On the centrality of blood to late medieval meditations on Christ, see Thomas Bestul, *Texts of the Passion: Latin Devotional Literature and Medieval Society* (Philadelphia: University of Pennsylvania Press, 1996), 26–68.

76 Mechthild of Magdeburg, for example, describes her first "greeting from God" as coming unbidden and without any special preparation. In part sparked by a desire to emphasize the freedom of God's gift to the soul, the refusal to discuss the 'works' of the body and the soul also highlights human freedom. See Mechthild of Magdeburg, *Flowing Light*, bk. 4, chap. 2.

77 See Judith Butler, "Melancholy Gender/Refused Identifications," in *The Psychic Life of Power: Theories in Subjection* (Stanford, Calif.: Stanford University Press, 1997), 132–50; and Sigmund Freud, "Mourning and Melancholia," in *On Metapsychology*, trans. James Strachey (New York: Penguin Books, 1984), 245–68. Although Freud distinguishes mourning, in which loss is avowed and worked through, from melancholy, in which loss is disavowed through incorporation, ultimately the two categories collapse into each other, with all mourning appearing melancholic. And although Freud does not make it explicit, as long as the objects lost are gendered, the nature of their incorporation will be tied to gender and to the gendering of identity. On the gendering of melancholy, see Juliana Schiesari, *The Gendering of Melancholia: Feminism, Psychoanalysis, and the Symbolics of Loss in Renaissance Literature* (Ithaca, N.Y.: Cornell University Press, 1992).

78 Sigmund Freud, "The Ego and the Id," in *The Complete Psychological Works*, 19:25–26. On the bodily ego, see also Kaja Silverman, *The Threshold of the Visible World* (New York: Routledge, 1996), 9–37; and Sarah Beckwith, "Passionate Regulation: Enclosure, Ascesis, and the Feminist Imaginary," *South Atlantic Quarterly* 93 (1994): 814.

79 Drew Leder, *The Absent Body* (Chicago: University of Chicago Press, 1990), 69–99; and Elaine Scarry, *The Body in Pain: The Making and Unmaking of the World* (Oxford: Oxford University Press, 1985), 27–59.

80 Butler is right, I think, to associate subject formation with the process of melancholic incorporation and with experiences of pain. However, we should distinguish between bodily pain (illness and other forms of physical pain that help the child articulate a bodily morphology) and psychic pain (at the loss of a desired object), despite the fact that the two experiences can probably never be fully disentangled. Both are inevitable aspects of embodied existence and affect all human beings, regardless of sex difference (although the ways in which we experience them are perhaps inevitably gendered).

81 Beckwith, "Passionate Regulation," 817.

82 Ibid., 818.

83 Beckwith uses Foucault's aphorism at the opening of her essay: "The soul is the prison of the body." See Beckwith, "Passionate Regulation," 803.

84 Beatrice's abjection of the body alone arguably distinguishes her from Angela of Foligno, who abjects herself both body and soul in identification with the abject body of Christ.

85 This use of hagiographies is made evident by the manuscript tradition for Beatrice's own vita. Of the four known manuscripts, one is contained in a collection of spiritual writings produced at the request of John of St. Trond, a monk in Villers, when he was the chaplain of the Cistercian convent at Vrouwenpark in Wezemaal. The manuscript, completed in 1320, was presumably collected for the edification of these Cistercian nuns. Examination of this and similar manuscript collections might further elucidate how hagiographies were read in relationship to other forms of religious writing. For the manuscript information, see LBN xxi. The influence of hagiography is suggested by the development of autohagio-graphical genres. When women's spirituality comes under more stringent ecclesiastical

scrutiny, women repeat these hagiographical gestures in their own texts. See Amy Holly-wood, *The Soul as Virgin Wife: Mechthild of Magdeburg, Marguerite Porete, and Meister Eckhart* (Notre Dame, Ind.: University of Notre Dame Press, 1995), 201–6.

86 It is worth mentioning that Beatrice had early contact with beguines, women who wished to live religious lives in the world. The beguines' rejection of enclosure and their desta-bilization of the boundaries between inside and outside played a key role in reactions against them. A comparison of the *Ancrene Wisse* with Julian of Norwich's *Showings* in light of Beckwith's reading of the former text would clarify to what extent the anchorite rule was enacted in the ways Beckwith suggests.

87 Judith Butler, *Bodies That Matter: On the Discursive Limits of "Sex"* (New York: Routledge, 1993), 76; cited in Beckwith, "Passionate Regulation," 818.

88 Beckwith, "Passionate Regulation," 818–19.

89 I cannot speak here to the situation of women south of the Alps. For the complexities of northern Europe, see Hollywood, *Virgin Wife*, 201–6.

90 Although arguably Marguerite's annihilation of the soul itself occurs through the suffering deployment of love. See Amy Hollywood, "Eckhart's Apophatic Ethics," *Eckhart Review* 10 (2001): 35–46.

91 Irigaray's inattention to the history of women's struggles against male dominance is re-flected in the paucity of reference to women and women's writing within her work. Other than "*La Mystérique*," her only engagement with women's texts that I know of are brief dis-cussions of Simone de Beauvoir, a conversation with the biologist Hélène Roach, and a review of Elizabeth Schussler-Fiorenza's *In Memory of Her*. See JTN 9–14, 37–44; and Luce Irigaray, "Equal to Whom?" *Differences* 1 (1989): 59–76. Irigaray's inability to see women's historical resistance to male dominance is tied to her acceptance of the terms set by psy-choanalysis, at least for the past. On the limits of psychoanalysis for understanding certain historical moments, see Page duBois, *Sowing the Body: Psychoanalysis and Ancient Representations of Women* (Chicago: University of Chicago Press, 1988).

92 Grace Jantzen rightly suggests that some women mystics can be reread in this light, al-though the centrality of death, loss, and trauma in the work of most of these women would also need to be taken into account. See Grace Jantzen, *Becoming Divine: Towards a Femi-nist Philosophy of Religion* (Bloomington: Indiana University Press, 1999).

93 On the relationship between hysteria and melancholy, see SA 78–87; SO 66–73.

94 See Schiesari, *Gendering of Melancholia*.

95 For some of the most interesting of these discussions, see Patricia Huntington, *Ecstatic Subjects, Utopia, and Recognition: Kristeva, Heidegger, Irigaray* (Albany: State University of New York Press, 1998); Jantzen, *Becoming Divine*; and Christine Battersby, *The Phenomenal Woman: Feminist Metaphysics and the Patterns of Identity* (New York: Routledge, 1998). Huntington and Battersby, in particular, are aware of the limitations of Irigaray's deployment of sexual difference, although they do not ask where it comes from, as I have tried to do here.

96 See, for example, Sharon Patricia Holland, *Raising the Dead: Readings of Death and (Black) Subjectiv-ity* (Durham, N.C.: Duke University Press, 2000), esp. 1–9.

97 Is the denigration of fetishism a valuing of "knowledge" over desire and belief? If so, then in finding the fetish in Irigaray's argument we find the true site of her desire.

98 In other words, we need to distinguish analytically sex–gender differences from sexuality: hence the centrality to feminist theory of the projects of queer theory, which always

point to the complexities and multiplicities of bodies and desires, complexities that are often forced to find a place for themselves within a two-sex system, but that, nonetheless, constantly resist those constraints and point to multiple ways of thinking about sexuality. In order to critique the continuation of phallic modes within it, queer theory also needs feminist theory (hence the continued relevance of the Irigarayan critique of Bataille and Lacan). For queer readings of medieval mysticism, see Karma Lochrie, "Mystical Acts, Queer Tendencies," in *Constructing Medieval Sexuality*, ed. Karma Lochrie, Peggy McCracken, and James A. Schultz (Minneapolis: University of Minnesota Press, 1997), 180–200; Dinshaw, *Getting Medieval*, 143–82; and Amy Hollywood, "Sexual Desire, Divine Desire; or Queering the Beguines," in *Queer Theology: New Perspectives on Sex and Gender*, ed. Gerard Loughlin (Oxford: Basil Blackwell, forthcoming).

99 For Irigaray the originary trauma is sexual differentiation itself. As reconfigured by a new imaginary, she suggests, there would be no originary trauma, a suggestion that points again to the utopianism of her project (SA 72; SO 61).

100 Françoise Meltzer, "Re-Embodying," in *God, the Gift, and Postmodernism*, ed. John Caputo and Michael J. Scanlon (Indianapolis: Indiana University Press, 1999), 267–68.

101 See Caroline Walker Bynum, "Why All the Fuss about the Body? A Medievalist's Perspective," *Critical Inquiry* 22 (1995): 1–34; and Amy Hollywood, "Transcending Bodies," *Religious Studies Review* 25 (1999): 13–18.

CONCLUSION

1 Of course, one still wonders why it is necessary for this first, primary caregiver to be figured necessarily and only as female. On the possibility of reconfiguring models of kinship through meditation on the figure of Antigone, see Judith Butler, *Antigone's Claim: Kinship between Life and Death* (New York: Columbia University Press, 2000).

2 Irigaray rejects melancholic incorporation as a cannibalistic assimilation of the other. Instead she favors bodily memory, in which the otherness of the (m)other is never forgotten. She rejects incorporation as the end toward which bodily memory and repetition work, yet at the same time she suggests that bodily memory, reconfigured as a memory of the body's pleasures, can serve as the imaginary and symbolic support of feminine subjectivity. This attempt to avoid the Freudian collapse of mourning and melancholia depends ultimately on the rejection of both as crucial moments in subject formation. Preferable, I think, is Derrida's move to articulate the deep ambiguity of mourning and melancholy as an "unfaithful fidelity" in which "success fails" and "failure succeeds." If we fully interiorize the other, we fail to remember him or her as other; only in interiorizing the other as other than, and greater than, one's self does one really mourn. See Penelope Deutscher, "Mourning the Other, Cultural Cannibalism, and the Politics of Friendship (Jacques Derrida and Luce Irigaray)," *Differences* 10 (1998): 159–84; Dennis King Keenan, "Eucharistic Sacrifice" (paper presented at the annual meeting of the American Academy of Religion, Nashville, Tenn., November 2000); and Jacques Derrida, *Memoires: For Paul de Man*, trans. Cecile Lindsay, Jonathan Culler, and Eduardo Cadava (New York: Columbia University Press, 1986), 35.

3 See Juliana Schiesari, *The Gendering of Melancholia: Feminism, Psychoanalysis, and the Symbolics of Loss in Renaissance Literature* (Ithaca, N.Y.: Cornell University Press, 1992), 64–66.

4 Angela of Foligno, *Il Libro della Beata Angela da Foligno*, ed. Ludger Thier and Abele Calufetti

(Grottaferrata: Editiones Collegii S. Bonaventurae ad Claras Aquas, 1985), 338; Angela of Foligno, *Complete Works*, trans. Paul Lachance (New York: Paulist Press, 1993), 197. This is just one of many similar images of abjection found throughout Angela's *Memorial*. See *Libro*, 144, 206–8, 242, 302–4; *Works*, 128, 150–51, 162–63, 184–85.

5   Irigaray thus attempts to avoid the association of femininity with trauma, which she argues is inscribed within phallocentric psychoanalysis. For an analysis and critique of the tendency within feminist politics and theory to define political identities in terms of injury and trauma, see Wendy Brown, *States of Injury: Power and Freedom in Late Modernity* (Princeton, N.J.: Princeton University Press, 1995), esp. 52–76. For an analysis of contemporary culture as a "wound culture" in which identity is defined in terms of injury, see Mark Seltzer, *Serial Killers: Death and Life in America's Wound Culture* (New York: Routledge, 1998), esp. 253–92. As Hal Foster notes with regard to contemporary theoretical and artistic redefinitions of experience in terms of trauma, trauma serves the agendas both of a poststructuralist dissolution of the subject and the nostalgia for the real that has recently questioned this "postmodern turn": "On the one hand, in art and theory, trauma discourse continues the poststructuralist critique of the subject by other means, for again, in a psychoanalytic register, there is no subject of trauma; the position is evacuated, and in this sense the critique of the subject is most radical here. On the other hand, in popular culture, trauma is treated as an event that guarantees the subject, and in this psychologistic register the subject, however disturbed, rushes back as witness, testifier, survivor. Here is indeed a traumatic subject, and it has absolute authority, for one cannot challenge the trauma of another: one can only believe it, even identify with it, or not. *In trauma discourse, then, the subject is evacuated and elevated at once.* And in this way trauma magically resolves two contradictory imperatives in culture today: deconstructive analyses and identity politics. . . . Here the return of the real converges with the referential." Hal Foster, *The Return of the Real* (Cambridge, Mass.: MIT Press, 1996), 168.

6   Seltzer, *Serial Killers*, 137. We return full circle to the fantasies that engender a film like *Snuff*. A number of contemporary fiction writers, perhaps most intensively Dennis Cooper, follow Bataille in attempting to think through the complex relationships between desire, violence, fantasy, and the real. Cooper suggests that fiction is redemptive in that it provides the space for fantasy to flourish without danger to bodies. Seltzer's analysis raises the question of whether these types of distinctions still hold up within our contemporary "wound culture." See, especially, Dennis Cooper, *Frisk* (New York: Grove, 1991).

7   See Suzanne Guerlac, *Literary Polemics: Bataille, Sartre, Valéry, Breton* (Stanford, Calif.: Stanford University Press, 1997), 22–37.

8   Poets, not surprisingly, have done the most to think about loss and mourning from a feminist perspective. See Melissa F. Zeiger, *Beyond Consolation: Death, Sexuality, and the Changing Shapes of Elegy* (Ithaca, N.Y.: Cornell University Press, 1997), esp. 135–68. Within modern Western culture, Zeiger argues, women tend to refuse to let go, to "accept loss," and so fail to incorporate fully the lost other, thereby engaging in forms of traumatic repetition of loss that never reach the valorized forms of melancholy traditionally associated with men. The failure of incorporation suggests a gap between traumatic repetition and melancholic incorporation, a gap that someone like Beatrice of Nazareth attempts to overcome through forms of bodily incorporation. In calling for bodily memories of lost pleasures, Irigaray is

perhaps engaging in a similar move, although, as I have said, she is critical of the appropriative gestures of melancholy.

9 My thanks to Michelle Meyers for helping me articulate this point.

10 These formulations are indebted to a response given by Randall Styers to Ellen Armour's *Deconstruction, Feminist Theology,* and Tom Carlson's *Indiscretion* (paper presented at the annual meeting of the American Academy of Religion, Nashville, Tenn., November 2000).

11 Even if we accept the inevitability of death and its effects, should we still hold out for a utopia in which all violence—and so, under one set of definitions, all trauma—can be overcome? My sense is that both the deaths of others and our own deaths are often experienced as violence regardless of whether an agent can be identified. The danger with visions of utopic nonviolence is that the reality of loss is disavowed and/or repressed, and it inevitably returns in disruptive and debilitating forms.

12 Religion and mysticism are both deeply political and irreducible to politics in crucial ways. Hélène Cixous and Catherine Clément, like Kristeva, have theorized death, mourning, and their ties to gender and religion much more explicitly than has Irigaray. See Amy Hollywood, "Mysticism, Death, and Desire in the Work of Hélène Cixous and Catherine Clément," in *Religion in French Feminist Thought: Critical Perspectives,* ed. Morny Joy, Kathleen O'Grady, and Judith Poxon (London: Routledge, forthcoming).

13 Although she returns to a more Freudian conception of human drives—and so to closer links between body, affect, and language—Kristeva does not question the phallocentric nature of psychoanalysis, which accounts for the more ambiguous relationship of her work to both feminism and mysticism.

14 To similar arguments among historians that those dealing with the Holocaust will need to find a place for "ritual" and "acts of piety" within their work, Kerwin Lee Klein argues that what he detects as a "mystical" and "therapeutic" turn in Holocaust historiography is in danger of undermining the rational and critical basis of historical work. Again, I think the challenge is to find a place for both reason and affective discourses. Critical work will enable us to reflect on, among other things, how and if we can distinguish between traumatic repetition and "working through." See Kerwin Lee Klein, "On the Emergence of Memory in Historical Discourse," *Representations* 69 (2000): 127–50; Dominick LaCapra, *Representing the Holocaust: History, Theory, Trauma* (Ithaca, N.Y.: Cornell University Press, 1994), 207–23. Klein cites Michael Roth on the viewing of Claude Lanzmann's *Shoah* as a "ritual" and "act of piety." See Michael S. Roth, *The Ironist's Cage: Memory, Trauma, and the Construction of History* (New York: Columbia University Press, 1995), esp. 214–27.

abjection, 72, 345–46n. 9

absolute, the: the individual and, 129–30; women's desire for, 145

action: Bataille's rejection of, 63; contemplation and, 10, 11, 63, 115, 131, 298n. 27; on metaphysics and, 129–30

Aelred of Rievaulx, 337n. 30

Albert the Great, 246

analytic discourse, 179, 180; goal of, 150, 156, 157, 163, 164, 168

Angela of Foligno, 1, 6, 66, 68–75, 77, 78, 101, 275–76, 296–97n. 17; Bataille compared with, 91, 99; Bataille on, 64, 68–69, 114, 115, 148–49, 272; desire for mystical union with Christ, 71–72; desire to be all, 114; erotic mystical experiences, 68; experience of God, 1–2; identification with Christ's suffering, 91, 114; meditative practice, 71–72; Memorial, 68, 296n. 17; and ritual, 21; and servitude, 64; survival guilt, 91; wish to suffer with Christ, 95; writings of, as diaries/journals, 101–2

angels, 225–26

anguish, ecstatic, 95

anti-Semitism, 301n. 57

apophasis, 97–99, 108

apophatic memory, linguistic strategies of, 108

asceticism/ascetic practice, 96, 97, 99, 107, 254–55, 264; of Beatrice of Nazareth, 264–65; language of, 108

Atheological Summa (Bataille), 101, 114. See also *Guilty*; *Inner Experience*

Augustine of Hippo, 101, 103

autonomous women, 311n. 14

autonomy, 121, 196, 216–18, 266, 267

baroque, 162, 166

Baruzi, Jean, 319n. 50

Bataille, Georges, 116, 228, 273, 281n. 19; ambivalence toward mysticism, 63, 64; ambivalence toward the term "mysticism," 63–64, 114; on Angela of Foligno, 64, 68–69, 114, 115, 148–49, 272; Angela of Foligno compared with, 91, 99; anti-Hegelianism, 40; attempt to undermine phallic masculinity, 116; autobiographical readings of his work, 39–41, 45, 47, 48; Beauvoir compared with, 120; on catastrophe, 80; change in attitude toward writing, 293n. 57;

Bataille, Georges (*continued*)

"Coincidences," 44–45, 47, 48, 51, 52, 54; compared with other mystics, 101 (*see also specific mystics*); conception of mysticism, 113–14; conceptions of the mystical, 64; contingency of his survival, 80; contradictions in texts of, 108, 150; criticisms of, 27–33, 36–37, 41, 62, 321n. 8; on death, 105–6, 117, 139–45; as desiring to be all, 33, 35, 113; dualisms/dialectics in his work, 38, 57, 59, 63, 205; on ecstasy, 148; ecstasy, masochism, and his theory of religion, 56–59; erotic writings, 39, 42, 46; *Eroticism*, 39; on eroticism and religion, 298n. 34; eroticism and sexuality in writings of, 38–39, 48–50, 116–17; and ethics of catastrophe, 79–87; and fascism, 285–86nn. 4–5; Fautrier and, 310n. 9; "fleshy promiscuity" with his readers, 32–33, 35, 41; force of his desire, 88; gender dynamic in his texts, 114–16; on God, 64, 66–68, 104–5; how to approach his texts, 100; from image to text, 94–99; images of (Chinese) torture victim, 62, 81, 89, 90, 92, 93, 116, 276, 293n. 52, 297n. 18, 298n. 32, 303n. 2, 345n. 4; on interplay between communication and experience, 37; "The King of the Wood," 106–7; and Lacan, 149–50, 321–22nn. 11–12; language of virility, 114–16; life history, 61, 62, 286–87n. 9, 294–95n. 8; *Madame Edwarda*, 39, 116–17; meditation, traumatic memory, and, 75, 77–79; meditative practice, 56, 69–74, 89, 92, 94; mystic writing, 99–108; mysticism, history, and, 60–66, 295n. 10, 309n. 47; new mystical theology, 66–69; *On Nietzsche*, 33–35, 39, 57, 62, 82, 99, 100, 107, 204; on pedagogical purpose of his writing, 102; personality, 62; phallus vs. fetish in writings of, 47–51; on poetry, 114–15; prewar political

activities, 63; pseudonymity, 42, 45, 46; and psychoanalysis, 46–47; and the real, 63, 149–50; reality effects, 42–47; reflection on chance and ecstasy, 80; rejection of action, 63; relation between "experiential" and theoretical texts, 38–42; replies to Sartre, 33–35, 37, 288n. 15, 301n. 57, 307n. 33; resistance of his writings, 63; on ritual and desire, 21; and sacrifice, 204–5, 312n. 17; sadomasochism and, 51–56, 298n. 32, 303n. 2; Sartre's criticism of, 27–37, 67, 85, 88–89, 99, 113, 287–88nn. 12–15; self-annihilation and, 46, 47, 91; self-subverting quality of his appeal to experience, 40; sexual identity, 310n. 7; *Story of the Eye*, 39, 41, 42, 44, 45, 50–54, 58; style, 32; survival guilt, 91; "The Tale," 44–45, 47, 51, 53, 54; *Theory of Religion*, 39, 58, 117; trauma, photography, and the scandal of the real, 88–94, 301n. 59, 303nn. 1–2; turn to mysticism, 63; types of language used by, 36–38, 40–41, 59; violence in his work, 44, 47, 48, 57 (*see also* sadomasochism); wartime experiences and motivations for wartime writing, 61, 62; Weil and, 309n. 50; witnessing, 88, 89; on writing, 106; writing strategies, 99–100; writing trauma, writing desire, 108–10. See also *Guilty; Inner Experience*

Beatrice of Nazareth, 185–86, 244; asceticism, 264–65; desire for freedom, 263; Irigaray compared with, 268, 269; methods used against forgetfulness, 258–59; and the mystical body, 247–53; "On the Seven Manners of Loving God," 240, 247, 248, 257–58, 262, 265; on traumatic repetition, melancholic incorporation, and interiority, 257–66; and ventriloquizing orthodoxy, 253–57

Beauvoir, Simone de, 6, 315–16nn. 26–30; ambivalence, 128, 140; Bataille compared with, 120; beliefs regarding God, 125–

26; on body and its relation to femininity, 316n. 30; as Carmelite, 125; on Christian mysticism, 118; on Christianity, 130; criticism of psychoanalytic accounts of sexuality, 151, 176, 315n. 22; on death and responsibility, 26, 123, 139–45; despair and dissatisfaction with life, 144; divergence from Sartre, 135, 139–40; encounters and relations with other writers, 25–26; existentialist ethic, 134, 135, 137, 140; on faith, 141–42; on freedom, responsibility, and situatedness, 134–37, 140, 142–43, 145, 151, 317n. 37; gendering of religion, 310n. 8; on hysteria, 243, 246, 247; Irigaray contrasted with, 198–99, 209, 266; and Lacan, 323n. 15; life history, 25–26, 124–26, 314nn. 15–17; loss of faith, 125, 126; on love of self, 132–34; on male-female relations, 135, 266–67; on metaphysics and action, 129–30; nostalgia, 19; overvaluation of masculinity, 318n. 46; *The Prime of Life* (memoir), 25–26; Sartre influenced by, 318–19n. 49; Sartre's influence on, 140; *She Came to Stay,* 120–22; "she wanted to be everything," 120–23; "Situation and Character," 132–33; on Teresa of Avila, 19, 128–29, 131, 133, 137–40, 142–44, 208; on woman's love of man and love of God, 123–29, 132; on women and religion, 132–34. See also *Second Sex*

Beauvoirian culturalism, 176–77
Beckwith, Sarah, 262, 264
being-for-itself vs. being-in-itself, 121, 140
belief: deconstructing, 220–29; as dependent on concealment, 222; and mastery, 223; problem of, 206–11
Bernini, Giovanni Lorenzo, 202
Bersani, Leo, 54, 302n. 65
Bhabha, Homi, 90
Blanchot, Maurice, 66, 105
bodily limitation, experience of, 20

bodily practices, 20
Bonaparte, Marie, 175–76, 330n. 8
Borel, Adrien, 46
Breton, André, 32
Butler, Judith, 260–61, 264, 325n. 21
Bynum, Caroline Walker, 217, 257, 282–83n. 27

Cadava, Eduardo, 93–94
Caruth, Cathy, 79
castrated mother, 169, 290n. 29
"castrating" principle, 168
castration, 116–18, 133, 181, 277; Lacan on, 157–58, 165–66, 168, 234; masochistic submission to, 52–53
castration anxiety, 157, 175, 271
catastrophe, 66, 109; ethics of, 79–87
Cathars, 254, 256, 257, 351n. 61
Catholicism, 254, 256, 321n. 9
Certeau, Michel de, 147, 282n. 21, 283n. 33
Charcot, Jean-Martin, 161–62, 243, 347n. 22
Cheah, Pheng, 231–32, 335n. 17
Chow, Rey, 304n. 3
Christ, 95, 130, 131; abjection of, 72; Beatrice of Nazareth and, 258, 259; Cathars vs. Catholics regarding the body of, 254, 256; crucifixion, 72–74, 77–78, 91–93, 204, 262; eroticized/feminized relationship with, 131; feminine imagery inscribed on, 192, 198–203; as feminized aspect of the divine, 199–203, 206–8; identification with, 72, 91, 95, 114, 199, 263; and life of contemplation, 71; as little (object) *a,* 206; suffering, 72–74, 77–78, 87, 91, 114, 260, 262; union/unity with, 70–72. *See also* Eucharist
Christian mysticism, 9, 19, 66, 67; Bataille on, 114; Beauvoir on, 118; Irigaray on, 203–5 (*see also* Irigaray, on Christ and feminine imagery); twentieth-century fascination with, 20. *See also specific topics*
Christian tradition, and primacy of sexual difference, 218

Christina the Astonishing, 241–44, 248, 253, 256, 350n. 54, 351n. 60
Cixous, Hélène, 3–4
Clairvaux, Cistercian Bernard of, 8
Clément, Catherine, 3–5, 327n. 59
Clover, Carol, 51–53
communication, 31, 203, 327n. 57; and experience, 37, 120; laceration and, 300n. 52
"confessions," 101–3
contemplation, 66; and action, 10, 11, 63, 71, 115, 131, 298n. 27; life of, 71
Cooper, Dennis, 356n. 6
Copernican revolution, 152
Cornell, Drucilla, 231
cross-identifications, 52
crucifix, 93
crucifixion, 83, 130; of Christ, 72–74, 77–78, 91–93, 204, 262. *See also* sacrifice

darkness, encounter with, 69–70
death, 123; Bataille on, 105–6, 117, 139–45; Beauvoir on, 26, 123, 139–45; desire for, 251–52; desire to come to terms with, 20; encountering/confronting, 46, 47, 105, 145; Irigaray on, 20, 227, 268, 270, 274, 275; and loss of mother's body, 274; and responsibility, 139–45; of self, 123 (*see also* self-annihilation, Bataille and); sex, gender, and, 20–21, 270, 275. *See also* mortality
death drive, 75, 220
demonic possession, 246, 255–57, 347nn. 18, 22, 352nn. 66, 68. *See also* hysteria, ventriloquizing
Derrida, Jacques, 40, 41, 46, 281n. 19, 283n. 33, 309n. 1; "To Speculate—On Freud," 220, 224, 228
desire, 67; Bataille on ritual and, 21; to be all/everything, 113, 114, 118, 120–23, 140, 142, 161, 165, 182, 267 (*see also* Bataille, as desiring to be all; Lacan, on desire to be everything); to be with another, 140; object of, 104; related to

God, 139; will and detachment from, 13; writing, 108–10
detachment, 97; from desire, 13
determinism, 151
Deutscher, Penelope, 212–14, 216
Dionysius the Areopagite, 9, 283n. 31
divine/divinity(ies): female, 217; Irigaray on subjectivity and, 213–20; need for feminine avatars of, 181; self-subverting nature of, 70
divine Person, as male, 127
"divine women," 184
"Divine Women" (Irigaray), 206, 209, 213, 219–20, 229, 337n. 34
Dora, Freud's case of, 3
dramatization, 71
Drinka, George Frederick, 280n. 8
dualistic hierarchies, 134, 215, 216

Eckhart, Meister, 7, 234; on Bible and the divine, 9, 97, 99; Sermon 86, 10–11; on suffering, 307n. 26
ecstasy: object of, 81, 104. *See also specific topics*
ecstatic anguish, 95
ecstatic standing outside of the self, 81
ego, imaginary (bodily), 262–64
ego ideal, imaginary, 261
elements, 215
Encore (Lacan), 64–65, 181, 261; Bataille and, 149–50; and feminine sexuality, 152, 176; goal of analytic discourse in, 157; and phallic function, 156, 176, 204. *See also* Lacan
erotic and spiritual, conflation of the, 127
erotic experience vs. mystical experience, 68
eroticism: and mysticism, 121–22; and religion, 57, 298n. 34. *See also specific topics*
erotic love, gendered ways of experiencing, 121–22
erotomania, 127–29
escapism and mysticism, 10
essentialism, 190. *See also* Irigaray, as biological/bodily essentialist
"eternal now," 113–14

ethic, existentialist, 134, 135, 137, 140
ethical relation to the real, 79
ethics, 63; of catastrophe, 79–87
Eucharist, 92, 98, 226
existence, 104; justifications for women's,
    122, 126, 127, 130, 132, 143, 313n. 8
existentialism, 29
existentialist ethic, 134, 135, 137, 140
experience. See inner experience
exscription, 108
externality. See interiority and externality

faith, 141–42
fascism, 285–86nn. 4–5, 304n. 3
Fautrier, Jean, 310n. 9
female divine, 228, 229
female divinities, 217
female genitals, 116–17
female power, 156
female psychosexual development: Freud's
    theory of, 175. See also psychosexual
    development
female sexuality: Lacan and psychoanalytic
    theory of, 176; question/problem of,
    152
female subjectivity, 124, 133; Irigaray on,
    189–90, 192–94, 206, 213
female- vs. male-authored mystical texts, 98
feminine avatars of the divine, need for
    completely, 181
"feminine evasiveness," 115–16
feminine imaginary, 193, 194, 209, 237,
    267, 338n. 42. See also under Christ
feminine jouissance, 150, 159–66, 179, 192,
    194
feminine libido, 176, 179
feminine vision of the world, 130
feminine vs. masculine forms of mysticism,
    7–9
femininity, 150; and fluidity, 193; primary,
    178; theories of, 174; transcending,
    129–33, 136
feminism, 271, 356n. 5; ambivalent
    relationship between mysticism and, 5;

Irigaray on, 5, 6, 177, 180–82, 330n.
    16; Lacan and, 167–70; and loss, 356n.
    8; and psychoanalysis in France, 167,
    173–86; rituals and, 21
"feminism": criticism of the term, 177,
    330–31n. 16; problem with the term,
    338–39n. 47
feminist philosophy, 278; Irigaray on tasks of,
    180–82
feminist theorists, on fetishism, 241
feminist utopians, and evasion of history,
    266–73
femme, la, 169
fetish, 47–51, 94; phallus as, 237
fetishism, 95, 106, 184–85, 332n. 35;
    and belief, 236–41; Freud on, 237,
    239, 267, 344–45n. 4; and hysteria,
    241–47, 263–65, 344–45n. 4; Irigaray
    on, 236–47, 267–71; melancholic
    incorporation and, 261; as response to
    sexual difference, 239
fetishistic scopophilia, 52, 53
fetishization, 109, 184, 270, 346n. 9; of
    female sex, 117, 118; of the heterosexual
    pair, 238–39; and masochism, 52;
    mortality and, 272; of the other, 90–91;
    of sexual difference, 267, 270, 271; of
    suffering body, 94–95
Feuerbach, Ludwig, 210, 230, 235, 237;
    account of religion, 211, 218, 234–35,
    237; The Essence of Christianity, 214, 218–19,
    229–31; notion of humanity, 230, 231;
    notion of species being, 230–32, 234
Fink, Bruce, 163
Flowing Light of the Godhead, The (Mechthild of
    Magdeburg), 101–3
Foucault, Michel, 313n. 6
Fouque, Antoinette, 177–79
fragmentation, 72
fragmented body, 83
Franciscans, 71
Francis of Assisi, 243
freedom, 263; and death of spirit, 11;
    Teresa of Avila and, 134–35, 143. See

freedom (continued)
    also autonomy; Beauvoir, on freedom,
    responsibility, and situatedness
Freud, Sigmund, 75; *Beyond the Pleasure Principle*,
    220–25, 260–61, 342n. 28; and the
    body, 152–55; on fetishism, 237, 239,
    267, 344–45n. 4; Irigaray's criticisms
    of, 239–40; Irigaray's indebtedness
    to, 184; and language, 154; on
    masochism, 54, 292n. 45; model of
    sexual differentiation, 239; "Mourning
    and Melancholia," 353n. 77; on primal
    loss or threat of loss, 183; theory of
    psychosexual development, 174–75
future, unknowability of the, 105, 109

Garric, Robert, 126
gender: identifications across, 52; woman as
    a, 230–31. *See also specific topics*
gendered language, 207; of virility, 114–16
gendered ways of experiencing love, 121–22
gendering/division of mysticism, 7–12, 114
gender roles, 98
genitals, male and female, 116–17
Gerson, Jean, 8
Gilles de Rais, 338n. 37
God, 97, 104, 202, 209, 218; absence of,
    104–5; Angela of Foligno's experience
    of, 1–2; authors confessing to (*see*
    "confessions"); Bataille on, 64, 66–68,
    104–5; Beauvoir on woman's love of
    man and love of, 123–29, 132; death of,
    105; desire related to, 139; doubleness,
    164; gendered ways of experiencing love
    for, 121–22; Irigaray on, 198, 212, 214,
    216, 219, 236–37; Lacan on, 168; of the
    mystics, 67; as phallus, 133; as projection
    of human desire, 67–68; self-hatred, 67;
    union with, 68
goddess, 169
Godhead, 97
God-man, 69–70
Grosz, Elizabeth, 211, 212, 231–32, 335n.
    17

Guerlac, Suzanne, 293n. 53, 302n. 61
guilt, 78, 83; survival, 91
Guilty (Bataille), 57, 61–63, 66, 68, 80–
    82, 99, 101–3; death in, 105–6; and
    Nietzsche, 104; opening, 60–61; paradox
    of, 107
Guyon, Madame, 137–38, 317–18n. 40

Hadewijch, 95, 98–99, 207
Harvey, Van, 231
Hegel, Georg, 40, 230, 311–12n. 14, 343n.
    40
Heidegger, Martin, 224, 227, 342n. 30
Herman, Judith, 76–77
Hershey, John, 84
heterosexism, 190
heterosexual pair, 135, 266–67; Irigaray's
    fetishization of the, 238–39
heterosociality, 191, 212
hierarchies, dualistic, 134, 215, 216
Hiroshima, 301n. 60
Hiroshima (Hershey), 84
history: as (at least) double, 63; rationality vs.
    irrationality of, 309n. 47; as unfinished,
    105
Holocaust, 301n. 57, 357n. 14
homosexual, women as innately, 177–78
Horney, Karen, 175
horror films, 51–53
Huntington, Patricia, 182–83, 206, 231
hysteria, 183; Beauvoir's feminist analysis
    of, 243, 246, 247; Freud on, 243, 268,
    344–45n. 4; vs. mysticism, 128–29,
    131, 243; ventriloquizing, 247, 253–57
    (*see also* demonic possession)
hysterics, 3; medieval mystics vs. modern,
    20; vs. obsessives, 4. *See also* Beatrice of
    Nazareth; Madeleine

idealism, 106, 145, 232–33, 319n. 56
identification(s): across gender, 52;
    cross-identifications, 52; Irigaray's
    understanding of, 217; masochistic, 52,
    55, 93
imaginary, 157, 159, 166, 174, 181–83, 185;

feminine and masculine, 193, 194, 204, 209, 237, 267, 338n. 42; transformation of, 209. *See also* Irigaray, on the real, imaginary, and symbolic; Lacan, theory of the imaginary, symbolic, and real

imaginary (bodily) ego, 262–64

imaginary ego ideal, 261

immanence, 130, 132, 134, 139, 199, 207, 213, 313n. 7

impossible, the, 104

"impossible" other, 104

impotence, law of, 203, 206, 208, 278

Incarnation, 198, 199, 205

incorporation, 72

individual and the absolute, the, 129–30

inner experience, 81, 114–16; communication as possible only through, 120; defined, 64; as mode of action with ethical ramifications, 63; problem of, 36–42

Inner Experience (Bataille), 39, 64, 66, 68–70, 73–74, 82; Bataille's motivations for writing, 88; Beauvoir on, 25; Marmande on refractory power of, 63; opening, 99; Sartre on, 27, 29, 36–37, 67, 88–89; suffering in, 57–58, 82; temporality and ecstasy, 27

interiority and externality, 257–61, 264, 265, 268, 269, 271

intersubjectivity, 140, 213, 232

Irigaray, Luce, 179–80, 274–76, 278, 331nn. 28–29, 340n. 9, 341n. 20, 342nn. 26–30; analysis of Melusine story, 214–16; Beauvoir contrasted with, 198–99, 209, 266; on belief, 206–11, 218–30, 236–41, 344nn. 1–2; "Belief Itself," 219–20, 225, 230–31, 233, 236; as biological/bodily essentialist, 183, 185, 186, 188–90, 209, 232, 240–41, 269; on bodily memory, 274–75; on Christ and feminine imagery, 198–203; "Così fan tutti," 174, 180, 181, 192, 203, 204, 266; criticisms of, 186, 191, 240, 268, 270, 354n. 91; on

death, 20, 227, 268, 270, 274, 275; on Derrida's "To Speculate—On Freud," 220, 224, 228; "Divine Women," 206, 209, 213, 219–20, 229, 337n. 34; on divinity and subjectivity, 213–20; on feminism, 5, 6, 177, 180–82, 330n. 16; on fetishism, 236–47, 267–71; fetishization of, 240–41; fetishization of the heterosexual pair, 238–39; on Freud's *Beyond the Pleasure Principle*, 220–25, 342n. 28; on God, 198, 212, 214, 216, 219, 236–37; on hysteria, 241–47; *I Love to You*, 232, 233; on identification, 217; indebtedness to Lacan, 184, 192, 196; "La Mystérique", 194, 196, 198, 203, 208, 266, 335n. 19; on language, 196–97; on melancholic incorporation, 269, 270, 355n. 2, 356n. 8; metaphors, 195, 198; on mother-child relationship, 212–13, 274; on mystical encounter, 19–20; on mysticism, 187–95; "Questions to Levinas," 192; on the real, imaginary, and symbolic, 180–83, 185, 193–94, 204, 206, 209, 237, 269; on sexual difference, 20, 183–93, 210, 212, 213, 229–35, 266, 267, 269–71, 281n. 17, 332n. 31, 343nn. 39–42; *Speculum of the Other Woman*, 173, 174, 179, 181, 183, 192, 193, 204, 206, 277; tensions and paradoxes in her work, 206, 229, 270, 345n. 5; *This Sex Which Is Not One*, 174, 179, 188; two accounts of belief in her work, 184

James of Vitry, 244–45, 254, 255

Janet, Pierre, 2–3, 75–76, 279n. 5

Jantzen, Grace, 229

Jay, Martin, 40

Jesus Christ. *See* Christ

Jones, Ernest, 175

Jones, Serene, 211–12

Jonesian naturalism, 176

jouissance, 57, 149, 151; defined, 57; feminine, 150, 159–66, 179, 192, 194; phallic, 149, 160

Julian of Norwich, 93

Kepler, Johannes, 152
Kojève, Alexander, 295n. 10
Kracauer, Siegfried, 93–94
Kristeva, Julia, 277, 338–39n. 47, 345–46n.
9

Lacan, Jacques, 79, 321nn. 9–11, 323–24nn.
18–19, 325nn. 31, 33–35, 326nn.
38–39; and the baroque, 162, 166;
Bataille and, 149–50, 321–22nn.
11–12; Beauvoir and, 323n. 15; and
Catholicism, 321n. 9; on communication
and its referential function, 327n. 57;
on desire to be everything, 118, 161,
165; double-edged discourse, 160; on
feminine jouissance, 150, 159–66, 192,
194; on femininity, 119; and feminism,
167–70; on Freud and the unconscious,
152, 266, 323n. 17; Irigaray's criticisms
of, 173–74, 180, 184, 192, 203, 206,
237, 266; Irigaray's indebtedness to, 184,
192, 196; on language, 149, 153–55,
157, 163–65; on libido, 179; life history,
321nn. 9–11, 323n. 18, 328n. 63; little
a and the big *A*, 156–59, 164–69, 179,
182 (*see also* Christ, as little [object] *a*);
on love, woman, history, and mysticism,
64–66; on masculinity, 118; and mystics,
163; on the Other side, 159–69, 174,
179; and politics, 321n. 10, 323n. 14;
and psychoanalysis, 21, 149–51, 153,
156, 198 (*see also* psychoanalysis); and
psychoanalytic theory of female sexuality,
176; on sexual difference, 153–54;
on sexual relations, 203; theory of the
imaginary, symbolic, and real, 157,
322n. 13, 325nn. 31, 35, 330n. 16,
331n. 27. See also *Encore*
Lacanian psychoanalysis, 153, 166, 173;
Irigaray's critique of, 180, 194
lack: mystical ecstasy as fullness vs., 146–
51; and the real, 182; subjectivity
as grounded in, 206; women as

representing, 117–19, 267. *See also*
castrated mother; loss
language: bodily trauma and, 109; eruption
of affect in and through, 162; gendered,
114–16, 207; Irigaray on, 196–97; Lacan
on, 149, 153–55, 157, 163–65; loss of
the use of, 196–97; referential, 327n.
57; signifier function, 157, 163–64;
tendencies in, 149; trust in, 227–28;
visionary/cataphatic vs. apophatic, 98
Leiris, Michel, 25
"letting go," 97
Levinas, Emmanuel, 187–88, 192
libidinal repression, 54
libido, 176, 179
limitation. *See* desire, to be all/everything
loss: disavowing/refusing to accept, 234,
238–39, 356n. 8; feminism and,
356n. 8; Freud on, 183, 353n. 77;
Irigaray on, 238–40, 267–68, 270, 272,
274–75, 277; of mother's body, 228–29,
238, 239, 274; of self, 70, 267–68;
unrepresentability of women's, 277. *See
also* castration; lack
Louette, Jean-Francois, 30–31
love, 96, 97, 207; as divine, 208; erotic,
121–22; Lacan on, 169; of self, 131–34;
woman's love of man and love of God,
123–29, 132
Lu Xun, 303–4n. 3

Madeleine, 2–3, 279–80nn. 5, 7, 8
male-dominant cultures, 151, 157–58, 209,
215, 354n. 91
male-dominant symbolic, 159, 161, 164,
167
male fantasies of plenitude and wholeness,
65, 151, 156, 157, 159, 168–70,
224–25
male power, basis of, 151. *See also* wholeness,
male fantasies of plenitude and
male privilege, 134
male psychosexual development, 223–25,
228–29; Freud's theory of, 174

male subjectivity, 65

Marie of Oignies, 245, 254, 255–56

Marmande, Francis, 63

Mary, Virgin, 226

Mary and Martha, story of, 10–11

masculine and feminine forms of mysticism, 7–9

masculine imaginary. *See* imaginary, feminine and masculine

masculinity, 139; Beauvoir's overvaluation of, 318n. 46; Lacan on, 118. *See also specific topics*

masochism, 75, 110, 292n. 47; fetishization and, 52; primacy in Freud's understanding of sexuality, 54; projected onto female victims, 52; religion, ecstasy, and, 56–59. *See also* sadomasochism

masochistic identification, 52, 55, 93

master/slave relation, 136, 311–12n. 14

mastery, belief and, 223

Maurras, Charles, 314n. 14

McCallum, E. L., 261, 332n. 35

McClintock, Anne, 239

meaninglessness, 143, 145

Mechthild of Magdeburg, 100–102, 207

meditation, and traumatic memory, 74–79

meditative practice, 56, 262, 298n. 27; Angela of Foligno's, 71–72; Bataille's, 56, 69–74, 89, 92, 94; toward a new, 69–74; visions and ecstasies that follow, 11

melancholic incorporation, 260–65, 268–70, 332n. 35, 353n. 77, 355n. 2, 356n. 8

Melusine story, Irigaray's analysis of, 214–16

memory(ies), 71; bodily/traumatic, 75–79, 82, 109, 274–75; linguistic strategies of apophatic, 108; narrative, 75–78, 82, 83

metaphors, mystical, 195, 198

Michelet, 314n. 15

mirror image, 195, 200, 222–23

mirror stage, 157, 222, 223

Montrelay, Michèle, 178

mortality: embracing one's, 238; experience of, 20; and fetishization, 272

mother-child relationship, 175, 212–13; Irigaray on, 212–13, 274. *See also* male psychosexual development; Melusine story, Iragaray's analysis on

motherhood, 313–14n. 8

mother(s), phallic vs. castrated, 169–70, 290n. 29

mother's body, loss of, 228–29, 238, 239, 274

"Mourning and Melancholia" (Freud), 353n. 77

"Mouvement de libération des femmes" (MLF), 177, 179–80

Mulvey, Laura, 51

murder, 42–44

mystic, defined, 307n. 32

mystical, conceptions of the, 64

mystical discourse and practice, doubleness of, 278

mystical ecstasy, as fullness vs. lack, 146–51

mystical moments, three, 1–4

mystical theology, toward a new, 66–69

mystical works, instructions for reading, 100

mysticism: conceptions of, 113–14, 148–49; denigration of, 7–10; as desire for "what is there," 113–14, 116; as event/encounter, 19; and gender, 6–13; historical shift in meaning of the term, 147–48; and history, 60–66; origins of the term, 146–47; vs. pathology, 279–80n. 7; as temptation, 141. *See also specific topics*

Name-of-the-Father, 156–58, 206

Nancy, Jean-Luc, 108, 300n. 52

narcissism, 131–35, 320n. 57

Nazism, 61

Newman, Barbara, 242, 244, 246–47, 253

Newton, Isaac, 152

Nietzsche, Friedrich, 89, 99–101, 103, 104, 319–20n. 57; Beauvoir on, 320n. 57; fault/failure, 107, 308n. 44; how to

Nietzsche, Friedrich (*continued*)
  read, 100; Irigaray's interpretation of,
    204; mystical aspect of his writing, 307n.
    32. *See also* Bataille, *On Nietzsche*
nihilism, 62, 233
non-knowledge, 74. *See also* unknown
"not all/whole," 64, 65, 119, 160, 179–81,
    192, 202
nothingness, 27, 30, 38, 62, 69. *See also*
    unknown; void

"object-point," 73
objectification, 123
obsessive-compulsive persons, 4
Oedipus complex, 55, 174
One, desire for the, 165
Orient, European discussions of, 90
Origen, 146–47
other: demonized, 215–16; denial of the,
    121, 123; experiencing the real existence
    of the, 132; invoking the absent, yet to
    be born, 105; recognition of the, 132,
    134–39; refusal to acknowledge the,
    239. *See also* Lacan

pantheism, "black," 37
paradoxes, 106–8
patriarchy. *See* male-dominant cultures
penis, 132; relation to phallus, 155–56,
    158–61, 237
penis envy, 175
Petit, Le, 45
phallagocentrism, 180–82, 196, 266, 267
phallic jouissance, 149, 160
phallic law of impotence. *See* impotence, law
    of
phallic power, 176
phallic signifier, 151, 155, 158, 159, 170,
    179, 223
phallic symbolic order, 151
phallus, 277; and castration, 117; conflation
    of imaginary and symbolic, 155; as
    fetish, 237; Lacan on, 65, 118, 151, 153,
    155–61, 176; primacy, 65, 118, 151,
    153, 155, 156, 175; relation to penis,

155–56, 158–61, 237; in writings of
    Bataille, 47–51. *See also* castration
photography: death and, 91–92; trauma,
    scandal of the real, and, 91–94, 301n.
    59, 303nn. 1–2
poetry, 114–15, 356n. 8; trust in language,
    227–28
political and metaphysical, convergence of,
    122–23, 296n. 14, 357n. 12
politics, 84; Lacan and, 321n. 10, 323n. 14;
    vs. mysticism, 62–63, 296n. 14
Porete, Marguerite, 8, 12–13, 96, 207; *The
    Mirror of Simple Souls,* 96–100, 195, 265
pornography, 42–44; and antipornography
    debates, 43, 44; hard-core, 43–44
possession. *See* demonic possession
post-traumatic stress disorder (PTSD), 76–77
power, 150; male and female, 156
presence and absence, interplay of, 105–8,
    149; gender, sex, and, 117–19
presence (transparence), 105
primal scenes, 50
prostitutes, 116–17, 311n. 14
pseudo-Albert the Great, 246
Psychanalyse et Politique (Psych et Po), 177
psychoanalysis: aim/goal of, 149, 153, 162,
    166, 168; Bataille and, 46–47; Beauvoir's
    ambivalent attitude toward, 128; and
    Christianity, 162, 164; compared with
    mysticism, 164, 165, 167; as discourse
    through which feminine jouissance
    speaks, 179; as a double, 153; and
    feminism in France, 167, 173–86;
    Lacan and, 21, 149–51, 153, 156, 198;
    Lacanian, 153, 166, 173, 180, 194; as
    practice that elicits mystical jouissance,
    21. *See also specific topics*
psychosexual development, 223–25, 228–29;
    psychoanalytic theories of, 174–75,
    290n. 29
real, the: apprehension of, 65; associating
    it with lack and castration, 182; and
    Bataille's conception of heterogeneity,

149–50; Bataille's relationship with, 63; contemplation of, 66; defined, 150; emergence, 55, 150; ethical relation to, 79; feminine jouissance and, 166; as possibility, 182; shifting meanings, 322n. 13; specificity of, vs. narrative contextualization, 65; trauma, photography, and the scandal of, 88–94, 295n. 9, 301n. 59. *See also* Irigaray, on the real, imaginary, and symbolic; Lacan, theory of the imaginary, symbolic, and real

"reality," claims to, 58

reality effects, 42–47, 55

reason, 96, 103

reciprocity, 89, 123, 135

redemption, language of, 108

redemptive activity, 72

redemptive suffering, 94–96

religion, 227; gendering of, 310n. 8. *See also* belief; faith; *specific topics*

repetition, 72

repetition compulsion and compulsive repetitions, 75, 85, 109, 220, 260, 342n. 28

repression, libidinal, 54

responsibility. *See* Beauvoir, freedom, responsibility, and situatedness

Rimbaud, Arthur, 114–15

rituals, 20–21, 278

Rodowick, David, 51–52

Roudinesco, Elisabeth, 176–79

sacred, the, 103, 104, 117, 118

sacrifice, 56–58, 203–6, 274; Bataille and, 204–5, 312n. 17. *See also* crucifixion; Eucharist

sadomasochism, 51–56, 291nn. 38–40; Bataille and, 51–56, 298n. 32, 303n. 2. *See also* masochism

Said, Edward, 90

salvation, 67, 68, 72, 115–16, 130

Sartre, Jean-Paul, 25, 286n. 7; *Anti-Semite and Jew*, 301n. 57; on Bataille's *Inner*

Experience, 27, 29, 36–37, 67, 88–89; Beauvoir's divergence from, 135, 139–40; Beauvoir's influence on, 318–19n. 49; *Being and Nothingness*, 27, 29; conception of mysticism, 113; criticism of Bataille, 27–37, 67, 85, 88–89, 99, 113, 287–88nn. 12–15; on idealism and Christianity, 319n. 56; influence on Beauvoir, 140; on inner experience, 37–38; life history, 28; *Nausea*, 27; "A New Mystic," 28–32; on value, 145

scopophilia, fetishistic, 52, 53

Second Sex, The (Beauvoir), 128, 132, 137, 139; and sexual liberation, 127, 176; and subjectivity, 124, 134, 138, 140; and Teresa of Avila, 142; on women's desires, 122, 145

self: absence/death of, 105; absence of God and contingency of the, 104–5; conceptions of internalized, 265; death of, 123; loss of, 70, 267–68

self-abdication, 140

self-annihilation, Bataille and, 46, 47, 91

self-denial/self-negation, 40, 103, 121

self-differentiation, 234

self-dissolution, 56, 74, 75, 85, 86, 166

self-emptying, 200

selflessness, 140

self-love, 131–34

sensibility, sovereign, 84–85

sensible ecstasy, 4–6

sensible transcendental, 199, 207, 334n. 10

servile sentimentality, 84

servitude, 64

sexual difference, 174; and the body, 151; Christian tradition and the primacy of, 218; concept of, 284n. 42; effacement and denial of, 227; fetishism as response to, 239; fetishization of, 267, 270, 271; fluidity of, 196; as function of language, 151, 154; Irigaray on, 20, 183–93, 210, 212, 213, 229–35, 266, 267, 269–71, 281n. 17, 332n. 31, 343nn. 39–42; Lacan on, 151, 196, 237; mysticism and

sexual difference (*continued*)
  the primacy of, 187–93; obsession with, 239; and psychosexual development, 174–75, 223–25, 228–29; from species being to, 229–35; transcending, 131–33, 136, 190
sexual differentiation, 239
sexual relations, 203
sexual signifiers, 149, 151–56
signifier function of language, 157, 163–64
signifiers: sexual, 149, 151–56; signified, significance, and, 163–65, 182. *See also* transcendental signifier
Silverman, Kaja, 155–56
slavery. *See* master/slave relation
Snuff (film), 42–44
solipsism, 138–40; spiritual, 62
soul, 12–13, 96, 265; Lacan and the, 167
species being, 230–32, 234
spectacle, 46
speech, loss of the use of, 196–97
speechless body, 83–84
subjectivity, 65, 142; and divinity, 213–20; as grounded in lack, 206; inauthentic, 140; Irigaray on divinity and, 213–20; men's recognition of women's, 136; transcendent, 127, 131; universal "truth" of, 167. *See also* female subjectivity; intersubjectivity; *specific topics*
sublimation, 54
suffering, 70, 97; in Bataille's *Inner Experience*, 57–58, 82; of Christ, 72–74, 77–78, 87, 91, 114, 260, 262; desire to come to terms with, 20; Eckhart on, 307n. 26; embracing and intensifying, 96; Irigaray's rejection of, 337n. 34; meanings attributed to, 93; redemptive, 94–96; self-dissolution and representations of, 56; valorization of, 95; witnessing another's, 86–87
suffering body, fetishization of, 94–95
Suleiman, Susan, 45, 114–15
surrealism, 287n. 10
Surya, Michel, 45

Sweetman, Robert, 242
symbolic, the, 157, 166, 168, 181–83, 185, 204, 237; conflation/unity of the imaginary and, 181, 183, 193–94, 206, 329n. 70. *See also* Irigaray, on the real, imaginary, and symbolic; Lacan, theory of the imaginary, symbolic, and real

Taylor, Mark, 169
temptation, mysticism as, 141
Teresa of Avila, 99, 137, 138, 317–18nn. 38–41, 319n. 54; Beauvoir on, 19, 128–29, 131, 133, 137–40, 142–44, 208; as existentialist hero, 144; and freedom, 134–35, 143; gender of her mysticism, 134; and hysteria, 3, 4, 128, 243; Irigaray on, 202; overcoming her femininity/sexual difference, 136; power of her belief, 208; reform movement, 318n. 45; totalizing autonomous subjectivity, 142
Thomas of Cantimpré, 242–46, 254, 255, 257
torture, 72–75, 82, 83, 86. *See also* Bataille, images of (Chinese) torture victim; Christ
totalitarian thought, 29, 33, 35, 295n. 12
totality, 35. *See also* desire, to be all/everything
transcendence, 121, 122, 127, 128, 130–31, 134, 135; Beauvoir on, 198–99, 209, 313n. 7; of bodily limitations, 190, 278 (*see also* sexual difference, transcending); as discontinuity, 58; Irigaray on, 198–99, 209, 213, 225, 227, 232; men's desire for absolute, 139
transcendental, sensible, 199, 207, 334n. 10
transcendental signifier, 149, 153, 182; phallus as, 151, 155, 158, 159, 170, 179, 223
transcendent subjectivity, 127, 131
transcending: femininity, 129–33, 136; sexual difference, 131–33, 136, 190
transformation, 69; of world, 134–39
trauma, 277, 301n. 60; displaced from body

to language, 109; femininity, feminism, and, 356n. 5; Lacan on, 166, 295n. 9; and masochism, 110; psychotherapeutic treatment of, 76; victims, onlookers, and, 300n. 49; writing, 108–10. *See also under* Bataille

trauma discourse, 356n. 5

traumatic repetition, 260, 268, 356n. 8

Turner, Denys, 320n. 1

unconscious, Lacan on the, 152, 323n. 17

union/unity: with Christ, 70–72; desire for and experience of, 113; with God, 68. *See also* Christ, union/unity with

unknowability of the future, 105, 109

unknown, the, 27, 30, 109. *See also* non-knowledge; nothingness; void

utopianism, 183, 240, 357n. 11

utopians, feminist: and evasion of history, 266–73

victimization, 75. *See also* crucifixion; torture

victims, onlookers, and trauma, 300n. 49

violence, 42–44, 202, 204–5, 357n. 11; in Bataille's work, 44, 47, 48, 57 (*see also* Bataille, images of [Chinese] torture victim). *See also* sadomasochism; torture; trauma

virility, gendered language of, 114–16

virtues, 96

visionaries, 320n. 2; discussion of their experience, 305n. 14

void, 27, 70, 74. *See also* nothingness; unknown

war, and mysticism, 60–61, 301–2nn. 59–60

Wartofsky, Marx, 231

Weber, Alison, 138

Weil, Simone, 309n. 50

wholeness, 113, 168; fantasy of (lost), 203, 310n. 8, 336n. 22; male fantasies of plenitude and, 65, 151, 156, 157, 159, 168–70, 224–25. *See also* mystical ecstasy, as fullness vs. lack

will, annihilation/renunciation of, 13, 227

Williams, Linda, 42–44, 289n. 13

witches, witch hunts, and hysteria, 3

witnessing, 86–89

woman, as a gender, 230–31

women: of action, 131; attitude regarding their body, 130; becoming the phallus, 161; desire for the absolute, 145; "divine," 184; identification as man's other, 122; identification with nature, 215; as innately homosexual, 177–78; love of man and love of God, 123–29, 132; men's recognition of their subjectivity and autonomy, 135–36; projection of immanence and the body onto, 139; religiosity, 122; as representing lack for men, 117–19, 267; role of, 98; self-justification/justifications for existence, 122, 126, 127, 130, 132, 143, 313n. 8; transcending their femininity (*see* transcending, femininity). *See also specific topics*

women mystics, neglect of the influence and contributions of, 6–11

women's body, objectification of, 117

women's position, doubleness of, 160–61

"wound culture," 356nn. 5–6

writing: and death, 89, 106; trau- matic/traumatized, 109

writing desire, 108–10